Solvay

C000132725

History of a Multinational Family Firm

KENNETH BERTRAMS

Fonds National de la Recherche Scientifique and Université Libre de Bruxelles

NICOLAS COUPAIN

Solvay S.A.

ERNST HOMBURG

Maastricht University

Coordinated by Ginette Kurgan-van Hentenryk,
with the partnership of Philippe Mioche

CAMBRIDGE
UNIVERSITY PRESS

CAMBRIDGE
UNIVERSITY PRESS

32 Avenue of the Americas, New York NY 10013-2473, USA

Cambridge University Press is part of the University of Cambridge.

It furthers the University's mission by disseminating knowledge in the pursuit of
education, learning and research at the highest international levels of excellence.

www.cambridge.org
Information on this title: www.cambridge.org/9781107436930

First published 2013
First paperback edition 2014

A catalogue record for this publication is available from the British Library

Library of Congress Cataloguing in Publication data
Bertrams, Kenneth.
Solvay : history of a multinational family firm / Kenneth Bertrams, Nicolas Coupain,
Ernst Homburg.
p. cm.
Includes bibliographical references and index.
ISBN 978-1-107-02480-9 (hardback)
1. Solvay Chemicals – History. 2. Chemical industry – Belgium – History 3. International
business enterprises – Belgium. 4. Solvay, Ernest, 1838–1922. 5. Philanthropists –
Belgium. I. Coupain, Nicolas, 1978– II. Homburg, Ernst, 1952– III. Title.
HD9656.B44S653 2012
338.8′8766–dc23 2012025227

ISBN 978-1-107-02480-9 Hardback
ISBN 978-1-107-43693-0 Paperback

Contents

PART 2 THE YEARS OF CRISIS (1914–1950): THE MAKING AND UNMAKING OF INTERNATIONAL ALLIANCES
Kenneth Bertrams

PART 3 THE ERA OF DIVERSIFICATION AND
GLOBALIZATION (1950–2012)
Ernst Homburg

Tables

Charts

Figures and Maps

Abbreviations

2,4-D	sodium salt of 2,4-dichloro-phenoxy acetic acid
ADL	Arthur D. Little
AEI	American Enterprise Institute
AG	Aktiengesellschaft (joint-stock company)
AIP	Application Integrity Programs
ARG	Aethylen Rohrleitungs-Gesellschaft
BAP	Société Bourguignonne d'Applications Plastiques
BEF	Belgian franc
BGB	Banque Générale Belge
BOI	Board of Investment (Thailand)
BPCC	By-Products Coke Corporation
CCPC	Corpus Christi Petrochemical Company
CEFIC	Conseil Européen des Fédérations de l'Industrie Chimique
CEO	chief executive officer
CFC	chlorofluorocarbons
CH	Swiss franc
CKA	Castner-Kellner Alkali Company
CKV	Chlor-Konventionsvertrag
CNSA	Comité National de Secours et d'Alimentation
COIG	IG Farben Control Committee
COO	chief operations officer
CPC	Chemical Products Corporation
CRB	American Commission for Relief in Belgium
CRT	cathode-ray tubes
DCE	dichloroethane
DCSI	Direction Centrale des Systèmes Informatiques
DCT	Direction Centrale Technique
DGC	Direction Générale Commerciale
DGT	Direction Générale Technique
DM	Deutschmark
DMP	Direction des Matières Plastiques
DNF	Direction Nationale pour la France
DPC	Division des Produits Chimiques
DSA	Departement Santé Animale (animal health)
DSC	Daehan Specialty Chemicals Co. Ltd.
DSW	Deutsche Solvay Werke
EBIT	earnings before interest and tax
EBRD	European Bank for Reconstruction and Development
EC	European Community

ECTFE	copolymer of ethylene and chlorotrifluoroethylene
EDC	ethylene dichloride
EEC	European Economic Community
EPA	Environmental Protection Agency (United States)
ERT	European Round Table of Industrialists
ESW	Ebenseer Solvay Werke
EVC	European Vinyl Corporation
EVOH	(poly)ethylene vinylalcohol
FCF	Filatura Corti Fratelli
FDA	Food and Drug Administration (United States)
FEX	fabrication expérimentale
FF	French franc
FFC	Federal Furnace Corporation
FMC	Food Machinery and Chemical Corporation
FNRS	Fonds National pour la Recherche Scientifique (Belgian National Fund for Scientific Research)
GBU	global business unit
GmbH	Gesellschaft mit beschränkter Haftung (limited-liability company)
HCCH	hexachlorocyclohexane
HCFC	hydrochlorofluorocarbons
HDPE	high-density polyethylene
HFC	hydrofluorocarbons
IACS	International Association of Chemical Societies
ICI	Imperial Chemical Industries
IG	Interessengemeinschaft
KC	Kali-Chemie
KPIC	Korea Plastics Industry Corp.
LDPE	low-density polyethylene
LTM	Latéma
MCPA	sodium salt of 2-methyl 4-chloro phenoxy acetic acid
MEA	membrane-electrode assemblies
MES	Maison d'Ernest Solvay
MFA	copolymer trifluoroethylene and perfluoromethylvinyl ether
MHRA	Medicine and Healthcare products Regulatory Agency (UK)
MSD	Merck, Sharp & Dohme
NAFTA	North American Free Trade Agreement (United States, Canada, Mexico)
NAS	North American Solvay Inc.
NBD	New Business Development
NKF	Nederlandse Kabelfabriek
NoH	Neder-over-Heembeek
NSW	Nestomitzer Solvay Werke
NYSE	New York Stock Exchange
OLED	organic light-emitting diodes
OMV	Oesterreichische Mineralölverwaltung
OPV	organic photovoltaic
OSW	Oesterreichische Solvay-Werke Betriebsgesellschaft
OTC	over-the-counter (pharmaceuticals)
PAN	polyacrylonitril
PE	polyethylene
PET	polyethylene terephtalate

PFA	perfluoroalcoxy
PO	propylene oxide
PP	polypropylene
PPS	polyphenylen sulfide
PS	polystyrene
PTFE	polytetrafluoroethylene
PUR	polyurethane resin
PVC	polyvinyl chloride
PVDC	polyvinylidene chloride
PVDF	polyvinylidene fluoride
RAF	Red Army Faction
RBU	regional business unit
REBIT	recurrent earnings before interest and tax
RM	Reichsmark
ROE	return on equity
ROI	return on investment
RWM	Reichswirtschaftsministerium
SA	Société Anonyme (joint-stock company)
Sabed	Società Bario et Derivati
SAC	Solvay American Corporation, successor to SAIC
SAIC	Solvay American Investment Corporation, predecessor of SAC
SAIGS	Società Anonima Industriale Gomma Sintetica
SBA	Société Belge de l'Azote (et des Produits Chimiques du Marly)
SBB	Société Belge de Banque
SBE	Société Belge d'Electrochimie
SBU	strategic business unit
SEA	Solvay (South East Asia) Pte, Ltd.
SGB	Société Générale de Banque
SIR	Système d'Information Rapide
SPC	Solvay Process Company (United States)
SSC	Semet-Solvay Company (United States)
STMP	Société de Transformation des Matières Plastiques
TEL	tetraethyl lead
THAN	Thompson-Hayward Agriculture & Nutrition Company
TNT	trinitrotoluene
TQM	total quality management
TrB	Direction (Transformation) Bâtiments
TrC	Direction (Transformation) Calandrage
TrE	Direction (Transformation) Emballage
TSAC	The Solvay American Corporation
UAC	United Alkali Company
UCB	Union Chimique Belge
ULB	Université Libre de Bruxelles
VC	vinyl chloride
VC_2	vinylidene chloride
VCM	vinyl chloride monomer
VF_2	vinylidene fluoride
VUB	Vrije Universiteit Brussel
WCC	Wyandotte Chemicals Corporation

FIGURE I.I. Four generations of Solvay leaders: Ernest (1838–1922), Armand (1865–1930), Ernest-John (1895–1972), and Jacques (1920–2010). (Solvay Archives.)

Introduction

In his authoritative history on *The Chemical Industry 1900–1930*, the economic historian L. F. Haber summed up the role of the Solvay company: "Solvay's own enterprises were relatively small, but their interests and connections within Belgium as well as outside were extensive." He continued: "A comprehensive history of Solvay is badly needed and would fill a major gap in our knowledge of the development of the European chemical industry."[1] This book fills that gap.

Solvay and its history stand out for several reasons. During most of its 150 years of existence Solvay remained one of the leaders in its fields, but, more interesting, it also was one of the earliest multinational, or "polynational,"[2] groups, as well as being a family-controlled firm up to the present time. These two features taken together make the company unique in the chemical industry, and perhaps even among businesses more generally. Moreover, the influence of the Solvay family – as well as the company – extends far beyond the realm of business. Solvay has lent its name to a number of initiatives in the field of science and education, particularly to the famous international conferences on physics and chemistry that have been organized since 1911. In its home country Solvay is an icon, being one of the last independent crown jewels from when Belgium was the second most industrialized country in the world. The large number of institutes, schools, and streets named after Solvay in Belgium illustrates the enduring impact of Solvay's legacy to that small nation. Paradoxically, the resilient tradition of secrecy that lay at the core of the company's technological success has long hindered a better understanding of its multiple lives. The present book aims to end that obscurity.

Although Solvay is a Belgian-born enterprise, it has encompassed diverse national cultures and has mostly acted at the local level as an indigenous firm. Since the first year of its existence (1863), international expansion of its ammonia-soda business was at the core of Solvay's strategy. As the primary raw material for soda ash – salt – was absent from Belgium's subsoil, Solvay soon had to cross national borders. Furthermore, the industrial patents on which the enterprise was founded had to be implemented quickly in major industrialized countries, to avoid seeing them copied or circumvented by powerful

---

[1] Haber (1971), 307; see also Metzner (1955), 92–5.
[2] The expression is from Christian Jourquin, Solvay's CEO from 2006 to 2012; interview Christian Jourquin, 28 Sept. 2010.

competitors. Within a few decades, Solvay elaborated a unique model of international expansion, one based on a combination of wholly owned factories, subsidiaries, and partnerships with foreign entrepreneurs, rooted in their own markets: France and Britain in 1872; Germany, Russia, and the United States during the early 1880s; and followed by the Habsburg Empire and, later, Spain, Italy, and many other countries. This multinational network appeared to be an asset for the continuous improvement of the ammonia-soda process, which long remained the core of Solvay's technical expertise. Indeed, geographical diversification contrasted sharply with the single-product orientation that characterized the company during the first half of its history.

Operating as a multi- or "poly"national not only was an asset but also often a concern, especially when European geopolitics started to become instable after 1914. During World War I, Solvay's plants were on both sides of the front line. As a result of the war and the Russian Revolution, the group lost its Russian factories, and its control over its American business. During the interwar period the company tried to compensate for those losses by maneuvering itself into the heart of a complex network of international cartel agreements in the chemical industry, which then were politically allowed. World War II brought a new blow, though, to the powerful international position of the company. After the war, all assets in Central and Eastern Europe were nationalized by the new regimes.

The period after 1945 showed another aspect of Solvay's multinational character. As surprising as it may seem, the processes of European integration and globalization partially undermined the polynational strongholds of the group. For historical reasons, Solvay had many small and medium-sized production sites, well tuned to local demands and relying heavily on national networks. During the past twenty-five years the company has had to reevaluate fundamentally that strategy. Many plants were closed down and others scaled up. For a company that tended to prefer the word *evolution* to *revolution*, and for which traditions had great importance, this was a painful process.

Solvay's other major characteristic is that of being a family business. Whether the emphasis is on capital control, managerial leadership, or organizational style, the firm has deliberately kept this distinct character through the waves of history. That is not as obvious as it may seem. Although many family-owned or family-controlled companies have gained international status, only a few have stemmed from the creation of an inventor-entrepreneur and even fewer have been able to survive over six generations. In Solvay's case, the overwhelming influence and charisma of the patriarch could well have jeopardized the development of "his" brainchild after his death in 1922. But this threat did not materialize: a succession crisis was avoided, and the challenge of changing generations was largely overcome.

Ernest Solvay's heirs have carefully striven to cultivate the long-lasting family character of the enterprise. Effective succession planning was part of the strategy. It entailed reaching out to the most promising members among the groups of descendants, in-laws, as well as, albeit more scarcely, to outside partners. Also, a significant role was given to the upper management (e.g., technical general managers, plant managers, national general managers), most of whom did not belong to the family. In practical terms, their activity went largely beyond the levels of merely assisting and informing decision makers. That said, the imprint of the Solvay family on Solvay & Cie, even when it became a listed public company in 1967, remained an undisputed and undisputable hall-mark of the company throughout its history. Whether such family ingredients have undermined or enhanced the company's performance is an issue that is addressed in the present volume – for there is no doubt that the evolution of the firm is closely intertwined with the history of the Solvay family.

Solvay kept its initial form of a limited partnership for more than a century. The managing partners (*gérants*) were fully liable for their total private assets. Publication of annual results was not mandatory; profits were kept secret. In such a family business, the relationships among associates remained largely permeated by a family atmosphere and close personal contacts. Paternalistic values also prevailed in the relations of the *gérants* with the managers, employ-ees, and workers, particularly with plants that were often at distant locations, isolated from the outside world. The governance of the group therefore diverged significantly from that of the archetypical Chandlerian multinational and mul-tidivisional group, with salaried managers and relative openness to multiple stakeholders.[3] It was only during the last fifteen to twenty years that Solvay has gradually become more similar to other large public companies, without entirely losing its family character.

As mentioned already, Solvay's success initially rested completely on its innovative ammonia-soda process, "rediscovered" during the early 1860s by the twenty-three-year-old apprentice manager Ernest Solvay while working in his uncle's gas factory. Only around 1950, after more than eighty years as a producer of alkalis only, did the company embark on a diversification process. Chemicals, plastics, and pharmaceuticals became the firm's sectors of develop-ment in a globalizing economy. When we started to write this fascinating history in 2007, the company firmly stood on three legs of about equal size: chemicals (soda ash, caustic soda, peroxides, and fluorinated chemicals), plastics (PVC, special polymers, fuel tanks, pipes and fittings), and pharmaceuticals (cardio-vascular, hormones, gastroenterology). Since then, the company has changed dramatically. Writing the last two chapters of this book was like shooting at a constantly moving target: in 2009 and 2010 the pharmaceutical activities were sold and the company divested its fuel tanks and piping businesses; in 2011 it took over the French multinational Rhodia. If some may doubt the dynamic character of family firms, Solvay's recent history completely falsifies this notion.

We conclude this introduction by making some remarks on our sources and by thanking those who were of great help to us. Although a few books and brochures about the history of the group already existed, they were not based on comprehensive research in the company archives. It was Daniel Janssen, honorary chairman of Solvay SA, who took the initiative to ask Solvay to com-mission a thorough history of the group at the occasion of its 150th anniver-sary, in line with the long scientific tradition of the company. He then asked

---

[3] See Chandler (2004).

Ginette Kurgan-van Hentenryk to set up an international team of historians. This book therefore presents the first scholarly study of Solvay, mainly based on company archives, private papers, interviews, and the general literature. We are very grateful to the members of the Industrial Committee, who from the start have taken a great interest in our work and have made possible our full access to relevant sources, and with whom we could discuss several issues in great openness. Of them, next to Daniel Janssen, Aloïs Michielsen and Jacques Lévy-Morelle have been most helpful in opening doors for us inside the company and in bringing us into contact with relevant interviewees. Jean-Marie Solvay, in his turn, has given us access to the precious private archives of his family at La Hulpe, which was of great importance to our work.

Most of the archives relating to the general strategy of the company are kept by the Corporate Secretariat at Brussels. These archives, which also contain several dozen meters of files on the national organizations, on the different subsidiaries and plants, and on legal issues, have been the corner-stone of our enterprise. Archives on the financial, social, commercial, and technical aspects were opened to us by the corresponding departments at the Solvay headquarters. We also made use of specific archives of sites and plants, kept locally by the company or in public depositories. In addition, more than thirty interviews have been held with present and past top managers and experts, from different departments and national organizations of Solvay, who worked for the company during the past five decades. We are very grateful for the invaluable information we received from them and for the great openness of our conversations. Without forgetting the contributions by the others, we would like to mention in particular – in addition to the members of the Industial Committee – Christiane Baleux, Michel Bande, Félix Bloyaert, Pierre Casimir-Lambert, Hervé Coppens d'Eeckenbrugge, Robert Friesewinkel, Auguste Gosselin, Cyril Van Lierde, Jacques Van Rijckevorsel, Paul Washer, and Pierre Weekers, each of whom also supplied valuable documentation in writing.[4]

We also received help from many other people, both inside and outside the company, too numerous to name them all. From Solvay Brussels, Belgium, we would like to mention in particular the central archivist Fabienne Delhalle, as well as several others from the Corporate Secretariat (Philippe Van Loey, Guy Fautré, Nathalie Gérard, Gaëlle De Vos, Françoise Frédéricq, Michel Defourny, Jenny Campion, Isabelle Cosaert, Nicole Van Pée, and Ariane Maurissen). Additional help at Brussels was received from the Communication Department (Marie-Jeanne Marchal, Erik De Leye, Isabelle Chaerels, Katrien Delanote, and others); from Corporate Development (Michel Washer); from the Financial Department (Michèle Laemont and Stéphane Collignon); from the Shareholders Department (Annunziata Menolascina and Anne Tilkens); from the Intellectual Assets Management Department (Thierry Depireux, Valérie Lecharlier, Patrick Marichal, and Stephanie Missoten); from the Human Resources Department (Véronique Depauw); from the Science and Technology Department at Neder-over-Heembeek (Francis Cauwbergh, François Carette, and Jean-Marie

---

[4] A full list of archives and interviews can be found at the end of the book.

Marchal); and from the team of the Maison Ernest Solvay (managed by Catherine Jouniaux).

In Germany (Bernburg, Hanover, and Rheinberg) we were assisted by Anja Rupprecht, Ingo Schierhorn, and Frank Schneider; at Torrelavega, Spain, by Eliza Solorzano, Luis Hervela, and Oscar Mariner; at Tavaux, France, by Jean-Pierre Schrayen, Christian Clerc-Girard, and Michel Grzelczyk; at Rosignano, Italy, by Silvano Benvenuti; and at Syracuse, New York, by Cara Burton and her team at the Solvay Public Library.

Special words of thanks are due to Suggie Casey (Solvay Houston), who put much effort in translating the chapters of Part 1 of the book; to Professor Philippe Mioche, who produced two valuable reports that were used for writing of several chapters; and to the two anonymous referees, who gave several useful suggestions. Last but not least we express our great gratitude to Professor Ginette Kurgan-van Hentenryk, from the Université Libre de Bruxelles, who coordinated the project and who was of invaluable help during all stages of our work.

Brussels and Maastricht, February 2012
Kenneth Bertrams, Nicolas Coupain, and Ernst Homburg

PART I

THE PIONEERING YEARS (1863–1914)

The Quest for Leadership and the First Stages of the Internationalization

Nicolas Coupain

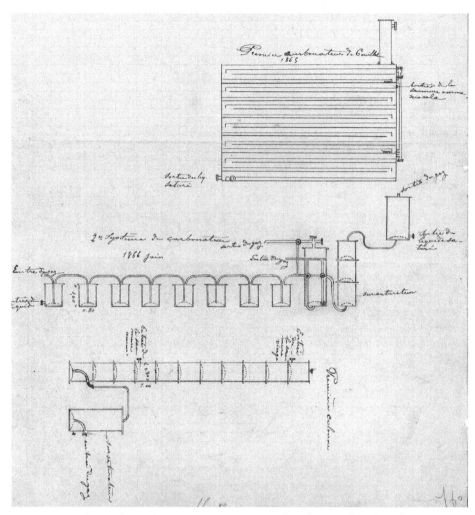

FIGURE 1.1. Successive carbonation apparatus tested at the Couillet plant from 1865 to 1869, drawn by Louis-Philippe Acheroy on the eve of the company's twenty-fifth anniversary. (Solvay Archives.)

I

First Steps

When Vision and Reality Meet

Solvay was launched as a limited partnership in 1863 to operate the ammonia-soda process. This groundbreaking method for producing soda ash had been tested earlier without success by several inventors, leaving the old Leblanc process to dominate the alkali industry. Solvay was the first company to succeed in industrializing the ammonia-soda process, after a handful of individuals joined forces to transform a simple idea into a lasting economic and technical success. Ernest Solvay and his brother Alfred, age twenty-five and twenty-three, respectively, from a middle-class family in a rural area, earned the trust of a few private investors to launch their risky venture. Many challenges lay ahead: gathering funds, receiving government authorization to erect works, and salt tax exemptions, registering a patent, and above all, scaling up the process to the industrial level and conquering the domestic market.

The central character in this story, Ernest Solvay, remains ingrained in the collective imagination as the archetype of the mid-nineteenth-century entrepreneur-innovator. The image of him that has been conveyed is of a brilliant handyman who, without advanced formal education and almost by chance, discovered a revolutionary chemical process. Owing to this accomplishment, he earned the right to join the pantheon of heroic inventors, even being described by his biographers as "a model for future generations."[1] However, a few nuances bring more depth to the analysis of this image. First, innovation is never born of nothing. In the mid-nineteenth century, scientific information became accessible to a wide public. The Belgian legislative, economic, ideological, and technological environments were such as to stimulate invention. Second, although one can fail alone, success often comes through teamwork. The human and social attributes of individuals are as crucial as their capacity to surround themselves with the right people. As a matter of fact, Ernest Solvay's life experience as a self-taught, self-made man often overshadowed his role as leader. Certainly, he developed his process autonomously. But in great part, the accomplishment resulted from his force of persuasion and his ability to adapt to (or even invent new) rules of the game, so that his enterprise was able to cross the boundary between failure and success.

---

[1] For the construction of the myth surrounding Ernest Solvay, see Devriese and Frederic (1997), 321–44.

1.1 INSPIRATION AND IMPLEMENTATION

Initial Human Capital

The Solvay family was among the local bourgeoisie at Rebecq-Rognon, a small village in the province of Walloon Brabant. Located halfway between the financial and commercial center of Brussels and the coal basins of Charleroi and Borinage, this rural region was not under the direct influence of either the former or the latter. The primary economic activities centered on small-scale agriculture (including the mill of the family of Louis-Philippe Acheroy, future head of production for Solvay), quarries, breweries, as well as chicory, tobacco, and thread factories.

During the period under French rule (1793–1814), Alexis Solvay, a man of republican leanings and grandfather of Ernest and Alfred, had opened a boarding school. Several Solvay family members worked there as teachers. Others managed the farm next to the school and the lands that the family had acquired over time. Nearby, the porphyry quarries of Quenast became the major economic activity. Alexandre Solvay (1799–1889), Ernest and Alfred's father, left his post of educator at the boarding school to operate one of these quarries from 1830 to 1850, a period of consolidation of the first industrial revolution in Belgium. There, he developed a commercial network that extended as far as Paris. In 1850 his local fame led him to sit in the Chamber of Commerce at Nivelles alongside Guillaume Nélis (1803–1896), doctor and paper manufacturer at Virginal-Samme and the future cornerstone of the supervisory board of Solvay. Guillaume Nélis represented one of the Solvays' few connections with the upper middle class in business and politics. After the sale of his quarry, Alexandre Solvay built a salt refinery on his property, before ending his professional career as a merchant of colonial commodities. As Ernest Solvay himself enjoys recalling in his memoirs, it is in his father's office that he came into contact with sodium chloride.[2]

Typical bourgeois values governed the relationships and behavior of the Solvay family members.[3] Discipline, merit, and respect of family were set forth as fundamental principles. Opinions were liberal. Ernest and Alfred's uncles Florimond Semet and Léon Hulin were Freemasons, although the Catholic religion was practiced and Christian morality was part of daily life. Charity was given to the poor, and women were expected to be good homemakers, educating their children and managing the household accounts. Matrimonial alliances with other local families ensured maintenance of the landed wealth and the perpetuation of values. Thus, the Solvays, the Semets, and the Hulins, all rich landowners, formed a small inner circle through several marriages, including Alexandre Solvay with Adèle Hulin and Florimond Semet with Elisa Hulin. As for Ernest Solvay, he took as his wife his cousin Adèle Winderickx, daughter

---

[2] Solvay (1904), 108.
[3] For an in-depth analysis of the human and social capital of the Solvay brothers, see Gubin and Piette (1997), 95–136.

of Flore Hulin. Alfred (1840–1894) married his second cousin Marie Masson. The Solvay daughters chose husbands with stable and profitable situations, whereas the sons were guided toward strong, upwardly mobile careers. The appetite for risk and the spirit of adventure were not an evident part of Solvay family values, judging from the sober response of the Solvay brothers' parents during uncertain times (see Section 1.2).[4]

The Solvay brothers also had three sisters, whose husbands would play important roles in the company. Aurélie, the eldest, married the doctor Léopold Querton, who practiced in the coal mines of Grand-Hornu. The couple served as guides and confidants for the brothers, especially during the laborious launch of the business. Alphonsa united with Alphonse Delwart, a lawyer who brought to the company his expertise in inheritance and real estate matters. Elisa married Louis Semet (1844–1920), future *gérant* (managing partner) and inventor of a coke oven system that guaranteed the ammonia supply to Solvay. All of these people made up the first close-knit Solvay family circle; they were engaged in the work of the Solvay brothers and would share in the benefits of the company's future success.

Ernest and Alfred were enrolled in primary school at the family boarding school along with Louis-Philippe Acheroy. According to Acheroy, "Ernest showed great intelligence, but was of a very nervous temperament.... Alfred was calmer, more relaxed, the darling of all his friends."[5] The brothers were then placed in the Christian boarding school, Frères de la Doctrine Chrétienne, at Malonne, where their report cards demonstrated that they were gifted students.[6] It was there that Ernest "developed a taste for mechanics, chemistry and especially physics. Starting at this age, he invented, he combined all types of things that were good to do, but that we found had already been invented when we consulted our book."[7] It seems that his professor, Brother Macardus, was the one who instilled in him the taste for chemistry.[8] Although his father pushed him to study engineering at the University of Liège, Ernest's plans changed drastically when pleurisy forced him to bed and required him to continue his education by self-study.[9] Immobilized for several months between the ages of seventeen and eighteen, he never went back to his former degree plan. Alfred, for his part, obtained a diploma in geometry and land surveying. He then began chartering ships in Antwerp while Ernest resigned himself to learn accounting to keep the books for the family business. Dissatisfied with the prospect of a modest career, Ernest declared quickly that he was not ready "to

[4] ACS-O, 1001–1, Alexandre Solvay to Guillaume Nélis, 5 Oct. 1865 and 8 Nov. 1865.

[5] HC, Louis-Philippe Acheroy, Notes sur les commencements de la fabrication de sel de soude par le procédé Solvay, 1887, 1.

[6] PPSF, Box Ernest No. 1, School report cards and awards. Ernest Solvay won most of the science awards and ranked high in all disciplines.

[7] HC, Acheroy, Notes sur les commencements de la fabrication, 1.

[8] Van Belle (2010), 17–23.

[9] Among the many publications that appeared, especially upon the death of Ernest Solvay, is the biography written by two of his friends: Héger and Lefébure (1929).

remain a coffee merchant all his life"[10] – already "the Universe was occupying all of his thoughts."[11]

The initial human capital of Ernest Solvay did not ensure him an extraordinary destiny; he had no university degree and no extended network. Neither did it close any doors to him. It determined only in part his future evolution, which would be influenced by his experience – his values and education – and by his innate composition of perseverance and ambition. Soon his life would take a decisive turn with the invention of a new process for the low-cost production of soda ash, a particularly widely used and highly demanded industrial good.

The Alkali Industry in the Mid-Nineteenth Century

Soda ash has been used in its natural state since antiquity for producing glass, bleaching textiles, and making soap. In the eighteenth century, European natural soda ash, also called barilla, came especially from Alicante in Spain and Provence in France. In Brittany and Great Britain, it was brown algae, or kelp, that was used as a source of soda ash. Countries and regions that did not have these natural resources (e.g., Russia, Scandinavia, North America) imported them or replaced them with potash, which was obtained from wood ash. The unreliable supplies and growing demand added urgency to the industrial production of synthetic soda ash. The Frenchman Nicolas Leblanc (1742–1806) was the first to propose a successful means of producing soda ash from sea salt, in 1790. He achieved the direct calcination of sodium sulfate with coal and calcium carbonate through the addition of limestone in the proper proportions.

The so-called Leblanc cycle was in reality a combination of interdependent batch processes. The first phase required salt in its raw state and sulfuric acid, often made on-site. These two substances were put into a reaction in two steps in cast-iron furnaces to yield sodium sulfate (Glauber's salt) and hydrochloric-acid gas. The sodium sulfate could be used in that state by glassmakers or could be transformed into black ash by firing it with limestone and coal or coke. The black ash had to be washed with hot water to obtain a soda ash solution. This was then evaporated to obtain the soda crystals (washing soda). From these crystals, anhydrous soda ash or sodium bicarbonate could be derived, for use in the kitchen or for personal grooming. Caustic soda, with its multiple degreasing and bleaching uses, was obtained through the causticization of soda ash with lime.

As a result of the integration in one place of so many different productions, the Leblanc process became synonymous with the heavy chemical industry.[12] The French had been pioneers in the field, but from 1840, English chemical engineers contributed lasting technological advances in Great Britain, which

[10] HC, Acheroy, Notes sur les commencements de la fabrication, 2.
[11] Masson-Solvay (1915), 14.
[12] Bensaude-Vincent and Stengers (1993), 209.

TABLE 1.1. *Worldwide Leblanc Soda Ash Tonnages and Prices (1810–1863)*

Year	Total production (in tons)	Price per ton (in francs-or)
1810	10,000 to 15,000	1,500
1850	150,000	700
1863	300,000	450

Sources: Haber (1958), 10; Duchene (1995), 286–7.

rapidly became the worldwide center for soda ash.[13] In the early 1860s, 120 large and small manufacturers operated in Great Britain, clustered together near raw material sources and communication routes. The black-smoke-saturated districts of Tyneside, Merseyside, and Clydeside exported their white powder throughout all of Europe, Russia, and the United States.[14] Domestic demand was also strong because of the early industrialization of the United Kingdom. The means of transport, all of which converged toward the port of Liverpool, gave access to all the markets and enabled the importation of pyrites, from which sulfur was extracted. Coal, limestone, and salt, which had been tax exempt since 1825, were abundant and less expensive than on the Continent. The price of British soda ash dropped by approximately 66 percent between 1824 (£25) and 1861 (£8).[15] Taxes and customs duties on raw materials and processed products played a major role in international commerce. When they were high, they favored the rise of local manufacturers, whereas during laissez-faire periods, they enabled the dominant country to supply other territories. This was one of the elements that the Solvay company would later master to secure its own international domination.

The Leblanc process required a great deal of coal and was a heavy polluter, as a result of the escape of a large amount of hydrochloric acid fumes into the air and solid waste that contained sulfur compounds. Pressure from public opinion in response to this serious pollution led the British government to pass the Alkali Works Act in 1863, to abate the harmful emissions. This measure promoted research for by-product recovery processes, which would finally reinforce the competitiveness of the Leblanc manufacturers. Notably, the question of sulfur recovery attracted the attention of a young German chemist, Ludwig Mond (1839–1909), who succeeded in 1861 in selling a process for this purpose to a plant at Widnes, Great Britain, before leaving the Leblanc industry in the 1870s and becoming one of Solvay's most powerful partners, and thus the primary competitor of the Leblanc producers in Great Britain (see Chapter 2).[16]

---

[13] The Leblanc process was constantly improved thanks to engineers such as William Gossage, James Mac Tear, Henry Deacon, John Glover, and Walter Weldon. See Haber (1958), 10.

[14] Warren (1980), 39–49.

[15] Warren (1980), 41–4.

[16] Reader (1970), 39–40.

In the middle of the century, after several decades of domination by the English Leblanc soda ash, several researchers tried to develop a new process that was both an alternative and an improvement: production of soda ash with ammonia. In 1811, the French physician Augustin Fresnel had established the theoretical base for the reaction: "by treating a solution of sodium chloride with bicarbonate of ammonia, sodium bicarbonate is precipitated, while ammonium hydrochloride remains dissolved in water."[17] The Londoners Harrison Grey Dyar and John Hemming are recognized as having implemented the first application of the process on an industrial scale.[18] In 1838 and 1839, they took out patents in England and France. They established a small plant at Newton, near Liverpool, with the help of the industrialist James Muspratt, who had introduced the Leblanc process to Great Britain. The original absence of a device for recovering ammonia was rectified in a second patent granted in 1840. Dyar and Hemming had well understood the benefits of reusing the by-products of the process, but they were not able to figure out how to avoid waste, which led to the failure of their enterprise.[19] In the 1840s and 1850s, no fewer than ten entrepreneurs and chemists tried their luck.[20] In this war of patents, some of which were filed only several days apart, each one constituted a more or less important variable but none was completely successful. In most cases, it was the equipment design that was at fault, not the series of chemical operations. The primary advance during this period was the injection of carbonic acid under pressure by Henry Deacon at Widnes; however, this had to be abandoned, because he could not convince his financial partners to continue to invest.[21] In contrast to the Leblanc process, the ammonia process had to function continuously and was thus more difficult to put into operation.

In 1854, a particularly fertile year for experimentation, Théophile Schloessing and Eugène Rolland filed a patent that combined the principles of continuity, regularity, and automation of the process. To exploit it, they erected a plant at Puteaux, near Paris, which was in operation until 1858. This was the most highly developed attempt before Solvay's. Financially backed by the salt maker Ernest Daguin, they achieved a promising production rate of twenty-three

[17] Lunge and Naville (1881), 167.
[18] A. Vogel had mentioned the reaction in a memo of 1822 in Germany, and J. Thom was probably the first to produce handcrafted ammonia soda in 1836 in the Turnbull and Ramsay plant near Glasgow. See Mond (1885), 529.
[19] ACS-O, 1001-1, 1887–1889, *Mémoire sur la fabrication de la soude par le procédé dit à l'ammoniaque, par Charles Violette, E. Cornut, Poiré*, 1887. This memoir was written at the request of Ernest Solvay by independent French experts in 1887, in response to an attack by French Leblanc producers and in an effort to demonstrate that his process was distinguished from prior work on ammonia soda and could lead to economic rewards. The scientific committee in charge of studying the question sided definitively with the Solvay process.
[20] Louis Kunheim at Berlin in 1840, Paul Seybel at Vienna in 1840, Alfred Canning at Paris in 1840, an anonymous industrialist at Vilvoorde in Belgium in 1842, Henri Waterton in 1840, William Chisholm in 1852, Bowker in 1854, William Gossage and Henry Deacon in 1854 and 1855 in Great Britain, Louis Grimes at Marseilles in 1852, and Sébastien Türck near Nancy in 1854.
[21] Haber (1958), 88.

tons per month.[22] Unhappily for them, though, their process required 180 kilograms of salt per 100 kilograms of soda ash produced, compared to 150 kilograms in the Leblanc process. The process generated salt waste that was not reusable but nonetheless was taxed. A request for the repeal of this tax by Rolland to the French Public Works and Trade Ministry met with a clear refusal.[23] However, according to contemporary experts, the tax alone did not explain the lack of profitability. The design of the reaction equipment, the true heart of the process, did not enable sufficient yields.[24] Thus, between 1858 and 1861, the emergence of a profitable ammonia-soda industry no longer seemed feasible. Ernest Solvay began his work in 1859–1860, apparently unaware of what had already been accomplished by his predecessors.

Ernest Solvay as Individual Inventor

Ernest Solvay started his career thanks to support from his circle of family and friends. Guillaume Nélis, a close family friend with no children of his own, made an attractive proposal to the two brothers to take over his paper mill, to get them started. Nevertheless, a second offer made to Ernest by his uncle Florimond Semet to enter the gas company of Saint-Josse was the one he finally accepted.[25] For his part, Alfred embraced a commercial career in Hull, England. Ernest Solvay, who was expected to replace his uncle as the head of the plant, was given the job of apprentice-manager in 1859, in charge of ammonia waters and their use. He invented a means of concentrating the waters to facilitate their transportation, as well as a system of production of ammoniacal liquor (volatile alkali) based on the distillation of the concentrated waters with lime.[26] Between the ages of twenty and twenty-two, he continued his self-taught education in chemistry by reading specialized magazines, attending public courses and conferences, and visiting the Musée de l'Industrie at Brussels. One of the numerous letters he sent to his parents sheds light on the sources he used to gain information, as well as provides a description of his daily schedule, which was probably exaggerated in an effort to conform with his parents' expectations:

> I get up at 6:15 AM and am at the plant at 6:30 where I remain until 7:30. I eat with my uncle and aunt, I read a bit of the newspaper and at 8:15 I am back

---

[22] Throughout this book, the word "ton" refers to the metric ton (one thousand kilograms).

[23] *Les Soudière réunies* (1955), 12–13.

[24] Mond (1885), 530; ACS-O, 1001-1, 1887–1889; *Mémoire sur la fabrication de la soude par le procédé dit à l'ammoniaque*, 1887, 26.

[25] Since 1817, Brussels was the first city in continental Europe to light its streets using gas. The gas came from the distillation of coal, which generated ammoniacal liquors, among other by-products. At the time, the local administration was the legal entity in charge of gas distribution. The limited partnership Semet & Cie had been in existence at Saint-Josse since 1845, became a joint-stock company in 1873, and was one of the last local companies to be absorbed by a large gas group after the First World War, the Compagnie Générale du Gaz pour la France et l'Étranger. See Brion and Moreau (2005), 197.

[26] Solvay (1904), 109. Ammoniacal liquors could be used as such for washing wool, dyes, printing, degreasing fabrics, pickling of metals, production of soap, and so on.

at the plant. I work until 11:00 either inside the plant or with the workers. At 11:00 we take lunch. At noon, I am at the plant where I read works on gas, or work with chemistry until 1:00 PM. From 1 to 5:00, I oversee the workers or do office work. From 5 to 6, we eat dinner. At 6, I am back at the plant until 8. From 8 to 10, I finish reading whatever interests me in the papers (Echo du Parlement, Étoile belge, Industrie & Commerce belges, Belgique industrielle, Journal du Gaz, Science pour tous, Bulletin du Musée de l'Industrie and several others). Needless to say, I am far from having the time to contemplate politics and to read about all the murders and other newspaper items.... In the evening, I sometime go to the theater or I attend concerts of the Grande Harmonie...or I go to Mr. Robin's Gymnase polytechnique (where there are electrical machines) or sometimes I attend industrial chemical classes with Mr. Masson, or I go see the lighting devices.... On Sundays, I get up like every other day and go to the plant until 9:30 AM. I then go to mass.... In the afternoon, I take walks on the boulevards or go to the Musée de l'industrie (where I have a permanent list).[27]

While experimenting with the manufacture of sesquicarbonate of ammonia, Ernest Solvay noticed that the substance reacted with sodium carbonate to form bicarbonate of soda. It was on this occasion that he "discovered," by the end of 1860, the principle of production of soda ash with ammonia, which in fact had already been the subject of many experiments, as we have seen. On 15 April 1861, he excitedly filed his first patent, "Industrial production of soda ash with sea salt, ammonia and carbonic acid." In a style inspired by his scientific readings, he described the series of chemical reactions and the state of the substances while not being especially precise about the methods used to carry this out. However, he was already planning for uses for each of the by-products:

I send a current of ammonia gas into a concentrated solution of sea salt contained in a closed container.... Then I saturate this double solution with carbonic acid in any bubbler device.... The precipitated sodium bicarbonate is then separated from the solution by decanting, dripped, washed with clear water and then pressed to remove any water. Then it can be dried and used commercially in this state or converted into neutral soda ash through calcination in a lightly heated retort oven. The carbonic acid gas which is emitted in this case is then used for a new operation. As for dissolution of ammonium hydrochloride, it is used to reform caustic ammonia, by its mixture with lime.... I produce the carbonic acid necessary for these operations by calcination of calcium carbonate in a retort oven or an ordinary lime kiln.... The lime produced in this manner is used constantly for production of ammonia gas.... As for the sodium bicarbonate wash water, it is added to the water used to dissolve the sea salt. I reserve the right to process my liquid residue of calcium chloride.[28]

The patent was the instrument used by individual inventors to secure their discoveries and hopefully to disseminate them, through licenses or through

---

[27] PPSF, Ernest Solvay to his parents, 29 Mar. 1859.
[28] Excerpts from Belgian Patent No. 10692, filed by Ernest Solvay, dated 15 Apr. 1861.

their proprietary use. At the time, national patent systems varied greatly from one country to another. They constituted tools for economic policy, enabling each country to promote national innovation by arbitrating between protection of the inventors and dissemination of the discoveries. The Belgian patent law of 24 May 1854 gave great latitude to inventors while also requiring them to implement the discovery within a year of the patent's filing, after which it became null and void. The new patent law required no prior examination, in contrast to the situation in Great Britain, the United States, Russia, and Austria-Hungary. The person filing the patent thus claimed an invention at his own risks and perils, much like the French model. The patent publication process provided more or less discretion to inventors: some countries ensured rapid and integral publicity of innovations through official journals, whereas others, such as Belgium, simply provided access to the research and published only summaries, three months after the filing.[29]

It is rather surprising that, despite his habit of reading scientific literature and his frequent visits to the Musée de l'Industrie, Ernest had not discovered any prior patents. Scientists who were contemporaries of Solvay wrote that they found this impossible to be the case.[30] Even if doubts could legitimately subsist, there is no proof that calls into dispute Ernest Solvay's good faith when he claimed not to have been aware of the other attempts. On the contrary, he later regretted his lack of knowledge in his private correspondence.[31] Perhaps he lacked the systematic research habits of a university scholar. An additional handicap was that the patents were filed very inefficiently, without an index.[32] Moreover, the ammonia-soda process, though known, did not show up in the general chemistry treatises.[33]

An Entrepreneur Surrounded

Ernest Solvay easily convinced his brother Alfred to abandon his job in England, where he sometimes considered local commercial practices immoral. Steps were taken with the provincial administration to construct a testing station in a vacant plant on Gaucheret Street at Schaerbeek, close to Brussels. Alexandre Solvay advanced a great part of the funding necessary. Florimond Semet, who foresaw in this venture an outlet for his unused ammonia water, did not oppose the project.[34] In September, Ernest Solvay wrote to the minister of finance to obtain a salt tax exemption of up to twenty-five thousand kilos per month, to level the playing field with the Belgian Leblanc producers, who were benefiting

---

[29] Edmond Picard and Napoléon D'Hoffschmidt, *Pandectes belges*, tome 14; Brussels: Larcier, 1885, col. 399ff.

[30] Schreib (1906), 10.

[31] PPSF, Ernest Solvay to Léopold Querton, 13 Sept. 1865.

[32] ACS-O, 1001–1, Notes sur la fabrication de la soude par M. Pirmez: Historique de l'affaire, 23 June 1887, 5–6.

[33] HC, Acheroy, Notes sur les commencements de la fabrication, 2.

[34] AES, Box Z; Masson-Solvay (1915), 18.

from this exemption. His argument shows the extent to which he had already become familiar with the fundamental structure of the market:

> One understands the great importance of this soda ash production when one considers that it is used to produce sodium bicarbonate, sodium chloride (hypochlorite), caustic soda; that are used in great quantities in manufacturing of soaps, degreasing of wool, in economic household laundry, and in large proportions in the production of glass, along with sodium sulfate. All the glassmakers confirm that they would completely replace sulfate in this industry if we were able to lower the price to a certain extent. In fact, it is far more efficient since, to replace 135 kilos of sulfate in the production, all you need is 100 kg sodium carbonate and the latter can in all instances be used in place of sulfate.[35]

At the end of December, the equipment was ready to start up and Ernest Solvay wrote to his brother-in-law Léopold Querton:

> About the success of the operation in itself and the great advantage that there would be in implementing it industrially, I never once doubted and now doubt even less than before. What I cannot promise . . . is to see all of the combinations succeeding at the same time.[36]

Ernest Solvay's unshakable faith in his process is striking. However, although he was already anticipating some obstacles, he probably did not yet realize how difficult it would be to master the multitude of technical, administrative, legal, and interpersonal details to make it work. Aside from development of the process, the questions to be solved in the testing station would require numerous skills: management of supply of raw materials (e.g., salt, lime, coal, ammonia), the design, ordering and repair of mechanical devices, claims to defaulting suppliers, calculation and projection of optimal cost prices, control of operating expenses (e.g., locomotive, boiler, assistant's salary, patent rights), and so on.[37] In May 1862, his old neighbor and classmate Louis-Philippe Acheroy gave up his monastic life and entered into the service of Solvay. He became the kingpin for all the experiments, alongside Alfred Solvay. At this time, Ernest was still employed at the Gaz de Saint-Josse.

In September, production had reached scarcely three tons per month, and Alexandre Solvay's investment of BEF 35,000 ($6,650) had already been swallowed up by experiments. The plant was often shut down, and the equipment proved unreliable. The cost price was BEF 58 for one hundred kilograms of soda ash, far from the BEF 34 achieved with the Leblanc process at the time. According to Ernest's speculative calculations, a cost price of BEF 26 was feasible if the losses in ammonia could be reduced from 20 percent to 8 percent; if the distiller, drier, and decomposition equipment could be made to work

---

[35] Ernest Solvay to the minister of finance, 27 Sept. 1861. Since the 1850s, the majority of glass was made with sodium sulfate, which had supplanted the previously used sodium carbonate. Sodium carbonate was no longer used except for high-quality glass and crystal. The drop in price of sodium carbonate, due to the ammonia process, would reestablish the previous situation. See Lunge and Naville (1881), 195.

[36] HC, Ernest Solvay to Léopold Querton, 28 Dec. 1861.

[37] AES, Box Z, "Notes, citations, calculs, expériences, plans, etc. 1860–1861-1862."

FIGURE 1.2. Solvay & Cie's main initiators: on the left (from the top down): Ernest Solvay (1838–1922), Alfred Solvay (1840–1894), Louis-Philippe Acheroy (1837–1911). On the right (from the top down): Guillaume Nélis (1802–1896), Eudore Pirmez (1830–1890), Valentin Lambert (1810–1886). (Solvay Archives.)

together harmoniously; and if economies of scale could be realized through a higher production volume.[38] Reaching this cost thus remained largely conditional. Up to then, no expert had yet made a pronouncement on the viability of the industrial project.

His spirits dampened by what still seemed a pipe dream, Alexandre Solvay did not wish to continue as the sole investor. It was at this point that a second set of relations became necessary. Ernest turned to Guillaume Nélis to find not investors but industrialists who could buy and implement his process. Nélis, fifty-nine years old, a member of the House of Representatives, and a well-connected industrialist, used his network to put Ernest Solvay in contact with potential partners. The Van der Elst brothers, manufacturers of chemical products, were not interested in soda ash. Louis Denayer, a papermaker at Willebroek, thought it over and declined. Solvay had proposed transferring the patent to him and had guaranteed a cost price as low as BEF 22, in exchange for assurance of using the process on an industrial scale (three thousand tons per year), hiring his brother Alfred as production manager, allowing management by the acquiring firm of the foreign patents, participating in the earnings, and being reimbursed for costs already incurred.[39] It was finally Henri Henroz, manager of the Compagnie de Floreffe, Fabrication de Glaces et de Produits Chimiques, a Leblanc producer, with whom the negotiations went further. Before they could be concluded, Ernest Solvay had to certify the validity of his invention. He and Nélis felt it was wiser to formally ascertain that there were no previous patents on the process. After technical and commercial skills, legal services were required. Nélis advised Ernest Solvay to contact his liberal colleague in the House of Representatives, Eudore Pirmez (1830–1890), who would be one of the major forces in constitution of the company.

Ernest Solvay met Eudore Pirmez at the start of 1863. From a bourgeois family in the region of Charleroi, Pirmez had begun a career as a corporate lawyer in which he had forged a solid reputation. Among the cases that he had handled was one regarding hydrochloric acid pollution by the Floreffe Company; during that case he became familiar with the alkali industry. Although he would dedicate considerable time to the development of Solvay throughout his life, he would also distinguish himself by board memberships in railroad and coal companies, and especially as director of the Banque Nationale (1877–1890), as member of Parliament (1857–1890), as minister of the interior (1868–1870), and as minister of state (1884–1890).[40] His financial and legal expertise, as well as his political connections, would serve the cause of Solvay, even if his differences in viewpoints with Ernest Solvay on industrial and financial questions would erupt from time to time to disturb the normal course of business (see Chapter 3).

---

[38] AES, Box Z, memo from Ernest Solvay, 30 Sept. 1862.
[39] AES, Box Z, draft of a contract with the Denayer Company, handwritten by Ernest Solvay, n.d. [1862].
[40] Delaet and Montens (1996), 515–17.

New research into the collections of the Musée de l'Industrie finally revealed the existence of previous patents from Sébastien Türck and from Harrison Grey Dyar and John Hemming.[41] The lack of validity of Solvay's initial patent caused an immediate rupture in relations with the Compagnie de Floreffe. The story would of course have been different if Ernest Solvay had simply sold the rights for the process to that firm. He became even more demoralized when he discovered the bankruptcy of Schloessing and Rolland, the first ones to truly attempt industrial application of the process. Eudore Pirmez, though, found a reason for hope: "If someone risked 1,500,000 francs [US$285,000] to implement this reaction, the success would be of great value," he alleged.[42] Because selling a nonprotected process was no longer an option, the solution was to create a company, based on a new patent drawn up so as to protect the succession of equipment and operations rather than the principle itself. That was the advice that Pirmez gave to Solvay,[43] who diligently began describing in scrupulous detail his system by comparing it with those of his predecessors. The elements of the gas being absorbed by a liquid, pressure, conveying distance, gas division, inverse operation of the gas and liquid, absence of a vacuum in the equipment, and cooling all made the second Solvay patent untouchable.[44] It was filed successively in Belgium (12 September 1863), in France (12 November 1863), and in England (11 December 1863).

Ernest Solvay was aware of the difficulty of raising the funds needed for an enterprise this risky. At the request of Nélis, he estimated the capital necessary at about BEF 100,000 (US$19,000), which would soon prove inadequate. The trio immediately set out to find investors. The chemist Louis Melsens, professor at the veterinary school of Cureghem, seemed to be interested but could not come up with the money.[45] Approached about being hired as a salaried chemist, he never formally entered the service of Ernest Solvay, but he kept up technical correspondence with him for more than twenty years. The powerful glassmaking and chemical company of Saint-Gobain refused any interest in the process despite approaches by Pirmez, which is quite ironic, as Solvay would later become one of the most feared competitors of the French company.[46] Eudore Pirmez remained convinced of the potential of the business and would not give up. He persuaded his colleague Gustave Sabatier (1819–1894), liberal deputy of Charleroi, as well as several members of his family to contribute to start-up capital. His father, Léonard Pirmez (1798–1866); his aunt Hyacinthe Pirmez (1805–1879); and his father-in-law, the glassmaker Valentin Lambert (1810–1886), also joined in. The Solvay family remained on

[41] Solvay (1904), 110.

[42] ACS-O, 1001–1, Notes sur la fabrication de la soude par M. Pirmez: Historique de l'affaire, 23 June 1887, 7.

[43] PPSF, Eudore Pirmez to Ernest Solvay, 7 Sept. 1863.

[44] Significantly, Ernest Solvay, in his Belgian Patent No. 14995, dated 12 Sept. 1863, "for equipment practically realizing direct production of soda ash," described his invention as follows: "the patent that I claim does not focus on this reaction . . . known for a long time, but rather on the equipment that enables its advantageous use on an industrial scale."

[45] PPSF, Guillaume Nélis to Ernest Solvay, 3 July 1863.

[46] Daviet (1989), 124–48.

its guard, following the advice of uncle Florimond Semet, who was in the best position to judge the feasibility of the project and saw absolutely no chance of success.[47] Formation of capital was thus fairly typical for a small company in an underdeveloped sector. Solvay would not be propelled by Brussels high finance but by the bourgeoisie of the Charleroi region, who were in one way or another familiar with the alkali business. Established and wealthy even before the Industrial Revolution, the Lambert and Pirmez families stemmed from the glassmaking tradition. Nélis was involved in papermaking, and Sabatier was a champion of economic liberalism, combining political duties and board memberships in iron, coal, and railroad companies.[48] The Solvay brothers did not exactly belong to this set. Their father was active in small business and quarries, activities peripheral to the Industrial Revolution.

The choice of land for the building of the plant naturally went toward the Charleroi area – the stronghold of the main investors. At first, Jemappes, in the Borinage basin, had been considered for its proximity to the limestone quarries.[49] Léopold Querton and Adèle Solvay might have helped the Solvay brothers with their knowledge of the region. However, it was the site of Couillet, near Charleroi, that was selected. The site offered direct access to roads, railways, and the Sambre River, and it was located at the heart of one of the world centers for window glass, which exported up to 95 percent of production.[50] Aside from salt, raw materials were close at hand. The immediate industrial environment, composed of ironworks and coal mines, gave the region the look of a dense and productive cluster. Valentin Lambert, an established industrialist, often served as a relay and adviser on practical issues regarding construction of the plant, coal supplies, and building relationships with local authorities.[51]

A final obstacle had to be overcome before the constitution of the company: the salt tax, from which the Leblanc producers had been exempt. The exemption was indeed granted to Solvay as a result of the good relations that Nélis, Pirmez, and Sabatier had with the powerful liberal finance minister Walthère Frère-Orban, and despite the notice issued by his administration that the enterprise had been declared "devoid of any chance of success."[52]

Solvay & Cie was formally founded on 26 December 1863, in a favorable economic context and a wide-open national market. On the one hand, economic liberalism promoted the creation of numerous enterprises in many industries.[53] On the other hand, the Belgian chemical industry was underdeveloped until the 1850s or 1860s, in contrast to other key sectors of the Industrial Revolution such as mining, textile, iron, and glass. At the most, the chemical

[47] Masson-Solvay (1915), 21.
[48] Kurgan-van Hentenryk (1996), 539–40.
[49] PPSF, Eudore Pirmez to Ernest Solvay, 7 Sept. 1863.
[50] Delaet (1986), 119.
[51] As is shown in his correspondence with Ernest Solvay (ACS-O and PPSF).
[52] ACS-O, 1001–1, Notes sur la fabrication de la soude par M. Pirmez: Historique de l'affaire, 23 June 1887, 8.
[53] Gadisseur (1981), 51–70.

industry was an auxiliary one characterized by a largely negative commercial balance.[54] Most imports of soda ash and rock salt came from Great Britain, through the port of Antwerp. The shipments from the Rhine entered through Liège, and the Kuhlmann Company supplied the French border region from Lille.[55] The major Belgian manufactured goods, designed for the local market, were sulfuric acid from roasting of pyrites, soaps, alum from la Meuse, and the gas produced from the distillation of coal. Chemical factories more closely resembled disorganized industrial kitchens than true plants.[56] The industrial census of 1846 revealed that less than thirty out of the 417 chemical factories had a steam engine and that the average number of workers per plant was only 3.5.[57] Some modestly sized Leblanc plants, often combined with plate-glass works, had been erected after 1840 at Moustier, Aiseau, Vedrin, Floreffe, and Saint-Gilles.[58] In 1850, they were producing four thousand tons a year of soda ash, or 2.5 percent of worldwide production. In terms of raw materials, Belgian subsoil was rich in coal, minerals, and limestone, and the gas plants could furnish ammonia, but the country lacked rock salt, which posed a significant problem for the development of an alkali industry. This situation made it difficult to launch a business in the chemical sector, but it did have the advantage of an open field in terms of competition. Solvay thus had time available for trial and error. The company would probably not have survived in the shadow of a giant like the one it would become.

Solvay was set up in the form of a limited partnership (*société en commandite par actions*).[59] It was only a start-up, though, and available funds were still too limited to even imagine a joint-stock company, the creation of which was still subject to government approval. In a partnership, the *gérants commandités* (managing partners) risked their own personal fortunes, whereas the *commanditaires* (silent partners) limited their losses to the venture capital they invested. A favorable but not anticipated consequence of this type of family-owned private company was that it did not require that the annual figures be published. This enabled Solvay to grow discreetly, without revealing to the world the extent of its earnings.

According to estimates by Ernest Solvay, the start-up capital amounted to BEF 136,000 (US$25,840), with 136 shares each worth BEF 1,000 divided into two categories. The Solvay brothers received 34 shares financed in exchange

---

54 Duchene (1995), 289.

55 Haber (1958), 43.

56 Landes (2003), 185–6.

57 Duchene (1995), 287.

58 Hauzeur de Fooz (1951), 1.

59 In 1863, there were three types of companies possible: a private company (*société en nom collectif*), in which all the associates together were liable; the limited partnership (*société en commandite*), contracted by active partners who were liable with their own fortunes and sleeping (or silent) partners, who provided financial backing but whose responsibility was limited to the amount they contributed; and a joint-stock company (*société anonyme*), in which each associate's liability was limited to his or her contribution, and in which the liability of the managers was also limited to the execution of the mandate received.

for their tangible (receivables and debts from the testing station) and intangible (patents and process) contributions. The silent partners divided up 102 shares of preferred stock. Among them, Guillaume Nélis held the largest individual portion (25 shares), but the Pirmez and Lambert families together held 49 percent of the company (20 shares for Hyacinthe Pirmez, 23 for Léonard Pirmez, 12 for Eudore Pirmez, and 12 for Valentin Lambert). Sabatier took 10 shares. The initial contract, drawn up by Eudore Pirmez and based on proposals by Ernest Solvay, allocated a monthly salary of BEF 2,500 (US$475) to Alfred for his active management. Ernest, who remained manager of the Gaz de Saint-Josse, did not receive any compensation. A supervisory board composed of Pirmez, Nélis, and Sabatier was established to audit the books, but the board could not modify the articles of association without the votes of a *gérant*. A share-withdrawal clause prohibiting access to third parties locked the shareholding structure of the company. The spirit of the articles of association aimed to reward the *gérants* proportionately to their success. They received progressive percentages of earnings, as well as the right to subscribe to one share on three in case of a new issue, beyond their normal rights as shareholders. Distribution of earnings was done in four stages: the silent partners' shares were first, taking 8 percent of earnings; 8 percent then went to the *gérant* shares; the progressive percentage was granted to the *gérants* in a third stage;[60] and the remaining income was then distributed equally among all shares. For the *gérants*, the risk was high, with fixed compensation relatively low and their economic and social success strongly tied to the process.

1.2   A DIFFICULT START FOR THE COUILLET PLANT

Workshop Culture and Empirical Method

The Solvay plant at Couillet developed on the basis of a workshop culture, far from the images of a science-based industry that are sometime projected by the key sectors of the so-called Second Industrial Revolution, such as organic chemistry, electricity, and telecommunications. It would be misleading to take the early days of the ammonia-soda industry as a case history of this new business model that would implement industrial research to introduce new processes, in the style of the German dyestuffs industry at the end of the nineteenth century. In other words, the Solvay brothers started out not in a laboratory wearing white coats but rather amid grease and smoke. They proceeded largely by trial and error, much like Nicolas Leblanc three-quarters of a century earlier. The new process was more in keeping with an extension of the first wave of industrialization. It constituted an improvement – radical,

---

[60] The managing partners were given one-tenth of earnings that exceeded 10 percent of capital, two-tenths of earnings that exceeded 20 percent of capital, and three-tenths of earnings that exceeded 30 percent of capital.

to be sure – of an existing process, and Solvay would try desperately to improve all the details. However, their initial attempts almost ended in bankruptcy.

The daily correspondence between Alfred at Couillet and Ernest at Saint-Josse is the best record of the litany of setbacks during the first year of the company's existence. Moreover, Ernest's letters sent to his sister Aurélie and his mother serve as a barometer of the stakeholders' confidence. It is fascinating to observe the Solvay family's romantic and romanticized version of the two brothers' struggle, from the brothers' own narrative. The image of heroic inventor was not only constructed ex post but also in real time by the principal protagonists. This image was reinforced by the fact that the family and business correspondence were completely integrated. Private letters contained production figures and health reports, technical details, and family events. Even the important dates coincided: Ernest Solvay married a few weeks after the establishment of the company. His daughter Jeanne was born at the start of construction of the first plant, and his son Armand was born just before a crucial decision to abandon or continue with the business.

The first stone at the Couillet plant was laid on 14 March 1864, but the first technical tests did not take place until January 1865. Meanwhile, the expenditures had already exceeded forecasts. An additional payment of BEF 39,000 (US$7,400) was requested from partners. New capital was injected by Jean Pirmez, uncle of Eudore; Arthur Hochereau, nephew of Sabatier, manager of the mechanical construction shop of Haine-Saint-Pierre, and supplier of Solvay; and Léopold Querton, brother-in-law of Ernest Solvay. At the plant, the steam engines, turbines, buckets, lime kilns, drier, and distiller did not prove reliable. There was frequent turnover in the poorly trained personnel, who struggled to understand instructions from the *gérants*.[61] There was still a considerable amount of ammonia lost and an uncertain supply of it, despite a contract that had been entered into in 1863 with the gas plant at Brussels. In addition, the primary concern was the central equipment, which carbonated the ammonia brine. The baffles that made up the equipment were supposed to enable a long conveyance for the reactive substances, but the horizontal trajectory of the liquid resulted in the formation of carbonate agglomerates, which systematically clogged the equipment and blocked the entire process. Repeated shutdowns ruined any hope of mass production. After several months, production rose to three hundred kilograms of soda ash per day, far from the twelve tons per day expected by Ernest Solvay.[62]

In spite of this, the absolute confidence of Ernest Solvay in the quality of his process did not wane. His power of persuasion was still intact in mid-1865. He already envisioned, in a report to the supervisory board, the construction of plants in France and England, once the process was perfected.[63] However, the company's prospects of success were scarce. Pirmez had proposed to his parliamentary colleague Édouard Jaequemyns that he issue an opinion based

[61] AES, Box Z, Ernest Solvay to the Conseil de Surveillance, 27 June 1865.
[62] HC, Acheroy, Notes sur les commencements de la fabrication, 3.
[63] AES, Box Z, Ernest Solvay to the Conseil de Surveillance, 27 June 1865.

on an expert report by the prominent chemist Jean Stas. Their judgment on the venture was final:

> In sum, what do you have? A principle that cannot be patented, equipment which is patented but which, without exception, is unreliable. There remains the hope of perfecting the equipment, but to do this, it must be made larger and more complex. Let us assume that success will be obtained at this price, which seems extremely doubtful to me. But even in this case, I do not predict a lasting success, due to the probable increase in the price of ammonia.[64]

Despair finally prevailed in October and November 1865. Attempts to entice new investors – the industrialists Hector Sadin and Jules Letoret from Borinage and the glassmakers Casimir Lambert and Dominique Jonet from Charleroi – had failed again. A debt of BEF 115,000 (US$21,850), for which the *gérants* were personally responsible, had accumulated, unbeknownst to the family. Florimond Semet, unhappy about the time Ernest was spending on his own business, relieved him of his duties at Gaz de Saint-Josse, thereby making Ernest's financial situation precarious. Ernest Solvay confided in his sister:

> My situation is comparable to that of a man who is loaded with a 100-kilo sack and finds himself in the middle of a swamp with no exit in sight, sinking up to his knees and from which he absolutely has to escape. I have no more determination, honestly.[65]

Suicide was even feared by his relatives.[66] Confidence was eroding among the associates. The partners balked at signing blank checks in the absence of tangible results: "you have to understand that your hesitations contributed in no small part to putting off your backers and that you would need a success to inspire confidence in them."[67] Ernest Solvay, low on means, felt abandoned by his shareholders and blamed himself for having voluntarily underestimated the amount of initial capital: "the process will break through, about that I have no doubt, but perseverance is still needed . . . Success depends uniquely now on the financial backers."[68]

The Pirmez family was also putting pressure on Eudore, who had brought his relatives along into the venture. Bankruptcy was considered, despite the stain that it would leave on the reputation of the partners' families. Ernest Solvay's mother, in charge of the family accounts, resigned herself to organizing the failure in a way that would not compromise the future of her other children.[69] But when the Solvay parents learned that their sons were personally responsible for the debts incurred, it was agreed with the partners to try "a final test

---

[64] Édouard Jaequemyns to Eudore Pirmez, 22 Sept. 1865. Pirmez had insisted that Jaequemyns, his wealthy liberal colleague in Parliament and former chemistry professor, give an enlightened opinion on the process, to interest him in the affair and possibly to entice other investors through his support.

[65] PPSF, Ernest Solvay to his older sister Aurélie, 15 Nov. 1865.

[66] Masson-Solvay (1915), 34.

[67] PPSF, Valentin Lambert to Ernest Solvay, undated [around Oct. 1865].

[68] PPSF, Ernest Solvay to Léopold Querton, 3 Oct. 1865.

[69] PPSF, Adèle Hulin (Ernest's mother) to Aurélie Solvay, 29 Sept. 1865.

before bankruptcy." The silent partners got the upper hand in negotiations, and Alexandre Solvay had no other solution to reduce the debt than to pay out BEF 41,000 (US$7,800) borrowed from Hyacinthe Pirmez. Contributions from the silent partners would serve to acquire equipment with new designs. The associates, heavily involved despite their respective individual careers, had been making great efforts for several months to design a practical solution to the primary technical problem. There was the idea to replace the inefficient reaction equipment with small bubblers in series, thus allowing separate washing and no longer requiring a complete shutdown of the system. According to several sources, Nélis, Pirmez, Acheroy, and Ernest Solvay contributed to the design of this collective innovation, which proved a determining factor in the company's survival.[70] This equipment, arranged horizontally, was later stacked vertically: the famous Solvay column.

The new arrangements of the company had to be part of an updated contract for association. Whereas the articles of association of 1863 were full of optimism (compensation proportional to earnings, which were considered immediate), those of 1866 reflected a more defensive posture. To reduce the amount of debt on the balance sheet, it was agreed, not without bitterness, that twenty-four shares would be withdrawn from the *gérants*.[71] Their rights of subscription in the case of new issues of shares would be limited to one-sixth instead of one-third. In contrast, fixed compensation and a lodging allowance were granted. The *gérants* would also collect 19 percent of the earnings and maintain a graduated percentage. Any distinction between shares had ended. The capital was increased to BEF 205,000 (US$39,000) through the increase of Alexandre Solvay's holdings to 20 percent (41 shares of 205) and by Édouard Fauconnier, an industrial neighbor in Couillet and friend of the Pirmez family, who invested BEF 5,000. The Pirmez and Lambert families together held the majority of the shares (114 of 205). The supervisory board included Valentin Lambert and Édouard Fauconnier, chosen because of their industrial knowledge and geographic proximity.

The Light at the End of the Column

After the painful start-up (1864–1866) came four years, from 1867 to 1870, of fragile stabilization, during which doubts were only slowly overcome. Ernest Solvay worked daily at the plant at Couillet, together with his brother Alfred, Louis-Philippe Acheroy, and a half dozen workers.[72] The latter were poorly qualified and poorly paid, and it was difficult to establish their loyalty, given the low wages.[73] No respite was allowed: the cost price had to drop enough

---

[70] PPSF, Guillaume Nélis to Ernest Solvay, 11 Feb. 1865; ACS-O, 1001–1, Notes sur la fabrication de la soude par M. Pirmez: Historique de l'affaire, 23 June 1887, 38–9; Memo from Ernest Solvay to Édouard Jaequemyns on improvements to be made to the process, 4 Sept. 1865.

[71] Masson-Solvay (1915), 29.

[72] ACS, Register of employee records from Couillet 1867–1920.

[73] ACS, AG, Gérance report 1867.

to become competitive with Leblanc soda ash and to establish Solvay as a major producer of ammonia soda. The Kunheim Company of Berlin, a failed experimenter with the ammonia process in the 1840s, showed interest in 1866 in taking out a Solvay license for Prussia. It was too soon. Ernest Solvay did not wish to export his method before it was perfected.[74]

At Couillet, the implementation of bubblers in a horizontal series was temporarily effective, but the generally poor quality of the other equipment still caused shutdowns. Complete refurbishing of the equipment was required, despite the heavy investments needed and the limited resources available. It was at this price that the output regularly improved: from one ton per day in April 1866 to one and a half tons in June 1867, two tons in January 1868, and three tons in December 1868.[75] The problems of obstruction in the bubblers were finally resolved by stacking them in a vertical, ringed column, in which the ammonia brine was introduced and came into contact with the ascending carbonic acid gas for a longer period of time. The different stages were separated by convex and perforated screens, thus enabling good diffusion of the gas.

Columns had been used to distill alcohol and ammonia, but they never had been applied to the production of soda ash. This was a critical factor in fixing the technical superiority of the Solvay process over those of competitors. Indeed, during the following two decades, rival ammonia soda processes were invented. The designs of Jules Boulouvard in France, of James Young in England, and especially of Moritz Hönigmann in Germany were implemented, but without attaining a similar yield.[76] The development of the Solvay column was far from immediate: it took several years to refine the concept and regulate the device. The progress made in the areas of mechanical construction, air pumps, and metal alloys went hand in hand with these incremental developments. A second production unit, financed by the issue of thirty-one shares each worth BEF 1,500, began in 1870. With five columns, the production at Couillet leapt from 941 tons to 1,855 tons annually between 1869 and 1871.[77]

In addition, fears about ammonia supplies were resolved with the construction, wherever possible, of concentration workshops adjoining gas plants. This method ensured a continuous supply to Solvay while reducing transportation costs, as a watery solution was no longer sent, only concentrated ammonia. The first supply plant was built in the city of Brussels in 1867, although the neighbors had filed a claim for damages. A second plant was erected at Forest the following year, and then a series of others at Tournai in Belgium, and at Saint-Omer, Valenciennes, Dunkerque, Cambrai, and Arras, in the north of France.[78]

---

[74] ACS-O, 1001–1, Historique de la Société Solvay, Ernest Solvay to Guillaume Nélis, 18 May 1866 and 25 Oct. 1866; ACS, AG, Gérance report, 25 May 1868.

[75] HC, Acheroy, Notes sur les commencements de la fabrication, 4–5.

[76] Schreib (1906), 135–53.

[77] ART-PDO, Solvay & Cie.

[78] ACS, AG, Gérance reports from 1867 to 1870.

Technical stabilization in the process was also achieved through early relationships between Ernest Solvay and renowned scientists. In the same manner that Ernest Solvay had often reaped the benefits of his partners' political, industrial, and commercial relationships, he knew to surround himself with industrial consultants before doing so had become a widespread practice. It has already been noted that he came to know professors at schools and public conferences, that Louis Melsens had become a regular correspondent, and that he consulted with Jean Stas and Édouard Jaequemyns. Ernest Solvay had also informed Henri Bergé of the progress of his work. This chemistry and physics professor at the public school in Brussels, and future rector of the Université Libre de Bruxelles, had conducted some quality control tests on the soda ash produced in the first years of the company.[79] The famous German chemist August Kekulé, founder of the first research laboratory at a Belgian university, exchanged several letters with Ernest Solvay in which the attraction was clearly mutual. In March 1867, Solvay had taken the initiative to contact the scholar, then professor of chemistry at Ghent. Two years later, Kekulé, having returned to Bonn, indicated his intrigue with the mysterious Solvay, who seemed to have succeeded in his ammonia-soda process. Kekulé, with sufficient credibility so as to obtain information, inquired about the development of the company. Solvay, not wanting to miss the opportunity, responded: "if the relationships that you must have abroad (England, Prussia, France) put you in a position to be able to inform me about companies which would be most likely to use my process, I would be extremely grateful."[80] At this stage, these relationships had more to do with personal connections than with a systematic collaborative enterprise. Nonetheless, they were part of a gradual convergence, under the influence of the German model, of the science of universities and industries; they laid the groundwork for the first forms of applied research.[81]

In 1868, Solvay was already the primary soda ash manufacturer in the country, but the flow of casks of soda ash remained problematic. The commercial strategy was elaborated parallel to an increase in tonnage. The Leblanc soda ash, whose price had regularly dropped over the decades, was well positioned in the market. Also, at the beginning, Solvay produced only soda ash, whereas the Leblanc manufacturers also produced sulfate, soda crystals, caustic soda, bicarbonate, and chlorine. The higher purity of the Solvay soda ash was only a relative advantage, to the extent that some of the smaller industrial customers valued price over quality.[82] The absence of causticity was also an obstacle to the introduction of Solvay's soda ash with bleachers and papermakers, who were obliged to causticize it before use. The English soda ash producers thus continued to supply the Belgian market, particularly the Flemish textile

---

[79] AFi, Livre journal 1865; PPSF, Ernest Solvay to Henri Bergé, 22 Sept. 1868; Bolle (1963), 122–3.

[80] PPSF, Ernest Solvay to August Kekulé, 16 Jan. 1869.

[81] Bertrams (2006), 50–2.

[82] ACS, AG, Gérance report 1867.

sector.[83] The glassmakers, who still preferred sodium sulfate over sodium carbonate, also had local suppliers, the small Belgian soda ash works next to the glass factories, such as Floreffe, Sainte-Marie d'Oignies, and Moustier. Solvay entered the Belgian market by articulating his commercial policy around two factors: the demonstration that his soda ash could advantageously replace the old product in various productions and an obsessive policy of dropping cost and sale prices.

Communication with professionals was first done through personal contacts, especially by Ernest Solvay and Guillaume Nélis, and was later complemented by local sales agents, who served as intermediaries, thus depriving the supplier of a direct contact with the consumer industries. Among the first Solvay customers were the papermaker Denayer; the glassmakers Baudoux, Herbutte, Jonet, Casimir Lambert, and Moustier; and the Fabrique Belge des Laines Peignées at Verviers.[84] On another level, Solvay started to show at national and international industrial fairs, the most prestigious media of the times. The company was present at the 1867 World's Exhibition in Paris, the fourth of its kind. Solvay obtained an encouraging bronze medal but attracted little attention, as the report of the international jury forgot to mention the company, assessing that "the attempt by which it was hoped to directly and economically produce soda ash by working with sea salt and ammonium carbonate, appears to have been abandoned."[85] Schloessing and Rolland neither knew anything about the Belgian inventor nor mentioned him in their memoir on the production of ammonia soda of 1868.[86] Accolade would have to wait.

The cost price began to drop rapidly: from BEF 265 per ton in 1866 to BEF 210 in 1867. The sale price followed the same curve, going respectively from BEF 345 to BEF 290 per ton.[87] That was only the start. The differential left an appreciable margin. In financial terms, losses were entirely offset to allow for the first earnings, of BEF 1,181, in 1867. In 1868, earnings of BEF 5,582 enabled payment of the first dividend of BEF 50 per share, compensating the patience of the shareholders. The next year, on earnings of BEF 61,000, BEF 42,000 were put in reserve and the associates shared BEF 19,000. Working capital was constituted. This was the inauguration by the *gérants* of a policy to reinvest a great part of the earnings into the business, through depreciation and reserves, instead of realizing immediate profits. The amount of debt was brought down to reasonable proportions, but borrowing from bankers was still considered excessive by the supervisory board. From then on, the firm would have greater independence from banks, preferring direct borrowing from corporate associates. The silent partners agreed with this conservative strategy of self-financing, because they felt the consequences would be great. Ernest Solvay, who had to accept unfavorable conditions for the *gérants*

[83] ACS-O, 1001–1, Historique de la Société Solvay, Ernest Solvay to Guillaume Nélis, 24 June 1868.
[84] AFi, Livre journal 1865 à 1868.
[85] *Exposition Universelle de Paris* (1868).
[86] Schloessing and Rolland (1868), 5–63.
[87] ART-PDO, Solvay & Cie; ACS, AG, Gérance reports 1866 to 1871.

during the renegotiation of the contract in 1866, had regained the psychological advantage. The share of the capital held by the Solvay brothers and their family (30 percent of BEF 250,000 in 1869) would gradually increase (see Chapter 3). In 1870, finances were stabilized and confidence had returned. Solvay was ready to take the next step: the conquest of the industrialized world.

FIGURE 2.1. Syracuse works of the Solvay Process Company (United States): the first ammonia soda plant on American soil started its production in 1884. In this picture (ca. 1913), Syracuse had already become the largest soda ash plant in the world. (Solvay Archives.)

2

A Multinational Pioneer

Even before success in its native country was assured, Solvay aspired to establish itself on the major European markets.[1] At the start of the 1870s, the ammonia-soda process was functional but not exactly mature. The company had no experience in either mass production or international commerce. Because it preferred borrowing from its few silent partners, its financial resources were limited. Nonetheless, the company had already been forced to think about transnational possibilities. Its competitors in Belgium were English, and the race to file patents would be an issue in all industrialized countries. Also, the ammonia-soda industry's fundamental basis was different from the Leblanc industry's. England was the country ideally suited for Leblanc, given its concentration of know-how and capital, and especially the advantageous conditions for maritime transport and raw materials. In the case of the ammonia-soda process, sulfur did not enter into consideration, and fuel consumption was less by almost half. It was just the opposite for salt, of which large amounts were needed; finding a location near a salt deposit was a top priority, whereas the distance from other sources seemed hardly as important.[2] In this new configuration, competing ammonia-soda processes could emerge in other countries. Solvay thus had no alternative but to protect its invention everywhere simultaneously and to quickly enter into production on the major markets.

Between 1870 and 1890, Solvay became one of the first multinational companies to be established in Continental Europe, Great Britain, Russia, and the United States, all at the same time. This early internationalization took place in two clearly identifiable phases. In the 1870s, Solvay turned toward countries that bordered Belgium, which were primary worldwide markets. In France, the company built its own plant; in England, it began operations through licensing; in Germany, it took over an existing plant. These three tactics would prove at times slow and costly and at other times uncertain. On the basis of these initial hesitations, Solvay changed its strategy in the 1880s and opted for the constitution of companies in fairly close partnerships with local entrepreneurs in Russia, the United States, and Austria-Hungary, and it turned to this solution in England and Germany. This new expansion model proved much more rapid, efficient, and profitable. Its backbone was continuous research to achieve technical supremacy in the area of soda ash, because without maintaining its

---

[1] AES, Box Z, Note from Ernest Solvay to the Conseil de Surveillance, 27 June 1865.
[2] Warren (1980), 103.

technical advantage, the fortress could easily turn into a house of cards. All other issues were relegated to second place, especially production of chlorine and caustic soda, as well as the administrative and commercial organization. Among all the competences required, engineers took precedence over chemists, financial managers, and lawyers.

2.1   EXPERIMENTING WITH THREE STRATEGIES OF INTERNATIONALIZATION (1870s)

Dombasle, the Model Plant

Shortly before the outbreak of the Franco-Prussian War on 19 July 1870, the Solvay brothers and Eudore Pirmez had begun preliminary research on installation of a soda ash plant in France.[3] Aside from the geographic proximity and cultural similarities, interest in their large neighbor stemmed from the rich salt deposits and the significant demand for soda ash by the glass and soap makers. At this time, about thirty small Leblanc plants, spread throughout northeastern France and in the region of Marseilles, were producing between fifty thousand and sixty thousand tons of alkalis. The major plants were held by Saint-Gobain, the Soudières du Midi, and Kuhlmann. The war, which ended on 19 May 1871, deferred but did not stop the Solvay project. After multiplying contacts and exploring land near Lyons and Nancy, the Belgian entrepreneurs opted for the town of Varangéville-Dombasle in Lorraine. Its location appeared to be particularly advantageous, in terms of both raw materials and means of communication. The salt deposits scattered across the region were exploited through underground mines at Varangéville or by pumping brine at Dombasle and at La Madeleine. The Lorraine salt market was controlled and locked by a cartel of ten salt makers, created in 1863 at Nancy. From the start of its activities at Couillet, Solvay had been supplied Lorraine salt, in particular through Daguin & Cie.[4] This supply would continue until Solvay began purchasing its own concessions in the region and established its own saltworks at Flainval (1879), Crévic (1882), and Haraucourt (1902). The company thus added an activity to its portfolio by upstream integration, and at the same time it stirred up the defensive reflexes of the saltworks already in place. In fact, the cartel tried every way possible, both direct and underhanded, to oppose Solvay's initiatives in the salt industry. This was in vain, though, because the Belgian company offered a significant national market for Lorraine salt and consequently received the support of the national authorities. Investments in salt deposits also offered to Solvay a way to dissuade, or even retaliate against, the salt producers that had harbored the idea of establishing rival soda ash plants.

---

[3] This section on France draws largely on Mioche (2008).

[4] AFi, Livre journal 1865 à 1868. Daguin & Cie and Solvay were on good terms. In February 1870, Daguin provided Solvay with a series of communications on the competition and raw materials in the Nancy region. PPSF, Box Ernest Solvay 2, Dombasle, Ernest Daguin to Ernest Solvay, 14 Feb. 1870.

In addition to salt, the lime necessary for the production of soda ash was available in quarries located within a radius of fifty to sixty kilometers, and German coke could be brought in from Sarrebruck by rail and water. Early on, the ammonia was produced in a small gas plant built on-site. The location, connected to roads and to the Paris-Strasbourg rail line and the Marne-Rhine canal, was ideally situated. The Meurthe, a free-flowing river, could be used for spillover of waste. A final criterion for location was only partially fulfilled: proximity with industries that consumed soda ash. Although Dombasle was in fact near Lorraine glassmakers, the primary centers of French consumption were in Paris, Lyons, and Marseilles.[5] Dombasle would thus be doing business long distance.

To finance the considerable investments needed for this giant plant, the *gérants* proposed that they get the capital needed through two successive loans of BEF 600,000 (US$114,000) from the silent partners. The partners, reassured by the progress of the business, agreed to the loans without blinking an eye. This contribution proved necessary, as the budget, first estimated at BEF 300,000, was nearly tripled (BEF 861,000, or US$163,500) for construction of the plant in its initial dimensions. The job of construction and development was given to Prosper Hanrez (1842–1920). This mining engineer had begun his career in the family's mechanical workshop, Hanrez & Cie, in the region of Charleroi. He had then worked as an engineer with the Chemins de Fer du Centre, and later as a manager at the Société des Charbonnages Unis at Couillet. As an inventor, he had filed several patents for coal driers, boilers, and train-coupling systems. He met the Solvay brothers when they called on Hanrez & Cie to construct their plant at Couillet. He was hired by Solvay on 24 March 1873 at a salary of BEF 10,000 (US$1,900) per month, plus 2 percent of the plant's earnings and costs associated with his job.[6] Under his impetus, Dombasle became, for a while, the largest soda ash plant in the world. From the beginning of the project, it was designed to hold up to eight production units in parallel; Couillet had only two.[7] Hanrez designed the plans for the plant, worked with local authorities to ensure smooth implementation, and rapidly established a working network of Lorraine decision makers. The installation file was approved by the French authorities about ten months after the application request, which had been introduced by Ernest Solvay on 4 October 1872. As Philippe Mioche points out, this rapid response illustrates the determination of the public authorities to support Lorraine industrialization.[8] Afterward, Hanrez turned out to be a pivotal figure in Solvay's international development. He took over the design of the foreign plants and the different financial structures for each subsidiary, over which he exercised real authority, alongside the Solvay brothers. De facto *gérant*, he was formally acknowledged in this post in 1880, receiving as

---

[5] ACS, 1029–18, La politique commerciale des frères Solvay, 1938.

[6] PPSF, Box Ernest Solvay 2, Contrat Prosper Hanrez, 24 Mar. 1873; Brion (1996), 350–1.

[7] ACS, AG, Gérance report, 26 May 1874. After the start-up of the first unit in December 1874, the following units came on line at regular intervals: August 1876, April 1877, March 1878, October 1879, September 1880, and October 1882.

[8] Mioche (2008), 13.

additional remuneration, 2 percent of the overall earnings. He held that position at Dombasle until his repatriation to the Central Administration in Brussels in 1883. Other engineers at Dombasle would become major players, too. Among them was Édouard Hannon (1853–1931), hired in 1876 as a technical engineer in Lorraine before going to Brussels in 1883 to organize and become the head of the Central Technical Department. He was appointed *gérant* in 1907 and held that position until 1925.

Solvay rapidly carved out a lion's share of the French soda ash market, with production at Dombasle surpassing twenty-five thousand tons in 1880, fifty thousand tons in 1884, and one hundred thousand tons in 1889.[9] Approximately 70 percent of the production was sold domestically. The rest was exported, which enabled France to reinstate a positive trade balance for soda ash. Some competitors reoriented their activities or merged. In the middle of the 1880s, eight Leblanc producers remained in operation (Saint-Gobain, Kulhmann, Pechiney, Hautmont, Maletra, Cie Générale des Produits Chimiques du Midi, Rio Tinto, and Grimes). Additionally, the salt maker Daguin & Cie purchased the Société des Produits Chimiques de l'Est and erected the La Madeleine plant in 1881, near Nancy, implementing the Schloessing and Rolland ammonia process (see Chapter 1). Solvay, through a pricing war and an increase in volume, acquired a dominant position in France, which would enable it to conclude agreements to its advantage, and to oversee the gradual demise of the Leblanc plants and prevent the entry of new competitors into the sector (see Chapter 3). The soda ash plant at Dombasle maintained its special importance in the Solvay group because of the volume of its production, but also because of its role as a model plant and in training several key men in the enterprise.

Ludwig Mond, Industrial Friend

The rapid internationalization of Solvay greatly benefited from the support of foreign entrepreneurs, first and foremost in England. At the dawn of the 1870s, Solvay did not have adequate human and financial resources to develop all markets simultaneously. The ammonia process began to be known in industrial circles, and letters of inquiry began to flood into Couillet. Among those looking for information was Ludwig Mond (1839–1909). This German chemist came from a Jewish middle-class family in Germany. From the age of fourteen, he had taken scientific courses at Cassel Polytechnic. From the age of sixteen, he had studied chemistry at the Universities of Marburg and Heidelberg, notably under the chemist Bunsen. He interrupted his studies at nineteen, before getting a degree, and was hired at a German Leblanc soda ash plant, near Cassel, in 1860. After this first experience, he channeled his energy to recovering sulfur in the calcium sulfide waste from the process, for which he filed a patent in 1861. Flush with his university background and the credit received for his patent, he acted as consultant for chemical companies in the Netherlands before returning to Great Britain, homeland of Leblanc soda ash, which offered numerous

[9] ART-PDO, Solvay & Cie; Haber (1958), 110.

opportunities for a gifted chemist. Hired by the Hutchinson company, he applied his sulfur-recovery process there while granting patents to English and European competitors. It was in this company that he met his future associate, John Tomlinson Brunner (1842–1919). Mond moved to Widnes in 1867 and rapidly began looking for new opportunities. Because his prosperity was directly linked to the recycled waste products from the Leblanc process, he considered the emergence of the ammonia-soda method a threat, as it did not generate the same sulfurous residue.[10] With the help of the eminent English chemist Henry Deacon, Ludwig Mond sent a request for information on the process at Couillet to Henri Henroz, manager of the Compagnie de Floreffe, and he made inquiries to Professor Van den Gheyn, of the University of Ghent.[11] After collecting all the information available on ammonia soda, including the Solvay patent of 1863, and an 1871 patent by James Young,[12] he still did not manage to figure out how Solvay could operate continuous production without incurring huge losses of ammonia. Mond then asked Ernest Solvay for permission to visit the plant at Couillet. Solvay hesitated but finally agreed to receive Mond on 22 April 1872, on condition of his promise not to divulge what he would see there and not to build a competing ammonia-soda plant.[13] The correspondence between the two men and their respective associates showed that this four-day visit was the beginning of a relationship of mutual admiration and shared enthusiasm.[14]

Mond rapidly understood the advantage of developing the Solvay process in England. For his part, Ernest Solvay saw in Mond a brilliant chemist who could very likely perfect his invention, as well as an entrepreneur capable of competing with Leblanc manufacturers on their own turf. That battle posed some challenges, as England had less favorable conditions for the ammonia-soda industry: cheap coal and sulfur minimized the savings realized on these materials, and ammonia was more expensive, thus exacerbating the question of losses.[15] An agreement in principle was concluded between the two men, but a written accord was not signed until five months later. In the meantime, Mond, already convinced of the conclusion of the agreement, began earnestly working with John Brunner to assemble the funds, choose the land, and secure the patent. It was this latter point that proved so valuable for Solvay. Mond pressed Ernest Solvay to file a new patent integrating the column (18 May 1872) and thus barely beat out, by a matter of days, the English chemists James Young and Walter Weldon, both of whom had been getting ready to patent similar processes. Afterward, he remained a keen observer of evolving trends in Continental Europe, especially in Germany, where intellectual property laws varied

---

[10] Reader (1970), 37–42; Watts (1923), 20–1.

[11] Lischka (1985), 81.

[12] James Young was assistant to Henry Deacon when the latter was experimenting with ammonia soda ash with Holbrook Gaskell at Widnes. Young conducted research on a small scale in the laboratory and filed a first patent on 28 Sept. 1871. See Lischka (1985), 82–3.

[13] ABM, DIC/BM 1/2, Agreement between Ernest Solvay and Ludwig Mond, 22 Apr. 1872.

[14] ACS-O, 1001-1, Historique de la Société Solvay, Correspondence Ernest Solvay-Guillaume Nélis, 1872; Lischka (1985), 85.

[15] Warren (1980), 103–20.

widely, before they were standardized by the law of 1877 and the creation of
the Reichspatentamt. Mond relied on the services of two patent specialists: the
lawyers Mardsen Latham for England and Carl Pieper for Germany. He also
got a great deal of information from the Leblanc producer Robert Hasenclever,
head of Rhenania.[16]

Brunner and Mond had great troubles in pulling together the needed capital.
They lacked half of the £10,000 necessary. Mond proposed to the shareholders
of Solvay that they participate financially in the creation of the English company. Pirmez saw an opportunity for Solvay to gain entry into England other
than by granting a license, and one that involved no ties to capital. Several
possibilities were discussed: a loan with a share in earnings, establishment of a
Solvay plant with Mond as plant manager, and constitution of a limited company in which the Solvay shareholders would contribute proportionally to their
holdings in the Belgian company. This latter solution was chosen as a basis for
negotiation. Ernest Solvay, morally committed to Mond and counting heavily
on him to export his process to England, sided with Mond in the negotiations
more often than with his silent partners:

> A wealth of reasons obliges me to recommend an arrangement with Mond by
> our company, and if we do not do this, we very simply will lose several years in
> England, because I do not see any other way to handle this other than through
> the intermediary of a man that can do everything without our help and who
> has the chemical capabilities of Mr. Mond. And it must be kept in mind that the
> question of loss of ammonia has not been resolved and that it is the most important
> issue.... Once this question is resolved, we will scarcely need chemists any longer,
> but we must be patient.[17]

Ernest Solvay proposed for Mond remuneration similar to that enjoyed by
the *gérants* at Solvay, based on gradual percentages taken from the earnings.
In addition, he asked that one-fifth of the English shares be granted to himself
and his brother. Pirmez acted as representative for the Solvay partners. He felt
that Mond, who was bringing nothing more to the table than his license, hardly
deserved such advantageous treatment, to the detriment of the financial backers, who would thus come under double jeopardy in their dividends. Mond,
seeing that he had the support of Ernest Solvay, did not temper his demands,
and negotiations for a direct participation of the Belgian shareholders of Solvay
ended in failure.[18] This divergence of views among the partners of Solvay was
one of the first conflicts that would trouble the relationship between the Solvay
brothers and their silent partners (see Chapter 3).

The agreement between Mond and Solvay was signed on 23 September
1872. The partners came to agreement on the principle of a simple license

[16] PPSF, Box Ernest Solvay 2, Correspondence with Mond, 1872–1874; Lischka (1985), 91.
[17] ACS-O, 1001-1, Histoire de la Société Solvay, Ernest Solvay to Guillaume Nélis, 2 Aug. 1872.
[18] Van Belle (2008), 2008, 84–7; ABM, DIC/BM 1/1, Ludwig Mond to John Brunner, 2 Aug.
1872; ABM DIC/BM 7/18, Ludwig Mond to Ernest Solvay, 2 May 1872, 3 May 1872, and
12 May 1872.

for the patents of 1863 and 1872. Mond had to settle for a fixed fee of eight shillings per ton of soda ash produced, which would be in place until the patents expired in 1886. According to Eudore Pirmez, the contract "left a little to be desired, but there was no time for second thoughts. It provided an income that could be substantial . . . and it left to the partners [of Solvay] the capital they needed to establish the plant at Dombasle, without recourse to third parties."[19] The contract provided for a complete exchange of plans, instructions, and improvements. It would become null and void if construction of the plant had not started up within a year and was not producing soda ash within two years. Solvay maintained the right to erect its own plant in England, and it could grant other licenses there with a minimum licensing fee of twenty shillings per ton.

Brunner and Mond finally found, in the person of Charles M. Holland, an English partner who enabled them to establish Brunner, Mond, on 28 February 1873. His participation amounted to £5,000, compared to £4,000 for Brunner and £1,000 for Mond.[20] The plant of Brunner, Mond was built in Northwich, "like a cannon threatening the Leblanc fortresses."[21] It went on stream in 1874. The launch was tedious and beset by technical problems of all kinds, given the weakness of some of the equipment, for which Mond had thought he could fudge a little on the specifications.[22] Louis-Philippe Acheroy, production head for Solvay at Couillet, was sent for weeks at a time to help regulate the equipment.[23]

During the same period, a second project for a Solvay plant would emerge in England in a fairly singular way. Among the candidates for the funding of Brunner, Mond was the chemist James Richards, friend of Brunner, and his financiers John H. Kearne and Butler Gasquoine. After three months of talks in 1873, during which Mond exposed all the production details to the investor candidates, the candidates broke off negotiations. Mond ignored the reason for the rupture, but Solvay was well aware. Richards had, in the meantime, gone directly to Solvay to obtain a license. Keeping Mond completely in the dark, Solvay granted a license to Richards, as it had every legal right to do, for a fee of twenty shillings per ton. Solvay had decided to hedge its bets, just in case Mond failed. As one can imagine, these maneuvers did not make Ludwig Mond happy, as he saw a potential financial backer transformed into a direct competitor. In addition, the information-exchange clauses possibly involved communications on process developments from Mond to Richards, via Solvay. Mond did not hide his scorn: "I regard these gentlemen [Richards, Kearne, and Gasquoine] as thieves and I do not wish that they should profit from whatever improvements I shall make on your process."[24]

[19] Van Belle (2008), 83.
[20] Watts (1923), 23; Lischka (1985), 94.
[21] Ernest Solvay (1904), 115.
[22] ACS, AG, Gérance report, 26 May 1874.
[23] PPSF, Correspondence Louis-Philippe Acheroy-Ernest Solvay, Jan. 1874.
[24] Lischka (1985), 101; Reader (1970), 48.

This episode, illustrating the fine line between industrial trust and economic reality, led to the establishment in 1876 of a plant at Sandbach, in Cheshire. Richards had access to technical assistance from Solvay to build his plant, similar to the one at Couillet. He never managed, however, to make a profit from it, given the steep fees he owed to Solvay, but also because of the lack of engineering skills. Solvay reproached him for not paying enough attention to all the "details, the little things that ended up being more important than the big ones."[25] In a desperate attempt, Richards promised his customers volumes that he could not deliver and slashed prices, selling at a loss. In 1878, Richards offered Solvay the opportunity to buy his plant, a proposal favored by Eudore Pirmez. The transaction never took place. Taking his revenge, Brunner, Mond took over the plant through a lease agreement, using it as a large-scale laboratory financed by Richards, Kearne, and Gasquoine, before purchasing it in 1881.[26]

After Mond and Richards, Solvay still granted several other licenses, although these would have far less impact than had been the case with Mond. In 1874, Charles Delsart, engineer at the École Centrale de France, and Émile Savoye, a chemist at Lille, signed a license contract to build a plant in England, with a fee of twenty shillings per ton. Nothing ever came of it. The following year, Solvay concluded the same type of agreement with a certain Christian Wahl of Chicago, to establish a plant in the United States and Canada.[27] After these fruitless attempts, Solvay finally turned away from this mode of free but passive expansion.

Delayed Presence in Germany

Direct establishment of Solvay in Germany had been considered since 1873. The soda ash industry there was less concentrated than in England or France. Production was nominal before the 1880s, and the Leblanc producers were modest in size.[28] However, an ammonia process inspired by that of Solvay and patented by Moritz Honigmann, a chemist from Rhenania, had begun to take hold there. Honigmann began a plant at Würselen (Aachen) in 1870. He then granted free licenses, which enabled several small ammonia-soda plants to emerge at Schalke, Nuremberg, Rothenfelde, Salzuflen, Duisburg, and Trotha, and a little later at Montwy, Stassfurt, and Dieuze.[29] In 1873, BASF and Verein Chemischer Fabriken Mannheim approached Solvay to build a soda ash plant together on the Neckar River. It seems that Solvay's claims discouraged the German firms. Verein then called on Honigmann independently to set up a plant at Heilbronn, which came on stream in 1881.[30]

---

[25] ABM, DIC/BM 7/18, Ernest Solvay to James Richards, 16 May 1876.

[26] Lischka (1985), 102–4.

[27] PPSF, Box Ernest Solvay 2, Contract Solvay-Delsart & Savoye, 12 Mar. 1874; Contract Solvay-Wahl, 20 Nov. 1875.

[28] Haber (1958), 122.

[29] ACS, Eilsberger (b) (1930), 27, 138.

[30] Haber (1958), 122–3; Van Belle (2008), 90. ADSW, Neckar, Situation sur le Neckar en Wurtenberg, travel report from Alfred Solvay and M. Baesjou, Oct. 1879.

In the meantime, Solvay began exploration in the German Alsace-Lorraine region. The salt deposits that supplied Dombasle extended across the border. Solvay at first considered the Sarre territory. E. Poncelet, Solvay's commercial representative in the area, was put in charge of preparations for the establishment of a plant at Sarralbe. The request for concession was filed in February 1874 with the Imperial Government of Alsace-Lorraine. Following numerous delays and administrative concerns, the project was put on hold for almost ten years. The government asked for, among other things, the complete plans of the Couillet plant, and it made it clear that it reserved the right to interrupt production at any time if excessive amounts of waste were observed being dumped into the waters of the Sarre.[31] The delayed solution to these problems, in favor of Solvay, kept the soda ash plant from opening until 1885, after the company had acquired other locations in the country.

A second option was also considered: the takeover of an existing plant located at Wyhlen, in Baden, about six kilometers upstream from Basel, on the Rhine. This new modus operandi would encounter another type of problem, negotiation for purchase. In 1874, Salzwerk Wyhlen A.G. had established a salt plant, a sulfuric acid manufacturing unit, and an ammonia-soda plant using the Bolley process, which borrowed elements from a variety of other methods. Despite considerable investments, the company had never reached the level of profitability and was being liquidated. Solvay was approached for any interest in acquisition. Having interest only in the soda ash plant and the portion of the salt concession likely to supply it, Solvay purchased those assets for a price of BEF 600,000 (US$114,000) in the early part of 1878. Pflüger, a representative of Salzwerk and a deputy in the German Reichstag, had to obtain numerous government permits necessary for division of the concession and for use of the salt. During a meeting with Pflüger, Ernest Solvay, Pirmez, Hanrez, and Charles Van Ouwenhuysen, it appeared that Salzwerk had attempted to swindle the buyers. The concession that contractually should have covered five hundred hectares had been cut up in such a way as to allocate to Solvay 90 percent of the non-salt-producing area. Solvay took the case to the courts in Freiburg, but it was rejected, because the contract had been signed. Before filing an appeal, a financial settlement was reached, by which Solvay purchased all the installations, at the considerable sum of nearly BEF 1 million (US$190,000).[32]

The soda ash plant was almost entirely rebuilt under the supervision of Prosper Hanrez. A new permit was required. As for the other establishments, the question of environmental impact was raised. Hanrez included in his request a report that aimed to prove the benign aspect of the Solvay process compared to the Leblanc process, using as an example the low impact of the plants at Couillet and Dombasle, located on rivers with lower flow rates than the Rhine.[33] Solvay further reinforced its position, when in a new concession

---

[31] ACS-O, 1101 Sarralbe, Correspondance relative aux demandes d'autorisation d'usine.
[32] ACS-O, 1155 Wyhlen, Création de l'usine; ACS, AG, Gérance report 1879; Van Belle (2008), 90; ACS, Eilsberger (b) (1930), 69–74.
[33] ACS-O, 1155 Wyhlen, Création de l'usine, demande d'autorisation, 1879.

obtained in June 1880, the state of Baden committed itself not to grant any
other new concessions in the future in the surrounding area unless the conces-
sionaire agreed to pay a fine to Solvay and not to establish another soda ash
plant within twenty kilometers of the Wyhlen wells.[34] Charles van Ouwenhuysen took over as manager of the plant in 1880. This soda ash plant, once
started up, was well positioned to supply the local market in southern Germany
and Switzerland, but Solvay could hardly claim to have cornered the German
market.

2.2   EMERGENCE OF A TRANSATLANTIC GROUP
OF SOLVAY COMPANIES (1880s)

Change of Scale in England

After the failures of Dyar & Hemming and Deacon in using the ammonia
process, the English Leblanc manufacturers had looked with skepticism at the
arrival of Brunner, Mond. They did not become alarmed immediately, as the
prices charged initially by Brunner, Mond were adjusted to market prices.
However, Brunner, Mond generated a much higher margin, which was kept
secret. After the difficult technical implementation, profits climbed rapidly.
The poorly financed private partnership of the early years was transformed
into a limited company in 1881, with capital of £600,000, represented by
thirty thousand ordinary shares and thirty thousand preferred shares. Initially,
thirty-six thousand shares were issued, including eighteen thousand ordinary
shares and eighteen thousand preferred shares. During the intense negotiations
that preceded this transformation, Mond, as well as Solvay, Pirmez, and Hanrez, proved tough negotiators. The Solvay *gérants* had not entirely abandoned
the idea of starting their own production on English soil, and they compared
the options at hand, especially in terms of maximizing their profits. Mond
fought point by point to ensure that Solvay would not enter into competition
with him. The solution that seemed to come out of the talks was to transform the temporary licensing fee into a permanent licensing fee of one shilling
per ton. Brunner and Mond, after leaning toward this solution, finally opted
for the transfer of one-fifth of the shares to Solvay, in exchange for abandoning
the fee, the transfer of English patents, and noncompetition clauses on British
territory. Solvay needed Mond's expertise too much in this difficult market to
make a competitor out of him. In fact, he became his close ally in the fight
for mastery of the world's soda ash market. Alfred Solvay was named to the
supervisory board. After having sold its preference shares in 1885, Solvay's
participation into Brunner, Mond fluctuated around 13 percent until its incorporation, in 1926, in ICI (Imperial Chemical Industries). The first dividend on
ordinary shares was 15 percent and increased constantly until it reached 35 percent in 1900, thereby generating abundant financial returns for Solvay.[35] New

[34] ACS, Eilsberger (b) (1930), 73.
[35] ACS-O, 1242 Brunner Mond, Boxes 1B and 3B; ACS, 1241-40-1A ICI, Échange d'actions BM
    contre actions ICI.

installations were erected at Northwich, alongside the old plant, and expanded several times, to the point of surpassing the capacity of Dombasle as of 1887. The plant at Sandbach, initially kept in check, also soon made up for lost time. The 1880s became the battleground for a veritable soda ash war, between Brunner, Mond and the Leblanc manufacturers, which would eventually lead to a merger in 1891, with forty-eight of them going to United Alkali Co. (see Chapter 3).[36]

Founding of Deutsche Solvay Werke A.G.

In the early 1880s, Germany had no fewer than twenty-three soda ash plants, fourteen of which used the Leblanc process; five, the Honigmann process; and four, mixed.[37] For Solvay, Wyhlen had no possibilities to become a large plant, and the Sarralbe project was on hold. The *gérants* knew that they had to expand their position in Germany by occupying a more central position: "should we then let our competitors take hold or should we seize the opportunity so that those who want to imitate us find that the position is already taken?"[38] As in other countries, a key person was needed to whom oversight of operations could be delegated. Carl Wessel (1842–1912) showed interest in this mission and was recruited by Solvay in 1880. Wessel was a graduate of Realschule at Elberfeld. Having had commercial experience in a silk export firm, Metzger & de Bary, he was hired in 1864 as a sales representative for the chemical firm E. Matthes & Weber A. G. at Duisburg. In 1868, Wessel founded his own commercial company that imported Scandinavian wood. He abandoned this activity to begin work for Solvay. He immediately became responsible for sales in Germany, Austria, Scandinavia, Poland, and Russia, until Solvay established other subsidiaries that took over most of these territories.[39] Mandated by Solvay, Wessel set out on a quest for a location that would combine all the criteria desired for installation of a soda ash plant of a size comparable to that of Dombasle. The locality of Bernburg, in the duchy of Anhalt, was perfectly situated and met every requirement. It had access to a navigable river – the Saale – and to a railway. It was located near large lime quarries, lignite mines, rich rock-salt beds, and saltworks that could furnish brine. Wessel set his heart on obtaining a property that belonged to the Anhalt authorities in the city of Bernburg. The project encountered significant opposition. The inhabitants of the city, led by their mayor, united forces against Solvay, fearing that the land would be destroyed and that toxic pollutants would be emitted. Some even feared the growth of a working class that would threaten the peaceful middle-class city with depraved behaviors and an increased burden on the public budget.[40]

---

[36] Reader (1970), 104–7.

[37] ACS, Eilsberger (b) (1930), 211.

[38] ACS, AG, Conseil de Surveillance report 1879.

[39] Carl Wessel would become manager of the Bernburg plant in 1883 and chairman of the *Vorstand* of the Deutsche Solvay Werke AG in 1889. Elected to the city council at Bernburg in 1889, he was chosen chairman of the council in 1903. That same year he was elected to the Reichstag. ACS, Eilsberger (b) (1930), 440–75.

[40] ACS, Eilsberger (b) (1930), 81.

Residents of the towns bordering the Saale and Elbe rivers downstream from the plant feared water pollution and joined in the protests. The opponents took every possible action to stop the process. In 1881, the decision to grant the concession came under the jurisdiction of the regional industrial committee, the Kreisdirektions-Kollegiums in Gewerbesachen, whereas the decision to sell the land came under the jurisdiction of Anhalt's Parliament. The government of the duchy of Anhalt was favorable to the installation, primarily for tax reasons. Several of its members were convinced by the lobbying efforts of Carl Wessel of the opportunity presented to the region by the establishment of a soda ash plant. Passing by a single vote, the Anhalt Parliament authorized sale of the property and the concession was granted shortly afterward, in July 1881.[41]

Plans for the soda ash plant at Bernburg were drawn up at Brussels with the active collaboration of an engineer named Eugen Frey, who had been brought to Brussels from Dombasle. The raw materials were available locally, whereas the ammonia would be purchased from gas plants at Rome, Hamburg, Mannheim, and Trier, and then concentrated by Solvay in its own installations adjoining these plants. Production began in 1883, and the plant rapidly reached its cruising-speed equivalent of two-thirds of the tons produced at Dombasle and Northwich.[42] Two years later, the soda ash plant at Sarralbe finally went into production. As the business in Germany for Solvay was expanding considerably, the question of creation of a separate company with its own management was considered. Agreeing that this was an acute need, Carl Wessel first submitted to Solvay the idea of constituting a mining company (*Gewerkschaft*) by reaching out for German capital. The integration of national partners would have enabled Solvay to counteract nationalist criticism from public opinion in Anhalt.[43] Recourse to banks was not required, because two known industrial partners of Solvay, the Röchling brothers at Sarrebruck and Vopelius at Sulzbach, declared themselves willing to participate financially. During negotiations, the concept of a mining company evolved into a plan for transformation into a unique limited company encompassing all the German installations of Solvay. Deutsche Solvay Werke Aktiengesellschaft (DSW AG) was constituted on 13 May 1885, with its corporate headquarters at Bernburg. It was founded against a backdrop of reflection on the form the Solvay group was to take and the manner in which to reinforce the ties among all its parties (see Chapter 3). Concerning the choice of wording for the corporate name, Carl Wessel declared: "it is not at all necessary to add onto the name what product you make, because we are already known. This name really sounds good. You feel the force of it."[44] Carl Wessel, at the time manager of Bernburg, took over as head of *Vorstand* for oversight of current operations, alongside Eugen Frey,

[41] ACS-O, 1152 Bernburg, Relations adm. publ; ACS, Eilsberger (b) (1930), 75–93.
[42] ART-PDO Solvay & Cie, DSW, BM&Co.
[43] ACS, Eilsberger (b) (1930), 157–8.
[44] Carl Wessel to Ernest Solvay, 3 Mar. 1883, quoted in ACS, Eilsberger (b) (1930), 164.

new manager of Wyhlen, and Joseph Masson, manager of Sarralbe. A supervisory board was set up to handle the books and provide general supervision to the business. It was originally composed of the Solvay brothers, Prosper Hanrez, Louis Semet, and Carl Röchling. Solvay and its *gérants* together held about 84 percent of the capital of M 10 million. Ludwig Mond was part of the supervisory board from 1886 to 1888. He personally held a 2 percent share, as did John Brunner.[45]

In 1886, total consumption of soda ash in Germany amounted to 120,000 tons, the production of which was spread out among the three plants of DSW (42,000 tons), the Honigmann plants (40,000 tons), and the Leblanc plants (38,000 tons).[46] In Germany, the Solvay process had taken considerable time to develop, and Honigmann had succeeded in installing several operational plants there, though of more limited capacities. The competitive battle thus would be, more than elsewhere, triangular (see Chapter 3).

A Step into the Steppe: Lubimoff & Cie

Installation in Russia was not an immediate success. The tsarist country consumed little soda ash. Local production was very limited, as were imports of English soda ash, which were expensive because of high customs duties.[47] The Solvay process aroused the interest of the engineer-chemist Samuel A. Chapiro, who brought it to the attention of Ivan I. Lubimoff, a wealthy industrialist who owned saltworks at Perm, in the Ural Mountains. The industrialist proposed a partnership with Solvay in 1881. As was his practice, Solvay gathered a great deal of information about the potential partner, in this case from the Belgian consulate in Russia. Talks began in Brussels and ended with the constitution in February 1881 of the limited partnership Lubimoff & Cie, in which Solvay, as silent partner, held 50 percent of the capital of BEF 1.5 million (US$285,000), and Ivan Lubimoff, as managing partner, the remaining 50 percent. That same year the construction of the soda ash plant at Berezniki, on the Kama River, began. Lubimoff provided the land near his saltworks and had the equipment manufactured in his foundries and workshops at Perm. The very harsh climate in wintertime and the poorly developed means of communication placed Berezniki more than a week away from Moscow, by sleigh and boat, before the first bridge over the Volga River was built and the railway was constructed between St. Petersburg and Perm. Although in close proximity to salt and lime, the plant had to bring in ammonia from the gas plants at St. Petersburg, and it was far from the centers of consumption. It

---

[45] After several stock trades from 1885 to 1887, the distribution was as follows: Solvay & Cie, 72 percent; Ernest Solvay, 7 percent; Alfred Solvay, 4 percent; Prosper Hanrez, 0.5 percent; Louis Semet (new *gérant*), 0.5 percent; L. Mond, 2 percent; J. Brunner, 2 percent; Röchling brothers, 6 percent; Vopelius brothers, 4 percent; and members of the DSW *Vorstand* (Wessel, Frey, and Masson), 2 percent. ACS, 1151 DSW, Rapport général; ACS-O, 1152 Bernburg, Résumés divers.

[46] ACS, 1151 DSW, Rapport général.

[47] Haber (1958), 221.

was poorly built and poorly managed by Chapiro. Lubimoff & Cie accumulated losses in 1883, the date it began production, and through until 1886.[48] Lubimoff, as managing partner, was solely responsible for the conduct of the business, and Solvay was in no way obligated to bail him out beyond his initial layout. Lubimoff expressed the desire to resign from his position as manager, which Solvay refused. In February 1885, the *gérance*, by its own initiative, hired Albert Gyhra, an Austrian mechanical engineer from the Belgian company Zimmermann-Hanrez, to replace Chapiro. After acquiring experience at Dombasle, Gyhra was sent to Berezniki, where he took the production process in hand, trained workers, and reconfigured the plant. He obtained authorization to address questions, including technical ones, directly to Brussels, without first going through his Russian superiors. Gyhra was joined by Alfred Bruyère, former mechanical supervisor of the Belgian steel company Cockerill.[49] After having given complete free rein to Lubimoff, Solvay intervened authoritatively in the business of the Russian company.

In parallel with the Berezniki business, Solvay was quickly showing interest in the Donetz basin, which had a better location; was rich in salt; and was perceived by European entrepreneurs, especially Belgians, as a veritable El Dorado at the end of the nineteenth century.[50] After commissioning geological studies, Alfred Solvay and Édouard Hannon went to visit the location in 1885. They marked the site of Lysychansk, and Ernest Solvay himself went to visit it in August 1886. A second soda ash plant would be erected there in 1891. Meanwhile, it was necessary to resolve the disastrous situation with Lubimoff & Cie by transforming it into a joint-stock company. This solution enabled the integration of some new Russian partners and increased the influence of Solvay in the decision-making process through the board of directors, and at the same time it relieved Lubimoff of his day-to-day management duties. A first agreement was signed in Moscow in September 1886 between Lubimoff and Solvay. Each party contributed assets, considered equal, to the new company. At the beginning of 1887, Ivan Lubimoff, who probably received bad advice from his relatives, sent Solvay a draft of a modified contract in which he laid claim to new considerations. The letter set Ernest Solvay into a rage, although he had maintained confidence in Lubimoff until then, despite his disappointing management of the business. His firm response brought Lubimoff back to a more moderate stance.[51]

The new joint-stock company, Lubimoff, Solvay & Cie, was constituted in April 1887 with capital of R 3 million. In addition to the two primary shareholders (41.7 percent each) was the powerful trade company of Wogau & Cie, importer of chemicals in Russia (3.3 percent); Auguste Loutreuil, a French businessman well connected in Russian industrial circles (6.6 percent);

[48] Accarain (2002), 42–3; ACS-O, 1225 Lubimoff: Statuts et conventions d'origine.

[49] Accarain (2002), 55–6.

[50] Peeters and Wilson (1999), 35.

[51] ACS-O, 1225 Lubimoff: Statuts et conventions d'origine, Ernest Solvay to Ivan Lubimoff, 9 Apr. 1887.

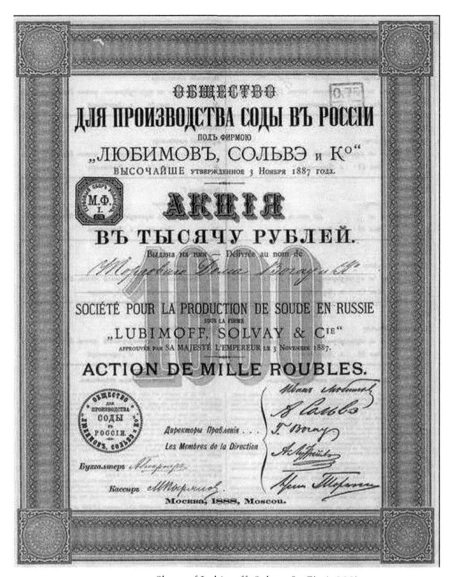

FIGURE 2.2. Share of Lubimoff, Solvay & Cie (1888).

and Charles James Thornton, an Englishman active in the wool industry.[52] Wladimir Orlow was named general manager. Under these new arrangements, Lubimoff Solvay, with its central headquarters in Moscow, would recover rapidly. Given the low levels of local production, Lubimoff Solvay faced its initial primary competition in the form of imports of soda ash from abroad. The increased tonnage at Berezniki and a new hike in customs duties ensured it an almost complete takeover of the market at the start of the 1890s, before

[52] Accarain (2002), 73–9.

new competitors appeared (Ouchkoff, Zombkowice, and Slaviansk), but their appearance did not imperil Solvay's leadership (see Chapter 3).[53]

Crossing the Atlantic: The Solvay Process Company

Until the start of the 1880s, soda ash consumption in the United States (160,000 tons in 1883) was largely covered by English imports. The only manufacturer in the country was the Pennsylvania Salt Manufacturing Co., which used a cryolite process and managed to produce scarcely a few thousand tons per year.[54] Solvay had protected its equipment in the United States by a patent filed on 4 March 1873. It was biding its time, waiting for American entrepreneurs to make the first step.

William B. Cogswell (1834–1921), a mining engineer, was director of a lead mine in Missouri, which belonged to Rowland Hazard (1829–1898), an industrialist from Rhode Island, active as well in the wool and textile industries.[55] During a meeting of the American Institute of Mining Engineers in Philadelphia in 1878, Cogswell found out about the existence of the ammonia-soda process.[56] As a native of the region around Syracuse, New York – "the Salt City" – where all the required raw materials were in ample abundance, he quickly saw an opportunity to import this manufacturing process to the region. Cogswell traveled to Europe to meet with the manufacturers who used the process. With the help of Julien Deby, an engineer at Rio Tinto living in Brussels, he made contact with Alfred Solvay, who at first put him off. Cogswell persisted and had letters of recommendation sent, signed by American personalities, who were able to change Solvay's mind.[57] Thus did the procedure begin. What followed was the site selection and source of raw materials, the financing structure, communication of plans, recruitment of American engineers, and the sending of several of them (William Neil, Edward Trump, Henry Cooper, and Nicholas Bodot) to Dombasle for practical training.[58]

The Solvay Process Co. (SPC) was founded on 12 October 1881. To limit the financial investment, Solvay subscribed to only one-third of the capital (US$100,000), but reserved half of the earnings beyond 10 percent of the capital paid. When production would reach fifty thousand tons annually, this right to half of the earnings would be exchanged for shares, so as to obtain half of them. Because Solvay was in a good bargaining position, it could

---

[53] ACS, *Solvay & Cie. Soude et produits chimiques.* Booklet published for the World Exposition of Paris (1889), 23; Haber (1958), 221.

[54] Cryolite, or glacial rock, is a rare mineral discovered in Greenland at the start of the nineteenth century. Treated with lime, it decomposes into different substances, one of which is soda ash. The cryolite soda process was used marginally in the Danish plant at Oeresund starting in 1858 and by the Penn Salt Co., at Natrona, starting in 1865 and until 1904. Lunge and Naville (1881), 167.

[55] ASPC, Biographies, William Cogswell and Rowland Hazard.

[56] There, Cogswell heard the speech made by the engineer Oswald. J. Heinrich. See Heinrich (1878–9).

[57] ACS-O, 1271 Solvay Process, Box 1A, letters from Andrew White, president of Cornell University; Rowland Hazard; and Charles Sedgwick from Syracuse.

[58] ASPC, Trump (1935).

be very creative in setting up the contract and imposing the most favorable terms. The remaining two-thirds of the capital was contributed by R. Hazard, president (US$100,000); Cogswell, general manager (US$95,000); and three other board members, William Sweet, Earl Alvord, and George Dana (US$5,000).[59]

The plant at Syracuse went into production in 1884. Despite sending over Belgian and French technicians and foremen, the first year saw a succession of technical problems of all sorts and even several fatal accidents.[60] This was the first ammonia soda installation on the American continent, and only a handful of engineers had ever seen these plants operating in Europe.[61] As of 1885, the major technical problems were overcome, and production skyrocketed. The share of SPC production in the total consumption of the United States was already 10 percent in 1884, and it reached 55 percent in 1892.[62] Syracuse would in fact become, in 1897, the largest soda ash plant in the world, due to an explosion of demand in the American market. In 1889, the Tully salt beds began being exploited by SPC, through a company created expressly for this purpose, the Tully Pipe Line Co.

New means were required to finance this rapid growth. Capital was increased to US$700,000 in 1885, US$1,200,000 in 1886, US$1,500,000 in 1889, and US$3,000,000 in 1891. On 1 January 1887, Solvay gave up its rights to half the earnings against shares, and Brunner, Mond made a striking entry into the shareholders of SPC. The American shareholders kept 42.8 percent of the shares, compared to 40.5 percent for Solvay and 16.7 percent for Brunner, Mond. In exchange for this English *intrusion*, R. Hazard obtained an agreement from Brunner, Mond to relinquish its voting rights, and at the same time he persuaded Solvay to surrender a small number of its rights as well, thus maintaining a majority of the votes in the assemblies in American hands.[63] The reason for the entry by Brunner, Mond was that, from 1885, the Belgian and English partners had shared the market, in accordance with the common commercial practices of the time. Continental Europe had gone to Solvay, whereas England and the United States had been granted to Brunner, Mond. The appearance of SPC thus constituted an indirect incursion by Solvay onto territory reserved for the English partners. Solvay, fearing a competitive battle between his two associates on American soil, required – or allowed – the entry of Brunner, Mond into the shareholding of SPC. In return, the commercial peace was organized by a series of successive agreements in which Brunner, Mond received a defined contingent of sales (see Chapter 3).

[59] ACS-O, 1271 Solvay Process, Box 1B. Résumés, Constitution of SPC; Contract Solvay-SPC, 12 Dec. 1881.

[60] ASPC, "Dr. L.C. Jones' Story of the Solvay Alkali Enterprises," in *Chemical Markets*, no. 24, 3 Mar. 1929.

[61] ASPC, Biographies, Edward N. Trump Notice, in *Sibley Journal of Engineering*, vol. 46, 1932, no. 9.

[62] ACS-O, 1271 Solvay Process, Box 1B, Soda ash in the United States, letter from Rowland Hazard, 1913.

[63] ACS-O, 1271 Solvay Process, Boxes 1A, 1B, and 2B.

After this initial setup period for SPC, internal power plays cropped up regularly among the three companies, with SPC determined to increase its margin of maneuver, and Brunner, Mond trying to slow down its loss of influence in the United States. Between the two, Solvay made efforts to maintain cohesion among all parties for the greater good of the group and in its own interest. It is to be recalled that Solvay held about 13 percent of Brunner, Mond and 40 percent of SPC in the 1890s. From a technical standpoint, however, the three parties committed through an agreement in 1885 to a complete and shared exchange of all their improvements.[64]

Partnering with Aussiger Verein in Austria-Hungary

For Solvay, Austria-Hungary was not a country to be ignored, even though it was not a top priority. The Austro-Hungarian Empire, having officially united the two monarchies since 1867, occupied the major portion of Central Europe. It extended in the north to Bohemia, Moravia, Silesia, and Galicia, and in the south to Croatia, Dalmatia, and Bosnia-Herzegovina. In the west, it encompassed the provinces of Austria and Kustenland (Trieste), and in the east, Transylvania and Bucovina. From an economic perspective there were great disparities between Austro-Bohemia, prosperous and industrialized, and the eastern, rural area.[65] The largest manufacturer of chemicals in the empire was Oesterreichischer Verein für Chemische und Metallurgische Production, founded in 1856 at Aussig, in the Sudetenland. A Leblanc manufacturer, it supplied to the country a major part of its soda ash, sulfuric acid, and bleaching materials. At its head was the renowned chemist Max Schaffner (1830–1907). Schaffner had patented, like Ludwig Mond, a sulfur-recovery process widely used in the Leblanc industry starting in the 1870s. Miller & Hochstetter at Hruschau and Wagenmann & Seybel at Vienna were the other major manufacturers of alkalis.[66]

According to a travel report written by Alfred Solvay and Louis Semet in September 1881, annual soda ash consumption in the empire was only thirty thousand tons. Despite high customs duties, imports represented 40 percent of this figure. The Bohemian glass industry was the main consumer, using more than one-fourth of the total. The decision to install a plant in Austria was made in 1881, mainly to prevent new competitors from seizing the market, as was pointed out in the report: "considering that imports are strong, it is likely that if we do not take our place, others will, as we have already heard about. There is thus reason to establish at Ebensee a plant of at least twenty tons a day, if the Government grants us serious and favorable conditions regarding salt and if we can find good property."[67]

---

[64] ACS-O, 1271 Solvay Process, Box 2A, Entry of BM in SPC 1886–1887, Voting rights 1895.
[65] Taylor (1961).
[66] Haber (1958), 51.
[67] ACS-O, 1184 Solvay Werke, Box 1, Études préliminaires, Travel report by Alfred Solvay and Louis Semet, Sept. 1881.

From the beginning, the location of Ebensee, in the Salzkammergut, was effectively considered the best choice, as it combined the greatest number of favorable points: rich salt deposits belonging to the state, a navigable lake connected to the Danube River, proximity to centers of consumption, and even a lack of local competitors. Among the other potential locations, Maros-Ujvar in Transylvania was also studied, but the "degree of culture" and the labor market were not favorable, and the distance from consumption centers was a disadvantage.[68] One would have to wait until 1895 before a small Solvay soda ash plant was built there to serve the local market.

In 1882, Austrian entrepreneurs had begun talks with Solvay to obtain a license to create a soda ash plant at Szczakowa, in Silesia. When Max Schaffner, of Aussiger Verein, learned of the existence of these maneuvers, he invited Ernest Solvay and Carl Wessel to a meeting in Dresden, to open parallel negotiations. Fearing the superiority of the ammonia process over that of Leblanc, Schaffner had been determined to be a part of its development in Austria-Hungary. Endowed with a certain prestige, he probably had little difficulty in convincing Solvay to opt for an exclusive partnership with Aussiger Verein.[69] In 1883, the partners founded the Limited Partnership of Oesterreichischer Verein für Chemische und Metallurgische Produktion & Co. Ammoniaksodafabrikation System Solvay. Capital of BEF 1,500,000 (US$285,000) was subscribed, half by Solvay, silent partner, and half by Verein, managing partner.

Key men in the Solvay group contributed their support and supervision to establishing the plant at Ebensee. Wessel organized sales distribution between DSW and Verein, whereas Hanrez kept control over the construction plans, which he drew up on the basis of topography reports sent by Schaffner, and integrated the latest improvements received from Northwich.[70] Schaffner took over coordination of the work, ordered the equipment, and acted as liaison with the persnickety imperial bureaucracy.[71] The latter required, among other things, complete communication of the plant's plans and technical specifications, which would then become accessible to the public. The Belgian and Austrian partners were clearly reticent about doing this. Schaffner made

---

[68] ACS-O, 1184 Solvay Werke, Box 1, Max Schaffner to Ernest Solvay, 22 Dec. 1882.

[69] [Gintl] (1906), 30–1. The soda ash plant at Szczakowa was nonetheless erected, with the name Erste Oesterreichische Ammoniaksodafabrik der Jaworznoer Steinkohlenwerke. It was bought by the limited partnership Solvay-Verein in 1907 and liquidated in 1909.

[70] ACS-O, 1184 Solvay Werke, Box 1, Plant Construction, Schaffner and von Woelfen (Verein's commercial director) to Solvay & Cie, 22 Jan. 1883, and Prosper Hanrez–Max Schaffner correspondence of 1, 5, 9, and 12 May 1883.

[71] It was not the first time that Solvay had to deal with the Austrian authorities. In 1873, following awards received at the Universal Exposition of Vienna, Solvay, to protect the validity of its Austrian patent, had to build a "fictional" plant to demonstrate to the government inspection commission that the process was being implemented in the country. It was Charles van Ouwenhuysen who was put in charge of this mission. The demonstration plant was set up with Seybel at Leising, the very ones who had tried unsuccessfully to process ammonia soda ash in the 1840s! PPSF, Box Ernest Solvay 2, Correspondence Charles van Ouwhenuysen-Ernest and Alfred Solvay 1873–1874.

arrangements to "simply provide a theoretical description of the process giving no concrete details about the equipment."[72]

The plant at Ebensee came on line at the end of 1885 and conquered a significant share of the market, without crushing the competition.[73] The managing partner did not aggressively go after the market with a policy of low prices, despite the repeated exhortations in this regard by Solvay. Aussiger Verein, which continued to produce soda ash using the Leblanc method, had greater interest in stabilizing the market than in annihilating the old process. Consequently, the plant at Ebensee did not drastically increase its tonnage. It stagnated at a production of ten thousand to fifteen thousand tons until the middle of the 1890s, and from twenty thousand to thirty thousand tons until 1913. The effect of this policy was to impede development of Solvay soda ash plants in the Austrian-Hungarian Empire, to prolong the existence of Leblanc plants (until 1911), and to stimulate new competition.[74] Thus, can it be said that the alliance with Aussiger Verein was a strategic mistake by Solvay? Not completely – the main goal was achieved of establishing a presence there and of taking advantage of Aussiger Verein's knowledge of the terrain.

Comparison of Contributions from the Associated Companies

Chart 2.1 shows the comparative tonnages of soda ash produced by each plant within the Solvay group. Until 1890, Dombasle and Northwich mainly took the lead, followed by Bernburg and Syracuse. The decrease of the relative weight of the Solvay plants in comparison with those of the associated companies illustrates the importance of the partnership strategy: from 63 percent in 1880, this proportion was only 24 percent in 1890. In 1890, Brunner, Mond ranked first in volume (33 percent), followed by Solvay & Cie (24 percent), DSW (21 percent), SPC (15 percent), Lubimoff (4 percent), and the Oesterreichischer Verein (3 percent). A look forward in 1913 confirms this trend, except that the SPC climbed to first place: in 1913, Solvay & Cie plants produced 19 percent of the total output, whereas SPC contributed 25 percent; Brunner, Mond, 22 percent; DSW, 20 percent; Lubimoff, 7 percent; and the Oesterreichischer Verein, 7 percent.[75] From a financial standpoint, the dividends distributed by the subsidiaries represented, from the early 1890s, 50 percent of Solvay & Cie's gross profit. This proportion remained until World War I (see Chart 2.2).[76]

[72] ACS-O, 1184 Solvay Werke, Box 1, Construction usine, Max Schaffner to Solvay & Cie, 16 May 1883.
[73] In 1900, the private partnership company Solvay-Verein held "only" 35 percent of the market.
[74] ACS, 1184-1-1 Solvay Werke, Vienne, Historique des usines Solvay du groupe de Vienne.
[75] ART-PDO Solvay & Cie, SPC, BM, SW, DSW, Lubimoff.
[76] ACS, AG, Annual accounts 1884–1914.

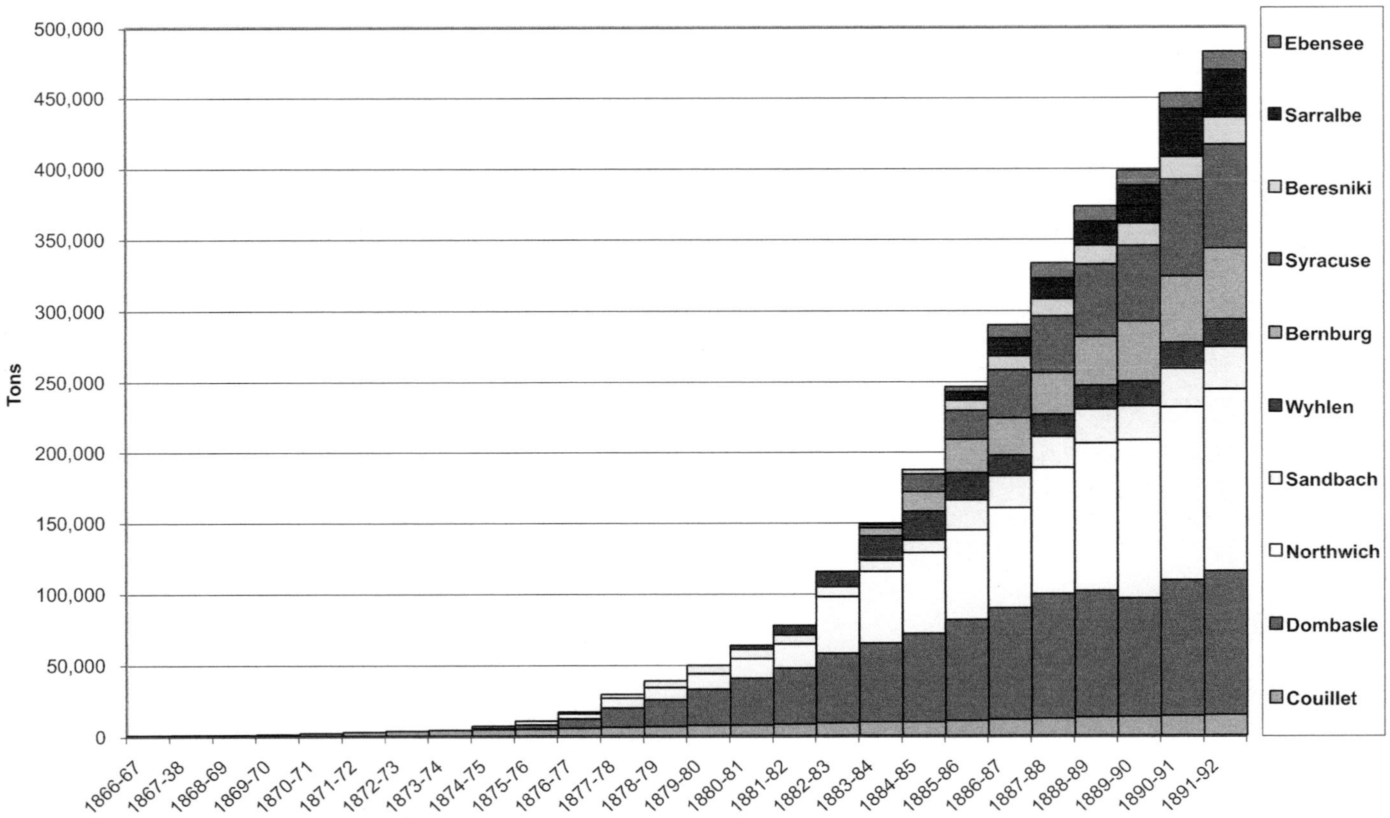

Tons
500,000
450,000
400,000
350,000
300,000
250,000
200,000
150,000
100,000
50,000
0
1866-67
1867-38
1868-69
1869-70
1870-71
1871-72
1872-73
1873-74
1874-75
1875-76
1876-77
1877-78
1878-79
1879-80
1880-81
1881-82
1882-83
1883-84
1884-85
1885-86
1886-87
1887-88
1888-89
1889-90
1890-91
1891-92
Ebensee
Sarralbe
Beresniki
Syracuse
Bernburg
Wyhlen
Sandbach
Northwich
Dombasle
Couillet

CHART 2.1. Production of the Solvay group's plants (1866–1892). *Sources:* ART-PDO Solvay & Cie, SPC, BM, SW, DSW, Lubimoff.

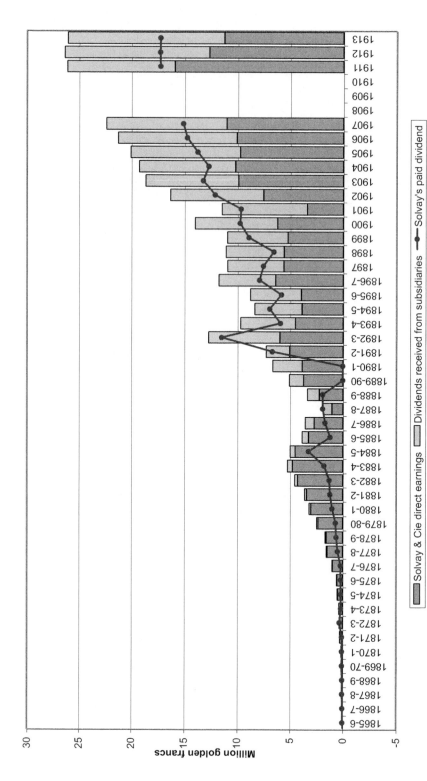

CHART 2.2. Earnings from Solvay direct activities, dividends received from foreign subsidiaries, and dividend paid by Solvay & Cie to its shareholders (1866–1913). *Sources:* ACS AG meeting minutes 1866–1873; ACS AG reports by the gérance 1874–1913.

2.3   A COMPANY OF ENGINEERS

In the middle of the 1870s, Solvay confronted with three considerable technical threats. First, the ammonia process was not Solvay's exclusive privilege. English, French, and German inventors continued to develop their own methods, to patent them, and to erect their plants in France and especially in Germany.[77] This frenetic activity was reinforced by confirmed success of the process, henceforth recognized in industrial circles and bestowed with medals at universal expositions.[78] Although competition with the lingering Leblanc process plants could wait, competition from new arrivals on the scene risked compromising development of Solvay. It would thus be imperative to maintain the technical advantages acquired and to consolidate know-how through organization and adequate technology scouting. This need was all the more important because protection offered by the patents was limited in time and subject to circumvention. Second, prospects for growth were threatened by the scarcity of ammonia on the market. The gas plants could not, alone, sustain an exponential growth in volume. Solvay simultaneously worked diligently to reduce waste and find a new supply source through a system of recovery coke ovens. Third, the Solvay process did not furnish, by nature, either chlorine or caustic soda, two products that were certainly less crucial at the time, but by which the Leblanc producers could increase their margins, thus prolonging all the longer the fight with Solvay. The research and development policy would be guided by these three challenges.

The Quest for Technical Supremacy

Through its quest for technical supremacy over the ammonia-soda process, Solvay acquired the image of a company of engineers rather than of chemists. In fact, the primary technical challenges had more to do with design and adjustments of mechanical equipment than of expertise in chemistry. The greatest strength of the nascent group was that it organized from the very start efficient circulation of technical information through a network of its plants, thus enabling rapid dissemination of technological innovation. Information sharing was institutionalized by industrial conventions signed between Solvay & Cie and each and every affiliated company: SPC in 1881; Brunner, Mond in 1882;

---

[77] In France, there was the plant at Sorgues (Vaucluse) that used the Boulouvard process as of 1878 and the plant at La Madeleine (Lorraine) using the new Schloessing and Rolland process as of 1881. In Germany, there were no fewer than about ten soda ash plants using the Honigmann process. Alongside these significant installations, there were numerous patents filed, with varying degrees of detail: Young in 1872, Hugo Müller in 1874, Laurent in 1875, Scherbacheff in 1875, Verzyl in 1875, Knab in 1877, Kuentz in 1877, Bernard in 1877, Wallace and Claus in 1877, the Count of Montblanc and Goulard in 1878, Jossinet in 1878, and Boutmy in 1879. See Lunge and Naville (1881), 223–9.

[78] Solvay & Cie, which had worked its way through in the shadows surrounded by indifference during its first ten years of existence, gained international recognition in 1873, when at Vienna, Ernest Solvay received a diploma of honor for his process. This distinction was followed by others that solidified the prestige of the company: gold medals and top prizes at expositions in Philadelphia (1876), Vienna (1877), Paris (1878), Sydney (1879), Melbourne (1880), Amsterdam (1883), Antwerp (1885), and others.

Verein in 1883; DSW in 1885; and Lubimoff in 1887. They stipulated the conditions of mutual and free communication of current and upcoming patents and improvements, complete reporting of activity, visit of plants by engineers, and so on. Some subsidiaries had these terms in their statutes; others signed additional conventions. From 1875, a system of comparative production tables was progressively set up: twice a month, all the group's plants communicated their technical operating data to corporate headquarters in Brussels. There the data were analyzed and compared, and the conclusions distributed to all the plants through technical reports. The nature of these data, as well as the measuring and reporting methods, was validated unanimously by the engineers of the companies affiliated with the Solvay system. In this way, each plant had at its disposal a selective report of key information coming out of all the operating sites in the group: quantities and composition of raw materials and outputs, temperatures, pressure and concentration in the various equipment, fuel consumption, volume of liquors, and levels of efficiency and waste. These comparisons also led to a certain healthy competition among the plants, each of which wanted to demonstrate its own efficiency. When a piece of equipment underwent an improvement, tests on an industrial scale were first done in two or three plants to take all parameters into account. The tests were then made available to the plants collectively. The main production engineers were encouraged to visit foreign plants and to meet together annually at Brussels.[79] Additionally, a certain degree of autonomy was given to each subsidiary in terms of development, to enable the plants to react to local competition while also preventing local competitors' emergence in other places.[80] The system, inaugurated in the 1870s, was consolidated subsequent to the creation in 1885 of the Direction Centrale Technique (Central Technical Department) in Brussels (or Section D), under the direction of Édouard Hannon. Before him, the position was held by Prosper Hanrez, who had been in that position since Dombasle but had never held the title officially. This section "had to control production and cost prices and... act as a mirror with the plants, reflecting information useful to them in every direction."[81] The section was also charged with mechanizing operations and making all the manufacturing steps continuous so as to reduce headcount and transform traditional duties of the worker into operations for control and measurement of production, limiting thus the risk of human error.[82]

Thanks to international cooperation, the process benefited rapidly from innovations coming from affiliated companies. Mond, obsessed by ammonia waste, patented in 1874, and then in 1883, continuous distillers, which

[79] ASPC, Trump (1935).

[80] As examples, Brunner, Mond focused its research on reducing ammonia losses because this raw material was expensive in England; in Germany, the appearance of a caustic soda cartel pushed Wessel to accelerate opening of the causticizing units.

[81] ACS, CdG, 24–28 Nov. 1930; Note no. 1249 of 24 Dec. 1930.

[82] ACS-O, Technical Committee, meeting minutes, 1889–1900, 29 Oct. 1897: Hannon observes that "reducing the number of daily hours will be justified by a decrease in cost price; that more intensive equipment operating more regularly will decrease the need for headcount but will increase the intellectual level of the workers needed, who will be more like overseers. That is the true philanthropy of the future."

enabled replacement of the intermittent distillation of ammonia liquors, which was labor intensive and costly in terms of materials. He introduced the use of milk of lime in place of bulk slaked lime, as well as cooling coils.[83] Likewise, the American Cogswell patented in 1887 a system for interior cooling of the columns that was later adopted everywhere. During the 1870s and 1880s, Ernest Solvay filed, through the work of his own teams and those of his subsidiaries, several patents for improvement. In particular, those of 1876 claimed about ten improvements, including an improved absorber, water pumps and filters, a brine density regulator, injection of virgin brine at the top of the column at the same time as injection of ammonia brine in the middle, introduction of solid salt in addition to brine to improve yield, and more.[84] Thus, the production underwent constant technical adjustments while still remaining fairly mysterious for outside observers. Secrecy was an integral part of the group's philosophy. Technical improvements were not necessarily patented immediately, and when they were, the descriptions remained hazy as to their concrete application.[85] Likewise, employees were contractually bound by traditional confidentiality clauses, and everything was done to retain them within the group. At the beginning of the 1890s, the process had reached its technical maturity. Ernest Solvay wrote to his technical managers: "We cannot cease to strive to do better than our competitors and since there are no longer any true revolutions to be waged for us, we must move toward secondary concerns."[86]

Industrial Research in Its Infancy

The early years of Solvay had been marked by a culture of the workshop based on self-teaching through empirical methods. Ernest Solvay, an archetype of the inventor-entrepreneur, had overcome a multitude of technical problems, surrounded by his brother and his friend Acheroy. Occasionally, he had fallen back on industrial consultants who were part of the academic world. Until 1875, no academically trained chemists were employed by Solvay. Improvements in the process and taking it to the next level were more often due to the work of mechanical engineers than to chemists. Ludwig Mond embodied,

---

[83] Watts (1923), 30; Lischka (1985), 97.

[84] English Solvay patents of 8 Mar. 1876 (no. 999), 5 May 1876 (no. 1904), and 20 May 1876 (no. 2143).

[85] In most of the chemistry manuals from the end of the nineteenth century and beginning of the twentieth century, one sees that their authors (e.g., Lunge, Wagner, Schreib, Sorel) are led to formulate hypotheses regarding the concrete operations of certain stages in the Solvay process. Some admit to a lack of recent information and rely on indirect sources. Thus, H. Schreib wrote in 1906: "In publications on the Solvay process, there appeared communications that were completely contradictory. This is explained quite easily by the fact that Solvay continually modified his process, making new improvements. On the other hand, he often indicated several different instructions for a single and same operation and this it seems was done to hide the process that he was actually using. Many of Solvay's instructions, for example in descriptions of a German patent of 27 November 1877, are very obscure and even incomprehensible for professionals"; and later: "For this device [the Solvay column] there were given so many different indications that it was hard to understand exactly how it was, in reality, to be employed." See Schreib (1906), 143–7.

[86] ACS-O, Technical Committee, meeting minutes 1889–1900, 12 Aug. 1892.

remotely, the first expert in chemistry, but his role immediately went beyond chemist to develop into that of a manager. It was in the middle of the 1880s that an embryonic internal industrial research organization emerged, characterized by creation of a central laboratory at Brussels interconnected with the plant and subsidiaries' laboratories. Academically trained chemists were hired to implement experimental scientific methods and to work on relatively long-term projects, although they were somewhat limited in their autonomy by the *gérants* and technical managers.

The first experimenter, appointed at the Couillet plant lab in 1874, was Arthur Brichaux, a college graduate. The following year, at the time Dombasle and Northwich entered into production and when Solvay became multinational, Ernest Solvay began looking for a chemist with a university degree "capable of carrying out and properly overseeing research work," not just a "simple analyst."[87] He turned to Professor Chaudelon of the Université de Liège, who recommended René Lucion, doctor of natural sciences with a specialty in chemistry. Lucion installed a rudimentary lab in the Brussels house that had served since 1875 as the company's offices. Ernest Solvay meant to have him test the validity of his new ideas: "What pleasant years we spent together starting and drawing up, bibliographically and experimentally, a host of questions of varying importance.... Lucion gave serious thought to everything I wanted to clarify."[88] Later, in each plant, at least one chemist was given analytical tasks of raw materials and outputs, as well as control over the production process. These employees were not intended to receive managerial positions.

This early organization was similar in structure to the system in place in the English Leblanc industry, which was characterized by the use of chemists, who did not necessarily have university degrees, to carry out most of the routine tasks of quality control and were involved only peripherally in research, which remained under the command of the owner.[89] The soda ash industry, strictly speaking, required less research than the dye industry, where the competition for speed to market of new materials determined economic success. In Germany, large chemical companies such as BASF, Hoechst, Bayer, and Agfa institutionalized their industrial research at the end of the 1870s by creating labs that were totally dedicated to research, independent of production, and staffed with a significant number of academically trained chemists.[90] Although Solvay cannot be compared to the companies mentioned here, the Belgian group distinguished itself by gradually moving away from the prevalent usages in the soda ash industry, in particular by interconnecting its production and research units through a network.

In addition to the analytical labs in the plants, a semi-industrial research lab was founded in Brussels in 1883, in the new buildings of the Central Administration. Lucion was joined there by Brichaux, then by a team of six chemists and lab assistants. The analytical tasks remained important, but increased attention

---

[87] PPSF, Box Ernest Solvay 2, Joseph Chaudelon to Ernest Solvay, 26 Apr. 1875.

[88] HC, Ernest Solvay's speech for the twenty-five-year career of A. Brichaux, R. Lucion, E. Hannon, 1901.

[89] Donnelly (1994), 100–28.

[90] Homburg (1992), 91–111.

was given to improvement of the process, valuation of its by-products, and the study of new opportunities. Electrolysis of salt was studied there in 1884 on a small testing installation.[91] In 1889, a technical committee was set up that aimed to hold weekly meetings of the research (Brichaux, Lucion, and Ortlieb) and technical (Hannon and Lemmonier) managers. Ernest Solvay occasionally attended these meetings or communicated his recommendations. Discussed at the meetings were the current and future experimental trials, reports from the subsidiaries, management of patents, and organization of the documentation system.[92] In 1889, a second laboratory, larger and better equipped, was built on the Rue de Neufchâtel, several hundred meters from corporate headquarters. Alongside this work, Ernest Solvay undertook, on his own, through Brichaux and Lucion, research that was not directly linked to the activity of the company (see Chapter 5).

In England, Germany, and the United States, the subsidiaries also had available to them small teams of chemists installed in the principal plants and who communicated with Brussels. At Northwich, the first university-degreed chemist, Gustav Jarmay, graduate of the Zurich Federal Polytechnic, was hired in 1877 to carry out routine analytical tasks and to work under the supervision of Mond on various problems such as loss of ammonia in the Solvay process, recycling of waste in production of hydrochloric acid, and production of synthetic ammonia by nitrogen fixation. Jarmay became plant manager at Northwich in the early 1880s. Like Solvay, Mond established and financed his own lab at London and had working there several collaborators from Brunner, Mond.[93] At Syracuse, the analytical lab was composed, in 1889, of the chemists Charles Pennock and J. A. Bradburn and three unskilled assistants. The majority of their tasks involved analysis of substances and control of the production process, but also the contribution of scientific know-how to the client industries that did not have chemists.[94] At Bernburg, the small laboratory of Heinrich Wilsing functioned in the same way in the mid-1880s. It did not become a true research laboratory until the end of the 1890s and proved crucial in the development of the electrolysis technology (see Chapter 5).[95]

Securing Supply of Ammonia

The problem of availability of ammonia was approached in two complementary ways: first, by reducing waste, in which Ludwig Mond played a big role with his continuous distillers, and second, by increasing availability. Until the mid-1880s, the Solvay soda ash plants were supplied limited volumes of ammonia from gas plants, which were sometimes far away. To reduce costs and uncertainty linked to this crucial raw material, Ernest Solvay delegated this question

[91] AES, Box V, Weekly reports from René Lucion to Ernest Solvay, here dated from 21 June 1884.
[92] ACS-O, Technical Committee, meeting minutes 1889–1900.
[93] Donnelly (1994), 116.
[94] ASPC, address by Charles Pennock at the occasion of the twenty-first anniversary of the Solvay Process Co, Solvay-Geddes, 1902.
[95] ACS, Eilsberger (b) (1930), 345.

to his brother-in-law, Louis Semet,[96] hired in 1876. Semet, having worked like him at the Saint-Josse gas plant, had shared his idea of developing a model coke oven for recovery of by-products.[97] The coke ovens served to distill the coal to obtain lighting gas or blast-furnace coke. Until then, the potential valuable waste, such as ammonia, benzol, and tar, had been allowed to escape. After six years of research, a small battery of six Semet-Solvay ovens were installed, in 1882, in a coal-mining installation belonging to the Société des Charbonnages de l'Ouest de Mons. The coke had to be instantaneously heated to a very high temperature. To do this, it was necessary to find a device enabling transmission of the heat through walls that were as thin as possible while still ensuring stability of the system. The Semet-Solvay ovens met these criteria and enabled rapid calcination and consequently strong production by the ovens. The seams were greatly reduced, and the yield in by-products was very high. In 1886, a battery of twenty-five ovens was built at the coal mine of Havré, belonging to the Société du Bois-du-Luc, which later bought it. These ovens underwent fantastic development, through the supply of both ammonia to the Solvay plants and coke to the metallurgic industry (see Chapter 5). The strategic and commercial success of these ovens enabled Louis Semet to become a *gérant* in 1887.

Toward a Broader Range of Products

Slow Growth in Caustic Soda

Until the start of the 1880s, Solvay remained determined to never undertake production either of caustic soda or of any other caustic salts and soda crystals used in domestic applications. Traditionally, caustic soda, combined with fatty acids, constituted an essential element in hard soap. In the liquid state, it could be dissolved and act as a degreasing agent. Its usages would multiply at the end of the nineteenth century, especially in the dye industry. In its informational brochures, Solvay exhorted the consumer industries to produce by themselves the caustic lyes from Solvay soda ash, for reasons of transportation efficiency.[98] It involved simply dissolving the soda ash in water, adding the proper proportion of quicklime and heating it. That was the process used in fact by the Leblanc manufacturers with their own soda ash. Watching the market grow and habits remain, Solvay decided to produce caustic soda by itself. Dombasle installed in 1883 a process for causticizing soda ash with lime. The plants at Syracuse (1888), Berezniki (1890), and Sarralbe (1891) followed close behind, without, however, producing on a very large scale, except for in the United States, where production quickly surpassed twenty thousand tons per year.

---

[96] Louis Semet (1844–1920) was the nephew of Florimond Semet, owner of the Saint-Josse gas plant where Ernest Solvay's career began. In 1874, he married Elisa Solvay (1851–1948), Ernest's younger sister. Thus, he was both his cousin and his brother-in-law. He entered Solvay & Cie in 1876 and became *gérant* in 1887, replacing Prosper Hanrez, until his resignation in 1907. He was also a member of the supervisory board (*Aufsichtsrat*) of DSW from 1885 to 1909.

[97] PPSF, Box Ernest Solvay 2, Handwritten note by Ernest Solvay: History of Semet ovens, 1889.

[98] ACS, Brochure Solvay & Cie published for the World Exposition at Paris in 1878.

When the lime was not of very high purity, a better choice was the Loewig process for causticizing soda ash by iron oxide. In 1883, Solvay purchased a license for this process through the intermediary of Wessel, who was eager to see the DSW produce caustic soda. In Germany, the threat existed of a syndicate forming that could weaken the general position of the DSW. He also wanted to be able to compete in caustic soda with the English Leblanc firms on the export markets. It would be the end of the 1890s before the process was mastered and installed in several plants (Berezniki, Sarralbe, Northwich, Couillet, and Donetz), in the form of a continuous process. Nonetheless, the process with lime maintained the upper hand. Solvay was late in increasing its tonnage in caustic soda. In Germany, caustic soda was not immediately part of a syndicate, thus allowing free access to unbridled competition. Soon electrolysis would offer an alternative and complementary method for the production of caustic soda, thus opening the door to new players in the sector (see Chapter 5).

The Unfulfilled Challenge of Chlorine Recovery

One of the weaknesses of the Solvay process was that it did not draw any profit from the chlorine contained in the sodium chloride. The data were simple: as long as this situation persisted, Solvay could not totally overcome the Leblanc manufacturers, which, thanks to improvements brought by the Weldon and Deacon processes, recovered hydrochloric acid in their fumes and converted it to chlorine for manufacture of bleaching powder used in the textile industry. There was no urgency in this, however, because supply outstripped demand. Already in 1872, Solvay and Mond were aware of this lacuna. Mond wrote to Solvay: "It would be very desirable for you to seriously study at a reasonable scale the production of muriatic acid [i.e., hydrochloric acid] with magnesia."[99] From this moment on, Solvay and Mond both threw themselves into a serious research program on chlorine and hydrochloric acid that lasted until the advent of electrolysis in the mid-1890s. Substitution of lime by magnesia came to nothing. Brichaux and Lucion investigated other methods. In theory, the most attractive idea was to be able to close the Solvay process cycle by recovering chlorine and hydrochloric acid from the waste product, calcium chloride. Several patents were filed in 1877 that aimed to blend calcium chloride with silica or alumina and to heat and dry the mixture. The chlorine that was generated could be used directly for the production of bleaching powder. At Dombasle, a process using copper chloride was also studied. In 1889 Solvay joined together with Professor Prosper De Wilde to test a process he invented that was able to obtain hydrochloric acid through decomposition of a blend of magnesium chloride and clay.[100] For his part, Mond perfected in 1883 a process for treating ammonium chloride with sulfuric acid to obtain hydrochloric acid and ammonium sulfate. In 1886, he obtained chlorine by passing the ammonium chloride vapors over nickel oxide and recovered ammonia that could be

---

[99] PPSF, Box Ernest Solvay 2, Correspondence with Mond 1872–1874, Ludwig Mond to Ernest Solvay, 8 Dec. 1872.

[100] ART, Unclassified files, Research on chlorine, hydrochloric acid, chloride of lime, 1879–1900.

reinjected into the ammonia-soda process.[101] All these efforts, seductive in theory and sometimes tested on an industrial scale, did not provide any economic returns and were abandoned when electrolysis came into use. For lack of anything better, a small part of the calcium chloride resulting from the soda ash production was marketed as an air dehumidifier and as a cooling vehicle in chill rooms.[102]

Attempts at Phosphates

Early on, the company thus attempted to recover the chlorine from the waste product generated by its process, calcium chloride. Because chlorine still had few market outlets, Solvay was interested in a patent that the Belgian chemist Prosper De Wilde had filed for enrichment of phosphate of chalk by hydrochloric acid to obtain precipitated phosphate, a fertilizer that performed as well as the superphosphate (obtained by treatment of the phosphate of chalk by sulfuric acid).[103] Thus, when chalk beds were discovered at Mesvin-Ciply in Belgium, Solvay purchased them, in 1882. This was not a high-risk move, as the beds could also provide natural rich phosphates. Under the direction of the engineer Alfred Lemonnier, exploitation was begun in 1884 in a plant opened at Mesvin, and research on enrichment was carried out there.[104] Solvay first ensured the monopoly of the Bouchez process for mechanical enrichment of chalk, and then developed internally the "Ortlieb-Solvay process" for this same purpose. This secondary activity had problems taking off, as a result of a collapse in phosphate prices in the 1880s.

However, the affair was reignited when the company had the opportunity to buy new beds in France. Ernest and Alfred Solvay remained in favor of developing phosphates, whereas Semet and Hanrez were doubtful, and the supervisory board considered this diversification a distraction that risked diluting their resources. Alfred Lemonnier was able to convince the first four of the opportunity offered by these rich beds and of the necessity of buying them quickly. Lemonnier had in fact paid a visit to the directors of Saint-Gobain to propose to them a joint acquisition, which they refused.[105]

Between 1888 and 1895, Solvay established nine plants for enrichment of phosphate of chalk in Belgium (Mesvin, Mesvin-Ciply, Ciply, and Spiennes) and in France (Hargicourt, Vaux-Eclusier, Curlu, Orville, and Beauval), as well as three plants for superphosphates, at Mesvin, Hemixem (Antwerp), and La Madeleine-Lez-Lille.

---

[101] Watts (1923), 35–8. This method was superseded by Carl Höpfner's process in which the chlorine was recovered as zinc chloride and then decomposed electrolytically. Mond then focused on the Höpfner process instead of following Solvay in the acquisition of the Castner electrolytic process. This explains the absence of participation by Brunner, Mond in Castner-Kellner Co., as is discussed in Chapter 5.

[102] ACS, Brochure Solvay & Cie published for the World Exposition at Paris in 1900.

[103] PPSF, Box Ernest Solvay 2, note by Ernest Solvay, 15 May 1879; Ernest Solvay to E. Carenon, 15 Mar. 1879.

[104] ACS, AG, Gérance and supervisory board reports, 1886.

[105] AHR, PD Alfred Lemonnier, "40 ans à la Société Solvay & Cie 1881–1921."

At the end of the 1880s, these plants provided up to fifty thousand tons of phosphate of chalk, thirty thousand tons of which were transformed into superphosphate of chalk.[106] This activity was abruptly abandoned in 1895, when Solvay sold the entirety of these beds to Saint-Gobain, in the context of an agreement in which Solvay ceased exploitation of phosphates while Saint-Gobain agreed not to begin production of ammonia soda.[107] By reselling this accessory activity, Solvay protected itself against competition in soda ash from its most serious French rival (see Chapter 3).

---

[106] ACS, Brochure Solvay & Cie published for the World Exposition at Paris in 1889.
[107] ACS-O, 1701 Saint-Gobain, Transfert des activités phosphates, 1895.

FIGURE 3.1. Offices of Syndikat Deutscher Sodafabriken GmbH and of Syndikat Deutscher Aetznatronfabriken GmbH erected at Bernburg in 1907. The German soda ash and caustic soda cartels were directly managed from DSW headquarters, which were also installed in this building. (Solvay Archives.)

3

Reaching a Dominant Position

At the dawn of the 1880s, Solvay had become a multinational group composed of wholly owned factories and partially held subsidiaries. Industrial conventions had institutionalized the circulation of technical information among its parties. Its plants, ideally located, had production capacities and technology superior to the Leblanc plants. In a sector in which products were hardly differentiated and in which manufacturers had little control over the volume of demand, these competitive advantages enabled the group to reach a dominant position. Solvay's competitive and commercial strategy became the second pillar of its power, the first being its technical predominance. To be effective, it had to conquer the increasingly protected national markets and overtake the residual international commerce. In these different economic spheres, Solvay and its partners entered into competition not only with the Leblanc manufacturers, which were solidly established and capable of supplying a broad range of soda and chlorinated products, but also with newcomers in the ammonia-soda industry. Everywhere, competitive battles broke out. Everywhere Solvay increased its output and reduced prices to force existing competitors to negotiate industrial ententes, a form of market organization in vogue at the end of the nineteenth century. These agreements enabled Solvay to stabilize its position while giving the Leblanc producers time to smoothly phase out their obsolete process.

Internally, the Solvay organization had simply followed along with international expansion. The hybrid structure established in the 1870s and 1880s underwent few changes, despite the numerous questions brought up about reinforcement of group cohesion. The headquarters took on greater importance, being the center for technical management that channeled know-how and the commercial department that dealt with the web of contracts and agreements. Sustained growth enabled both the significant remuneration of capital and a transition to almost exclusive self-financing. Also, new dynamics were established, following long negotiations among associates. The founding partners, now considered heroes, concentrated full decision-making power in their own hands and ensured for themselves and their family greater control over the company.

3.1   WAR AND PEACE IN SODA ASH INTERNATIONAL TRADE

Market Organization and Solvay's Commercial Strategy

During the first fifty years of its existence, Solvay witnessed changes in the reg-ulatory aspects of international trade, changes that overall proved to its benefit. As pointed out by the historian Paul Bairoch, protectionism was the rule rather than the exception during the nineteenth century and up to World War I. Great Britain was viewed as "a liberal island in an ocean of protectionism,"[1] which stemmed from increased nationalistic sentiments in the large nations aiming to develop their nascent industries. Only small countries such as the Netherlands, Denmark, Switzerland, Portugal, Belgium, and Sweden had fol-lowed the English model by adopting a resolutely liberal trade policy. Yet the period 1860–1879 was the only real free-market interlude in Europe. As of 1860, bilateral trade treaties, initiated by the Franco-English Cobden-Chevalier Treaty, momentarily relaxed tariffs and instituted the most-favored-nation clause. Solvay thus began its international expansion in a precise moment of tariff disarmament. In other words, it took advantage of the fact that the lax restrictions on English soda ash exports inhibited the development of this industry on the Continent.

This situation did not last. In 1879, Germany was the first country to rein-force its trade barriers, in the context of Bismarckian realpolitik. Through reciprocity and a domino effect, most European countries followed its lead. In France, the Méline Tariff of 1892 constituted the high point of this gradual return to European protectionism, which lasted until World War I.[2] This global trend was nonetheless mitigated by the more liberal policy of Great Britain and other smaller European countries, as well as by specific tariffs on certain prod-ucts. With respect to the United States, following other imperatives, including protection of domestic salaries, it was characterized throughout the period 1861–1913 as "the bastion of modern protectionism," with average duties estimated at 40 percent on manufactured goods.[3] It was during this period of a general return to protectionism that Solvay was fully expanding in the large markets. The group contributed significantly to making the countries in which it was located almost autonomous with respect to soda ash, a key product for several of their processing industries.

From the beginning of the 1870s, the ammonia process enabled achieve-ment of a cost price that was 20 percent to 30 percent lower than that of Leblanc.[4] Solvay had been the first to master this production process and thus had a competitive edge that it defended through its technical excellence. A rapid depreciation policy of its production equipment further increased this advantage. In the heat of competition, it gained the natural privilege of setting

---

[1] Bairoch (1999), 31–48.
[2] Dormois (2009), 89–98.
[3] Bairoch (1999), 53.
[4] Haber (1958), 101–2.

sales price. Its general policy was to let prices drop to promote soda ash consumption, to gradually extinguish the Leblanc process, and to avoid the arrival
of new competitors enticed by high profits. There is ample evidence that the
price of soda ash on the international market was three times lower in 1900
than in 1864, as a result of a battle generated by the arrival of the ammonia
process.[5] Prices were greatly depressed in the middle of the 1880s, at the time
when the competitive battles were at their fiercest. They climbed again after the
Leblanc manufacturers began their reconversion in the 1890s. In 1891, soda
ash produced by the ammonia process for a cost of 7.50 francs per one hundred kilograms was sold at 11.90 francs, which left Solvay with a gross margin
between 35 percent and 40 percent. Prices never fell below Solvay's cost price,
but they did fall well below the cost price of Leblanc manufacturers, which
were regularly forced to sell at a loss. Under these circumstances, quantities
of soda ash put on the market by the two types of manufacturers followed an
inverse curve (see Chart 3.1). The transfer of power from Leblanc to Solvay
took place between 1885 and 1890.

To maintain its position acquired in the national markets, which were
becoming increasingly impenetrable, Solvay had to learn to use to its advantage industrial ententes, an economic tool that had been in common use from
the 1880s. The purpose of these agreements among firms operating in a sector
was to influence production or distribution of goods or services by limiting
competition and sharing markets. Depending on the countries and the times,
these collaborative mechanisms had various names: *cartels, ententes, syndicats, comptoirs de vente, bureaux, Verband, Konvention, Gemeinschaft*, and
so on.[6] This form of cooperative capitalism is today considered an impediment
to free trade, as it restricts innovation, prevents the elimination of ineffective firms, keeps prices high to the detriment of the consumer, and favors
dumping in outside markets. In the second half of the nineteenth century, the
agreements were sometimes used by states as industrial and commercial policy
tools to ensure stability and surplus revenue not only for the manufacturers
but also for national economies. The cartels preexisted Solvay and often regulated its markets upstream (salt) and downstream (e.g., glass, soap). They
were tolerated in France, Belgium, Austria-Hungary, and Russia. They were
encouraged and legalized in Germany, the figurehead of the cartel movement,
where they numbered seven hundred in 1910.[7] Great Britain remained in an

---

[5] The data available on prices and cost prices of soda ash are hardly comparable from one
country to another over long periods. The calculation methods vary, depending on raw materials, transportation and customs costs, place of measurement (e.g., at the plant, port, customer), currency exchange rates, degree of purity of the soda ash, and the truthfulness of the
information put forward by the manufacturers themselves. We refer to the following internal
and external sources: ACS, 1029–18, La politique commerciale des frères Solvay, 1938; ACS,
1001-24-1 Politique des prix pratiqués par la Sté Solvay avant, pendant et après la guerre,
1932. Haber (1958), 101–2; Warren (1980), 39–49; Schreib (1906), 369–84; Lunge and Naville
(1881), 649.

[6] Hexner (1946), 9.

[7] Schröter (1996), 132–3.

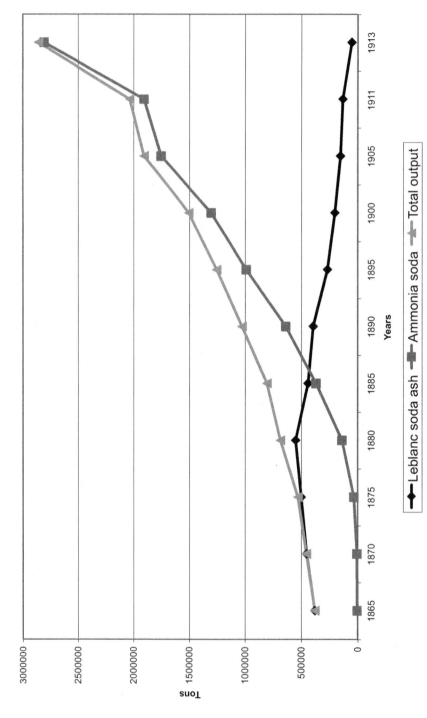

CHART 3.1. Worldwide soda ash production (1865–1913). *Source:* Te-Pang Hou (1947), 41.

ambivalent position, whereas in the United States, the Sherman Act of 1890 forbade any collusion among competitors.[8] Organized at first on a regional scale, the ententes became national, and then evolved into more elaborated forms of international cartels. This phenomenon reached its peak after World War I (see Chapter 9). In the chemical industry, international cartels were instituted in the gunpowder (1890), dynamite (1896), automobile fuel (1902), chloride of lime (1903), lime (1906), borax (1906), petroleum (1906), dyed silks (1907), saltpeter (1909), carbide (1910), superphosphates (1910), oleins (1910), and nitrogen fertilizer (1910) industries. In the glass industry, a primary Solvay customer, international cartels developed from the national ententes as of 1900.[9] Despite their multiplication, cartels were often fragile organizations put into place for short periods of time. Their efficiency assumed a simple product, high research-and-development costs, or a small number of firms active in the industry. Their internal organization required steadfast direction, with instruments available for control and retaliatory measures.[10] The alkali industry met most of these criteria. Even if no international cartel was recognized as such, in reality, one did exist from the end of the 1890s and was orchestrated by the Solvay group. To better understand the formation of this cartel, it is necessary to delve into the structure of each of the large national markets.

From Competitive Battles to Industrial Ententes in the National Markets

France, Primary Market and Group Apprentice

Since the start of the 1870s, France had become the primary market for Solvay and a source of rich commercial experience that was then disseminated to its other subsidiaries. The plant at Dombasle exported to the duty-free Belgian market, to compensate for the small size of the Couillet plant. The Paris office, created in 1876 and managed by Jules Bister, was in charge of all foreign relations. In reality this office was the veritable commercial headquarters of Solvay & Cie until the creation of Section C in 1885 in the Central Administration at Brussels.[11] In France, as elsewhere, the central office, along with local agencies and independent agents, was able to make the merchandise flow over long distances and to receive information on markets and competitors, which was then sent back to national managements and to Brussels.

Until 1881, France was still importing English soda ash. In the first half of the 1880s the battle intensified. Increased tariff duties and the rise in power of Solvay dried up the flow of imports and made France autonomous in soda ash (see Chapter 2).[12] Saint-Gobain, the largest Leblanc manufacturer, understood that its process was in peril and set up a semi-industrial ammonia-soda installation at Saint-Fons in 1881.[13] That same year, Daguin & Cie, a salt supplier for

---

[8] Motta (2004), 1–17.

[9] Dormois (2009), 63–5.

[10] Barjot (1994).

[11] Mioche (2008), 27; ACS, 1029–18, La politique commerciale des frères Solvay, 1938, 13.

[12] Haber (1958), 210.

[13] Daviet (1988), 286.

Solvay, acquired the Société des Produits Chimiques de l'Est, which had established an ammonia-soda plant at La Madeleine (Nancy), using the improved
process of Schloessing and Rolland. Solvay retaliated by lowering its prices
and filing a lawsuit against Daguin for infringement of its equipment patents.
A civil court nonsuited Solvay. Peace returned through the intervention of the
Leblanc manufacturers, worn down by the price war that had opposed the
two ammonia-soda producers. Solvay and Daguin abandoned the lawsuit and
concluded a first five-year accord for the sale of their products (10 December
1886). Solvay's position remained virtually untouched, as it obtained half of
the one hundred thousand tons produced annually in the country, as well as
any future increases and exports. Daguin was limited to a quota of thirteen
thousand tons and agreed not to establish any other plant.[14]

This first agreement instigated by the Leblanc manufacturers rapidly led to
a general entente among all the French producers, in the form of the Participation Soude, in January 1887. It called for sharing all of the soda ash products,
regardless of the manufacturing process used. Solvay and Daguin reached agreement there with the Leblanc manufacturers Saint-Gobain, Maletra, Kuhlmann,
Hautmont, Péchiney, Weiss, the Compagnie Générale des Produits Chimiques
du Midi, Rio Tinto (Marseille l'Estaque), and Grimès & Cie. In a dominating
position, Solvay received a minimum quota of nearly half of the total production, as well as exclusive attribution of later increases and exports, except for
four thousand tons of caustic salts. To administer the sales, the central offices
of the syndicate, located at Paris, were in charge of controlling the application
of quotas. Each participant nonetheless remained in contact with its customers,
giving the appearance of independence.[15] In reality, this entente marked the
death knell for the Leblanc process and prevented a ruinous and desperate
fight. Solvay also continued to conclude bilateral agreements with several of
its competitors, to further solidify its position. In 1894, an agreement with
five *fabricants du centre* (Saint-Gobain, Péchiney, Kuhlmann, Hautmont, and
Maletra) called for allocation by Solvay of an indemnity, known as the New
Year's gift (*cadeau de nouvelle année*), to the other companies in exchange
for their commitment not to oppose Solvay within the Participation Soude.[16]
A sales office for the Eastern soda ash makers, directed by Solvay, was also
inaugurated in 1906 to regulate shared sales of Solvay, Saint-Gobain, and
Daguin.

The general entente, renewable every five years, was extended without incident until 1895, when a brief but strong conflict pitted Solvay against Saint-
Gobain. It shed light on another weapon in the competitive arsenal: intimidation by the spectacular but temporary incursion into a competitor's territory
to provoke negotiations. This conflict broke out after a new attempt made by
Solvay to lower soda ash prices to fight against English imports and against

[14] ACS-O, 1001–49 Affaire Daguin; ACS-O, 1100–5/2 Affaire Daguin; ACS-O, 1100–13/14 Dombasle, Résumés divers.
[15] ACS-O, 1001–51 Contrats, "Résumé des engagements industriels et commerciaux contractés
par la Société Solvay & Cie envers les sociétés affiliées et réciproquement," Dec. 1888.
[16] ACS-O, 1001–51 Contrats, Contract of 15 Jan. 1894, extension on 24 Dec. 1900.

the emergence of new ammonia-soda plants in eastern France. Saint-Gobain, a representative for the Leblanc producers whose profitability was affected by this measure, opposed it. Given the danger implied by this refusal, Solvay purchased massive phosphate deposits in France and Belgium, a sector in which Saint-Gobain was increasingly investing.[17] Solvay itself had entered secondarily in this sector, in the 1880s (see Chapter 2). The two companies rapidly arrived at an arrangement, after which Solvay withdrew from phosphates and superphosphates and sold all its deposits to Saint-Gobain. In return, Saint-Gobain agreed not to construct an ammonia-soda plant for ten years and had to take part in the New Year's gift from Solvay to the other Leblanc manufacturers.[18] As indicated by Jean-Pierre Daviet, a Saint-Gobain historian, this agreement is important inasmuch it had a long-lasting effect on market sharing in the French chemical industry.[19]

The ententes rarely involved all the manufacturers. Some newcomers voluntarily remained outside them, in an effort to make their own place in the ammonia-soda industry or to resell their plants at a nice profit to Solvay or to the cartel. The ammonia-soda plants of La Meurthe and of Montferrand are two examples of this. The first was encouraged by salt makers and glassmakers. In June 1891, the Rosières-Varangéville salt maker was looking to create a soda ash plant, encouraged by the Eastern glassmakers' syndicate (Syndicat des Verriers de l'Est), which had complained about excessive prices of soda ash in France compared to the Belgian and German markets. Solvay replied by threatening to create a rock-salt mine with costs shared by the Participation Soude. Also, Rosière-Varangéville was excluded from supplies sent to Solvay and to Saint-Gobain. In November 1891, the ammonia-soda plant was established. Solvay put pressure on the Comptoir des Sels, the salt cartel of which it was a member, so that the new soda ash plant could not get supplies. Then Solvay carried out its threat to purchase an additional rock-salt concession at Crévic. In 1894, the new soda ash plant reached an operating rate of thirty tons per day. In a difficult financial situation, it tried in vain to join the Participation Soude. However, Solvay decided, via the Participation Soude, on a new drop in prices in 1895. Gasping for air, the Meurthe plant petitioned the authorities to protest Solvay's tactics against it, but without results. In June 1896, bent but not broken, it was admitted into the bilateral Solvay-Daguin agreement, with a quota of 8 percent, purposefully too low to enable it to reach profitability. In 1901, Saint-Gobain, which wanted to have an ammonia-soda plant despite its commitment of 1895, proceeded with the acquisition of the Meurthe plant, which would become final at the end of 1906, only after expiration of the agreement with Solvay. This movement stirred up new problems in the relationship between the two large firms. Solvay protested but refused to pursue the affair in court. It maintained combat on the economic level by purchasing the entire production of sulfuric acid produced by Vieille-Montagne in its plants at Baelen and Viviez, so as to reduce supplies to Saint-Gobain. This final

[17] Daviet (1988), 294.
[18] ACS, 1029–18, Politique commerciale des frères Solvay, 1938; ACS-O, 1701 Saint-Gobain.
[19] Daviet (1988), 354.

show of strength led to the signature of a special soda, acid, and phosphates agreement with Saint-Gobain. The tension issuing from this episode did not prevent repeated renewals of the Participation Soude until 1921.[20]

The competition against the Montferrand ammonia-soda plant marked a second chapter of the French story and had many implications. As of 1889, the Compagnie des Sels de Besançon had established a saltworks in the Franche-Comté area, three hundred kilometers south of Dombasle. An ammonia-soda plant was planned for the site. In the field, Louis Talvard, the new commercial manager for Solvay at Paris, and Adolphe Marquet, the plant manager at Dombasle, kept Brussels apprised of the project status while trying to discourage the competition's shareholders and managers through shrewd persuasion. Nonetheless, the ammonia-soda plant was constructed. Unable to prevent its establishment, Solvay reacted, resorting to the usual practices: dropping soda ash prices through the Participation Soude and salt prices through the Comptoir des Sels. Unable to withstand the financial pressures, the Montferrand plant rapidly shut down. It was then that Arthur Lambert, a Solvay engineer at Couillet between 1879 and 1886, took over the plant with the help of investors. Solvay's fear of seeing its process "pirated" by one of its own engineers was becoming reality. The five-year noncompete clause in Lambert's contract had ended, and most of the patents had fallen into the public domain in 1887. Lambert did not hesitate to threaten Ernest Solvay in person with publication of a detailed manual on installation of ammonia-soda plants. The plant resumed production in 1894, under the name La Soude Française. Ernest Solvay, taking a direct blow, recommended a forceful response. The Participation Soude once again dropped prices, preventing the Soude Française from becoming profitable. In 1896, the Participation Soude proposed to purchase the plant for a price of FF 900,000 (US$171,000). The proposal was rejected, and new capital was injected by industrialists from the North of France, the company Desprez, Paquet, Vincent, & Savary. A new company, the Soudière de Montferrand, took over assets from the previous company. It would take three more years of fighting before Solvay proceeded with the acquisition of the plant through the cartel at a price of FF 1,150,000 (US$218,500). The agreement stipulated that the selling company had to "dismantle the plant, sell the equipment, destroy everything so designated by Solvay and in case of future sale of the land, ensure that a soda ash plant could not be erected on the property for fifteen years."[21]

For Solvay, the Dombasle plant had long been adequate for meeting the demands of domestic consumption and exports to the ports in the Mediterranean (e.g., Italy, Spain, Algeria). Nonetheless, as of 1892, the company wanted closer proximity to the booming consumption center of the soap makers in Marseilles. It had already studied the region, but it was the multiplication of competing projects that finally prompted the decision to build. Several Leblanc plants had already been active there since the start of the nineteenth century. Since 1877, the Sorgues plant, taken over in 1878 by the Compagnie Générale des Produits Chimiques du Midi, manufactured ammonia soda using

---

[20] ACS-O, 1100-7-1/2/3 Soudière de la Meurthe; ACS-O, 1100–13/14 Dombasle, Résumés divers.
[21] ACS-O, 1100–1/3–1 Soudière de Montferrand et Affaire Lambert; Mioche (2008), 36–7.

the Boulouvard process. It was soon joined by the Compagnie des Produits Chimiques d'Alais et de la Camargue, which would come to be known as Pechiney, which tried to install the same process in its plant at Salin-de-Giraud. Things became even more urgent when in 1892, Saint-Gobain opened a huge plant at Sète, and Pechiney considered erecting a new Leblanc plant at Salin-de-Giraud in collaboration with the Marseilles soap makers. Following Solvay's actions indicating a possible price drop, the latter project was abandoned. In 1895, Solvay acquired from Pechiney about forty hectares at Salin-de-Giraud to build a plant there. The two firms agreed that Pechiney would supply Solvay with salt and cease its production of ammonia soda, on the condition that Solvay would not acquire interests in salt on the Mediterranean coast.[22] Salin-de-Giraud remained a midsize plant, working with sea salt instead of rock salt. By this second establishment, Solvay had consolidated its hold over the French market.[23] The last French Leblanc plant closed its doors in 1913.

Triangular Competition in Germany

In the Zollverein, and then in unified Germany, the trade policy on alkalis was clearly protectionist until 1873. A sharp drop in tariffs from M 4 to M 1.5 per hundred kilograms starting on this date had the effect of paralyzing the German alkali industry by favoring market penetration by English soda ash. Pressure exerted on the authorities by the industry led to an increase in customs duties to M 2.5 in 1879–1880. Imports of soda ash declined rapidly and Germany began to export. The production tripled in fewer than eight years, in part because of the rise in power of DSW. Germany became a net exporter of soda ash in 1884, of soda crystals in 1886, and of caustic soda in 1890. In 1880, the country numbered about twenty Leblanc plants, compared to five in 1901 and two in 1909.[24] Domestic consumers were unscathed by these protectionist measures, as the price of soda ash dropped from 17 to M 9 per hundred kilograms between 1878 and 1888.[25]

Solvay had been late in entering Germany, and the Honigmann ammonia soda process had made sharp inroads there (see Chapter 2). In the mid-1880s, before the competitive struggles were bound by agreements, DSW had achieved a market share of 35 percent, compared to 33 percent for the Honigmann plants and 31 percent for the Leblanc plants, for a total production of 120,000 tons.[26] Carl Wessel's task was thus all the more challenging, despite support from the *gérants*, members of the supervisory board of DSW, and their equilibrium policy between their French and German plants.[27] Like in France, it was the Leblanc manufacturers, worried about competition from Solvay, which initiated the agreement negotiations. Friedrich Engelhorn (BASF) and Robert Hasenclever (Rhenania) went to Brussels for this purpose in January 1884.

[22] ACS-O, 1001–51 Solvay-Péchiney contract from 24 May 1895.
[23] Daumalin, Lambert, and Mioche (2007).
[24] Warren (1980), 187.
[25] Schallermair (1997), 46.
[26] ACS, 1151 DSW, Rapport général.
[27] ACS-O, 1001–51 Contrats. "Résumé des engagements industriels et commerciaux contractés par la Société Solvay & Cie envers les sociétés affiliées et réciproquement," Dec. 1888.

Other meetings followed in Germany, assembling representatives from BASF, Rhenania, Griesheim, Verein Mannheim, and Dieuze as well as Carl Wessel himself. The negotiations failed systematically until 1886, in light of demands by Wessel to have 40 percent of consumption and all exports.[28] Wessel was not in favor of an agreement at any price, especially to preserve the image of DSW with its consumers: "we do not want it to be said later that it was us who wanted the agreement in order to get an increase in prices. This would make a bad impression on customers."[29] On the contrary, he was determined to increase output to up to two-thirds of domestic production, to naturally squeeze out the competition.[30] The negotiators had a great deal of leverage. Wessel and the *gérants* were able to depreciate the price of salt thanks to their saltworks at Sarralbe and Bernburg. They threatened to begin the production of by-products from the Leblanc process, in particular chlorinated products. They especially continued to lower the cost price of their soda ash. For their part, competitors attacked the interests of the whole Solvay group by increasing their exports to France, Belgium, Great Britain, and even the United States and Russia. The troubled situation in Germany thus generated instability in the world market, to which neither Brunner, Mond nor SPC was immune, and which pressed Carl Wessel to come to an agreement. It became clearer that peace would prevail only by granting all the German manufacturers an adequate share in international trade.

In 1887, a first step in this direction was taken with the constitution of the Syndikat Deutscher Sodafabriken Carl Wessel, which aimed to distribute soda ash from DSW and seven smaller manufacturers in the north of the country through a shared sales office.[31] Having failed to win over all the players at one time, Wessel had played both ends against the middle. Four years of open fighting were still necessary against the large producers of western Germany, in particular Rhenania, Verein Mannheim, Matthes & Weber, Griesheim and Dieuze, before the conclusion of a general agreement in 1891. The resistant plants were incorporated into the syndicate. The articles of association called for common sales of all types of soda ash. DSW held half of the votes in the general assemblies and was charged with day-to-day management. As expected, the amount of exports from the plants in the west forced Solvay, Brunner, Mond, and SPC to grant an export quota of 35,000 tons to German producers, to be allocated on approval by Solvay and according to prices set by Solvay. DSW received half of total production, estimated at 189,000 tons in 1891.[32] Four

---

[28] ACS, Eilsberger (b) (1930), 213.

[29] ACS, Eilsberger (b) (1930), 214.

[30] ACS-O, 1151 DSW, CS meetings, 25 Oct. 1886.

[31] These seven firms were Chemische Fabrik Buckau AG, at Magdeburg; R. Suermondt & Cie, at Montwy; Nürnberger Sodafabrik, at Fürther Kreuzung; Engelcke & Klause, at Trotha; Rothenfelder Salinen-und Soolbad AG, at Rothenfelde; AG Georg Egestorffs Salzwerke, at Linden; and Chemische Fabrik Schöningen, at Schöningen.

[32] Quotas were allocated as follows: DSW, 99,088 tons; Verein Chemische Fabriken, 21,294 tons; Suermondt & Cie, 15,895 tons; Buckau, 14,000 tons; Matthes & Weber, 11,676 tons; Dieuze, 9,017 tons; Rhenania, 8,697 tons; Chemische Fabrik Griesheim, 6,333 tons; Engelcke & Krause, 3,000 tons.

plants in the north were shut down and their owners indemnified by members. Several dissidents remained. They were gradually forced either to cease their activities or to integrate into the syndicate through special agreements.[33] The syndicate further reinforced its position by concluding an agreement with the German salt cartel, which included the Prussian national saltworks. From then, any new entrants could no longer be furnished salt without the permission of the soda ash cartel, thus making construction of new soda ash plants almost impossible. Thanks to the protections in the sector, the price of soda ash, which had dropped to M 9 per hundred kilograms in 1890, was temporarily brought back up to around M 12.[34] Alongside this cartel policy, which was also in the process of becoming a general rule in the German heavy-chemical industry (there were thirteen cartels in 1905), DSW put into practice other mechanisms that Solvay had already tried in France. It notably started the production of chromium (from 1892 to 1904) to counter four producers of alizarin – Neuhaus, Bayer, Leverkus, and Gauhe – that planned to erect a common soda ash plant to become autonomous.[35]

The takeover of the plant at Château-Salins, in German Lorraine, was a second telling episode, and one that had repercussions in France. It demonstrated the difficulty in reconciling the interests of a multinational company in two neighboring markets, each imbued with a certain nationalism. In 1896, a capitalist, Claudius Tillement, and a technician, Alfons Nicolas, built an ammonia-soda plant alongside a saltworks at Château-Salins. Carl Wessel, very influential in the Alsace-Lorraine salt association, requested that Tillement & Cie be prohibited from joining this association, and he threatened withdrawal of the DSW saltworks and eruption of a salt war if they were allowed to enter. At the end of 1896, the salt cartel was not renewed, and the fight for refined salt broke out. Since Tillement had begun operations with his soda ash plant, Wessel had generated a parallel drop in prices of soda ash through the syndicate. This conflict led to losses at numerous soda ash and salt plants, which strongly reproached Wessel for "being a bad German and ruining a national industry to the benefit of foreigners [Solvay]."[36] Under this pressure, Wessel proposed allowing the entry of Tillement & Cie into the salt and soda ash syndicates, but the *gérants* refused this option because they had just purchased the Montferrand plant in France and had concluded a balanced agreement with the Meurthe plant. Such overly favorable treatment given to Tillement in Germany could have called into question this agreement in France. Solvay thus persuaded Wessel to continue the price war, but contrary to their anticipations, Tillement & Cie did not back down and reinvested, all while threatening to establish a second ammonia-soda plant on the French side of the border. Attacked on its own territory, it was Solvay that then asked Wessel

---

[33] These were BASF, AG Heufeld, Moritz Honigmann, Hermania Chemische Fabrik AG, Schönebeck, Chemische Fabrik Heinrichshall, and Silesia Verein Chemischer Fabriken Saarau. ACS, Eilsberger (b) (1930), 210–75; ACS-O, 1151 DSW, CS meetings 1885–1892.

[34] Schreib (1906), 380; Haber (1958), 228; Krause and Puffert (2000), 309.

[35] ACS-O, 1151 DSW, Affaire Chrome; ACS, Eilsberger (b) (1930), 276–87.

[36] ACS, Eilsberger (b) (1930), 292.

to come to an agreement with Tillement. Wessel, at the head of the German syndicate, felt he could not backpedal, especially to preserve French interests. Detecting the momentary weakness of DSW, the Von Schmidt saltworks at Sarralbe rushed into the breach and announced a soda ash plant project, which finally forced Wessel to negotiate. DSW granted a small part of its salt quota to Von Schmidt and proposed that Tillement join the syndicates or sell its plant to DSW at the considerable price of M 2 million. Solvay was very reticent to propose such a price, fearing the fallout with other new investors. Tillement ably played on cross-border tensions and agreed to abandon its French project under the condition that DSW purchase the Château-Salins plant. This acquisition was approved in April 1900, to Solvay's great dislike. One of the clauses stated that Tillement and Nicolas could no longer be involved in any soda ash plant. Château-Salins became the fourth soda ash plant and the third saltworks for DSW.[37] The affair continued in France when Nicolas broke his word and set up the Soudière Lorraine in 1904 at Bayon, near Dombasle. Immediately, Solvay sued Nicolas, who defended himself by invoking the free trade and industry law. Solvay was defended by the illustrious attorney and future president of the French Republic, Raymond Poincaré, who had already been minister of education and of finance. The court concluded that Nicolas had acted in bad faith and precipitated the purchase of the assets at Bayon by the Participation Soude in 1907.[38]

Slow Penetration into Austria-Hungary

Despite the initial poorly developed Austrian-Hungarian market, Solvay was late in consolidating its dominance in the empire. This was largely because the Aussiger Verein (Aussig), its Leblanc associate, was not inclined to eradicate the old process and maintained a policy of high prices (see Chapter 2). The result was the appearance of several respectably sized competitors in the ammonia-soda field, supported in the various regions of the empire by local political and economic circles.

The startup of Oesterreichischer Verein's plant at Ebensee and of its rival's plant at Szczakowa in 1885 brought about a drop in prices and surplus production on the national market.[39] According to the contract of association between Solvay and Aussig, their Austrian joint venture could not compete with Solvay on external markets, which closed the door to exports. The Oesterreichischer Verein hence negotiated an agreement with the Austrian producers, which ended with the creation of a central sales office at Vienna in July 1888. The Syndikat der Oesterreichische-Ungarische Sodafabriken, presided over by Adalbert Brettschneider, from Aussig, determined the quotas to adjust production to national consumption and to raise prices.[40]

---

[37] ACS, Eilsberger (b) (1930), 288–305.
[38] ACS-O, 1100-2/3, 1100-3/1 Saline et soudière de Bayon 1904–1906; ACS-O, 1100-4 Affaire Solvay & Cie contre Nicolas 1906; Mioche (2008), 38–40.
[39] [Gintl] (1906), 33.
[40] Baumgarten and Mezlény (1906), 129.

In Hungary, rumors abounded about political intentions to facilitate the construction of a soda ash plant. Solvay and Aussig had already marked out the site of Maros-Ujvar, in Transylvania, but had initially considered the place of secondary importance. Negotiations were begun with the government. At the same time, in the north of Bosnia, a consortium of investors, Geiringer, Kantor, Rochter, and Landau, undertook efforts to build an ammonia-soda plant at Lukavac. The Bosnian government broadly supported them by allocating land, concessions, and raw materials at low prices. The soda ash plant at Lukavac, run by the Erste Bosnische Ammoniaksoda-Fabrik AG, began production in 1894. It rapidly achieved an advantageous cost price, which enabled it to go beyond the regional Bosnian market and to sell in Austria, Hungary, and Italy. The construction of a Solvay plant at Maros-Ujvar was consequently accelerated. It started up in 1895, under the control of the Ungarische Ammoniaksodafabrik (System Solvay), a new limited partnership company made up in parity between Solvay and Aussig. Modest in size, it remained devoted to the local market and avoided the onerous transportation costs between Ebensee and Hungary. Maros-Ujvar was incorporated into the syndicate, unlike Lukavac, with which the Oesterreichischer Verein had preferred to continue the fight. In 1896, the Lukavac group planned to start a soda ash plant in Russia with the group Vial and Pradel, thus threatening the position of Lubimoff and of the whole group. Solvay persuaded Aussig to include Lukavac in the cartel and sent Carl Wessel to accompany the negotiations. In 1901, the quotas of the Austrian syndicate were set as follows: Ebensee (23.5 percent), Szczakowa (18.8 percent), Lukavac (18.8 percent), Aussig (17.7 percent), Maros-Ujvar (10.2 percent), and Hruschau (11.1 percent). Fifteen years after its creation, the Oesterreichischer Verein thus held only 33.7 percent of the market, clearly less than the other Solvay subsidiaries. More alarming, other ammonia-soda plants were involved in the debate. The new-generation plants could provide 71 percent of the sixty-nine thousand tons anticipated, compared to 29 percent for Leblanc. The competition continued to proliferate. An ammonia-soda plant was built at Podgórze (Krakow), in the early years of 1900, by the Erste Galizistiche Ammoniaksodafabrik AG (originally B&W Liban), helped by two Lukavac renegades, the engineers Muller and Tempelhof.[41] To cut the competition, the Lukavac company was forced to buy it in 1907. For its part, Aussig finished by giving up on the Leblanc process in 1903. An ammonia-soda plant then became indispensable in Bohemia; it was needed to take up the slack. The plant at Nestomitz was built to this end by the Oesterreichischer Verein. Similar in capacity to Ebensee, the plant began production in 1908.[42]

Consolidation of the market took place in two steps as late as 1907–1908. Oesterreichischer Verein acquired the plant at Szczakowa and dismantled it. It also managed to acquire 51 percent of the Podgórze plant. The cartel was then composed of only three groups: Oesterreichischer Verein, Bosnische AG, and Hruschau. The first two merged in an effort to streamline their operations

---

[41] ACS, CS meeting 27 Dec. 1904.
[42] [Gintl] (1906), 54–9.

and centralize their administration at Vienna. A leasing company (*société fermière*) with a complex structure, Oesterreichische Solvay-Werke Betriebs-gesellschaft mbH (OSW), was created. It leased the four plants of Ebensee, Nestomitz, Lukavac, and Podgórze. Its capital was distributed among Solvay (34 percent), Aussig (34 percent), and Bosnische AG (33 percent). Only the plant at Maros-Ujvar remained formally separate, for political reasons. Its earnings, however, were distributed among associates. Following this merger, which brought together the primary Austrian interests, the syndicate was no longer needed, and it came to an end in 1909. Hruschau, the last Leblanc plant, was taken over by Aussig and shut down in 1911.[43]

Russia Locked Out

Despite its initial difficulties (see Chapter 2), Lubimoff, Solvay & Cie rapidly grabbed a large part of the Russian market, still only slightly developed and protected by imposing trade barriers. During the 1880s, Russia carried out a voluntaristic commercial and industrial policy characterized by protectionist measures and by the abolition of the excise tax on salt and the granting of development premiums for the national chemical industry. In 1885, the Russian Empire still imported about three-fourths of its consumption of alkalis. At the end of the 1890s, consumption had grown by 50 percent, but imports had become negligible.[44] Establishment of a plant at Berezniki coincided with a first hike in the trade tariffs. A second Solvay plant was built in 1891, at the same time as another hike was announced. Located at Lysychansk, in the Donets Basin, in the Ukraine, it was closer to the consumption center and rapidly became the larger of the two factories. It integrated at the start a causticizing unit using the Loewig process and would become a pioneer of electrolysis. A coal mine was also being operated by Solvay nearby as of 1900.

As in Austria-Hungary, the contract of association between Solvay and its Russian subsidiary called for nonencroachment on their respective markets. The sale of soda ash, soda crystals, and caustic soda by Lubimoff-Solvay was exclusively handled by the firm of Wogau & Cie in Moscow. In 1899, Lubimoff-Solvay was producing more than 80 percent of Russian soda ash, or sixty-eight thousand of the eighty-two thousand tons produced annually. At this time, new competitors appeared, but Lubimoff-Solvay, enjoying a dominant position, did not establish a Russian syndicate. It limited itself to bilateral agreements with its most serious rivals. In 1900, the Sud Russe company opened a plant using the Honigmann process at Slaviansk, sixty kilometers east of Lysychansk. It was financed by the group Vial and Pradel, which had considered a partnership with the Bosnian company of Lukavac. An agreement in 1900, renewed until 1915, granted it a quota of 16 percent of the market.[45] Two other minor agreements were implemented with Trampedach and Thalheim at Riga and Taguied at Baku. However, no arrangement was ever concluded with the Leblanc producer

[43] ACS, 1184-1-1 Historique des usines Solvay du groupe de Vienne; ACS-O, 1184 Groupe de Vienne, Rapport général.

[44] Warren (1991), 160.

[45] ACS-O, 1001–51 Contrats suite; Accarain (2002), 21–2.

Ouchkoff, which had concentrated on caustic soda and bleaching powder since 1893. Around 1900, Lubimoff-Solvay purchased the small caustic soda plant of Barnaul, in western Siberia. Its cost prices were high, but its distance made it competitive on its local market, delimited by Osmk and Tomsk cities. The other competitors came from the electrolysis field (see Chapter 5).

Great Britain, or the Battle on Enemy Territory

In Great Britain, the challenge was not to develop a new industry in a market protected by trade barriers but to grow in the shadow of the Leblanc producers that dominated the world scene. Conquest of the English market would especially allow Solvay and Brunner, Mond to take the reins of international commerce. Within the group, it was Brunner, Mond that had the broadest decision-making autonomy, as Solvay held only 13 percent of voting shares. However, the English partners broadly applied the competitive methods used on the Continent, in particular lowering costs and sales prices. Like elsewhere, this strategy pushed the Leblanc manufacturers to propose an agreement and prevented the emergence of significant adversaries in ammonia soda. This rise in power of Brunner, Mond was concomitant with the slowdown in English exports on the primary markets as of the mid-1880s, as these markets were gradually becoming autonomous as a result of the Solvay process. Brunner, Mond did not escape this circumstance, as the proportion of its exports to its domestic sales fell from 80 percent in 1880 to 64 percent in 1890 and 33 percent in 1900.[46]

For a long time, Brunner, Mond refused to enter discussions with its English competitors. Between 1875 and 1890, free trade and technical improvements on both sides led to a drop in soda ash prices of around 50 percent.[47] The Leblanc producers were divided on the issue and did not react when faced with the maturity of the ammonia-soda technology. It was only in 1891 that Brunner, Mond was constrained to accept negotiations for an agreement, following the formation of the United Alkali Company (UAC), which presented itself as a defensive grouping of 90 percent of the English Leblanc producers, or forty-eight firms, in a single company. Following other amalgamations realized in the 1880s (e.g., Salt Union, Dynamite Trust), UAC became the largest chemical enterprise in the world and the biggest industrial group in the United Kingdom. It had an increasing range of products outside of alkalis: sulfuric acid, salt and soon fertilizer, cyanides, precious metals, soaps, and so on. The foundation of this giant company brought Brunner, Mond to the negotiating table. It also precipitated in Germany the incorporation of holdouts in the large Syndikat Deutscher Sodafabrieken. However, UAC was a giant with feet of clay, slow to maneuver, despite its stated intentions at the beginning, to streamline and invest in research.[48] An entente, initiated by UAC, was concluded in 1891 following long debate. Under the agreement, UAC had to limit its production

[46] Warren (1980), 193.
[47] William F. Lawson Dick, *A Hundred Years of Alkali in Cheshire*, 1973, quoted in Warren (1980), 163.
[48] Warren (1980), 147–74; Haber (1958), 180–5; Reader (1970), 104–7.

of ammonia soda to 15,000 tons, and Brunner, Mond promised not to produce more than 165,000 tons of soda ash and 3,600 tons of bleaching powder, and not to produce caustic soda. This agreement began the gradual withdrawal of UAC from soda ash and toward alkalis of lesser importance at the time. This entente was renewed under similar terms in 1897, 1900, and 1907 up to the war. Until 1893, the prices of soda ash had temporarily gone beyond £6, before bottoming out at £4 s15. At this price, Brunner, Mond remained profitable, unlike UAC.[49] Thus, UAC continued to maneuver to reestablish its influence in the sphere reserved for its rival. In 1893, UAC erected an ammonia soda plant at Fleetwood and managed to get good results from it, thanks to the process developed by the Pole chemist Hawliczek. For its part, Brunner, Mond began the production of caustic soda using the Loewig process in 1895. It also increased its production of soda crystals, which it had started in 1888 at Northwich, in a new plant built at Silvertown in 1894.[50] The agreements did not prevent the signatories from developing on their own and only defined the situation at a given moment in time. The quotas set out in the agreement of 1907 illustrated quite well the evolution of market sharing. Brunner, Mond and UAC were granted, respectively, 125,000 and 18,000 tons of soda ash, 95,000 and 82,600 tons in soda crystals, and 31,000 and 4,000 tons in sodium bicarbonate. If these quotas were exceeded, between 70 percent and 85 percent of the surplus volumes were passed on to Brunner, Mond. Also, Brunner, Mond had to limit itself to 14,000 tons of caustic soda and 11,500 tons of bleaching powder while receiving half of later increases.[51] It was the rise of electrochemistry that would finally put UAC out of the alkali business (see Chapter 5).

Because the Leblanc manufacturers were gradually being phased out, Brunner, Mond focused on minimizing competition from new ammonia-soda plants. Most of them were rapidly acquired, for demolition or repurposing. Two of them had been erected by Leblanc manufacturers before the creation of UAC, at Middlewich (Cheshire Alkali Co.) and at Widnes (Mathieson & Co.). They never reached profitability and were closed in 1897 and 1898, respectively. In 1895, Brunner, Mond acquired and reconfigured the ammonia-soda plant of Murgatroyd & Co., built at Middlewich two years earlier and operating the Schloessing and Rolland process obtained from Daguin. In 1900, Brunner, Mond took over and demolished the Bell Brothers' ammonia-soda plant at Port Clarence (Middlesbrough), which had operated from 1884 using this same process, for which it had obtained a license from Maletra. That same year, Brunner, Mond again acquired the ammonia-soda plant of Bowman and Thompson at Lostock, refurbishing it in 1907. Finally, a last ammonia-soda plant, built by the Ammonia Soda Co. at Plumbey in 1908, was bought in 1916.[52]

[49] Haber (1958), 184.
[50] Watts (1923), 40.
[51] ACS-O, 1242, 1b Brunner Mond. Contracts.
[52] For further information on these various initiatives and their takeover by Brunner, Mond, see Reader (1970), 111–12; Warren (1980), 111–16.

Brunner, Mond showed the same intransigence toward its customers and suppliers aiming to venture out in soda ash as it had to its competitors. Thus, it arrived at a favorable agreement with the Salt Union in the early 1900s. The conglomerate had brought together sixty-four saltworks and had exercised, from 1888, a quasi monopoly on salt in England. Undermined by internal tensions, its financial results were poor. The accord imposed by Brunner, Mond stipulated that the Salt Union would have to dissuade any firm from building a soda ash plant in Cheshire, in exchange for which Brunner, Mond would promise not to support any firm that wanted to produce salt, an eventuality that in fact never occurred.[53] However, a long and resounding battle for influence pitted Brunner, Mond against the great soap producer Lever Brothers between 1907 and 1920. Lever unleashed hostilities by starting up the production of caustic soda for its own use. It threatened to put it on the market, despite an arrangement between the two firms. Brunner, Mond responded by purchasing two large soap makers, Joseph Crosfields & Sons and William Gossage & Sons. A temporary truce was concluded in 1913, but it had to wait until 1920 before the situation was completely diffused. As of that time, Lever was exclusively supplied by Brunner, Mond and absorbed the two competitive soap makers.[54]

Open Competition in the Anticartel and Protectionist United States

The United States remained overall protectionist up to World War I (and after). In the specific case of alkalis, the trade barriers were already high before the emergence of a national industry. When this became mature thanks to technologies imported from Europe, the Dingley Tariff of 1897 made the taxes prohibitive, taking them from 0.25 to 0.375 cents per pound of soda ash.[55] This evolution in American industrial and commercial policy especially benefited Solvay Process Co, at the expense of English producers, including Brunner, Mond, for which the United States was an essential market. In fact, in the middle of the 1880s, Brunner, Mond sold more soda ash to the United States than to Great Britain and held the position of market leader, with 37 percent of the market share, compared to 48.5 percent for all of the English Leblanc manufacturers.[56] An agreement of 1885–1886 with Solvay had reserved for itself this rapidly growing market. The rise in power of SPC modified the deal. The subsidiary of Solvay already held 25 percent of the market after three years of operations, and imports had fallen. Rather than initiate a useless competitive fight, Brunner, Mond and SPC came to an agreement, with the mediation of Solvay, on the gradual withdrawal of Brunner, Mond from the United States in exchange for 16.25 percent of SPC shares without voting rights (see Chapter 2). The portion of Brunner, Mond in its shared sales with SPC decreased from five-ninths in 1887 to one-third in 1895 and finally zero in 1905. In 1892,

---

[53] Haber (1958), 181.
[54] This important episode goes beyond our scope. See Reader (1970), 234–45, 293–8, 372–5.
[55] Haber (1958), 216.
[56] Reader (1970), 98.

SPC already provided 55 percent of total American consumption of soda ash.[57]

New competitors appeared in the mid-1890s. Most were financed by glass-making industries in the Northeast, unhappy with the control of SPC over their raw materials. Between 1892 and 1910, five large ammonia-soda plants were built in the Great Lakes region, rich in salt, and a sixth in Virginia. The latter, the Mathieson Alkali Works, started up in 1892 at Saltville, Virginia. Far away from the others, it was also independent of the glassmakers. Its founder, Neil Mathieson, had left Great Britain after having sold his ammonia-soda plant at Widnes to UAC. Two years later, Michigan Alkali Co. opened its ammonia-soda plant at Wyandotte (near Detroit). Soon, it became closely linked with the Edward Ford Glass Co., a glassmaking company created by the son of John B. Ford after the rupture of the Ford family with the Pittsburg Plate Glass Co.[58] In 1900, the latter financed Columbia Chemical Co. at Barberton, Ohio, despite efforts by SPC to dissuade it from doing so. In 1910, a fourth heavyweight competitor, the Diamond Alkali Co., settled in Painsville, Ohio, with support from a consortium of glass and soap manufacturers. Given this proliferation of new plants, American soda ash production doubled in the first decade of the twentieth century, to achieve one-third of world production.[59] In addition, four electrolysis plants entered into competition with SPC in caustic soda and bleaching powder (see Chapter 5). Having witnessed its market share in soda ash drop back down to 44 percent, SPC did not sit back. It first expanded its plant at Syracuse, New York, which became the largest soda ash plant in the world. It then constructed a second soda ash plant at Detroit, comparable in size to that of Syracuse, in 1896, after UAC itself had threatened to enter into operations there. In 1912, in Kansas it bought a small plant built five years earlier by the Hutchinson Chemical & Alkali Co. At this time, its market share had climbed back to 60 percent. It should be noted that the natural soda ash deposits in Wyoming, today the primary source for American soda ash, were already known and that SPC had already considered them, but their distance from the consumption centers made them unprofitable at the time.

On this highly competitive and rapidly growing market, SPC pushed its advantage further by increasing its output rather than controlling the market. The rare agreements concluded with competitors proved fragile and transitory, given antitrust laws and the American spirit of individualism. The first was concluded with UAC in 1894 for caustic soda; SPC received four-sevenths of the shared sales. However, UAC did not honor its obligations for long and proceeded with dumping on the American market. In response, SPC exported its caustic soda to the English market. It was then that UAC threatened to build an ammonia-soda plant at Detroit, which led to a new agreement.

[57] ACS-O, 1271, 1B Solvay Process Co, Soda ash in the USA, letter from Rowland G. Hazard, 1913.
[58] Haynes (1954), 488–90 (on Wyandotte Chemicals Corporation).
[59] ACS, 1271-065-001; Glasscock (1969), 36–67; Warren (1991), 171.

Another accord, with limited scope, governed the relations with Mathieson and Michigan between 1899 and 1901. Each one was forbidden to lower prices and to work with the other's customers. In contrast to what the other subsidiaries of Solvay had succeeded in obtaining from their competitors, there was no clause limiting exports from Mathieson and Michigan, which annoyed Solvay and especially Brunner, Mond. The accord was suspended until 1904, at which time it was renewed until 1907, but with a ban on exporting across the ocean.[60]

Overall, the industrial and commercial strategy fostered by Brussels' head-quarters seemed to be applied with less zeal by SPC than in the rest of the world. In terms of capital holdings, Solvay was a majority holder in SPC (42 percent, compared to 41.75 percent for the Americans and 16.25 percent for Brunner, Mond), but the abandon of voting rights on five hundred Belgian shares and on all English shares gave the American directors 58 percent of votes in the assemblies. Thus, Solvay could strongly suggest strategy but could not impose it. In fact, the American associates were sometimes too adventurous for Solvay *gérants*' liking. In 1891, Hazard proposed to create, in association with local partners, a large salt company to take over leadership in the sector. Solvay succeeded in convincing SPC to maintain its own saltworks, thus ensuring its autonomy, without aggressively going after other salt makers and without bringing new partners into the mix.[61] Later, Solvay became more and more concerned with the significant investments granted by SPC (and thus in part by itself) to allow intense expansion of the Semet-Solvay Co., to the detriment, according to Solvay, of the alkali business. The Semet-Solvay Co. was actually founded in 1895 to build and operate in America coke ovens invented by Louis Semet for recovery of by-products (see Chapter 5).

Taking Command of the International Soda Ash Trade

We have seen how Solvay and its subsidiaries penetrated, grew, and dominated each of the large national markets. Likewise, the group managed to organize to its advantage the residual international trade in three stages.

The first step was the distribution of sales zones, or *rayons*, among the group companies. From 1885 to 1887, several agreements between Solvay and Brunner, Mond divided the world into three *rayons*: Solvay (Continental Europe and Russia), Brunner, Mond (England, the British Empire, and North America), and the shared territory subject to negotiation (the rest of the world). In its own territory, Solvay concluded additional agreements with its sub-sidiaries as soon as they were able to supplant the parent company or the other subsidiaries. Accordingly, Solvay & Cie kept France, Belgium, Holland, Spain, Portugal, Italy, Malta, Greece, Turkey, Asia, and Africa (Mediterranean sea-ports), whereas DSW was given Germany, Poland, and Scandinavia. Lubimoff

---

[60] ACS-O, 1271, 1B Solvay Process Co
[61] ACS-O, 1271, 1B, Solvay Process Co., Saline à Syracuse.

and Oesterreichischer Verein remained mostly confined to their national market – Russia and the Baltic states for the former; Austria-Hungary, Romania, and Bulgaria for the latter – through their contract agreement with Solvay.[62] For its part, Brunner, Mond gradually abandoned the United States following the agreement in 1887 with SPC. It then turned toward Asia, especially China and Japan, as well as the British Empire.[63]

A second consolidation step took place when the national syndicates were formed in France, Germany, and Austria-Hungary. These were directed by Solvay Group companies and were incorporated in the group's internal agreements. For example, Lubimoff made arrangements with DSW and the German syndicate for sharing sales in Poland. In some cases, pressure from members of the national cartels constrained the Solvay companies to accept an increase in export quotas allocated to these cartels. The coordination of this dual national and international dimension often forced Solvay companies to walk a tightrope. They had to preserve peaceful relations with their national competitors while dissuading them from looking for outside markets. These agreements also instituted a complex system of compensation. When a Solvay company acquired a competitor whose exports had the effect of disrupting a sister company in another country, the former could be granted a new quota for export to the sister company's market, to compensate for the expenses generated by the acquisition.

The third step was the creation of what can be considered an international soda ash cartel, which resulted from the formation of UAC. Unifying almost all the English Leblanc manufacturers, UAC became a single negotiator for the Solvay Group. The agreement of 1891 between UAC and Brunner, Mond was a first decisive move, by which soda ash, soda crystals, and bicarbonate were practically acquired by Brunner, Mond in its territory, whereas UAC began its reorientation toward caustic soda and bleaching powder. Through the existing ties between Solvay and Brunner, Mond, this alliance with UAC represented a first partitioning of the global alkali market between Solvay and the Leblanc producers. Nonetheless, up to 1897, UAC was still free to sell on the Continent, even if it did so at a loss. It would not be until that year that Solvay, on its own behalf and on behalf of its German, Austrian, and Russian subsidiaries and syndicates, concluded a global agreement with UAC regulating sales and prices in Europe and in the European ports of the Mediterranean, for soda ash and caustic soda (18 October 1897). After that, UAC was blocked in its shared markets with Brunner, Mond and with the rest of the Solvay Group. This episode can thus be considered the institution of an international soda ash cartel, even if it was not formalized in an actual organization. The agreement was renewed in 1900, 1901, 1906, and 1907, and it was reworked to follow the evolutions of the markets and the means of production.[64]

---

[62] ACS-O, 1001–51 Contrats; ACS-O, 1001–51 Contrats Suite.
[63] On exploitation of markets in Asia and in the British Empire by Brunner, Mond, see Reader (1970), 175, 224–7, 335–47.
[64] ACS-O, 1001–51 Contrats; ACS-O, 1001–51 Contrats Suite.

3.2 EVOLUTION OF MANAGEMENT STRUCTURES

Until World War I, Solvay was perceived by the outside world as having great continuity. Its seemingly simple, self-financed limited partnership organization reinforced its secretive nature, and its growing and unassailable control over its primary market gave it a certain prestige. Internally, however, relations among associates underwent some turbulent times. For the most part there were disagreements about control of the company and the use of its financial resources. The origin of these dissensions went back to the first years of the company. In 1866, although the enterprise seemed closer to failure than to success, defensive statutes had replaced the optimistic contract of 1863. To expunge certain debts, the Solvay brothers were forced to give up twenty-two of their thirty-four shares, and their father Alexandre had been obligated to borrow to subscribe to forty-one of them (see Chapter 1). This situation, considered humiliating by Ernest Solvay, instilled in him an ardent desire for independence, which would manifest time and again, in particular during successive renegotiations of the company statutes.

Shaping of Financial and Management Principles (1866–1882)

From the beginning, the associates had agreed that in case of success, the prerogatives and compensation for the *gérants* would go hand in hand with the financial results. Now, these results were brilliant. The Solvay brothers, through their own merits, had earned a sort of moral authority to regularly promote their ambitions. In 1871, when an increase in capital was necessary to finance expansion, Ernest Solvay proposed that his shareholders simulate successive issues of shares rather than just a single issue. Through this artifice, the *gérants* could, at each issue, exercise their statutory right to receive for free one-sixth of the new shares, in addition to those that they were authorized to take on the basis of a prorated amount of their existing (small) number of shares.[65] This request was accepted by the silent partners as encouragement. Following this episode, the portion of shares held by the Solvay family grew from 27 percent to 41 percent, 16 percent being held by Ernest and 8.9 percent by Alfred (see Table 3.1). This new distribution was enacted in the statutes of 1873, as was the increase in capital, to BEF 1,200,000 (US\$228,000).[66]

The same year, a Belgian law (18 March 1873) made it mandatory for partnerships limited by shares to publish their results. Solvay & Cie, which had been created in this form (*commandite par actions*), was transformed into a limited partnership company (*commandite simple*) in 1874 to keep secret the profits it drew from the ammonia-soda process. This further accentuated the closely held, family nature of the business, a concept ingrained in both the associates and the employees' minds. The partnership shares (*parts*), were still nontransferable to third parties and could not go outside the intimate social

---

[65] ACS-O, 1001–1, Historique de la Société Solvay, Ernest Solvay to Guillaume Nélis, 27 Nov. 1871; Van Belle (2008), 73–7.

[66] ACS-O, *Statuts successifs Solvay & Cie de 1863 à 1889*, 1890.

TABLE 3.1. *Partnership Shares (with voting rights) Held by the Family Groups (1863–1966)*

	Solvay Family	Pirmez Family	Nélis Family	Lambert Family	Other Associates
1863	25%	40.4%	18.4%	8.8%	7.3%
1864	10%	53.6%	16.6%	11.3%	8.5%
1866	27.4%	42.1%	13.2%	8.8%	8.8%
1873	41%	33.4%	10.9%	7.4%	7.4%
1882	63.8%	20.9%	7%	4.4%	4%
1888	63.9%	22.8%	7.8%	2.4%	3.1%
1966	61.1%	21%	7.6%	6.2%	4%

Source: ACS-O, *Statuts successifs Solvay & Cie de 1863 à 1889*, 1890.

circle. This legal statute also enabled avoidance of taxes on companies in Belgium until after World War I, whereas in France, a law of 1872 set a flat-rate tax at 5 percent of the capital.[67] Solvay's equity was maintained at an extremely low level until 1882, not only to limit the French tax burden but also to have maximum effect on the progressive percentages of profits for the *gérants*. Indeed, the statutes of 1874 had set the dividends as follows: in the first place, the "suitable" depreciation had to be done before declaring the net earnings. Then 10 percent had to go into a reserve fund; 19 percent of the surplus was then allocated to the *gérance* and 1 percent to the supervisory board. Of the 80 percent remaining, the *gérants* collected progressive percentages of the profits (10, 20, and 30 percent on amounts reaching, respectively, 10, 20, and 30 percent of the capital). The rest was attributed to the partnership shares. As long as the progressive percentages system persisted, the capital was kept at low levels. The statutes of 1874 also initiated a mechanism of retained earnings in the company, which became a privileged partnership (*commandite privilégiée*). It had to be used to finance French expansion and came to an end in 1882. The deferred earnings gave shareholders the right to collect an annual interest of 5 percent, payable before distribution of dividends. No voting rights were associated with them. Before this system could bear fruit, two debenture loans of BEF 600,000 (US$114,000) each were subscribed to again by the silent partners, in 1874 and 1875. After this date, Solvay & Cie's intense policy of self-financing would really begin; the shareholders would no longer have to untie their own purse strings. The company functioned in this manner until 1882. During these eight years, the *gérants* retained three-quarters of the total earnings in the company, instead of the half called for in the statutes, or BEF 11.5 million of 15.3 million (US$2,185,000 of US$2,907,000). As Eudore Pirmez observed:

> Without doubt, this distribution already gave a splendid dividend and the associates could only congratulate themselves for having thus developed the equity. It is not without interest, however, to note that very few associates were met that would not have yielded to the temptation of immediate gains, since especially the

[67] ACS, AG, Gérance report, 31 Dec. 1918.

partnership contract gave that right of distribution. Though there are few examples of similar prosperity, there are fewer still perhaps of unanimous consent to leave within a company such a great portion of the earnings.[68]

In addition, the plants were depreciated for exaggerated amounts, which came back to retaining an already-large part of the profits realized. The holdings in the subsidiaries, as well as the salt concessions and the patents, were shown as assets on the balance sheet only for symbolic amounts; they were not representative of their true value. Furthermore, the debt to third parties, especially banks, was held at a very low level so as to reinforce independence. This creative accounting was the expression of the extremely cautious financial policy of a fast-growing enterprise. It was facilitated by the closed structure of the company. It was not, however, unique in the chemical industry of the nineteenth century. Some large German dyestuff companies such as Hoechst and BASF resorted to the same mechanisms.[69]

Change in Internal Dynamics and Debates on the Group's Structure (1882–1905)

Since the company had reached a certain stage of development, new dynamics had taken place in the corporate bodies, and tensions among associates surfaced. In 1879, Prosper Hanrez entered his name as a third *gérant* alongside the founding brothers. He was unanimously recognized as the key person in the success of Dombasle and the conquest of the French market.[70] In this respect, he could claim rights to the highest functions within the company. He wrote to Ernest Solvay of his desire to "reach a dominant and truly independent situation in our business."[71] No one was opposed. As a *gérant*, he received 2.2 percent of shares and 2 percent of earnings, to which was added a "gift" of an additional 2 percent from the Solvay brothers from their own percentages. Hanrez joined the Central Administration at Brussels in 1881. For his part, Alfred Solvay had established his quarters there, after having left the direction of the Couillet plant in 1879. He was the primary architect of the commercial strategy, and especially the conclusion of contracts, alliances, and ententes.[72] Ernest Solvay, victim of overwork and sometimes precarious health, retired from daily management, although he continued to supervise the overall technique and strategy. Between 1884 and 1887, he took several cures far from Brussels, on the recommendations of his friend Doctor Paul Héger.[73] After recovering to an improved physical condition, he increasingly devoted himself to his personal scientific projects (see Chapter 5). Prosper Hanrez and Alfred

[68] Van Belle (2008), 102.

[69] Abelshauser, von Hippel, Johnson, and Stokes (2004), 97–102; Haber (1971), 123.

[70] PPSF, Box Ernest Solvay 2, Note by Ernest Solvay on Prosper Hanrez, 25 Jan. 1884; Van Belle (2008), 98–9.

[71] AES, Box V, Prosper Hanrez to Ernest Solvay, 10 June 1879.

[72] ACS, DS 40, Aperçu historique sur la Gérance de Solvay & Cie et considérations relatives à une transformation éventuelle de notre Société en S.A., par Armand Solvay, 9 Jan. 1928.

[73] Héger and Lefébure (1929), 62.

FIGURE 3.2. Garden party at Ernest Solvay's house in Ixelles, gathering the Solvays, Semets, van der Straetens, Delwarts, and Quertons (around 1885). This family clan would soon experience the turmoil of management structures changes. (Solvay Family Archives.)

Solvay, often overshadowed by the figure of Ernest, in reality played a pivotal role in the consolidation of the company's success. Recall that it was only in the 1880s that the fight against the Leblanc manufacturers tilted in favor of Solvay and that the bases for a long prosperity were established.

At the same time, a renewal of the statutes was required because the privileged partnership would expire in 1882. It was the subject of intense negotiations. Eudore Pirmez was still chairman of the supervisory board and the legal counsel of Solvay, in addition to his political mandates and his position as director of the national bank. He drew up a draft of the statutes, but these were rejected by Ernest Solvay, who required almost-unlimited expansion of power of the *gérants*. This divergence of views led to the retirement of Pirmez from the matter and the constitution of a commission for the revision of the statutes, composed of the three *gérants* and representatives of the silent partners. The commission did not reach consensus. The *gérants* remained firm and ended up obtaining, through the statutes of 1882, a considerable increase in power and fortune: the progressive percentages of the Solvay brothers, limited to the duration of their effective management, were converted into shares with voting rights. Thus, a temporary stipend was transformed into a perpetual and inheritable income. The Solvay family in that way acquired the absolute majority of the ten thousand shares with dividends (63.8 percent). Ernest alone held

35.4 percent, compared to Alfred's 18.7 percent (see Table 3.1). As modest limitations to this expansion of power, their personal voting rights in the assemblies were limited to 15 percent, whereas the majority needed for modification of the statutes was taken to four-fifths of the votes. It was also agreed that the company would be transformed within five years into a joint-stock company (*société anonyme*) presided over by Pirmez, to allow the shareholders who so desired to sell their shares. Also, the system of retained earnings was extended. It took the form of ten thousand shares with interest of BEF 1,000 (US$192) without voting rights, to be funded through retained earnings, against payment to their holders of an annual interest of 5 percent.[74]

This revision of the statutes marked a watershed in the relations of the associates from the early days, as well as their families, within which shares had begun to be transferred or inherited. In their memoires and their correspondence, Pirmez and Nélis spoke plainly about the broken friendships, even if courteous relations periodically resumed among the protagonists.[75] Under the regime of the new statutes, the *gérants* had rights that were greatly superior to those typically granted to managers in a limited partnership. They could mortgage all the goods of the company, call for considerable retained earnings, and create and acquire other companies. With the general assembly in which they were majority holders, they could also modify the headquarters and the legal structure of the company, decrease the capital to reimburse shares with interest, and modify the estimates of the equity.[76] Their preponderant influence was further accentuated following several nominations. As of 1882, the role of legal counsel, always held by Eudore Pirmez, was passed to the attorney Edgard Hulin, a cousin of the Solvay brothers. On the supervisory board, Léopold Querton, brother-in-law of the *gérants* and a supporter from the first moment, received one of the two additional seats called for in the new statutes. For his part, Nélis expressed the desire to retire from the board following the dissension of 1882. Ernest Solvay paid him glowing homage for the services rendered but did not retain him.[77] In virtue of the new distribution of the shares, it was Gustave Herman, attorney and brother-in-law of Ernest Solvay's spouse, who was appointed. The *gérants* thus had free rein to direct their enterprise without internal constraints.

In compliance with what had been concluded among the associates in 1882, the draft for transformation into a joint-stock company was studied between 1882 and 1885, under the direction of Prosper Hanrez. This form of company, more open and appropriate to an enterprise of Solvay's size, offered the advantage of share liquidity for shareholders and broader access to capital, even though this was still largely provided by self-financing. While Ernest Solvay and

---

[74] ACS-O, 1001–1, Historique de la Société Solvay, Folder 14, Révision des statuts; ACS-O, *Statuts successifs Solvay & Cie de 1863 à 1889*, 1890.

[75] ACS-O, 1001–1, Folder 15, Guillaume Nélis to Ernest Solvay, 4 and 16 Mar. 1891; Van Belle (2008), 102.

[76] ACS-O, *Statuts successifs Solvay & Cie de 1863 à 1889*, 1890; Van Belle (2008), 124.

[77] ACS AG, 2 July 1883.

Eudore Pirmez were at the start partisans of a single global corporation, Hanrez recommended the creation of a joint-stock company in each country in which Solvay held a majority, all placed under the control of a Belgian parent joint-stock company. This solution aimed especially to integrate national investors into the subsidiaries to take advantage of their network and to "counter the spirit of rivalry among nations which had increasingly developed."[78] A first step was taken with the creation of Deutsche Solvay Werke AG, assembling all the German assets (see Chapter 2). It was at the same time that the new offices of the Central Administration were inaugurated in Brussels (1883) and that the Central Technical Department was created there (1885), thus reinforcing and formalizing the general organization of the group.

In 1885, while his health kept him at a distance from the business, Ernest Solvay opposed continuation of the transformation. His fears were many. He did not want to see the financial details of the enterprise unveiled before the public, nor did he want to have to deal with new shareholders. He finally feared that the entity that he called his "industrial masterpiece" would be put in peril by the creation of companies likely to become more independent.[79] Although most of the shareholders stood behind Ernest, Prosper Hanrez remained determined to carry out his project. Alfred Solvay, who in all circumstances followed the lead of his older brother, tried to play the intermediary, but each of the two men stood their ground. Prosper Hanrez consequently offered his resignation. Faced with the seriousness of the announced departure of this valuable leader, Ernest Solvay declared himself ready to create a French joint-stock company, which Hanrez would manage.[80] This offer did not change Hanrez's mind, and his resignation was accepted by the general assembly in July 1886. He withdrew from industrial life to start a political career. He remained, however, a large shareholder and still participated, as such, in the life of the company, which remained a limited partnership for eighty more years. To replace Hanrez, the *gérants* proposed the nomination of their brother-in-law, Louis Semet, already linked to Solvay since he had begun to develop his coke ovens in 1876. He took the position in 1887, with compensation greatly superior to that of Hanrez, but with clearly fewer prerogatives than those of the Solvay brothers, who had decided to remain masters of their ship.

Although having obtained from the shareholders the concessions proportional to his immense success, Ernest Solvay wanted to take an additional step. Perhaps feeling that he was in the autumn of his life, even though he was not yet fifty years old, the perpetuation of his "industrial masterpiece" tormented him. On 10 June 1887, he sent a letter from Carlsbad to Pirmez, in which he proposed simply that the non-Solvay family shareholders exchange a portion of their shares with dividend against shares with interest and without voting rights, to leave to him four-fifths of the voting rights. He also asked for the end

---

[78] Van Belle (2008), 127.

[79] PPSF, Box Ernest Solvay 2, Folder "Anonymat," Ernest Solvay to Ludwig Mond, 28 Sept. 1885.

[80] AES, Box V, Eudore Pirmez to Prosper Hanrez, 7 June 1886, and Prosper Hanrez to Alfred Solvay, 7 July 1886.

of the limitation of voting rights to 15 percent, so as to obtain total control of the company and the possibility, over time, of leaving it in one block to his heirs.[81] Confronted with the strong defiance of Pirmez and his allies, Ernest Solvay did not insist, and the distribution of voting rights remained untouched. In 1888, the company could celebrate its first quarter century with great pomp. It was just a break in the clouds.

Arguments became even more heated in 1889, when the *gérants* made a new proposal that was, to say the least, poorly received by the non-Solvay family partners. They intended to purchase all shares with interest by holding back the net earnings from 1889 and 1890. In other words, this meant a decrease in dividend to buy back long-term bonds. The stated goal was to decrease the financial charges of the company. The silent partners, resolute to no longer give in, vigorously opposed the proposal and filed a lawsuit in the commercial courts of Brussels. They were nonsuited through an article (no. 11) of the statutes interpreted in favor of the *gérants*.[82] An appeal was going to be filed, but a financial settlement took place. The *gérants* agreed that the shares with interest were to be only gradually reimbursed, and only after a dividend of BEF 200 (US$38.4) per share had been paid.[83] Eudore Pirmez did not witness this agreement. He had died prematurely at the age of sixty, on 2 March 1890. At the height of the suit, he had written several documents in defense.[84] He had also united the partners outside the Solvay family (including Prosper Hanrez) in an "association de défense" of their interests.[85] This perhaps would have been dissolved if Pirmez had lived, but his death made his defensive initiatives a sort of "sacred legacy."[86] The association persisted and until 1903 systematically opposed any proposal by the *gérants* requiring four-fifths of the votes. Such proposals included, among others, in 1893 the transformation of DSW into a limited liability company (in order not to publish the balance sheet) and the constitution of a contingency fund through retained earnings. Without these funds, the *gérants* again had to exaggerate the depreciations.[87] Willing to mediate the situation, Guillaume Nélis came out of retirement in 1895, at the age of ninety-three, to return to the supervisory board, but he died the following year. In 1894, the company was also traumatized by the untimely death of Alfred Solvay (at the age of fifty-four), which dealt a heavy blow to Ernest's morale. He was the sole surviving founder. It was Armand Solvay (1865–1930),

---

[81] Correspondence quoted in Van Belle (2008), 150–60.

[82] ACS; Eudore Pirmez, *Mémoire sur l'interprétation des statuts de la Société en commandite Solvay & Cie*, Brussels, 1891.

[83] ACS-O, 1001-40 Finances; ACS-O, 1001-1, Historique de la Société. Folder No. 12. Procès Solvay contre associés, 1891, Transaction.

[84] These are his well-documented "Historique de la Société Solvay" and "Mémoire sur l'interprétation des statuts." They were written to demonstrate that Pirmez and his allies were properly interpreting the law. Previously confidential, parts of this material have been published in Van Belle (2008). They ought to be recast in this context of conflicting interests.

[85] ACS-O, 1001-1, Historique de la Société. Folder No. 12, Convention du 14 avril 1890 entre associés afin de défendre leurs droits.

[86] ACS, DS 40, Aperçu historique sur la Gérance de Solvay & Cie..., par Armand Solvay, 9 Jan. 1928.

[87] ACS-O, 1001-1, Historique de la Société, Folder No. 5, Fonds de prévision 1895–1896.

TABLE 3.2. *Profits and Self-Financing Mechanisms of Solvay & Cie: Equity, Debts, Earnings (including dividend received from foreign subsidiaries), and Paid Dividend (1863–1913) (in thousand gold francs)*

Year	Capital (all types of shares)	Reserves and Provisions	Debts	Earnings	Dividend Received from Foreign Subsidiaries	Distributed Dividend
1863	136	0	n.a.	n.a.	0	0
1864	151	0	n.a.	n.a.	0	0
1865	175	0	11	−28	0	0
1866	205	3	76	0	0	0
1867	205	8	7	6	0	13
1868	219	42	83	48	0	19
1869	250	10	152	77	0	29
1870	250	175	278	108	0	38
1871	250	364	259	238	0	49
1872	250	364	238	295	0	265
1873	1,186	266	0	321	0	12
1874	1,186	266	955	450	16	152
1875	1,186	561	1,549	527	28	16
1876	1,186	919	1,542	957	33	177
1877	1,186	1,697	1,054	1,516	108	444
1878	1,186	2,820	1,020	1,620	112	59
1879	1,186	3,950	1,987	2,414	134	657
1880	1,186	5,861	1,826	3,128	181	961
1881	1,186	8,258	2,346	3,562	198	1,176
1882	12,947	251	4,708	4,507	285	1,240
1883	15,563	981	6,346	5,203	470	1,723
1884	18,807	2,825	8,151	4,966	498	3,212
1885	20,000	3,438	6,874	3,802	609	1,171
1886	20,000	5,960	5,519	3,528	862	1,644
1887	24,000	6,152	4,528	1,825	840	1,858
1888	24,000	6,689	3,591	3,309	1,119	1,868
1889	24,000	6,516	2,599	5,048	1,363	0
1890	24,000	6,456	3,124	6,603	2,782	0
1891	24,000	7,887	3,491	7,254	2,254	6,659
1892	24,000	8,463	4,580	12,666	6,725	11,458
1893	24,000	9,007	9,542	9,675	5,216	5,885
1894	27,000	10,123	6,895	8,340	4,513	6,901
1895	27,000	11,623	7,554	8,729	4,822	5,791
1896	27,000	13,905	8,240	11,712	5,368	7,878
1897	27,000	17,405	8,509	10,879	5,294	7,515
1898	27,000	20,484	11,528	11,053	5,495	6,524
1899	31,500	21,199	14,613	10,915	5,715	8,901
1900	31,500	22,199	13,898	13,962	7,796	9,740
1901	31,500	25,929	13,878	11,432	8,092	9,639
1902	31,500	27,274	12,431	16,230	8,740	12,073
1903	40,000	23,956	14,188	18,576	8,709	13,192
1904	40,000	28,855	13,347	19,200	9,049	12,663
1905	40,000	35,505	14,774	20,006	10,307	13,700

Year	Capital (all types of shares)	Reserves and Provisions	Debts	Earnings	Dividend Received from Foreign Subsidiaries	Distributed Dividend
1906	40,000	41,505	15,740	21,219	11,194	14,711
1907	40,000	48,505	15,847	22,329	11,354	15,073
1908	40,000	n.a.	n.a.	n.a.	n.a.	n.a.
1909	40,000	n.a.	n.a.	n.a.	n.a.	n.a.
1910	40,000	69,505	16,812	n.a.	n.a.	n.a.
1911	40,000	78,505	20,332	26,065	10,218	17,195
1912	40,000	87,505	21,859	26,310	13,675	17,212
1913	40,000	96,505	20,423	26,033	14,837	17,192

Note: In 1897, only eleven months are shown. As of 1897, the accounting periods corresponded with the calendar year, instead of 1 May to 30 April. In 1889–1890 and 1890–1891, distribution of earnings was suspended, following the lawsuit filed by the minority partners. The balance sheet of 1873–1874 is only partial, following the change in statutes and system. Finally, the balance sheet of 1908 and 1909 could not be found. N.a. = not available. The difference between the annual earnings (net until 1889, then gross) and the distributed earnings (dividends plus progressive percentages plus interest from partnership shares) gives an idea of the self-financing mechanism. From 1874, the earnings that were not distributed to the shareholders and *gérants* were used to increase the privileged partnership, then the partnership shares with interest (making up part of the capital), as well as reserves and several contingency funds and additional depreciation to the normal plant depreciation (not shown on the balance sheets). The debt (that included special funds in favor of personnel from the 1890s) was limited during the entire period, aside from the first decade, during which self-financing could not yet be put into place. Between 1874–1875 and 1881–1882, earnings from foreign subsidiaries derived only from the license granted to Brunner, Mond. After creation of BM Ltd. in 1881, the license was converted into shares with dividends. Then dividends from other subsidiaries (i.e., SPC, DSW, Oesterreichischer Verein, Lubimoff) were added. These dividends were an integral and increasing part of the annual earnings.
Source: ACS AG meeting minutes 1866–1873; ACS AG reports by the gérance 1874–1913.

Ernest's son, gifted with a great instinct for compromise, who succeeded his uncle in the position of *gérant* (see Chapter 5). At the start of the 1900s, relations began to ease. The supervisory board, then presided over by the conciliatory Léon Mondron (Lambert family), accepted the constitution of a

TABLE 3.3. *Conversion of Currencies Before 1914*

	1 pound =	1 dollar =	1 gold franc =	1 gold mark =	1 kroner =
In pounds	1.00	0.21	0.04	0.05	0.04
In dollars	4.85	1.00	0.19	0.24	0.20
In gold francs	25.22	5.20	1.00	1.23	0.95
In gold marks	20.43	4.21	0.81	1.00	1.18
In kroners	24.02	4.95	0.95	0.85	1.00

Note: Before 1914, exchange rates were based on the gold standard. In the framework of the Latin Union, the Belgian franc was equal to the French and Swiss francs.

contingency fund in 1903. The association of silent partners soon dissolved in 1905, thus enabling the return to more harmonious relations.[88]

During the period separating the abandon of the first transformation project into a joint-stock company (1885) and World War I, the question of reinforcing the Solvay Group's unity regularly appeared on the agenda. Should it continue to act in a fragmented way, form a truly unified international trust, or reinforce ties among affiliated companies within a federation that would be more flexible than a single trust? For a long time, Ernest Solvay had warned his associates about the "obsolescence and decline inherent in any industry," and he pleaded in favor of a single company, considering that "the whole should be greater than the sum of its parts."[89] During a trip to the United States in 1885 – one of his only pleasure trips, with his daughter Hélène – Ernest Solvay had been impressed by the constitution of giant trusts concentrating horizontally entire sectors of American industry.[90] The Nobel Dynamite Trust was another source of inspiration. On several occasions, Edgard Hulin was charged with studying the "tightening ties among the companies of the Solvay process." Federation, trust, pool, and merger projects among Solvay, DSW, and Brunner, Mond were all examined.[91] None was carried out, mainly to avoid being out of step with the national governments. In reality, the bundles of contracts of association, industrial and commercial agreements among the group companies, and protected leadership in its markets had provided Solvay with a sufficiently stable and comfortable position, in the absence of any major upheaval (e.g., war, technological breakthrough). Solvay & Cie., still the keystone of the group, remained a hybrid company mixing Belgian and French (and later Spanish and Italian) establishments; a German joint-stock company; and holdings in English, American, Russian and Austrian companies. From 1890 to 1913, dividends from these holdings made up 50 percent to 60 percent of gross earnings.[92] During this entire period, group cohesion was very strong, despite the relatively flexible formal ties. In a fairly original style, the structure of the Solvay Group adapted to its industrial strategy.[93]

In a letter of 1902 sent to the president of SPC, Armand Solvay summarized the business vision that had been passed along to him by his predecessors:

> In industry, unity makes strength;[94] our role is confined to maintaining this intimate union, this cohesion in our industrial family and this role is made easy for us by the confidence that has been placed upon us. We do not intervene directly in any business, it is only by consensus that we act, from discussions based on the general principles that serve us as guidelines.... In the United States, trusts

---

[88] ACS, DS 40, Aperçu historique sur la Gérance de Solvay & Cie..., par Armand Solvay, 9 Jan. 1928.

[89] Discours d'Ernest Solvay à l'occasion du 25ᵉ anniversaire de Solvay & Cie, 1888.

[90] Héger and Lefébure (1929), 61.

[91] ACS-O, 1001–44 Projet de Fédération des sociétés du procédé Solvay, Pourparlers concernant la fusion des sociétés du procédé Solvay.

[92] ACS, Financial accounts, 1890 to 1913.

[93] According to the structures-follows-strategy concept elaborated by Alfred D. Chandler Jr. in Chandler (1962).

[94] "Strength through unity" is also the national motto of Belgium.

were built too quickly, by financiers, on financial bases and not on sound industrial principles: capital was too great and the resulting competition will lead to a catastrophe. But after the current phase, trusts will go in the right direction, the one which you and our subsidiaries have followed for many years. Reasonable capital, prices never exaggerated to discourage competition, well-located plants kept on the cutting edge of progress in their industry by an organization profiting from the many developments contributed by each and every one, etc. etc. The trusts conceived in this way will turn into real economic progress from which the entire society will profit.[95]

[95] ACS-O, 1271, 4B, Armand Solvay to Rowland Hazard, 20 Dec. 1902.

FIGURE 4.1. Children of workers playing in the streets of a colony of Deutsche Solvay Werke near the plant at Bernburg, around 1920. (Solvay Archives.)

4

Labor Organization, Social Policy, and Societal Vision

Solvay elaborated its social policy based on endogenous and exogenous motivations. On the one hand, it shaped its labor force to achieve massive and continuous production. On the other hand, it adapted to the sociopolitical context of the time, managing to maintain maximum independence, from both the states and from workers' organizations. After a quarter century of relative social passivity, Solvay set up a highly developed paternalistic organization, garnering for the company the image of a socially advanced enterprise. In this chapter, we try to identify the determining factors of the company's social policy before approaching its different mechanisms and assessing its results in terms of social peace and productivity.

4.1 ELABORATION OF AN INDUSTRIAL RELATIONS STRATEGY

From the beginning, the Solvay process was designed to ensure continuous and massive production relying on advanced mechanization. Development of compressors and air pumps dedicated to each department as well as the use of reserve columns enabled the factories to function twenty-four hours a day, seven days a week. Because these devices were only profitable in large-scale factories, Solvay built larger soda plants and employed more workers than did its competitors.[1] The introduction of a continuous process upended the traditional work organization. As was the case in other sectors that had adopted processes of this type (e.g., steel, glass), the Solvay technique required fewer workers with craftsman's skills and more operators with diagnostic skills.[2] It also necessitated an organization that was capable of ensuring cooperation between teams working in sequence in an integrated process, governed by the rate of the machine. Although this framework was conducive to the application of scientific management, Solvay did not implement Taylor's methods, such as time measurement, until the middle of the 1920s.[3]

From a worker's viewpoint, a job in a Solvay soda plant was an advantageous alternative to the risky work in the mining or metallurgy industries, despite the possible contact with hazardous substances (e.g., lime, ammonia, gas, boiling

[1] ASPC, Trump (s.d.), 20; Schreib (1906), 140.
[2] On the image of the American steel industry, see Nuwer (1988), 808–38.
[3] ACo, 4.1.1 Organisation, ART, Ocna Muresului; Mioche (2009).

water).[4] The jobs were not as hard and were less dangerous than in the Leblanc plants, where handling of the salt cake, finishing of the caustic soda, and packaging of the bleaching agents were particularly unhealthy.[5] Even though, after the appearance of the Solvay process, the Leblanc industry improved its mechanization to increase productivity, to adapt to new safety standards, and to lift process-control responsibility from the workers, Solvay had clearly pushed the rationale much further, from the very beginning.[6]

The situation was different in the production sites attached to soda plants. In the coal and salt mines, just as in the lime quarries, much of the labor was done manually and was sometime heavy (e.g., busting rocks, loading salt onto barges, handling lime trolleys), because highly developed mechanization of the extraction sites was not immediately deemed to be profitable.[7] Likewise, some secondary productions, such as soda crystals, were not manufactured continuously but were custom made. There again, it was necessary to wait longer for certain manual jobs to be automated (e.g., raking and discharge operations, handling lye, packaging).[8]

Beyond the nature of the work itself, the location of the production sites, near salt beds, influenced social policy. Because the great majority of plants were isolated in the countryside and located in the vicinity of agricultural villages, finding and establishing a loyal workforce was a problem. In consequence, Solvay developed company towns fully equipped with social services.

Along with these determining factors peculiar to the alkali industry, external influences came into play. The company had begun its activities in a climate of absolute social laissez-faire. The Industrial Revolution had already generated its perverse effects by plunging a large working-class population into poverty: inadequate housing, long workdays, minimum wages, total social insecurity. The only social initiatives came from the private sector and the goodwill of certain "social patrons" of the textile, coal, and metal industries, who voluntarily made available lodging and other charitable institutions for their workers. Strikes were outlawed and, when they occurred, were brutally repressed. The first workers' organizations were not structured well enough to counterbalance the power of the omnipotent owners.

In this context, Solvay did not at first establish any formal social policy, as is seen in its responses to the inquiry from the Belgian Work Commission in 1886.[9] The major challenges it had to confront and overcome at first were on the technical and commercial levels. Additionally, the *gérants* deplored the

---

[4] The nature of work-related accidents is a testimony to this, even though we lack information for the years before 1914. The logbook at the Couillet plant shows that out of 181 work-related accidents occurring in 1925 and 1926, 33 percent were accidents in the quarry, 30 percent were for mechanical reasons, 16 percent to falls, 13 percent to handling accidents, and only 9 percent from burns or poisoning from contact with chemicals. ACo, 4.6.2.1 Accidents.

[5] Haber (1958), 236.

[6] Donnelly (1994), 118.

[7] ASPC, Trump (s.d.), 24, 99; Toca (2005), 182.

[8] ACo, 2.6.2.1 Copies lettres section A, Main d'oeuvre aux cristaux, 11 Dec. 1899.

[9] At this time, Solvay had not yet established in Belgium the mutual aid funds. The salaries it paid were within industry standards and had dropped following the crisis. It still employed about a dozen children. The workday remained at twelve hours. See Gubin and Piette (1997), 129.

fact that the workforce in the early years was composed of workers who were "generally not very intelligent and thus, poorly paid and disloyal."[10]

The 1880s witnessed the beginning of changes to come in most of the industrialized countries. In Belgium, where a prolonged recession held sway (1874–1895), the violent riots of 1886 acted as a catalyst among the progressives – Liberals and Catholics – and generated embryonic social legislation: ban on seizure of salaries (1887), protection of women and children (1889), and workers' compensation insurance (1890). Despite everything, Belgium brought up the rear compared to its neighbors, which had earlier adopted similar laws. In Germany, especially, Bismarck had set up the first state social security system to short-circuit the rise to power of the Social-Democrat party. The workers there benefited from mandatory health insurance (1883), workers' compensation (1884), and old-age pensions (1889). The movement was launched in the industrialized countries, thus making the climate favorable for business owners to invest in social economy and welfare programs, including housing, pension funds, health insurance, leisure, and education. Sporadic experiments that occurred during the first wave of industrialization were expanded and institutionalized by many companies. Solvay was part of this second wave of paternalism, at the very time when the word was turning into a pejorative synonym for neo-feudalism. The theoreticians of this system, Frédéric Le Play and his disciples, preferred the term *patronage*. The challenge, according to them, was to reassure the traditional world and to adapt the labor force to industrial work without harsh force, but rather by relying on their disposition, to orient and channel them in a direction that was beneficial to the company.[11]

Solvay was even one of the most representative firms of this movement, in every country where it had a direct or indirect presence. Working conditions for laborers in its plants were at first very disparate, depending on the location, the local labor market, legislation in place, and the status of the competition. Questions were settled pragmatically, on a case-by-case basis. At the turn of the twentieth century, an underlying harmonization of its social policies became nonetheless perceptible. Moreover, the entrepreneurs associated with Solvay implemented similar policies, probably through a game of mutual motivation. In the United States, the Hazard family was already well known for the social initiatives set up in its textile factories in Peacedale, Rhode Island.[12] It confirmed this reputation by adopting highly developed welfare schemes and establishing company towns at Syracuse and Detroit. In Austria-Hungary, Schaffner's Aussiger Verein applied the same type of enlightened policy in its plant in Bohemia.[13] It had no problem adapting to the Solvay vision for its jointly held plants at Ebensee, Maros-Ujvar, Lukavac, Nestomitz, and Podgórze. Likewise, Brunner, Mond was looked on as a progressive company in instituting

[10] ACS, AG, Gérance report, 1867.
[11] Noiriel (1988), 17–35; see also Reid (1985), 579–607; Nelson (1995); McCaffray (1987), 951–65; Perrot (1979), 154.
[12] Nelson (1995), 101.
[13] [Gintl] (1906), 68–71.

one of the most extensive social programs of the entire British chemical industry.[14]

Ernest Solvay's biographers often established a direct link between his own philosophy and the social policy in force within the company. However, we know little of his ideas in terms of actual industrial relations.[15] The most credible interpretation is that he effectively impregnated the company culture with his moral principles but left to the executive managers the task of defining practical social policy. Indeed, by the time Solvay & Cie formalized its paternalistic policy, Ernest Solvay had already left the day-to-day company management. The other *gérants* (e.g., Alfred Solvay, Fernand Van der Straeten, Edgard Hulin, Armand Solvay, Louis Solvay) played a significant role to that effect. The nonfamily *gérants*, such as Hanrez and especially Hannon, as well as the national managers in direct contact with the reality on the ground (e.g., Wessel, Marquet, Toeplitz, Bourriez, Alban) also strongly contributed to shaping this social policy.

Nonetheless, we cannot infer that Ernest Solvay's ideas were antipathetic to these policies. As a progressive-liberal, he attributed a social mission to his role of business owner. Influenced by the positivism of Saint-Simon and Auguste Comte, he was convinced that human progress would be achieved through the triumph of pure science. A man of systems, convinced of the power of deductive force, he firmly believed that a unique law could simultaneously govern the movements of the universe; the physiological functioning of individuals; and by extension, social relations (see Chapter 5). His social organization theories, which he mostly communicated during his terms as Belgian senator (1892–1894 and 1897–1900), are indicative of his vision of industrial relations. Easily mixing disciplines, Ernest Solvay applied the law of conservation of energy, recently revealed as a fundamental principle of thermodynamics, to the study of the human body and societies. According to him, and to the German chemist Wilhelm Ostwald, a human being should be considered a machine or a motor, to which energy is supplied and from which yield is produced. From this postulate comes his theory of social energetics and productivism, which has the ultimate goal of maximizing social yield and human well-being through the maximum production of goods.[16] Although criticized for his extreme determinism, especially by the sociologist Max Weber, Ernest Solvay never departed from his view:

> Society, like individuals, acts automatically. The laws that it obeys and that regulate social movement are precisely those that constitute what I called "energetics" or "social productivism," coming together in the human and physiological law of "search for a better existence" that in itself is no more that a veiled expression of the physical-chemical law of "maximum work."[17]

[14] Haber (1958), 249; Reader (1970), 233–4.
[15] As is rightly emphasized by Gubin and Piette (1997), 127.
[16] Ernest Solvay's doctrine of social energy was beautifully put into context in Rabinbach (1992), 179–82. See also Stengers (1997), 149–65 and Crombois (1997), 209–20.
[17] Solvay (1900), 164.

In this thought system, each individual should be compensated according to his or her productivity capacity, that is, his or her usefulness. To arrive at that, Ernest Solvay argued for vocational training for the unemployed (*capacitariat*), the passage of an inheritance tax to eliminate the heritage of large fortunes benefiting nonproductive heirs, and state participation in creation of companies and a free socialization of goods. He went as far as proposing the elimination of currency for a system of social accounting (*comptabilisme*) that would allow drawing up a productivity balance sheet for each individual and recording any financial transaction with a centralized organization.

To meet the great social challenges of his time, Solvay promoted a reformist and progressive liberalism that he sometimes assimilated with scientific socialism. He rejected completely the revolutionary socialism likely to shatter the established order, as well as the "obscurantist conservatism."[18] Although aspiring to "equality at the start," Ernest Solvay was also convinced of the natural inequality among mankind. He then argued for a modernized version of enlightened despotism in which a government of social savants would guide society based on rational science. There is found here certain fundaments of the paternalistic logic, legitimizing the maintenance of a strict hierarchy in the work organization, the principle of redistribution directed by the most able and the intellectual, and material elevation of each in a goal toward social peace and collective prosperity.

4.2   THE MULTIPLE FACETS OF SOLVAY'S SOCIAL RELATIONS

An Industrial Empire, Diverse Work Conditions

During its first half century of development, the Solvay Group acquired a vast and complex structure. Both the countries directly dependent on Solvay (e.g., Belgium, France, Italy, Spain) and the German, English, American, Russian, and Austrian joint ventures were equipped with a complete organizational structure, with their own administrative, technical, and commercial facilities. The soda plants, located at the heart of the production system, were of varying sizes. The largest (e.g., Dombasle, Bernburg, Syracuse, Northwich, Lysychansk) employed up to 3,000 workers in 1913. Laboratories and secondary production lines (e.g., refined salt, soda crystals, bicarbonate, caustic lye) were also attached to these plants. On the contrary, the headcount of the small soda plants had no more than several hundred workers (300 at Wyhlen, 430 at Couillet, 450 at Salin-de-Giraud, and 700 at Sarralbe). Around its soda plants, Solvay worked salt mines, limestone quarries, and sometimes coal mines (e.g., Donetz, Lieres, Osternienburg, Micheln). In Germany, productions were more diversified, with potash from Solvayhall and cement from Bernburg. For transporting goods, the company organized navigable river fleets. The Solvay Group, including all entities, already employed 6,000 blue-collar workers and 500 white-collar employees in 1888. A quarter of a century later,

---

[18] Solvay (1879); *Notes, lettres et discours* (1929), 463–80.

headcount had surged to 20,000 blue-collar workers and 5,000 white-collar employees.

A Paternalistic Relationship

In the paternalistic system, the patron assumed the authority and duties of a father with respect to his "salaried children." He provided for their well-being in exchange for their respect and obedience. In the large companies, and particularly in multinationals, the link between the personnel and the production tool owner tended to slacken. Solvay made great efforts to conserve it, even if the tie became more symbolic than practical. Starting around 1880–1890, at the time when Solvay became solidly established in its primary markets, the company set up a large-scale paternalistic policy. Busts of the founding brothers were distributed to all of the sites. Anniversaries became excellent opportunities to celebrate the familial and private nature of the interpersonal relationships. Regular visits from upper management were organized in each plant to maintain contact with the base. But beyond these practices, the managers remained very personally involved in social questions, even minor ones. The minutes from the *gérance* meetings are peppered with mention of individuals taking retirement, special bonuses for good and loyal service, appointments and replacements of employees and workers, indebtedness troubles of a particular employee, diplomatic settlements of conflicts between engineers, and so on.[19] Until 1879, Alfred Solvay had continued to manage, on site, the plant at Couillet, to such a degree that upon his death, his employees described him in these filial terms: "our venerable leader had a good and compassionate nature. Seeing people suffer caused him great pain, and helping others was his greatest happiness. His goodness knew no limits."[20] At the local level, plant managers and department heads ensured that the patronage system was maintained:

> Each department head assumes the role of the patron with his subordinates. He has a personal relationship with each of the workers who report to him and he knows them individually: their personality, their professional value, their family situation, their sorrows and their joys should all be very familiar to him. He treats them with respect. He instructs them. The plant organization is thus set up for this purpose. Each department head has the power he needs to assume the role of a little owner; he has access to direct information from the secretariat, the doctor, the social workers. In an effort to prepare its cadres for this social function of their duties, the company provides training for each engineer or manager that it hires.[21]

The plant managers were given great latitude, including financial, to carry out philanthropy with regard to regional works or institutions. That was the case for Carl Wessel in Germany and Prosper Hanrez in France. Hanrez's

---

[19] ACS, RdG, 17 Dec. 1891, 6 May 1892, 9 Aug. 1907, 10 Dec. 1907, 3 April 1908, 28 April 1908, 29 Nov. 1910, and so on.

[20] ACS, *Obituaire d'Alfred Solvay: Discours au nom des ouvriers de l'usine de Couillet, lu par M. Bruyère, ouvrier*, 1894, 16.

[21] AHR, *Ernest Solvay et ses réalisations sociales à la Société Solvay & Cie*, 1943.

successor, Adolphe Marquet, for example, convinced central management to create in 1895 a mutual aid fund for the whole Meurthe department ("La Prévoyance nancéenne"), not just for the area around the plant, and to fund it significantly (FF 150,000), to once and for all shut down the xenophobic accusation often aimed at Solvay.[22]

Hierarchy and Recruiting

As in the rest of the industry, the distinction between white-collar employees and blue-collar workers was evident at Solvay. Early on, engineers, chemists, accountants, statisticians, designers, attorneys, and doctors enjoyed solid protection and received a variety of benefits. Senior management paid very close attention to their recruiting. Their skills were taken into account, but also their personality, their reputation, and their morals.[23] Hiring decisions were based on information gathered from candidates' former professors, former employers, and the residential housing authority. The highest positions (e.g., plant managers, technical managers, process engineers) were exclusively given to engineers. The chemists were relegated to a lower rung, including the manager of the central laboratory, René Lucion. In the plants, chemists were mainly assigned the tasks of analysis (titrations) and process control, whereas engineers had to be free to innovate. Solvay was looking to foster emulation and avoid development of strict, insulated specializations within the company, as Édouard Hannon notes in a retrospective:

> We must not departmentalize each engineer into one specialty, in which he will be engaged his entire career, because then we only have troops and we lose sight of the need to create leaders, with deeper experience. It is from among these leaders alone that can rationally be recruited our future managers. The company technicians will never be specialists in anything but soda ash, which is the specialty of Solvay.[24]

At the intermediate level, the foremen constituted important links between management and workers. Control of their discretionary powers made up a key element of paternalistic management.[25] According to Daniel Nelson, the role of foremen tended to diminish in industries that implemented continuous processes.[26] Nonetheless, in the case of Solvay, they continued to play a predominant role in the work organization. Each step of the production process (e.g., distillation, lime kilns, rotating dryers, causticizing, maintenance, workshops) remained controlled and managed by an experienced foreman. The foremen recruited and trained the workers under their jurisdiction. They

---

[22] ACS, 1100 61–2A, La Prévoyance Nancéenne, cited by Mioche (2008), 69–71.
[23] For example, ACS, RdG 25 July 1911: an in-depth inquiry was done by the manager at Couillet on the engineer Cornille, who, despite a capricious nature and socialist past, seemed to be suited for the job.
[24] ACS, Édouard Hannon, Note sur le principe d'une participation ouvrière, April 1928.
[25] Reid (1985), 582.
[26] Nelson (1995), 36.

enjoyed a stable position and received a monthly salary. They maintained discipline by meting out punishments and fines, instituted to maintain order in the workshop.[27] The production engineers or plant managers could be brought in for possible conflicts, but Solvay meant to preserve the authority of the foreman. Thus when in 1910, the French management planned to increase the social role of the engineers by giving them more latitude to dismiss workers, Georges Chardin – general technical manager and son-in-law of his predecessor, Édouard Hannon – emphasized:

> The danger inherent in reforming current practices through an official memo, which, among other problems, would diminish the prestige of the foremen and discourage some of them who currently take to heart the duty of maintaining a strict discipline among the workers. It stands to reason that there would be great benefits if the punishments and dismissals were controlled by the engineers, and that the workers knew that they were subject to them, through the intermediary of the foremen; but we must proceed slowly, by persuasion and consensus among the foremen.[28]

The blue-collar workers obviously represented the greatest majority of the workforce, around 90 percent of the personnel in the plants, and they were almost all male. They were divided into two categories. On the one hand, the soda ash workers, or production operators, worked in continuous shifts, seven days a week. Among them were about twenty different skills and about a 30 percent range in salaries. On the other hand, the yardmen worked during the day, six days a week. They were assigned to the mechanical construction (e.g., boiler works, foundry, metal framing), cooperage, carpentry, bricklaying, masonry, packaging, and general services departments. Solvay also employed workers for the mines and the quarries. Table 4.1 gives a summary of the duties, salaries, and work schedules of the workers in the soda plants around 1910.

During the early years, the great majority of the workforce had low skill levels and the rate of turnover was high. Solvay often had difficulties in recruiting workers, in terms of quality as well as quantity. By definition, it was impossible to hire experienced personnel when the group built a first ammonia soda plant in a new country. Also, most of the plants were located in rural areas, outside the large labor pools. The workforce in these areas often comprised agricultural laborers not trained to work in a modern chemical industry. A number of workers were peasants who viewed factory work as income that was used to supplement, not supplant, their farm income. Numerous witnesses at the time emphasized this fact. In his memoirs, Wladimir Orlow described the early workers at Berezniki as "men barely out of serfdom, used to constraint, capable of great effort but not too inclined to steady work. On the equipment, the fear of reprimands made them resort to cheating."[29] At Syracuse, most

---

[27] ACo, 4.1.01.04 Workshop guidelines established in compliance with the law of 15 June 1896. The memoirs of Wladimir Orlow provide helpful information on the role of foremen: Accarain (2002), 148–50.

[28] ACS, RdG 30 Aug. 1910.

[29] Accarain (2002), 139.

TABLE 4.1. *Qualifications, Salaries, and Schedules of Blue-Collar Workers (1908–1912)*

Job	Couillet (1908) Salary Per Day (BEF)	Couillet (1908) Hours Per Week	Lysychansk (1912) Salary Per Day (BEF)	Lysychansk (1912) Hours Per Week	Berezniki (1912) Salary Per Day (BEF)	Berezniki (1912) Hours Per Week
Shift men						
Machinist	4.0	8 × 7	4.6	8 × 7	2.8	8 × 7
Lubricator, oiler	3.8	8 × 7	4.6	8 × 7	2.8	8 × 7
Pumper	4.0	8 × 7	4.6	8 × 7	2.8	8 × 7
Stoker, supplier, feeder	4.3	8 × 7	4.6	8 × 7	2.8	8 × 7
Generator heater	4.2	8 × 7	4.6	8 × 7	2.8	8 × 7
Coal driver	3.6	8 × 7	4.6	8 × 7	2.8	8 × 7
Lime kiln	4.1	8 × 7	4.6	8 × 7	2.8	8 × 7
Lime work	4.0	8 × 7	4.6	8 × 7	2.8	8 × 7
Distiller	4.2	8 × 7	4.6	8 × 7	2.8	8 × 7
Measurer	4.0	8 × 7	4.6	8 × 7	2.8	8 × 7
Filtration chief	5.2	8 × 7	4.6	8 × 7	2.8	8 × 7
Filterer	4.2	8 × 7	4.6	8 × 7	2.8	8 × 7
Column washers	3.8	8 × 7	4.6	8 × 7	2.8	8 × 7
Column testers	3.5	8 × 7	4.6	8 × 7	2.8	8 × 7
Drier monitors	4.3	8 × 7	4.6	8 × 7	2.8	8 × 7
Heater	4.2	8 × 7	4.6	8 × 7	2.8	8 × 7
Grinder	3.9	8 × 7	4.6	8 × 7	2.8	8 × 7
Adjuster	5.0	8 × 7	4.6	8 × 7	2.8	8 × 7
Input and output	3.5	8 × 7	4.6	8 × 7	2.8	8 × 7
Cleaner	3.5	8 × 7	4.6	8 × 7	2.8	8 × 7
Yardmen						
Heavy labor	3.6	9.5 × 6	2.5	9 × 6	2.2	9 × 6
Adjuster	4.9	9.5 × 6	5.0	9 × 6	4.1	9 × 6
Blacksmith	5.2	9.5 × 6	8.6	9 × 6	4.1	9 × 6
Hammer man	3.9	9.5 × 6	4.5	9 × 6	2.3	9 × 6
Carpenter	4.9	9.5 × 6	5.9	9 × 6	3.6	9 × 6
Mason	4.6	9.5 × 6	4.0	9 × 6	3.6	9 × 6
Assistants and handlers	3.8	9.5 × 6	3.9	9 × 6	2.2	9 × 6

Sources: ACo 2.6.2.1 Copies lettres 1908–1910; ART, Moscou, Correspondence 1912.

of the workers originally came from farms in the region and the surrounding saltworks. A great number of them were unskilled European immigrants (e.g., Irish, Italian, Polish, Ukrainian), which made the plant resemble the tower of Babel.[30] At Dombasle, the plant manager Adolphe Marquet regularly pointed out to management "the difficulty he had in finding workers for the plant and the benefits there were to be had in keeping them."[31] For his part, Ludwig Mond had to resort to Irish and Welsh workers because he could not find enough people in Cheshire capable of working in his plant at

[30] West (1981), 8; Cominolli (1990).
[31] ACS, RdC, 3 Mar. 1892.

Northwich. He wrote in 1874, at a delicate time: "You cannot find a good experienced fitter and yet you have to say thank you to these inexperienced drunkards when they turn up at all, and have to pretend that they are really working."[32]

The workers from this period thus received on-the-job training, until a certain worker elite was formed, whose loyalty then had to be won. After a first generation of plants had been established, Solvay organized the transfer of competences from the existing sites to the new ones, just as it had done for the transfer of its technologies (see Chapter 2). Men were transferred between Dombasle and Salin-de-Giraud, and were then sent to Spanish (Torrelavega in 1907) and Italian (Rosignano in 1913) plants. Both engineers and experienced foremen were transferred short- or long-term to new production facilities, whereas a lesser number of Spanish and Italian technicians were brought in for training at Belgian, French, and German sites. The most promising local workers could thus receive training that was more practical than theoretical and possibly climb the corporate ladder.[33] Such transfers also took place between Belgium and Russia, where Belgian engineers, foremen, and blue-collar workers spent part of their careers.[34] On the contrary, in the case of America, it seems that transfers occurred only from west to east. The first American engineers came for training in Europe, but there is no trace of employees sent by Solvay across the Atlantic.

Discipline, Schedules, and Wages

As with all the large mechanized plants of the time, management maintained strict discipline to promote stability of the production process. This was the repressive side of the paternalistic relationship. The workshop rules provide us with several illustrations.[35] All workers were subject to the orders of foremen, production managers, and head operators. Those who did not follow the rules were subject to fines, which were then donated to a savings account for needy workers. The workers could be dismissed in case of an egregious fault but also when production was interrupted by a strike. Punctuality was strictly enforced. Being ten minutes late was punished by a fine of two hours' wages. The fine was doubled if the offense was repeated. Any worker who had a moment of free time had to use it for maintenance of the equipment found in his work area. The worker who had completed his tasks had to immediately ask his foreman for additional work. He could be asked to do any job outside his usual duties. Any worker caught idle had to be punished by a fine of fifty centimes; if he was found asleep, he could be fined 5 BEF, in addition to losing his day's pay and possible dismissal. The worker was held responsible for wear and tear on the tools and machines on which he worked. Deviant behaviors

---

[32] Letter from Mond to Hasenclever on 28 Jan. 1874, cited by Lischka (1985), 119–20.

[33] For the Spanish case, see Toca (2005), 176–94; for Salin-de-Giraud, see Daumalin, Lambert, and Mioche (2007), 11–12; for Russia, see Accarain (2002), 55 and 108.

[34] Accarain (2002), 55, 108.

[35] ACo, 4.1.01.04 Workshop regulations established in compliance with the law of 15 June 1896.

such as alcoholism, gambling, and assembly were obviously forbidden. Workshop rules, related to payment of salaries and work schedules, were posted on the walls of the plants and contained provisions that had the force of a contract.

The Solvay Group very early introduced an eight-hour workday and a third shift for the production operators. The eight-hour day was one of the battle cries of the labor movement in all the industrialized countries. The First International had had it on its agenda since 1866. However, it was not written into national law until after World War I. At Solvay, until the very start of the twentieth century, the shift workers were still working in two shifts of twelve hours each, from 6:00 A.M. to 6:00 P.M. and from 6:00 P.M. to 6:00 A.M. They had no established days off (neither Sundays nor holidays), nor did they have a fixed time for meals; they matched their schedule to the machine's rhythm. The company organized operations to ensure them periodic breaks. The yardmen also worked twelve-hour days for six days, with Sundays off. Brunner, Mond innovated in this field as early as 1889. The workweek for shift operators was reduced to fifty-six hours, which raised labor costs by more than 20 percent and necessitated recruitment of three hundred additional men. To limit the impact of this increase, Brunner, Mond cut salaries by 10 percent, but the following year, they were restored to previous levels as a result of the significant increase in productivity per worker.[36] In 1895, the British company reduced the work schedules of the yardmen to forty-nine hours and fifteen minutes. At Solvay & Cie, the upper management had mixed feelings on the issue. Ernest Solvay had some reservations: "It can't be a question of outright charity or of curtailing each person's right to work. It is the nations who have the least expensive working day compared to the others who will carry the day. There are only artificial barriers."[37]

Reduction in work hours was possible only at the price of a corresponding increase in productivity. Stimuli coming from the plants led Solvay to adopt the system of three eight-hour shifts at the group level. In Russia, Sigismond Toeplitz, the plant manager at Donetz who was inclined to listen to workers' claims, applied the system in 1897 without informing the management at Moscow or Brussels. He was determined to demonstrate that the gains in productivity would compensate for the increased costs in wages.[38] Ten years, however, were necessary for the measure to be adopted everywhere, without cuts in salary. As of 1 April 1907, the shift workers were divided into three teams working in eight-hour shifts (6 A.M. to 2 P.M., 2 P.M. to 10 P.M., and 10 P.M. to 6 A.M.). On Sunday, operations were handled by two teams each working twelve-hour shifts (6 A.M. to 6 P.M. and 6 P.M. to 6 A.M.). The third shift thus enjoyed twenty-four hours of rest while the first two worked twenty consecutive hours. The yardmen saw their daily schedule go to nine and a half hours and later to nine hours.

[36] Watts (1923), 69–70.
[37] ACS-O, Technical Committee, Meeting minutes, 1889–1900, 29 Oct. 1897.
[38] Accarain (2002), 165–6.

Solvay once again was looked on as a precursor when, on its fiftieth anniversary in 1913, it instituted paid leave for workers. They received six or seven paid days off annually with double wages. Brunner, Mond had beat them to it, as it had introduced a week off with regular pay in 1884 and then added double wages in 1902.[39] As for the Solvay white-collar employees, they received two to three paid weeks of vacation, depending on their job and their seniority. In 1892, the workweek for white-collar employees at Central Administration had been limited to forty-two hours per week, and in 1909, they obtained Saturday afternoons off, the result of a petition.[40]

With regard to salaries, different random observations show that they were generally higher than in the rural region around the plant but remained in the middle range of salaries in the industry. The various levers of paternalistic policy enabled Solvay to maintain average salaries and preserve its competitiveness. Significant wage disparities existed among the countries, and even among different plants in the same country, depending on the local labor markets. Thus, around 1910, the average daily salary of a worker was the equivalent of US$0.52 at Berezniki, US$0.76 at Salin-de-Giraud, US$0.81 at Couillet, US$0.86 at Donetz, and US$1.14 at Dombasle,[41] and when the plant at Torrelavega came on stream, the salaries there were lower than those of other plants in the group but higher than the Spanish average.[42] Workers were paid according to time worked (hourly or daily) because compensation by task or by yield was not appropriate in the framework of a soda plant. Salaries of white-collar employees and foremen were paid monthly, whereas compensation of the general managers was set on a yearly basis and included variable bonuses (percentages). Thus, in 1910, the technical manager earned BEF 35,000 (US$6,650) per year, compared to BEF 30,000 (US$5,700) for the commercial manager, the financial manager, and the *gérants*, with the variable bonuses of the latter being proportionally greater.[43]

Town Planning and Industrial Architecture Dedicated to Productivism

At the end of the nineteenth century, availability of worker housing became a subject of increasing concern in most of the industrialized countries. Blue-collar worker residences singularly lacked comfort, space, and hygiene, and rents were proportionally expensive, both in the cities and in the towns surrounding the plants. From the worker's standpoint, the opportunity to receive or to rent healthy lodging at a low price constituted an enormous factor in the choice of a place to live and work. Without this, many of them voluntarily left in search of better wages. By procuring residences for workers whose services they valued, some industrials, including Solvay, accomplished what they considered their

---

[39] Watts (1923), 69.
[40] ACS, RdG, 29 Oct. 1892, 29 Nov. 1910.
[41] ACo 2.6.2.1 Copies lettres 1908–1910, ART, Moscou, Correspondence 1912; Mioche (2008), 66; Haber (1958), 242–6.
[42] Toca (2005), 184.
[43] AHR, Rémunération des cadres dirigeants. A Belgian franc of 1910 had the same buying power as €3.40 or US$4.40 in 2009.

social obligation while at the same time promoting their productivity objectives. Company towns represented the most efficient tool to lock in the labor force, improve health and hygiene conditions, moderate salaries, stabilize production flow, and exercise social and moral control over the worker population. A memo from Édouard Hannon written during a visit to the plant at Donetz illuminates the pragmatic way in which Solvay perceived the question of lodging:

> The workforce derives mainly from the inhabitants of the village. These villagers, to increase prices, prevent, through the raising of rents and through harassment, the influx of foreign workers. It would thus be of interest to create lodging in adequate numbers. The skilled workers that have to come in from outside complain loudly about the situation. An essential factor is to lodge all the foremen, skilled workers, adjusters, blacksmiths, etc. as close to the plant as possible, for example in lodging built at the edge of Donetz. They can then be on call for any emergency repairs occurring during the night. Currently, precious time is being lost searching the village for the men necessary. This leads to very costly plant shutdowns.[44]

Solvay constructed its first company housing at Dombasle in 1873, to lodge workers who had to be on call. These first cottages, each composed of two tiny rooms, constituted only a stopgap solution. Soon villas were built for managers, engineers, and cadres. The company town then developed apace: there were 106 residences in 1883, 263 in 1889, 460 in 1909, and 600 in 1910. The different neighborhoods of the company town were named after the managers and partners, to create a symbolic link between the workers and the company owners: Hanrez town (built in 1873 and named in 1893), Nélis town (1876), Pirmez town (1879), Semet town (1881). In 1909, a third of the workers were housed at the plant; another third in the village of Dombasle, which had become an industrial town; and the other third in the surrounding areas. Financial pressure on rental costs due to the regular increase of the population encouraged Solvay to continue building housing.[45]

The town-planning know-how gained by Solvay developed at the same time as its industrial activity. The initiatives taken at Dombasle were replicated and sometimes improved at other sites. At Brussels, the Central Bureau of Auxiliary Constructions (Bureau Central des Constructions Complémentaires) was in charge of designing the cities, and several soda ash engineers lent their talents. Édouard Hannon himself designed some of the housing models. All the sites were provided with a series of houses, if not complete towns. The most highly developed were those of Dombasle, Rosignano, Torrelavega, Donetz, Sarralbe, and Salin-de-Giraud, which was completely isolated from the outside world. The period 1890–1914 witnessed a harmonization of the industrial territories shaped by Solvay across the continents. Everywhere, the same logic was applied. The size and look of the housing reflected the position the inhabitant held in the company. Housing was classified into categories by size: the smaller the

---

44 ART, Moscou, Notes de Mr. Hannon, Visit by Édouard Hannon to the plant at Donetz, May 1893.
45 ACS, Brochure from the Exposition of Nancy 1909; Mioche (2008), 82–91.

house and the farther away it was from the production site, the lower the person's position was in the social hierarchy. Gradually, the architecture began to reflect the image of the company. The top standing of the plant managers' homes reflected the prestige of the firm. The offices were located in sumptuous buildings. The village recreational halls (*casinos*), with beautiful architectural details, were designed to reinforce camaraderie and esprit de corps.[46]

Hygiene, Education, Leisure, and Morality

In concordance with the hygiene theories in vogue in the middle of the nineteenth century, Solvay provided its towns with sewage systems, water purification, and residential distribution. It also provided public baths and gaslights. Availability of plowed and fertilized agricultural land, as well as allotment of little gardens attached to the workers' homes, aimed to provide a healthy pastime for the workers and to supply extra food for the household. Additionally, the satisfaction of working the soil was supposed to offer a respite from the hard work at the plant. In the same vein, several plants had farms that produced meat, grains, and vegetables that were sold at the company store, the company restaurant, and the cooperative.[47] Solvay encouraged and subsidized the formation of cooperatives administered by employees and workers, subject to oversight and control by the company. These internal commercial interests were supposed to meet the needs of distributing foodstuffs at affordable prices in the absence of local networks, prevent worker indebtedness, and anticipate the expansion of collective reflexes accompanying the cooperative movement.

To further reinforce the economic attractiveness of the towns, the white-collar employees and foremen were housed for free, whereas the workers benefited from rental discounts based on seniority and the number of dependent children: 25 percent for the worker with seven years of service and two children or one year of service and three children, and 100 percent for twenty-seven years of service and two children or six years of service and seven children.[48] By thus encouraging large families, the Solvay towns became incubators for future workers. Loans were also given at preferential terms for construction or purchase of a house, thus further reinforcing the link between employer and wage earner. Along the same lines, an internal savings bank offering 5 percent interest was set up in 1877, to encourage frugality and savings.

Despite the anticlerical leanings of its founder, Solvay also financed the construction of churches and paid Catholic priests to live on its lands, considering it "a duty for any company to give its personnel the freedom to worship, if they

---

[46] The objectives of Solvay's industrial architecture are broadly comparable to those of other large companies at the time, such as Schneider at Creusot or General Electric in the United States. See Littmann (1998), 88–114.

[47] At Syracuse, Tully Land Farm thus employed more than 250 workers. For functioning of the La Lorraine cooperative in Dombasle, see Chiousse (1901), 54.

[48] AHR, *Ernest Solvay et ses réalisations sociales à la Société Solvay & Cie*, 1943.

FIGURE 4.2. Employees doing gymnastics at the facilities of the Lukavac plant in Bosnia. (Solvay Archives.)

so desire."[49] According a fundamental importance to instruction and worker education, Solvay organized and subsidized day care and primary schools in most of its towns, often in agreement with local authorities, relieved of this burden by the company, sometimes even by legal obligation, as in Russia. For the adults, the company organized evening courses in arithmetic, the mother tongue, history, and civics, as well as public lectures on moralizing themes: frugality, the evils of alcohol, progress, the role of the woman in education, and so on. Homemaking schools taught wives sewing, ironing, and household budget management. In the United States, Americanization classes were organized for foreign workers and their children. At Syracuse, a mechanics school officered, as of 1907, two-year programs that taught operations of all the Solvay Process Co. and Semet-Solvay Co. branches.[50] In a later phase of its development, Solvay tried to encourage the upward mobility of some of its workers by granting scholarships to the most gifted among them, staying in line with the doctrine of meritocracy of the enlightened patrons. The Ernest Solvay Fund in Russia (100,000 rubles) and the Fund Édouard Hannon in Belgium and France (BEF 5 million, or US$950,000) were created for this purpose in 1913.

---

[49] ACS, RdG, 22 Oct. 1909. Restoration of the Barcarin Church at Giraud. Comments by the *gérant* Fernand Van der Straeten, son-in-law of Ernest Solvay.
[50] West (1981), 12.

The company also provided numerous facilities for leisure activities, thus promoting social peace, identity, and cohesion. Some aimed to create unity among all the workers, regardless of status: theaters, music clubs, theatrical troupes, and sporting clubs and equipment. The gymnastics club could even be used to prepare young men for military service. Other types of leisure activities mirrored the social hierarchy of the plant: while the workers had a café (where religious or political discussions were forbidden) and a popular library, the cadres gathered in higher-standing clubhouses.[51]

An Internal Social Security System

Supplemental health and insurance initiatives constituted another important aspect of Solvay's social policy. The first priority was to establish health facilities in close proximity to the plants, for the workers and their families. The first health-care services appeared in 1878. The first complete hospital began in 1890 at Dombasle. It was followed by others, providing free services to workers and their families for general medical needs, surgery, home nurses, maternity, dentistry, and so on.[52] In cases when the plant did not have complete installations, agreements were concluded with nearby hospitals. The doctors, due to their permanent and intimate contact with the working population, played a primary social role and constituted a privileged link between the plant management and the personnel. Solvay also covered drug costs of the workers who had more than two years' seniority and paid half their salary during lost time due to sickness. Employees getting treatment under a certain ceiling were reimbursed to up to two-thirds of their medical and pharmaceuticals expenses.[53] For major operations, the reimbursement levels were subject to the discretion of the department heads. Following enactment of the French law of 1898 on work accidents, the company insured all of its working personnel against accidents with outside insurance companies (e.g., Assurances de Zurich, de Winterthur). Accident victims received reimbursement for damages from half their salary to their entire salary, depending on the family size and seniority.[54]

Another facet of social protection was through the setting up of contingency funds, either outside of any government intervention or in accord with nascent social legislation, depending on the country. Bismarck's Germany was the first to establish a national system of social protection. It was rapidly imitated by Austria-Hungary. In these two countries, Solvay was thus obligated to finance, as were all industrials, a health insurance fund for its workers, a workers' compensation fund, and a pension fund for employees and workers. In other countries it was a free savings system based on voluntary decisions and without public financing that prevailed longer. The local and then national mutual aid

[51] Mioche (2008), 81.
[52] AHR, *Ernest Solvay et ses réalisations sociales à la Société Solvay & Cie*, 1943; Mioche (2008), 71–3; Perales (2004).
[53] ACS, RdG, 4 July 1913.
[54] AHR, *Ernest Solvay et ses réalisations sociales à la Société Solvay & Cie*, 1943; ACS, RdG, 31 May 1907.

associations used to play a major role. Heirs of the guilds and corporations, they had grown out of the companies, local collectivities, trade unions, and religious associations.[55] In the case of companies, the mutual funds were often managed at the discretion of the employer. They offered nontransferrable benefits and linked workers to their job.[56] In some ways, the funds were instruments used to win the loyalty of workers after having enticed them to join the company.[57] Joint management of the funds often became the subject of workers' claims.

At Solvay, a pension fund was created in 1879–1880 for Belgian, French, and German employees and foremen, before the transfer of the latter to the German fund in 1885. Supplied exclusively by the company, these funds granted to employees a sum at the time of their retirement, at the age of sixty. Each worker had an individual account, and the equity was converted into treasury bonds.[58] Solvay & Cie, like DSW, used the pension fund as a way to retain employees in the group, by anniversary service awards or increasing percentages (from 10 percent to 30 percent, depending on seniority). If the employees voluntarily left the company, and especially did not respect the noncompete clause for five years, management committee could decide to give them nothing, because the amount in the accounts remained company property.[59] The savings and pension fund in Russia was established in 1890 following the same principle. Subsidies in the case of retirement, death, or illness were given on a case-by-case basis, depending on seniority, good conduct, and the seriousness of the case. It was not a pension that was acquired but a subsidy that the plant could withdraw at any time.[60] In addition to the funds for employees, special funds were instituted at Solvay and DSW for upper cadres, except for top managers, whose profit sharing was separately regulated. Payments were based on evolution of earnings.[61]

Pension funds were extended to workers in 1889, with mandatory participation. Workers age twenty-five years and older, married, and widows with children working more than three years for Solvay without interruption were the beneficiaries. Dues, of 1.5 percent withheld from a salary along with a 3 percent match by the company, were paid to national pension funds, guaranteed by the state (in Belgium and France, and then in Spain in 1913). Here again, seniority was compensated by additional payments after ten years of uninterrupted service. Funds were managed by the plants through a committee composed of two company representatives and three workers. After thirty years of service, the affiliates earned a pension (minimum BEF 400, or US$76 per year in 1910) with rights to it at age sixty. They could nonetheless continue to work after this age, sometime after seventy, at a time when life expectancy

[55] Dreyfus (1995), 92–102; Conrad (1990), 531–63.
[56] Reid (1985), 583–4.
[57] Trempé (1995), 390.
[58] Sirjacobs (1997), 314.
[59] ACS, Eilsberger (b) (1930), 409–14.
[60] Accarain (2002), 23 and 127.
[61] ACS, Eilsberger (b) (1930), 426.

scarcely reached fifty.[62] For the "old workers," who had been hired before the establishment of pension funds and considered particularly deserving, Solvay filled in the gap for them to be able to have a reasonable pension.[63]

Alongside the pension funds, auxiliary mutual aid funds were often set up in the plants, designed to support the worker from cradle to grave, in a spirit of charity. Special funds, such as the Fund Alfred Solvay (1894) and the anniversary funds (twenty-five years for DSW), reinforced on occasion this action. Assistance and subsidies were granted for childbirth, scholarships, funeral costs, compensation during military service, help for the needy, for widows and orphans, and adjustments for the cost of living. This philanthropy reached its zenith during celebration, in 1913, of the fiftieth anniversary of the company, when special funds were released to pay bonuses and increase contributions from the company to the pension fund (6 percent of the salary instead of 3 percent).

Public Relations and Philanthropy

At the turn of the twentieth century, Solvay had become a synonym for a powerful and progressive company in a modern and fast-growing industry. While it kept its financial results and production processes absolutely secret, it eagerly presented to the public the scope of its social programs to enhance this flattering image. This reputation contributed to its prestige with the general public, its customers, and its competitors, but also with the labor market. It relied on its favorable reputation in relations with local and national public authorities, in particular for obtaining salt concessions; in competition with national firms; and even for the attribution of honorary titles for some top managers, such as the French Legion of Honor for Hanrez and Chardin.[64] Édouard Hannon – again – summarized in retrospect the way Solvay viewed public relations:

> Public opinion becomes favorable if you respect morals, customs, if you get involved in the country by doing good works, giving gifts, subsidies, subscriptions to public utility works, . . . by serving ones personnel through large social and other institutions, by leading rather than following the national companies. You thus create useful and loyal support. And you get good press.[65]

[62] ACo, 4.5.05 Pensions; AHR, *Ernest Solvay et ses réalisations sociales à la Société Solvay & Cie,* 1943.

[63] ACS, RdG, 28 Mar. 1891, 7 June 1907, 3 Aug. 1908, 24 Sept. 1912, and so on.

[64] For example, when the University of Paris asked Solvay to make another donation to equip its chemistry lab, it was decided to "stall a little while . . . given what we have done, and quite recently. If we wait a bit (competition), the moment will perhaps be more favorable to provide this act of generosity" (ACS, RdG, 2 Feb. 1912). The following year, Solvay made a large donation and asked the university rector, in return, to help Georges Chardin receive the Legion of Honor (ACS, RdG, 18 July 1913). In 1910, support from the chemist Albin Haller, beneficiary of a subsidy for the University of Nancy, had been requested in the same vein (ACS, RdG, 27 Sept. 1907).

[65] ACS, NdG 1925–1949, La politique de Solvay & Cie, 31 Oct. 1926.

When the first truly universal exposition of social economy took place in 1889 in Paris, Solvay received a gold medal for its worker housing, alongside a handful of other industrials.[66] Likewise, the La Lorraine cooperative at Dombasle received a silver medal during the exposition of 1900.[67] The brochures published on the occasion of these events dealt broadly with all the social institutions of the company. The anniversaries of 1888 and especially of 1913 were also occasions to extend generosity and at the same time make the company known.[68] The largesse of the gifts made by Solvay compared to other subscribers often impressed observers. Its contributions to the foundation of chemical and electric institutes of the University of Nancy in 1897–1898 were as much as five to ten times greater than those of other industrials (e.g., Pont-à-Mousson, Saint-Gobain). We see here a desire to become deeply integrated into French territory by possibly acting in a more patriotic spirit than the national companies.[69]

The patronage of the company and the Solvay family sometimes crossed paths. Personally, Ernest Solvay, the "Belgian Carnegie,"[70] distinguished himself by the scope of his generosity, especially toward scientific institutions. He financed the construction, in the very heart of Brussels, of a veritable scientific city and institutes that are still renowned, with the dual intent of encouraging scientific progress and verifying his own scientific theories (see Chapter 5). As an enlightened but not dogmatic liberal, he also granted special attention to educational works for the worker population and had close relations with several Belgian socialist leaders such as Émile Vandervelde, Édouard Anseele, and Louis Bertrand. His largest gift was the million Belgian francs allocated to creation of a worker education institute attached to the Maison du Peuple (People's House) of Brussels and the creation of an office of social legislation under the auspices of the Belgian Workers' Party.[71]

Aiming at Social Peace

A limited number of strikes were recorded during the first fifty years of the company's existence. It is true that the chemical industry, in general, was less hit than other sectors by worker unrest.[72] In 1886, when violent strikes broke out near the plant at Couillet, it continued to operate – likewise in 1913 – despite a general strike against the soaring cost of living. When, despite everything,

---

[66] Among the medalists were Schneider & Cie, the mining companies of Anzin and Blanzy, and the coal mines of Bois-du-Luc and Marimont-Bascoup, Vieille Montagne. See Cacheux (1891), 135; Godineau (1989), 71–87.

[67] Chiousse (1901), 54.

[68] Aside from special measures taken in favor of its workers, in 1913 Solvay made a series of large gifts. The recipients in Belgium were the Institut Bordet (BEF 500,000); the vocational school at Charleroi (BEF 250,000); the school for the disabled at Charleroi (BEF 300,000); the National League against Tuberculosis (BEF 100,000); and the welfare offices at Couillet, Montignies, and Jemeppe (BEF 35,000). Abroad it gifted to the University of Paris (BEF 500,000).

[69] Mioche (2008), 92–5.

[70] As he was sometimes called by the Belgian press. Underlined by Héger and Lefébure (1929), 83.

[71] Despy-Meyer and Montens (1997), 230–45.

[72] Abelshauser et al. (2004), 108.

signs of independent labor organization were beginning, the company reacted rapidly, often granting additional benefits. Thus, when rumors surfaced about possible creation of a labor union at Dombasle in 1910, management authorized the plant manager to raise salaries.[73] When, in 1909, Spanish workers tried to set up their own autonomous mutual aid fund, the plant at Torrelavega financed its own fund, as well as health services.[74] Several strikes broke out nonetheless. In the agitated context of Russia at the start of the twentieth century, workers, members of the Social-Revolutionary Party, were able to block the plant at Berezniki for five days in March 1905. The army intervened, and the situation was brought under control by the new plant manager, Émile Dévien. Later, the scope of the social programs at Lubimoff Solvay & Cie in favor of its workforce – the "Solvayski" – more or less insulated the plant from penetration by Marxist theories, such that its administrator Wladimir Orlow was told by one of the agitators, "You are our worst enemy."[75] The following year a violent strike erupted at Salin-de-Giraud. In this remote plant, labor was composed of 40 percent single men, more inclined to revolt than married workers with children. From the outside, the Confédération Générale du Travail (CGT) came in to distribute its revolutionary message. The strike lasted two months, until heavy-handed intervention by the army brought it to an end. Solvay proved particularly intransigent in resolving the conflict, not hesitating to fire all of the union members on information from the foremen and threatening to shut down the plant completely. In all, the plant was shut down for five months, during which its production was supplemented by other soda plants in the group.[76] The same year, several strikes broke out at Sarralbe over requests for a salary increase. However, DSW rejected the request, arguing that the wages were already higher than those offered by the competitors (Dieuze). After some violent riots and halts in the operations, 192 workers were fired. Further negotiations led to the adoption of the eight-hour day, Sarralbe becoming the first German plant to implement it.[77] Finally, at Torrelavega, a strike broke out in September 1910 to protest the failure to implement an eight-hour workday, given the lack of skilled labor. The conflict was resolved in favor of the workers, and, quickly, additional measures were taken: construction of new housing, a club and a washhouse, replacement of fines by suspensions, and an increase in overtime pay.[78]

The goal of establishing a patiently formed labor force was fulfilled in the plants offering better working conditions. As an illustration, figures from the German plants show significant differences in turnover rates depending on the sites. For the period 1911–1913, worker turnover was the lowest in soda plants established for a long time and/or with an infrastructure beneficial to workers (15 percent at Bernburg, 9 percent at Sarralbe, 6 percent at Château-Salins, and 25 percent at Rheinberg). By contrast, the rate was

[73] ACS, RdG, 30 Sept. 1910, 6 Oct. 1910.
[74] ACS, RdG, 29 June 1909.
[75] Accarain (2002), 252.
[76] Daumalin, Lambert, and Mioche (2007), 22–8.
[77] ACS, 1151, DSW AG, Résumés divers no. 38.
[78] ACS, RdG, 2 Sept. 1910, 3 Feb. 1911.

high in soda plants acquired more recently and in the process of restructuring (56 percent at Montwy and 60 percent at Wurselen), as well as – surprisingly – in the small plant at Wyhlen (49 percent). The salt, potash, and lignite mines and plants, which did not constitute the core business of Solvay, had turnover rates that also proved high: 43 percent at Borth, 46 percent at Solvayhall, and 59 percent at Osternienburg.[79] These figures, though fragmentary, confirm the difficulty of and need for establishing a stable labor force and the priority given to workers of the soda plants.

Overall, Solvay's progressive social policy was crowned with notable success. Aside from providing to its employees work and living conditions that were significantly above average, the social policy enabled the company to maintain total independence with respect to the states, such as workers' organizations. By anticipating social legislation and being among the leading companies in social matters, Solvay systematically defused any claims, generating almost uninterrupted social peace and, consequently, a stable production.

[79] ACS, DSW, Annual Reports 1911, 1912, 1913.

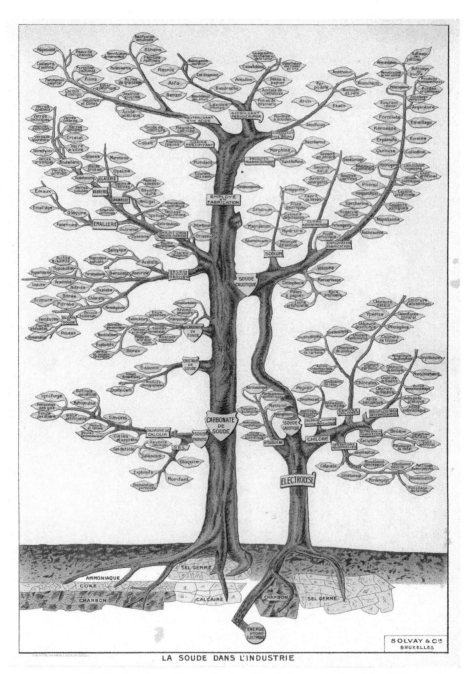

FIGURE 5.1. The "soda ash tree" was displayed by Solvay at industrial exhibitions. In the soil the raw materials are depicted. Trunks represent the main products, whereas branches symbolize the subproducts and derivatives. The numerous leaves show the multiple uses of soda ash. After 1900, a second trunk grew beside the main one, announcing the coming of electrolysis, another method of producing caustic soda, with chlorine and hydrogen as by-products. (Solvay Archives.)

5

The Consolidation of Power

At the turn of the twentieth century, Solvay appeared as a cohesive group, dominant and sure of itself. Its industrial and financial power derived especially from its consolidated leadership in soda ash. However, the enterprise began – or continued – other productions either as opportunities arose (e.g., potash, phosphates), stemming from its own needs (e.g., ammonia), or from an evolution of the market (e.g., caustic soda, chlorine, coke by-products). In most cases, these endeavors were the result of defensive diversifications aiming to increase pressure on competitors threatening to begin development in soda ash. A second objective was to achieve closed and extensive chemical cycles, by optimal valuation of by-products from the Solvay process. This implied, consequently, a development of markets. This industrial logic led Solvay to pursue, almost by accident, the manufacture of three types of fertilizers (phosphate, potash, and nitrogen based) and to enter the field of electrochemistry, which promised to be revolutionary. In terms of revenue, these activities were secondary. The first priority remained the deployment of the Solvay process in all countries in which demand justified it. New plants were thus built in Spain and Italy by Solvay & Cie, and in Germany, DSW strengthened its position both by acquiring existing plants and by building new ones.

These prewar years were both a breathing space and a transition period in the history of Solvay & Cie. The industrial power achieved by the first generation was consolidated by application of proven recipes, almost through inertia. Passing the baton to the second generation started with the death of Alfred Solvay in 1894 and the definitive retirement of Ernest from day-to-day management. However, Ernest's influence remained predominant even after his successors had taken over the reins of the company. Removed from industrial life, Ernest Solvay had time to devote himself to science, his "fifth child."[1] However, although his scientific patronage had wide and deep reverberations, his personal work remained, at best, misunderstood.

5.1 OPPORTUNISTIC DIVERSIFICATIONS: POTASH AND COKE OVEN BY-PRODUCTS

After an incursion into the phosphate fertilizer sector between 1882 and 1895 (see Chapter 2), Solvay was induced to manufacture and market potash-based

---

[1] AES, Documents remis à M. Purnal, no 6, Voeux et désirs exprimés à mes enfants, 1911.

fertilizers, following the discovery of potash beds in Germany. Nitrogen-based fertilizer was produced as well, which provided a market for the recovery of by-products from its coke ovens.

German Investments in Potash

From 1861 to 1918, Germany benefited from a world monopoly on potassium chloride, an especially precious resource for fertilizer production. Stassfurt, a town neighboring Bernburg, made up its historical nerve center. After abandonment of the salt monopoly by the Prussian state in 1868, access to the sector increasingly expanded into private companies, which cooperated closely with one of the first German cartels, the Deutsche Kali Syndicat (1876).[2] Because potash was considered a key resource for the national economy, this cartel was even enforced by law in 1910.

As early as 1882, Carl Wessel had launched exploratory drillings in the area of Bernburg, to secure its own supplies of rock salt. During these explorations, potash salt was discovered below the layers of common salt. Well aware of the higher market value of this resource, Carl Wessel was relentless until he convinced the Solvay leaders to continue investment in the search for potash. Solvay was reluctant to stray from its original plan of action on soda ash and dilute its limited financial resources, all the more because the major competition for potash mainly came from the Anhalt and Prussian governments. The Belgian company considered the exploitation of potash only a defensive weapon against potash producers that would try to enter the soda ash market. However, through the impetus of Carl Wessel, the activity began to expand. The salt beds of Roschwitz I (1890), Plömnitz I (1890), Plömnitz II (1899), Peissen (1902), and Roschwitz II (1905) provided rock salt to the soda factory at Bernburg as well as potash salts (e.g., carnalite, sylvinite, kainite). The processing plant of Solvayhall was started up in 1890 for the production of potassium chloride and derived products such as potassium sulfate, bromine, hydrochloric acid, magnesium, potash fertilizers (or mixed salts), potassium bromide, and ferrous oxide. The exploitation of potash finally generated significant earnings for DSW before World War I, a result, among other things, of the protection offered by the German cartel. On the eve of conflict, potash installations represented 14 percent of the value of DSW's industrial assets and generated between 20 percent and 25 percent of its revenue.[3] Solvay & Cie could finally be very pleased that, despite initial hesitations, it followed Carl Wessel's vision.

Coke Ovens and Their By-Products

As of the mid-1880s, the Semet-Solvay coke ovens not only generated sizable earnings for Solvay with their by-products but also ensured its supply of ammonia to the soda plants (see Chapter 2). Although Solvay & Cie sold its first four

[2] Schröter (1994), 75–92.
[3] ACS-O, 1151 DSW, Annual reports 1912–1913–1914.

coke ovens of Bois-du-Luc in 1888, it maintained the plant at Havré-Ville and appointed as its manager the engineer Edmond Bautier, a nephew by marriage of Ernest and Alfred Solvay. The ammonia water was concentrated there before being sent by tank car to the soda ash plants. The plant also manufactured ammonium sulfate (a nitrogen-based fertilizer), anhydrous ammonia, and ammonia hydroxide. Following experiments performed by the chemist Jean Ortlieb around the end of the 1880s, the plant began the distillation of other by-products, tars and hydrocarbons, which it sold under different forms of benzol. In Belgium, the markets for ammonium sulfate and benzol were regulated, like many other products, by cartels and cross-border agreements.[4]

Although not the only type of recovery oven,[5] the Semet-Solvay system enjoyed tremendous development across the world. In 1890, there were 115 units; in 1900, 1,800 units; and in 1913, more than 5,000 units. Solvay marketed its ovens using participation contracts developed by Edgard Hulin (successor to Eudore Pirmez in the position of legal advisor and *gérant* from 1907 to 1919) and Louis Semet (designer of the ovens and *gérant* from 1887 to 1907). Typically, Solvay built batteries of ovens at its own cost at the customers' facilities in the different countries and was reimbursed by a fixed fee and, often, by valuation of the by-products. Coke, the principal product, remained the property of the industrial partner. For administration of this rapidly growing activity, a special Section F was organized in the Central Administration, initially managed by William Kirkpatrick and supervised in the *gérance* by Fernand van der Straeten.[6]

During the first decade of the twentieth century, competition changed in the European coke-oven sector. As in France and Germany, powerful corporations were built up in Belgium with the support of the large banks. This was the case with the Coppée Group in 1908, supported by the Société Générale, and the Piette Group in 1911, financed by the Banque d'Outremer, the Société Française de Banque et de Dépôts, and the Banque de Paris et des Pays-Bas. Industrial clients began to show interest in cash payments for the ovens to exploit the by-products themselves, which scarcely satisfied Solvay's needs in ammonia. In an effort to keep the activity competitive and to enable it to conclude partnerships autonomously, Solvay transformed its Section F into the Société Anonyme des Fours à Coke Semet-Solvay in May 1912. Its capital of BEF 16 million (US$3,040,000) remained wholly owned by Solvay & Cie. The board of directors was made up of *gérants* of Solvay & Cie, except for Ernest Solvay. Fernand van der Straeten became the head of the company,

[4] ACS, RdG 16 Feb. 1909, 4 May 1909; Lucion (1908).

[5] The Semet-Solvay system was one of the dominant models for recovery furnaces, alongside the systems by Simon-Carvès (F), Hüesnner (ALL), Seibel (FR), Otto-Hoffmann (ALL), Koppers (ALL), Coppée (B), and so on. See Mott (1936).

[6] ACS, Brochure Solvay & Cie, Paris Universal Exposition, 1889, 29–32, ACS, Enquête sur l'activité de la Société Fours à Coke Semet-Solvay pendant l'occupation 1914–1918, notes from M. Kirkpatrick; ACS, CS annual report 1902; ACS, AG Gérance report 1909; ACS, DS 40, Aperçu historique sur la Gérance de Solvay & Cie..., par Armand Solvay, 9 Jan. 1928, 8–13; ACS, *Fours à coke à récupération des sous-produits, système Semet-Solvay*, booklet published for the exhibition of Liège, 1905.

TABLE 5.1. *Development of Semet-Solvay Coke Ovens in 1913*

	Number of Industrial Clients	Number of Ovens	Annual Production of Coke (tons)
United States	21	1,713	4,485,000
England	24	1,389	1,972,000
Belgium	22	1,314	1,939,000
France	6	285	378,000
Japan	5	241	326,000
Germany	4	173	273,000
Italy	2	82	118,000
Australia	1	66	120,000
TOTAL	85	5,263	9,611,000

Source: ACS, S.A. *Fours à coke Semet-Solvay*, booklet published for the exhibition of Ghent, 1913.

after his forced resignation from the *gérance* of Solvay & Cie because of a family misunderstanding and divergent viewpoints that were irreconcilable on the managerial level.[7]

In the United States, SPC was equally very dynamic in developing these ovens, the first of their kind on the American continent. In 1895, SPC established the Semet-Solvay Co., a wholly owned subsidiary. According to the licensing contract put into place, the SSC would have to pay Solvay & Cie 15 percent of the earnings from the coke ovens, without any expiration date. Solvay then repaid this sum to Louis Semet. Between 1900 and 1911, the cumulative fees amounted to no less than US$370,000. The contract was transferred to the Belgian Société Anonyme des Fours à Coke Semet-Solvay in 1912. The SSC, managed from Syracuse, expanded considerably, and even finished by surpassing in size its parent company. Within SPC, it was said that the Semet-Solvay Co. was like "the tail wagging the dog."[8] Although in Europe Solvay let its customers operate the ovens themselves, the Semet Solvay Co. integrated its activities vertically, manufacturing and commercializing the coke to the metal industry, as well as all the by-products, especially town gas, tar, and benzol. At many occasions, Solvay & Cie showed reticence and criticism on the high investments made by SPC to grow in this capital-intensive sector instead of focusing on the alkali market. To limit expenses of Solvay and SPC, a satellite organization, the By-Products Syndicate, was created in 1902 to take charge of a series of operations linked to by-products. Solvay & Cie held only 10 percent of the shares. In 1905, it was transformed into a company, the By-Products Coke Co., and continued its expansion in close collaboration with the Semet-Solvay Co., which was becoming more and more independent of Solvay & Cie.[9]

---

[7] ACS, CdS, 23 Apr. 1912; ACS, AG, note by the gérance, 6 May 1912; PPSF, Box Armand Solvay 1, Folder 27.

[8] ASPC, Address by W. H. Blauvelt at the occasion of the twenty-first anniversary of the Solvay Process Co., Solvay-Geddes, 1902, 47.

[9] ACS-O, 1271, 2A By Products Syndicate; ACS-O, 1271, 3A By Products Coke Corporation.

5.2 BEING A PART OF THE ELECTROCHEMICAL REVOLUTION

Salt electrolysis constituted a technological breakthrough in the history of the alkali industry. This technique of passing an electrical current through simple salt brine enabled production, without undesired by-products, of caustic soda and chlorine in almost equal proportions, as well as hydrogen. Although the hydrogen, which was not used initially, could be released into the atmosphere, the caustic soda (a corrosive liquid) and chlorine (a toxic gas) posed storage and transportation problems and thus required a balanced demand of the two products. Because the chlorine end uses (mainly transformation into bleaching powder, by passing chlorine gas over slaked lime) were less plentiful than those for caustic soda, there was the risk of overproduction. Consequently, salt electrolysis could only be attractive, from an economic standpoint, if demand for chlorine increased significantly. Although electrolysis did not fundamentally alter Solvay's business plan, it dealt a fatal blow to the Leblanc producers that had specifically turned to chlorine and caustic soda. England, the land of Leblanc, was a primary target, as it produced at the end of the nineteenth century two-thirds of the world's chlorine using the Deacon and Weldon processes.

The producers of ammonia soda, Solvay at the head, had understood that this was not an urgent situation and continued to concentrate their efforts on capturing market growth in soda ash and on a gradual phasing out of the Leblanc process. Nonetheless, scientific literature from the time announced electrochemistry as the starting point of a major upheaval, even though few observers were capable of predicting where and when it would happen.[10] The theoretical bases for the electrolytic process had been established in the lab by Humphrey Davy (1807) and Michael Faraday (1834), but another half century would elapse before a cluster of innovations and scientific progress (e.g., electrical engineering, dynamo, physical chemistry) made it possible on an industrial scale. The first reliable generators appeared in the 1870s. The first experiments with salt electrolysis were thus not undertaken until the 1880s, and the inventions and development necessary were not achieved until around 1890. Aside from the alkali sector, the nonferrous metals industry became very interested in electrolysis for production of sodium and aluminum.

Two electrolysis technologies emerged simultaneously: diaphragm cell and mercury cell. Each process used a different method to keep the chlorine produced at the anode separate from the caustic soda and hydrogen produced at the cathode. The diaphragm cell was used for the first time in 1886 by Chemische Fabrik Griesheim in Germany, for production of chlorine and caustic potash.[11] Mercury-cell electrolysis, more expensive but producing a purer caustic soda, became a stable process following the pioneering and independent work of the American Hamilton Castner (1858–1899) and the Austrian

---

[10] Lunge (1893).
[11] Hardie (1959), 60–2.

Carl Kellner (1850–1905), from whom Solvay was able to obtain licenses after long and painstaking negotiations. In 1888, Castner had founded the Aluminium Co. at Oldbury, but its profits plummeted following introduction of electrolytic processes for production of aluminum. The Aluminium Co. then turned to electrolysis of salt, using a mercury cell from 1892 on. For his part, the Viennese Carl Kellner was active in the Austrian paper industry. Between 1892 and 1894 he patented several types of mercury cells to produce chlorine for wood pulp bleaching. The two inventors discovered each other during the summer of 1894, when Castner, wanting to patent his process in all the industrialized countries, ran up against a patent filed by Kellner in Germany and Russia.[12]

In the meantime, Solvay had not sat idly by. Although its two production processes for caustic soda began to pay off, chlorine was still not part of the portfolio (see Chapter 2). The company therefore initiated a long and interesting innovation process, mixing acquisition of external technologies, in-house development, and international cross-fertilization to set up a long-lasting electrolytic process. The Technical Committee perused the literature, scrutinized the competition, and inquired about developments abroad thanks to uninterrupted contacts with the subsidiaries.[13] Eventual adoption of an electrolysis process was considered in all cases only as a defensive measure, both to dissuade the Leblancs from opening ammonia soda plants and to prevent a coalition of bleaching powder producers that would have enabled them to sell caustic soda at very low prices.[14] At any rate, Solvay did not have the means to prevent competition from flourishing in electrolytic alkalis, as it had been able to do for the ammonia soda process.

Additionally, motivations varied sharply among the group's companies. Ludwig Mond was betting on a zinc process for chlorine recovery and put forth serious doubts about the imminent success of electrolysis. In the United States, SPC remained passive, as electrolysis was out of the scope of its activity. By contrast, Carl Wessel once again demonstrated his leadership ability. Informed by Max Schaffner of Aussig, he inquired into the success of Griesheim. His attention was also drawn to the installation of an aluminum plant using hydraulic power from the Rhine at Neuhausen.[15] Wessel pushed Solvay to take a position. He wanted to have chlorine available to ensure the domination of DSW in Germany and to fight against English soda makers internationally. He made contact with Ignatz Stroof of Griesheim, formerly of Aussig, and he sent his engineers Emil Gielen and Asmus Jabs on an assignment to observe the two pioneering firms. Joint-venture projects were examined, but no agreement was reached. Backed by Solvay and Mond, DSW thus decided in 1893 to develop its own diaphragm-cell electrolysis with asbestos. Heinrich Wilsing, head chemist at the soda factory in Bernburg, was given the assignment. His work bore fruit, and construction of a one-hundred-horsepower pilot plant at Osternienburg

[12] Hardie (1947), 2–6.
[13] ACS-O, Technical Committee, Meeting minutes, 1890–1892.
[14] ACS-O, CS, 15 June 1894.
[15] ART, Electrolyse, procédés divers, 1890–1893.

near Bernburg was agreed on in the summer of 1894, the same summer during which the Castner and Kellner patents collided.[16]

Ludwig Mond, who had visited the plant at Oldbury, recognized the quality of the Castner process. His positive opinion encouraged Ernest and Armand Solvay, along with Hannon and Wilsing, to visit the plant as well, in October 1894. After that, Solvay no longer showed interest in any process other than the mercury cell. The company's big English competitor, UAC, had been offered the Castner process one year earlier, but its central lab brushed it aside. This rejection of electrolysis by the leader of the Leblancs is considered the fatal decision that led to its inevitable decline.[17]

Simultaneous negotiations with Kellner and Castner proved difficult. Solvay feared an alliance between the two inventors in an aim to raise the price of the patents and the licenses. Wessel and Gielen rapidly convinced Kellner to sell his patent to Solvay & Cie for M 1 million, for all countries except Austria. In contrast, the Castner process belonged to Aluminium Co. for all countries except the United States, where a license was granted to Mathieson Alkali Co. Pressure intensified when Aluminium Co. granted a new license to Agfa in Berlin. Solvay had to act quickly, but the situation was complicated because Mond, in an effort to preserve his understanding with UAC, did not wish to proceed with the purchase. In July 1895, Mond even tactlessly suggested to Solvay a mutual purchase of the Castner process with UAC, considering that commerce in chlorine was a sort of English prerogative.[18] Solvay took no offense but separated from its English partner on this question and continued negotiations on its own with Aluminium Co., even though doing so could mean entering into competition with Brunner, Mond in chlorine and caustic soda in England.

An agreement was reached in October 1895 by which Solvay & Cie and Aluminium Co. exchanged the Kellner and Castner patents and divided up the markets so that caustic soda went to Aluminium Co. in England and to Solvay on the Continent. The sale of chlorine remained open. The American market was excluded from the accord, as the two firms had American subsidiaries that competed with one another.[19] This agreement appeared to be a beneficial deal for Solvay, because application of the Kellner process posed technical problems that did not exist with the Castner process. The Kellner process was thus never later put into application. At the most, it could enrich the Castner process through an electric device that gave way to the Castner-Kellner process.[20] With hindsight, the Kellner process was used primarily as a bargaining chip for acquisition of the Castner process, which was technically superior but legally blocked on the Continent by patents from the former.

---

[16] ACS, Eilsberger (b) (1930), 197.
[17] Reader (1970), 119.
[18] Reader (1970), 120.
[19] ACS, Expired Contracts, Agreement concluded with the Aluminium Company, 7 Nov. 1895.
[20] Kellner's device of electrically short-circuiting the soda cell to promote decomposition of the amalgam was added to the Castner system to give birth to the Castner-Kellner process. See Hardie (1959), 63.

Industrial use of the Castner-Kellner process was undertaken by Solvay group companies in continental Europe, and by a new company, the Castner Kellner Alkali Co. (CKA) in England. This company was formed in 1895, with a capital of £300,000, one-third of which was subscribed by Aluminium Co. and the rest by the public.[21] Brunner, Mond did not participate in the capital, but because the shadow of Solvay hovered over the affair, CKA was perceived as a company friendly to Brunner, Mond and became the primary competitor of the UAC in chlorine and caustic soda. Becoming aware somewhat late of the success of the CKA, Brunner, Mond ended up acquiring 25 percent in 1916 and took total control in 1920.[22] In 1895 CKA built its electrolytic plant at Weston Point (Runcorn), and the pilot facility of Oldbury was transferred to the DSW site at Osternienburg to be developed there by Heinrich Wilsing and to serve as a base for the first electrolytic plant in the Solvay Group. Coming on stream in July 1897, it first produced caustic potash lye before being converted to the production of caustic soda. Wilsing brought all his experience to Solvay & Cie for construction, as of 1897, of its Belgian electrolysis plant at Jemeppe-sur-Sambre, near Charleroi.[23] A third unit was erected in 1901 at Lysychansk (Donetz) following the same plans as Jemeppe, and then a fourth in 1913 at Torda, near the plant of Maros-Ujvar (see Chapter 7).

Although they had not themselves developed the mercury-cell process, Solvay's engineers contributed significantly to its improvement. Within the first year of operations, Brichaux and Wilsing had developed a new type of cell at Jemeppe. Although Castner's rocking cell made the mercury cathode flow by imparting a slow, rocking movement to the cell, the long and stationary Solvay cell made it flow continuously along the bottom of the slightly inclined, elongated trough. This type of "long" mercury cell was adopted by CKA in 1902 and by all the new mercury electrolysis units from then on. Since then, the evolution of the mercury cell has been a history of cumulative minor improvements, mainly directed toward increasing its electrochemical efficiency.[24]

In 1900, there were already more than forty electrolysis plants in the world, half of which produced alkalis.[25] Aside from the Castner-Kellner process, the cell developed by Griesheim was the most widely used, either proprietary or under license (e.g., at Bitterfeld, Rheinfelden, Ludwigshafen, Flix, Slaviansk, Zombkowice). In the United States, electrolysis units proliferated, especially near powerful hydroelectric sources, such as the Niagara Falls. The principal ones became competitors, either small or medium, of SPC, notably Mathieson Alkali Co., Hooker Chemical Co., Niagara Alkali Co., and Pennsylvania Salt Manufacturing Co.[26]

---

[21] The directors of DSW (Wessel, Gielen, Frey, and others) as well as, probably, those of Solvay & Cie, participated personally in the capital of CKA. AHR, PD Carl Wessel, letter from Wessel to Schaffner, 25 Jan. 1897.

[22] Reader (1970), 254, 329.

[23] ART, Osternienburg, Electrolytic plant, Correspondence 1900–1901, Notes from Wilsing on Jemeppe.

[24] Hardie (1959), 63.

[25] Warren (1980), 178.

[26] ACS, 1271–065-001; Warren (1991), 171.

In the area of electrolysis, Solvay remained a medium-sized player on the global level, in line with its defensive posture. Before the war, its electrolysis plants maintained a limited capacity (3,000 to 4,000 tons of caustic lye and 6,000 to 7,000 tons of bleaching powder in 1913). In all, Solvay's continental companies produced in 1913 only 11,000 tons of electrolytic caustic soda compared to 140,000 tons by causticizing their soda ash.[27] Because of the lack of various markets, the chlorine was almost exclusively converted into bleaching powder until the end of the 1920s, at the time when products were becoming more diversified (e.g., liquid chlorine, hydrochloric acid, sodium hypochlorite).[28] Additionally, Osternienburg and Jemeppe produced, from 1907, compressed hydrogen used in the production of artificial silk. Despite its limited production, Solvay used electrolysis to increase pressure on its competitors and conclude agreements in caustic soda and bleaching powder as it used to do with soda ash. A price war brought about an advantageous balance of power: on entry into production of CKA, Solvay & Cie and the new German syndicate of electrolytic alkali producers (including DSW) purchased all its production for three years. They poured product into the English market at low prices, to demonstrate to UAC, and to Brunner, Mond, that the continental companies were able to come in and disturb the English players on their own market. Solvay and DSW in fact believed that Brunner, Mond had a tendency to be too accommodating to the UAC.[29] From 1900, this demonstration of force led to the signature of the first international agreements for bleaching powder among the major producers (e.g., UAC, Griesheim, Solvay, CKA).[30]

5.3 A NEW ROUND OF GEOGRAPHICAL EXPANSION

In addition to opportunistic diversification and a strategic positioning in electrolysis, Solvay's policy during the period 1900–1914 was characterized by securing the positions acquired in soda ash and by a search for new markets. Priorities for the *gérance* could be summarized as follows: (1) to ensure an adequate balance between supply and demand to systematically capture all the growth in the sector; (2) to renegotiate national and international agreements under advantageous terms, having them cover more of the products derived from soda ash, so as to ensure accurate forecasting of markets and revenue; (3) to dissuade everywhere any projects for new soda plants;[31] and (4) to examine the opportunities for expansion, by increasing the size of plants and by constructing new soda plants anywhere it was economically pertinent to do so. At the very time when Brunner, Mond was being forced to go out and look for new growth engines in China, Japan, and the British Empire, Solvay & Cie

---

[27] ART, PDO, Solvay & Cie, DSW, Lubimoff & Cie.

[28] Osternienburg produced liquid chlorine in small quantities starting in 1905 (one hundred to five hundred tons per year).

[29] ACS, CS, 5 Nov. 1897; Haber (1958), 226.

[30] ACS-O, 1001–51, Contracts, Agreement on bleaching powder, 21 Dec. 1900.

[31] In particular when they were supported by renegades from the Solvay plants who circumvented their noncompete agreements, such as Muller and Tempelhof in Austria (1904–1907), Nicolas at Bayon (1904 to the end of 1907), and Lambert at Montferrand (1896).

was focusing its expansionist efforts on Southern Europe. For its part, DSW was working toward territorial conquest in the German Empire.[32]

Introducing Heavy-Chemical Industry to Spain

A report of 1893 from the technical section (and not, as one would expect, from the commercial one) on the evolution of alkali consumption in Europe had already clearly demonstrated the advantage for Solvay of erecting soda plants in Spain and in Italy, rather than supplying these countries from its Belgian and French plants.[33] Because these territories fell within the sales radius of the Belgian parent company, it was the responsibility of the parent to conquer them. With strong experience in the construction of plants in foreign territory, Solvay & Cie logically preferred direct installations instead of local partnerships.

Spain, cut off from its former colonies (i.e., Cuba, Puerto Rico, and the Philippines) after the Spanish-American War in 1898, witnessed some embryonic industrial development. The Restoration favored foreign investments, in particular in mines and metallurgy. However, the Leblanc process had not taken root there, leaving the alkalis sector totally open to imports. Solvay was one of the first foreign chemical companies to show interest in Spain, together with Nobel and Griesheim. The Belgian company had filed a patent there for ammonia soda in 1895 to prevent competition from filing it first. The company sent its first emissaries, Robert Desguin and Léon de Harven, in 1896, to inventory the list of resources and the means of transportation available in Cantabria. The area had good connections with the Basque and Catalan textile industries. The region of Torrelavega was considered very favorable in terms of proximity to raw materials, as well as in terms of access to the ocean, local demand in growth, and availability of a largely rural work force.[34] The decision to build a plant there was not made until 1902, following two trigger events: the construction of a rail line linking Torrelavega to the Asturias mining basin and the announcement of the introduction of three electrolysis plants in Spain around 1900, by Electroquímica de Flix (subsidiary of Griesheim), Electra del Besaya (subsidiary of the French Thomsom-Houston), and the Compañía General de Productos Químicos de Aboño.[35] To become independent of Spanish suppliers, in 1903 Solvay purchased the coal mine of Lieres (Asturias) from La Fraternidad, as well as the salt mines of Polanco and the lime quarry of Rinconeda.[36] The soda plant did not begin production until 1908, or nearly fifteen years after the first investigations were made. Average in size (forty thousand tons per year of soda ash and sixteen thousand tons per year of caustic soda in 1913), its objective was to supply the domestic market in soda ash and to take a leadership role in caustic soda. Headed up by the former engineer of operations at Salin-de-Giraud, Paul Alban, the plant was largely run

---

[32] ACS-O, 1242–1B, Brunner Mond, Negotiations with Brunner, Mond on sales areas, Sept. 1901.
[33] ACS, 1482–1-1 B, Report on the state of the soda ash industry, Dec. 1893.
[34] ATo, Report from Harven to Hannon, Bilbao, 15 Aug. 1896; Mioche (2009).
[35] Toca (2005), 83–91.
[36] Sánchez Landeras (1998); Álvarez Quintana, Surez Antuña, and Caso Roiz (2003).

by Belgian, French, and German technicians. A company town and different social amenities, typical for the group but advanced for Spain at the time, were rapidly set up there (see Chapter 4). A sales office was established the following year at Barcelona, where the nascent Spanish chemical business community was concentrated.[37] The international agreement of 1907, concluded between the Solvay Group and United Alkali Co., immediately eliminated the small contingent of one thousand tons of soda ash exported up to then by UAC to Spain, while its contingent of twelve thousand tons of caustic soda had to be reduced each year, on condition of financial compensation, up to its elimination in 1912.[38] Solvay's foremost competitor in caustic soda became the electrolysis plant of Flix, with the two other rivals being forced to close their doors because of lack of profitability.

Italian Investigations

In the liberal Italy of Giolitti, the situation proved comparable. Industrial production in general, and the chemical industry in particular, witnessed rapid growth at the start of the twentieth century, attracting German, English, and Belgian capital. The country did not yet have soda plants, and salt remained a monopoly of the state. The customs duties on alkalis were consequently very low, which enabled Solvay to provide two-thirds of the fifty-three thousand tons of soda ash consumed in Italy (in 1907) from Dombasle and from Salin de Giraud. Two electrolysis plants had been established, at Brescia and at Bussi, the first operating a mercury-cell license from Solvay. Solvay made a passionate plea for self-sufficiency in soda ash to the minister of finance and was able to convince the Italian authorities to give it the right to explore the salt beds in 1907.[39] The geology of the country was still poorly known, but the company knew that it had to be based not far from the two primary consumer regions, Piedmont and Lombardy. Léon de Harven was again part of a prospecting team, along with Maurice Bodart, manager of Spanish coal mining at Lieres. Concessions were obtained at Volterra and at Rosignano in 1909. The work at the Rosignano plant began in 1913, and a sales office was established at Milan in May 1914, but the outbreak of the Great War marked a significant setback in the initial development plans (see Chapter 7).

Staying Ahead in Germany

In Germany, DSW, still dynamic, fought to strengthen its national domination. Between 1900 and 1914, the German chemical industry was in a boom period, employing 180,000 people in 1913. Outside of inorganic chemistry (e.g., alkalis, potash, acids), several branches of organic chemistry witnessed impressive growth, in particular dyes and other specialties (e.g., pharmaceuticals,

---

[37] Puig (2007), 368–400.
[38] ACS-O, 1001–51 Contracts, Solvay/UAC sales agreement for the countries of Europe and the United States, July 1906.
[39] ACS-O, 1130 Italy, soda ash plant projects.

photochemicals, synthetic essences).[40] The alkalis sector was nonetheless undergoing intense turmoil. The empire continued to send out rumors regarding ammonia soda plant projects (e.g., Stade, Schönebeck, Lünebourg, Saarburg, Burbach, Bremen, Halle [Saale], Wesel, Stadtilm), encouraged by numerous discoveries of salt beds. Often, DSW was solicited by entrepreneurs or financiers initiating soda plant projects in an aim to resell them for a fortune. It took all of Carl Wessel's might to nip most of these projects in the bud through intimidation, takeovers, and other economic pressures. Control over the soda ash syndicate, and thus over the setting of sales prices, was in this respect a formidable means of dissuasion.[41] Another good way to consolidate its position was to ensure the ownership of new soda plants. In Silesia, DSW purchased, in 1901, Steinsalz-& Sodawerke AG at Montwy (Inowrocław/Hohensalza). The latter held a soda ash plant and a salt works and was sponsored by the bank R. Suermondt & Cie. It had been a member of the German syndicate since 1887, with a quota of 6 percent. Later, DSW increased Montwy's output until it reached 10 percent of its total volumes.[42] In a more symbolic way, DSW ended up purchasing the Honigmann plant at Würselen in 1912, where the principal ammonia process in competition with Solvay had been developed (see Chapters 2 and 3). For lack of profitability in soda ash, Honigmann relied on caustic soda (by direct causticizing) as of 1894 and had become the largest manufacturer in the German Empire. Resistant to any agreement with the syndicate, Honigmann represented a constant thorn in the side of DSW. After long negotiations, he agreed to sale of his plant, for the price – colossal for the time – of M 16,250,000. This acquisition greatly strengthened the position in caustic soda of DSW, which thus instantly doubled its market share.[43]

Finally, the construction of a plant at Rheinberg seemed an industrially audacious project. Since the start of the 1890s, Carl Wessel was attracted by the rich beds of salt and coal in the lower Rhine. The spot was ideal for installation of a soda plant, given the transportation vector offered by the Rhine. However, beyond that, he had the vision of creating on that spot a vast complex for mining of salt and coal. Indefatigable, he financed costly exploratory drilling in the region, guided by the Belgian geologist for Solvay, Jean Ortlieb. Incidentally, these drillings were instrumental in frightening away competitors that were recalcitrant to join the syndicate. Multiple technical problems, and then the onset of the war, considerably slowed the establishment of immense salt mines at Borth and Wallach, which did not go into operation until 1926. The soda plant at Rheinberg started up in 1906, under the leadership of the prior manager of Wyhlen, Ludwig Frohnäuser.[44] On the eve of the war, Rheinberg was producing 40,000 tons of soda ash per year and was a midsize plant for DSW, and still clearly smaller than Bernburg (150,000 tons per year) and

[40] Haber (1971), 108.
[41] ACS, 1151 DSW, AG & Bernburg – Summaries.
[42] ACS, Eilsberger (b) (1930), 374–6; ART-PDO, DSW.
[43] ACS, 1151 DSW, Rapport général, 47. Production of caustic soda by processing of soda ash from Rheinberg, which made up the only activity of the plant at Würselen, was completely shut down in 1931 and the tonnage taken over by Rheinberg. The plant was demolished.
[44] Rupprecht (2007).

TABLE 5.2. *Sales Quotas within the German Syndicates in 1913*

Firms	Soda Ash (%)	Caustic Soda (%)
DSW	68.6	54.4
Verein Chemischer Fabriken – Mannheim	7.9	8.3
Sodafabrik Stassfurt – Buckau	7.9	5.7
Matthes & Weber – Duisburg	5.3	4.4
Dieuze	4.8	2.2
Kalk and Vorster & Gruneberg	3.9	4.8
Rhenania	1.8	14.4
Griesheim	1.8	7.9
TOTAL	100	100

Source: ACS, Eilsberger (b) (1930), annexes, 22–7.

Sarralbe (85,000 tons per year). It increased in power from the mid-1920s, following the loss of several plants by DSW (Sarralbe, Château-Salins, and Montwy) at the end of the conflict (see Chapter 7). Given its three additional plants, DSW had definitively locked up the alkalis sector by 1913 (see Table 5.2).

5.4 ENSURING CONTINUITY: THE RISE OF THE SECOND GENERATION

Internally, the period 1894–1914 was characterized by the gradual transition between the first and second generations of *gérants*, following the confirmation of the definitive victory of Solvay over Leblanc. Solvay's financial success and its focus on a unique field allowed it to buck the trend of transforming the large family firms into joint-stock companies with an open and splintered shareholding structure, to more diversified fields, led by salaried managers who were not part of the founding families.[45] As with all companies strictly held by families, Solvay would be able to enjoy the benefits of this model (e.g., long-term vision, strong identity, less bureaucracy, continuity, financial independence) while also exposing itself to the inherent risks (e.g., inhibition of technological and organizational innovation, path dependency, less proactive strategy, succession challenges).[46] The state of the company as presented in a speech by Ernest Solvay in 1913 was edifying in this regard. It sounded like a mission being conferred to his successors:

> Our company is a closed company.... With us, financial considerations do not exist.... Perfection is attained only when the capital and the work are adequately remunerated with long and continuous assurances on security.... The true problem has never been for us about the capital to be remunerated, but rather a process to be created and continuously perfected, strengthened and globalized,

[45] The DuPont chemical company being a prime American counterexample. See, e.g., Chandler (2004), 170–92.

[46] Literature on family companies is abundant. For an overview of the question, see Colli (2003).

which necessarily brings with it the proper and continuous remuneration of grow-ing capital.[47]

In the delicate area of succession planning, Ernest Solvay exercised predom-inant moral authority, both with timing and with the choice and training of the successors. The problem of continuity of his work preoccupied him early on, as witnessed by his numerous notes and "interim wills."[48] He attached special importance to the intimacy of the group formed by his family and his industrial partners, and he staked his bets for the future on a preeminence of family managers. If direct heirs from the two founders did not provide a big enough pool, posts would be proposed to nephews and in-laws brought in through the framework of a well-organized matrimonial strategy. Interestingly enough, he did not exclude salaried managers or high-level technicians from access to the highest positions. He was the one who introduced to the *gérance* Prosper Hanrez and Édouard Hannon, successive masters of the Solvay tech-nique. They remained, however, the only two nonfamily *gérants* until 1967 (see Chapter 16).[49] This aspect of the moral heritage of the founder was, it seems, later forgotten:

> I sincerely hope that it [the management] can continue to be made up of direct progeny or of the closest alliances and especially the most capable, and gifted heirs of the two founders, initiated in advance, at the same time as by the most capable and tested members of the company's personnel, in the higher interest of the company.[50]

In delicate health, Ernest Solvay could never have guessed that he would live to see eighty-four years and that he would be the last survivor of the "heroic" founders. His brother Alfred did not enjoy this same longevity. He died at fifty-four years, apparently spent by the weight of his responsibilities after Ernest distanced himself from the management to tend to his own work:

> He accepted every task to take the burden off of his brother. Very fatigued, he, who rarely took any time off, left for Cannes in 1893, and died there of pneumonia on 23 January 1894. It was an immense loss, with general desolation, . . . and poor Ernest, what a blow! His brother, with whom he had worked since the first day of his invention, on whom he relied so completely, he had died on the job! He had not seen it clearly, he had let his brother get run down, become exhausted. What remorse![51]

The loss of Alfred Solvay quickly brought to a head the crucial question regarding succession mechanisms for the highest posts in the company and

---

[47] *Cinquantenaire* (1913), 81–3.

[48] AES, Documents remis à M. Purnal.

[49] It seems (but is hard to confirm) that Carl Wessel had imagined one day joining the *gérance* of Solvay & Cie, as recompense for his major successes in Germany, but that access was denied him. Consequently, he abandoned the presidency of the *Vorstand* of DSW in 1908 to stay with the Supervisory Board, alongside the managers of Solvay & Cie. ACS, DS 40, Aperçu historique sur la Gérance de Solvay & Cie. . ., par Armand Solvay, 9 Jan. 1928.

[50] AES, Documents remis à M. Purnal, Voeux et désirs exprimés à mes enfants, 1911.

[51] ACS, DS 40, Aperçu historique sur la Gérance de Solvay & Cie. . ., par Armand Solvay, 9 Jan. 1928.

reaffirmed even more the choice of an independent family company. The future *gérants* had to have engineering or legal degrees, do internships at the plants and in the offices, and carry out travel assignments abroad. Armand Solvay, the oldest son of Ernest, had begun his apprenticeship with the company in 1890, immediately after getting his mine-engineering degree from the University of Liège. First sent on an internship to the plants of Dombasle, Bernburg, Northwich, and Syracuse, he returned to work at the Central Administration in 1891, when he became to some degree the private secretary of his uncle Alfred. The brother of Armand, Edmond, did not seem to have the same abilities and remained outside the family business. Ernest Solvay supervised Armand's apprenticeship and offered him good sense advice for management of a multinational company, as seen in this letter from 1891:

> I sincerely hope that you will get up to speed in English, telling everyone who would like to speak French with you that my express desire is that you speak only English or German, because German is also spoken in the B.M. & Co business. Take note also of any particularities that distinguish production from one country to another, from industrial and commercial aspects to personnel, workers, cultural ideas, etc, etc. All of these observations will serve you well later and will give you a healthy appreciation of the facts and actions that constitute an active and productive life. You must know the behavior of the people deriving from the morals and customs of a country to properly judge their actions.[52]

Upon the death of Alfred, Armand was moved to the post of *gérant*, at the age of twenty-eight. On this occasion, the *gérance* was expanded from three to four members, to the benefit of Fernand van der Straeten, a thirty-eight-year-old who had been working for the company for several years and was the son-in-law of Ernest Solvay. Louis Semet and Ernest Solvay had removed themselves from the day-to-day business, which rested primarily on the two new arrivals, assisted closely by Edgard Hulin, full-time legal adviser. The collaboration between Armand Solvay and Hulin on the one hand, and van der Straeten, on the other hand, proved difficult, as detailed in a journal written by Armand of their repeated differences in opinion both on methods and on strategy. Armand Solvay reproached van der Straeten for "his particular way of conceiving of and discussing affairs, always looking at the small aspects before first asking questions about the overall impact, like Hulin and I do. His way of thinking always leads to long and painful discussions that are exhausting and waste our time."[53] Because the situation was showing no signs of improvement, van der Straeten was diplomatically removed from the *gérance* and given the presidency of the Société Anonyme des Fours à Coke Semet-Solvay, created in 1912. In 1906, it was Armand Solvay's turn to undergo temporary health problems. It became time to rejuvenate the *gérance* by the addition of young family members. Thus, the *gérance* was expanded to seven members the following year. It was once again Ernest Solvay who appointed his colleagues. Louis Semet gave up his seat to Louis Solvay, engineer from ULB, thirty-one years old

---

[52] PPSF, Box Armand 1, Ernest to Armand Solvay during a training trip to Northwich, 22 June 1891.
[53] PPSF, Box Armand 1, Folder 27, Nov. 1904–March 1905.

and the only male heir of cofounder Alfred Solvay. He was joined by Georges Querton, doctor of law and son of Léopold Querton and Adèle Solvay, already active in the commercial section and the secretariat since 1899. Edgard Hulin and Édouard Hannon were also brought into management as compensation for their merits. Ernest Solvay was planning for the future when he wrote in 1911:

> I have no doubt that Émile [Tournay, son-in-law of Alfred Solvay] and Emmanuel [Janssen, husband of his granddaughter Paule van Parijs] will do likewise, the first dealing especially in the law of which Edgard [Hulin] is a master and the second in general business for which he appears to have an exceptional gift. In personnel, Chardin seems to be a valuable successor to his master Hannon, his predecessor at the general technical management, and Huaux a man of great worth and future. Our family company thus has a reserve [of talent] and good chances at continuing the traditional conditions that generated its power.[54]

Thus, it is not surprising that Armand Solvay asked himself, in the final years of his life: "For how many years will the shadow of my father hover above us and succeed in keeping our family, that had become so numerous, together?"[55]

The questions of succession were naturally posed at other levels of the group organizational chart, in which it was also necessary to ensure continuity. On the Supervisory Board, the number of commissioners had been expanded from three to five in the revised bylaws of 1882. Two were from the Solvay family, alongside two representatives from the Pirmez family and one representative from the Lambert family, alternating with a representative from the Nélis family. As of 1903, the number of members expanded to seven: three Pirmez, two Solvay, one Lambert, and one Nélis. Allocation of seats was negotiated privately and bilaterally within the family branches.[56] The function of commissioner was highly prized because it was prestigious and paid well, though without effective power. Indeed, since the overturn of the shareholders of 1888, the Supervisory Board no longer exercised firm control over the all-powerful *gérance*. Its several annual meetings were limited to a superficial examination of current business affairs and an agreement on the dividend. The silent partners had never been so aptly named until the start of this period. Even the request of an annual balance sheet by a silent partner during the general assembly meeting was perceived as an act of defiance toward the *gérance*. Nevertheless, relations between *gérants* and silent partners had once again become cordial by 1903, when the Association de Défense formed by the silent partners had agreed to the constitution of a contingency fund (see Chapter 3).

Passage of the generations in the affiliated companies constituted a potential risk as well for the group's unity. The problem did not come up in the German, Russian, and Austrian subsidiaries, led by salaried managers controlled by the family board members of Solvay & Cie. At Brunner, Mond, heirs of the

---

[54] AES, Documents remis à M. Purnal, Vœux et désirs exprimés à mes enfants, 1911.

[55] ACS, DS 40, Aperçu historique sur la Gérance de Solvay & Cie..., by Armand Solvay, 9 Jan. 1928.

[56] PPSF, Box Armand 1, Folder 3.

founders continued to be a part of the management and board, but the salaried managers had a more marked influence than at Solvay & Cie, in particular in daily management. At the start of the twentieth century, there were four Brunners and three Monds on the Board, but just a single descendant of each founder in the management (Alfred Mond and Roscoe Brunner).[57] By opening up its top management to senior salaried executives, Brunner, Mond was an exception in Victorian industrial capitalism.[58] For its part, the American SPC remained under the influence of Cogswell (1834–1921) and the Hazard family, despite the presence of professional managers. Rowland Hazard, deceased in 1899, was replaced in the presidency of the enterprise by his son Frederick (1858–1917). His second son, Rowland Gibson Hazard (1855–1918), replaced Cogswell as vice president in 1916. The English and American heirs had been initiated into the Solvay Group's philosophy and had had amicable relations with the Belgian descendants. The second generation was still sufficiently steeped in the founding principles to guarantee continuity. History would be different with the third generation (see Chapter 7). Among the three heads of the Solvay group (United Kingdom, United States, and Europe), only the Belgian parent remained almost exclusively directed by family managers.

5.5 THE NONINDUSTRIAL LIFE OF ERNEST SOLVAY: *SCIENTIA VINCERE TENEBRAS*

During the early part of his life, Ernest Solvay restrained his youthful attraction to science, to concentrate on his industrial enterprise.[59] Once this was solidly established, his immense fortune allowed him to give free rein to his overwhelming passion. Both in private and in institutionalized ways, he aspired to revolutionize several areas of scientific knowledge. His journey was guided by his intuitive nature, along with an ambition sometimes bordering on megalomania: "At a very young age [1857], I clearly had the vague but nonetheless profound intuition that I could be called on to later play a role in reforming human knowledge, by restoring the foundation and creating great guidelines."[60] Flush with his industrial success, which had originally been met with great skepticism, Solvay had developed the idea that his intuitions, even when rejected by the majority, would sooner or later prove right. A free spirit, he maintained a

---

[57] Alfred Mond (1868–1930) was the second son of Ludwig Mond (who retired from management in the 1890s). He was part of the active management, in the sales area, from 1894 to 1906, when he became a member of Parliament. He was also a member of the board of directors, which he left briefly in 1916 to return from 1923 to 1926, after his political career had collapsed. Roscoe Brunner (1871–1926), the youngest son of John Brunner, in addition to being a managing partner, became director in 1901 and succeeded his father in the role of chairman in 1918. Reader (1970), 92–4, 218–21.

[58] Chandler (2004), 271–2.

[59] "Overcome darkness with science" is the motto of the Université Libre de Bruxelles, to which Ernest Solvay was closely linked.

[60] AES, Documents remis à M. Purnal, Note from Ernest Solvay, "Du prolongement nécessaire, pour après moi, de mon action en science pure et appliquée: raisons, buts, voies et moyens," 20 Aug. 1918.

certain distance from the science of his time, which did not fail to elicit criticism from his contemporaries:

> I must say that my work was done freely.... I worked thus, because I did not have the leisure of going back to the classic sources and immersing myself in a field of science of which I knew little and whose theories did not always seem relevant. Additionally and especially, I wanted to maintain complete independence of thought and investigation without in any way being influenced by pre-established systems.[61]

To test his ideas, Solvay never hesitated to solicit advice from the great scientific authorities, both Belgian and foreign (e.g., Becquerel, Frémy, Stas, Kamerlingh Onnes, Lorentz). On top of this, he surrounded himself with a permanent team of scientists and engineers, personally compensated by him to try to demonstrate the validity of his intuitions. Some of them, more or less convinced by the theories of their patron, became academic relays that Solvay used as a basis to then develop his own system of patronage.[62] The industrialist was imbued with the scientism of the Belle Époque. He believed that science and reason would elucidate metaphysical darkness and govern the world on the basis of rational and positivist, almost mechanical, laws. His great dream was to establish a general order by uniting three scientific fields: physico-chemistry, bio-physiology, and sociology. The law of conservation of energy, discovered in the middle of the nineteenth century, would link these three disciplines together. According to Solvay, the progression of the universe should be attributed not to either a vital force or matter endowed with a soul but to energy transformations. The sequence appeared completely logical to him: if a great universal law existed to explain the movement of the planets, the mechanics of living beings and the functioning of societies, it should be possible to declare an energetico-productivist scientific law and to govern the world on the basis of a purely rational order. However, what the science of his time would demonstrate was in fact the absence of such a law that would be valid in all frames of reference. The uniqueness of his objective contrasted singularly with the diversity of his work, which can, in retrospect, be considered somewhat scattershot. He pursued many paths, bouncing from one discipline to another, never academically mastering any of them. A prolific author, he published around sixty articles, letters, and discourses on scientific questions, alongside 139 writings on political and social issues.

Solvay thought he could revolutionize classic physics, a science that was still limited in its theoretical arsenal.[63] His first focus of research, which he called in his own jargon the *gravito-matérialitique* theory, aimed to review

---

[61] Quote from Héger and Lefébure (1929), 77.

[62] In the center of this network was Paul Héger, physiologist and personal doctor for Solvay; Émile Tassel, chemical engineer and professor of physics at the Université Libre de Bruxelles; and Charles Lefébure, engineer and future secretary to King Albert I. Also part of this network were the scientists and engineers Camille Wissinger, Georges Hostelet, Paul Warnant, Édouard Herzen, Émile Waxweiler, Auguste Slosse, Georges Barnich, Gustave Caudelier, Robert Goldschmidt, Léon Gérard, Eugène Lagrange, Arthur Brichaux, and René Lucion.

[63] See Vanpaemel (1999), 55–69; Marage and Wallenborn (1999), 70–94.

the notions of the constitution of matter, gravity, and cosmogony. In a paper published in 1894, he delivered a unitary but speculative theory on energy and matter. The objective was to formulate an updated version of Newton's law of gravity "by putting it in the context of modern ideas on energy and its transformations."[64] The scientists to whom he submitted the paper decried his lack of rigor. In fact, as has been well demonstrated by Isabelle Stengers, Solvay selected certain theories prevalent at the time to reinforce his own vision and then extrapolated them carelessly. At the same time, he arbitrarily discarded any that infringed on this optimistic outlook (the second principle of thermodynamics, in particular).[65] Despite general disapproval, Solvay never lost his self-confidence and continued along this path until the end of his life.

He constantly went back and forth between purely theoretical concepts to research on practical applications. In the 1880s, in several Parisian workshops, in the lab at Couillet and then in his own private lab in Brussels, he invented experimental devices designed to validate his own physico-chemical theories: a gyroscope, a device with rotating disks producing a vacuum, a vacuum tube modeling the earth's atmosphere, a pyrometer, an impact machine designed to calculate the material equivalent of heat, a device designed to use the action of inertia to record displacements, a booster device, and a mechanical generator of extreme temperatures. The latter actually led to some promising results. By 1872, Solvay got the idea into his head of "producing an absolute cold $(-273°$ C)."[66] His tests focused especially on liquefaction of gases using standard industrial equipment and without having recourse to high pressures. Several patents were filed in 1885 for devices with successive expansions, enabling attainment of a temperature of $-93°$ C. Ernest Solvay observed his competitors in the field and corresponded, among others, with Heike Kamerlingh Onnes (to whom he gave a subsidy for his cryoscopy lab in Leiden). After the Bavarian Carl von Linde succeeded in liquefying gases by successive compressions and expansions in 1895, Solvay halted his investigations. Nor did he follow up with the proposal made to him in 1900 by George Claude, the French founder of Air Liquide, who tried to interest him in his undertaking.[67]

Ernest Solvay also explored the study of meteorology, atmospheric phenomena, and the earth's magnetism. He published several papers on the subject, starting with a paper filed at the Académie des Sciences de Paris in 1873, which resulted in correspondence with Henri Becquerel and Edmond Frémy. He then delegated research on this question to his collaborators Camille Wissinger and Charles Lagrange. His most ambitious project in this area was the design of a machine capable of condensing steam contained in the ambient air to produce electricity. As revolutionary an invention as it was, it was totally unfeasible because it was contrary to the second principle of thermodynamics.

---

[64] *Gravitique: De la gravité astronomique de la matière et de ses rapports d'équivalence avec l'énergie.* Paper completed in 1887, filed in 1888 at the Académie des Sciences de Belgique and published in 1894. Jean-Charles Houzeau, Jean Servais Stas, and Gustave-Adolphe Hirn, to whom Solvay submitted it first, expressed very critical opinions.

[65] Stengers (1997), 149–65.

[66] HC, letter from Ernest Solvay to Gustave Cauderlier, 29 Sept. 1872.

[67] Tassel (1920), 89–95; see also Baillot (2010); Dienel (2004).

Gradually, Solvay became interested in biology and physiology. Conceiving each living being as a "chemical-electric-mechanical device" and the brain as a "polar organ produced by organic electricity," Solvay considered electricity as having a predominant role in the phenomenon of animal life.[68] His convictions evolved following repeated contact with several physiologists including Paul Héger, who also became his personal doctor. With the latter acting as intermediary, Solvay's passion for science developed into scientific patronage of a scale and posterity unequaled in Belgium.[69] Solvay sometimes confided that the industry had never been more for him than a means of acquiring the independence necessary to devote himself to science. In a memo from April 1880, he admitted, for the first time, his desire to "create a scientific institute designed to affirm or contradict" his theories.[70] However, he waited until 1887 to enter academic territory with the granting of a first subsidy of BEF 5,000 (US$950) to the physiology laboratory of Paul Héger, and later a second payment of BEF 25,000 (US$4,750) in 1888. The movement had begun. The subsidies evolved into a project for the establishment of an institute, for which the two men drew up a research program. Although Solvay wished to focus on electrophysiology, Héger intended to go beyond this framework and significantly expand lab experimentation. Finally in 1893, a dual institute was founded, one for basic research and the other for teaching and research. With it was born the first pillar of a veritable *cité scientifique*, located in the Parc Léopold in Brussels.[71] In total, during his lifetime, Ernest Solvay donated about BEF 5 million (US$950,000, equivalent to more than US$20 million in 2010) for the construction of multiple institutes in this *cité scientifique*.[72]

In his systemic view, Solvay considered sociology of great importance, its purpose being to "organize world society in a fair and rational way" based on physico-chemical and physiological laws. To develop his social theories (see Chapter 4), Solvay created in 1894 the Institute of Social Sciences and appointed as its directors Hector Denis, Guillaume de Greef, and Émile Vandervelde, three figures in the Belgian socialist movement. This first attempt ended in failure: in 1901, Solvay ousted the three directors following conflicts over financial considerations and theoretical disputes.[73] It was only a minor setback, however;

---

[68] *Notes, Lettres et Discours* (1929), 130: "Observations générales sur le rôle de l'électricité dans les phénomènes de la vie animale en vue du programme expérimental de l'Institut Solvay," Speech given by Ernest Solvay, 14 Dec. 1893.

[69] The practice of financing academic institutes through patronage was in full bloom at this time. The Clarendon physics labs at Oxford (1872) and Cavendish of Cambridge (1874), the Institut Montefiore at the Université de Liège (1883), the California Institute of Technology (1891) financed by Andrew Carnegie, and even the Nobel Foundation (1901).

[70] Tassel (1920), 30.

[71] Héger then solicited Alfred Solvay and the bankers Georges Brugman, Fernand Jamar, and Léon Lambert to create the Institut d'Hygiène, de Thérapeutique et de Bactériologie. Héger also approached Warocqué for financing of the Institut d'Anatomie. A true *cité scientifique* thus took shape, through the collaboration among private patrons, the city of Brussels (via its liberal burgomaster Charles Buls) and the Université Libre de Bruxelles. See Viré (1974), 86–180; Brauman and Demanet (1985).

[72] Viré (1974), 151–7; Despy-Meyer and Montens (1997), 239.

[73] AES, Box S, Conflit survenu à l'occasion de la création de l'Institut, 1901.

in 1902 at the heart of the new *cité scientifique*, the Solvay Institute of Sociology was erected, under the leadership of a new gray eminence, Émile Waxweiler, engineer and liberal progressive from Ghent. Like the Institute of Physiology, the work done there gradually distanced itself from the theories of Solvay, who agreed to give some latitude to the specialists.[74,75]

Financial support to the university institutes continued through the foundation in 1903, within the *cité scientifique*, of the Solvay Business School. Émile Waxweiler became its director and thus assured its liaison with the other institutes, as Solvay wanted. The goal of the *école*, which is still one of the most renowned European business schools, was to train elites, "managers that could comprehend both the flow of business and society in general."[76] This meant bringing the discipline from empiricism to science. In general, Solvay remained very involved in the life of Université Libre de Bruxelles, for which he had been named a permanent member of the board in 1891 and received a doctorate honoris causa in 1898.[77]

Curiously enough, although physics and chemistry were at the heart and the origin of his undertaking, these sciences were the last ones to which Solvay dedicated institutes. It would not be until 1910 when he met men who submitted convincing projects to him. In physics, it was Walter Nernst, famous German physico-chemist, who persuaded Solvay to organize at Brussels an "international scientific council to elucidate questions of current interest on molecular and kinetic theories."[78] In fact, the physicists of the time were aware, as was Solvay, that a new era was beginning, by deeper exploration into new concepts, promoted mainly by Max Planck (quantum theory) and Albert Einstein (restrained relativity). The first Solvay Council of Physics, held in 1911 at Brussels, remains iconic in the history of science. It initiated for physics the principle of the international scientific colloquium, in the form of a private meeting bringing together the greatest minds of the time. Among the twenty renowned physicists, eleven were or would become Nobel laureates. During the opening ceremony, Ernest Solvay submitted his *gravito-matérialitique* theory that he had been refining ceaselessly up to then, in the hope that it would

---

[74] Crombois (1997), 218.

[75] Additionally, Ernest Solvay furthered his intervention in the social sciences field by creation of the Ecole des Sciences Sociales of the Université Libre de Bruxelles as well as an Institut d'Education ouvrière directed by Émile Vandervelde and financial support to various political and social organizations such as Vooruit of Ghent, the People's House of Brussels, the Office of ethnography, etc. Finally, to ensure dissemination of his social doctrine, Ernest Solvay acquired in 1901 a bankrupt liberal historical Belgian newspaper, "l'Indépendance belge," that he used as a propaganda medium for his social work.

[76] Quoted in Constas, Devriese, and Oosterlinck (2003).

[77] Solvay's support to the university also exceeded the Brussels framework because, in his international perspective, he largely subsidized (personally or through the company) the Electro-Technical Institute at Nancy, the chemical lab at the Geneva University, the Imperial Institute of Chemistry at Berlin, the Conservatoire des Arts et Métiers de Paris, the scientific research lab at Mont Rose, the Institut Marey at Paris, Wellesley College (Massachusetts), the bacteriological lab at Léopoldville (Congo), and so on, which earned him numerous prestigious academic distinctions.

[78] Pelseneer (1975), 7.

FIGURE 5.2. The first Solvay Conference of Physics of 1911 gathered the most brilliant minds of the time (Nernst, Planck, Brillouin, Rubens, Sommerfeld, Lindemann,
Lorentz, De Broglie, Knudsen, Warburg, Perrin, Hasenohrl, Wien, Curie, Jeans, Ruther-
ford, Poincaré, Kamerlingh Onnes, Einstein, Langevin, together with Belgian organizers
Solvay, Goldschmidt, Herzen, and Hostelet). This picture remains an icon in the history
of sciences. (Picture by Benjamin Couprié.)

be discussed. This did not happen. However, progress was elsewhere. This
"witches' Sabbath," as Albert Einstein described it, is still considered as the
event that enabled emergence of quantum physics.[79] Following this success,
Robert Goldschmidt, who had introduced Nernst to Solvay, suggested that the
latter create the International Institute for Physics. Lorentz, who had presided
over the first council to general satisfaction, accepted the task of establishing the
foundation of this institute to encourage fundamental research worldwide and
to promote, in Belgium, the development of the scientific movement. Except for
several interruptions due to political events, the institute continued to organize
prestigious councils. The one in 1927, venue of the famous debate between
Niels Bohr and Einstein, remains the most symbolic.

In chemistry, a similar project was under discussion with Wilhelm Ostwald
and William Ramsay, president of the International Association of Chemical
Societies (IACS). It was delayed further. Solvay was not satisfied with their proposals to create a sort of bibliographic institute specialized in chemistry. Backed
by Lorentz, he envisioned the creation of a chemistry council similar to the one
that had just been established for physics. Albin Haller, chemistry professor at

[79] Marage and Wallenborn (1999); Lambert (2010), 159–73.

Nancy, was brought into the discussions that resulted in the founding of the International Solvay Institute for Chemistry fashioned after the physics institute and endowed, like it, with BEF 1 million (US$190,000). Consequently, the secretariat of the IACS was established at Brussels in 1911, and it took over scientific direction of the institutes. The first Council of Chemistry, delayed by the war, was not organized until 1922.[80] In contrast to the Institutes of Physiology and Sociology initially designed to develop and disseminate Solvay's theories, these two institutes were assured from the start of total independence.[81]

In the autumn of his life, Ernest Solvay was confronted with an impressive amount of scientific work that had been started, paths that had been cleared, and impasses that had not been overcome. With a feeling of urgency and of work not completed, he organized his Comité de Prolongement between two climbs in the Alps.[82] For each discipline, he tried to contractually bind the services of his collaborators, with very large compensation. Émile Tassel, who no longer believed in the *gravito-matérialitique* theory, politely declined the offer.[83] Ernest's sons, Armand and Edmond, and two of his grandsons, Ernest-John and Emmanuel Janssen, backed by the faithful Lefébure,[84] were tasked with seeing that the patronage be continued and that his research be furthered:

> They shall hold dear to their hearts the honorable accomplishment by their father/grandfather, even after his death, and using a small part of their fortune, carry on the task that he had initiated for the benefit of humanity, a task presented to them in advance, around 1880. Science for him was like his fifth child that had to be nurtured and reared.[85]

---

[80] Pelseneer (1975), 72–85; Van Tiggelen (1999).

[81] The institutes are still active today; see http://www.solvayinstitutes.be.

[82] Ernest Solvay, preferring solitary meditation to mundane dinners, discovered a passion for mountain climbing in his fifties. In 1921, at the age of eighty-two, he scaled Diavolezza (Switzerland) for the last time. He offered to the alpinists' community a famous mountain hut (at 4,003 meters) on the Matterhorn, which bears his name.

[83] AES, Documents remis à M. Purnal, no. 26, letter from Tassel to Solvay, 14 Oct. 1918.

[84] Charles Lefébure (1862–1943), an engineer working both for the company and on Ernest Solvay's personal experimentations, became his most intimate collaborator and personal secretary. Having collected his confidences and ideas up to his mountain trips, he consequentially received the charge to monitor succession issues after his death.

[85] AES, Documents remis à M. Purnal, no 6, Voeux et désirs exprimés à mes enfants, 1911.

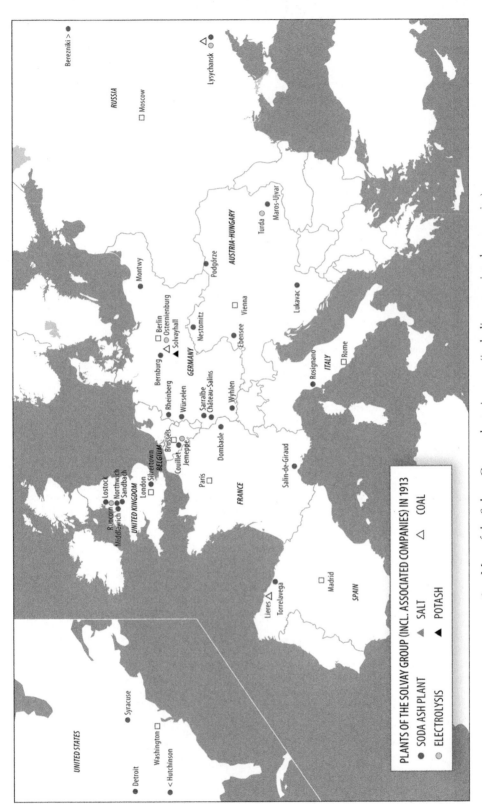

PLANTS OF THE SOLVAY GROUP (INCL. ASSOCIATED COMPANIES) IN 1913

● SODA ASH PLANT   ▲ SALT   △ COAL

○ ELECTROLYSIS   ▲ POTASH

FIGURE 6.1. Map of the Solvay Group plants 1913 (including associated companies).

6

Conclusion of Part 1

In 1865, when the small plant at Couillet was beset by problems, experts consulted by Eudore Pirmez had declared: "In sum, what do you have? A principle that cannot be patented, equipment which is patented but which is unreliable. There remains the hope of perfecting the equipment, but to do this, it must be made larger and more complex. Let us assume that success will be obtained at this price, which seems extremely doubtful to me. But even in this case, I do not predict a lasting success, due to the probable increase in the price of ammonia."[1] From the comfortable vantage point of hindsight, it is easy for the historian to refute this dire prediction. Let us ask the question again in 1913: in sum, what do we have? A mature, protected, and permanently improved process; a cost price continuously going down; domination of the world alkali business; annual profits for the parent company of BEF 26 million (almost US$5 million), which enabled both self-financing of the necessary investments and distribution of generous dividends to the close circle of family associates; thirty-two plants (only eight of which were wholly owned), employing twenty-five thousand people, producing nearly two million tons of alkalis, and making the Solvay group the most international and the largest chemical group worldwide in terms of employees and output.[2] Without falling into the realm of hagiography, the history of this first half century of existence is one of immense success of an enterprise that was able to take astute advantage of a technical and commercial opportunity at the international level.

6.1 CAPITALIZING ON A TECHNOLOGICAL BREAKTHROUGH

Solvay's success relied, above all, on the optimal valorization of a process that constituted a major technological breakthrough in the history of the chemical industry. It has been long established that Ernest Solvay did not discover the fundamental reaction – nor was he the first to try to develop the ammonia soda process. However, he and his close collaborators (Alfred Solvay and Louis-Philippe Acheroy) can be considered the first to have technically and economically succeeded in scaling up this gas-liquid reaction in a continuous process. This technical prowess was already a great achievement: the beginnings

---

[1] Édouard Jaequemyns to Eudore Pirmez, 22 Sept. 1865, quoted in Chapter 1.
[2] As indicated in Haber (1971), 161.

in the test station at Schaerbeek, and then in the plant at Couillet, were risky
ventures, based especially on empirical experimentation. The mid-nineteenth
century was a time when a young, imaginative inventor could still elaborate
a new heavy-chemical process in his private workshop and develop it on an
industrial scale, thanks to some good personal connections. The development
of the Solvay process relied on a mastery of principles that would today fall in
the realm of chemical engineering: continuous production, increasing mechanization, constitution of closed cycles, savings in energy (especially coal) and
raw materials, waste reduction, research on valorization of by-products, control of reactions and mastery of their parameters (e.g., pressure, temperature,
flows, purity). This technical excellence proved Solvay's essential competitive
edge. Because the patents would eventually enter the public domain, the company favored a cult of secrecy regarding the actual functioning of the operation
rather than systematically patenting its equipment in detail. Once the process
was mature, at the start of the 1880s, Solvay aimed to conserve its technological advantage through systematic research on incremental improvements
stimulated by networking and the cross-fertilization of all its plants, whether
they were wholly owned or part of a joint venture. This practice was illustrated
by the meticulous elaboration of the comparative production tables for review
by the Central Technical Department and the dispatching of innovations as of
1875. This preeminence in technology and mechanical engineering over pure
chemistry conferred on Solvay an image of a company of engineers. The by-
product coke ovens for recovery of ammonia, the electrolytic mercury cell, and
the causticizing processes developed or improved internally were among the
other technical successes achieved by Solvay.

6.2   A HYBRID MULTINATIONAL ORGANIZATION

For lack of real diversification, growth efforts focused on geographical expansion. In a time span of twenty years, Solvay became one of the first multinational
chemical companies, relying on a network of plants extending from Michigan to
the Urals, going through the Mediterranean and the Caucasus, all connected to
Brussels. Considering the threat of independent establishment of ammonia soda
plants in other countries, Solvay felt very early the need for internationalization
(a stated objective as of 1865). In contrast to the Leblanc industry that dominated the international alkali trade from England, Solvay played the national
card everywhere. It selected sites that combined a salt mine and direct access to
secondary raw materials (e.g., lime, coal), lines of communication, and a consumer market. The return to protectionism at the end of the nineteenth century
and the erection of trade barriers confirmed the relevance of this multinational
strategy. In its conquest of the world, Solvay did not have a model to follow.
Initially lacking experience and resources, it proceeded through trial and error.
During the 1870s it built a giant plant in France with its own funds while it
granted licenses in England and bought an existing plant in Germany for reconversion. Observing the lack of efficiency with these latter two methods, Solvay,
in a second expansion phase (in the 1880s), turned to associations with local
partners in Russia, Austria-Hungary, and the United States, providing them

with its know-how. The group eventually adopted a mixed profile of wholly owned establishments in Belgium, France, Italy, and Spain; a fully owned subsidiary in Germany; and joint ventures elsewhere. The international networks of engineers, financiers, and lawyers proved essential for the apprenticeship of national cultures and for the integration into varied territories. Adopting the principle of think globally, act locally, the Central Administration in Brussels tried to manage the entire network with rigor and diplomacy. It reined in wayward partners and worked at a good balance between strategic centralization and operational decentralization. The Belgian *gérants* were more than once subjected to the contradictory desires of their partners. Take, for example, the determination of Carl Wessel to diversify into costly activities (e.g., potash, salt, chrome, cement); the independence of Ludwig Mond; the self-indulgence of the American partners who were more worried about rapid growth than controlling their production costs; the lack of experience of Ivan Lubimoff in managing a chemical company; and the divergence of viewpoints with Aussiger Verein, associated with Solvay while remaining an important Leblanc producer. Conversely, Solvay & Cie sometimes seemed a conservative parent company, holding back its partners in their frenetic attempts at conquest. But Solvay wished to stay the course and enforce its principles forcefully while still leaving the door open to suggestions. Thus, it was on the advice of its foreign directors that Solvay entered into electrolysis (after the insistence of DSW) and adopted early on the eight-hour workday (first tested in Russia) and a week of paid leave (inaugurated by British partners). This multinational model, limiting the efforts of operational management while generating abundant profits, enabled organic growth at limited costs, in accord with the principle of financial self-sufficiency.

6.3　AN UNSHAKABLE LEADERSHIP

Another pillar of the Solvay edifice, less often brought to light but still just as important, was the rigor of its commercial management and its means of dominating the competition. At this time, soda ash was a basic chemical products most in demand by the glass, textile, paper, and soap industries, to name just a few. Demand, already great, was about to explode parallel with the drop in price enabled by the ammonia process. The challenge for Solvay hence was to capture the growth of this demand while slowly pushing its competitors out of the market, to forge worldwide leadership. To do this, the competitive fight had to be won both in the national markets and in international trade. In both spheres, the Solvay companies entered into competition with the Leblanc producers, solidly established and capable of furnishing a wide range of soda and chlorinated products, as well as with the new arrivals in the ammonia-soda business. In each market, competitive fights burst open, bringing about a drop in prices. Solvay's competitors, incapable of attaining competitive cost prices, were constrained to enter into agreements and often join sales syndicates led by the Solvay companies. A second phase then opened up, in which prices and sales quotas were set to Solvay's advantage, the latter reserving for itself future increases. These practices of limiting the competition – common at the time in many sectors – ensured the company reliable and significant incomes and outlets and conferred on it a lasting, dominant position. For its competitors (e.g., United Alkali, Saint-Gobain, Rhenania, Honigmann), Solvay appeared to be a very well organized group, uncompromising in business affairs and almost unassailable on its reserved market. Upon hopeless confrontation, all preferred sooner or later a reconversion to other activities. On the one hand, the Leblanc producers, whose business was artificially kept alive, obtained the possibility of a soft phasing out of their obsolete process and reconversion to other products. Later development of Solvay in caustic soda, and then the appearance of electrolytic chlorine, finally put an end to the Leblanc process by removing its last market outlets. On the other hand, newcomers lured by the profitability of the ammonia process were systematically pressured by Solvay. Different methods could be deployed: price wars and selling at a loss, pressure via the soda ash and salt syndicates controlled by Solvay, lobbying public authorities and in professional areas, legal procedures for patent infringement and disrespect of noncompete clauses, and so on. At the turn of the century, each of the markets was under control. As of 1897, international agreements concluded between Solvay and United Alkali Co dictated international alkali trade, within an informal cartel controlled by a three-headed Solvay group, distributed over the European Continent (Solvay & Cie, DSW, Lubimoff, Verein), Great Britain (Brunner, Mond & Co.), and the United States (Solvay Process Co.).

6.4   THE LIFE OF A FAMILY BUSINESS

These technical and commercial accomplishments were inevitably coupled with a human dimension. The launch and development of the business took place only thanks to concentric circles of people who gravitated around the founding Solvay brothers. The first steps were supported by an early intimate circle, made up of the family (parents, sisters, brothers-in-law) and longtime friends (e.g., Louis-Philippe Acheroy, Guillaume Nélis). It is through Nélis, a true moderator and a connection to wider economic and political spheres, that a second circle of associates (e.g., Eudore Pirmez, Valentin Lambert, Gustave Sabatier) brought in not only capital but also legal, commercial, and industrial experience. Finally, international expansion rested on a third circle of individuals: Prosper Hanrez in France, Ludwig Mond and John Brunner in England, Carl Wessel in Germany, Rowland Hazard and William Cogswell in the United States, Ivan Lubimoff in Russia, Carl Schaffner in Austria-Hungary, and all their collaborators. One of the main strengths of Ernest Solvay was that he surrounded himself with talented men and delegated important tasks to them; he convinced financiers to trust him and to rely on international networks. In his somewhat autocratic exercise of power, he did not hesitate to enter into conflict or to cast aside anyone who called his authority into question. Thus, Prosper Hanrez, who did not hide his desire to run the company, was compelled to resign in 1886, despite his important contribution to the expansion of the group. Also, Eudore Pirmez, an eminent Belgian politician, was not able to avoid takeover of control by the Solvays to the disadvantage of the silent partners. The period of internal tension (1882–1905) did not end until after the new distribution of shares and organization of powers were fully accepted by the silent partners. The immense wealth generated by this closed family company gave birth to an industrial dynasty solidly implanted in the Belgian bourgeoisie, endowed with numerous political and international connections. Strict succession plans were put into place, at the level of both shareholding (right of preemption) and top executive positions. Prosper Hanrez and Édouard Hannon remained the only two nonfamily *gérants* until 1967. The overpowering figure of Ernest Solvay (and the early death of his brother) explains the strong identification of the company with his person. Retired from the daily management of the business from the end of the 1880s, his ideas, in particular the primacy of the intimate family group, the financial independence, and prevalence of industrial activity over speculation, nonetheless continued to influence his successors.

In social terms, Solvay was distinguished by its progressive policy, motivated by the quest for social peace, the worry about independence from the states and the labor organizations, economic pragmatism (plants in continuous operation), the need for finding and retaining a labor force, and a certain sense of social duty and philanthropy of the owners. This was translated into advanced paternalistic measures, aiming to reinforce the well-being of the workers while also moralizing and controlling them. Anticipating social legislation, Solvay forestalled any complaints, generating an almost-uninterrupted social peace and, consequently, a stable production. The paternalism instituted between 1890 and 1914 remained firmly anchored in the company culture. This longevity can certainly be explained by an absence of internal disapprobation, by the willingness to maintain know-how within the company, by the persistence of the family nature and the great continuity of views among the generations of leaders.

Having full knowledge of later events, it could be said that in 1913, the organization of the Solvay group was incubating the causes of future troubles: a nondiversified profile in a chemical sector that would soon burgeon into new areas, a significant presence into countries that would soon be prey to conflicts and territorial grabs, total independence at the eve of the creation of large national trusts. Nonetheless, the heavens were completely aligned at the time when the guests at dinners celebrating the fiftieth anniversary, dining on exquisite French cuisine and enjoying vintage wines, congratulated themselves in an atmosphere of family and business responsibility with a job well done.

PART 2

THE YEARS OF CRISIS (1914–1950)

The Making and Unmaking of International Alliances

Kenneth Bertrams

FIGURE 7.1. Results of the bombing of the Château-Salins soda ash plant on 24 July 1917. This was one of the few major destructions Solvay experienced during World War I. After the transfer of Alsace-Lorraine from Germany to France, the plant was transferred from DSW to Solvay & Cie. (Solvay Archives.)

7

The Multiple Fronts of World War I

The celebration of the fiftieth anniversary of Solvay in 1913 had amply demonstrated the magnitude of the company's internationalization. From the 1870s, the approach followed by Solvay combined a strong thrust for geographical expansion and constant efforts to adapt management capabilities and financial resources. The projects carried out during the year 1913 significantly showed that Solvay aimed to strengthen its presence in Continental Europe while becoming less dependent on outside sources; it included the construction of a plant in Rosignano (Tuscan coast) and the negotiations leading to the purchase of potash mines in Suria (Catalonia).[1] Unsurprisingly, the interplay between the expansion of activities and the centralization of command was at the core of Ernest Solvay's speech during the September 1913 jubilee.[2] According to him, striving for the upper hand in the world business of alkali meant seeking a dense coordination among the company's partners and subsidiaries. It also presupposed a sound and stable international political environment, the kind of which the war would shatter in pieces.

All hell broke loose in Europe during the summer of 1914. At first, like other companies, Solvay had to face the urgent mobilization of its workers and the chaos resulting from unplanned military schemes. But within a few weeks, it was getting obvious that the situation of the company would differ in many respects from the bulk of multinational businesses. First and foremost, the central administration of Solvay was located in occupied territory throughout the war. From 20 August 1914, when the German troops reached Brussels, until the early days of November 1918, it had to cope with the exile of the legal government in France and the involvement of a German military government in the conduct of the economy.[3] But the loss of Belgium's national sovereignty had implications for Solvay on the international scale; it meant that the central administration was partly isolated from other belligerent countries, and from its foreign subsidiaries. As a result, the tight chain of decision that had prevailed hitherto gave way to a more decentralized – and chaotic – model of information circulation. In the last months of 1914, the *gérance* decided to transfer the center of communication with countries belonging to the Triple Entente from Brussels

---

[1] ACS, RdG, 30 Sept. 1913.
[2] "Une affaire aussi vaste, aussi divisée, aussi diversifiée et néanmoins aussi continue que celle qui constitue la Société Solvay & Cie" (*Cinquantenaire* 1913, 78).
[3] De Schaepdrijver (2004), 69–79; Pirenne (1928); Van Langenhove (1927).

to Rotterdam, in the neutral Netherlands. One of the *gérants* – Armand Solvay – did spend most part of the war in Biarritz, from where he was able to assist his fellow colleagues in solving international commercial issues.

In some way, we tackle here a paradox of World War I: the obstacles raised by the war on the international stage would precisely reveal to Solvay the positive outcomes of its international organization. Instead of neutralizing the company's action, wartime circumstances unexpectedly strengthened the links among its subsidiary plants in France, Spain, and Italy, which were deeply committed to a state-driven economic mobilization in the name of patriotic duty. The production drive that took place at that time enabled Solvay to maintain and even increase its market shares in countries where competitors were eager to emerge as new leaders. Solvay's controlled companies, in contrast, also seized the war as an outstanding opportunity to increase their production figures. This was the case on both sides of the front, albeit with much less success in the German and Austrian empires, both of which were on the verge of collapsing. In the United States, the exceptional wartime growth experienced by the Solvay Process Company was proportional to its desire to dispose of their Belgian shareholders. This led to a tense and complicated relationship, which was only partially solved as the war drew to a close. Finally, the name of Solvay came out of the war with an unprecedented gain of prestige due to its involvement in the setting up of a relief organization in Belgium, whose ramifications extended on the international stage. And to this, we must turn.

7.1 FACING THE OCCUPATION, ORGANIZING THE RELIEF EFFORT

In the sparkle of the company's fiftieth anniversary, Louis Solvay asked his mother to write down her recollections of the very first years of the enterprise. Marie Masson-Solvay declined at the time but changed her mind three years later: "What I did not endeavor while everything was joyful, I am resuming now at the saddest hour, when the country is devastated and crushed by the winner, at the very moment that a zeppelin, that despicable symbol, purrs across the sky above Boitsfort."[4] Belgium was invaded by the German troops on 4 August 1914, in violation of the nation's independence and its commitment to neutrality. The march of the Kaiser's army had left the country in a state of disarray and anxiety. In cities like Brussels starvation was looming over the population. At the initiative of the mayor of Brussels, Adolphe Max, loads of flour, rice, and salt were purchased and stocked in warehouses owned by the different municipalities of the city. His action paved the way for the rapid spreading and generalization of *soupes populaires et scolaires* (populace and school canteens).[5] For this, he requested the financial help of Ernest Solvay, who replied by a donation of BEF 1 million. With this contribution, Ernest Solvay became committed to a wider action dedicated to the distribution of food supply in and around Brussels. With his grandson-in-law Emmanuel Janssen,

---

[4] Masson-Solvay (1915), 9.
[5] Rency (1920), 122.

who was by then general secretary of Solvay, they formed the hard core of what was about to be known as the Comité National de Secours et d'Alimentation (National Committee for Relief and Food), a private organization that would grow out as "a kind of government" during the course of the war, according to Ernest Solvay himself.[6] The innovation of this *Comité* was largely because of its composition as a network of industrialists, financiers, and statesmen, moving away from the traditional political cleavages. Its Executive Committee was headed by the energetic director of the Société Générale de Belgique, Émile Francqui, with the impulse of the leader of the multinational electrical holding Sofina, Daniel (Dannie) Heineman.[7]

On both the local and the international stages, important members of Solvay were closely associated to the tasks of the *comité*. Appointed vice president of the *comité*'s Executive Committee in September 1914, Emmanuel Janssen also held the key responsibility of chief of the Secours (benevolence) Department, which functioned with the profits resulting from the sales of imported food-stuffs to those who could still afford it.[8] This position gave him an outstanding bird's-eye view of the global economic activities taking place in Belgium during the war. Together with Heineman, the *gérant* Louis Solvay headed the subcommittee in charge of the overall control of the "municipal warehouses," whose role was crucial in dispatching food supply to the municipalities of Brussels. The presence of these men partly coincided with the rejuvenation of the company's management as well. In March 1916, Emmanuel Janssen stepped in the *gérance* with Alfred Solvay's son-in-law, Émile Tournay. Louis Solvay (b. 1876), Tournay (b. 1878), and Janssen (b. 1879) embodied a new generation of young *gérants*, whose wartime experience would be instrumental in the later development of Solvay.[9] Finally, no less than two members of Solvay acted as liaison officers with the municipalities: Édouard Hannon was responsible for Saint-Gilles, and the director of Solvay's financial department, Louis Huaux, organized his action in Ixelles.[10]

Considering his role at an early stage, Ernest Solvay served as chairman of the *comité*. One of his first initiatives as such had been to bear the relief action on the international political level. He therefore requested the patronage of two neutral countries as a way to avoid the intrusion of the occupants and benefit from their international caution. The American ambassador to Belgium, Brand Whitlock, and his Spanish counterpart, the Marquis of Villalobar, agreed to take on this role. These men convinced the first general governor to Belgium, Feldmarschall Colmar von der Goltz, to endorse the enterprise of the *comité* and leave it reasonable room to maneuver.[11] However, for the very reason that this private relief initiative contributed to the social stabilization of the

---

[6] During a meeting held on 15 Oct. 1914; see *Rapport général* (1919–1921), 368.
[7] Ranieri (2005), 81–2.
[8] Henry (1920), 66–7.
[9] On the rise of the second generation, see Chapter 5.
[10] NAB, CNSA, 3334, Minutes of the meetings, 1 Sept. 1914; NAB, CNSA, 3334, Minutes of the meetings, 3 Sept. 1914. I am wholeheartedly grateful to Michaël Amara for his help and guidance in the consultation of this archive material.
[11] Whitlock (1919), 194–5; Van Langenhove (1977), 20; Ranieri (2005), 84–5.

Belgian population, the British government expressed some reluctance vis-à-vis the *comité*'s action. Because Britain was controlling the blockade and Belgium was a net importer of foodstuffs, the disinclination of the Allied authorities had to be overcome. On 15 October, Ernest Solvay delivered a speech in which he confirmed that the issue of organizing a system of food supplying "from outside" was put under scrutiny.[12] The following day, he was present with Émile Francqui and Emmanuel Janssen at the American legation in Brussels to formally request that Brand Whitlock and the Americans intervene officially with the German and British authorities.[13] Von der Goltz made clear in a letter addressed to Whitlock that he "explicitly and formally [gave] the insurance that the provisions imported into Belgium by the Committee under the patronage of [His] Excellency for the maintenance of the civil population shall be free from requisitions on the part of the Military Administration and that they shall remain exclusively at the disposition of the Committee."[14]

The British approval was to be next. In this respect, the role of Herbert Hoover turned out to be pivotal. A wealthy American businessman based in London, Hoover had assisted his fellow citizens caught by the war to escape from Continental Europe. He seemed willing to help organizing the relief effort that had begun in and around Brussels. Portrayed as "a man of action" by Ernest Solvay,[15] Hoover was also an old acquaintance of Francqui, whom he knew from their early days in China, where they had been restlessly competing for the takeover of the largest collieries of the country.[16] Whatever their past rivalries and appetite for ambition, Hoover and Francqui agreed to collaborate. The American Committee for Relief in Belgium (CRB) was launched on 22 October with Herbert Hoover appointed as chairman and Dannie Heineman vice chairman.[17] The CRB had already acquired US$250,000 worth of foodstuffs, which had to be shipped to Belgium via Rotterdam with the backing of a group of US representatives. Interestingly, the intermediary of the *comité* to the CRB in the Dutch port was a man of Solvay. The assistant director of the Commercial Department, Jean Van den Branden, had been sent to Rotterdam by the *gérance* to enable the circulation of information between the company and its subsidiaries across the world.[18]

International in its organization, the *comité* thus extended its operation to the whole occupied territories of Belgium and, from April 1915, to the north of France. Considered the "largest philanthropic organisation that has ever been functioning" on Belgian soil,[19] the *comité* was also more than a mere

---

[12] NAB, CNSA, 3334, Minutes of the meetings, 15 Oct. 1914.

[13] Nash (1988), 24; Ranieri (1985), 118.

[14] NARA, RG 84, American Embassy, London, Correspondence, 1914, vol. 47, File 848 (Belgium), von der Goltz to Whitlock, 16 Oct. 1914 (Doc. No. 11) and Whitlock to Page, 16 Oct. 1914 (Doc. No. 27). I am indebted and most grateful to George Nash for providing me a copy of these clippings.

[15] NAB, CNSA, 3334, Minutes of the meetings, 1 Dec. 1914.

[16] Nash (1988), 26; Ranieri (1985), 98–102, 117–22.

[17] NARA, RG 84, File 848, Memoranda 22 Oct. 1914, Document Nos. 14–16.

[18] ACS, RdG, 24 Nov. 1911; NAB, CNSA, 12, General Report, First Semester 1915, 30 June 1915, 94.

[19] Rency (1920), 148; Ranieri (2005), 90.

relief agency. By the end of 1914, Jean Jadot, governor of the Société Générale, obtained from the government-in-exile the commitment that it granted the CRB a monthly allowance of BEF 25 million in exchange for the payment of a fraction of the state's remaining debts and the salary of unemployed civil servants.[20] This recurring budget followed a one-shot grant of BEF 5 million jointly given by the Belgian Ministry of Home Affairs and the British government. Finally, the National Bank of Belgium issued the *comité* a loan of BEF 15 million with the guarantee of a consortium of banks, among which the Mutuelle Mobilière et Immobilière.[21] The latter was created in January 1914 with the objective to become the financial instrument of Solvay's shareholders and *gérants*. By the end of the war, the turnover of the whole relief operation was estimated at BEF 2.4 billion in total (BEF 3.4 billion, with the inclusion of the North of France).[22] But the most important victory of the *comité* was fought in the political arena. It crystallized the resistance of the Belgian population and shared all the characteristics of a provisional government. The matter was stated unequivocally by the head of the Political Department to the general governor, Baron Oscar Von der Lancken:

> We must not hide the fact that the influence of the Committee on the Belgian population is sizeable.... The common opposition of all Belgians vis-à-vis the Germans is concentrated in the Committee. In other occupied enemy countries, political forces concentrate in secret societies; here, they are channelled by an organism born of economic distress, which the occupying power has had to tolerate to avoid catastrophe.[23]

7.2 THE CONDUCT OF BUSINESS IN OCCUPIED TERRITORY

Slow Production at Couillet, Standstill at Jemeppe

Among its many missions, the *comité* carried out an essential task – it provided work. The exile of workers, the privation of raw materials, the breakdown of means of communication were but some of the challenges faced by Belgian factories because of the occupation. Most of the plants had shut their doors or were functioning with a small workforce. The number of unemployed, insignificant before 1914, rose to half a million by 1917.[24] As a result, occupying authorities implemented a system of voluntary and forced labor in Germany that aimed to solve the problems of manpower in the German war industry. Despite a harsh opposition, deportations had indeed taken place from October 1916 onward. No fewer than 160,000 Belgian workers had been forcibly recruited by the end of the war.[25]

---

[20] Baudhuin (1946), vol. 1, 40; Van Langenhove (1927), 89. The amount of the funding rose to BEF 37.5 million by January 1917; six months later, it was taken over directly by the American government ($15 million).

[21] NAB, CNSA, 9, General Report, 1 Dec. 1914, 22.

[22] Henry (1920), 61.

[23] Quoted in De Schaepdrijver (2006), 31.

[24] Baudhuin (1946), vol. 1, 47; De Schaepdrijver (2006), 30.

[25] Thiel (2007), 76, 109–22.

In this context, the attitude of Solvay regarding its Belgian plants was twofold. After the shock of the invasion, it first consisted in preventing the German army from confiscating the products and the equipment. The flow of salt supplies coming from the mine of Borth in Germany, moreover, was interrupted. As a result, the works of Couillet and Jemeppe had immediately ceased production. In response to the distress call of the mayor of Brussels, the plant manager at Couillet, Ferdinand Bouriez, organized the securing and clearing of the seven tons of salt kept in the plant's stockpile.[26] Accordingly, salt was transferred into the communal warehouses, where it was sold at factory price. On 11 October sales were limited to one kilo per household per week.[27] However, in spite of these restrictions, reserves were drying up quickly: Solvay's stock of salt was reduced to a mere 1,217 tons by March 1915. It was at that moment that Solvay obtained from General Governor von Bissing the authorization to resume the importation of rock salt from the salt mine of Borth owned by DSW but officially handled by Syndikat Deutscher Sodafabriken. The *comité* proved instrumental in the negotiations.[28]

In May 1915 the plant of Couillet resumed its production of soda ash "in the sake of public hygiene."[29] At the request of Ernest Solvay, two specialists of international law ascertained that the restarting or closing of an industrial establishment located in occupied territory entailed no legal infringement.[30] The production of Couillet was planned to reach a maximum of twenty-five thousand tons yearly. The bulk of the output covered the needs of the Belgian industry (see Table 7.1). In June 1916, something unexpected happened: the German authorities, invoking the production shortage of the German soda industry, requested that a monthly allotment of 1,200 tons of soda should be sent to Germany.[31] The archives remain silent on the underlying motives of this demand, which seems rather surprising in view of the small amount at stake. It was taken very seriously, however. And the consequences of the decision, which cannot be reduced to a mere alternative between resistance and collaboration, were judged too important to be left to the responsibility of the company alone. That time, it was not legal counsel but political advice that was sought. Michel Lévie, Jean Jadot, Jules Hennin, and Paul Pastur, all prominent figures of the *comité* acting as "unofficial representatives of the Belgian Government," observed that, with regard to the lack of soap and cleaning products for the population, the suspension of the production of soda was out of the question for the time being.[32] By so doing, they gave their moral blessing in disguise.

---

[26] ACS-O, 1001–49, Couillet Correspondance, Marche de l'usine pendant la guerre, "Note mise à la disposition du Gouvernement Belge du stock de sel à Couillet," undated [1920].

[27] NAB, CNSA, 3334, Minutes of the meetings, 27 Sept. 1914 and 11 Oct. 1914; NAB, CNSA, 9, General Report, 1 Dec. 1914, 10; Rency (1920), 120; Henry (1920), 19.

[28] ACS-O, 1001–49, Couillet Correspondance, Marche de l'usine pendant la guerre, "Note mise à la disposition du Gouvernement Belge du stock de sel à Couillet," undated [1920]; Sougnez (1936), 7.

[29] ACS, RdG, 5 Dec. 1913.

[30] Sougnez (1936), 7–8.

[31] ACS-O, 1001–49, Couillet Correspondance, Note written by F. Bouriez, 24 Aug. 1920.

[32] ACS-O, 1001–49, "Note mise à la disposition du Gouvernement."

TABLE 7.1. *Production and Deliveries of Soda Ash at Couillet, 1915–1918 (in tons, rounded figures)*

	1915	1916	1917	1918	Total
Production	13,904	22,953	25,027	20,344	82,228
Deliveries					
Various industries	10,123	12,157	6,793	4,338	33,411
Cooperatives	–	2,917	9,671	7,847	20,435
Jemeppe plant	2,243	1,513	646	1,527	5,929
Occupied France	823	1,875	874	674	4,246
Netherlands	375	0	0	0	375
Germany	0	1,965	5,422	5,066	12,453
TOTAL	13,564	20,427	23,406	19,452	76,849

Source: ART, PDO, table 3; ACS-O, 1271, "Usine de Couillet: Relevé des expéditions de soude," undated [1920]; ACS-O, 1001–49, "Note mise à la disposition du Gouvernement."

According to the available statistics, the German authorities actually never claimed the portion demanded. The initial fraction decreased to a sheer 900 tons and then 500 tons monthly after the company had protested to the Rohstoffverwaltung that the German soda plants could "do a little effort" and increase their own production.[33] Among the German customers, Henkel & Company (Düsseldorf) was by far the most important – it accounted for 35 percent of the deliveries to Germany.[34] Besides soda ash, the plant of Couillet also produced a total amount of 1,100 tons of soda bicarbonate during the war, so as to make up for the lack of baking powder; 100 tons of pharmaceutical bicarbonate; and some 8,500 tons of calcium chloride, which was mostly sold to brewers, refrigerating industries, and well drillers located in Campine and on the banks of the Rhine River.[35]

Contrary to Couillet, the main production lines of Jemeppe (electrolytic caustic lye, chloride of lime, and compressed hydrogen) remained closed throughout the war. During a visit to the plant, Édouard Hannon and Émile Tournay had made sure to prevent the production of caustic soda and hydrogen. The newly installed mercury cells had been hidden, and the machines were partly sabotaged. For that reason, only a tiny proportion of caustic soda has been produced in Belgian factories, whereas nine hundred thousand tons had allegedly been imported from Germany and transferred to warehouses in Antwerp, Brussels, and Couillet, according to a source in 1924.[36] Nevertheless, in reply to the pressure exerted by the occupying authorities by the end of the war, the direction of the company had to switch its standstill strategy at Jemeppe. "In order to

[33] ACS-O, 1271, Folder 25, Joseph Famerie to Hermann Zeiss, Verwaltungschef bei der Generalgouverneur in Belgien, Abteilung für Handel & Gewerbe, Rohstoffverwaltung, 3 June 1916.
[34] ACS-O, 1001–49, Instruction judiciaire – Notes, "Solvay & Cie: Relevé des factures aux fournitures de soude au Syndikat Deutscher Sodafabriken à Bernburg pendant l'occupation," undated [1920].
[35] ACS-O, 1001–49, Instruction judiciaire – Notes, "Note sur la production de chlorure de calcium durant la guerre," undated [1920]; ART, PDO, Tables 8, 16, 18.
[36] ACS-O, 1271, Deliveries of caustic soda from Germany, 2 July 1924; Kerchove (1927), 139.

prevent the requisitioning of our machines and electrical appliances," said the head of the supervisory board Paul Misonne at a meeting in December 1918, "we had implemented a small carbide plant, while proceeding to the renovation of the electrolytic plant. This...was a huge success for, despite several attempts, we have not encountered any complementary requisitioning beside those...involving a small amount of mercury, platinum, and copper."[37]

Postwar Views on Wartime Attitudes

In comparison with other firms located in Belgium, whether they belonged to the chemical industry or to another branch, Solvay could stand the burden of the war. After all, the plants of Couillet and Jemeppe had not been destroyed or bombed during the war, nor had they been dismantled for the gain of the Germany industry by the efficient services of the Abbaugruppe.[38] Despite the Rohstoffverwaltung's intrusion in the company's commercial policy, the supply of soda partially met the significant demand of domestic consumption, as well as the massive needs of the national glass industry. The latter field, it must be said, enjoyed special privileges granted by the German authorities as it contributed to the war effort (construction of army camps and shelters).[39] Moreover, Solvay had taken measures to avert accusations of having an unpatriotic attitude. In the political climate of the postwar purge and the context of German hostility, aroused by press campaigns, some industrial companies were prosecuted for collaborating with the enemy. The coal producer Evence Coppée was one of them: he had been accused of systematically providing the German army and its Coal Administration (Kohlenzentrale) war-related products such as benzol, toluol, coal tar, and other coal derivatives, all of which resulted from the distillation of coal by-products.[40] As to Solvay, it fell under an investigation launched by the jurisdiction of Charleroi in the summer of 1920, but the procedure was dismissed after a couple of months.[41]

More painful, however, had been the prosecution brought against SA des Fours à Coke Semet-Solvay & Cie. Registered as a public company on 13 May 1912, and therefore legally distinct from Solvay (see Chapter 5), SA Semet-Solvay owned its largest plant of refining of benzol and tar distillation in Havré-Ville, near Mons. Contrary to Coppée, with which it shared many characteristics (they were both concerned with the recuperation of coal by-products), Semet-Solvay partly ceased its industrial activities (tar distillation) by December 1915 to avoid the intrusion of the Kohlenzentrale. In spite of this, Semet-Solvay was denounced by the lawyers of Coppée after the war. They had to prove that Coppée was just a scapegoat in a branch – the chemical industry – whose participation in the German war effort was perceived as a

[37] ACS, CdS, Minutes of the meetings, 11 Dec. 1918.
[38] Schaepdrijver (2004), 216–7; Baudhuin (1946), vol. 1, 67–9; Baudhuin (1946), vol. 2, 83–90.
[39] de Kerchove (1927), 51–61.
[40] Dubois (1985), 320.
[41] ACS-O, 1001–49, Clippings from local newspapers (*Le Rappel* and *Le Journal de Charleroi*, dated 6 Oct., 1920); Sougnez to gérance, 3 Nov. 1920.

commonplace. The instruction against Semet-Solvay started in April 1920, but no serious evidence was found so as to be able to file a lawsuit.[42] Even in Coppée's case, charges were dropped in July 1925 (they would occasionally reappear until 1936). Such exposure was a hard blow for the Belgian chemical industry. In 1927, an acute observer wrote, "The chemical products which were produced in Belgium were all, to a large extent, intended to be used for the German war industry."[43] Industrialists had to justify their wartime attitude by referring to a politics of lesser evil that largely prefigured the mechanisms of industrial activity in Belgium during World War II.[44] Solvay was largely spared by these polemics, although the members of the board of Semet-Solvay during the war actually were *gérants* of Solvay – and testified correspondingly as witnesses at the Coppée trial. In postwar Belgium, needless to say, the name of Solvay did not square with the claim of unpatriotic behavior.

7.3 EUROPE AT WAR: THE WESTERN SIDE

While the *comité* provided an informal network to help Solvay organize its industrial activities in occupied Belgium, no such tool existed on the European scale. Of course, the presence of both Armand Solvay and Jean Van den Branden away from the front lines smoothed things over a bit. But this could hardly overcome the isolation of Brussels. In general, in the traditional backyard market of the company – France, Spain, and Italy – individual contacts had to make up for the interruption of the usual mode of governance.

Coping with the Industrial Mobilization in France

The outbreak of the war was a serious blow to the French industrial elite, which lamented the technological domination of the German army. The French chemical industry was especially pointed to for its backwardness and lack of relationships with universities and technical schools.[45] As usual, the nationalist reaction was to accuse foreign companies on French soil of being responsible for this situation.[46] But these were but minor voices. What did prevail was a notable state-driven industrial mobilization, largely due to the drive of farsighted technocrats such as Albert Thomas, Louis Loucheur, and Étienne Clémentel.[47] They fostered especially the manufacturing of war-related products by building new plants (production of sulfuric and nitric acids, and dyestuffs) but paid similar

---

[42] ACS-O, 1271, Procès Semet-Solvay, Folders 1–18.

[43] de Kerchove (1927), 139–40.

[44] ACS-O, 1001–49, Folder 10, "Nous avons tout mis en œuvre pour ne prêter aucune aide aux Allemands," 21 Dec. 1923; "Comparaison entre la conduite de Semet-Solvay et celle de Coppée," undated.

[45] For instance, Moureu (1920). For a broader context, see Galvez-Behar (2008), 283–6.

[46] ACS-O, 1106, Paris, Relations avec les administrations publiques et les particuliers, "Extrait de *L'Humanité* du 12 août 1917," 24 Aug. 1917. See also Daumalin, Lambert, and Mioche (2007), 40–1.

[47] Chauveau (2006), 22–3; Kuisel (1981), 31–58; see also Godfrey (1987) and the contributions in Fridenson (1992).

attention to the development of existing chemical industries. With plants in Dombasle and Salin-de-Giraud, Solvay did not miss the opportunity to contribute to this industrial drive. This was not as obvious as it may seem: successive mobilizations deprived both sites from important numbers of workers and engineers.[48] Moreover, Dombasle was particularly vulnerable; it was located just seventeen kilometers from the front line. The plant had been bombed five times in July 1917 but had reported no prolonged interruption. Shortly after the war, French president Raymond Poincaré awarded the personnel of the factory a national distinction of merit (*citation à l'ordre du jour*) "for the greatest services it rendered the country during the hostilities in carrying on its patriotic duty throughout the war and in spite of the most violent bombings it had to face."[49]

Solvay's products did not pertain to the category of chemical weapons, neither explosives nor propellants. But large amounts of caustic soda were needed in the manufacturing of phenol, which led to the production of melinite (picric acid), the French army's favorite gas weapon. Hence, the production of caustic soda (through causticization) was scaled up to an impressive extent (see Table 7.3): by 50 percent in Torrelavega, 100 percent in Dombasle, and 400 percent in Salin-de-Giraud (in 1916 and 1917). As a result, the wartime contribution of Solvay to the total needs for caustic soda charted by the French army's Service des Poudres is estimated at 75 percent.[50] Nevertheless, Dombasle and Giraud continued to provide basic alkali products (e.g., soda ash, crystal soda, refined salt) to their usual customers (e.g., the glass and soap industries). But they did so with an impressive productivity, one that yielded results close to, and sometimes greater than, prewar levels. By doing so, Solvay did more than merely maintain its presence on the French alkali market; it significantly improved its market shares, which had been determined by the soda convention signed in 1905 with Saint-Gobain and Marchéville-Daguin. Table 7.2 shows that Solvay's volume of production during the war was such that it not only took over the quotas lost by the two French companies; it was largely sufficient to be exported, and most notably to the plant of Rosignano, which needed soda ash because of the British blockade.

The winning position acquired by Solvay on the French alkali market did not hinder the renewal of the 1905 sodium carbonate-acids-fertilizers convention between Solvay and Saint-Gobain, which was to expire by the end of 1916 (see Chapter 3). This time, however, Saint-Gobain wanted the convention to be complemented by an option for the purchase of a license of the Castner-Kellner-Solvay process, limited to the production of ten tons of chlorine per

---

[48] At the Dombasle plant, 1673 workers and employees were sent to the front (more than 60 percent of the work force) and only 529 were allowed to return to the factory. See "Discours de M. Armand Solvay," 4; "L'usine de Dombasle," *La Revue Solvay*, 2/1983, 3. On Giraud, see Daumalin, Lambert, and Mioche (2007), 41–6.

[49] ACS, CdS, Minutes of the meetings, 19 Dec. 1917; ACS, RdG, 30 Dec. 1918.

[50] Moureu (1920), 26; ART, PDO, table 6. According to Daumalin, Lambert, and Mioche (2007), 42: "Solvay répond aux trois quarts de la consommation totale de soude caustique (300 tonnes jour pour 400 au total) de l'armée française entre 1915 et 1918."

TABLE 7.2. *Production of Soda Ash at Dombasle and Giraud: Deliveries in France by Solvay & Cie, Saint-Gobain, and Marchéville-Daguin, 1913–1919 (in tons, rounded figures)*

	1913	1914	1915	1916	1917	1918	1919
Production							
Dombasle	230,698	157,691	174,748	216,697	225,000	166,700	167,300
Giraud	47,500	41,220	35,790	46,496	52,545	37,150	18,136
TOTAL	278,198	198,911	210,538	263,193	277,545	203,850	185,436
Total	244,254	189,058	210,011	286,127	296,861	210,053	149,872
deliveries							
whence:							
Solvay & Cie	176,130	145,835	169,933	240,310	256,410	181,547	120,446
St.-Gobain	26,024	15,248	19,468	23,698	20,254	7,309	8,446
[Quota]	[25,824]	[23,489]	[29,303]	[35,699]	[38,155]	[28,977]	[25,798]
Marchéville	42,100	27,975	20,610	22,119	20,197	11,197	20,980
[Quota]	[41,962]	[31,626]	[34,517]	[47,834]	[49,415]	[32,677]	[23,699]

Note: The quota figures refer to the sales agreements of soda ash concluded between Solvay & Cie and French competitors.

Source: ACS-O, 1701, St.-Gobain, Folder 4 – Entrevues avec M. Mayoussier en 1920, "Décompte définitif des contingents de soude perdus par St-Gobain & Marchéville-Daguin pendant les années 1914 à 1919," 19 May 1920; ART, PDO, table 3.

day. The deal had been prepared by a longtime acquaintance of the *gérance*, Félix Mayoussier, head of Saint-Gobain's Commercial Division of chemical products since 1890.[51] On Solvay's side, Armand Solvay had seized the matter with Louis Talvard, acting director of the Paris office. "Since it is impossible to communicate with Brussels on a regular basis," deplored Armand Solvay, "and despite the reports received from the Gérance, I am forced to take up responsibilities."[52] The prolongation of the convention for another ten years was signed hastily, and Saint-Gobain never materialized its option, for which it had agreed to pay half a million francs. The difficulties of communication that had surrounded the whole issue led to diverging interpretations of the agreement between both firms after the war.

The Mediterranean Connection

In neutral Spain, as well as in Italy, subsidiaries of Solvay & Cie first seemed stranded after the Belgian and French engineers responded to the mobilization for their homelands. But soon enough they counterbalanced their dependence on foreign technology and the isolation of the Brussels *gérance* by a series

[51] Daviet (1988), 555–6.

[52] ACS-O, 1701, St.-Gobain, Folder 4 (esp. files "Entrevues avec M. Mayoussier en 1920" and "Note from M. Armand (29 Dec. 1915)") and ACS, Contracts, Saint-Gobain, Renouvellement des contrats avec la Société de Saint-Gobain, Communication from Mayou [Mayoussier] (14 Dec. 1915), Note from Talmans [Talvard] (6 Jan. 1916).

TABLE 7.3. *Production of Soda Ash and Caustic Soda – Dombasle, Giraud, Torrelavega, 1912–1919 (in tons, rounded figures)*

| | Soda Ash | | | | Caustic Soda | | | |
	Dombasle	Giraud	Torrelavega	Total	Dombasle	Giraud	Torrelavega	Total
1912	218,705	50,570	40,055	309,330	26,651	11,191	16,625	54,467
1913	230,698	47,500	39,560	317,758	24,461	12,343	16,220	53,024
1914	157,691	41,220	42,760	241,671	17,505	10,960	13,907	42,372
1915	174,748	35,790	52,100	262,638	31,475	20,489	19,451	71,415
1916	216,697	46,496	61,900	325,093	60,136	39,541	23,642	123,319
1917	225,000	52,545	51,800	329,345	51,008	40,742	18,622	110,372
1918	166,700	37,150	67,000	270,850	23,560	26,214	23,308	73,082
1919	167,300	18,136	46,755	232,191	13,717	11,037	19,779	44,533

Source: ART, PDO, tables 3 and 6.

of initiatives.[53] A key figure in this respect was the French engineer Georges Chardin, head of the company's Central Technical Department. Although he had been mobilized as a former captain of artillery, he was granted a special deferment of his military obligations at the request of Auguste Fade, plant manager of Salin-de-Giraud.[54] Chardin consequently ensured the liaison between the plants of Giraud, Rosignano, and Torrelavega, on the one hand, and between them and the *gérance*, on the other hand. But his action went beyond the role of intermediary in the Mediterranean region. Before the newly appointed manager Albert Gonod joined him in Italy in June 1916, Chardin set up a provisional plant of causticization at Rosignano intended for the manufacturing of explosives (with soda coming from Dombasle or Syracuse, New York). By the end of 1916, the production had already reached 531 tons, 481 tons of which were delivered to the Italian Ministry of Munitions. These figures are not taken into account in the production statistics of Solvay, as the plant was officially declared "auxiliary" to the military aims of the Italian government as soon as 15 December 1915, after the country left the Triple Alliance to join the Triple Entente.[55] In Spain, Chardin also played an important role in helping Léonard Alban, plant manager of Torrelavega, to tame a general strike that had arose in February and March 1917 after seven workers and the leader of the workers' union La Fraternidad had been expelled.[56] These incidents notwithstanding, both sites had proved their usefulness in a time of crisis. Accordingly, the *gérance* was aware that they were about to play a major role in the postwar development of Solvay.

---

[53] Celati and Gattini (1993), 27; Toca (2005), 179–80. According to Toca, the first Spanish engineer in Torrelavega was recruited in 1923.

[54] Daumalin, Lambert, and Mioche (2007), 39–40; Sougnez (1936), 11.

[55] Celati and Gattini (1993), 40–3.

[56] ACS, CdS, Minutes of the meetings, 4 Apr. 1917; Toca (2005), 185–6.

Innovation and Profits at Brunner, Mond

Across the Channel, the war transformed Brunner, Mond into an overwhelmingly flourishing and profitable business, whose domination in alkali products led them to further expansion. In 1916, they not only took over the small but annoying rival works of Ammonia Soda Company at Plumbey (which had found an outlet in Italy); they also decided to take a 25 percent interest in the Castner-Kellner Company.[57] Brunner's position was largely due to the bold choice made by Lord Moulton, head of the Committee for Explosive Services, to mix pure TNT with ammonium nitrate (amatol) in the manufacturing of high-explosive shells used by the British army. By November 1915 Moulton had charged Brunner, Mond with tackling this problem on an industrial scale. This they did both at their works at Lostock through a treatment with calcium nitrate and at their plant at Sandbach, by substituting sodium nitrate for salt in the ordinary ammonia-soda process, as well as by crystallization from a solution of sodium nitrate and ammonium phosphate. The latter process was an innovation resulting from in-house research and was fully exploited in the premises of Swindon from September 1917 onward. With all works and production processes combined, Brunner, Mond ensured the manufacture of no fewer than 216,120 tons of ammonium nitrate until the end of the war. With caustic soda made at Northwich and sulfonate at Lostock, synthetic phenol was also produced on an average of ten tons daily between July 1915 and January 1919.

The important supply in war-related products only complemented the more traditional products Brunner, Mond continued to manufacture. The company's output of alkali products rose in the first two years of the war, with impressive growth observed at Northwich, Middlewich, and Sandbach. Profits increased especially in 1917 and 1918, when overall war production was at its peak. The figure for 1918 was £1,112 million, 44.6 percent greater than that for 1914. British legislation had introduced special tax measures to counter these exceptional profits resulting from the war economy. Overall, as W. J. Reader put it, "it seems fair to assume . . . that demands arising directly from the war, as well as stimulating Brunner, Mond's technical ingenuity, also contributed quite handsomely to their prosperity, though exactly how handsomely it is not now possible to say."[58] Solvay shareholders, therefore, reaped the benefits of Brunner, Mond's wartime activities, as the dividend rate ranged between 25 percent in 1914 and 27.5 percent at the end of the war.[59] Moreover, Solvay could count on Brunner, Mond's support in the unexpected fight that both companies had to engage in with their American partner, the Solvay Process Company (SPC).

[57] This section draws largely on Reader (1970), 282–99, and Watts (1923), 52–67; see also Chapters 3 and 5.

[58] Reader (1970), 287.

[59] ACS, CdS, Minutes of the meetings, 4 Apr. 1917 and 19 Dec. 1917.

7.4 EUROPE AT WAR: THE EASTERN SIDE

What was the perspective on the other side of the front line, across the German border? Although the impression of "Germany's undisputed superiority"[60] is in fact nuanced, it goes without saying that the level of development reached by the German chemical industry on the eve of World War I was outstanding in terms of capital concentration, technological innovation, organizational capabilities, and research-and-development potential. Its Austrian counterpart was more modest in scope and contrasted with its lack of concentration.[61] Impressive as they were, and precisely because of their domination, the Central European empires had a lot to lose from the war. For matters of convenience, we include the Russian case in this chapter, although the Russian Empire was a founding member of the Triple Entente.

DSW in a Changing Environment

According to a historian of chemistry, "war is a technological forcing house."[62] True, the absence of imported Chilean nitrates as a result of the British blockade sparked one of the most important innovations during the war in Germany, namely the production of synthetic ammonia (or the Haber-Bosch process). However, this innovation reminds us that most of the German chemical manufacturers were largely dependent on foreign imports for the supply of raw materials and intermediates. By the same token, the dyestuffs industry's world leaders – Bayer, Höchst, BASF, and Agfa, to name but a few – were cut off from their international export market, which had accounted for 82 percent of their turnover in 1913.[63] This vulnerability was a source of unrest between the industry and the military administration of the Kaiserreich. In the chemical industry, the designated institution was Kriegschemikalien AG, established in September 1914 with the impetus of Walther Rathenau and Wichard von Moellendorff, both from AEG (Allgemeine Elektricitäts-Gesellschaft). In its campaign for industrial concentration, however, the state could rely on the previous patterns initiated by the industrialists themselves. As soon as 1905, a "little IG" (or "Dreibund") had been constituted as a profit-sharing agreement between Bayer, BASF, and Agfa. Later on, another bloc was formed in the dye industry among Höchst, Cassella, and Kalle – the so-called Drei(er)verband. Finally, with an eye on the postwar reconfiguration of the dye industries, these concentrations brought about the creation of an expanded IG in 1916, with all the former participants and a few smaller ones.[64] Therefore, it seems reasonable to concede to the Germans, and to a lesser extent, their Austrian neighbors, an initial advantage in comparison with the Allied chemical industry.[65]

---

[60] Aftalion (2001), 102.
[61] Johnson (2000); Johnson (2006), 2–4; Szöllösi-Janze (2000), 99–102.
[62] Haber (1971), 184.
[63] Plumpe (1990), 50–2, 69–82; Abelshauser, von Hippel, Johnson, and Stokes (2004), 151–7; Kobrak (2002), 60–6.
[64] Plumpe (1990), 45–9, 66–7, 96–106; Abelshauser et al. (2004), 127–34, 171–3.
[65] Johnson (2006), 15.

TABLE 7.4. *Production of Soda Ash – DSW, 1912–1919 (in tons, rounded figures)*

	Bernburg	Wyhlen	Rheinberg	Sarralbe	Ch-Salins	Montwy	Total
1912	150,400	41,660	31,945	85,000	20,070	32,726	361,801
1913	151,525	43,880	39,200	85,500	20,200	38,010	378,315
1914	150,780	41,095	40,518	61,117	12,080	22,756	328,346
1915	163,490	37,725	52,060	64,190	7,545	33,556	358,566
1916	192,500	42,625	62,420	71,204	17,255	37,012	423,016
1917	186,600	38,765	55,275	63,250	9,405	33,175	386,470
1918	174,400	30,990	53,935	56,105[a]	–[a]	26,188	341,618[a]
1919	134,950	12,696	42,885	31,330[a]	–[a]	–[a]	190,531[a]

[a] From 1918, Sarralbe and Château-Salins were transferred to Solvay & Cie (France), and Montwy joined the newly created society Zakłady Solvay w Polsce in 1920.
Source: ART, PDO, DSW.

Deutsche Solvay Werke (DSW) was estimated to provide up to three-quarters of the ammonia-based soda ash consumed in Germany, and it accounted "perhaps [for] one-half of the caustic soda" made in the Reich[66] – there is no doubt that it contributed to the overall war effort. The precise nature of its contribution, however, remains difficult to assess in the light of available evidence. Nor can we tackle, for the same reason, the issue of the relationships between DSW and Solvay during the war. As far as we know, continuity in governance persisted throughout. The composition of the *Vorstand* – Emil Gielen, Ernst Eilsberger, and Arnold Bongardt – remained untouched between 1909 and 1920. As to the *Aufsichtsrat*, it was still in the hands of the *gérance* – the only modifications were substitutions because of Georges Querton's death in 1914 and the departures of both Louis Semet (1909) and Fernand van der Straeten (1912). Despite the fact that Solvay was by far the main shareholder of the firm, the independent German legal status of DSW prevailed. As a result, the various plants it owned were not sequestered throughout the war, although they seemingly fell under the surveillance of a "high civil servant."[67] From the annual reports of activities the DSW administration in Bernburg compiled for the *gérance*, it appears that the bulk of its supplies in ammoniac from 1916 onward came from Kriegschemikalien AG, in Berlin.[68] The production of soda ash during the war shows a general trend of progress (see Table 7.4). The total output of DSW was more important than that of Solvay's – this had been the case since 1909 but was never to be reproduced after 1918 (except for a brief period during World War II). The production of caustic soda, however, was strained because of the increasing competition (and the corresponding economy of scale) exerted by the future IG Farben. At the plants of Würselen and Sarralbe (causticization), as well as at Osternienburg (causticization and electrolysis), the production levels – and the sales – dropped 10 percent each year between 1913 and 1919.[69]

[66] Haber (1971), 114; Aftalion (2001), 103.
[67] Sougnez (1936), 9.
[68] ACS, Administration Centrale Bernburg. Annual Report (1916), 10–2.
[69] ACS, Administration Centrale Bernburg. Annual Reports (1912–1919).

Another source of concern in the early stages of the war had been the huge shrinkage of potential outlets for the potash industry, over which the Germans had a monopoly. This, of course, affected DSW and its potash Solvayhall plant at Roschwitz near Bernburg. But after serious drops in 1914 and 1915, the decline proved milder than Brussels had expected. The bombing of Château-Salins on 24 July 1917, during which the plant was hit by 108 shells, was the only major destruction Solvay experienced during the war.[70] Overall, therefore, things had gone mostly smoothly in Germany. The sustained domestic demand for basic alkali products and electrolysis derivatives (e.g., calcium chloride, liquid chlorine, chloride of lime), which went on through the war despite the increase of prices,[71] yielded significant returns. Net annual profits fluctuated between DM 4.7 million and 6.4 million and proved more stable than the growth patterns of the firms that would constitute the future IG group.[72] From the point of view of production and financial results, DSW did not feel the burden of the Reich's defeat. It was the loss of its plants located in Alsace-Lorraine and Poland that brought it back to the reality of politics.

Challenges in Austria-Hungary

Postwar geopolitical transformations had even wider implications in crumbling Austria-Hungary, where Oesterreichische Solvay-Werke Betriebsgesellschaft mbH (OSW) organized its activities. Although the Vienna office of Solvay Werke was spared by the war, the eastern front line actually crossed the regions of the plants of Lukavac (northern Bosnia) and Podgórze (Galicia). The factories were not damaged but had to suspend production and could resume work only intermittently. In comparison, the rival Monfalcone found itself in the line of fire and was almost completely destroyed.[73] Solvay Werke also owned an electrolytic unit in Turda, close to its soda plant in Maros-Ujvar, in regions that still belonged to Hungary. It had been set up in 1912 from a former cellulose plant for the Hungarian government to facilitate the production of chlorine and to prevent the emergence of competition in the region. After parallel commercial arrangements, the *Vorstand* of OSW had planned a production capacity of 12,000 tons of chloride of lime and 6,000 tons of caustic soda, but the *gérance* had curbed this initial enthusiasm to 6,800 tons and 3,100 tons, respectively.[74] The plant, however, proved largely unsatisfactory. It gave way to important delays in the delivery of chloride of lime, which forced Verein Aussig to compensate. Difficulties in the supply of natural gas (methane) were first mentioned, but a team of technicians sent from Brussels shortly before the war broke out did not agree. During their visit, they recorded, "With the exception of three

[70] ACS, CdS, Minutes of the meetings, 10 Dec. 1915 and 19 Dec. 1917.
[71] ADSW, 594, "Rapport historique," 1919.
[72] ACS, Administration Centrale Bernburg, Yearly Reports (1912–1919); Plumpe (1990), 94–5.
[73] ACS, CdS, "Note sur la marche des usines," undated [Feb. 1915] and minutes of the meetings, 10 Dec. 1915.
[74] ACS-O, 1202, Roumanie, Turda, "Turda: historique de la fondation" (Note from Vienna, 13 May 1930) and "Turda" (note from the Secrétariat Général, 3 June 1930).

TABLE 7.5. *Production of Soda Ash – SW, 1912–1919 (in tons, rounded figures)*

	Ebensee	Maros-Ujvar	Nestomitz	Lukavac	Podgórze	Total
1912	28,690	21,884	27,287	22,030	21,406	121,297
1913	30,875	23,334	27,817	23,396	20,112	125,534
1914	27,451	27,388	28,947	16,072	4,893	104,751
1915	34,574	25,352	25,417	13,515	–	98,858
1916	36,401	24,629	28,432	19,639	14,277	123,378
1917	25,733	20,826	22,006	20,403	16,542	105,510
1918	13,769	17,619	10,635	7,685	9,599	59,307
1919	12,531	5,505	20,617	3,460	11,532	42,113

Source: ART, PDO, SW.

foremen who went to Jemeppe, no member of the current personnel has ever been in touch with electrolysis; hence, nobody seemed to be convinced that the meticulous attention to detail was the undisputable condition for success."[75] Later, as Aussig was increasing pressure, OSW sought comprehensive technical expertise to slowly overcome its problems.

In the face of these obstacles and the instability of the whole region, the production effort of OSW was of great importance during the war. The start and (especially) the end of the conflict had proved difficult for all its plants, but the situation had otherwise been under control. The works of Ebensee, Nestomitz, and Maros-Ujvar could make up for the sporadic failures at Turda and, to a lesser extent, at Lukavac and Podgórze.

The Loss of Lubimoff, Solvay & Cie

Further east, in Russia, the Bolshevik Revolution put an end to one of the fastest-growing and profitable enterprises of the Solvay Group. Lubimoff, Solvay & Cie had started from scratch in 1883 in a huge but underdeveloped market, which it was to dominate five years later for soda ash and eleven years later for caustic soda.[76] After the death of the main partner I. I. Lubimoff in 1899 and the settlement of a long struggle for his succession, Solvay owned exactly 71.3 percent of the company from 1907. When the war broke out, director Wladimir Orlow had left for Bavaria and reached Moscow only in December 1914. Shortly thereafter, he was struck by a cerebral hemorrhage that considerably weakened his condition and prevented him from working as he had previously.[77] The technical director Sigismond Toeplitz assumed the transition and became the de facto executive director of the company. With the help of French engineer Émile Devien, who was transferred from Berezniki

---

[75] ART, Turda, Instructions & Contrôle, Fabrication, Notes et Rapports – 1914, "Rapport sur la situation actuelle de l'usine de Torda, 5–10 juin 1914," by R. Lucion and L. Clément, 16 June 1914.

[76] ACS-O, 1225, Lubimoff, Société Lubimoff Solvay & Cie, Tableaux statistiques de la production et de la vente des marchandises, 1 Aug. 1930, tables 7 and 16.

[77] Accarain (2002), 82, 92–3.

TABLE 7.6. *Production of Caustic Soda – SW, 1912–1919 (in tons,*
rounded figures)

	Podgórze	Maros-Ujvar	Lukavac	Nestomitz	Torda	Total
1912	3,220	3,160	3,072	93	0	9,545
1913	3,618	3,662	3,154	3,312	113	13,859
1914	2,331	4,178	3,144	5,059	1,281	15,993
1915	704	3,458	1,814	4,314	1,747	12,037
1916	2,902	3,271	3,157	3,983	2,016	15,329
1917	2,285	3,832	3,371	–	1,804	11,292
1918	1,627	4,869	2,730	–	1,310	10,536
1919	1,874	3,169	560	1,709	176	7,488

Source: ART, PDO, SW.

to the Donetz plant in 1916, he attempted to adapt the production organization to wartime conditions. The output of caustic soda (both processes) increased slightly from 1914 to 1916, yielding approximately 26,000 tons per year at Donetz (4,000 tons from the electrolytic plant) and 15,000 tons per year at Berezniki. The production of soda ash, however, mildly declined from the (substantial) prewar levels, largely because of technical hindrances. At the Donetz plant, the production of soda bicarbonate increased from 5,000 tons in 1913 to 7,736 tons in 1916, when it represented 12 percent of the total sales of the company. This was not too bad, taking into account the increasing competition that Lubimoff, Solvay had to face in the empire, notably the chemical firms of the Dynamite Nobel group.[78]

Besides business as usual, a remarkable drive for the production of chemicals to be used in the war took place in Russia after a brief phase of inertia. Just like in France and Germany, the wartime combination of scientists, industry, and the military was seized as an opportunity to make the country's chemical industry less dependent on foreign suppliers.[79] However, contrary to France, in Russia it was judged preferable to organize the production in existing factories rather than to build new plants. General Vladimir N. Ipatiev, professor of organic chemistry at the Artillery Academy of St. Petersburg, was the initiator of this strategy. He was well known to both scientists and industrialists in and outside his country.[80] But Ipatiev was also instrumental in 1917 in helping building near the Donetz electrolytic works a pilot plant of products aimed at chemical warfare: picric acid, chlorine, and a small amount of phosgene (see Table 7.7).[81] This was the only time a Solvay-related planted produced chemical gas during the war.

---

[78] ACS-O, 1225, Lubimoff, Société Lubimoff Solvay & Cie, Tableaux statistiques, tables 1, 9, 21 and 32; ACS, CdS, "Note sur la marche des usines," undated [Feb. 1915].

[79] Brooks (2006), 79.

[80] In April 1915, the research director at Coppée, Gustave Brichant, met Ipatiev to discuss a contract to supply benzene, toluene, and xylene (ACS-O, 1272, Semet Solvay, File 2, Olivier Piette to Emmanuel Janssen, 20 June 1924).

[81] Accarain (2002), 224–7; Brooks (2006), 86, 93.

TABLE 7.7. *Production of Picric Acid, Chlorine, and Phosgene at Donetz, 1915–1917 (in tons converted from pouds, rounded figures)*

	1915	1916	1917
Picric Acid	318	1,578	1,375
Chlorine	171	1,713	1,327
Phosgene	–	–	36

Source: ACS-O, 1225, Lubimoff, Société Lubimoff Solvay & Cie, Tableaux statistiques, table 33.

In the first days of the October Revolution, workers seized the Berezniki plant. Admiral Koltchak's counterrevolutionary army followed in 1918, and the plant was eventually reoccupied by the Bolsheviks at the end of 1919. The situation at Donetz was even more confused: the plant was successively occupied by the Bolsheviks between January and April 1918, then by the Germans, the (independent) Ukrainian troops of Symon Petliura, the Ukrainian troops of Anton Denikine, and ultimately the Bolshevik troops again in December 1919.[82]

7.5   THE DECLARATION OF INDEPENDENCE OF SOLVAY PROCESS COMPANY

Growing Apart

When the war broke out, Solvay urged the Solvay Process Company to supplement the supply of alkali products to France, Italy, and the Netherlands, which had traditionally pertained to its market. Evidently, Solvay feared that the occupation of Belgium would be an opportunity that competitors (or even governments) would seize to supersede it in Continental Europe.[83] As a result, production ran at full scale, and output figures soared between 1914 and 1917: SPC almost doubled its production of soda ash and calcium chloride (liquid and solid), tripled its output of caustic soda, and increased by 40 percent its production of sodium bicarbonate.[84] This was largely good news for SPC, as its domestic market shares had been stagnating around 60 percent for some years because of the presence of a new wave of competitors in the soda business (see Chapters 3 and 5).

More than its industrial strategy, though, it was the attitude of SPC that irritated Brussels. By early summer in 1914, Solvay, with Brunner, Mond's blessing, sparked what the American associates later referred to as "the French Revolution," which mainly consisted of getting rid of the Semet-Solvay Company (SSC) shares owned by SPC and strictly separating their activities so that SPC and SSC were transformed into two independent companies. The reorganization also entailed changes in management: Henry Handy, head of SSC, was

---

[82] Accarain (2002), 26, 106, 128–9.
[83] ACS, CdS, Minutes of the meetings, 10 Dec. 1915.
[84] ART, PDO, SPC.

FIGURE 7.2. Solvay Process Company top executives and board members a few years before World War I. (*left to right*) John M. Wing, J. W. Smith, Rowland G. Hazard (vice president), John D. Pennog (in the back), Fred Hazard (president), William B. Cogswell (vice president), unidentified (in the back), Edward N. Trump (general manager), and Andrew H. Green. (Solvay Archives.)

pushed out of the SPC board, and the Hazard brothers were friendly but firmly reprimanded.[85] These decisions hurt many feelings on the American side. With the outbreak of the war, Handy and other dissidents, frustrated by what they deemed an intrusion of European shareholders in their expanding business, did not wait too long to ignite a counterrevolution.

A first signal was given by a circular dispatched by SPC on 28 October 1915. Shareholders were asked to mark their agreement regarding the complete purchase of the assets of the Federal Furnace Co. (Chicago) by the By-Products Coke Corporation, a holding controlled by SPC since 1902, when the company started its vertical integration. An increase of authorized capital from US$5 million to US$10 million was called on in this respect by the Hazard brothers.[86] The underlying idea was to pursue the process of vertical integration that SPC had started several years earlier, aiming to control the market from coal recuperation to steel manufacturing. Solvay, needless to say, was dubious about the move, which it considered remote from its core activities ("Are they planning to build additional plants in the metallurgy branch with coke ovens?" asked a

[85] ACS-O, 1271, 3B; Reader (1970), 292.
[86] ACS-O, 1271, 4A, Enclosed circular in Van den Branden (Rotterdam) to gérance (Brussels), 17 Nov. 1915.

baffled *gérance*). But Solvay was especially reluctant about the suggested amount of the authorized capital increase. The deal could be solved, they argued, with a contribution of US$235,000 after the exchange of shares; there was thus no reason to double authorized capital.[87] Whatever the reservations expressed by Solvay, Fred Hazard considered the operation "not only logical but absolutely necessary" for the growth of the By-Products Coke Corporation, and he went ahead with the approbation of other shareholders. To him, the merger was just the appetizer of a multicourse meal.

The Revolt against European Shareholders

At the same time (October 1915), in the midst of growing communications problems, SPC suggested a new incorporation for SSC. Giving as a pretext the modification of the corporation legislation regime, Hazard proposed raising the capital of SSC from US$4 million to US$10 million. From that amount, only US$2 million (twenty thousand shares) had to result from an issue of stock, the bulk of the operation consisting of a mere accounting transfer (from the old to the new SSC). Still, from a mere financial standpoint, it yielded a profit of US$4 million, as each stock issued was sold at 200 percent of the old shares' face value. Despite Solvay's protest, Hazard's statement was obvious: "the increase has been approved and will be executed accordingly."[88] More than the nature of the decision, the tone and the mechanisms of the operation were appalling to the *gérance*. The management of SPC had not only justified the increase by an expansion of the demand and the need for fresh capital; they also claimed that their exceptional business growth had suffered from the exceptional deliveries made to Europe. "The American shareholders," explained Fred Hazard at the meeting of SPC's General Assembly of 1916, "could blame us" for supplying the European continent at war because it "has prevented us from adopt[ing] an aggressive policy" in the American soda business.[89]

Since the "French Revolution" of 1914, it seemed odd that Hazard discussed so enthusiastically an issue that concerned the sole development of SSC. Sticking apparently to the terms of the revolution, the SPC board had decided in June 1916 not to subscribe to the capital increase. But herein was the underlying idea of the combination: preventing Solvay (and Brunner, Mond) from further intruding in the course of action of SPC and transferring part of the ownership to SSC, which was not controlled by European shareholders. The financial arrangement consisted of three steps, which were, in the terms of the *gérance*, "a bit weird, one must confess."[90] According to Brussels, the wild capital increase seemed like a conspiracy orchestrated by Handy and others to

[87] ACS-O, 1271, 1B, RH 33, Memo SPC – By-Products C.C. (Fusion de la BPCC avec la FFC), undated [1916]; ACS-O, 1271, 4A, Gérance to Van de Branden, 27 Nov. 1915.

[88] ACS-O, 1271, 4A, F. Hazard to Van den Branden, 28 Dec. 1915.

[89] ACS-O, 1271, 4A, Memorandum by F. Hazard, General Assembly meeting, 30 Aug. 1916.

[90] ACS-O, 1271, 3B, R.H. 0 and R.H. 2, Notes Capital increases SPC, undated [1912]; ACS-O, 1271, 4D, Notes Sougnez, SPC 1916 capital increase, 19 Oct. 1916.

diminish the influence of Solvay and Brunner, Mond.[91] Even after the transaction, however, the former still owned 62,500 shares (of 167,390) of SPC
(37.6 percent) and the latter held 23,886 shares (14.3 percent). Their loss was
thus 4.3 percent and 1.6 percent, respectively.[92] From Biarritz, Armand Solvay,
probably informed by Edgar Hulin, was particularly irritated that the shares
issued had not transited by an ordinary rights issue to existing shareholders, in
conformity with the disposals of the 1881 convention between Solvay and SPC
regarding shareholders' preemption. In a letter to Brunner, Mond in which he
pressed the idea of an allied opposition, Armand expressed his bitterness: "there
is no doubt that the board of SPC is trying to free itself from all European influence.... I believe that it is trying to profit by our difficulties ... to seize upon a
large part of the world's market."[93] Ironically, Solvay had precisely turned to
SPC during the war to preserve its trade, not to overturn it. Brunner, Mond,
however, had as much to lose as Solvay in terms of commercial distribution
from an unbound SPC.[94]

Until the end of the war, despite the difficult circumstances of the war,
Solvay and Brunner, Mond struggled to come back to the status quo ex ante.
The fight was essentially fought on legal grounds, but there some unexpected
events occurred. The deaths of Fred Hazard (27 February 1917) and his brother
Rowland (23 January 1918) triggered an attempt to bring together the American shareholders' voting power – the Hazard voting trust – whenever they had
to cast their vote. This proved a counterproductive measure: some shareholders
expressed their mistrust in this voting system, and their withdrawal contributed
to its failure. When the war ended, after some concerns with the US Alien Property Custodian had been cleared up thanks to the effective intercession of the
Belgian minister of foreign affairs, Paul Hymans, the legal advisers of Solvay
urged Solvay and Brunner, Mond to reach a compromise with SPC and avoid
a lasting legal procedure. An agreement followed suit whereby SSC handed
over to Solvay and Brunner, Mond some 10,000 shares of the 17,390 it had
obtained in 1916. A modification of the constitution of SPC was also made
to avoid repeating the issue of stock.[95] The underlying objective was to not
impede the spectacular growth of SPC, which had brought its shareholders
considerable profits (net profits soared from US$1.8 million in 1914 to US$8.9
million the following year and to US$8.2 million in 1916).[96]

Thus, the situation Solvay faced eventually turned out to its advantage.
However, the atmosphere was then thick with mutual suspicion. The financial
engineering of the Hazard brothers with the complicity of SSC's upper management prefigured the transformation of the landscape of the chemical industry
after the war. As soon as December 1915, Armand Solvay had expressed his
fears: "I am still haunted by the complications which might affect our whole
business after the war and the importance we therefore should have to always

[91] ACS-O, 1271, 4A, Service financier 33–36, Gérance to Van den Branden, 11 Nov. 1916.
[92] ACS-O, 1271, 4A, Service financier 33–36, Armand Solvay to Brunner, Mond, 7 Nov. 1917.
[93] Quoted in Reader (1970), 292.
[94] ACS-O, 1271, 4D, SPC – Création d'une usine au Canada, undated [1917].
[95] Reader (1970), 293.
[96] ACS, CdS, Meetings of the fiscal years 1915–1917.

assure an agreement in a country where our interests are so substantial."[97] The intuition applied originally for France, but it was true more generally as well. For Solvay, the end of the war gave way to unexpected worries. Whereas the worst predictions had concentrated on its plants in northwestern Europe in the summer of 1914, Cassandra's pupils proved wrong. Despite the painful occupation of Belgium and the inevitable loss of Russia, the company came out of the war safe and sound. The United States, on the contrary, had been eager to help launch the offensive against the Central European empires in the first months of the war but had showed signs of nationalism. Everywhere else, uncertainty and pessimism dominated.

[97] ACS-O, 1701, St.-Gobain, 4 – Entrevues avec M. Mayoussier en 1920, Note from M. Armand, 29 Dec. 1915.

FIGURE 8.1. Solvay executives visiting the Wieliczka salt mine, near Krakow, Poland (1921). In front row (*from left*), the *gérants* Émile Tournay and Louis Solvay. Next to them is Sigismond Toeplitz, head of the Zakłady Solvay. (Solvay Archives.)

8

From the Ashes, 1918–1922

Looking with hindsight on the immediate postwar years, one is struck by the sharp contrast between the promising prospects of the future and the everlasting burden of the past. World War I had created a new stage in the history of mankind. It had mobilized sixty-five million men across continents, had killed more than eight million, wounded another twenty-one million, and transformed those remaining into survivors.[1] Europe was especially affected. Nowhere else did the feelings of despair and disillusion grow so wild. They would soon be converted by revolutionary pushes from the Left (as in Russia, Finland, and Germany) or by reactions of order and authority embodied by forces of the Right (Admiral Horty's anticommunist and antidemocratic regime in Hungary paved the way for many similar experiments). In large parts of Europe, stretching from Finland and Lithuania to Greece and Turkey, there was actually a prolongation of the war. Extreme ideological movements followed on each other with rapid pace. In Italy, the revolutionary red wave of the years 1919 and 1920 (*biennio rosso*) gave way to the nascent years of Mussolini's fascism (*biennio nero*, 1921–1922). In countries where democracy was not challenged, political and social measures were taken to harness the possible upsurge of revolts. Quite aptly, the Czech politician Tomas Masaryk described postwar Europe as "a laboratory atop a graveyard."[2]

In this context of instability, the *gérance* was determined to examine the most important questions concerning the future development of the company. Among them was the position of Solvay in the current international chemical industry. The occupation of Belgium had impeded upper management from keeping up with competitors. Also, the world chemical landscape was being transformed at rapid pace. Initial stagnation gave way to quick recovery. Industrial concerns were emerging, especially in the United States, but many uncertainties remained as to the fate of the former chemical power – Germany. How, then, could Solvay narrow the competitive gap it was threatened to face worldwide? Chapter 9 covers the challenges posed by the upcoming of giant chemical companies. This chapter, in contrast, examines how Solvay responded to two major outcomes of the war: nationalist streams and aspirations for social justice.

---

[1] Audoin-Rouzeau and Prochasson (2008), 13–19.
[2] Quoted in Mazower (1999), ix–x.

8.1   THE REORDERING OF EUROPE

Instability and *nationalism* were key words of the period. The consecutive collapse of the autocratic empires of Romanov Russia, Habsburg Austria-Hungary, Hohenzollern Germany, and Ottoman Turkey led to a huge makeover of Europe's map. Through various treaties that espoused US President Wilson's claim that international peace could be achieved through self-determination, a series of successor states emerged from the imperial ashes. Fueled with nationalism, they were wary of anything that resembled multinational companies, such as Solvay. Although they could not proceed to forced nationalization, they resorted to the available soft tools of state bureaucracy – higher fiscal burden, protectionist measures, ad hoc legislations, paperwork controls – as a way of legitimizing their existence. As a matter of fact, the war economy had clearly paved the way for state intervention in all belligerent countries in Europe, winners and losers.

Solvay was far from unaware of the ongoing geopolitical transformation that swept over Europe. At a meeting of the supervisory board held just one month after the signing of the Armistice, Paul Misonne summed up the situation:

> The profound modifications resulting from the war for some countries will have obvious repercussions for some of our subsidiaries [*filiales*]. For the DSW plants, Saaralbe and Château-Salins should be removed; on the other hand, Würselen and Rheinberg are located in the occupied zone by the Allied army in Germany. We cannot anticipate whether and to what extent they could continue their activities. The plant of Hohensalza, of which DSW owns almost all the shares, and that of Podgórze, owned by the Austrian Solvay-Werke, will undoubtedly join the independent Poland. In Austria, the plant of Nestomitz is located in the Czech Republic, that of Lukavac will probably be tied up to Serbia, and finally the works of Maros-Ujvar and Turda should be part of Romania. It is impossible to tell you at the present time what we or our subsidiaries [*filiales*] are going to do; we have to wait until the definitive constitution of all these new States.... But it goes without saying that 1918 as well as the following year will be deeply influenced by the upheaval we have witnessed.[3]

Details notwithstanding, this description corresponded to redrawing of borders that took place in the following years. In fact, with the exception of Ebensee, all the plants Solvay owned in the Habsburg Empire were affected by the Treaty of Saint-Germain-en-Laye (September 1919) and confirmed by the Treaty of Trianon (June 1920). If Solvay had factories in six countries in Continental Europe in 1914 (including Austria-Hungary), that number doubled in the 1920s.[4] This surely demanded loads of energy and diplomatic skills in the art of legal engineering. For what could be obvious for Solvay was by no means as clear to its fellow associates. Deutsche Solvay Werke and Oesterreichische Solvay-Werke believed that they were actually losing plants – which they did to a large extent.

---

[3] ACS, CdS, 11 Dec. 1918.
[4] Haber (1971), 325; Bolle (1963), 120–1, map.

Germany, from Defeat to Confusion

"The real problem with the Versailles Treaty," argues historian Niall Ferguson, "was not that it was too harsh, but that the Allies failed to enforce it."[5] The provisions of the Versailles Peace Treaty, signed in June 1919 and considered by the Germans as a *Diktat*, stipulated not only important losses of territory but also economic sanctions. There were two sets of economic pressures. First, the German industry was subject to Allied restrictions, particularly in terms of reparations, some of which were paid in chemicals. The other set of economic constraints was not per se the offspring of the Versailles Treaty but the attitude of Allied governments and companies in implementing policies, which promoted domestic industry at the expense of the German chemical industry (e.g., property seizures, technical missions, patents infringements).[6] Solvay exerted the first pressures directly and relied on its English and American associates for the second. The latter concerned especially the outcomes of the Haber-Bosch ammonia-soda process for which "inspection missions" had been organized as a way to spur creative inspiration, as is seen in Chapter 9.[7]

The relation of Solvay with DSW, however, was more complex. On the one hand, the *gérance* had to prove to the administration of the Reparations Commission that DSW plants were actually controlled to a large extent by Belgian capital; on the other hand, it had to avoid to overly increasing the burden on the *Vorstand*'s shoulders. The fact that French and Belgian political delegations claimed the highest amounts of reparations surely did not help. As Belgian-German relations reached their nadir, the only viable strategy for the *gérance* was to place all its confidence in the managers and workers of DSW. That is exactly what Emmanuel Janssen and Louis Solvay did when they visited Würselen and Rheinberg in late December 1918, just after it was taken over by Belgian troops. In agreement with French colonel Louis Audibert, they insisted on carrying on production despite the meager supplies of raw materials and the difficulties of transportation.[8] But everything was pending until the decisions of the great powers were known. Hence the first meeting between the *gérance* and the *Vorstand* of DSW took place at Krefeld (sixteen kilometers south of Rheinberg) on 8 July 1919, ten days after the signing of the Versailles Treaty. It focused, among other issues, on the conditions of the transfer of Sarralbe and Château-Salins to France, as well as on that of Hohensalza/Montwy to Poland.[9] These questions crystallized the issues at stake. Business interests, military purposes, and political agendas were overlapping.

Before the provisions of the peace treaty were made public, Solvay thought it could avert the sequestration of Sarralbe and Château-Salins. In a letter to the minister of foreign affairs, Paul Hymans, the *gérance* urged the Belgian government to "preserve from all harsh measures a group of plants represented

[5] Ferguson (2002), 106.
[6] Steen (2000), 324.
[7] For a general picture, see Johnson and MacLeod (2006), 223–7.
[8] ACS, RdG, 30 Dec. 1918.
[9] ACS, 1542–1-1A, Notes, Voyage à Crefeld, 8 July 1919; ACS, CdS, Report of the gérance, 25 July 1919.

by Belgian capital, run by Belgians, and which, all in all, constitutes a part of our national heritage beyond our borders."[10] That DSW was financially controlled by Solvay was irrefutable: since the General Assembly meetings of 6 May and 5 October 1904, Solvay had owned 94 percent of the capital, whereas Brunner, Mond held 4 percent. The remaining 2 percent was broken down as follows: Carl Wessel and his legacy owned 480 shares (1.2 percent), and the former director Eugen Frey had 160 shares, as did the widow of Joseph Masson.[11] Nevertheless, article 297 of the Versailles Treaty stipulated that "the Allied and Associated Powers reserve the right to retain and liquidate all property, rights and interests belonging at the date of the coming into force of the present Treaty to German nationals."[12] Because Eugen Frey was of Swiss origin and Masson's widow of Belgian nationality, DSW was thus "German," though for a mere 1.2 percent.

Despite the argument, the French government was not disposed to waive Solvay from the obligation to liquidate Sarralbe and Château-Salins. As a way to anticipate litigation, the *gérance* proposed to cope itself with the sequestration, but suggested also plant manager of Dombasle Albert Tasté or plant manager of Sarralbe André Cattenoz. The latter was finally selected. A former engineer at Dombasle, Cattenoz was perceived by the *gérance* as "a fine albeit not very energetic" personality.[13] In fact, he had been considered by the French administration because of his French nationality. Ironically, the same nationalist feelings would apply for the plants of Sarralbe and Château-Salins: the *commissaire* of the French Republic at Strasbourg (and future president of the republic), Alexandre Millerand, demanded that they adopt the French status and refused to adopt the German currency as a guarantee for the liquidation.[14] In spite of the importance of Solvay plants in the French chemical industry and the role of the company in supplying caustic soda to the French army during the war, the authorities valued the transfer for an amount estimated at DM 73,920.[15] The *gérants* were unanimously furious.

This prompted them to call for the assistance of the Belgian minister of economic affairs, Henri Jaspar, who had favorably followed the role of Solvay in the wartime relief programs. Arguing that DSW was "not strictly speaking a German company," the *gérance* sought for diplomatic arbitration.[16] Through

---

[10] ANOH, Folder "Visite de M. Louis Solvay au Ministre de Serbie (Paris)," Gérance to Paul Hymans, 11 Dec. 1918.

[11] ACS, DSW, Rapport général, Historique du capital, table 4; ACS-O, 1101, Folder "Séquestre Sarralbe et Château-Salins," Document No. 32, undated.

[12] http://www.firstworldwar.com/source/versailles264–312.htm (accessed 18 Oct. 2009).

[13] ACS, RdG, 30 Dec. 1918.

[14] ACS-O, 1101, Folder "Séquestre Sarralbe et Château-Salins," Document No. 16, Cattenoz to the gérance, 10 Oct. 1919.

[15] The calculation was the following: Wessel's participation was of DM 480,000 DM (480 shares at DM 1,000) and the plants of Sarralbe and Château-Salins contributed approximately 7 percent of the overall weight of DSW. The market value of DSW shares was estimated at 220 percent of their nominal value (ACS-O, 1101, Folder "Séquestre Sarralbe et Château-Salins," Document No. 26, gérance to Cattenoz, 5 Nov. 1919).

[16] ACS-O, 1101, Folder "Séquestre Sarralbe et Château-Salins," Document No. 33, gérance to Henri Jaspar, 14 Nov. 1919.

Jaspar, other key experts of the Belgian delegation at the Reparations Commission were asked for mediation. George Theunis, the rising star in the management of public and private affairs, was the most active among them. A close collaborator of Jaspar, Theunis was also known to Emmanuel Janssen, who he had met when responsible for the London-based Belgian Commission for Supplies during the war.[17] When Janssen visited Theunis in his Paris office to report on the sequestration, Theunis was convinced that "personal intervention rather than purely administrative involvement" would bring the whole issue to an end.[18] His assumption proved right. After Theunis asked Gaston Gourdeau, his acquaintance and high civil servant in the Ministry of Commerce and Industry, to contact his best friend Édouard Estaunié, who was president of the Higher Committee for the Liquidation of Sequestrated Goods, the matter was solved – at least diplomatically. Of course, it took more than a year to sort things out in terms of administration and legal issues (the authenticated deed of the transfer was signed on 20 January 1921). On the whole, the transfer question had brought out three important points: first, nothing ought to be taken for granted; second, Solvay had to make extensive use of its networks of industrialists, academics, and officials around the world; third, the multinational company had to face the unforeseen implications of sharp nationalism. "In spite of what we did for France during the war," lamented the *gérance*, "let us never forget that we are [treated as] foreigners and, more than that, foreigners owning and running a web of international plants."[19]

For DSW, whatever the fate of its "lost plants," the situation was grim.[20] All factories ran out of combustible and of feedstocks. From July 1919 until January 1921, Wyhlen had to cease its production because of the lack of coal. The Versailles Treaty forbade Bernburg, Wyhlen, and every plant to the east of the Rhine to export their production. "It seems we should work something out with the Germans," wrote the *gérance*, bemused. "Their sales price is fifty percent cheaper than ours."[21] Anyway, the protective tariffs raised by Allied countries made it almost impossible for German firms to get the funds needed to ensure reparations payments. Depending exclusively on the unstable domestic consumption, sales fluctuated. During the occupation of the Ruhr area by the French and Belgian armies in 1923, the production of Rheinberg was reduced by 50 percent and by 75 percent at Würselen.[22] At a meeting at Basel, Emil Gielen and Ernst Eilsberger reminded Emmanuel Janssen that they expected the Belgians to put an end to their pressure in the Ruhr area. They also complained about the unfair competition made by United Alkali Co., which exported to

---

[17] Depoortere (1996), 574–6; see also Tilman (2006), 234–6.

[18] ACS-O, 1101, Folder "Séquestre Sarralbe et Château-Salins," Document Nos. 43–44, Visit to M. Theunis – Visit to M. Goudeau, 2 Dec. 1919.

[19] ACS, CdS, Report of the gérance, 18 Jan. 1923.

[20] Unless otherwise noted, data are compiled from the yearly *Report Activities* provided by the central administration at Bernburg (1919–1925).

[21] ACS, CdG, 7 July 1921.

[22] It should be borne in mind that the west bank of the Rhine was under military occupation starting in December 1918. Belgian troops occupied Rheinberg and Würselen until February 1926. Rupprecht (2007), 47–52.

Germany at relatively low prices. Last but not least, the hyperinflation that affected the Weimar Republic in 1923 was such that DSW recorded a seventeen-digit turnover for that year. By January 1923, Solvay decided to take over the reparations costs of the mining pits of Borth and Wallach and to provide DSW monthly allowances of DM 1 billion (raised to DM 4 billion in May and DM 10 billion in July). But this was worthless. Louis Huaux observed that these payments lost half their worth by the time they reached Bernburg, eight days later. "Our current policy is to save our [German] plants from a catastrophe," warned the _gérants_ to their silent partners.[23]

This account could give the impression that DSW depended on aid from Solvay for its survival. But this interpretation is to be nuanced. First, the financial stability of DSW had been confirmed through two operations of capital increase (19 September 1922 and 9 November 1922), which raised the capital from DM 120 million to DM 500 million. After the period of currency depreciation and suppression of the _Papiermark_, the sum was reevaluated at 75 million _Reichsmark_ (in parity with the _Goldmark_). As a token of confidence and recognition, members of the _Vorstand_ had been allowed to subscribe. The "German" part of DSW accounted thus for 1.84 percent. Second, except for some years largely depending on the political context (1919–1920 at Bernburg, Wyhlen, and Osternienburg; 1923 at Würselen and Rheinberg), the production always reached, or even exceeded, its prewar levels.[24] Third, Solvay intended to have an active role in the reorganization of the German chemical industry in the 1920s as part of its wider international objectives. DSW was expected to become the bridgehead of this strategy. The year 1924 was a fresh start in this respect.

Solvay-Werke after Austria-Hungary

The creation in 1908 of the central, Vienna-based Österreichische Solvay-Werke Betriebsgesellschaft mbH, resulting from the merger of the silent partnership Oesterreichischer Verein für Chemische & Metallurgische Produktion AG (Aussig)–Solvay with the Erste Bosnische Ammoniaksoda-Fabrik AG Lukavac, was a fine work of institutional and financial engineering. But it was nonetheless a suitable configuration in comparison with the Kafkaesque reorganization process that took place after the war. The Habsburg monarchs had adopted the strategy of playing one ethnic group against another as a way to consolidate their authority, but this had the unexpected outcome of accelerating the pace of the empire's disintegration along "national" lines.[25] In view of the creation of four successor states, which included six plants, the _gérance_ wondered right away whether it was still relevant to maintain the framework

---

[23] ADSW, Archiv I, 526, E. Eislberger to Solvay & Cie, 7 Nov. and 3 Dec. 1923; ACS, CdS, Report of the gérance, 5 Dec. 1923; ACS, CdG, 16 Feb., 27 April, 4 May, 27 July, and 10 Aug. 1923.

[24] ACS, DSW, Rapport général, Historique du capital, tables 5–6. For the production data, see ibid., Usines et mines, passim.

[25] See Taylor (1961).

of the Solvay-Werke holding. That issue would pop up on and off at the top of agendas until 1925.[26] In the meantime, a mapping effort was needed to grasp the situation. By the end of 1918, instability still prevailed. The impression was that Maros-Ujvar and Turda would no longer belong to Hungary, nor to the Ungarische Solvay-Werke for that matter; that Lukavac would join Great Serbia; and that Podgórze (Erste Galizistiche Ammoniaksoda-Fabrik AG) would form an independent Polish group with the plant of Montwy-Hohensalza, 97.6 percent of which was owned by DSW (Steinsalz- und Sodawerke GmbH).

The difficulty of the whole operation came up against a paradox: on the one hand, there seemed to be no single solution, given the variety of national interests at stake; on the other hand, some uniformity had to be provided, as the ghost of the Austrian empire still haunted these regions, and the partners. When they visited Serbia in July 1919, Louis Solvay and Émile Tournay had to slalom between industrialists and financiers, officials and jurists, finally realizing that they were confronting contradictory judgments. Backed with diplomatic assistance, they still had to wait until June 1920 to buy from the Verkehrsbank (former Hungarian bank) the final shares of Lukavac to own it entirely with the Verein.[27] The situation was not any clearer in Romania, whose troops were busy marching in Transylvania, where two Solvay plants were located. To get some information, the *gérance* relied on the former representative of the Commission for Relief in Belgium in Brussels, Fernand Baetens, who had been mandated by the Société Générale to investigate its subsidiaries. By March 1920, Turda and Ocna-Muresului had both been transformed into a single national Romanian company, Uzinele Solvay din Transylvania, in which Solvay and Verein had equal shares. However, the new Romanian administration had demanded 12 percent of the capital, as well as the integration of Romanians into the board. In the following years, the increasing nationalist pressures in Romania would become difficult to cope with.[28] Further north, Poland faced a political turmoil. The fears of a civil war between the fractions belonging previously to Russia, Germany, and Galicia were provisionally overcome by the patriotic drive inspired by Marshal Piłsudski and the "wars of federation" he waged against Lithuania and Bolshevist Russia.[29] But quite extraordinarily, the situation appeared more stable there. This was partly because of the transfer of DSW shares in Montwy/Hohensalza to Solvay, shortly before the same applied for Sarralbe and Château-Salins (20 December 1920), but it was also the result of the people involved. As it happened, Zakłady Solvay w Polsce, set up on 19 May 1921, was largely managed by a network of directors and engineers

---

[26] For instance, ACS, RdG, 3 June 1919; ACS, CdG, 27 Apr. 1921; ACS, Vienna, 1184-37-3A, Minutes of the meeting in Vienna, 28 May 1923.

[27] ANOH, Folder "Voyage à Belgrade de MM. L. Solvay et Tournay, juillet 1919," passim; ANOH Lukavac, Folder "Politique industrielle," Note sur l'industrie de la soude en Yougoslavie (remise par Mr. Delcoigne, Ministre de Belgique, à M. Nuitchitch, Ministre du Commerce, 11 June 1920); ACS, RdG, 18 July 1920; ACS, 1201-1-1A, Folder "Historique de la fondation de l'usine de Turda," 3 June 1930.

[28] ACS, RdG, 4 Apr. 1919; ACS, CdG, 25 May 1923.

[29] Snyder (2003), 57–65.

who had formerly been active at the Donetz and Berezniki plants – Sigismond Toeplitz, Émile Devien, Heinrich Kulakowski, and Wladimir Tolloczko.[30]

The nationalization of the plants jointly owned by Solvay and Verein Aussig was a hard blow, but it was to be expected given the political atmosphere. After all, intense negotiations coupled with a dash of organizational imagination eventually allowed the business activities to resume.[31] Serious worries came from another front, that of the associates and alleged friends. During two meetings in The Hague on 28–29 May and 12–13 September 1919, Louis Solvay, Émile Tournay, and Emmanuel Janssen were surprised by the eagerness with which the members of Verein's *Vorstand*, Josef Benes, Alfred Herzfeld, and James Landau, proposed transforming Nestomitz into an independent company and thus breaking up the 1883 limited partnership company of Ebensee. According to Josef Benes, fiscal reasons prompted Verein (which, in the meantime, had dropped its Austrian origin to be granted Czechoslovakian nationality) to do so.[32] But this was just partly true. The other reason was that the desire expressed by Verein to run directly (and exclusively) the more rentable plant of Nestomitz was inversely proportional to its influence in the region, which had largely vanished. Hence the double speech it held with the *gérance* in matters of reorganization. By 1920, Solvay, perhaps more preoccupied with its American issues, saw no evil. But when Verein struck back the following year to suggest another transformation of the limited partnership contract, it became unacceptable. "One can wonder," wrote Édouard Hannon, "if the origins of the disagreement that separates the Verein with us for so long do not lie in M. Benes' pretention to be the sole master and to avert consulting us for matters which concern the limited partnership."[33] Nevertheless, in the sake of mutual interests, Solvay was not disposed to quarrel with its allies. The convention drafted in November 1921 gave Verein leeway in the management of Ebensee and Nestomitz; Solvay, in contrast, was given a free hand in the other plants (Zakłady included). Robert Desguin, assistant to Jean Vanden Branden at the Commercial Department, was appointed general manager of Maros, Torda, and Lukavac. The underlying motive was that he should stay in Vienna as a way to keep an eye on sales. Janssen had made a concluding comment to his colleagues: "the current agreement is provisional – maybe for long."[34] This proved wrong, as the trust between the two companies was withering.

[30] Accarain (2002), 128–9n65, 159–64, 185, 195n95, 224–5n108; ACS, Rapport Zakłady, 1, 8.
[31] With the exception of the Zakłady, Solvay & Cie and Verein did have an equal number of shares in the new nationalized companies, although, for political reasons, the official presentation was 55–45, in favor of Solvay & Cie. A series of modifications in the agreements of mutual interests (6 Nov. 1935 and 17 Feb. 1936) ensured Solvay & Cie a majority of 51 percent (ACS, Binder Zakłady – Groupe de Vienne, Historique des usines, Nov. 1951, 14).
[32] ANOH, Folder "Visite de M. Louis Solvay au Ministre de Serbie (Paris)," Benes to gérance, 2 Apr. 1919; ANOH, Folder "Lukavac – Administration. Entrevues de La Haye des 12 et 13 septembre 1919"; ACS, CdS, Report of the gérance, 25 July 1919.
[33] ACS, Vienna, 1184–37-2A, Solvay Werke, Unknown gérant [Édouard Hannon?] to Louis Solvay and Émile Tournay, 9 Nov. 1921.
[34] ACS, Vienna, 1184–37-2A, Solvay Werke, Report of M. Desguin, 22 Nov. 1921; Session of the gérance, 29 Nov. 1921; Report of J. Vanden Branden (Vienna, 4–8 March 1922), 18 March 1922.

In the following months, Solvay realized that the convention had perhaps satisfied and appeased its associates, but it was not responding to its own expectations in terms of production capacities, and it did not guarantee the confidentiality of the technological process, as Verein was able to dispatch its engineers to Nestomitz. A special agreement, set forth at Solvay's request on 20 July 1922, had modified the repartition of license rights, which were henceforth controlled from Brussels.[35] But it was the general organization that was ineffective. Obviously, the *gérance* wanted to return to the centralization of business operations. During a meeting in Vienna, Louis Solvay, Émile Tournay, and Emmanuel Janssen reported their views to Joseph Benes, who understood their arguments but wanted some form of compensation – he wished to "save the pride and prestige of Aussig."[36] The compensation was Poland. Through the voice of Dr. Max Meyer, a former student of Carl Bosch and presumed successor of Benes as general manager of Aussig, Verein wanted equal participation in the Zakłady instead of its 10.5 percent. The *gérance*'s reaction was scathing:

> The Peace Treaty has profoundly transformed the conditions in which the industry we have in common with you should now be run.... The legal form to adopt for our conventions should not be considered on the point of view of the individual advantages they could theoretically bring out, but rather on the point of view of its conformity with reality.... [As to Poland] we should aim at reorganizing the best we can our mutual interests, and not at modifying them.[37]

The next steps consisted in transforming Ebensee and Nestomitz into a limited partnership company and adopting a framework of "community of interests" (31 December 1923) for the plants of the former Habsburg Empire. This was made possible by establishing a delegation (11 October 1923) composed of three representatives from Verein and three from Solvay (reduced to two each in 1928).[38] The liquidation of the Solvay-Werke holding and the consecutive creation of the Sodabetriebsgesellschaft mbH on 23 October 1925, with a capital of 20,000 Austrian schillings, was considered a pure formality with fiscal motives.[39] However, with the exception of commercial amendments for special products (e.g., dichromate, calcium chloride), this new montage lasted until 1935. It was notably able to deal with the growing demands of Romaniazation exerted by the Brătianu administration throughout the 1920s.[40] This thus was a proof of stability to the standard of *Mitteleuropa*.

35 ACS, 1184-1-1, Vienna, Suite à la note sur l'établissement de Vienne, Jan. 1928.

36 ACS, CdG, 6 Apr. and 25 May 1923; ACS, Vienna, 1184–37-3A, Solvay Werke, Report of the meeting in Vienna, 28 May 1923.

37 ACS, Vienna, 1184–37-3A, Solvay Werke, gérance to Benes, 5 July 1923.

38 ACS, Folder "Groupe de Vienne," Note sur l'Etablissement de Vienne, Sept. 1926.

39 ACS, Vienna, 1184–38-10: Solvay-Sodabetriebsgesellschaft, Minutes of the meetings of the Delegation, 23 Oct. 1925. By that time, Eudore Lefèvre had replaced Robert Desguin, who resigned in May 1926 because of health problems.

40 ACS, Binder Zakłady – Groupe de Vienne, Historique des usines, Nov. 1951, 12–3; ACS, CdG, 25 May 1923; ACS, Vienna, 1184–37-3A, Minutes of the meetings in Vienna, 25–26 Oct. 1923. The headquarters of the Uzinele Solvay din Romania was transferred to Bucharest in 1926 to avert the conditions of nationalization set by the Economic Commission in Transylvania. A

Strengthening Leading Position in France

The control of the French alkali market had always been a priority for the *gérance*, especially among its most experienced members. The anxiety over losing its position after the war and during the conflict was accordingly high (see Chapter 7). Local competitors (Saint-Gobain and Kuhlmann, in particular) had benefited from the support of the government in adapting their production facilities. At first sight, the geopolitical context was largely favorable to Solvay. Contrary to expectations, though, the takeover of Sarralbe and Château-Salins was not greeted with cheerful optimism by Solvay. The reasons were twofold. First, the two factories were in bad shape. At their visit to Sarralbe in December 1918, the *gérants* were sure that there had been some "fiddling" with the machines during the war.[41] Château-Salins had been severely bombed; it was more a burden than a real asset. As a result, alkali production was interrupted and machines were dismantled. Mulling over both plants' future development, the head of the Central Technical Department, Georges Chardin, thought to make Château-Salins into a kind of branch (*succursale*) of Dombasle; Sarralbe would specialize its production in derivatives of caustic soda.[42] The second source of worry was more general. It concerned the changing equilibrium in the distribution of alkali in the French chemical industry. The transfer of Alsace-Lorraine increased the French production quota by some 130,000 tons (i.e., 80,000 tons for Sarralble; 20,000 tons for Château-Salins; and 25,000 tons for the soda ash plant of Dieuze, owned by the Salines Domaniales de l'Est).[43] For a few years, the conditions imposed on Germany under the Treaty of Versailles (especially by article 268(a), stipulating a five-year open-door policy for products made in Alsace-Lorraine and exported to Germany) could alleviate the pressure. But this was provisional – and everyone knew it.

How would it be possible, then, to harness the changing industrial environment? The first answer came from Kuhlmann. Largely spared by the war and willing to expand,[44] Kuhlmann made an unfriendly acquisition of Dieuze in May 1920. After Solvay replied with a substantial price cut, a deal was reached whereby Solvay bought Dieuze for FF 5 million and offered to supply Kuhlmann in soda ash at a 15 percent reduction from the market price (valid for thirty years).[45] The move was not addressed to Kuhlmann but to Saint-Gobain, with which relations were particularly strained since the participation of the Mutuelle Mobilière et Immobilière in the creation of the International Company for Mechanical Glassmaking in April 1921.[46] The International Company

---

lawsuit was filed against the company for unauthorized capital increase. The issue was finally settled in 1929 after negotiating with the government.

[41] ACS, RdG, 30 Dec. 1918.

[42] ACS, CdG, Minutes of the meetings, 7 July 1921.

[43] ACS, Binder Comité des industries chimiques de France, Rachat de Dieuze. On the history of Dieuze, see also http://www.mairie-dieuze.fr/saline/saline-exploitation-17.htm (accessed 17 Sept. 2008).

[44] Langlinay (2006).

[45] ACS, RdG, 9 June 1921.

[46] ACS-O, 1701, Saint-Gobain, Folder "Entrevues avec M. Mayoussier en 1920, Exposé de la politique de Solvay & Cie," passim.

had been set up for the use in Europe of the Libbey-Owens process in view of producing flat-drawn glass, which was able to threaten the plate-glass market, led by Saint-Gobain. By 1923, it branched out into the Société Franco-Belge pour la Fabrication Mécanique du Verre (Mécaniver Franco-Belge), in partnership with the French bottle-making company Souchon, and it included board representatives from the Gillet group and Péchiney (Alais, Froges, and Camargue).[47] As a result, Saint-Gobain was infuriated by the purchase of Dieuze. At a meeting in Paris on 9 December 1921, Emmanuel Janssen learned from the directors of Saint-Gobain's Commercial Department of Chemical Products, Félix Mayoussier and his son Henry, that the French company intended to break its alkali contract with Solvay and buy half the shares of Société de la Grande Paroisse, which had a potential alkali output through the production of synthetic ammonia via the Claude process (see Chapter 9).[48]

Armand Solvay was most irritated by the situation in France, where the intrusion of political views in industrial issues was at its peak. The nationalist reaction against Solvay was nothing new. But since the war, what had been the sole expression of extremist opinions had started to work its way in official circles.[49] Although the issue with Saint-Gobain was solved by November 1922, with the renewal of the alkali convention more or less along previous lines,[50] this highlighted the fact that the predominance of Solvay was not unreservedly accepted anymore. Moreover, to the competition of private firms was added the possible competition of the French state, which did not want to see its role reduced to mere intervention.[51] Armand's intuition of political interference was soon confirmed by the French government's desire to reactivate the soda ash plant Société d'Études et de Produits Chimiques, in Mouguerre, near Bayonne. A proposition of law had been submitted in the sake of national defense by the minister of war, André Maginot, in July 1922. This was a direct threat for Giraud, as well as a useless duplication of efforts. After unsuccessful attempts to negotiate with French chemical companies and political networks (Minister Jaspar had been again sought for mediation), a feeling of dismay prevailed within the *gérance*: "To sum up, there is nothing to do with the Ministry [of War], and even less with diplomatic leverages. We have been dumped [*lâchés*]. Let us defend ourselves."[52] The following year the French government granted the Société d'Études FF 8 million (and the supply of coal exploited in the Ruhr area). The determined opposition of a high civil servant in close

---

[47] Daviet (1988), 427–8, 561.

[48] ACS-O, 1701, Saint-Gobain, Folder "Rupture du contrat," Minutes of the meeting of 9 Dec. 1921, 10 Dec. 1921; ACS, CdG, 12 Dec. 1921; ACS, 1106–49-2/3, Consultation de Me Guist'hau c/o Grande Paroisse.

[49] ACS-O, 1106 Paris, Folder "Relations avec administrations," Armand to Ernest-John, 12 Aug. 1917.

[50] The quotas were as follows: 71.5 percent for Solvay & Cie, 13.5 percent for Saint-Gobain, and 15 percent for Marchéville. The latter had remained a staunch ally of Solvay & Cie. ACS-O, 1701, Saint-Gobain, Subfolder "Renouvellement du contrat," passim; ACS-O, 1106, Paris, Subfolder "Anciennes conventions," passim; ACS, Binder Comité des Industries Chimiques de France.

[51] Haber (1971), 236–8; Kuisel (1981), 59–92; Carls (2000).

[52] ACS, 1107–29-1A Bayonne, Meeting of the gérance, 20 Dec. 1922.

relation with Solvay's rivals – Georges Patart – had been instrumental in the whole issue.[53] Quite ironically, five years later the Société d'Études was facing financial difficulties, and Solvay was asked to join in. However, the heyday of state-owned chemical works was largely over by 1927. Solvay had accepted considering the deal at its own conditions.[54]

Potash Supply: The Acquisition of Suria

Another case worth mentioning in the immediate postwar period is the intense energy expended by Solvay to secure and control its position in the supply of potash. The worldwide monopoly exerted by the German Kali Syndikat (Stassfurt) since 1888 had prompted American and European companies to explore alternative sources. Shortly before the outbreak of the war, the Spanish engineers Viader and Macary found a deposit in the north of Barcelona. They eagerly sold the option to the Compagnie Bordelaise des Produits Chimiques, which proposed selling it to Solvay in November 1913. During the course of the war, Solvay ordered the execution of preliminary drillings in the region; twelve of thirteen tests confirmed the presence of potash-based ores.[55] The other side of the coin, though, was that the defeat of Germany entailed the transfer of Alsace-Lorraine, that is, the end of Kali Syndikat's monopoly. Needless to say, Solvay, which had already invested some BEF 12 million ($2.3 million) in the business, was willing to sell Suria or, at least, was looking for a partner.[56]

At this stage, two mining engineers played an important role. The first was René Étienne. Trained at the École Polytechnique, Étienne was appointed professor at the École des Mines de Saint-Étienne in 1900, then at the prestigious École des Mines de Paris.[57] After having acted as intermediary between Emilio Viader and the Mathieu family (of Bordelaise) for the sale of the potash concessions, he executed the drillings and approached Solvay to take over the option.[58] When the director of Solvay's Paris office, Louis Talvard, died in November 1919, the *gérance* appointed Étienne as his successor, given his expertise and contacts in the French chemical industry.[59] The second engineer whose role was instrumental was Herbert Hoover. After his leading accomplishment as director of the Committee for Relief in Belgium, Hoover had coordinated relief programs in Central and Eastern Europe. Meanwhile, he had set up with his counterpart of the Comité National, Émile Francqui, a series of academic and scientific foundations Belgium. One of them, the CRB

---

[53] Patart was head of the Service des Poudres from 1919 until his retirement in 1925, and then was appointed director at the Compagnie Nationale des Matières Colorantes (controlled by Kuhlmann), board member of Ugine (Société d'Électricité, d'Électrométallurgie et des Aciéries Électriques), and consulting engineer at DuPont. ASC, Binder Bayonne SEPC, passim; Langlinay (2006), 159–60.

[54] ASC, Binder Bayonne SEPC, passim.

[55] ASC-O 1126 Suria, Cie Bordelaise, Options sur le gisement, passim; Binder Suria, Historique de la société.

[56] ACS, RdG, 19 June 1919: "In order to sell the [Suria] business without loss nor profit, we should get at least 20 million."

[57] http://www.annales.org/archives/x/etienne.html (accessed 21 Oct. 2009).

[58] ACS-O, 1126 Suria, 4/1, Correspondance Bordelaise – Étienne, passim.

[59] ACS, RdG, 5 Dec. 1919; ACS, CdS, Report of the gérance, 12 Dec. 1919.

Educational Foundation (set up in April 1920), was designed as an exchange program between American and Belgian university students. The foundation was run by former CRB delegates, most of them American engineers based in Brussels – Edgar Rickard, William Hallam Tuck, and Millard Shaller, to name but a few.[60] Taking into account that Americans were the largest consumers of potash, the *gérance* was eager to benefit from the advice of such a network. While in New York with their associates of Brunner, Mond in April 1919, Hannon, Tournay, and Janssen seized the opportunity to consult Edgar Rickard and Prentiss Gray on this issue. Back in Brussels, another meeting took place among Hoover, Tuck, and Hannon. Hoover seemed to be interested but insisted that complementary drillings be carried out before any further investment. The *gérance* gave him an option of acquisition valid between 30 October and 31 December 1919.[61]

In spite of the efforts – and the appointment of William Tuck as Solvay's consultant for American affairs – the deal with Hoover's business partners (Captain T. T. C. Gregory and John Agnew) never materialized.[62] The *gérance* sought instead to attract the group of Syndicate Managers (future Allied Chemical & Dyes), which was busy integrating the Solvay Process Company (see Chapter 9). Shortly after, the operational company Minas de Potasa de Suria was set up on 25 September 1920, with the help of local notables; Emmanuel Janssen became its general manager.[63] Simultaneously, a tentative agreement was reached whereby the American consortium was given a one-year option to acquire the company (then estimated at BEF 50 million, some US\$3.7 million), taking effect 1 November 1920. At any rate, the Americans immediately took over the 18 percent stake that the Compagnie Bordelaise had put in.[64] It did not take a year for Orlando Weber, general manager of Allied, to announce that he was not willing to raise the option. The *gérance* was stunned. Seven years had passed since the first drillings, millions had been squandered, and the Americans – Solvay's new associates – were then wary of a business opportunity for the supply of potash.[65] In an impulse of pride, the *gérants* unanimously decided to pay Allied's shares back (approximately US\$1.1 million) so as to own and manage Suria "without foreign control." To their silent partners,

[60] Bertrams (2010); *Belgian and American CRB Fellows* (1950).

[61] Hoover's underlying intentions were a mystery to Solvay & Cie. A cryptic telegram he sent to the *gérance* on 19 October 1919 did not help clarify his position: "If it helps matters, it can be argued that financial arrangements must meet my approval." ACS-O, 1126 Suria, 3, Folder "Notes sur la cession éventuelle de Suria aux Américains," handwritten annotation to the "Note au sujet du Capitaine Grégory," Document No. 7, undated.

[62] The reasons for this turnaround remain quite unclear. In a pivotal sixteen-page memorandum from 7 February 1921, Janssen says that the *gérance* turned down two offers made by John Agnew and Colonel John Beaty because of the interest expressed in February 1920 by the leaders of the future Allied. ACS-O, 1126 Suria, 9 (a), Folder "Pourparlers de vente de Suria aux Américains," Subfolder 6/5, "Voyage de MM. Janssen et Tuck aux Etats-Unis," Notes sur l'option concernant les concessions de Suria, 7 Feb. 1921, 6.

[63] ACS, CdG, 12 May 1921; ACS-O, 1126 Suria, 4/2, Correspondance with Marquis de Hoyos and with Marquis de Villalobar.

[64] ACS, RdG, 20 April 1920; ACS, CdS, Gérance report, 18 Sept. 1920; ACS, Binder Suria, Historique du capital.

[65] ACS-O, 1126 Suria, 9 (a), Folder "Pourparlers de vente de Suria aux Américains," Subfolder 6/5, Minutes of the meeting with O. Weber, 16 Feb. 1921.

though, they were not able to hide the setback. The sale of Suria had been announced months earlier as a means to increase Solvay's cash assets without having to resort to shareholders' funding assistance. A year later the situation was completely reversed.[66] Despite the capital increase decided on 3 June 1921 (fully subscribed to by Solvay), it took more than two decades – and the prowess of Solvay's financial engineering – for Suria to become profitable.[67]

8.2   FACING SOCIAL UPHEAVAL

Even before the signing of the Armistice, scattered social revolts burst out across Europe. Whether triggered by the outbreak of the Bolshevik Revolution or, usually, spontaneous, these movements had significant consequences in at least two ways. They surely affected the continuation of industrial activities at the level of the factory, but above all they exerted a pressure on the conditions of labor activities on a more global scale, which gave way to the slow enforcement of state-driven social legislations. In spite of the elaborate social guarantees Solvay provided its workers and employees (see Chapter 4), Solvay was caught up in the waves of postwar social upheaval. After witnessing the development of social unrest, plant managers alarmed the *gérants* of the organization of a series of strikes shortly after the war. At Couillet, strikes took place between March and June 1919 in solidarity with the workers of metallurgical plants in the region; a thirty-four-day strike erupted at Sarralbe in October 1919, after workers protested against the lower social standards they were given as a French factory and because they opposed layoffs of German workers.[68] Social tensions reached a peak in Italy. After a first strike was terminated in April 1919 at the satisfaction of the personnel of Rosignano (with a 25 percent raise in salary and other social benefits), the mining workers of the Acquabone quarry started a strike on 17 December 1919, which lasted no fewer than four months and completely blocked the activities of the soda plant.[69] More generally, the industrial activity of Solvay's plants was largely affected by the instability occurring on both sides of the industrial chain, upstream and downstream. Giraud was regularly paralyzed because of the strikes of dockworkers and soap producers in Marseilles; Dombasle, as well as the Ebensee and DSW plants, had to cope with social unrest in the coal basins.[70] Things were less clear in the successor states. Toeplitz was struck by the "dreadful misery" of the Polish population he observed in Warsaw. When he arrived at Lukavac in November 1920, Desguin was immediately passed a list of demands by the workers' delegation. Contrary to his first expectations, though, he deemed the bulk of them were reasonable and legitimate.[71]

---

[66] ACS, CdG, 16 Mar. 1921; ACS, CdS, Minutes of the meetings, 2 May 1921.

[67] ACS, Binder Suria, Historique du capital, Situation financière.

[68] ACS, RdG, 17, 24, and 29 June 1919; ACS, CdS, Report of the gérance, 25 July and 12 Dec. 1919. There was, however, no uniformity: contrary to Rheinberg, Würselen did not apply the eight-hour workday. ACS, RdG, 30 Dec. 1918.

[69] Celati and Gattini (1993), 155–84; Paolini (2007), 40–5.

[70] Daumalin, Lambert, and Mioche (2007), 67–71; *DSW Report activities* Bernburg, 1919–1925.

[71] ANOH Warsaw, Administration, Toeplitz to gérance, 25 Aug. 1920; ANOH Lukavac, Instructions & Contrôle, Personnel: Ouvriers, Desguin to Chardin, 25 and 27 Nov. 1920.

ZAKŁADY SOLVAY W POLSCE T.Z.O.P.

Mątwy
Kolonja Robotnicza

FIGURE 8.2. A workers' colony of Zakłady Solvay at Montwy, Poland. Workers' and employees' houses were built in a rural area and represented high building standards for the time. (Solvay Archives.)

Whatever the variety of their expressions, there was a general pattern in the workers' demands – the implementation of a social package focusing on the eight-hour workday and ground rules of the industrial democracy. With respect to the first issue, Solvay had already applied these things in most of its plants by 1907–1908. The *gérance* strove to generalize the measure to all positions but insisted that local particularities be taken into account. By the same token, the adaptation of wages to postwar living standards was done on an individual case basis (e.g., through allowances and wartime indemnities), without losing sight of the effort for competitiveness.[72] Conversely, the gospel for industrial democracy was more of a concern to the *gérance*. In Italy, France, and Belgium, it was a source of growing tensions between the employers and

[72] For the telling case of Dombasle, see ACS, RdG, 4 Jan. 1919.

the workers' representatives. The cornerstone of the disagreement was the preemptive determination of Solvay's management to not address social issues with unrecognized trade unions.[73] The principles of systematic collective bargaining implied for the company a form of institutionalized cooperation, which largely undermined its labor programs and social schemes.

Overall, the postwar period witnessed a difficult balance between public and voluntary welfare, shifting from private initiatives to state-controlled generalization. It was not construed in terms of social security but rather as a comprehensive form of private-public partnership to assist workers and their families.[74] Solvay adapted its regulations to the provisions set out in national legislations. Sometimes, this consisted in minor adjustments, as was the case for the new regime of labor contracts (Belgian law of 7 August 1922); on other occasions, it led to substantial transformations of previous dispositions, such as the system of pension schemes imposing the use of a retirement fund partly controlled by the beneficiaries and the creation, for the personnel of DSW, of the special Ernest and Alfred Solvay Fund.[75] In the same vein, Solvay had to meet the new fiscal measures that national governments were setting forth as a way to alleviate their public debts. All these external requirements implied the mobilization of proper knowledge and its transformation into adapted solutions. The *gérance*, in other words, needed to adapt its own administrative structure so as to capture – and produce – the corresponding expertise. As a result, the Conseil de Gérance had been set up in December 1920 as a way "to narrow the relations between the members of the *gérance* and their principal collaborators, on the one hand, and among these collaborators, on the other."[76] The Legal Department (Section Spéciale du Contentieux) followed suit some months later; it was headed by the jurist Paul Vander Eycken.[77]

8.3   DEATH OF THE FOUNDING FATHER

Ernest Solvay passed away on 26 May 1922. Until his last days, he carried on research projects on the scientific conversion of his reflections and theoretical insights (see Chapter 5). The outbreak of the war, however, was about to completely transform the international scientific community into two "hostile political camps." As a result, German (and Austrian) scientists were excluded from the scientific meetings until the Fifth Solvay Conference, in 1927 (which

---

[73] "As a rule, we have started to discuss the interests of our fellow workers only with those who are effectively working in our plants. We have pushed away energetically the intrusion in our business of foreign elements to the personnel.... Workers in our Belgian and French plants are attempting to merge their demands in an international entente. If the latter develops, we will have to cope with an organization willing to unify the concerted movements with the workers of our factories across the world." ACS, CdS, Report of the gérance, 20 Apr. 1920.

[74] Hong (1998), 114–40; Mazower (1999), 4–8.

[75] ACS, CdS, Report of the gérance, 22 Dec. 1921, and 7 May and 5 Dec. 1923; *Cent ans de droit social* (1987), 48–9, 81.

[76] ACS, CdG, 24 Dec. 1920. Less than two years later, the Conseils de Gérance were reorganized to hold meetings with "essentially pragmatic and concrete" proposals, "establishing a community of point of views." ACS, CdG, Nov. 1922.

[77] ACS, CdS, Report of the gérance, 2 May 1921.

saw a seminal confrontation between Albert Einstein and Niels Bohr).[78] This brutal intermingling between science and politics had led to a brief disagreement between the founder of the institute and its scientific chairman, the Dutch physicist Hendrik Antoon Lorentz, a fervent pacifist. But when Solvay confirmed to Lorentz that the continuity of the institute's activities was not endangered, their association resumed and remained fruitful.[79] By the time of the war, Ernest Solvay had also charged his collaborator Georges Barnich with reorganizing the Institute of Sociology, which he had created in 1902 along the initial lines of his current theories. The project was greeted with mixed feelings by the community of researchers, most of whom were professors at the Université Libre de Bruxelles. The issue was left until Ernest Solvay's death in 1922. Following his father's wish, Armand Solvay suggested that the Institute of Sociology be absorbed by the League of Nations or by the International Labor Office; the Institute of Sociology had close ties and contacts with both (Émile Vandervelde and Ernest Mahaim). The operation never took place, and the institute eventually joined the Université Libre de Bruxelles.[80] It prolonged the impressive series of gifts and donations that the legacy of Ernest and Alfred Solvay had granted to this academic institution throughout the 1920s.[81]

But ever since the war, the name of Solvay was not confined to industrialists or scientists – Ernest had become a living legend in Belgium. For his eightieth birthday, in the midst of the war, the delegates of the *Comité National* distributed a biography notice of Solvay "to read and comment" in school classes of various levels on 16 April 1918.[82] Acknowledging his role, King Albert I visited him on the very first day of his return to Brussels at the end of the hostilities, on 22 November 1918. Later on, Armand told King Albert that the day was "one of the greatest and most joyful of the entire live" of his father.[83] For his involvement in the relief program, Ernest Solvay had received the honorific title of *ministre d'État*. But he wanted also to exert an influence on the social and political context after the war. To another *ministre d'État*, his friend Émile Vandervelde, he confided that the burden of the postwar turmoil compelled him to intervene.[84]

[78] Kevles (1971), 47–60.

[79] Noord-Hollands Archief, Haarlem, Lorentz Papers, File 158: Lorentz to Lefébure, s.d. and File 153, Lorentz to Solvay, 6 Sept. 1918; PPSF, Box Armand Solvay No. 2, Folder 34: Instituts Internationaux de Physique et Chimie, Lorentz to Lefébure, s.d. [April 1926]. For more details, see Bertrams (2012).

[80] PPSF, Box Armand Solvay No. 1, Folder 12: Institut de sociologie, passim (see especially the memorandum drafted by Georges Hostelet, "De l'utilité du rattachement de l'Institut Solvay à la Société des Nations," undated [Feb. 1923]); ACS, 1001–28-23, Institut Solvay, Visite de M. Vander Eycken à Genève, June 1923. See also Crombois (1994); Van Daele (2005).

[81] Despy-Meyer and Montens (1997), 243–5.

[82] NAB, CNSA, 373, passim. Apparently, this birthday gift was a result of socialist representative Louis Bertrand's initiative.

[83] PPSF, Box Armand Solvay No. 1, Folder 5, A. Solvay to King Albert, 1 June 1922.

[84] PPSF, Box Armand Solvay No. 1, Folder 8, E. Solvay to E. Vandervelde, 15 Sept. 1918.

FIGURE 9.1. A rare picture of Orlando Weber (in profile on the right), taken in 1935, after his retirement as chairman of Allied Chemical & Dye Corp. His suspicion of journalists and photographers led the *Life Magazine* to call him the "mystery man of Wall Street," in an article of 1938. (Photograph by Robert Boyd, *Milwaukee Journal.*)

9

The Making of International Alliances

By the end of the war, there was no doubt that the international economy was about to encounter the same kind of upheaval that the European political order was confronted with. Solvay, as we saw in the previous chapter, was not immune to the profound changes caused by the rise of nationalism and state interventionism. But other developments, also deeply rooted in the war economy, tended to transform the very nature of industrial production. First, the postwar context enhanced the movement toward bigger units of production attempting to reduce costs and dominate the market by vertical integration, from feedstock to finished products.[1] Second, the dynamics of the international economy had shifted to a point at which financial and industrial arrangements between firms – the so-called horizontal axis – took place worldwide, whatever their strength and variety.[2] Third, the interaction of science, technology, and industry, whose result lay at the core of Solvay's own industrial development, was embedded in a complex web of patent and licensing systems influenced by interfirm agreements, national and transnational legislations, politics, and other extraindustrial considerations. It required professional expertise, to say the least.

For all these reasons, the return to normalcy – that is, to the prewar conditions of industrial relations – was a mere illusion. By 1914, Solvay was considered an undisputed master in its league – the alkali industry. It could count on the excellence of its process as applied in its plants in Belgium, France, Spain, and Italy. It enjoyed a privileged situation in its subsidiaries in Germany, Austria, the United Kingdom, and the United States – and, from there, the world market at large. Its international position actually made the difference. The postwar economic order was actually on the verge of breaking this hard-fought-for equilibrium – challengers were transformed into leaders, loyal friends into competitors, and advantages into constraints. The *gérance* realized these issues as they were unfolding. If left unaddressed, these challenges could become major threats for Solvay's rank, and growth, in the world chemical industry. In this sense, upper management was forced to take the initiative.

---

[1] Chandler (2004).
[2] A contemporary scholar defines the cartel as a "voluntary, potentially impermanent, business relationship among a number of independent, private entrepreneurs, which through co-ordinated marketing significantly affects the market of a commodity or service" (Hexner 1946, 24).

9.1 IG AND ALLIED: COPING WITH GIANTS

Although industrial cartelization was certainly nothing new in Europe before World War I (see Chapter 3), observers tend to acknowledge that the interwar period witnessed the peak of the cartel movement. The war had generated an accumulation of emergency-based surplus production, which proved difficult to meet the demand after the conflict. Ammonia, dyestuffs, and other chemicals were clearly affected by the imbalance between production and consumption. Politically, cartelization was also considered, by industrialists and public officials alike, as the appropriate institutional blueprint to ensure national self-sufficiency economies and to induce the changing patterns of international political relations. By the mid-1930s, in the wake of the Great Depression, national legislations would even favor industrial arrangements as a convenient way to regulate the market and embark on interventionist policies. As we shall see, the structure of the world chemical industry illustrated with striking evidence the recasting of boundaries between competition and cooperation.[3]

At the General Assembly meeting of December 1919, the *gérance* warned Solvay's silent partners that the company's power rested on a "more adequate orientation toward the important mergers of interests and great industrial concentrations which are currently occurring everywhere."[4] On this occasion, shareholders were duly reminded that industrial strategy was deeply connected with financial resources – and Solvay urgently needed to be financially scaled up for it to play a role in the negotiations to come. The problem, however, was that, despite fairly good production levels, its available funds were scarce because of the instable political and monetary context. Shortly after the Armistice, the adjustment of Solvay's capital to the real worth of its plants had been endorsed by the General Assembly. Following Edgard Hulin's calculation, the social capital was raised from BEF 40 million to BEF 200 million (from US$2,952,000 to US$14,760,000), which contrasted with the doubling of capital of SPC and Brunner, Mond at the same time.[5] This proved not enough, though. Still confronted with major parts of the funds tied up in foreign plants, the *gérance* opted for a step-by-step increase in social capital until the figure reached BEF 300 million (some US$14 million) in 1924 – and BEF 330 million (US$9.2 million) in 1928.[6] In the company's scaling-up process, the Mutuelle Mobilière et Immobilière, which had been created as an investment fund restricted to the Solvay family, played an ever-increasing role. Through the diversification of its participation (beyond the realm of alkali products) and the extension of its financial capacities, the Mutuelle gradually became Solvay's financial holding and pivotal instrument in the management of its international industrial relations (hence its name change to Mutuelle Solvay in 1927).[7] This gave way to

---

[3] Schröter (1996); Wurm (1994); Smith (1992).

[4] ACS, CdS, Report of the gérance, 12 Dec. 1919.

[5] ACS, NdG, "Étude sur les modifications à apporter à l'organisation de la Société Solvay & Cie" by E. Hulin, 24 Oct. 1918; ACS, CdS, Information to the CdS, 12 Dec. 1918.

[6] ACS, "Extraits des statuts successifs," Feb. 1956, "Variations du capital de Solvay & Cie," 26 Nov. 1952.

[7] *Mutuelle Solvay* (2000).

FIGURE 9.2. Some of the Solvay *gérants* visiting salt mines at Borth (1926). From left, Louis Solvay is the second; Emmanuel Janssen, fifth, and Ernest-John Solvay, seventh. (Solvay Archives.)

a series of interrelated events, whose intimate connection would not be fully perceptible before the 1930s (this is covered in-depth in Chapter 10). By 1918, however, the focus was – once again – on Germany.

Securing the Haber-Bosch Process

Among the issues Solvay had to deal with after the war, the Haber-Bosch process for nitrogen fixation was undoubtedly a salient one. The process invented by Fritz Haber and industrialized by Carl Bosch for the Badische Anilin und Soda-Fabrik (BASF) shortly before the war exerted considerable interest during the conflict itself, especially for its ability to produce nitric acid – an essential compound for the manufacture of explosives. After the war, the vigorous drive to conquer the nitrogen fertilizer market and change the habits of farmers only reinforced the concern about the ammonia-synthesis process. Warfare and welfare aims converged so as to prompt the Allies to include the free use of German patents under the provisions of the Versailles Treaty (article 306), which also required the yearly delivery of thirty thousand tons of ammonia to France during three years for the sake of reparations.[8] The treaty also allowed Allied forces to carry out inspection visits to German plants. In May and

---

[8] Travis, Homburg, Schröter, and Morris (1998); Haber (1971), 93–5, 213; Abelshauser et al. (2004), 183–4, 190–1.

June 1919, Lieutenant Colonel G. P. Pollitt, director of Brunner, Mond, took part in such a mission under the aegis of the British Department of Explosives Supply. His destination was the BASF works at Oppau, which several French engineers and chemists had already toured.[9] When, together with Brunner, Mond representatives, Pollitt met Édouard Hannon and Emmanuel Janssen on 22 August 1919, he could not hide his enthusiasm. He was literally "amazed" by the Haber-Bosch process, which he considered "remarkable and completely fit" for industrial purposes.[10]

Although this was a confirmation of what Solvay knew for some time, it was not likely what it wanted to hear. For more than a year, the *gérance* had received alarmist reports on the threats posed by the Haber-Bosch process and even by its forerunner in the production of synthetic nitrogen – the Frank-Caro process operated by the Bayerische Stickstoffwerke (an offspring of the Cyanidegesellschaft) as soon as 1908. During the war, the co-inventor Nicodemus Caro had contacted Emil Gielen of DSW to start a joint venture for the production of ammonium chloride (frequently referred to as muriate NH_4Cl), which could be obtained as a by-product of the synthesis of cyanamide. Later on, an exchange of shares between DSW and Bayerische Stickstoffwerke was suggested. Both projects were carefully put on hold until the end of the war.[11] In fact, the underlying motivation behind Caro's move was to compete with BASF in the production of ammonia-based soda carbonate. In its new facility eighty kilometers south of Bernburg – the Leuna works – BASF intended to build a large-capacity ammonia plant. When the war ended, the project was not fully completed, but Solvay did not want to take a chance.[12] After having collected the indications from Professor Albin Haller, a personal acquaintance of Ernest Solvay, and a technician from Brunner, Mond, A. W. Tangye, it was decided to investigate thoroughly the implications the Haber-Bosch process could have on the production of soda ash. Through the Paris office, Solvay's head of research René Lucion obtained the copy a confidential report on the synthesis of ammonia drafted by Camille Matignon, professor at the Collège de France and member of a recent mission at Oppau. The so-called Matignon Report contended that the high pressure involved in the Haber-Bosch process enabled the manufacturing of soda ash as a natural – and simple – by-process of the synthesis of ammonia. In other terms, the prospect of a specific "ammonia soda-ammonium chloride" process endangered the technical supremacy of the Solvay process.[13]

In a short note from May 1919, Édouard Hannon pointed out the "serious threat" posed by the Haber process both for coke-oven factories and soda

[9] Reader (1970), 328–9, 353–5.
[10] ACS, 1542–1-1A, Folder 1, Minutes of the meeting in London, 22 Aug. 1919.
[11] Haber (1971), 88–90; ACS, 1542–1-1A, Folder 1, "Note relative aux négociations pour l'achat du procédé Haber," undated [Oct. 1919].
[12] Abelshauser et al. (2004), 168–70.
[13] ACS, 1542–1-1A, Folder 1, "Rapport confidentiel sur la synthèse de l'ammoniaque" by Camille Matignon, 18 May 1919.

plants. He advised reaching some form of ententes to avoid unpredictable competition and market turbulence.[14] In the summer of 1919, another of Brunner, Mond's men, Henry Glendinning, shed a commercial light on the technical information Solvay had already gathered: he estimated that, provided there was a full exploitation of the combination between synthesis gas and ammonia synthesis, the reduction in production costs could reach 49.9 percent per ton of ash. The founder of Air Liquide, Georges Claude, spoke of a "revolution in the soda industry."[15] Thus, there was a growing atmosphere that tended to present the production of ammonium chloride enabled by the Haber-Bosch process as a direct, rather than potential, threat for the ammonia-soda process. Of course, not everyone at Solvay shared this feeling: Emil Gielen, for instance, trusted that the market prospects for a wide diffusion of ammonium chloride as fertilizer remained largely uncertain. But his view was isolated. A "memorandum relative to the negotiations for the purchase of the Haber-Bosch process," drafted at the time of the first negotiations (October 1919) and, therefore, intended to justify the strategy, contained the words *fears*, *dangers*, and even *anxieties* when referring to the issue of ammonium chloride. The conclusion was balanced, though. It emphasized that "chloride, according to [the] information obtained [was] a good fertilizer and might be substituted for sulfate of ammonia"; it carefully acknowledged also that the process still needed to "be widely advertized," as cultivators were "generally acting by routine and being very conservative."[16]

Solvay's reaction was also influenced by the international context. Alternatives to BASF ammonia technology were emerging (Claude in France, Casale and Fauser in Italy, and Cederberg in Sweden), but Badische had reached first-mover momentum, which it was keen to exploit when it went to license its process to foreign companies.[17] The French case was of particular interest. Under the impulse of the minister of industrial reconstruction, the flamboyant Louis Loucheur, a group of French industrialists headed by Joseph Frossard (Kuhlmann) and Émile Lambert (Société Lambert, Rivière & Cie) gathered into a consortium to negotiate the purchase of the Haber-Bosch license. Solvay was asked to join in this Société d'Études but declined the offer after Emmanuel Janssen overtly discussed the issue with Henry Mayoussier (Saint-Gobain). Janssen suspected the consequences of the French state's interventionist approach; Saint-Gobain, however, was busy negotiating with Air Liquide for the creation of the Société Chimique de la Grande Paroisse, which

---

[14] ACS, 1542-1-1A, Folder 1, Note de M. Hannon, May 1919. "Caveat consules!" were his final words.

[15] ACS, 1542-1-1A, Folder 1, J. H. Gold [BMC] to Solvay & Cie, 5 Mar. 1919; "Rapport confidentiel sur la synthèse de l'ammoniaque" by Camille Matignon, 18 May 1919; George Claude, "Une conséquence importante de la synthèse de l'ammoniac," *Chimie et industrie*, 8 Aug. 1919.

[16] ACS, 1542-1-1A, Folder 1, Entrevue avec Monsieur Gielen, 16 Sept. 1919; "Note relative aux négociations pour l'achat du procédé Haber," undated [Oct. 1919].

[17] Homburg and van Rooij (2004), 224-8.

intended to exploit the alternative Claude process.[18] Both companies, therefore, adopted a wait-and-see policy, which turned out to be very opportune. The
licensing agreement granting the French government exclusive rights to BASF
processes within French territory was symbolically completed on Armistice Day
in 1919; it allowed the French to produce up to one hundred tons of ammonia
daily. However, negotiations between the Service des Poudres and French chemical companies gathered into the provisional Compagnie Nationale de l'Azote
would drag until April 1924 before the Office National Industriel de l'Azote
came into being in a plant located in Toulouse. Solvay, which was represented
by the director of its Paris office, took a step out of these discussions as early as
March 1920 and withdrew completely by July 1922, when it was clear that the
adoption of the Haber-Bosch process would not survive nationalist attacks.[19]
For the time being, the French lead was not privileged, but it had contributed
to disturb Solvay's strategy in securing the ammonia synthesis technology.

In view of the nationalist atmosphere of the time, the *gérance* had trusted
that the best way to negotiate with BASF was to start discreet but direct contacts with the upper management. As a result, at their first meeting with DSW
managers since the war in July 1919, the *gérants* asked Gielen to approach
Carl Bosch on the matter. A meeting was planned for September. In the meantime, Hannon and Janssen consulted their British partners. Brunner, Mond,
whose enthusiasm for the Oppau facility we have mentioned, also considered
the Haber-Bosch process worth a meeting. They were urged by the Ministry
of Munitions to put up a plant of synthetic ammonia at Billingham with a
BASF license granted from the British government (allegedly as the result of a
confiscation under the Versailles Treaty) and, in terms of know-how, with the
findings and plans brought back from the Pollitt mission at Oppau. For this,
Roscoe and Jack Brunner had sought to meet with Sir Harry McGowan, chairman of Explosives Trades Ltd. (soon to become Nobel Industries Ltd.). The
company was eventually registered on 3 June 1920 under the name Synthetic
Ammonia & Nitrates Ltd. The company had many flaws – it was expensive,
unclear, and a bit reckless – but the patriotic and moral imperatives had overcome Brunner, Mond's early hesitations.[20] Then again, it gave Solvay the free
hand to negotiate with BASF.

The meeting with Carl Bosch took place in Aachen on 17 September 1919.[21]
The leader of BASF had asked his associate in the "little IG," the head of Bayer,
Carl Duisberg, to join. As impressed they might have been, the *gérants* adopted

[18] Baillot (2010), 215–20.

[19] Chadeau (1992), 100–2; Daviet (1988), 483–6, 493–500; Abelshauser et al. (2004), 184; Carls
(2000), 176–83; Godfrey (1987), 177–9; ACS, 1542-1-1A, Folder 1, Voyage à Paris (MM.
Talvard & Janssen), 24 June 1919; "Compte-rendu de la visite à M. Loucheur" by René
Étienne, 19 Dec. 1919; ACS, CdS, Minutes of the meeting, 7 Dec. 1920; Memo "Ammoniaque
synthétique: France," Appendix to Procédé Haber – Résumé, undated.

[20] ACS, 1542-1-1A, Folder 1, Minutes of the meetings in London, 22 Aug. 1919 and 26 Aug.
1919; Reader (1970), 355–8.

[21] ACS, 1542-1-1A, Folder 1, Minutes of the meetings in Aachen, 17 Sept. 1919 (Solvay & Cie's
representatives were Armand and Louis Solvay, and Emmanuel Janssen); "Note relative aux
négociations pour l'achat du procédé Haber," undated [Oct. 1919].

from the onset a global strategy: they defined their position as a multinational company with large interests in all countries where BASF was willing to expand. Hence, Solvay could act as the intermediary par excellence to negotiate Haber-Bosch licensing agreements all over the world (except, of course, in the German commercial area), whether with public or private interests. For Carl Bosch, this was an interesting proposal. But it was just a proposal among others – there was no reason for him to rush. When Armand Solvay reminded Carl Bosch of the close partnership Solvay had with Brunner, Mond and how, in that respect, they were able to work the Haber-derived process on their own, the reply of the BASF leader was straightforward: there was no way – or at least not without considerable loss of time and money – that another company could operate the ammonia process on an industrial scale without the know-how of the Badische. Bosch was so persuaded by his technical superiority that he invited the *gérants* to visit the BASF facilities. In return for its collaboration, BASF would take about 30 percent of profits resulting from the exploitation. After being ensured that an agreement on soda ash could easily be reached – it was a "secondary issue," according to Bosch – Solvay decided to consult its British and American partners. Bosch, in contrast, was on his way to fight hard against the French state's seizure of BASF's license rights. The *gérants* were not aware of the full underpinnings of these negotiations, just as they were ignorant of the fact that, in his home country, Bosch was confronted with the threat of socialization of the Leuna works.[22]

The Allied Way

An essential outcome of the Aachen meeting had been that the collaboration of Americans was not merely desirable – it was indispensable. Since the end of the war, Solvay had worked out all its diplomatic skills to make sure that SPC and, to a lesser extent, Semet-Solvay Company would pay allegiance to Brussels after their failed putsch (see Chapter 7). It seemed that everybody was eager to bury the hatchet and move on. Drawing on a political metaphor, Armand Solvay even suggested to a SPC manager that the network linking Solvay with its subsidiaries acted as a "small League of Nations" with its own principles[23] – and its own difficulties, no doubt. In April and May 1919, Janssen, Hannon, and Tournay stayed in the United States, where they discussed the full reorganization of SPC with its top executive managers – E. L. Pierce and Judge Nathan Miller. According to the *gérants*, these men were fit to prepare the post-Hazard era and bring SPC back to its prewar performance. The immediate outlook was not bright, though. SPC had only 38 percent of the market share in alkali in the United States (versus 70 percent for Solvay in Europe). Even more worrying, its leadership was disputed by challenging competitors. These were especially Columbia Chemical and Diamond Alkali, both of which were in close connection with local glassmakers. But other smaller businesses were also coming to the fore – Michigan Alkali, run by

[22] Abelshauser et al. (2004), 185–6.
[23] ACS, Binder SPC 1918–1919, Armand Solvay to N. T. Bacon, 3 Apr. 1919.

the Ford family at Wyandotte, Michigan, and Mathieson Alkali, located at Niagara Falls and using an electrolytic Castner's cell.[24]

This changing industrial landscape was further enhanced by other factors. American alkali companies could not count on the impossibility of British manufacturers to ensure their exports anymore. The end of the war had brought them back to the international trade markets, ruining the American expansion. Trade restraints might have worked things out but were prevented by the Sherman Act. American legislators, nevertheless, showed their fellow industrialists tireless compassion; they crafted another piece of law (the Webb-Pomerene Act of 1918), which exempted from the Sherman Act associations exclusively engaged in the De export trade. Put differently, what this law favored for American exporting firms was categorically banned when taking place within the United States. This led to the formation of the US Alkali Export Association (Alkasso), whose objective was to make worldwide trade arrangements with British manufacturers. From the start SPC joined Alkasso, to the dismay of Brunner, Mond, which, after all, still controlled about 80 percent of the joint British-American alkali world exports. The difficulty, however, was that Brunner, Mond's efforts were precisely in exports markets, whereas this segment represented no more than 5 percent for the Americans.[25]

Under these circumstances, how could Solvay & Cie set up a consortium of Solvay, SPC, and Brunner, Mond in the innovative field of synthetic ammonia? There were two variables to that equation. The first was the family business DuPont, and the second was the result of a previous merger incorporated in 1899, General Chemical Company. During the talks in Aachen, Bosch had been keen on emphasizing that, contrary to Solvay's initial statement, DuPont was not "merely interested in explosives." As a matter of fact, the Wilmington-based company, which had reaped the harvest of the war, intended to purchase the Haber-Bosch license from the US government's Chemical Foundation and was seeking technical assistance from BASF to start a big nitrates plant.[26] General Chemical was testing its original process "for converting atmospheric nitrogen into a compound containing combined nitrogen," designed by engineer Frederik W. De Jahn. And it had already approached SPC about a joint investment in launching a test plant to industrialize it.[27] When all parties eventually gathered in Brussels from 13–17 October 1919, it soon appeared that the foundations of the consortium sought for by Solvay were shaky indeed. Pierce and Miller, in particular, opposed strongly any agreement with DuPont. They were standing for General Chemical, whose participation they foresaw as the nexus of a wider holding composed of SPC, General Chemical, Semet-Solvay Company, Barrett Company, and National Aniline & Chemical Company. The latter company already consisted of a joint dyestuffs project incorporated in 1917; the enlargement of scope of these companies' activities seemed a "natural consequence,"

[24] ACS, NdG, Voyage aux États-Unis (octobre-novembre 1925) by E. Janssen, Nov. 1925; Haber (1971), 177.

[25] Glasscock (1969), 45–6; Haber (1971), 263–5; Reader (1970), 344–5.

[26] ACS, 1542-1-1A, Folder 1, Minutes of the meetings in Aachen, 17 Sept. 1919.

[27] For a later version of De Jahn's process, see http://www.freepatentsonline.com/1832102.pdf.

according to Miller.[28] The *gérants* agreed with this interpretation. They did so not only for the sake of SPC; they also trusted that the holding could strengthen their position in the following round of negotiations with Bosch. This proved wrong for several reasons. First, they underestimated how far along Pierce, Miller, and William H. Nichols – head of General Chemical – were in their planned partnership: an agreement had been reached between SPC and General Chemical to launch Atmospheric Nitrogen Corporation without Solvay's knowledge. Second, their assumption that General Chemical would drop De Jahn's process in favor of Haber's was unrealistic. Third, they had constantly privileged an agreement with DuPont, which was not to the liking of their American associates. Overall, the triangle negotiations turned into a dilemma: either a strong DuPont-BASF axis safeguarding Solvay's alkali position or the formation of a multiproduct American conglomerate with SPC – and thus Solvay – at its core.[29]

When Emmanuel Janssen realized during his stay in the United States in February 1920 that BASF had double-crossed Solvay by negotiating technical agreements directly with DuPont, he immediately advised the other *gérants* to suspend talks with Bosch. As a result, the consortium strategy collapsed like a house of cards. The other side effect of this turnaround was that it gave Nichols the upper hand in setting up the American consolidation. Pulling strings, however, was the financier Eugene Meyer Jr. His fortune and social prestige had grown immensely during the war; he had served as head of the War Finance Corporation, a government corporation established by Woodrow Wilson to pool financial resources for the US war economy. He was also the owner of the banking firm that served the interests of W. Beckers Aniline, which became part of the National Aniline. In the winter of 1918, he teamed up with Nichols to establish a voting trust as the financial backbone of that company. Shortly thereafter, he named a certain Orlando F. Weber board member, and subsequently general manager, of National Aniline. A cunning businessman, Meyer knew that the collaboration of National Aniline was most wanted, and he was willing to push up the bidding. After dragging negotiations, a compromise was finally reached whereby National Aniline became the fifth company of the consolidation. The chairman of SPC, E. L. Pierce, had to

---

[28] ACS, 1542-1-1A, Folder 1, Minutes of the meetings in Brussels, 13–17 Oct. 1919; Minutes of the meeting in Paris, 28 and 30 Oct. 1919. National Aniline & Chemical Co. grew out of the amalgamation in May 1917 of W. Beckers Aniline, Standard Aniline, Schoellkopf Aniline & Chemical, National Aniline, and parts of Benzol Products Company – itself the result of a merger of Semet-Solvay Co., Barrett Co., and General Chemical Co. See ACS, Binder BMC/SPC 1920, "Memorandum in regard to the Formation and Present Status of National Aniline & Chemical Co," by H.H. Handy, 23 Feb. 1920, enclosed as appendix C in J. H. Gold's "Report on visit to America, Feb.-March 1920," 20 Apr. 1920; Haber (1971), 187; "The Semet-Solvay System of By-Product Coke Manufacture," *Solvay Life*, 5 (3–5), Mar.–May 1921.

[29] ACS, Binder SPC 1918–1919, Nathan Miller to Solvay & Cie, 6 Dec. 1919; ACS, 1542-1-1A, Folder 1, Procédé Haber – Résumé, undated; ACS, 1542-1-1A, Folder 1, Subfolder Azote – Résumé de M. Ebrant (Procédé Haber Résumé, undated; Nomenclature dossiers Azote/Amérique/1920, Aug. 1933; Formation de l'Allied – Nomenclature des notes de voyage et d'entrevues préliminaires, undated).

concede that SPC had to pay a "high price" for this participation, literally and figuratively.[30]

Allied Chemical & Dye Corporation was incorporated on 16 December 1920 with William Nichols as chairman of the board and Orlando Weber as CEO. Pierce was vice president, as were Semet-Solvay Company's Henry Handy and William Nichols's son Charles W. Nichols. The new company was certainly a well-established, multiproduct corporation, but unlike DuPont, which was similar in its financial outlook, it was not oriented toward consumer-goods industries. Then again, Allied was the first American company to start ammonia synthesis on the basis of the Atmospheric Nitrogen Corporation's development. A onetime bicycle champion and energetic, if not autocratic, person, Orlando Weber had promised an important reorganization of the company along the lines he had already applied at National Aniline: rationalization of production costs, compression of the personnel, and a strict adoption of Taylor's scientific management principles. The *gérants* did appreciate the program but wanted to see its application. From owning 41 percent of SPC and 12 percent of Semet-Solvay Company's, Solvay held 16.66 percent of the share capital of Allied. They thus had reasons to make sure that they received the proper information in due time, as the fear of a loss of influence grew stronger among the managing partners.[31]

Sent to New York in January 1921, Emmanuel Janssen and Hallam Tuck's first impression of Orlando Weber was "excellent." The latter had announced that drastic measures were to be taken in the sales department of SPC, which had long been its Achilles' heel. "We have never been told that SPC was reduced to represent a mere thirty-five percent of the US overall production," claimed Janssen and Tuck, as they insisted on being relieved of the responsibility of this declining power.[32] In the following months, though, several signs showed the violence of Weber's practices: workers and employees from all ranks were laid off without notice, welfare work was dropped, industrial research largely neglected, wages were cut by 15 percent, and works eventually closed (e.g., the Hutchinson plant, some potash ventures). At SPC plants, the number of the personnel dropped from 6,221 in October 1920 to 3,209 the next year. With a hint of irony, the press would later call this illustration of labor management Weberism. Methods of downsizing aside, Solvay and Brunner, Mond were especially worried by the reckless dismissal of technical staff, which had been in close contact with Solvay's know-how. This conflicted strikingly with Solvay's longtime tradition – and contractual stipulations – of secrecy. In no time, engineers and skilled technicians went to competitive ammonia-soda concerns. According to a report drafted in 1927, there were two of them at

[30] ACS, Binder BMC/SPC 1920, "Memorandum in regard to the Formation and Present Status of National Aniline & Chemical Co," by H. H. Handy, 23 Feb. 1920; Pierce to Solvay & Cie, 4 Sept. 1920; ACS, RdG, 10 Nov. 1924 (account of E. Janssen's trip to the United States).

[31] ACS, Binder SPC/Allied Chemical 1921, Brief Summary of Transactions of organization meeting, 21 Dec. 1920; Haber (1971), 314–15.

[32] ACS, CdG, 12 May 1921; ACS, Relations Solvay & Cie-Allied, Résumé des entrevues (1921–1932), undated [Sept. 1932].

Michigan Alkali, four at Diamond Alkali, six at Columbia Chemical, and three at Mathieson Alkali. Whatever small in quantity, the impact of this brain drain was certainly not insignificant. In some cases, former SPC engineers even began a second career: Harold Alquist designed and rebuilt a soda plant in Japan after he did the same for the new works of Mathieson Alkali at Saltville, G. J. Lee was in charge of the Yung Lee plant in China, and another American director reactivated a soda plant in Donetz.[33]

In spite of these difficulties, the *gérants* gave Weber their full support for the organizational reforms he was undertaking. Allied's profits increased 11.9 percent in 1922 and 14.6 percent in 1923. Of a total of US$15.377 million during the latter year, SPC accounted for no less than US$5.4 million. Dividends, needless to say, followed suit. As a way to reward Weber's efforts, Solvay, Brunner, Mond, Nichols, and Meyer agreed after long negotiations to transfer him fifty thousand shares of Allied worth a total of US$3.8 million, provided that he promised to remain in command of Allied for at least five years (starting in January 1921). Solvay contributed 52.5 percent to this complementary payment.[34] Was this what Pierce had in mind when he acknowledged two years before that SPC, Semet-Solvay, and other companies were paying Weber's National Aniline a high price? Whatever the costs, it seemed that it was a price Allied's main shareholders were willing to pay. Besides, by that time, Pierce had already been dismissed.

Providentia: Reaching a Deal with IG

Talks with Carl Bosch had been suspended because of a divergent approach on the American question; they resumed, however, after sorting out the French case. Solvay had followed for some time the state-driven Compagnie Nationale de l'Azote, which was supposed to organize the license rights of the Haber-Bosch process for the French market. The project was finally dropped under nationalist pressures, thus legitimating the diffusion of the Claude process. Through its stake in the Société Chimique de la Grande Paroisse, Saint-Gobain was satisfied with the course of events, and it did not miss the opportunity to let Solvay know about its leading position. Negotiations had started at Armand Solvay's request, but the mutual distrust was overwhelming. "We have the impression that St-Gobain seeks to use the Claude process as a scarecrow

---

[33] ACS, 1271-33-1 A, Folder Personnel Solvay Process Cie (Documentation sur la réorganisation), "Réorganisation de la SPC après la creation d'Allied," 25 Jan. 1927; "Résumé de la situation dans l'industrie des produits sodiques," 6 July 1931; ACS, 1271-33-2, Folder 'Réorganisation Solvay Proces, Correspondance 1921', Nicholson Report (BMC), 24 Oct. 1921; Nichols to Solvay & Cie, 2 Dec. 1921; Solvay & Cie to Weber, 11 Jan. 1922; ACS, 1271-33-4 A, Folder O. Weber, Correspondance et Notes, Extract from the *NY Journal & American*, 19 Jan. 1938; Glasscock (1969), 37.

[34] By the end of 1922, the price of an Allied share had climbed from US$35 to US$85. ACS, CdG, 3 and 10 Nov. 1922, 29 Dec. 1922, 16 Nov. 1923; ACS, 1271-33-4 A, Folder O. Weber, Correspondance et Notes, Note pour la gérance – Rémunération du Président A.C.D., 27 Dec. 1922.

against us," said Janssen.[35] Consequently, René Étienne brought the *gérance* another option. This was to run the synthetic ammonia Casale process in partnership with mining companies and Alais, Froges & Camargue (Péchiney) Company, all of which shared the desire to move away not only from public initiatives but also from Saint-Gobain's excessive pretentions. Solvay did not oppose to have an eye in this new process, but its participation was meant to be seen as a leverage against Claude and for Haber. Although Solvay was growing skeptical about the industrial outcome of the former, it had not yet given up hope on securing the former. For some fortunate reasons, Bosch reached out at the same time (1 April 1922); he had heard that Solvay was part of the French consortium attempting to take hold of the Haber-Bosch process. Although this was already ancient history, the *gérants* did not deny it. They wanted a meeting with BASF, and a meeting they had.[36]

Since the first discussions with Bosch in September 1919, the political and industrial circumstances had considerably changed – and so had both companies. Solvay's position in the fast-growing but extremely protected American market was strengthened, and IG's recovered leadership had proved wrong Keynes's, pessimistic predictions of the "economic consequences of peace."[37] Just as BASF – and the constituents of IG for that matter – had a view on the international sphere, Solvay sought to contain BASF's market penetration in alkali products. As it happens, Gielen had insisted for several months that DSW, which was straining on the domestic market, needed a strong German partner. Janssen finally met Bosch in Berlin on 6 October 1922. During his stay, he was authorized to visit the Leuna works (the Oppau plant was still severely damaged after the explosion of September 1921). A preagreement was in the air: a community of interests between DSW and IG through a mutual exchange of shares (after a capital increase) and a commercial agreement. The basic principles of the latter were that the components of IG restricted their production of soda ash to the sole manufacturing of nitrogen products in Germany and to buying from DSW – at a discounted price – the alkali needed for other purposes in Germany. Bosch had initially hoped to obtain a direct participation in Solvay's capital, but the suggestion was immediately turned down by the *gérants*.[38]

At a meeting in Cologne on 20 November 1922, Janssen, Tournay, and Bosch agreed that the proportion of mutual exchange would be on the basis of 25 percent of DSW. This represented an amount of shares estimated at no less than DM 125 million (nominal value). After calculations, it was to be exchanged for DM 132 million worth of IG shares (nominal value). The lag was due to the difficult montage in IG's constituent companies. As a result, six

[35] ACS, CdG, 12 Dec. 1921; ACS, 1542-1-1A, Folder 3, Minutes of the meeting with Grande Paroisse and Saint-Gobain, 14 Dec. and 29 Dec. 1921; Memo "Ammoniaque synthétique: France," appendix to Procédé Haber – Résumé, undated.
[36] ACS, 1542-1-1A, Folder 4, Visite de Monsieur Étienne, 3 Apr. 1922; Bosch to Gielen, 1 Apr. 1922; Gielen to Bueb (BASF), 2 May 1922.
[37] Keynes (1920).
[38] ACS, 1271-33-1 A, File Communauté d'intérêts avec l'IG – Résumé, undated; ACS, CdG, 3 and 10 Nov. 1922; Abelshauser et al. (2004), 197–201.

firms agreed to exchange the counterpart of 5 percent of their capital (BASF, Bayer, Höchst, AGFA, Griesheim, and Weiler-ter-Meer). To compensate the apparent discrepancy of this financial transaction, it was agreed that IG would operate through its Swiss subsidiary Providentia AG, based in Schaffhausen. Solvay was to act as the legal transferor for its German subsidiary. The financial contract was eventually signed on 27 August 1924.[39] A couple of years later, Providentia was transformed into a holding company equally owned by Solvay and IG Farben. It became a successful financial vehicle for both concerns, despite that Solvay regretted being underinformed about its organization and activities. Among the main investments made until World War II, Providentia's portfolio held shares of Norsk-Hydro, which were exchanged to control 19.5 percent of Kali-Chemie's capital. This acquisition, focused at the time on the potentialities for alkali, and caustic soda in particular, proved decisive for Solvay's postwar diversification strategy (see Chapter 18).[40]

The separate commercial contract, also drafted by Paul Vander Eycken, confirmed basically the initial project whereby IG limited its production of soda ash to the manufacturing of nitrogen-related products and depended on DSW's deliveries for the remainder at a fixed price of 10 percent less than the German market price (the amount of the discount was inspired by previous business deals in France, as well as the contract between Brunner, Mond and Lever Brothers). In return, Solvay agreed not to manufacture in Germany any of IG's core products. This was, anyway, not likely to happen. At this occasion, the IG family members were all present (Cassella and Kalle, two pharmaceutical satellites of Höchst, had joined the others). By and large, the patterns of the 1924 soda ash agreement served as a blueprint for the conclusion of another commercial understanding between DSW and IG Farben in May 1927. It concerned the manufacturing of caustic soda – either by causticization or electrolysis – and gave way to a repartition of sales between both companies (54.5 percent for DSW and 45.5 percent for the IG group) in an ad hoc syndicate that they established and controlled – the Syndikat Deutscher Aetznatronfabriken GmbH.[41] Although the agreement specified that IG Farben could not sell more than twelve thousand tons of caustic soda per year, it explicitly

---

[39] ACS, 1151-37-13, Communauté d'intérêts IG-DSW (Folders 1A + A), varia; ACS, 1142-51-1, Folder Correspondance Entente financière IG-Solvay & Cie; Paul Vander Eycken, "Note concernant l'exécution de la Convention Financière…" 24 Oct. 1924; ACS, 1151-51-3, Convention financière Providentia-Solvay & Cie, 27 June 1924 (Brussels), 29 Aug. 1924 (Schaffhausen); Binder Contrats et conventions.

[40] ACS, 1142-51-1, Folder Convention financière Providentia-Solvay & Cie, "Note succincte sur Providentia A.G. et ses opérations," 3 Apr. 1933.

[41] ACS, 1151-51-4, IG–Convention soude caustique entre la DSW et l'IG, 19–20 May 1927; ACS, 1151-51-2, Soude caustique – Contrat syndical, Acte constitutif du syndicat soude caustique, 19 Oct. 1927; Contrat de livraison entre le Syndicat soude caustique et ses membres, 21 Nov. 1927. In conformity with their bilateral agreement, DSW and IG Farben respectively held 36.35 percent and 30.16 percent of the sales of caustic soda within the syndicate at the moment of its creation. Other members were Kali-Chemie AG (10.26 percent), Chemische Fabrik Kalk (9.72 percent), Sodafabrik Stassfurt GmbH (8.08 percent), and E. Matthes & Weber AG (5.43 percent).

left aside IG Farben's consumption for its own plants (section 7 – *Selbstverbrauch*). However, when the company accelerated the pace of expansion of
its organization in the following years, it was no longer clear what would fit
in the category of *Selbstverbrauch* – IG Farben had become such a sprawling
concern that it could be confounded with the German chemical industry as a
whole.

The situation posed by the 1927 agreement would thus have irremediable consequences for DSW's positioning in the market of caustic soda (see
Chapter 11). By then, though, such outcomes were not a source of unrest.
At Solvay, Georges Chardin was the only one who expressed some doubts
about the arrangement. Referring to both IG and Allied, he feared a dilu-
tion of the company in these giant chemical conglomerates. The *gérants* held
the opposite view. Not only were they convinced that Solvay had reinforced
its international position; they also felt that these agreements did not pre-
clude the company from establishing other partnerships outside Germany.
Besides, that was precisely what they had done in France. In December 1923,
shortly before the IG deal came into force, they finally followed René Étienne's
enduring advice to take a 13.3 percent stake in the Société Ammonia, to
exploit the Casale process. As mentioned, the Société Ammonia resulted from
an association between French coal-mining industries and Péchiney, which
intended to focus on coke-oven derivatives. Applying the principles of Pas-
cal's wager to commercial purposes, Solvay trusted that it had a lot to gain
from these agreements and little to lose. Rather than being the deliberate purpose, the Casale process was, in its understanding, a timely excuse to get
closer to big French chemical groups. It was clever indeed: six months later,
in June 1924, Kuhlmann announced its intention to work the Casale process and set up the Société des Produits Chimiques Anzin-Kuhlmann through
a participation in Ammonia.[42] "Our role," the *gérants* unanimously stated,
"is to become designated intermediaries in the changing orientations of the
chemical industry, in the international reorganizations which we are observing
everywhere."[43]

9.2   THE TWISTS AND TURNS OF INDUSTRIAL DIPLOMACY

What did Carl Bosch have in mind when he resumed negotiations with Solvay
leading to the Providentia deal? "Allied, most certainly," was the reply given by
Emmanuel Janssen. During their early meetings, Bosch had repeatedly alluded
to the activities of the American conglomerate. He believed that National Aniline was the only company capable of manufacturing decent dyestuffs – apart
from IG, of course. In a conversation with Janssen, he even sought to get
a slice of Solvay's share of the Allied pie, but he was not successful. As a
result, BASF had started direct negotiations in Great Britain and the United
States, respectively, with British Dyes Corporation (as soon as May 1922)

---

[42] ACS, 1700-1-1A, Minutes of the meetings on 20 Nov. 1923, 12 Dec. 1923, and 12 June 1924.
[43] ACS, CdG, 30 Nov. & 14 Dec. 1923, 4 Jan. 1924; ACS, 1151-51-3, Convention commerciale
   Providentia-Solvay & Cie, 7 June 1924; Binder Contrats et conventions.

and Allied (as soon as January 1923). Because it was in the interest of the *gérants* to foster an Allied-IG partnership, they preferred to inform Weber about the course of discussions between Solvay and IG.[44] During their stay in the United States, Janssen and Tournay also arranged a meeting between Weber and Bosch. The summit took place in New York on 26 October 1923, before the Providentia agreements were ratified. There was no uncertainty about the concrete outcomes. Suggestions had emerged throughout – the exchange of shares between National Aniline or Atmospheric Nitrogen, and IG; the proposal of a Swiss holding; repartition of market shares – but apparently without any result. It seemed that Duisberg, on the German side, and Nichols, on the American one, were especially reluctant about a partnership. Duisberg, in particular, held privileged contacts with the American dyestuffs producer Grasselli Chemical. Bayer and Grasselli concluded an agreement in June 1924, leading to the formation of Grasselli Dyestuffs Corporation, later known as General Aniline, and General Aniline & Film after the US government takeover of the corporation on the eve of World War II.[45] Weber and Bosch got along quite well. In spite of depicting Weber as a "financier" with an "American mentality whose main objective is to make dollars," Bosch had a good impression of the manager of Allied.[46] But although Bosch and Weber were quite skeptical about achieving any form of concrete combinations with each other, some of the *gérants* held a rather optimistic view. "To make it brief," said Janssen, "we have the impression that an agreement will be reached, but it is still difficult to see how." More symbolically, the meeting between the leaders of Allied and BASF was interpreted by Solvay as a victory for Weber. He had eclipsed DuPont in Bosch's eyes. Moreover, he was, according to the *gérants*, in "full community of views" with theirs.[47] This was about to change.

The Tripartite Agreement: A Fragile Precedent

Since the end of the war, Solvay's tactics with regard to international alliances had been to place special emphasis on the technological aspects of negotiations as a way to safeguard its commercial leadership and strengthen its industrial position. It was a forward-looking defensive strategy, which seemed to pay off in the early 1920s. Its first expression was to be found in the suggestion, shortly after the war, to launch the Committee for the Protection of the Solvay Process (Comité de Défense du Procédé Solvay) together with Brunner, Mond and SPC. The committee's guiding principles were to facilitate the circulation of technical

---

[44] ACS, 1151-37-13, IG: Communauté d'intérêts IG-DSW, Correspondance avec Weber, passim; ACS, CdG, 22 Feb. 1924; ACS, 1271-37-8 bis, Janssen to Weber, 27 June 1922; ACS, 1271-33-1 A, File Communauté d'intérêts avec l'IG – Résumé, undated, 14–6; ACS, Relations Solvay & Cie-Allied, Résumé des entrevues (1921–1932), undated [Sept. 1932].

[45] Baptista and Travis (2006); Stokes (2004), 49–57; Wilkins (2004), 238–9.

[46] ACS, 1151-37-13, Minutes of the meeting in Basel, 11 Jan. 1924.

[47] ACS, RdG, 12 Nov. 1923; ACS, CdG, 16 Nov. 1923; ACS, 1271-33-1 A, File Communauté d'intérêts avec l'IG – Résumé, undated, 19–27; ACS, Relations Solvay & Cie-Allied, Résumé des entrevues (1921–1932), undated [Sept. 1932].

innovation and know-how within the network of industries running the Solvay process. This made perfect sense in the context of the time. Solvay not only wanted to overcome the technological lag resulting from the occupation of Belgium, but it also had to face the imminent danger posed by the Haber-Bosch technology. Solvay's British and American partners greeted the initiative with measured enthusiasm at the Brussels meeting of October 1919. Since the focus was on industrial research, it was decided, at Lieutenant Colonel Pollitt's suggestion, to rename the project as the Study Committee for the Solvay-Process Companies. Its aim, generally accepted, was to establish "an international laboratory, which will accept at a later stage Germans and Austrians, a center of scientific documentation, and a center for social studies."[48] It was, in other words, the first experience of international alliance Solvay initiated after the war – an alliance with friends rather than competitors under the sign of scientific exchange.

Back home, however, British and American partners started to revise the committee's initial framework. Brunner, Mond started off by suggesting that the technical information pertaining to the manufacture of synthetic ammonia (or its by-products) by whatever process ought to be excluded from the agreement. It was not, needless to say, a minor addendum but undermined completely the scope the committee was aiming at. On the American side, the project suffered no criticism whatsoever until the formation of Allied. From then on, it appeared that the Study Committee was running counter to the provisions of the Sherman Act. The matter was discussed during Nichols and Pierce's stay in Europe in May and June 1921.[49] The upper management of Allied brought substantial revisions to the text, which led to the drafting of another agreement, proposed by E. L. Pierce on 5 August 1921. Solvay was stunned: the agreement "had nothing to do with the Study Committee" anymore; it merely reproduced the initial "contract of association" of 1881 between Solvay and SPC. More important, Pierce went on by asserting that "naturally" this new proposal would replace "all past agreements, taken or proposed" between Solvay and its European subsidiaries and its American subsidiaries. It was purely and simply a rejection of the original contract of 1881, which had been prolonged until 2010 long before the war broke out. As Solvay's General Secretary Ernest Sougnez put it, "The Sherman Act is the shield behind which our associates take convenient shelter."[50]

The Tripartite Agreement, as it was then called, was finally ratified by Brunner, Mond and Solvay on 8 July 1922. Although some salient aspects

[48] ACS, 1542-1-1A, Folder 1, Minutes of the meetings in Brussels, 13–17 Oct. 1919; Procédé Haber – Résumé, undated; ACS, CdS, Report of the gérance, 12 Dec. 1919. A copy of the bylaws of the Study Committee is in "Contrats intervenus avec la Solvay & Cie et qui sont périmés" (hereafter "Contrats périmés"), "Amérique," 15 Oct. 1920.

[49] ACS, CdG, 12 May 1921; ACS, Relations Solvay & Cie-Allied, Résumé des entrevues (1921–1932).

[50] ACS, 1271-51-2, Convention tripartite, Pierce to Solvay & Cie, 5 Aug. 1921; ACS, Binder SPC/Allied 1921; "Note Commission d'études," by E. Sougnez, 25 Aug. 1921; Note SPC, by E. Sougnez, undated; Solvay & Cie to SPC, 4 Oct. 1921; Janssen to Weber, 17 Feb. 1922; correspondence exchanged in binder "Contrats périmés – Amérique."

included in the former draft had been cut off (as it happens, there was no mention of a committee with its fixed seat in Brussels anymore), it was a major agreement, as it combined the conditions of exchange of technical information with the commercial repartition of each party's territory. Solvay's share was Continental Europe; Brunner, Mond's, the United Kingdom, the British Empire (exclusive of the Dominion of Canada), and the Far East; and Solvay Process Company's, North America.[51] Whether the agreement was binding and effective was, of course, another question. SPC was not sending its semiannual production costs charts to Solvay anymore; Brunner, Mond was reluctant to inform about the technicalities of its production of electrolytic caustic soda and chlorine, synthetic methanol, and other products; Solvay forgot to mention to SPC the three Casale-run units exploited by the Semet-Solvay & Piette controlled by the Mutuelle.[52] The fact that Weber had developed his own style of confidentiality management did not encourage Solvay to be proactive in terms of technology transfers. Another case in the point was the Amherstburg plant in Canada. It had been incorporated by Brunner, Mond in 1916 under a special agreement with the holding Brunner, Mond Canada Ltd., which was in fact 60 percent owned by SPC. After the consolidation of Allied and in accordance with the commercial provisions contained in the tripartite agreement, Weber wanted total control (with the intention of shutting the factory). To his surprise, Brunner, Mond opposed no firm resistance and offered to be Allied's interest for US$2.5 million, an amount that included trademark rights.[53] What Weber interpreted as a moral triumph was actually the result of a form of lassitude, a mutual desire to drift away from each other's control. Instead of smoothing things over, the tripartite agreement had triggered off a chain reaction of trilateral suspicion.

Becoming Designated Intermediaries

Upon return from a long stay in the United States in November 1925, Emmanuel Janssen reported to his fellow *gérants* that the "general situation [had] completely changed from last year" and was "serious" ("l'heure est grave").[54] First and foremost, in five years, Orlando Weber had turned a "collection of empty bottles" into one of the most successful businesses.[55] He had become the unchallenged ruler of an expanded empire. His "administrative technique," upon which he took unlimited pride, had contributed to enhance the production capacities of Allied's constituent companies. The market share

[51] ACS, 1271-51-2, Convention tripartite, Solvay & Cie, Brunner, Mond, and Solvay Process Company – Agreement, 3 Aug. 1921.

[52] ACS, CdG 18 Apr. 1924; ACS, RdG, 2 May 1924; ACS, 1271-37-8 bis, C. Lutkins to Janssen, 8 Jan. 1925; Roscoe Brunner to Weber, 18 Aug. 1925, and Weber's reply, 4 Sept. 1925; ACS, Relations Solvay & Cie-Allied, Résumé des entrevues (1921–1932).

[53] ACS, 1271-37-8 bis, Brunner, Mond to Weber, 16 Dec. 1924. The deal was finally settled by May 1925; see Reader (1970), 334.

[54] ACS, NdG, "Voyage aux États-Unis, octobre-novembre 1925" by Emmanuel Janssen, Nov. 1925.

[55] ACS, RdG, 2 Dec. 1925.

of SPC had progressed from 38 percent to 43 percent, production costs had declined, and sales prices were reaching prewar levels. The consortium's financial outlook was even better; reserves were high, and the investment strategy had been thriving. Allied had become the major shareholder of US Steel, whose market value was soaring. Thus, why was the situation so "serious"? As Allied's main shareholders, Solvay need not to complain. But as associates, times were rough. Weber's hubris had followed Allied's ascending profit curve. On the one hand, he was asking for freedom of action in the export business; on the other hand, he constantly referred to the Sherman Act to turn down international alliances. His anger focused especially on Brunner, Mond's alleged lack of trustworthiness. He was furious about the close contacts Brunner, Mond had with Allied's home competitors – Mathieson Alkali Works and Niagara Electro-Chemical Company – since their takeover of Castner-Kellner Alkali Company. The opposition of style between Weber and Roscoe Brunner (and later Sir Alfred Mond) had turned into a series of personal conflicts. But the mistrust had rubbed off on Solvay, whom Weber accused of being overtly conciliatory.[56]

In his seminal note of November 1925, Janssen was alarming: "Our great organization, which has yielded undisputable results for more than sixty years, is on the brink of being violently shaken, seriously threatened."[57] He suggested three possible strategies: first, the formation of a pan-European chemical group including Solvay, Brunner, Mond (and potential British partners), and IG, which would fight against Allied on equal terms; second, a closer partnership with Allied allowing the Americans to have a straightforward interest in Solvay; third, creation of a global holding in which Solvay would bring in its foreign portfolio – Brunner, Mond (12 percent), Allied (16 percent), DSW (70 percent), and IG (5 percent) – in combination with Brunner, Mond's participation in Allied (5 percent).[58] Janssen, needless to say, favored the last combination, which was the only one that could avoid at the same time losing Solvay's control and starting off a head-on war with Weber. When the latter paid Solvay a visit in Brussels in January 1926, the *gérance* cast no doubt on his intentions – he wanted the break free from any binding contracts. That he had in view the tripartite agreement was quite obvious. To Armand Solvay's son, Ernest-John, who had done a – quite restrictive – internship at Allied's headquarters between November 1924 and April 1925, Weber had not concealed his opinion to "get rid once and for all of contractual ties" with Solvay and Brunner,

[56] Reader (1970), 229; ACS, Relations Solvay & Cie-Allied, Résumé des entrevues (1921–1932); ACS, 1271-37-8 bis, Janssen to Weber, 19 Dec. 1925 and Weber's reply, 15 Jan. 1925; ACS, NdG, "Voyage aux États-Unis, octobre-novembre 1925" by Emmanuel Janssen, Nov. 1925 and "Considérations au sujet des prétentions de M. Weber" by Émile Tournay (Nov. 1925). Tournay was convinced that Weber's attitude was essentially fueled by his opposition to Brunner, Mond.

[57] ACS, NdG, "Voyage aux États-Unis, octobre-novembre 1925" by Emmanuel Janssen, Nov. 1925.

[58] ACS, NdG, "Voyage aux États-Unis, octobre-novembre 1925" by Emmanuel Janssen, Nov. 1925, 17–20.

Mond.[59] He urged Sir Alfred Mond to leave Allied the South American market, which represented sixty thousand tons of alkali and had been split among Brunner, Mond, UAC, and Alkasso. Solving these issues called for an all-around renegotiation.

Solvay elaborated its reaction following a two-step method – in dialogue with Brunner, Mond's upper management and among *gérants* exclusively. Concerning international market share, the *gérants* prompted their British partners to give up on their pretentions on Central and South America. What outraged Brunner, Mond was less the specific issue of the Americas than its underlying motivation. Sir Alfred Mond was convinced that Weber was pursuing a strategy of hegemony in alkali products. After South America, he argued, what would be the next concession?[60] Taking a more distant view, Armand Solvay paid particular attention to the initial contract of 1881, which dealt with the reciprocity of technical innovation rather than with market sharing, which was determined by commercial agreements that were easily modifiable. Weber ought to make the proper distinction, he argued, when he wrongly referred to the Sherman Act for prohibiting the exchange of technical information as laid out in the tripartite convention.[61] Weber, of course, could not have cared less. During a brief stay in Brussels in May 1926, he made clear that he wanted total freedom for the trade in the Americas and, presumably, for other parts of the world. In the same vein, he was quite reluctant about the creation of a three-party holding, which could be extended to a four-party agreement including IG in the future.[62]

This last aspect was of utmost importance. Since the organizational transformation of IG into a formally single unit – IG Farbenindustrie AG – in December 1925, the world chemical industry had shared an apprehensive mood about what to expect from this gigantic corporation: a partner or a competitor? Both, was the most likely answer. Solvay's reaction was instantaneous: "It will be more interesting for us to have a part of the whole rather than a fraction of the constituent companies."[63] At Brunner, Mond, rumors about "a major reorganization" became clearer. True, this was not only because of the formation of IG Farben; the British company had been deeply affected by a long-lasting quarrel with Lever Brothers concerning an alkali agreement, which culminated with the announcement of a public trial in November 1925. The litigation was only just avoided by settling the deal for a million British pounds and the revision of the contract.[64] Brunner, Mond needed to move on. Mergers were

[59] ACS, Relations Solvay & Cie-Allied, Résumé des entrevues (1921–1932); ACS, NdG, "Aide-mémoire pour la visite de M. Weber" by Ernest-John Solvay, 7 Jan. 1926.

[60] ACS, RdG, 21 April & 29 May 1926.

[61] ACS, NdG, "Note sur l'Allied" by Armand Solvay, 25 May 1926; ACS, RdG, 4 and 29 May 1926.

[62] ACS, 1271-37-7, Voyage aux États-Unis (Dec. 1926–Jan. 1927), Notes de W. H. Tuck, May–June 1926; ACS, "Relations Solvay & Cie-Allied, Résumé des entrevues (1921–1932)."

[63] ACS, CdG, 3 Apr. 1925; Abelshauser et al. (2004), 214–15; Reader (1970), 321.

[64] ACS, RdG, 6 & 17 Apr. 1925, 2 Dec. 1925, 10 Mar. 1926; CdG, 2 Apr. 1926; Reader (1970), 374–5.

in the air; the stand-alone attitude was not an option anymore. But what kind of coalition should be put up?

The *gérants* cleared up the matter by focusing primarily on what they did not want. Drawing on Janssen's note of November 1925, they ruled out his proposal of a global holding combining Solvay's foreign interests. "That formula's biggest inconvenient," went the argument, "is that it would turn Solvay into the intersection of different – if not divergent – interests."[65] At a joint meeting between Solvay and Brunner, Mond on 26 May 1926, it was further understood that a separate IG-Allied agreement should be prevented. Although it seemed quite obvious for the participants, it was a radical shift from Solvay's initial international alliance strategy. Above all, it illustrated that their objective of becoming designated intermediaries was compromised. When the heads of Brunner, Mond and Solvay gathered in La Hulpe, Belgium, on 9–11 August 1926 to prepare their counteropposition, they faced the cruel paradox of elaborating a strategy of containment based on a mechanism of integration. The *gérant* Édouard Hannon believed the solution was the business equivalent of the Locarno Pact, which had been recently ratified by the British, the French, and the Germans as a sign of appeasement. However inspiring, Hannon's *bon mot* was quite useless under such circumstances. In the spring of La Hulpe, everyone stood firm: none of the participants had something innovative to offer, but there was a strong commitment not to give way to Weber's diktat. The long-awaited frank explanation with the general manager of Allied took place in mid-September 1926 in New-York. It turned into a violent clash. As expected, Weber strongly rejected the status quo that Solvay and Brunner, Mond wished to preserve in both commercial and technical realms. Weber asked to terminate the tripartite agreement with immediate effect. To Solvay and Brunner, Mond, this was hardly a surprise. What they had not anticipated, however, was that, by the same token, Weber also demanded cancellation of the historical agreements on the grounds of the Sherman Act. This completed the declaration of independence initiated during the war. From now on, the *gérants* and Allied would communicate only through legal experts.[66]

ICI and the Creation of Solvay American Investment Corporation

One man was less puzzled than the others by the course of events. Emmanuel Janssen had been waiting in ambush for a while. He knew Weber too well to be truly affected by his fits of rage. After his global holding proposal had been swept away by his colleagues, Janssen had seized the standstill opportunity of La Hulpe to test another formula. The Mutuelle, he went on, not Solvay, could provide the hoped-for institutional vehicle enabling the international alliance driven by Solvay to take place. In Janssen's views, the Mutuelle could, after a necessary increase of its capital from BEF 100 million to BEF 300 million

[65] ACS, RdG 21 Apr. 1926; ACS, NdG by Ernest-John Solvay, 27 Aug. 1926.
[66] ACS, 1271-51-3, Convention tripartite du 3 août 1921 – résiliation; ACS, Binder "contrats périmés"; ACS, NdG, "Voyage aux Etats-Unis, septembre-octobre 1926" by E. Janssen, 28 Oct. 1926.

entirely subscribed by Solvay, absorb substantial portions of Allied, Brunner, Mond, and IG. Its portfolio expressed in Belgian Francs would thus be broken down as follows:[67]

Solvay & Cie	140,000,000
Shareholders Solvay & Cie	60,000,000
	Subtotal: 200,000,000
Allied	50,000,000
Brunner, Mond	25,000,000
IG Farben	25,000,000
	Total: 300,000,000

In spite of its untraditional approach – or maybe because of it – this plan received a frosty reception from the *gérants*. Armand Solvay did not recognize the opportunity of a method whereby "the Mutuelle would have interests everywhere and Solvay only in their plants."[68] His thirty-year-old son, Ernest-John, who had joined the *gérance* upon return from an internship in the United States, in May 1925, did not conceal his opposition. There was, he argued, a real danger in Solvay abandoning 71 percent of its total assets to the Mutuelle, which was after all a distinct (albeit friendly) company. Conversely, foreign associates could own through the planned Mutuelle up to 8 percent of Solvay & Cie's new capital (after increase of BEF 100 million) or 11 percent of its old capital (before the increase). It represented, he concluded, a financial detail for Allied and IG but a substantial amount for a company the scope of Solvay's. He was backed, without further arguments, by Louis Solvay and Émile Tournay. [69] Édouard Hannon, in his inimitable prose,[70] was perhaps less reluctant about the plan but nevertheless considered it hardly effective. What lay behind this unanimous antagonism was also the fact that some shareholders of the Mutuelle (the families Janssen, Hannon, and Hulin) did not have stakes in Solvay & Cie in the same proportion. Studying the question from a legal perspective, the counselor Paul Vander Eycken admitted some years later that the different shareholdings of both companies induced "delicate" issues.[71]

The plan was thus – provisionally – dropped. Its author remained convinced of the necessity to find some agreement with Allied. This he shared with

[67] ACS, NdG by Emmanuel Janssen, 3 Sept. 1926.

[68] ACS, NdG, "Note de M. Armand Solvay sur la situation internationale actuelle au point de vue de Solvay & Cie," 18 Nov. 1926.

[69] ACS, NdG, "Remarques concernant la situation actuelle de Solvay & Cie," by E.-J. Solvay, 4 Nov. 1926; ACS, RdG, 12 Nov. 1926.

[70] "On n'insiste pas, avec raison, sur le peu d'importance financière pour chacun, de cet arrangement. Ce serait, évidemment, un peu comme une réunion de parents pauvres réunis autour d'une petite table de la Mutuelle pour grignoter les miettes du plantureux dessert servi aux grandes tables voisines. Mais ce serait le moyen, plus sérieux, de se voir, se parler et discuter paisiblement." ACS, NdG, "La politique de Solvay & Cie," by Edouard Hannon, 31 Oct. 1926.

[71] ACS, Notes juridiques Paul Vander Eycken, "Note au sujet des dividendes à distribuer désormais par la Mutuelle," 29 Oct. 1928; "Note sur l'augmentation du capital du 26 novembre 1928," 20 Nov. 1928; ACS, "Note de Louis Solvay relative à l'augmentation de la participation de Solvay & Cie dans la Mutuelle," 19 May 1928.

Solvay's recently appointed counselor in the United States, Hugh D. Auchincloss, who had thoroughly analyzed Solvay's position in Allied.[72] Janssen and Auchincloss were reinforced in their belief by an important event: the newly formed British Allied (*dixit* Sir Alfred Mond), which was eventually called Imperial Chemical Industries (ICI), announced its intention to sell its Allied shares. The formation of ICI was, partly at least, the result of Weber's unilateral cancellation of the tripartite agreement. It was the last of a long series of vexations that persuaded Sir Alfred Mond to abandon the consortium deal with Allied and IG Farben and reconsider Nobel Industries' Sir Harry McGowan's project for a "big British combine." According to historian W. J. Reader, the agreement leading to the final formation of ICI was reached aboard the *Aquitania*, on return from America. The project was designed as a merger of Brunner, Mond, Nobel Industries, UAC, and British Dyestuffs Corporation, all of which developed diverse products and processes and, financially, pursued different investment strategies. Accordingly, the combination completely modified the outlook of Anglo-American relations in the chemical industry. Because of the long history of cooperation between Nobel Industries and DuPont, ICI was from its inception more predisposed to collaborate with the latter rather than with Allied (Sir Harry McGowan early on aimed to obtain a bigger stake in DuPont). Conversely, Brunner, Mond's sizable interests in Allied (about 5.3 percent) would sooner or later become a sensitive issue with respect to the new direction ICI would have to tackle if it wished to get closer to DuPont.[73]

The *gérance* of Solvay heard about the creation of ICI on 15 October 1926, shortly before an official announcement was made. From its 16 percent control of Brunner, Mond, Solvay was about to own a mere 6 percent of ICI's shares.[74] To some extent, it was caught short by this setup. However, this gave Emmanuel Janssen a sudden legitimacy to set forth other versions of the plan.[75] Back in the United States to attend Allied's annual board meeting for Christmas 1926, Janssen confronted Weber's dismay for the wide-range reorganization of the chemical industry in Europe. When Janssen submitted to him the latest edition of the plan, he threatened to set up an Americans-only voting trust, which would oppose Solvay and Allied's other foreign shareholders. Moreover, Weber resorted to a threat he was eager to use from time to time, namely to export directly to the European market Allied's major base products, as well as coal-tar derivatives and inorganic acids.[76] He was infuriated by the lack of subordination that Solvay and Brunner, Mond had been displaying since he demanded total freedom of action. In the following days, Janssen started to

---

[72] ACS, RdG, 19 Nov. 1926.

[73] Reader (1970), 460–4; Reader (1975), 23; Haber (1971), 296; Wilkins (2004), 244–5. On ICI's predecessor firms (e.g., United Alkali), see also Chapter 3.

[74] ACS, 1241-40-1A: Solvay & Cie to Brunner, Mond, 11 Jan. 1927; ACS, RdG, 15–16-20-21 Oct. 1926, 18 Nov. 1926.

[75] ACS, RdG, 22–23 Nov. 1926.

[76] This contradicts the common view that Allied "did not seek to establish itself abroad, and took part only in those international agreements that protected its home markets" (Aftalion 2001, 141).

elaborate on Weber's idea of a voting trust but at Allied's expense. He therefore conceived, with Tuck and Auchincloss, the design of the Solvay American Investment Corporation (SAIC), whose prime objective was to give Solvay the upper hand in the control and management of its U.S.-based participations.[77] Appointed chairman of SAIC was James H. Perkins, a financial expert graduated from Harvard, who served as president-elect of Farmers' Loan and Trust, the banking institution that was then responsible for Solvay's US interests. The other members of the board were American, with the exception of Armand Solvay and Emmanuel Janssen.

The creation of SAIC, needless to say, ushered in a period of tensions in the long history of relations between Brussels and New York. As an illustration, we can turn to private correspondence engaged in during the first months of 1927 by the two wise business leaders Armand Solvay and William Nichols. To Armand Solvay, who expressed his dearest wish "to reconcile the interests at stake in the great chemical consortiums created since the war," Nichols's reply was unambiguously nationalist:

> The Allied Chemical and Dye Corporation, notwithstanding its very large foreign ownership, is an American concern and it must conform to American laws; these laws, while they do not forbid size in industry, do forbid all material restriction of competition, and all kartels [sic] and consortiums such as you favor and as are freely formed in Europe.... I may frankly say that your large interests in the German kartels [sic], in the great new English merger, and in other chemical companies in other lands, coupled with your evident desire for a world consortium that would give all the world's trade, outside America, to other than Allied – all this does give us considerable anxiety. We are led to feel that perhaps you regard these other interests as more important to you than this company, which to us is all important.[78]

Unexpected as they were, Nichols's arguments demanded proper refutation, but this would take several months. Officially, Armand was taking some rest in the south of France; in fact, his reply was carefully revised by an armada of legal advisers. As Hugh Auchincloss put it, "The letter written by Armand Solvay . . . is so admirable in form and substance that under ordinary circumstances we would not hesitate to send it at once to Dr. Nichols." These were, however, no ordinary circumstances, and it was judged "wiser" by Vander Eycken and Auchincloss to suggest some adjustments. Most of them consisted in denying the insinuations contained in Nichols's letter and leaving out a few passages perceived as sensitive to American corporate legislation. Nevertheless, what was not added or removed was Armand Solvay's proposal of resignation, as well as Emmanuel Janssen's, as members of the board of Allied. Upon

[77] ACS, 1290–1-1A, Création de la SAIC, passim; ACS, 1271–37-7, Notes envoyées aux États-Unis, Folder "Lettres de M. Janssen et notes des diverses entrevues avec M. Weber"; ACS, RdG, 28 Jan. 1927; ACS, Relations Solvay & Cie-Allied, Résumé des entrevues (1921–1932), undated [Sept. 1932].

[78] ACS, 1271–37-1A, A. Solvay to W. Nichols, 22 Dec. 1926 and Nichols' reply, 10 Jan. 1927.

receiving the letter, Nichols unsurprisingly declined the offer and asked to cease the controversy, as mutual opinions had been "frankly shared."[79]

For Solvay's industrial and financial position in the United States, SAIC was a breakthrough in many respects. First, it was essentially an American company composed of a majority of experts in US corporate law; members of the board could not only denounce Weber's claims of foreign ownership but also carefully crosscheck his usual arguments referring to antitrust legislation. Second, SAIC provided Solvay with an appropriate – and visible – institutional platform for expanding its contacts and filling in its address book overseas. Janssen, Tuck, and Auchincloss had been keen on linking the American market boom they witnessed with the expected outcomes of SAIC's social network multiplier in that country. Finally, and most important, SAIC was a welcome financial instrument. As a holding trust, it enabled Solvay to undertake low-tax financial operations in the United States, which were wholly guaranteed on their US-based interests. Hence, this allowed SAIC to convert a US$10 million loan it had issued on the American market in 1920, which had necessitated the caution of Solvay's assets in Europe and the assistance of Brunner, Mond.[80] It did so as soon as January 1927 through the issue of a US$15 million US bond offering raised by the Boston investment bank Lee, Higginson & Co., which had already redeemed the 1920 loan three years earlier (without great public success). The reason for this haste was that proceeds of the operation were not solely used to lend US$10.5 million to Solvay; they were also planned to acquire a substantial amount of shares in the American Libbey-Owens Sheet Glass Company.

Libbey-Owens and the Reordering of the French Alkali Industry

The purchase of the American Libbey-Owens Sheet Glass Company had been planned by Emmanuel Janssen during the first days of his exceptionally productive business stay in the United States. In the midst of difficult relations, he had even asked Weber whether he and Allied would take part in the deal, which he presented as "very promising."[81] Weber finally agreed; the move was, indeed, opportune. On the one hand, it enabled Janssen to diversify the interests of SAIC and make it less dependent on Allied; on the other hand, it strengthened the position of Libbey-Owens's, European affiliate – the Compagnie Internationale pour la Fabrication Mécanique du Verre (Mecaniver) – which had been controlled by the Mutuelle Solvay since 1921. The introduction in 1928 of Henry Ford's Model A, which contained a windshield of laminated glass, gave the Libbey-Owens plant in Toledo, Ohio, an even stronger impulsion. It set stage to the merger of the Libbey-Owens Sheet Glass Company with

79 PPJS, Box Armand Solvay No. 1, Folder 3, E. Sougnez to A. Solvay, 24 Feb. 1927; Marshall & Auchincloss to Solvay & Cie, 18 Mar. 1927 (including revisions); A. Solvay to W. Nichols, 2 Apr. 1927; ACS, 1271-37-1A, W. Nichols to A. Solvay, 27 Apr. 1927.

80 ACS, CdS, Minutes of the meetings, 18 Sept. 1920. The loan was due to cover the expenses of Suria after Allied had reconsidered its participation.

81 ACS, 1271-37-7, "Lettres de M. Janssen et notes des diverses entrevues avec M. Weber," Minutes of the meetings, 15 Dec. 1926 and 5 Jan. 1927 (Allied HQ).

the Edward Ford Plate Glass Company in 1930, and the resultant creation of Libbey-Owens-Ford Glass Company.[82]

The variety and subtlety of the operations undertaken in New York at the turn of 1926 and 1927 were diversely commented on by the *gérants* left in Brussels. In the rush of the events, though, they decided not to interrupt the scheme that was leading to the shaping of the American corporation. Ernest-John Solvay and Émile Tournay, accompanied by Paul Vander Eycken, joined Janssen and eventually gave their approval to the launching of SAIC and its intended participations. Emmanuel Janssen, however, had not completely given up his design to set up an international consortium based on a pool of shares from IG Farben and ICI through the Mutuelle. He was even favorably considering its extension to a French group or to Allied. At the same time, Solvay was asked by the head of French metallurgical company Schneider, Jules Aubrun, to join an entente setting up a Bergius-like process to convert coal into liquid fuel. Sicol, as it was called, was intended to be a French, Belgian, and Luxembourg variant to the German Bergius syndicate. This was, of course, quite timely. Numerous chemical and oil companies sought to compete with the first comer in the field, IG Farben, in searching for valid hydrogenation processes. For the sake of observation, Solvay eventually accepted to participate to the extent of 7 percent in Sicol's capital.[83] More than anything, however, the strategy was to use Sicol as a Trojan horse in the complex landscape of the French chemical industry. If companies like Pechiney, Kuhlmann, and Saint-Gobain were potential partners in the international trust Solvay was currently building, it was above all a way to test their attitude and eventual loyalty toward the Brussels-based multinational. There was no doubt that these French companies were lacking the international dimension Solvay could offer. Conversely, Solvay needed allies in a country where it was busy reinforcing its industrial activities through the planned – but confidential – takeover of the Bayonne works and, most of all, the building of an electrolytic plant in Tavaux (see Chapter 10).

Emmanuel Janssen discovered with contentment that Solvay's international network in the alkali industry, as well as its extension in the glass industry, could weigh effectively on their presence in France. Could Solvay finally give the impetus toward the strong industrial concentration they hoped for in a country where they had substantial interests and serious contenders? For once, noted Janssen, discussions with the upper management of Saint-Gobain, Lucien Delloye and Robert de Voguë, were easy.[84] They paved the way for the creation of the Société d'Études et d'Applications Chimiques, whose objective was to start joint research programs and establish a common industrial laboratory. The newly constituted company Rhône-Poulenc and the Gillet family business group were also asked to join in. The Société d'Études was a further opportunity for another financial montage due to Janssen – the Mutuelle Industrielle, a

---

[82] See http://www.utoledo.edu/LIBRARY/canaday/exhibits/oi/OIExhibit/Syrup.htm.
[83] Petri (1994); ACS, RdG, 14, 16 Feb. and 23 March 1927.
[84] ACS, RdG, 25 Apr. 1927, 7 and 25 May 1927; ACS, 1290–40-4/1 A, Janssen to Perkins, 17 June 1927.

holding grouping of all French-based interests from the Mutuelle that proved difficult to undo.[85] The *gérants* looked forward to the changes they initiated in France. "If matters follow a logical course," they said to their IG partners, "the Société d'Études could, in the long run, become the chance for a merger in the French chemical industry at large."[86]

Nevertheless, this rosy picture was about to fade. To a large extent, tensions with the French chemical industry stemmed from the transformations that took place in the American glass industry. For example, SAIC's control of the Libbey-Owens Sheet Glass Company triggered a panicked reaction from the French leader, Saint-Gobain, which decided to take control of the Marchéville soda plant. Later on, the disclosure of Saint-Gobain's interests in Werra-Werke, a modest, family-run soda plant close to Eisenach (Germany), contributed to undermining the relations. Saint-Gobain's counterattack not only voided the alkali convention in France; it also ushered in a period of confrontation in the glass industry at large. Solvay threatened to step in directly to the glass industry and push for the building of a Libbey-Owens plant in Belgium if the Convention Internationale des Glaceries (dominated by Saint-Gobain) did not refrain from producing soda ash beyond its immediate needs. In fact, Janssen was actually thinking it was a good opportunity for Solvay. But the other *gérants* preferred to move carefully with their most valuable customer in France. After months of enduring negotiations, during which stakes in alkali and glass industries were closely intertwined, a compromise was finally reached by December 1927, with the prolongation of fairly similar production allotments (Solvay controlling 65 percent of the production of soda ash, and the remainder being split into equal parts between Saint-Gobain and Marchéville).[87]

The contract was eventually ratified in July 1928. It waited for the real truce in the glass industry to take place; Libbey-Owens's, affiliate Mecaniver (controlled by the Mutuelle) and the Convention Internationale des Glaceries neutralized each other in securing their respective position. Quite interestingly, the entente was echoed in the United States by a similar understanding between Libbey-Owens Sheet Glass Company and the Pittsburgh Plate Glass Company.[88] But Solvay wished to go further. To secure its dominant position in Germany, Solvay had DSW take over Werra-Werke. This did not consist merely in buying out the allotments of the convention; it was designed to take over the plant itself. When he visited the premises in January 1928, Emil Gielen of DSW had a favorable overall impression. It was a small factory whose industrial activities, quite limited in scope, had been slow to come on stream. However, parts of the factory required for urgent repair works, and the accounting showed important debts. The production of soda ash was reactivated at the start of 1930; it only accounted for 2 percent of the total production of DSW.[89] More than any other investment, the significance of Werra-Werke's takeover

[85] ACS, RdG, 19 Sept. and 9 Nov. 1927.

[86] ACS, 1142-40-15, Minutes of the Berlin meeting of E. Tournay, E.-J. Solvay, and Dr. Schmitz (IG), 9 July 1927.

[87] ACS, 1701-38-1 (1), Minutes of the meeting, 27 Dec. 1927.

[88] ACS, 1707-17-1, Saint-Gobain, passim; Daviet (1988), 412–17.

[89] ACS, 1157-1-1, Visite des Werrawerke, 3 Jan. 1928; Eilsberger (1930), 301–3; ADSW, Archiv I, Statistiken: Kapazität und Erzeugung, 1 May 1930.

was twofold for Solvay: underlining its growing responsiveness to potential threats in the soda and glass industry, and showing its French counterparts its ability to mobilize swiftly their foreign networks. International integration, needless to say, was Solvay's hallmark, and it was precisely what the Convention Internationale des Glaceries was lacking – and longing for. Conversely, the integration between soda and glass businesses remained an unresolved strategic issue for the *gérants*. By 1928, it seemed obvious that, on this matter at least, the company was at a crossroads.

9.3 EXPLORING ALTERNATIVES IN AMERICA

As the rationalization of the French chemical industry proceeded with tempered efficiency, Solvay could not help but notice that its German and English partners were pulling in the opposite direction. Since the creation of SAIC early in 1927, IG Farben and ICI had been eager to slow any form of consortium from taking place at the initiative of Solvay. Their attitude was not explicitly directed against the latter; it was rather the expression of a reorientation of priorities that was slowly coming to the fore. At IG, Carl Bosch was currently preparing the important hydrogenation agreement with Rockefellers' Standard Oil, which took place in 1927 and set the stage for the creation of the holding American IG Chemical Corporation in April 1929 and the subsequent joint venture Standard-IG in November 1929.[90] Though largely determined by technological matters rather than financial stakes, the operation of Standard-IG shed light on the shifting of strategy and the corresponding evolution of power of IG Farben in the United States since the first meeting Bosch had with Weber in October 1923. As to the American policy of ICI, the drifting away from Allied and toward DuPont was first considered a remote influence of Sir Harry McGowan. However, as McGowan's leadership on the board grew stronger, it became clear that Orlando Weber's company was not listed at the top of ICI's agenda. This, among other things, precipitated the ultimate burial of Emmanuel Janssen's scheme for an international trust with the Mutuelle acting as a "pivot."[91]

Allied: Strengthening Control, Lacking Information

In November 1928, ICI executed the agreement that had been concluded to give Solvay the preference for the acquisition of 100,000 shares of Allied (of a total of 115,916) previously owned by Brunner, Mond. This could be both interpreted as a proof of ICI's distrust of Weber's management and as a gesture of a friendly relationship with Solvay. At any rate, the question was not whether Solvay would raise the option but how it would finance the operation, which amounted to some US$25 million (ICI asked for US$235 per share, which was less than the market price, and Solvay willing to offer a maximum US$228).[92]

[90] Abelshauser et al. (2004), 227–30; Wilkins (2004), 241–2; ACS, 1142-40-15, Minutes of the meeting of E. Tournay, E.-J. Solvay, and H. Schmitz (Berlin), 9 July 1927.
[91] PPJS, Box Armand Solvay No. 1, Folder 3, E. Janssen to E.-J. Solvay, 10 July 1927 and E.-J. Solvay's reply; ACS, RdG, 27 Apr. 1927.
[92] ACS, 1241-40-3 A, RdG, 12 Nov. 1928.

Far from reducing its interests in Allied, which is what they could have done after the creation of SAIC, Solvay intended to reinforce its holdings, upping them from 16 percent to 21 percent (i.e., 466,488 shares). The problem, though, was that SAIC had already contracted a US$15 million loan. Adding an extra loan might have hampered its financial position with financial establishments in the United States. Moreover, an important portion of Solvay's capital was tied up in plants in Europe. A report by the jurist Georges Janssen, a cousin to Emmanuel Janssen, in late December 1928 concluded that the financing implied substantial financial transfers, either from Solvay alone or through the mediation of SAIC or the Mutuelle Solvay.[93]

The *gérants* hesitated for six months. Weber, who had been kept unaware of the transaction, claimed that he had the priority on these shares as soon as he heard about it. After long and painful negotiations, it was finally decided to issue special non-voting rights SAIC shares bearing nondetachable warrants, which entitled the bearer to convert four SAIC shares for each Allied share. By this complex mechanism, designed by Janssen, Tuck, and SAIC's executive vice president Félix Notebaert, Solvay could sell one hundred thousand shares of Allied to SAIC in exchange for its current debt. In other words, this enabled Solvay to keep absolute control on SAIC. However, the disadvantages of the operation were that it not only aggravated SAIC's liabilities but also hindered the necessary diversification of its portfolio, the bulk of which was made up of Allied shares. Notwithstanding these criticisms, the issue took place on August 28, 1929 – the share of Allied at the New York Stock Exchange was then selling at a peak of US$345, a "quite abnormal value" according to Tuck.[94] Because of its scope, the transaction prompted the assistance, together with Lee, Higginson & Co., of the J. P. Morgan investment bank. This led to changes on the board of SAIC, namely the resignation of its chairman, John H. Perkins, who was by then director of Solvay's traditional financial broker – the National City Bank. As a result, Emmanuel Janssen advocated setting up the Mutual Solvay of America, which – in conformity with the legacy of the other Mutuelle banking organizations – was designed to become a large financial vehicle that could include investors foreign to Solvay's, including top-of-the-range American investment banks like J. P. Morgan.[95]

Yet the most dramatic effect of these changes was elsewhere. The *gérants* had to give in that neither the creation of SAIC nor the purchase of ICI's one hundred thousand Allied shares exerted any kind of influence on Weber's reluctance to share information on Allied's financial situation. All the way

---

[93] ACS, DS 37, Étude financière de Georges Janssen, Solvay & Cie-Mutuelle, 31 Dec. 1928.

[94] ACS, 1241-40-3 A, appendix to RdG, 16 July 1929 and RdG, 17 July 1929; ACS, RdG, 28 June 1929.

[95] J. P. Morgan was preferred to the Farmers' Loan and Trust Company, which had been the financial broker of Solvay & Cie in the United States. Early in 1929, Farmers' Loan merged with National City Bank, after which the new investment bank became the leading underwriter of the May 1, 1929, US$30 million bond offering of the holding between Standard Oil and IG Farben (American IG). As James H. Perkins was also director at the new National City Bank, he trusted the choice of J. P. Morgan as an expression of a new banking strategy and consequently offered his resignation. ACS, RdG, 5 Mar, and 7 Aug. 1929, and 2 Dec. 1930.

through, Orlando Weber had been irritated by Solvay's tendency to speculate on the sale of the shares. He felt that the operation had been directed against him personally, and he was determined to put an even greater strain on its major shareholder. As the cold war got warmer, Solvay was resolved to find fresh American allies. Among them, quite logically, the name of the Morgan group came to mind. The prestigious investment bank had been of valuable assistance, and its financial and industrial connections were prominent both in the United States and in Europe. Morgan's representative in Europe, George Whitney, was even approached by the *gérance*.[96] The scheme, however, had to be put on hold. The collapse of the New York Stock Exchange in October 1929 was so sudden and brutal that it surprised the most placid investors, and SAIC was not in a comfortable position, with its heavy debt and uniform portfolio. Shortly before the stock market crash, Janssen and Auchincloss had hastily attempted to spread the risks by buying high-yielding stocks like American International Corporation (close to the National City Bank) and Kreuger & Toll bonds. Both choices, the latter especially, were a terrible mistake: the Swedish holding Kreuger & Toll did not stand the Depression and collapsed (Ivar Kreuger's suicide in March 1932 was a staggering event in the financial milieus).[97] In this difficult financial context, SAIC was depending on Allied's ability to survive the slump. The crash had obviously increased SAIC's reliance on Weber.

As it turned out, Allied's general manager was quite satisfied with the situation. According to him, the company was thriving and willing to pay its US$6 dividend per share. Moreover, the crisis had provided a wonderful opportunity for low-priced investments, which Weber told Ernest-John Solvay and Emmanuel Janssen at a meeting with IG Farben's Carl Bosch and Hermann Schmitz in Paris in the summer of 1930. He wished to inform his European competitors of his new design – the building of a nitrogen plant in France. The operation was interpreted as purely defensive by some observers. Janssen, for instance, saw it as both a countermeasure to IG Farben's increasing penetration of the American market and a sequel to the Nitrogen Cartel (Convention Internationale de l'Azote), which had led to production restrictions and sales quotas in close cooperation with Chilean producers.[98] Ernest-John Solvay, though, had a different opinion. The project was, according to him, the latest expression of Weber's everlasting hubris: "It would be logical to say to M. Weber that we do not intend to accept his implementation in Europe just like he refuses to see Europeans expanding in the United States."[99] Ernest-John

[96] ACS, RdG, 28 June and 20 Aug. 1929; ACS, Relations Solvay & Cie-Allied, Résumé des entrevues (1921–1932), undated [Sept. 1932].

[97] ACS, DS 97, "SAIC – Profits et pertes sur placements Solusa depuis sa création," Aug. 1931; ACS, 1271-37-4 A, M. Notebaert (SAIC) to Solvay & Cie, 26 Apr. 1930; ACS, 1271-37-3, G. Auchincloss to Solvay & Cie, 14 Oct. 1931. As of 31 July 1931, the market value of AIC dropped 72 percent and that of Kreuger dropped 44 percent. Core industrial investments were also at the brink of financial collapse: Libbey-Owens shares lost 63 percent between their purchase by Emmanuel Janssen (and Orlando Weber) in July 1928 and January 1932.

[98] ACS, RdG, 12 Aug. and 29 Aug. 1930. For the CIA, see Devos (1992), 118–21; Haber (1971), 276–7.

[99] ACS, Relations Solvay & Cie-Allied, Résumé des entrevues (1921–1932), undated [Sept. 1932].

Solvay's exasperation grew even stronger when Weber specified that the future plant would not take Solvay's soda ash because it was too expensive.[100] As a matter of fact, the project never materialized. On the basis of later evidence, one could even suggest that Weber never intended to launch such an enterprise at the turn of the 1930s. Whatever the seriousness of his French ambition, Weber appeared in the eyes of his Belgian associates to be a reckless gambler. His friendly claim that "Allied and Solvay's mutual interests are like those of two brothers," though asserted three years before, seemed to belong to another age. What was left between Allied's general manager and Solvay's managing partners was an ocean of misunderstanding. And the solutions to fill the gap were scarce.[101]

By 1931, the *gérants* not only contested Orlando Weber's inability to share information but also condemned his inappropriate leadership. The harsh price struggle between Michigan Alkali (Ford family) and Diamond Alkali (Evans family), let alone with Columbia Chemical and Mathieson Alkali, was such that Allied was losing ground in the utterly competitive soda domestic market. An independent study dedicated to the world alkali industry pointed out in 1933 that "the dominant position once held by SPC (in the production of soda ash) in the U.S. has now faded away after the dissemination of sensible information." The latecomers had been keen on reaping the harvest of technical knowledge. By 1937, the production of alkali was broken down as follows: Allied peaked at 45 percent, followed by Michigan (22 percent), Diamond (16 percent), Columbia (11 percent), and Mathieson (6 percent).[102] In addition to the domestic pressure, the Chilean competition in the sodium nitrate business did not help Allied in increasing the productive capacity and the distribution output of its Hopewell plant, of which Weber was so fond. Last but not least, the effects of the Great Depression had finally hit the American chemical industry, and Allied, at its core. Suffering from exhaustion, Weber's bad condition led him to leave the direction of Allied for three months. When he recovered from his burnout in April 1931, he realized that Solvay had made its way in successfully mobilizing some of Allied's unhappy American shareholders. Quite surprisingly, Charles W. Nichols was at the forefront of the anti-Weber clan. He was dissatisfied with Weber's autocratic manner and his assurance that Allied should keep on its strategy of price struggle with competitors in time of crisis. Nichols, therefore, did not rule out the possibility of voting against him at the next meeting of the board.

This, however, was a step the *gérants* hesitated to take. Weber was, after all, concentrating all the power and responsibility. With the pressure on his shoulders, he might as well have withdrawn naturally. Thus, during their annual trip

---

[100] ACS, RdG, 29 Aug. 1929.

[101] For Weber's quote, see ACS, 1271–37-4 A, "Note on my visit to M. Weber," by M. Notebaert (SAIC), 3 June 1927. On Weber's plan to build a nitrogen plant in France, see ACS, 1271–37-9 A, "Conversation avec M. G. Wells," by M. Notebaert, 19 Dec. 1934.

[102] ACS, 1290–38, Mutual Solvay of America Information, "Examen de la situation mondiale des produits sodiques," 23 Nov. 1933, 44–50. See also ACS, 1482-1-6, "The Alkali industry of the U.S. of America," by P. C. Allen and C. R. Pritchard (ICI), part 2, Mar. 1932, 18–32. Production data for 1937 in ACS, NdG, "L'industrie de la soude et du chlore" by René Boël (19 July 1937), 8.

to the United States in April 1931, Emmanuel Janssen and Ernest-John Solvay (accompanied by Hallam Tuck) did not openly object to Weber's reelection. They merely insisted that Hugh Auchincloss become a member of the board of Allied. This rather lukewarm reaction surprised Nichols and other anti-Weber American shareholders. Contrary to what they assumed, the decision of the *gérants* did not result from fear or plain indifference. It was duly advised by SAIC's new legal adviser, John Foster Dulles. A senior partner at the law firm Sullivan & Cromwell, Foster Dulles had solid experience in both corporate law and international diplomacy. As former economic adviser to Woodrow Wilson at the Versailles Peace Conference, he had developed an expertise in – and an irrepressible admiration for – German private and public affairs. His reputation and his networks were well established in Wall Street circles.[103] At first purely incidental, his collaboration with Solvay became significant as difficulties with Weber went public.

Ousting Weber

At the start of 1932, Solvay's situation in the United States could be summarized as the outcome of an ongoing dilemma. Ever since Weber's breach of the Tripartite Agreement in September 1926, the *gérants* had been dithering over the strategy to follow. As shareholders, they had nothing to complain about Allied's impressive earnings and dividends. As partners, however, they were kept in the dark and did not have a say. Somehow, they had favored financial interests over industrial control. But this was to end after their trip to New York in March 1932. The delegation was composed of the regular emissaries, Emmanuel Janssen and Ernest-John Solvay. But it also included two recently appointed *gérants*, Robert Gendebien and René Boël. The latter, in particular, was about to give Solvay a new impetus in the orientation of their American business. Janssen, it must be said, was not part of the *gérance* anymore (see Chapter 10), although he had agreed to join the delegation at his former colleagues' request. This large group agreed on the aims – getting information from Weber and naming Auchincloss to the board of Allied – but diverged on the means. Janssen (supported by Tuck) felt this should be presented to Weber as a sheer recommendation; the other *gérants* considered it an ultimatum. As expected, Weber strongly opposed what he considered a diktat. He would never appoint another member at "his" Board under these circumstances. The result was a direct and formal resignation of Solvay's delegates at the board of Allied. Practically, the decision did not alter much of the picture: Émile Tournay (who had replaced Armand Solvay after his death in February 1930) was hardly present, and Emmanuel Janssen had finally accepted Weber's suggestion to stay on an independent basis. An unexpected side effect was to be found elsewhere: Hallam Tuck offered the *gérants* his resignation as consultant of Solvay for American affairs. He felt this would be in contradiction with his recent appointment to the board of Allied.[104]

[103] Lisagor and Lipsius (1989), 69–95.
[104] ACS, 1271-53-2, Voyage aux États-Unis, Feb.-March 1932, notes et annexes, passim; Nomination of G.A. at the Board of Allied, 8 Feb. 1932; ACS, Dossiers spéciaux (DS), 164, Janssen to Solvay & Cie, 5 Apr. 1932.

In some way, Janssen's position forestalled the full exploitation of the symbolic effect that Solvay had wished to create around Allied after the collective resignation. There was still some confusion that needed to be cleared up. René Boël was the designated man for the job. At only thirty-three years old, the eldest son of one of Belgium's steel industry dynasties had shown an exceptional ability to negotiate and find solutions. A civil engineer graduate with qualification in mining technology, Boël was eager to enter this minefield.[105] During his stay in New York in September and October 1932 (fewer than six months after the previous visit), Boël's list of contacts included personalities from major banks (e.g., Federal Reserve, First National Bank, National City Bank, Chase) and other industries (e.g., US Steel, National Steel, Owens Illinois). Underlying these meetings was the idea to cultivate new alliances, which would grow out as a constructive opposition to Weber. "We should clearly realize," Boël reported to the *gérance*, "that Solvay & Cie and Allied's respective policies are in opposition. . . . And for that very reason, while defending ourselves as industrialists, we should move ahead [*manoeuvrer*] in the United States with Americans in order to resume the influence we are entitled to as shareholders."[106] According to these guidelines, Boël met twice with John B. Ford Sr. and his son John Ford Jr. In the glass industry, the Fords were natural partners to Solvay through their mutual interests in Libbey-Owens-Ford Glass and its related financial holding, Libbey-Owens Securities; in the soda ash business, though, they were competitors as owners of Michigan Alkali (Wyandotte). On both sides, Boël soon learned, the Fords were not pleased with Weber's unconditional low-price strategy and his aggressiveness over the Alkasso international exports policy. They told him they were relieved that Solvay was willing to seize the matter.[107]

Once he got back to Brussels, René Boël had all the information he needed to schedule another mission to the United States. He departed on 24 March 1933 for a lengthy four-month stay. Émile Tournay, senior managing partner, joined him. The plan for action was simple: to form a shareholders' committee that would force Weber to withdraw as general manager of Allied. Apart from the contacts he had developed under Foster Dulles's guidance, Boël relied on an unexpected group of allies: the president-elect Franklin D. Roosevelt's brain trust and their program of financial regulation embodied by the Securities Act of 1933. This piece of legislation called for public disclosure to potential investors of any significant information, ranging from the supply of a company's financial statement (bookkeeping) to detailed information about its structure.[108] As Allied was not a shining example of transparency, it fell in the line of fire of the law's prescriptions. Weber, quite predictably, refused to give in. By doing so, he did his opponents a great favor: the New York Stock Exchange authorities

---

[105] Dutrieue (1996), 62–3.

[106] ACS, DS, 203, Summary of the trip to the United States, appendix to the meeting, 22 Nov. 1932.

[107] ACS, 1271-37-11, Minutes of the meetings with the Fords on 24, 25 and 27 Oct. 1932; ACS, DS, 207, RdG, 20 Dec. 1932.

[108] Douglas and Bates (1933).

struck Allied from the trading list, but this also legitimized SAIC's longtime complaint that Weber was withholding information from stockholders. As a result, Boël and Foster Dulles successfully managed to gather a shareholders' committee representing, directly or by proxy, no less than a million shares of Allied's stock (about 40 percent). Together with the Nichols family, SAIC was leading the revolt. Boël persuaded Emmanuel Janssen to withdraw from the board of Allied. The tension reached a climax when the group of stockholders attempted to force the nomination of four new directors to replace Weber's closest hirelings. "Paths are diverging between us," warned the irritated general manager. He felt it was ironic, to say the least, that a company like Solvay, whose hallmark was secrecy, was spearheading a group calling for transparency.[109]

Although unsuccessful, the dethroning operation gave way to some reforms: Weber promised to conform to the requirements of the law and to make room at the board for two directors. But this was above all a psychological victory for Solvay. If Weber had resisted, his seat would have appeared shaky. New allies had emerged by joining the uprising, some of whom had never thought of opposing the head of Allied. In a desperate effort to win more support, Weber argued in the press that "the American Chemical industry [was] fighting to maintain [the American] market for American capital and American labor against the organized, combined and ruthless attacks of foreign competition." Solvay American Investment, Weber went on, had bought one hundred thousand shares of Allied previously owned by ICI and used the stock "largely for the purpose of building European chemical plants which compete with your company in the markets of the world."[110] Asserted in another context, such a statement would have been felt as a deliberate attack. This time, however, the *gérants* did not pay attention and preferred to focus on the coming steps delineated in the memoranda Boël had drafted during and shortly after his stay.[111]

In conformity with Foster Dulles's advice, the main idea was to proceed with extreme caution with regards to Weber. The dreadful economic situation had entailed a widespread feeling of protectionism within American industry and the US population. In his last address, Weber had judiciously attempted to strike a nationalist chord. An untimely move would put the entire operation in jeopardy. As a result, Solvay oriented its action on two different levels. First, in terms of coalition building, the *gérants* reached out for DuPont as a way to foster new partnerships in the United States. It did so after consulting Harry McGowan and Lord Melchett of ICI, as well as George Whitney of J. P. Morgan. Despite their intermediation, however, this proved arduous and ineffective. The project was soon dropped.[112] On a second and more original level, Solvay intended to restore its image in the American public opinion.

[109] ACS, 1271-37-5 and 1271-37-7, Voyage de MM. Tournay et Boël aux États-Unis, Mar.–July 1933, various excerpts; Lisagor and Lipsius (1989), 124–5; *Time*, 12 June 1933.
[110] "Weber hits back," *Time*, 26 June 1933.
[111] ACS, DS, 221–7, Aug.–Sept. 1933.
[112] ACS, 1271-37-14, Solvay & Cie to J.F. Dulles, 5 Aug. 1933; ACS, 1271-37-14 (ACS, DS, 244), Entrevue avec M. Dulles à Paris, 15 Dec. 1933.

Foster Dulles suggested that the *gérants* resort to an expert in public relations, Ivy Lee, who had already provided some help to the shareholders' committee in June 1933 and was contributing to a campaign for the reassessment of IG Farben in the United States.[113] To the attention of Boël, Lee drafted a kind of teaser – *The American Chemical Industry* – in which he pointed out the role of the president of the Chemical Foundation, Francis P. Garvan, in propagating rumors about alleged foreign domination in the American chemical industry.[114] Propaganda, however, was exactly what Ivy Lee did best and better than anyone. But when he outlined his "publicity" program in Brussels, the *gérants* expressed no enthusiasm and asked him to focus instead on the preliminary work of the program: "a thorough study about the activities of Solvay around the world."[115]

Nevertheless, more crucial for Weber than Lee's controversial activities was the second draft of the corporate regulation enactment – the Securities and Exchange Act of 1934 – which required the owner of more than 10 percent of any registered security to file "a statement showing the extent of his ownership." As it also included the spreading of registered companies' officers' salaries and stockholdings, the legislation called for far more complete disclosure than the previous edition.[116] This was too much for Orlando Weber. At the General Assembly meeting of April 1934, he designated his close associate and former secretary of the company, Henry F. Atherton, to replace him as CEO of Allied. Weber himself became chairman of the board. Orchestrated as it was, the substitution did not discourage dissenting shareholders, who were ready to embark on another round of contestation. An uneasy cohabitation prevailed for a full year. Then on 16 May 1935 came the news of Weber's sudden resignation of Allied Chemical. *Time* magazine's coverage of the event sounded like an obituary: "Complaint is sometimes made that the titans have departed from U.S. business. But for the past fifteen years business has had at its core and centre the legendary equal of any of the 19th Century myth men – Orlando Weber. Last week, without ever having found out much about him, U.S. business lost him."[117] But nobody was fooled by the real motivations of his withdrawal. For at the same time, the company officially announced its intention to apply for permanent registration on the New York Stock Exchange under the provisions of the Securities and Exchange Act. As the *Wall Street Journal* put it, "the financial community saw a direct connection between the two events."[118] In other words, the last thing this mystery man wanted for his retirement was to have his fortune publicly exposed.

[113] Hiebert (1966), 229–93; ACS, 1271-37-14, Minutes of a meeting with J. F. Dulles and C. W. Nichols, by F. Notebaert, 27 July 1933; ACS, DS, 221, RdG, 1 Aug. 1933.

[114] ACS, 1271-37-14 (f. 1), Lee to Boël, 19 Sept. 1933; Wilkins (2004), 812nn255–6.

[115] ACS, 1271-37-14 (f. 2–3), RdG, 30 Jan., 1 Feb. and 2 Feb. 1934.

[116] ACS, 1271-37-14 (f. 3), Notebaert to Solvay & Cie, Appendix: Note concerning special aspects of the Securities Exchange Act of 1934, 12 July 1934; ACS, 1271-37-14, J. F. Dulles (Sullivan & Cromwell) to Solvay & Cie, 20 Sept. 1934.

[117] "Weber withdraws," *Time*, 27 May 1935.

[118] *The Wall Street Journal*, 16 May 1935. See also the clippings of the *New York Times*, *New York Herald Tribune*, *Investment News*, and the *Journal of Commerce* in ACS, 1271-37-14 (f. 4).

For many, Weber was still active behind the scenes, leading a company he had largely and tirelessly contributed to develop. According to Solvay's man in New York, Félix Notebaert, the newly designated CEO and chairman of Allied, Henry Atherton was less a successor to Weber than his straw man. The *gérants*, he warned, should not be naive in this respect.[119] As a result, they reached out once again to Foster Dulles and strictly followed his recommendations. The first instruction Foster Dulles gave was to keep quiet for some time while making sure that sufficient friendly shareholders could be mobilized. During their New York trip in September and October 1935, Tournay, Ernest-John Solvay, and Boël managed to convince Nichols that he, as son of Allied Chemical's founder, should send a circular to the company's stockholders pleading for more independence on the board and asking in return for their full support. The letter, signed by Nichols, was drafted by Foster Dulles. The subterfuge allowed Solvay to get a clear visual on its sympathetic network without being overly exposed.[120] But it also led the company to switch from "outside to inside action," as Foster Dulles put it when he met the *gérants* in Paris in January 1936. Finally, the time had come to push for a Solvay candidate on the board of Allied. Only on such a condition would Allied's major shareholder approve the new management. Here again was Foster Dulles right on target. Although he was the one that the *gérants* deeply wanted to see on board, Foster Dulles declined and suggested an old friend of his – George Murnane.[121]

A former partner at Lee, Higginson (which went down after underwriting Kreuger & Toll bonds worldwide), Murnane was back on track with another of Foster Dulles's acquaintances from the 1919 Versailles Treaty, the French jurist Jean Monnet. Murnane and Monnet had recently teamed up in a new law firm, which was determined to live down its past failures.[122] Guarantee was given that Murnane was competent and reliable but would not hamper Solvay's freedom of action. Under Foster Dulles's pressure, the appointment of George Murnane as director of Allied took place at an extraordinary board meeting on 7 April 1936. The election was then ratified at the General Assembly meeting three weeks later. Solvay had successfully put an end to a ten-year battle. It had preserved its control in the company and had saved the bulk of its interests in the United States. For the sake of convenience and security, however, Foster Dulles recommended that SAIC's financial vehicle, Mutual Solvay of America (by then renamed Amusol), be transferred out of New York, and if possible outside the United States. This paved the way for Losanac Ltd., a company incorporated in Montreal, Canada. It was a first and important step in Solvay's geographical diversification in the Americas.

[119] ACS, 1271-37-14 (f. 6), Notebaert to Solvay & Cie, 28 Jan. 1936.

[120] ACS, 1271-37-14 (f. 5), Voyage aux États-Unis (21 Sept.–23 Oct. 1935), with an appendix of Nichols's open letter.

[121] ACS, 1271-37-14 (f. 6), Meetings of the gérance with J.F. Dulles, 21 Jan. 1936 (Paris) and 31 Jan. 1936 (Brussels).

[122] Mioche (2007), 60–8; Lisagor and Lipsius (1989), 124–5.

FIGURE 10.1. North side of the prestigious Avenue Louise of Brussels. The building on the right side was bought by the Mutuelle Solvay in 1927 for its headquarters. The building at the left corner was built in 1928 by the Mutuelle to house the Banque Générale Belge. In 1929, the Mutuelle bought the shares of Wiltcher's Hotel, next to the building on the right side, which became the headquarters of the Union Chimique Belge. In 1931, the Mutuelle and the Banque Générale Belge swapped their buildings and crossed the street. (© 2012 – Edmond Nels / Copyright SOFAM – Belgium.)

10

Family and Finance through the Crisis

Shortly before taking some rest in Biarritz in January 1928, Armand Solvay felt the need to leave his colleagues of the *gérance* a lengthy letter, with all the characteristics of a testimony. Beginning with a recollection of the heroic origins and early development of the family business, Armand then addressed the challenges the company had tackled since the Great War and the outstanding prosperity it eventually reached. However, as the letter unfolded, its content became more pessimistic. Armand started to cast some doubts on the company's ability to maintain its rank without undergoing profound changes. The legal form of Solvay, he went on, was not adapted to the patterns of the world chemical industry anymore. And he swiftly pointed out the parallel advantages of a public company in terms of capital circulation, ownership flexibility, and investment strategy. If Solvay were to be created that day, he observed, it never would have been established under the provisions of a limited partnership company. The transformation of the corporate regime had been considered several times before – a smooth modification was even foreseen in the company's bylaws. This time, though, it did not primarily focus on shareholders or exogenous funding. What Armand had in mind was the pursuit of managerial leadership and management efficiency. "I was struck to observe," he noted, "how a public company like the Mutuelle was able to ensure the proper training of our family members whose desire was to work.... They are not all meant to become business leaders, but to all of them one can provide the opportunity to develop their specific capabilities. And the future leaders would be recruited among those who have proved themselves worthy."[1]

Of course, the transformation of the corporate regime did not automatically entail a revolution in the management of organizational capabilities. Examples abound of family-owned public companies in which inheritors and their relatives kept control of the management (Brunner, Mond, which became a public company in 1881, is a fairly good example). Conversely, Solvay had already included two outsiders at the level of the *gérance* – the engineers Prosper Hanrez and Édouard Hannon. The choice proved successful in both cases. For

---

[1] ACS, DS 40, "Aperçu historique sur la Gérance de Solvay & Cie et considérations relatives à une transformation éventuelle de notre Société en société anonyme" by Armand Solvay, 9–14 Jan. 1928.

decades, the mechanisms of recruitment of the *gérants*, as well as the underlying discussion between family owners and salaried managers, had remained one of the *gérance*'s ultimate prerogatives. Although an inheritor himself, Armand Solvay knew too well that such a decision could never be taken for granted. The matter was utterly sensitive. It required skill and diplomacy with the different branches of the shareholders' families. But most of all, it required a cohesive and unanimous board. Hence, Armand's plea for a public company did not focus only on the expansion of competence; it also concerned the process of decision making, which was largely determining the industrial orientations of the company. Collective capability, he could have stressed, presupposed a consensual federation of individual initiatives and opinions. This, however, was not the case at the *gérance* at the turn of the 1920s and 1930s. And it was precisely what preoccupied the founding father's eldest son on the eve of his death.

10.1 MANAGERIAL LEGACIES

The year 1930 was a bad one for the inheritors at the command of the large chemical industry. Armand Solvay and Alfred Mond, First Lord Melchett, both passed away that year, the former in February, the latter shortly after Christmas. Despite some major differences – Mond had dedicated a fair amount of his time to national politics (he even served as minister of health for eighteen months in a postwar coalition government led by Lloyd George) – the two men shared several characteristics: they belonged to the same generation, not only in terms of time frame (Armand Solvay was born in 1865, Alfred Mond in 1868) but also, and above all, in terms of business culture. They embodied the second-generation leaders of a family business that happened to be an international chemical empire (see Chapter 5). In this respect, they committed their lives (partly for Mond, fully for Solvay) to the survival and growth of the company they inherited. This means they had been designated by the founders and had prepared to take over their role within the family and the company (Alfred Mond, again, was Ludwig Mond's youngest son). But they also had a name and a rank with which they had to stand for in the society at large. Another common trait of the second-generation business elite, therefore, is university education. Alfred Mond received his formal training at St. John's College, Cambridge, and at Edinburgh University, where he obtained his law degree (in contrast to his father's predispositions in the natural sciences), and Armand Solvay studied engineering at the Mining School of the University of Liège. Academic training was closely associated with the ascending social status they acquired from their fathers and the resultant combination of knowledge credentials, sociality, and legitimacy. Interestingly, recent findings suggest that the proportion of university-educated business leaders in Europe was quite even between inheritors and salaried managers.[2] Last but not least, Armand Solvay and Alfred Mond had witnessed the closing of an age and the dawn of

[2] Cassis (1999), 132–8.

another one. They had been raised in the former but were still in command during the latter. They had to cope with the upheavals of the war and the emergence of giant corporations, both of which had proved uneasy challenges for the company. The parallel between the two experiences seems to fade away, as their differences tend to outweigh similarities.

Whereas Brunner, Mond was but one part of a powerful amalgamation named ICI, Solvay remained an independent player in a worldwide system governed by agreements covering products, prices, and markets. Because of their common history and interests, Solvay could claim good relationships with ICI. But the dynamics of the interaction had nothing to do with the relationship it enjoyed with Brunner, Mond before the constitution of ICI in 1926. By and large, Solvay had become a mere shareholder of ICI – albeit the largest one, with almost 6 percent of the ordinary capital. With the deaths of Armand Solvay and Alfred Mond, both companies were about to lack their most intimate link: the interpersonal dimension. Here again, the war had swept away the traditional sociological framework. The postwar economic environment had favored the rise of professional managers. No wonder Armand Solvay had stressed in his letter the disappearance of the Hazards and the Brunners from the industrial stage while "new men, important, highly capable have come to the fore, like Weber and McGowan" (he could have added IG Farben's Carl Bosch and Carl Duisberg to the list). Harry McGowan, obviously, was the most emblematic incarnation of this new breed of salaried managers, just as Armand Solvay and Alfred Mond were of the inheritors. With a working-class background, McGowan was an exception in the landscape of the British business elite (he would eventually be raised to the peerage as Baron McGowan in 1937). The architect of the all-British amalgamation, he initially agreed to become ICI's first president while Alfred Mond was appointed chairman. Regardless of their divergent social origins and business views, their cohabitation seemed to never have resulted in "any serious dissension on fundamentals." Already a leading figure during Mond's chairmanship, McGowan became "the unquestioned head on earth of ICI" when he was unanimously elected "Chairman and Managing Director of the Company and of the Board" on 31 December 1930.[3]

On Solvay's side, by contrast, Armand's death triggered changes at the top of the company that were less automatic. One could not say, however, that the event caught the *gérants* by surprise. Armand Solvay had been ill for a long time and had relied on his colleagues to take care of day-to-day business affairs since the mid-1920s (with the exception of the French affairs). Yet, foreseen as it was, it was not an event the managing partners had been prepared for. In comparison to their British counterparts, the *gérants* had willingly postponed or avoided difficult discussions concerning the succession at the summit of the management. They did so almost in spite of Armand's attempt to initiate such debate, as his letter has shown. He had been chairman of the *gérance*, less in the formal sense of the word (for the office carried quite a modest power

[3] Reader (1975), 22–3, 133.

according to the company's bylaws)[4] than in its moral understanding – as a natural and uncontested figure who was able to stay above the fray. To some extent, his loss unveiled how essential Armand's presence, long eclipsed by his father's gleam, had been to the unity of the company.

As far as seniority was concerned, Louis Solvay was next. The son of Alfred Solvay – the other founder, as he readily reminded – was not someone one would call a natural-born leader. Appointed *gérant* in 1907, his industrial vision for Solvay was utterly conservative; he disapproved of any form of development that could divert the company from its core business. Producing alkali, he asserted, was what Solvay did best and ought to focus on. Vertical integration, either forward or backward, was out of the question (he was more evasive about horizontal integration). Louis justified this strategy for the sake of tradition. As did Armand Solvay, he took pride in belonging to the second generation but unlike his cousin he kept referring to the founders' principles, or what he called the "esprit de Rebecq" (in allusion to the hometown of the Solvay brothers).[5] What this esprit was really about is rather unclear, or so it seemed to the youngest *gérants* whose recollection of the pioneering times was narrow, if not inexistent. Louis used this past reference as a convenient argument to promote and, most of all, to discard new ideas. He was, for instance, against the project delineated by Armand of transforming Solvay & Cie into a joint-stock company. The problem was not that he opposed it but that he refused to discuss the matter further on the basis of the company's inalienable family culture.[6] With the exception of Émile Tournay, who stood almost instinctively on Louis's side, the *gérants* were puzzled by this attitude. Although Armand insisted that the "joint-stock company option [remained] the most logical and secure solution" for the future,[7] the *gérants* eventually gave in: Solvay would continue to be a limited partnership company until 1967.

The episode was less anecdotal than it appears at first sight. Not all issues could wind up with a compromise. As a matter of fact, it was rather emblematic of the uncomfortable climate at the top management in these years. "Why the mechanisms of the gérance are not functioning anymore? Why have the feelings of trust and union among its members faded away?" lamented Armand Solvay.[8] This was hard to understand, let alone explain. What had started as the sporadic manifestation of natural divergences in views between managing partners turned out to affect the running of day-to-day business. One

---

[4] ACS, Notes de Paul Vander Eycken, "Statuts de la Société Solvay & Cie – Rôle du Président de la Gérance," 25 Nov. 1929; "Pouvoirs que doit posséder le Président de la Société," 19 Oct. 1931.

[5] Louis Solvay coined the term in a letter he addressed to the president of the Supervisory Board (ACS, Viscount Guy de Jonghe Collection, Louis Solvay to Paul-Casimir Lambert, 30 Dec. 1931).

[6] He also alluded to Edgar Hulin's postwar note "Étude sur les modifications à apporter à l'organisation de la Société Solvay & Cie," (ACS, NdG, 24 Oct. 1918), which concluded with the necessity to preserve the limited liability partnership.

[7] ACS, DS 39, Armand Solvay to gérance, 8 Feb. 1928.

[8] ACS, PPSF, Box Armand Solvay, 2, Armand Solvay to gérance, 20 Mar. 1928.

could trace its first expression to the disagreements surrounding Solvay's international strategy and the role of the Mutuelle in structuring a transnational
consortium with Allied, Brunner, Mond, and IG Farben. As we know from
the previous chapter, the "Mutu-plan" promoted by Emmanuel Janssen was
eventually turned down, and as far as Solvay's interests in the United States
were concerned, this paved the way for the creation of the Solvay American
Investment Corporation (SAIC) in late 1926. Of course, the organization of
foreign policy was a major question that entailed confronting opinions. Instead
of smoothing things over, however, the debate had nurtured or reactivated tensions on various fronts. Among them, the development of the Mutuelle, which
we will come to shortly, was undoubtedly the most predominant source of
dissent. But other issues grew silent until Armand's death. They crystallized
around managerial hierarchies and organizational structure – two aspects that
have been highlighted as salient constituents of the modern business enterprise
in the United States and, to a lesser extent, in Western Europe.[9]

Recasting Leadership

During Ernest Solvay's era, conflicts of power and authority had occurred
between the *gérants* and (some of) the silent partners. They had been solved
both formally and informally, so that the *gérance* ultimately became the undisputed seat of executive power in Solvay's two-tier system (see Chapter 3). It
was organized rather smoothly, which rendered its action relatively efficient
for an international company this size. If there was one tradition, therefore,
that Louis Solvay was about to undermine as he took over the chairmanship, it
was precisely the collegial principle adopted by the *gérance*. The concentration
of power he was longing for did not match the guidelines that had prevailed
hitherto at Solvay. Herein lay a certain paradox for, in spite of the successive statements made by Ernest-John Solvay, Robert Gendebien, and Philippe
Aubertin requesting that Louis be formally designated chairman, he repeatedly
wiped out the suggestion.[10] But it was only a prima facie paradox: the three
gérants sought to reduce the risk of an autocratic management style, which
was in vogue in the 1930s (e.g., McGowan at ICI), whereas Louis did not want
to see his authority hampered by codified prescriptions. As a result, there was
considerable discussion about the prerogatives of the position, which went as
far as calling on the expertise of jurists outside the company. A compromise
was reached whereby the oldest *gérant* present could chair the meeting, but it
was short lived.

The misunderstanding between managing partners, which resulted in an
enduring crisis of leadership, was further enhanced by another factor. For
some years (at least since the failure of the international Mutu-plan he had
vigorously fostered), Emmanuel Janssen had expressed his desire to withdraw

---

[9] For an overview, see Chandler (2004), 14–46.
[10] ACS, PPSF, Box Armand Solvay, 2, "Déclaration de M. Louis Solvay," 22 Dec. 1927; ACS, DS
46-1, 5 Dec. 1929.

from Solvay and devote his time to businesses adjacent to Solvay that he had spurred on. His colleagues asked him to adjourn his decision for a while – and he did. Nevertheless, the perspective of Armand Solvay's death and Emmanuel Janssen's resignation called for a reinforcement of the *gérance*. The ideal candidate had been picked in early 1929. René Boël was, according to his father-in-law Armand Solvay, "the only one who represented a recognized and admired figure in industrial milieus at present times"; his recruitment was therefore "desirable for the sake of general interest."[11] Louis, by contrast, felt that the admission of a new *gérant* was premature. His argument was twofold. First, as an unexpected supporter of Taylor, he advocated a "merciless reduction of the number of gérants, based on a rational organization of labor."[12] Second, for some more obscure reason (perhaps fear of replicating Thomas Mann's *Buddenbrooks* dynamics of family management decline), he took very seriously the divide between second- and third-generation business executives. And he trusted that the *gérance* had already amply indulged the rejuvenation of its members. Born in 1899 and grandchild of the founder of a powerful steel industry, René Boël was definitely part of the third generation following Louis's criteria.[13]

The final confirmation of René Boël's recruitment dragged on for months. It yielded a painful conflict within the top management of the company. After the matter was brought before the supervisory board at the initiative of its President Paul-Casimir Lambert, the idea came to call on the arbitration of the *Comité de Famille* especially made up for the occasion. Composed of representatives of the different branches of the shareholders' families (Baron Fernand Van der Straeten, Edmond Solvay, Valentin Delwart, and Pierre Bautier), its recommendations were submitted in April 1930. First, Boël would become full member of the *gérance* after a one-year training and committing to focus exclusively on Solvay's activities; second, further recruitments had to be put on hold until Emmanuel Janssen's effective withdrawal; third, the *comité* insisted that a precise set of "interior regulations" within the *gérance* be drawn.[14] Despite these unambiguous guidelines, it took another year before things could be settled. The official statement of Emmanuel Janssen's resignation was made to the shareholders in May 1931. In the meantime, he had agreed with the *gérants* on the various positions linked with Solvay he would continue to assume to ensure a transition (e.g., Mutuelle, SAIC, Suria, Allied).[15] As to René Boël, the one-year probation he had to endure sufficed to convince the doubting Thomases of his potential for, and loyalty to, the company. Adding a hardworking temperament to multifaceted knowledge and social intelligence, Boël was perhaps the best counterexample to offer to the depiction of third-generation deterioration.

[11] ACS, DS 42, Armand Solvay to gérance, 27 Apr. 1929.
[12] ACS, PPSF, Box Armand Solvay, 2, "Déclaration de M. Louis Solvay," 22 Dec. 1927.
[13] Dutrieue (1996).
[14] ACS, DS 46–11 (folders (a) to (g)); ACS, DS 46–12, 4 Apr. 1930.
[15] ACS, DS 71, 7 Mar. 1931; ACS, DS 73, 18 Mar. 1931; ACS, DS 74, Emmanuel Janssen to Louis Solvay, 22 Mar. 1931; ACS, DS 81–82, 9 May 1931; ACS, DS 86, 16 May 1931; ACS, RdG, 2 & 6 June 1931, 4 Aug. 1931.

The Formalization of Organizational Structures

The business historian Alfred Chandler has made himself famous by singling out the role of management in the development of industrial capitalism and by shedding light on the close interconnection between corporate strategy and business structure. He notably drew a sharp distinction between the multifunctional form of an enterprise (where functions are broken down into departments under the narrow control of a single body), on the one hand, and the multidivisional structure (where diversification and decentralization prevail), on the other hand. As we know it, the Chandlerian thesis tends to consider the multifunctional structure as a first, provisional step toward the multidivisional form of organization, characteristic of the multiunit modern corporation. But there is a long way to go between such model and the universality – as well as superiority – it claims.[16] Moreover, the concepts have gradually become attractive catchwords, which hardly depict the real mechanisms of intrafirm decision making. For instance, one can cast some doubt on the assertion according to which Saint-Gobain, an offspring of the highly centralized French corporate culture dating back to Colbert, would have pioneered a multidivisional structure "as early as 1905."[17] Another example that should make us cautious is provided by ICI. In June 1929, the British chemical group promulgated a new organization chart that brought recognition to eight groups (called Service Departments) on the basis of product similarities. Hence, ICI was moving away from its patterns of centralization and closer to a multidivisional-like structure in tune with the so-called American scheme applied at DuPont, for instance. On a practical stance, however, McGowan's system of supreme control annihilated any form of decentralized management. His absolute direction hardly met any opposition, especially so "in the dictator's own circle" as Reader put it.[18]

With this critical reminder in mind, we can turn our attention to Solvay & Cie. After the war, the organization of labor within the *gérance* had required some readjustments in line with the allocation of competence and interests of its members. Basically, the idea had come to adapt, rather than resist, the structure implemented in the 1880s. Solvay's initial model of governance had been based on patterns of centralization of strategic planning together with a decentralization of operational management. This overarching layout set out by the first generation *gérants* was left unchanged. With it, Solvay amounted to what has been designated by Chandler as a multifunctional enterprise: six sections were controlled by a single body of managers. In May 1925, Louis Solvay sketched an organization chart that summed up the company's decision-making process. It was inspired by two major considerations – functions and sections, and plants and countries – but revealed a certain unbalance in the distribution of competence among *gérants*. Although some of them (Armand

[16] Chandler (1990), 164–8.
[17] Lévy-Leboyer (1980), 119.
[18] Reader (1975), 27–30, 138–44; Hannah (1980), 57.

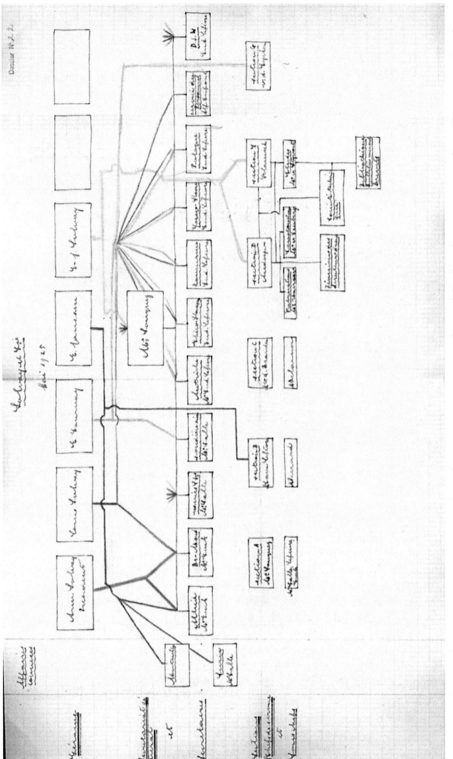

FIGURE 10.2. During the interwar, the *gérance* experienced many attempts to rationalize and divide tasks among its members. This organizational chart was drafted by Louis Solvay in 1925. (Solvay Archives.)

Solvay and Louis Solvay) only seemed to focus on countries, a third one supposedly dealt with specific functions (Ernest-John Solvay for Sections D, Technical, and E, Research), and two others were active on both sides (Emmanuel Janssen and Émile Tournay). The document was primarily theoretical for it could not cover the evolution of day-to-day management. Ernest-John Solvay, for instance, was going to be the one in charge with ICI affairs. Anyhow, with the successive recruitments of Robert Gendebien (1926) and Philippe Aubertin (1928), it became obvious that the mechanisms required profound revision.

In May 1928, a new organizational scheme was introduced at the top of the company. The repartition between functions and countries was maintained, but in contrast with previous editions, it was henceforth delineated between junior and senior managing partners. "In principle," went the document, "for each country and each function, a junior *gérant* carries out the daily job while a senior *gérant* provides the former of his advices.... The running of day-to-day management operations is left to the initiative of junior *gérants*."[19] Although the procedure bore the signature of Robert Gendebien, it made no doubt that the idea stemmed from Louis Solvay, who was continuously striving for the distinction between second- and third-generation *gérants* in Solvay's organizational patterns. Quite insidiously, the reform brought on this other front the generational issue that was going to shake the underpinning of the company's leadership for some years. The conclusive recommendations of the Comité de Famille notwithstanding, the core principles of this organization chart were applied until May 1931. A new and lasting set of "internal rules" within the *gérance* was elaborated in November 1931. The distinction between second- and third-generation managers was dropped and gave way to the notion of *gérants titulaires*, in charge of specific tasks and countries (see Table 10.1). In return, Louis Solvay got the upper hand on the personnel management (*service du personnel*), which included the crafting of social policy and the allocation of subsidies. The latter aspect was about to be reorganized from the vantage point of a new foundation – the Maison Ernest Solvay – whose design was to act as a federation of existing philanthropic foundations (see Chapter 12).[20]

Research and Technology: Independence versus Coordination

The attribution of roles and duties, albeit explicitly laid out in an organization chart, was still far from obvious as seen from the perspective of on-the-job practices. The weight given to some sections especially, in other words, could make the whole decision-making system irrelevant. Nowhere was this discrepancy more visible than at Sections D and E, and more precisely in their interplay. The difficult interaction between the technical direction and research

---

[19] ACS, NdG, "Solvay & Cie, organisation interne" by Robert Gendebien, 31 May 1928.
[20] ACS, DS 137, RdG 28 Dec. 1931; ACS, DS 144–145, RdG 11–12 Jan. 1932. It was first thought to call it the Fondation Alexandre & Adèle Solvay.

TABLE 10.1. *Repartition of Responsibilities among* Gérants *(November 1931)*

Functions	*Gérants* in Charge	Countries	*Gérants* in Charge
Section A (Central administration)	R. Gendebien E.-J. Solvay	Germany (Providentia)	E.-J. Solvay R. Boël E. Tournay
Section B and Mutuelle (Finance)	E.-J. Solvay R. Boël	Belgium	E.-J. Solvay R. Gendebien
Section C (Commerce)	E. Tournay R. Gendebien P. Aubertin (France only)	Spain (except Suria)	P. Aubertin R. Gendebien
Section D (Technical Direction)	R. Boël P. Aubertin E.-J. Solvay	United States	E. Tournay E.-J. Solvay R. Boël
Section E (Research)	R. Boël P. Aubertin E.-J. Solvay	France	P. Aubertin E.-J. Solvay
Section F (Legal Department)	R. Gendebien E. Tournay	United Kingdom	E.-J. Solvay R. Boël
Personnel management	L. Solvay P. Aubertin	Italy	R. Gendebien E. Tournay
		Poland	P. Aubertin R. Boël
		Switzerland	E. Tournay R. Boël
		Suria	E.-J. Solvay P. Aubertin
		Vienna group	R. Gendebien E. Tournay

Source: ACS, DS 126, Règlement d'ordre intérieur de la Gérance, 12 Nov. 1931.

laboratories was not a particularity of Solvay. The mechanisms of reorganization of research-and-development activities during the interwar have been the subject of an important literature. To a large extent, these studies confirm that the drive for industrial innovation witnessed until the late 1920s was either the result of important reorganization of in-house research structures (set up at DuPont, ICI, and Rhône-Poulenc, for instance), the consequence of ambitious interfirm technical knowledge exchange resolutions (e.g., the DuPont-ICI Patents and Processes Agreement of 1929), or the effect of the intense dynamics between academics and the industry (IG Farben).[21] It is also generally acknowledged, however, that the emergence of a fresh impetus for basic and industrial research after World War I gave way to interesting partnerships with public or private foundations. Although it could not match with the magnitude of the Kaiser-Wilhelm-Gesellschaft, the Belgian National Fund for Scientific Research was a successful innovation in this regard. Set up in

---

[21] See, e.g., Caron, Erker, and Fischer (1995); Hounshell and Smith (1988), 98–110; Marsch (2000); Abelshauser et al. (2004), 230–3; Haber (1971), 352–75; Reader (1975), 50–4.

1928 with a colossal financial contribution from the Solvay group and family, it also included the joint Science-Industry Committee that intended to stimulate university-based research in view with the needs of the industry. Keeping alive the family legacy of endowment for scientific research, Armand Solvay, and Ernest-John after him, became vice president of the board of the National Fund for Scientific Research.[22]

Nevertheless, off-site research activities were not among Solvay's preferred options. Working with universities could certainly yield opportunities, but it was even more effective to keep them at a reasonable distance. If in-house research structures were given priority, they were also a considerable source of preoccupation. Suffice it to say, in our limited framework, that the friction of institutional boundaries between both Technical and Research Departments (Sections D and E) stemmed as much from the usual overlap between quasi-similar tasks as from the difficulty to assign these tasks a clear definition. Since the replacement of Georges Chardin by Charles Audoyer at the head of the Technical Department in 1925, Section D began to act as an overarching department – a Central Technical Department – which was only given informal recognition.[23] This extension, which limited the scope and autonomy of the central and plant research laboratories, triggered another round of intense discussions between *gérants*. For historical reasons, Louis Solvay was opposed to any reorganization leading to the curbing of the central research laboratory's strong independence; the other *gérants* (especially those in charge with the functions of research and technology) feared an increasing dispersion of efforts. One of the collateral effects generated by these debates was the sudden elimination of the Technical-Commercial Service, an original administrative machinery set up under the impulsion of R. Boël, P. Aubertin, and R. Gendebien to foster coordination among Sections C, D, and E.[24] Eventually, the *gérants* decided to bury the hatchet by leaving the full autonomy to Sections D and E, defining precisely their attributions, and strengthening the overarching supervision by the *gérance* itself.[25] Opportune as it was, this compromise would only slow down the inexorable imperialism of the Technical Department, whose preeminence in Solvay's institutional setting for industrial innovation became obvious shortly after World War II.

10.2 THE COLLAPSE AND REBIRTH OF THE MUTUELLE

Since the early 1920s, the financial situation of Solvay & Cie became closely associated with the development of the Mutuelle. Created in 1914 as a public

---

[22] Bertrams (2006), 216–34. See also PPSF, Malle Armand Solvay, File 31, Armand Solvay to Charles Nichols, 25 Jan. 1928.

[23] ACS, DS 45 & 45 bis, "Organisation du service technique," various notes, 7 May 1925–25 May 1932.

[24] ACS, DS 246, Service Technico-Commercial, 19 Dec. 1933; ACS, DS 251, RdG 31 Jan. 1934, 4; ACS, DS 269, Meeting between R. Boël, Ch. Audoyer, L. Flamache, 13 Aug. 1934.

[25] ACS, DS 276, "Organisation des rapports la Gérance d'une part et les Sections D & E d'autre part" by R. Boël, 16 Oct. 1934; ACS, DS 276, RdG, 23 Oct. 1934.

company with a capital of BEF 5 million (US$965,000), the Mutuelle rapidly grew from a small-scale private bank dealing with the investments of the Solvay family into the financial backbone and banking subsidiary of the Solvay company. In 1920, it was decided that shareholders outside the family were authorized to take part in the various capital increases, after which the capital of the Mutuelle reached BEF 30 million (US$2,214,000). This expansion was part of a wider plan: Solvay intended to rely on the Mutuelle for strategic investments, both upstream and downstream their traditional production activities. The first step taken was the early internationalization of the Mutuelle's portfolio. A series of investments made, among others, in the successor states of the Habsburg Empire shortly after the war, yielded important profits, although the level of risk was particularly high.[26] Second, the *gérance* agreed to the full transfer to the Mutuelle of the shares owned by Solvay in the coke-oven industry. Consequently, the Mutuelle controlled 28.75 percent of the Société Semet-Solvay (renamed Société des Fours à Coke Semet, Solvay & Piette after the absorption of a related company in 1925). A third, and more decisive operation consisted in the introduction of Solvay in the glassmaking industry in 1921 through a leading position in the company running the Libbey-Owens process in Europe, the Compagnie Internationale pour la Fabrication Mécanique du Verre (Mecaniver). Both investments, as we have seen, had important outcomes on Solvay's international relations, whether with their American partners (Allied Chemicals) or with their French competitors (Saint-Gobain especially). As a result of all these endeavors, the Mutuelle was thriving. But its strategy did not seem to match with its limited financial capacity. To fuel the bank's feverish expansion, another capital increase was called for in August 1923. In view of both companies' overlapping interests – three-quarters of the Mutuelle's holding were said to be "contiguous" to Solvay's interests – the direct subscription of Solvay to the recapitalization of the Mutuelle amounted to no less than 40 percent.[27] Their fate seemed to be bound, for better or for worse.

From Finambel to Finabel

It is not unfair to say that, from its beginning, the Mutuelle was Emmanuel Janssen's brainchild. His contribution to the expansion of Solvay's banking company was widely acknowledged. Still, this intimate association was not without risks. In times of crisis, it would expose him to harsh criticisms by the very same who praised him in periods of prosperity. Janssen, therefore, strove to temper his eagerness for business setups. During a stay in the United States in the fall of 1925, he conceived the idea to transfer a portion of the Mutuelle's

[26] The bulk of the direct investments made in countries from former Austria-Hungary were in the banking sector: Österreichische Boden-Credit Anstalt, Bank of Bosnia, Croatian-Slovenian Mortgage Bank, Malopolski Bank, and Zivnostenska Banka. They totaled BEF 11.6 million in 1923, 84 percent of which was for Boden-Credit Anstalt alone. See ACS, RdG, 7 Aug. 1923.
[27] *Mutuelle Solvay* (2000), 6.

portfolio to a new holding company, the Société Financière Américano-Belge (Finambel). Basically, 70 percent of its capital was controlled by American groups (most of which belonged to the glassmaking industry and the banking sector), the remainder being equally held by the Mutuelle and the Philippson investment bank, an active Jewish private bank based in Brussels.[28] The creation of Finambel was the result of both the pressure exerted by some of the Solvay family shareholders to divest stakes of the Mutuelle and the strategy followed by Janssen to diversify the sources of funding while enabling the building of new industrial-financial networks (e.g., with the Ford family). Nonetheless, if he had taken into account the warnings put forward by some shareholders, Emmanuel Janssen had not anticipated the divergences of financial culture between both sides of the ocean.

By 1927, as tensions escalated between Allied and Solvay, American shareholders demanded that Finambel be listed on the stock exchange. Unsurprisingly, their European counterparts strongly opposed the idea. A third option was found after difficult negotiations. Through his private and business contacts with the head of the Antwerp-based international trade company, Édouard Bunge (who turned out to be Hallam Tuck's father-in-law), Emmanuel Janssen managed to have Finambel absorbed by a joint-stock bank, the Banque Générale Belge. Quite modest in scope at its creation in 1901, the Banque Générale Belge had experienced an impressive growth since the end of the war with the decisive assistance of the Bunge Company and the Anglo-South-American Bank Ltd. In 1925, Bunge had successfully convinced Janssen to have the Mutuelle become a shareholder of BGB. Three years later, it was Janssen asking Édouard Bunge and his partners at BGB to take over Finambel. Among the outcomes of this financial operation was the agreement, later confirmed by a contract (February 1928), allowing for an important transfer of customers from the Mutuelle to the Banque Générale Belge.[29]

Emmanuel Janssen did not remain inactive in the meantime. Although the ultimate version of his Mutu-plan was turned down shortly after Christmas 1926 (see Chapter 9), he continued to have high expectations for the Mutuelle, and its potential role in sparking off a consortium of chemical industries. Shifting from international to national scale was perhaps the best way to make it come true. Under his impulsion, the Semet, Solvay & Piette Company became the cornerstone of a merger operation in the Belgian chemical industry, which resulted in the launching of a new company, Union Chimique Belge (UCB).[30]

---

[28] On the Franz M. Philippson & Company, see Kurgan-van Hentenryk (2009), 221–3; Schreiber (1996).

[29] ACS, DS 58, RdG, 2 Dec. 1930; Brion and Moreau (2008).

[30] Beside the Société des Fours à Coke Semet, Solvay & Piette, the constituent companies of UCB in 1928 were Société Générale Belge de Produits Chimiques, Société Anonyme de Produits Chimiques de Droogenbosch, and Produits Chimiques et Pharmaceutiques Meurice. The initial capital was 175 million BEF. The next year, UCB absorbed another series of small-scale Belgian chemical plants: Société ostendaise Lumière et Force motrice, Produits réfractaires de Saint-Ghislain, Compagnie belge de Produits Chimiques de Schoonaerde, Cuivre, Métaux et Produits chimiques d'Hemixem, Compagnie Progil belge et Extraits tannants et colorants d'Hemixem,

The move was important in many respects for the Mutuelle held 12.54 percent of the new company's capital and 24.14 percent of the voting rights. From the perspective of the industrial landscape, it implied that Solvay became a new actor in the soda-consuming sectors, especially in nitrogen and superphosphate fertilizers. This was not to everyone's liking. Saint-Gobain immediately demanded – and obtained – to enact a clause in the renewal of its soda contract with Solvay, whereby the latter agreed to sell its interests in UCB if its position in superphosphates became a threat to Saint-Gobain.[31] On a financial standpoint, the UCB merger witnessed the strengthening of the Mutuelle's relations with Belgium's leading mixed joint-stock bank, the Société Générale de Belgique, from which the Mutuelle was already a minor shareholder. Their first strategic encounter dated from their mutual interests in Mecaniver, which led to the formation of a voting trust. The deal with UCB entailed a retrocession of forty thousand UCB privileged shares held by the Mutuelle for their countervalue in shares from the Société Générale.[32]

The Mutuelle was a flourishing business at the beginning of 1928. And there was no reason, for its main pilot, to hold back its ascension. Emmanuel Janssen always seemed to move forward on a triple interrelated front, guiding the Mutuelle simultaneously toward the chemical industry, the soda-consuming industry, and the banking sector (one could add to the list the thriving real estate division, which was run by Egimo, a subsidiary of the Mutuelle). In line with this optimistic agenda, the artificial silk industry, which relied heavily on caustic soda, was next on the list of acquisitions. In partnership with the French textile industrialist Edmond Gillet (already associated to the Mecaniver combination), Janssen got hold of two Belgian companies (Soie Artificielle de Tubize and Soie Artificielle d'Obourg) and an Italian one (Supertessile). The proximity with the Lyons-based Gillet group, close to the Crédit Lyonnais, reinforced the connection with the French private banks, especially the Haute Banque Vernes & Cie. The Mutuelle, the Gillet group, and Vernes & Cie teamed up to launch the Mutuelle Industrielle, whose aim was to become a financial holding niche for joint projects in the chemical and artificial silk industries in France.[33] The intention here was to counterbalance the financial networks and willingness of expansion of both Saint-Gobain and Rhône-Poulenc in their own courtyard, so to speak.

Parallel to this international branching out, Janssen made no secret of his intention to recast the influence of the Société Générale within the Mutuelle. Although a key ally, the Société Générale was somehow too powerful to become the Mutuelle's only financial partner (it had pursued its strategy of

Nouvelles Industries Chimiques de Nieuport, Franco-Belge Nadox. See Baudhuin (1946), vol. 2, 87–8.

[31] ACS, RdG 27 Dec. 1927; ACS, NdG, "Note sur la reprise de Chiminbel" by R. Boël, 13 Jan. 1937; ACS, 1323-40-5 A, File 412/b, "Participation dans la Société 'Union Chimique Belge', II, 10 July 1950.

[32] Kurgan-van Hentenryk (1997), 228; Brion and Moreau (1998), 267–8.

[33] Cassis (2010), 104, 171; Plessis (2009), 135–9; [Pardon] (2000), 6. On the Gillet family, see Joly (2010).

concentration by absorbing the Banque d'Outremer in February 1928).[34] Hence, he started informal discussion with the Société Générale's utmost rival and challenger, the Banque de Bruxelles. Underlying Janssen's preliminary talks with the Banque de Bruxelles was the idea to neutralize both these financial giants' respective power and to prevent the slightest possibility of a hostile takeover. Obviously, next to this rather defensive stance was also the aim to take advantage of their multiple interests grounded in different industrial, financial, and social networks. Last but not least, the current standing of the Mutuelle forced it to keep up with the pace of business affairs, which was booming. In ten years' time, the Solvay family investment house was turned into Belgium's third largest financial holding. And this generated some obligations of prestige, for example, making investments that went far beyond the scope of a family bank dedicated to the development of a chemical company.

More prosaically, the designs called for another capital increase of the Mutuelle, the fifth since the war. This time, however, the increase intended to reflect the scale of ambitions – from BEF 100 million to BEF 300 million (US$8,357,000). Among the different options considered, the *gérants* decided on 14 February 1928 that Solvay would entirely subscribe. However, because both companies had different shareholders, a special modus operandi was found: half the capital raised would be released back to Solvay in view of a retrocession to shareholders of the Mutuelle.[35] As such, therefore, the operation slightly affected the budget of Solvay. But the psychological impact was huge as Solvay was to control 80 percent of the Mutuelle, which officially remained a distinct public company. For some shareholders of Solvay, the deal amounted to a quasi takeover that exceeded Solvay's corporate prerogatives set forth in its bylaws. This was made clear by Fernand Van der Straeten in a letter he addressed to leaders of the Mutuelle just a week before the organization of its extraordinary General Assembly meeting on 20 March 1928. In the electric atmosphere of the time, Van der Straeten's assertion triggered a dramatic chain of events within the various branches of the family shareholders.[36] After some hesitation, also in the ranks of the *gérance*, the assembly eventually endorsed the capital increase, but the agreement seemed conditional. Some voices expressed that some Solvay shareholders would no longer accept taking part in similar operations. Among the *gérants*, Louis Solvay was leading the protest. Profoundly averse to the risk and the speculative nature of investment banks, he considered the existence of a strong Mutuelle an "opportunity of secondary order" and even a "dissipation of efforts" for the development of Solvay.[37] Unsurprisingly, Emmanuel Janssen took these comments, as well as the reluctance of a group of shareholders, as personal criticisms against his actions. Although he urged his colleagues at Solvay to "clarify" their position

---

[34] Kurgan-van Hentenryk (1997), 239–44.

[35] PPSF, Malle Armand Solvay, 1, Folder 31, Report of activities of the Mutuelle, undated [20 Mar. 1928].

[36] PPSF, Malle Armand Solvay, 1, Folder 31, "Note sur l'Assemblée Générale Extraordinaire de la Mutuelle le 20 Mar. 1928," by Robert Hankar, 2 Apr. 1928.

[37] ACS, NdG, L. Solvay, 19 May 1928.

concerning his and the Mutuelle's situation in this context, he received confusing, if not contradictory, information on both issues. This awkward state
of affairs, quite instructive of the crisis of leadership affecting the company,
lasted for a couple of years (until Janssen's formal resignation in May 1931).[38]
With hindsight, it is not doubtful that the episode of the March 1928 capital
increase can be seen as a watershed in the relations among family members,
and in Solvay's history in general.

At any rate, a consensus seemed to emerge that fostered a "lighter" Mutuelle
as the only viable solution. Janssen himself had already investigated in this
regard. Less inclined to reiterate the 1925 Finambel experience, he logically
strove for a joint French-Belgian enterprise. With a group of associates that
included the former partners of the Banque Générale Belge deal (Bunge,
Philippson, and Anglo-South American), the Belgian financial holdings (Société
Générale, Banque de Bruxelles) and the Banque de Paris et des Pays-Bas
(Paribas), Janssen set up the investment bank Compagnie Financière et Industrielle de Belgique (Finabel) in April 1928. The portfolio of Finabel consisted
mainly of assets previously owned by the Mutuelle, with the notable exception of industry and banking stocks considered essential to the development of
Solvay (e.g., chemicals, glass, artificial silk). Finabel started investing in a wide
array of promising areas, ranging from the automobile industry (it notably
backed the venue of Ford Motor Company in Belgium) to electricity and gas
industries.[39] The Mutuelle, by contrast, still held 7 percent of Banque Générale
Belge and some 14 percent of Finabel (notwithstanding the fact that both of
them had substantial cross-holdings) after this stabilizing operation.

Through the Slump: the Creation of the Société Belge de Banque

Although the creation of Finabel substantially reduced the burden of the
Mutuelle, the bank's figures were put under close scrutiny. Diversification
efforts had surely yielded significant results, but the portfolio still suffered
imbalance and revealed the major influence of banking assets, the bulk of
which came from Belgium-based joint-stock banks and financial holdings (see
Chart 10.1). Since the collapse of the New York Stock Exchange, this was a
source of concern as the panic threatened to spread. Beside the composition of
its portfolio, the Mutuelle's balance sheet showed another worrying discrepancy: the gap between cash flow and liabilities was growing wider. If Janssen
nuanced the importance of current liabilities in a dynamic yet secure company
like the Mutuelle, he could not deny that the figure had tripled since 1923,
reaching the symbolic amount of BEF 100 million (US$2,785,000). Even a
moderate *gérant* like Ernest-John Solvay called for a radical "unloading" of
the portfolio – and the promise to carry out a careful strategy.[40] When he had
asked a year earlier (April 1929) for the Mutuelle to continue divesting part

---

[38] ACS, DS 35, E. Janssen to the gérance, 11 June 1928; ACS, DS 74, E. Janssen to L. Solvay, 22
     Mar. 1931.
[39] ACS, DS 58, RdG, 2 Dec. 1930; Brion and Moreau (2008).
[40] ACS, DS 58, RdG, 2 Dec. 1930; ACS, DS 61 bis, "Note à propos de la Mutuelle Solvay" by
     E.-J. Solvay, 16 Jan. 1931.

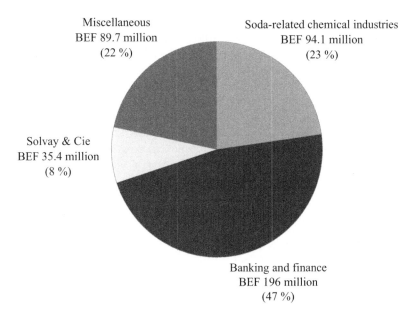

Miscellaneous
BEF 89.7 million
(22 %)

Soda-related chemical industries
BEF 94.1 million
(23 %)

Solvay & Cie
BEF 35.4 million
(8 %)

Banking and finance
BEF 196 million
(47 %)

CHART 10.1. Overview of the portfolio of the Mutuelle Solvay (November 1930). *Source:* ACS, NdG, "Note sur la reprise de Chiminbel" by R. Boël, 13 Jan. 1937; ACS, DS 60, "Situation financière de la Mutuelle" (November 1930), 23 Dec. 1930.

of its investments, Janssen told him that the unfavorable context of the stock market precluded them from doing so. If selling was not appropriate in April 1929, by late 1930, the financial situation was even worse. In this respect, the structure, and not only the context, ought to take the blame. A substantial portion of the Mutuelle's industrial investments could not be easily paid up; they were either completely tied up or dependent on resolving specific commitments (voting trusts, conditional or blocking agreements with Mecaniver, UCB, and Finabel). In a memo drafted at the *gérance*'s request in March 1929, Georges Janssen had singled out the eventual perilous outcomes for the Mutuelle considering the restricted circulation of its capital, as well as the eventual shortage of its cash flow.[41] The warnings had come true. With the further threat of unpaid debts from clients, the perspective was rather grim indeed.

In view of the nature and composition of the Mutuelle's portfolio, difficulties were expectable on several fronts. Eyes were turned to Finabel, but the staggering blow came from the Banque Générale Belge (BGB), whose situation was deteriorating faster than any other financial house. Its liabilities amounted to a total of BEF 475 million (US$13,255,000), whereas its cash flow did not exceed BEF 170 million (US$4,744,000). A credit crunch was looming. The impressive fall of diamond prices in the late winter of 1931 affected directly the banks of the Antwerp region and the BGB in particular, which had an important stake in the market of diamond industry. In a few weeks' time, rumors spread that

---

[41] ACS, DS 42 bis, "Note sur la situation financière de la Mutuelle Solvay" by Georges Janssen, 25 Mar. 1929; Reaction by E.-J. Solvay on 13 Apr. 1929.

BGB was on the verge of backsliding into bankruptcy – an allegation that was vigorously denied by the bank's authorities.[42] By April 1931, however, the situation was desperate. Even the head of the National Bank of Belgium, Louis Franck, was worried about the drought affecting the bank's cash assets. Unsurprisingly, he called for the quick setup of a rescue plan driven by a consortium of banks, which the Mutuelle, as a shareholder, was to be part of. Under pressure and in spite of Louis Solvay's soft reluctance, the Mutuelle accepted to pledge for a maximum guarantee of BEF 100 million (US$2,786,000), intending to give way to the National Bank's intervention. Other institutional shareholders of BGB (including Bunge, Philippson, and Lambert) were naturally asked to join in but declined the offer. The *gérants* were upset by this attitude. They felt that the absence of solidarity in times of crisis was a bad omen for further collaboration. If the rescue plan finally saved the BGB from collapse, it was at Solvay's own expense.[43]

Meanwhile, the financial turmoil was getting hold of the Mutuelle. In late December 1930, Emmanuel Janssen had once again suggested splitting the portfolio and transferring major stakes to an investment bank partly controlled by the Mutuelle. He envisaged the setup of a new financial combine with Paribas, Banque de Bruxelles (through its financial subsidiary Compagnie Belge pour l'Industrie), and the electrical engineering and financial company Sofina.[44] The other *gérants* seemed skeptical. Then again, they did not provide a real counterproposal, nor did they show any sign of enthusiasm for the alternatives suggested by Janssen, which, they trusted, were prone to market risk. These circumstances precipitated his withdrawal from the *gérance*, although he remained closely connected to the web of Solvay via his positions in Allied, SAIC, and Suria, among others.[45] He became vice president of the Mutuelle, which was under the direct control of the *gérants*. They appointed one of Armand Solvay's sons-in-law, Robert Hankar, executive head. His first assignment was to conduct, together with Georges Janssen and René Boël, a drastic operation of divesting the Mutuelle's portfolio. Solvay wished to get rid of no less than BEF 200 million (US$5,571,000) worth of assets, which represented 44 percent of the total value. The operation was designed to concern all sectors, with a special focus on the glass and artificial silk industries (and the notable exception of the coal sector); the project included the loss of majority stakes in two companies – Finabel and UCB.[46]

[42] Brion and Moreau (2008).

[43] ACS, DS 79, Special meeting on the situation of the BGB, 26 Apr. 1931; ACS, DS 79, RdG, 27 and 28 Apr. 1929; ACS, DS 79 bis, "Rapport sur la situation de la Banque Générale Belge..." by Albert-E. Janssen, 22 May 1931.

[44] ACS, DS 58, RdG, 2 Dec. 1930.

[45] ACS, DS 73, RdG, 18 Mar. 1931; ACS, DS 74, E. Janssen to L. Solvay, 22 Mar. 1931; ACS, DS 82, L. Solvay to E. Janssen, 9 May 1931; ACS, DS 86, E. Janssen to L. Solvay, 16 May 1931; ACS, DS 92, RdG 6 June 1931; ACS, DS 94, RdG 9 June 1934.

[46] ACS, DS 87, "Note pour MM. Solvay & Cie" by G. Janssen, 18 May 1931; ACS, DS 90, Gérance to G. Janssen, 21 May 1931. Other major divestments suggested (less than or equal to 50 percent) were Brufina, Mecaniver, Soie Artificielle de Tubize, Hydro-Electric, Supertessile, Carbochimique, Métallurgique de Hoboken, Sogechim, and the Wiltcher's Carlton Hotel.

But what were the options for alleviating the Mutuelle's heavy burden? If Solvay did not want to rush, the continuing drop of the stock market was running counter to them. The first intuitions had come to strengthen the Mutuelle's interests in BGB or Finabel through an exchange of shares. Yet the fragile state of the former and the depreciation of the latter's portfolio (Finabel recorded a 27 percent loss in July 1931) made the option hazardous. Emmanuel Janssen had whispered an alternative: regrouping some of the Mutuelle's industrial assets, especially in the artificial silk sector, into a financial trust organized around the International Holding & Investment Company (of which the Mutuelle was already a shareholder). But then again, Janssen had to abandon the project under the pressing advice of Belgium's business éminence grise, Émile Francqui.[47] A third and ultimate lead, also investigated by Janssen, consisted in creating a new financial company. Seductive as it was, this scheme rested on a range of difficult technical premises, which René Boël and Ernest-John Solvay were asked to explore. Both *gérants* concluded that the only viable way was threefold: enabling the merger between BGB and Finabel; organizing the subsequent transfer of the package of the Mutuelle assets into the new combination resulting from the merger (28 percent of which was controlled by Solvay); and setting an exchange of shares between the Mutuelle and the new company, so that the Mutuelle would be fully owned by Solvay. Emmanuel Janssen had not expected this last stage; he had never envisioned a clear-cut distinction between Solvay and the bulk of investments he had made since 1920 for the sake of the Mutuelle (and, thus, Solvay). The eagerness with which Boël and Ernest-John Solvay intended to break with the past was best seen in their suggestion, enclosed in their report, to get rid of the Mutuelle Solvay in due course. Although this was eventually turned down by their colleagues – a lighter Mutuelle (its capital was to be reduced by a third) was still useful as a financial intermediation – this revealed a major shift of approach.[48]

The three-step method adopted by Boël and Ernest-John Solvay in their report formed the blueprint for the setup of the Société Belge de Banque (SBB), officially launched on 5 January 1932. Its heterogeneous portfolio contained assets from the former BGB and Finabel, as well as the substantial package of holdings from the Mutuelle divested by Solvay (whose estimated value had lost another 30 percent since May 1931). The birth had not been painless; it had also taken place in the worst economic context ever. Still, the creation was groundbreaking in many respects. First, it clarified the complicated relations between Solvay & Cie and the Mutuelle, the firm and its investment bank. After years of intense expansion followed by a rapid downturn, the Mutuelle had

---

[47] ACS, DS 79, RdG, 7 July 1931; ACS, DS 98, RdG 10 Aug. 1931 (appendixes 1–3).

[48] ACS, DS 99, RdG, 13 Aug. 1931 (including the report written by Boël and E.-J. Solvay); ACS, DS 100, RdG, 21 Aug. 1931; ACS, DS 104, RdG, 2 Sept. 1931 (including notes by E.-J. Solvay and P. Vander Eycken); ACS, DS 146, RdG, 14 Jan. 1932; ACS, RdG, 15 Jan. 1932. The outline of the administrative reorganization of the new Mutuelle Solvay can be found in ACS, DS 190 bis, Programme MutuSol, 27 Sept. 1932. It should be noted that, in the wake of the Belgian legislation separating depository from investment banking institutions (the counterpart to the US Glass-Steagall Banking Act of 1933), the Mutuelle became on 8 August 1935 a limited partnership company under the corporate name Solvay, Tournay, Hankar, Boël & Cie.

become, to the eyes of some *gérants*, an unbound financial vehicle. By 1932, the equation "Mutuelle equals Solvay" had prevailed; it had definitely put an end to the autonomist patterns of Solvay's banking subsidiary. Moreover, it paved the way for the transfer of the Solvay group's overall financial resources to a centralized financial holding based in Switzerland, Gefucin.[49]

But the process leading to the creation of SBB was also a turning point for Solvay's own strategy. The idea, once promoted by Janssen, to use the Mutuelle as a pivotal nexus in an ambitious consortium failed on both national and international scales. Although it terminated Solvay's claim to become designated intermediary in the world chemical industry, it did preserve the company's capital and strengthened its leadership in the alkali business. The choice between their becoming a financial venture and an industrial company had been made at the expense of the former. A third and final outcome of the SBB operation concerned the future of Emmanuel Janssen's role. Inasmuch as the drastic rationalization plan of "his" Mutuelle differed from the design he had laid out in August 1931,[50] it eventually prompted the dawning, as the Société Belge de Banque, of a series of formally separate, albeit financially connected, business activities from those of Solvay, which were under his direct control. The whole question amounted to evaluating the extent to which they were indeed separate and parallel.

These conflicting territories later led to some difficulties between Solvay and Union Chimique Belge's respective management, when UCB was facing an important economic downturn and unable to pay its debts in November 1934. Emmanuel Janssen, then, requested that his former colleagues intervene, which they did, reluctantly, until Solvay held 28.4 percent of UCB.[51] A year later, however, tensions reached their peak as Janssen intended to fully reorganize the business activities of his family around UCB and proceed to an important expansion of its activities and financial capacities. The *gérants* had mixed feelings about the strategy to adopt: on the one hand, their stake in a wider UCB could help Solvay keep in touch with a whole range of crucial chemical and chemical-based products (e.g., nitrogen, pharmaceutics, glass, synthetic fibers); on the other hand, Janssen's proposal – the merger between UCB and the financial holding company controlled by the Janssen family, Chiminbel – would have deprived Solvay of its veto power, which was limited to shareholders owning at least 25 percent of the capital.[52] After a full year of argument, both

---

[49] Standing for Gesellschaft für Beteiligungen und für Unternehmungen der Chemischen Industrie, Gefucin was initiated by René Boël in August 1932 to unify the taxation regimes between outright-owned plants and subsidiaries through the perception of common license rights. By December 1934, the international holdings of the Solvay group (including ICI, Solvay USA, Suria, Providentia, and Aussig but not DSW) channeled through Gefucin. ACS, DS 187, 9 Aug. 1932; ACS, DS 279, Notes by R. Boël, Dec. 1934.

[50] ACS, DS 98, "Note pour MM. Solvay & Cie" by Georges Janssen, 6 Aug. 1931.

[51] ACS, 1323-40-5 A, Union Chimique Belge, Document Nos. I and II, 10 July 1950; ACS, DS 277, Various notes, Nov.–Dec. 1934; ACS, DS 282, RdG, 1 & 8 Mar. 1935.

[52] ACS, NdG, "Note sur la reprise de Chiminbel" by R. Boël, 13 Jan. 1937; ACS, NdG, "Remarques à propos du projet de fusion de Chiminbel" by E.-J. Solvay, 25 Mar. 1936; ACS, DS 302, UCB-Chiminbel File, 29 Feb.–28 May 1936;

companies finally came to an agreement in March 1937: through an exchange of shares, Solvay & Cie (via the Mutuelle) obtained 109,987 new shares of UCB-Chiminbel (approximately 23 percent) with the promise to keep its say in the strategy of UCB.[53] This episode, one could say, was the last far echo of the troubled period (starting in March 1928) that saw the confrontation of divergent visions about the family company's strategy and management.

---

[53] ACS, 1323-40-5 A, "Participation dans la société 'Union Chimique Belge'," Document No. II, 10 July 1950.

FIGURE 11.1. Casks of caustic soda, increasingly produced through electrolysis of salt in the 1930s. (Solvay Archives.)

The Electrolytic Industry

As the 1930s unfolded, one could legitimately wonder how Solvay, confronted internally with financial and managerial difficulties and externally with uneasy partnerships (most notably with Weber's command of Allied), was actually in a state to maintain its dominant position in the world alkali production. At first sight, the industrial pattern the company had set in the 1920s largely corresponds to the traditional picture of the Roaring Twenties. By 1922 at the latest, Solvay's plants and subsidiaries worldwide (without taking Solvay Process Company into account) had caught up – and sometimes exceeded – their prewar figures in all alkali products (mostly for political reasons, Deutsche Solvay Werke [DSW] had to wait until 1925). Between 1922 and 1929, the production figures of soda ash increased by 80.5 percent and that of caustic soda (through causticization) by 78.3 percent. Interestingly, the performance was especially remarkable for Solvay's own factories in Belgium, France, Spain, and Italy. There, the progression between 1922 and 1929 amounted to 85.2 percent and 136.3 percent for soda ash and caustic soda, respectively.[1]

A downward trend followed this period of exceptional growth. In view of the intensity of the Depression and the internationalization of its production and market organization, there was no way Solvay could remain unaffected by the slump. The reduction of prices that was called for could only partly make up for the weak demand and the general overcapacity. Because of a lack of financial evidence, we must rely on sales figures. As long as Solvay's outright own plants were concerned, the company experienced a drop of sales during the first three years of the 1930s. Between 1929 and 1932, alkali sales slid by 21.84 percent. The level of 1929 – a record-breaking year in the company's history in terms of output – was not reached until 1936 (see Table 11.1).

In contrast, in comparison with ICI and IG Farben, which were more diversified, Solvay's resistance seemed to have been stronger.[2] After the crisis and the years of recovery, Solvay could still benefit from an upward economic trend. The performance was largely due to the increase in caustic soda production. Looking at the sites of production, the impetus for caustic soda seemed once again more sensible in facilities directly controlled from Brussels than in the

---

[1] ANOH, Production figures compiled from tables "Carbonate de soude" (BIB total) and "Lessive caustique concentrée" (DCDE, caustic soda, 97.5 percent). See also ACS, 1482–1-8, "A Survey of World Alkali Situation," 23 Nov. 1933.

[2] Reader (1975), 116–22; Plumpe (1990), 433–50; Abelshauser et al. (2004), 239–42.

TABLE 11.1. *Evolution of Sales of Solvay in the 1930s*

Year	Sales (in tons)	Sales (1929 = 100)
1929	1,014,850	100.00
1930	915,480	90.21
1931	842,614	83.03
1932	793,234	78.16
1933	844,423	83.21
1934	910,683	89.74
1935	993,266	97.87
1936	1,032,309	101.72
1937	1,077,387	106.16
1938	1,016,958	100.21
1939	1,225,723	120.78

Source: ACS, 1001–28–19, Capacité de production des Usines Solvay & Cie, various years. Figures do not include deliveries from Bayonne plant (Soudière de l'Adour), which accounted for approximately twenty thousand to twenty-five thousand tons per year.

Solvay group as a whole.[3] However, drawing the conclusion that this was the deliberate result of a strategic drive for caustic soda launched by the *gérance* would be misleading for various reasons.

11.1   MISSING THE ELECTROLYTIC MOMENTUM

First, Solvay did not go unchallenged throughout these years. The crafting of alliances, trusts, and other combinations in the 1920s was not only designed to protect corporations from the instability of markets; it was also aimed at taming the outbreak of unexpected competitors. But it could not prevent competition from occurring in general – especially in a context where economic growth seemed unrestrained and boundless. Second, electrolytic caustic soda is missing from this statistical sketch, and it was precisely in the field of electrolysis that important changes were taking place as the demand for caustic soda was soaring after World War I under the influence of artificial silk producers and the more traditional consumption of soap makers.[4] Next to caustic soda, chlorine might well have been considered as the other by-product of electrolysis.

---

[3] In comparison with overall production of caustic soda (expressed in terms of "Lessive caustique concentrée" – caustic soda, 97.5 percent) in the Solvay group, the weight of Solvay & Cie's facilities (in Belgium, France, Italy, and Spain) grew from 35.8 percent in 1922 to 41.2 percent in 1939 (whereas the production of soda ash accounted for a permanent 35–36 percent during the interwar period). See production figures compiled from ANOH, "Carbonate de soude" (BIB total) and "Lessive caustique concentrée" (DCDE, caustic soda, 97.5 percent). See also ACS, 1482–1-8, "A Survey of World Alkali Situation," 23 Nov. 1933.

[4] Between 1909 and 1935, the artificial silk (or rayon) industry enjoyed yearly growth rates between 10 percent and 20 percent. This expansion was largely driven by changes in technological systems. After World War I, both the viscose and acetate-based productions superseded Chardonnet's nitrocellulose process, as well as Fremery and Urban's cuprammonium process (1897). See Coleman (2003), 934–5; Plumpe (1990), 296–7.

Yet with the increasing use of chlorine as a bleaching agent in the paper industry and the sudden outburst of new organic compounds, the balance between both products was about to be inverted, and the production of chlorine soon fully absorbed by the huge development of synthetic rubber and polyvinyl chloride in view of World War II.[5]

How, then, did Solvay respond to the industrial aggiornamento posed by the electrolytic process? Basically, the underpinnings of Solvay's electrolytic strategy were guided by the need to safeguard the positions acquired in caustic soda, which essentially was obtained through causticization. After Brichaux and Wilsing's technological breakthrough and the successive creation of electrolytic plants in Jemeppe, Osternienburg, and Lysychansk before 1900 (see Chapter 5), a wait-and-see attitude had followed, interrupted only by the building of Turda (1911) in what became Romania. After the war, and in spite of the loss of Lysychansk and the difficult start of Turda, the pursuit of an electrolytic program was not a priority. In contrast, efforts concentrated on rigorous cost-reducing schemes in existing causticization equipment. Several reasons were put forward to justify the stalled development of electrolysis: the intensive start-up capital required, the variability of the electrical power resources, and the more unpredictable yield of the process in terms of Solvay's engineering capabilities. One could add to the list that Solvay had no staff dedicated to the selling of chlorine and was thus deprived of a reliable network of customers.[6]

By October 1927, though, the head of Solvay's Technical Department, Charles Audoyer, started to show some signs of anxiety. As he stressed "the probable increase of chlorine consumption in various industrial branches," he trusted that Solvay should enter firmly in the electrolytic business. Relying on a thorough comparative study prepared by Section D, Audoyer intended to demonstrate the potentialities for the company of a "rapid and considerable" expansion in the demand for chlorine and chlorine derivatives (chloride of lime, especially). "Although [this trend] remains difficult to assess with precision," he concluded, "what we already know about it suffices to say that there is an opportunity we should seize *without delay*."[7] Beside market prospects, Audoyer cleverly touched on a core and sensitive issue – production costs. According to some estimates, the production of electrolytic caustic soda was cheaper than Solvay's traditional causticization process (especially if energy costs were low). Although the argument convinced the *gérants* to double the production capacity of electrolytic caustic soda at Jemeppe (up to forty tons per day), Audoyer dashed to Tavaux, Solvay's brand-new site in France, which he had located in the summer of 1925 with his uncle Albert Gonod, to "leave a sufficient room for the building of an electrolytic unit (running sixty t./d.)."[8]

[5] "For every ton of chlorine, about 1.1 ton of caustic soda is made. Until Hitler's war caustic soda was more important, and there was generally a surplus of chlorine. Since then the picture has been reversed." Haber 1971, 76n1.

[6] ACS, 1001–24-5, Politique industrielle – Produits chlorés (Section D, No. 3259), 22 May 1939.

[7] ACS, CdG 21 Oct. 1927; ACS, 1001–24-5A, "Note sur le développement de l'industrie électrolytique et la position à y prendre" (Section D, Note No. 516) by Ch. Audoyer, 24 Nov. 1927 (Audoyer's emphasis).

[8] ACS, RdG, 1 Sept. 1925, 25 Nov. 1927, and 27 Nov. 1927; Ducordeaux et al. (2005), 9–12.

Meanwhile, the debate on the comparative advantages of the electrolytic process went on. The former *gérant* Édouard Hannon, who never missed an occasion to enable his fellow associates to benefit from his experience and wisdom, was more skeptical. Historically, he argued, Solvay had gained a foothold only "moderately" in the electrolytic business as a means to exert pressure on a possible competition in caustic soda. For Hannon, there was no reason to change this winning strategy.[9] His opinion found an unexpected support from ICI. In July 1928, discussing the future of electrolysis at a board meeting of the British combine, Ernest-John Solvay learned from Lieutenant Colonel George Pollitt that ICI was still wondering about a proper strategy for its production of electrolytic chlorine. Pollitt suggested that Solvay attempt to extract chlorine from the calcium chloride resulting from its ammonia-soda process (and for which it had a very limited outlet at the Jemeppe plant). Coincidentally, Orlando Weber had made a similar recommendation to Emmanuel Janssen during his stay in New York.[10]

The most decisive blow to Solvay's entry in the electrolytic business in the 1920s came from its own Commercial Department (Section C). In what in many respects looked like a counterinvestigation of Audoyer's survey, G. Piérard and his assistants came to the conclusion that Section D had overstated the outlet opportunities for chlorine while neglecting the financial productivity and the amount of start-up investments in building an electrolytic plant (especially in taking into account the requirements of tied-up capital in a foreign country). Focusing especially on the French and Belgian markets, within which the causticization process turned out to be quite resilient, the study advised a cautious increase of the electrolytic production capacity and the signing of a series of price and production agreements with existing and future competitors in the field. These findings clashed completely with Audoyer's views. In a separate note appended to the memorandum, he refuted some elements of the analysis but regretted more profoundly that the electrolytic industry was considered a "reluctant option" only. As long as the chlorine market's capacity of consumption was not exceeded, Audoyer concluded with a feeling of bitterness, electrolysis was a "really interesting business."[11]

Solvay, as a result, did not engage fully and frankly in the electrolytic industry during the 1920s, a decision that was primarily justified as a way to safeguard the leadership in caustic soda. Looking at the matter with hindsight – which is a rather comfortable position, the historian should admit – the *gérants* not only missed a moment; they were about to lose their leadership in caustic soda precisely because of their choice not to take the electrolytic turn as soon as 1928. In June 1933, Piérard gave in that the production (and consumption) of electrolytic caustic soda accounted for 63 percent of the total increase of

[9] ACS, NdG, "Electrolyse" by Ed. Hannon, 26 Dec. 1927.
[10] ACS, 1001-24-5, ICI Board Meeting, 12 July 1928; ACS, CdG 6 Sept. 1928.
[11] ACS, 1001-24-5A (Section C), "Note au sujet du développement de l'électrolyse en France et en Belgique." by G. Piérard, 10 Sept. 1928, and "Complément à la Note," by Ch. Audoyer, 16 Sept. 1928.

caustic soda production between 1925 and 1931.[12] The outcome was quite logical. As Chart 11.1 clearly indicates, Solvay was forced to witness its market shares in caustic soda vanish into thin air because of their lagging behind in the electrolytic business. Obviously, the defensive strategy the *gérants* had conveyed had not been defensive enough; it had consisted in keeping up with causticization for the sake of antidiversification, despite available information pointing otherwise.

When they realized their alkali stronghold was under threat, the *gérants* converted to another rationale in their electrolytic policy – catching up by all means necessary. Concretely, the process followed two steps, depending successively on the levels of development of the electrolytic industry and the nature of Solvay's presence in national markets. In France and Germany, where urgent threats had to be faced, they took a path once taken with soda ash through the conclusion of ententes on prices and products. They did so by joining the movements of chlorine cartelization, which was already organized in function of national circumstances. At a later stage, from about 1934, the strategy was to gain a strong foothold in the electrolytic industry by building new plants (Torrelavega in Spain, Povoa in Portugal, Linne-Herten in the Netherlands, and Rosignano and Ferrara in Italy), taking over existing ones (Hallein in Austria, Ponte Mammolo in Italy, Westeregeln in Germany, and Aspropyrgos in Greece), and pursuing the rationalization of the electrolytic market at an international level (with IG Farben, ICI, Aussig, and even DuPont). In all cases, however, national policies and international issues were closely intertwined, both formally and informally. For Solvay, this implied making sure that conducting negotiations at these overlapping levels did not induce a mismatch of priorities.

11.2 THE TRANSNATIONAL CARTELIZATION OF THE CHLORINE INDUSTRY

Reordering the international chlorine export market was certainly not ranking high in Solvay's agenda in the early 1930s, but it was a most valuable doorway to access the community of producers, a convenient means of pressure on existing national groups, and a necessary option to set the stop-gap operation into motion. Unsurprisingly, Solvay mobilized its international networks in alkali products to obtain a privileged observation point in the chlorine business – a field in which it was deprived of its technical and commercial know-how. Just like the international movement for nitrogen cartel understandings, which started approximately at the same time, the cartelization of chlorine was multilayered and covered a wide range of related products. By and large, though, the situation differed according to the patterns of national markets. More than being strictly speaking international, therefore, the process is better characterized as transnational.

---

[12] ACS, 1001–24–5A, Réunion technico-commerciale du 21–22 juin 1933.

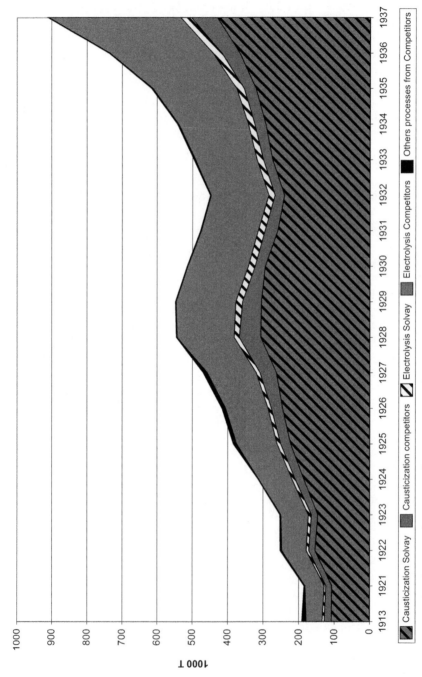

CHART 11.1. Production of caustic soda in Continental Europe (except Russia), 1921–1937. *Source*: ART-PDO Solvay & Cie, SPC, BM, SW, DSW.

France and the Entente Chlore

After World War I, several of the electrolytic units that had been built under the impulsion of the French government were dismantled. The remaining plants were selling their surplus of chlorine with great difficulty. By 1925, a third of the chlorine production derived from the manufacturing of hydrochloric acid, which was a key product for the glass industry. Quite ironically, it must be said, the introduction of the Fourcault process had entailed the conversion of Leblanc soda producers to the electrolytic process. Therefore, through their investment in the Libbey-Owens glassmaking processes (Mécaniver, 1921), Solvay had therefore spawned its own competition in caustic soda in France. If the chlorine industry was still burgeoning in France in the mid-1920s, it was nevertheless characterized by a significant increase in output (from 7,000 tons in 1921 to 22,500 tons in 1927). This rather small market in comparison with other industrialized countries was controlled by France's traditional chemical champions – Saint-Gobain, Péchiney, and Kuhlmann – with the addition of Electro-Chimie d'Ugine. After Péchiney and Saint-Gobain announced their intention to build new electrolytic facilities, chlorine producers demanded to settle a production agreement. Negotiations dragged on for months before the Entente Chlore was signed on 19 December 1927. It concerned only liquid chlorine, chlorate, and chloride of lime (bleaching powder); it did not cover the production of hydrochloric acid.[13]

Shortly thereafter, rumors spread that Solvay planned to set up "a very important unit of production of electrolytic caustic soda" in France. This was certainly not to the liking of the members of the Entente Chlore – and they intended to make themselves heard. Philippe Aubertin was the *gérant* in charge for the talks. Negotiations proved particularly painstaking, in fact disproportionally tense to the levels of production at stake (estimated for Solvay at 2,800 tons per year). The truth is that there was an important symbolic aspect to the whole issue. In spite of friendly political bilateral relationships between France and Belgium since the war, French chemical industrialists – Saint-Gobain in particular – did not approve much of Solvay's progression in their territory, especially when it came to company adopting a multinational attitude. To Solvay, however, the French case seemed, for historical reasons, as much a cultural and psychological affair as a business deal. Whatever the atmosphere of mutual suspicion, though, Aubertin insisted that industrial factors had to prevail. Inspired by the guidelines set out by the *gérance*, he aimed at safeguarding Solvay's domination in caustic soda in the French market. What he had in mind was the preservation of the company's interests in providing enough caustic soda to the enterprises gathered in the Comptoir des Textiles Artificiels controlled by the Gillet-Bernheim group (and to which Solvay was directly linked

---

[13] ACS, 1106–38-4A, File 1, "L'Entente Chlore et l'accroissement possible de la consommation," Section C, Jan. 1928, 7–8; 1001–24-5A (Section C), "Note au sujet du développement de l'électrolyse en France et en Belgique." The initial repartition was the following: Electro-Chimie d'Ugine (27 percent), Saint-Gobain (16.5 percent), Péchiney (16 percent), Bozel-Maletra (15.5 percent), Kuhlmann (15.5 percent), and Progil (9.5 percent).

through the holdings of the Mutuelle Solvay in Fabrique de Soie Artificielle de Tubize and some other participations initiated by Emmanuel Janssen).[14]

From 1932, Solvay obtained a quota of 11.19 percent of the overall French chlorine production (under the condition that the production of the entente did not exceed 23,800 tons per year). This was much after Electrochimie (19.94 percent); Saint-Gobain (15 percent); Alais, Froges & Camargue, Péchiney (14.15 percent); Kuhlmann (11.84 percent); and Bozel-Malétra (11.47 percent). But it was decisive enough to exert some influence through the new Tavaux plant, whose electrolytic unit had been on stream since September 1930.[15] Being the only understanding in the French chlorine industry, the Entente Chlore would continue, against all odds, until the outbreak of World War II. The whole time, Solvay's attitude remained quite passive, even indifferent. "To some extent," said the *gérants* in 1932, "we would see favorably the breach of the Entente Chlore as long as we are not pointed out as responsible of the rupture."[16] This proved slightly overconfident, for at the beginning Tavaux met a series of unexpected difficulties. Between 1930 and 1938, the plant ran on mere production of seven to nine tons of chlorine daily, whereas its capacity been estimated at twenty tons per day. During the war, several technical factors were put forward by Charles Guffroy (Section D) to explain this low performance, most of which could be categorized as being a discrepancy between the planning of the facility and the execution of the industrial command.[17] Fortunately for Solvay, Tavaux's disappointing start did not affect the positioning of the company in the French market of caustic soda. Hence, Guffroy could triumphantly claim that Tavaux had reached its prime and main objective: "Although we arrived last in France, we have now a foothold in this branch of the industry jealously controlled by our competitors."[18] It would be fair to add that the electrolytic industry never really took off in France during the interwar period. Solvay was thus able to reap the benefits of its leadership in the causticization process, in which it simply had no competition.

The Chlor-Konvention in Germany

With respect to the development of the electrolytic industry during the interwar period, Germany followed a completely different route than its French neighbor. Not only did the levels of production of caustic soda soar constantly throughout the period (including in the 1930s under the influence of chlorine production),[19] but also the bulk of the increase – 78 percent between 1929 and

---

[14] For a good overview of the international networks of artificial silk, see Plumpe (1990), 299–306.

[15] ACS, 1106-38-4A, File 2, Réunion de l'Entente Chlore, Direction Commerciale (Paris), 29 May 1933; Ducordeaux et al. (2005), 52–3.

[16] ACS, RdG, 24 May 1932.

[17] ACS, 1001-24-5, Politique industrielle – Produits chlorés, "Considérations générales sur notre politique Electrolyse," by Ch. Guffroy (Section D, No. 3618), 18 June 1942; and "Commentaires sur la note N° 3618" (Section D, No. 3621), 25 June 1942.

[18] ACS, 1001-24-5, "Considérations générales sur notre politique Electrolyse," 18 June 1942, 5.

[19] ACS, 1001-24-5, Direction commerciale – Documentation, World production of chlorine. Excerpt of *Die Chemische Industrie*, 29 May 1937.

TABLE 11.2. *Production of Caustic Soda in Germany, 1913–1937 (in 1,000 tons)*

	Causticization			Electrolysis (including Scandinavia)			Other Processes		
	DSW	Competition	Total	DSW	Competition	Total	Competition	Total	% Solvay
1913	38.8	19.4	58.2	3.2	23.1	26.3	12.0	96.5	43.5
1921	26.2	15.6	41.8	2.2	25.0	27.2	2.3	71.3	40.3
1929	33.1	52.7	85.8	4.0	89.1	95.7	2.0	180.9	20.5
1937	62.8	74.7	137.5	6.0	205.3	271.3	2.4	411.2	16.7

Source: ACS, 1001–24–5, "Le développement de la fabrication électrolytique de la soude caustique: Conséquences pour Solvay & Cie" (Section C, Service Technico-commercial), table B.91289, 29 June 1944.

1937 – came from the electrolytic production. Since the strategy of DSW vis-à-vis the electrolysis business came close to the patterns of Brussels, the outcome was simple: the contribution of DSW in the field was trivial. The production of its Osternienburg plant accounted for a modest 8.1 percent in 1921 and collapsed to the insignificant 2.2 percent in 1937. But there was more (or worse) to this: DSW also lost market shares in Solvay's technological stronghold – the production of caustic soda by causticization. From 65.5 percent in 1922, the proportion of DSW's production fell to 45.7 percent in 1937. This was caused by the emergence of competitors outside the alkali cartels, as well as by IG Farben's increasing production of caustic soda for its own consumption (*Selbstverbrauch*) in conformity with the dispositions of the industrial syndicate. The most pressing issue lay in the divergent interpretations given to the notion of *Selbstverbrauch*, which touched on the very definition of IG Farben as a *Konzern* in relation with its components and subsidiaries.[20] As a result of this double drop – in electrolysis and causticization – the share of DSW in the production of caustic soda was reduced from 40.3 percent in 1921 to 16.7 percent in 1937 (see Table 11.2).

The landscape of the chlorine market in Germany remained rather informal until the signing of the Chlor-Konventionsvertrag (CKV) on 26 November 1926, which intended to rationalize the agreements through production quotas and price fixing. On the basis of the average result of the years 1924–1926, DSW obtained a quota of 7.86 percent, whereas IG Farben controlled the

[20] Historical agreements in carbonate and caustic soda between DSW and IG Farben comprised the Vertrag über Natriumcarbonat (7 June 1924), on the one hand, and the contracts concluded in the framework of the Syndikat Deutscher Aetznatronfabriken (19 Oct. 1927), on the other hand. Many different versions were added to the latter, but the fundamental clause leaving IG Farben's consumption of caustic soda for its own plants out of the initial agreement was confirmed in a so-called *Schlussprotokoll* dated 24 Nov. 1932. As a result of IG Farben's boundless expansion and the corresponding elasticity of its *Selbstverbrauch*, DSW was thus losing outlets and market shares to IG Farben. Besides, with the entry of new members in the Syndikat (e.g., Kali-Chemie's Neu-Stassfurt from January 1935), DSW saw its production quota of caustic soda readjusted from 36.35 percent in 1927 to 33.34 percent (ADSW 560, Archiv-Raum I, Vorstand to gérance, 30 Sept. 1933, incl. "Note sur la consommation propre de l'I.G. dans le Syndicat de Soude Caustique," 9 Sept. 1933; ACS, 1151–51-2, Soude caustique – contrat syndical, "Accord du 13 décembre 1934," various letters; ACS, Binder "Recueil des contrats intervenus avec Solvay & Cie," Contrats DSW-Solvay & Cie-I.G, appendixes 1–3).

whole market, holding 50 percent.[21] The *Vorstand* of DSW, needless to say, was infuriated by this meager contingent. After several unsuccessful attempts to circumvent the agreements by finding new outlets for liquid chlorine and chloride of lime, Emil Gielen and Ernst Eilsberger faced the prospect of a complete harnessing of the electrolytic production at Osternienburg. The next round of negotiations that took place with CKV members in 1933–1934 – giving way to the so-called Special Chlorine Contract (Chlor-Sondervertrag) and the Chlorine Bloc-Contract (Chlorblok-Vertrag) – did not change much of the picture in spite of minor concessions (increase of the contingent of chlorine-based products from 280 tons to a maximum of 350 tons per month) and the promise to watch over the interests of Kali-Chemie's plant at Neu-Stassfurt in connection with those of DSW.[22] Considering these restrictions, one can wonder why DSW still remained aboard the CKV throughout these years. The answer to this question is twofold and slightly differs according to the range of priorities set by DSW and the Solvay group, respectively.

As already mentioned, underlying the action of DSW was fundamentally the need to maintain its positioning in the German caustic soda market and in the foreign markets it controlled (mostly in Scandinavia). The rapid increase of electrolytic units in Germany had not been considered a threat in that matter as long as the syndicate for caustic soda (Aetznatronsyndikat) could keep the upper hand among its members on production and sales. Over time, however, the strengthening of electrolytic caustic soda at the expense of causticization provoked a shift in the relationships between both kinds of producers. Since most of the members of the CKV also belonged to the syndicate for caustic soda, DSW could exert some form of pressure on its competitors from both sides. Within the CKV, Eilsberger was able to threaten for lower prices in caustic soda; alternately, within the syndicate, he could hold firm the important production quota of DSW. Therefore, using subtly the narrow interconnection of these two levels, the *Vorstand* of DSW managed to partly make up for its lagging situation in the electrolytic industry and have, relatively speaking, a greater say in national cartels.[23]

But there was also another side to the coin. Contrary to Bernburg's perspective, the priority scale as seen from Brussels was not, strictly speaking, national. In practical terms, the main objectives of the *gérance* were the protection of Solvay's industrial territory and the inclusion of the Solvay group in the international movement for chlorine cartel understandings. Both these goals, however, required the intermediation of the CKV, which in turn implied

---

[21] The remaining members gathered in Verteilungsstelle für Chlorkalk were Salzbergwerk Neu-Stassfurt (11.95 percent), Consolidierte Alkaliwerke-Westeregeln (11.95 percent), Feldmühle, Papier- und Zellstoffwerke (Formerly Königsberger Zellstoff-Fabriken und Chemische Werke Koholyt; 7.99 percent), Chemische Fabrik von Heyden (6 percent), and Chemische Fabrik Buckau (4.25 percent). ACS, 1151-51-101, Chlor-Konventionsvertrag, 1926–1933.

[22] ACS, 1151-38-230, "Note résumée sur la convention allemande du chlore," 27 Apr. 1934; ACS, 1151-51-101, Chlore – Contrat spécial et contrat de bloc, 1934–1936.

[23] ADSW 2417, Archiv-Raum I, Visite de MM. Eilsberger et Arendt, 22 Oct. 1934; "La prolongation des syndicats et des conventions," 19 Nov. 1935; ACS, 1151-38-230, Section C, "Situation de la DSW en ce qui concerne le chlore et les produits chlorés," 15 July 1932.

staying on good terms with IG Farben – not an easy task for Eilsberger and his colleagues at the *Vorstand* of DSW. Regarding the former concern, the best illustration was the so-called Brussels agreement among ICI, CKV, and Solvay on 30–31 December 1930. Basically, this safety deal limited the competition of ICI and CKV in Solvay's "preferred" markets for chloride of lime and liquid chlorine (e.g., Belgium, Spain, Portugal) and gave it some guarantees, in terms of quota or percentage allotments, for the export of its own chlorine-based production at Jemeppe to the Netherlands and the Scandinavian countries.[24] As a clear example of the interplay between international and national scales of negotiations was the fact that, in the wake of this understanding, Solvay achieved control of the Belgian domestic market in electrolytic caustic soda and chlorine-based products.[25]

11.3 FROM CAUSTIC SODA TO CHLORINE DERIVATIVES

Although the "Brussels agreement" enabled Solvay to obtain 8.5 percent of the European export market in chloride of lime and liquid chlorine in 1932, the bulk of the export volume remained in the hands of ICI and CKV (IG Farben, in particular). Together, British and German manufacturers of chlorine-based products controlled 73.3 percent of the European markets in 1932, which represented 63.8 percent of the world market.[26] The concentration of the international cartelization of chlorine went a step further in March 1931, when the two groups agreed to distinguish approximate zones of exports and to determine a proportional repartition of the volumes of trade, which eventually came down to 57 percent for ICI and 43 percent for the members of the CKV.[27] Six months later, this division of the world export market was opened to Aussig for a contingent of 5.56 percent converted in tons of chloride of lime. In view of this changing environment, Piérard's analysis concerning Solvay's export strategy in the chlorine industry was straightforward: "since we develop, in reality, an industrial policy, which is fundamentally opposed to that of ICI or IG [Farben], inasmuch as we aim at debasing the prices of chlorine as a way to prevent the development of electrolysis, while our colleagues have as prime and priority objective a more profitable yield, we have to act skillfully in order to put a stop to the conclusion of agreements with outsiders."[28] Yet such an approach could hardly be followed indefinitely. It proved especially ineffective

---

[24] ACS, 1001–24-7, "Historique de l'accord CKV-ICI-Solvay, Chlorure de chaux et chlore liquide," by G. Piérard, 27 Oct. 1937; black binder "Relations ICI-Solvay," Agreement No. 8. The Brussels agreement persisted until World War II but was subject to annual revisions, especially concerning the production quotas of chloride of lime.

[25] ACS, 1001–24-5, "Politique de Solvay & Cie dans le domaine de l'électrolyse," 5 June 1937, 20–1.

[26] ACS, 1151–51-101, "Note sur l'exportation mondiale du chlore liquide et du chlorure de chaux," by G. Piérard, 19 May 1933.

[27] ACS, 1151–51-101, Vorstand to gérance, Copy of the ICI-CKV agreement (14 Feb.–12 Mar. 1931), 2 Mar. 1933.

[28] ACS, 1151–51-101, "Note sur l'exportation mondiale du chlore liquide et du chlorure de chaux," by G. Piérard, 19 May 1933.

in a context of rapid growth of chlorine products under the influence of the bleaching industry.

Strategy, Plants, Products: Restarting the Electrolytic Engine

By 1935 and 1936, the world trade volume of liquid chlorine had exceeded by 100 percent the levels of 1929, an important part of which was absorbed by the Scandinavian countries. On the side of producers, the situation was especially impressive in the United States, where the annual average growth of production capacity was greater than 20 percent from 1927.[29] Besides, there was no indication that the upward trend would stall or drop in the following years – on the contrary. Everywhere in industrialized countries, national governments were inclined to stimulate industrial recovery, frequently by adopting protectionist measures and flirting with economic dirigisme or self-sufficiency (autarchy).[30] All of this called for a reorientation of strategy of the Solvay group as a whole with regard to the electrolytic industry. The driving force in this respect was undoubtedly René Boël. Since the withdrawal of Emmanuel Janssen in 1931, he was the *gérant* in charge of German affairs, where he had witnessed the irresistible rise of the electrolysis and the difficulties of DSW in coping with it. Moreover, through the Technical-Commercial Service he had initiated at the Brussels headquarters, he was in closer touch with Solvay's advisers who specialized in the field of the electrolytic industry (e.g., Audoyer, Flamache, Guffroy, Piérard).[31] These meetings, however episodic, were also an opportunity to overcome the potential divergent views expressed between Sections C and D, which had contributed to postpone the company's entry into electrolysis.

As he observed the continuous landslide of DSW's market shares in caustic soda and the complementary threat posed by the pending emergence of electrolytic units in Scandinavia, Boël insisted that DSW should not merely react from a commercial standpoint, namely from its position within the national cartel. Beyond the German subsidiary, another impulse should stem, he pursued, from a simultaneous effort in the research for new chlorine-based products, on the one hand, and a deepening of Solvay's participation in the electrolytic industry, on the other hand.[32] Whether the initial research directions concerned the making of chlorine without caustic soda – a process that was being put into operation by the Atmospheric Nitrogen Corp., a subsidiary of Allied, at its Hopewell plant in Virginia – or the experimentations with other by-products

[29] Hardie (1959), 41–3; ACS, 1001–24-5, Direction commerciale – Documentation, World production of chlorine; Excerpt of *Die Chemische Industrie*, 29 May 1937; "Le développement de la fabrication électrolytique de la soude caustique. Conséquences pour Solvay & Cie," 29 June 1944, 1.

[30] Berend (2006), 92–123.

[31] ACS, DS 246, Service Technico-Commercial, 19 Dec. 1933.

[32] ADSW 2417, Archiv-Raum I, "Réunion Hôtel Adlon – Berlin," 18 July 1934; "Voyage de MM. Boël et Masson à Copenhague," 12–15 Oct. 1934; "Visite de MM. Eilsberger et Arendt," 22 Oct. 1934; "Conversation avec le Vorstand des DSW – Paris," 27 Feb. 1935; ACS, 1001–24-5, Voyage de M. Boël à Bernburg, 3–6 Dec. 1935.

of the ammonia-soda ash process was not really essential. What did matter was that a new strategy had to be launched on the basis of findings that mobilized the R&D capabilities of Solvay, DSW, and ICI.[33] These technical exchanges generally confirmed that the electrolytic process had to be considered as the most efficient and economic. It was thus Solvay's "only means of defense against the chlorine industry." This implied a giant shift of perspective: building electrolytic units, rather than reducing the price of caustic soda by causticization, could hold back the inexorable competition that Solvay faced in the caustic soda market.[34]

Once the general guidelines were obtained from the *gérance*, it was possible to adjust the strategy of defense in function of the specificities of national markets. The mechanisms of cartels networking that had prevailed in France and Germany until then were pursued, but the focus lay essentially on the remaining countries, where a catching-up process was slowly but surely under way (in Spain, Italy, the Netherlands, Austria, Poland, Portugal, and Finland). A note from Section C outlined the underlying rationale in these top-priority countries: "our principle there is to 'move forward,' namely that, while we anticipate the development of the chlorine market, we prefer to carry out ourselves the increase of production capacity, rather than witnessing a competitor increase its contingent to our expense."[35] In contrast, such an ambitious program could not overlook local contingencies. As a result, it was decided to opt for a flexible mode of progression, which would adapt to national circumstances (see the Italian and Spanish cases later in this chapter) but would stick to the general patterns of Solvay's alkali policy. The spectrum of solutions was thus wide enough, ranging from the extension of Solvay's own electrolytic units to the setup of new plants and the adapted takeover of existing facilities (see Table 11.3).

Scaling Up the Know-How Exchange with ICI and DuPont

With this fully fledged industrial program, René Boël did not lower his expectations concerning the impact that could result from the innovation of chlorine-based products. For this, he relied on André Desoer from Section C (Commercial) and Léon Flamache from Section E (Research). In 1936, both of them were sent to ICI's General Chemicals Group at Northwich to gain some knowledge about chlorine derivatives, and trichloroethylene in particular (in accordance with the provisions of the ICI-Solvay Technical Agreement signed on 16 October 1933, which extended the previous exchange of technical information to "some chlorine-based products"). Another technical mission also took place in

---

[33] ACS, 1001–24-5, Visite de M. Breuer (DSW), Interview made on 14 Jan. 1936 (Section C, Service Technico-Commercial), 22 Jan. 1936; ACS, 1001–24-5, "Politique soude caustique et chlore," Production de chlore sans soude caustique, Minutes of the meeting of 13 Jan. 1936 with ICI (Alkali Division and General Chemicals Division), DSW, and Solvay & Cie, 6 Feb. 1936.

[34] ACS, RdG, 14 Jan. 1936.

[35] ACS, 1001–24-5, Section C, "Politique Solvay & Cie dans le domaine de l'électrolyse," 5 June 1937, 3.

TABLE 11.3. *Overview of the Development of Electrolytic Units (EU) in the Solvay Group (1928–1942)*

Creation of EU			Takeover of EU		
On its Own	Next to Soda Plant	Extension of Existing EU	On Stream in 1942	Almost Completed	Minority Participations
Tavaux (FR) 1930	Torrelavega (ES) 1935	Jemeppe (BE) 1928	Ponte Mammolo (IT) 1935	Hallein (AU) 1928–1940	Zabkowice (DE-POL)
Linne-Herten (NE) 1938	Povoa (PT) 1938	Osternienburg (DE) 1936	Westeregeln (DE)1939	Aspropyrgos (GR) 1939	Aetsa (FI)
Aniene-Ferrara (IT)1942	Rosignano (IT) 1941	Tavaux (FR) 1942			Boussens (FR)
	Lukavac[a] (YU)				
	Podgórze[a] (POL)				
	Zurzach[a] (CH)				

[a] Electrolytic units under construction (1942).

Source: ACS, 1001-24-5, Politique industrielle – Produits chlorés, "Considérations générales sur notre politique Electrolyse" by Ch. Guffroy, (Section D, No. 3618), 18 June 1942 and "Commentaires sur la note N° 3618" (Section D, No. 3621), 25 June 1942.

February 1937 at Zurich with Eugen Mayer from Aussig.[36] Desoer and Flamache drew the impression that chlorine-based solvents in general, whether as saturated hydrocarbons or as ethylenic hydrocarbons, were promised a great industrial future. In addition, these chlorine compounds were considered more profitable than the usual primary products, which Solvay had reduced its production to (e.g., liquid chlorine, chloride of lime, sodium hypochlorite, hydrochloric acids).

This persuaded Boël to give the manufacturing of chlorine derivatives a fresh impetus. Because he knew that the issue of products diversification was particularly sensible at the *gérance*, he strove to emphasize the logics of continuity between the long-standing production of alkali and the industrial extension to chlorine derivatives. The chlorine strategy was, as he implied, a consequence of the decision of the *gérants* to engage in the development of electrolytic units, itself an offspring of Solvay's belated entry in the electrolytic business.[37] To some extent, Boël sought to demonstrate that the production of chlorine derivatives could compensate, even partly, for the drop in Solvay's market

[36] ACS, CdG 19 Nov. 1936; ACS, 1001–25-17/3, Solvay & Cie Direction Commerciale, Service T.-C., "Echange de renseignements avec l'ICI et Du Pont sur les dérivés chlorés: Historique et situation actuelle," by A. Desoer, 29 Dec. 1942; ACS, 1001–24-6, Section E (L. Flamache), Rapport sur la visite à M. Mayer à Zurich les 26–27 février 1937, 9 Mar. 1937; black binder "Relations ICI-Solvay," Agreement No. 1.

[37] ACS, 1001–24-5, Réunion du Service Technico-Commercial, 14 July 1937; ACS, RdG, "Notre politique au point de vue produits chlorés," 9 Feb. 1937.

share in caustic soda. Far fetched as it was, the argument was not opposed by any of his colleagues. Without anyone really noticing, Boël had cleverly and discretely opened the door to product diversification. It all came down to benefiting from a favorable environment for technical information. As it happens, an unexpected opportunity came from the United States.

Just like Solvay, the American alkali producer Michigan Alkali (Wyandotte) was facing harsh competition in chlorine producers, which gave way to a fall in its market share in caustic soda. Contrary to Solvay, however, Wyandotte had no know-how, let alone any licenses, that would enable it to start out in the electrolytic industry – and it wished to do so. At the beginning of 1937, the management of Wyandotte contacted Solvay to obtain a license for the Solvay-ICI mercury-cell process, which it deemed the most appropriate for its industrial use. In view of its agreement with ICI, Solvay declined the offer. Of course, crucial to the decision was also that Wyandotte had become Allied's worst and more powerful competitor in alkali in the United States, holding some 22 percent of the domestic production (Allied's once hegemony had shrunk to 45 percent). With the blessing of Solvay, Wyandotte rang the doorbell of IG Farben, which used a somewhat similar version of the ICI-Solvay mercury cell after a deal concluded with Aussig. Shortly before Wyandotte and IG Farben signed the first draft of mutual agreement, word came that the understanding included, in addition to electrolytic chlorine and caustic soda, confidential information about the ammonia-soda process. This prompted ICI and Solvay to request that IG Farben interrupt negotiations with Wyandotte immediately. Obviously, the situation also underlined the urgency for an overarching clearing in the international electrolytic knowledge industry, which had been limited hitherto to trade agreements.[38]

Then again, solutions and problems were intertwined. Solvay and ICI certainly agreed on the aim to restrict IG Farben's power on American soil (especially so in the production of alkali), but they also needed to remain on good terms with the giant German concern, for different reasons. Hence, for the sake of industrial diplomacy, they were compelled to provide IG Farben with an alternative – and there lay the bone of contention. Since McGowan's arrival, ICI had made a strategic alliance with DuPont, whereas Solvay was still the major shareholder of Allied Chemicals. Favoring one would come at the other's expense. To make it even more complicated, Solvay saw with some enthusiasm a closer relationship with DuPont: it could diversify its American network beyond Orlando Weber and provide useful technical know-how, as in chlorine derivatives. How to exit this catch-22? John Foster Dulles had the answer.

The legal representative of Solvay's interests in the United States came to Brussels in the summer of 1937. Considering all options, he told the *gérants* it

[38] ANOH, Section E, Instructions et Contrôle, Administration, "Organisation de la surveillance des brevets nouveaux et de la documentation technique à la Société Solvay," by L. Flamache, 1 Aug. 1936; ACS, NdG, "L'industrie de la soude et du chlore," by R. Boël, 19 July 1937; ACS, black binder "Relations ICI-Solvay," Agreement No. 17; ACS, 1001–25-17/2, "Notes sur les accords conclus relativement aux informations concernant la cellule au mercure aux États-Unis" (trans. from ICI), 29 Nov. 1937.

was wiser for Solvay to talk with the management of Allied about the Wyandotte deal rather than ignoring them and bluntly switch alliances. Besides, doing so could also make a striking impression on the board of Allied. The *gérants* approved unreservedly; this could lead to a desirable reorganization of the international exchange of electrolytic knowledge.[39] While Foster Dulles and George Murnane were busy preparing the negotiations with Orlando Weber and Allied's general manager Henry Atherton, Solvay had to bring the matter to ICI. Ernest-John Solvay was in charge of announcing to McGowan the conditional approval of Solvay, namely that discussions among Solvay, ICI, and DuPont should include an extension of technical knowledge agreements to all chlorine derivatives. "The closer the relations between our companies are, the better they are," McGowan supposedly replied.[40]

Contrary to his initial doubts, Ernest-John Solvay was pleased to acknowledge that the stay he and René Boël had made in the United States in September and October 1937 had been incredibly productive. Technical difficulties had been smoothly overcome, thanks to the underground action of Foster Dulles and Murnane, but also because of the "extremely large and accommodating attitude of M. Jack Ford and M. Lamot du Pont."[41] In the following weeks and months, a series of joint agreements were concluded that gave way to increased liberalization of technical knowledge among foreign chemical companies focusing especially on the soda and chlorine industries.[42] But most of these bi- or trilateral agreements were superseded, on 12 December 1938, by the final ratification of the so-called Pool Agreement among ICI, IG Farben, Aussig, and the Solvay group. Through this overarching understanding, the four companies could exchange a wide array of technical information completely free of charge and determine together the strategy of transfer of knowledge to affiliates and nonmembers. The Pool Agreement also included a special appendix A, which delineated each group's respective commercial markets into exclusive or shared zones.[43] It amounted, in other words, to a clear-cut division of the world markets in the electrolytic business.

[39] ACS, 1271-37-14 (Folder 9), "Visite de M. Dulles," 2 Aug. 1937.

[40] ACS, 1001-25-17/3, "Echange de renseignements," 29 Dec. 1942, 2.

[41] ACS, NdG, "Le voyage d'Amérique," by E.-J. Solvay, 18 Aug. 1937; ACS, 1271-37-14 (Folder 9), RdG, 28 Oct. 1937.

[42] ACS, 1001-25-17/2, Solvay & Cie to ICI, 18 Dec. 1937; ACS, 1001-25-17/3, "Echange de renseignements," 29 Dec. 1942; ACS, black binder "Relations ICI-Solvay," Agreement No. 17; ANOH, Section E, Politique industrielle – Electrolyse, "Développement des produits chlorés. L'utilisation du chlore en chimie minérale et organique et le développement de son emploi," by L. Flamache, 1 Aug. 1936; ANOH, Section E, Concurrence – Chlore, "Étude économique comparative de l'électrolyse du chlorure de sodium et du chlorhydrate d'ammoniaque dans une grande soudière Solvay," 15 Apr. 1939.

[43] ACS, 1001-25-18 (Folder 16), Entente internationale ICI-IG-Verein-Solvay: Notes et correspondance relatives à la création des conventions pool, Dec. 1938; ACS, Binder Recueil des contrats intervenus avec Solvay & Cie, "Convention relative à l'échange de renseignements techniques concernant la fabrication de chlore électrolytique (ICI-IG-Verein-Solvay)," texte définitif, 28 Nov. 1938, and "Convention commerciale entre l'IG, Solvay et l'ICI relative aux produits sodiques et au chlore," texte définitif, 28 Nov. 1938; ACS, black binder "Relations ICI-Solvay," Agreement No. 13.

11.4 ELECTROLYSIS AND POLITICS: THE RISE OF AUTHORITARIAN REGIMES IN ITALY AND SPAIN

The 1930s were not only a period of economic and social crisis; they also coincided with growing political unrest. The Solvay group, which had been deeply affected by the postwar territorial reorganization in Europe, was about to face another side of the political turmoil generated by the war, less concerned with international geopolitics than with domestic politics. For different reasons, which cannot be detailed here, authoritarian groups were emerging everywhere in Europe, where they met with various success. The seedbed of contest lay in countries where the legacy of World War I was the most violently disputed and could not be tamed by weakened democratic regimes. This was clearly the case in Italy, where Mussolini and his black shirts had challenged the official authorities as soon as 1922. Spain, in comparison, had been rather isolated from the war. Nevertheless, after the country experienced the dictatorship of Primo de Rivera between 1923 and 1930, it was not able to contain rising social and economic tensions, which grew into a dreadful civil war in 1936. This section seeks to unravel how Solvay dealt with the changing political spectrum in these two countries, where it owned important soda plants and intended to start out in the electrolytic business.

Coming to Terms with Italian Fascism

From the mid-1920s, the progressive adaptation of Solvay's Rosignano plant to the capture of the political environment by the local section of the National Fascist Party would find many, and sometime averse, outcomes. In tune with the rising fascism found in the Italian society, the number of party members among the workers swelled from 12.5 percent in 1927 to 80 percent in 1941.[44] The works of Rosignano became shaped by the attributes of the regime. Especially striking was the setup of a wide program of social policy instruments designed to reinvigorate the spirit of the community among workers, most certainly after their working hours (*dopolavoro*). The overwhelming ideology found a direct and visible expression in the neoclassical architecture of the buildings (e.g., housing, school, theater, stadium, Casa del Fascio).[45] Boundaries between private and public spheres were blurred, and so was the relation between the management of the plant and the local section of the party. After showing and pretending indifference for a while, Belgian plant managers – Albert Gonod (1919–1926) and especially Clément Van Caubergh (1926–1936) – realized that they could not carry out their functions without coming to terms with these influential political forces. Consequently, and in agreement with Brussels, Van Caubergh authorized to make some donations to Rosignano's fascist organizations. These progressively grew into a politics of subventions, whose frequency and amount increased over time.[46]

[44] See Celati and Gattini (1998), 15–18.
[45] Mioche (2009), 28–9.
[46] ACS, 1130-49-11, Dossiers subventions, various files (1927–1939).

FIGURE 11.2. Balila's parade at Rosignano-Solvay under fascist regime (1930s). (Solvay Rosignano Archives.)

Taking these social transformations into account, Solvay's first encounter with the fascist regime from an industrial standpoint dated to the negotiations that led to the eventual takeover of the chemical company Adria, formerly owned by Austrians (Adriawerke). With a soda plant located in Monfalcone in the vicinity of Trieste, Adria was not considered a threat until it was given the status of *parastatale* by the fascist decree on 24 June 1926 related to industries "interesting [to the] national defense."[47] This, wrote Solvay's commercial

---

[47] ACS, black binder "Monfalcone," 18; Salvati (2006); Petri (2002), 58–69.

officer in Milan, Léon de Harven, means that it is "linked to the Government or that the Government might be interested in it."[48] But it also meant that Adria, though losing money, had gained the explicit support of Mussolini's minister of finance, Giuseppe Volpi. In Brussels, the *gérants* did not seem to pay much attention to the issue. They had already turned down de Harven's suggestion to take over Adria a year earlier, preferring to follow Hannon's advice, itself based on the founding brothers, not to hold a production monopoly in alkali in Italy.[49] In terms of domination, Solvay controlled the bulk of the soda ash market and provided 65.16 percent (46,139 tons in 1926) of the domestic Italian consumption of caustic soda. Its relation with other chemical companies in the Consorzio di Soda e Cloro was outstanding, and it benefited from a special contract with the important artificial silk producer SNIA Viscosa, which had absorbed 43.8 percent of Solvay's production of caustic soda in 1926.[50] Why, in this thriving context, would Solvay bother with this ill-functioning plant?

Aware of Solvay's lack of concern for Adria, the Italian government found a way to remind the *gérants* who was actually leading the country and its chemical industry. In July 1927, Léon de Harven was subtly told by a chief of the cabinet of Minister Volpi that the salt concession Solvay had gained in 1911 for Rosignano was not meant to last forever. Volpi sought to get rid of the Adria burden on Solvay's shoulder. As investor in the Società Adriatica di Elettricità (SADE), he might have had personal reason to do so.[51] At the same time, Emmanuel Janssen was approached by his friend, the artificial silk industrialist Edmond Gillet, who offered him an investment in the Società Chimica dell'Aniene, his group controlled through the holding company CISA Viscosa. He had in mind a joint investment with Solvay (and probably UCB) in this company, which included a small electrolytic unit at Ponte Mammolo, near Rome. The manager of Aniene was a certain Baron Alberto Fassini. Besides his successful debut performance in the movie industry as producer of the blockbuster *Quo Vadis* (1912), Fassini happened to be "one of Mussolini's five lieutenants," according to Janssen.[52] This sudden flow of information, needless to say, called for a complete reorientation of the *gérance*'s strategy in the Italian chemical industry. First and foremost, however, it implied that the company had to find its way in the vortex of the fascist bureaucracy.

The *gérants* agreed on two issues: first, in both cases "the question was rather political than industrial," strictly speaking; second, the man at the core of the problem could also provide the solution, and this was Giuseppe Volpi.[53] To reach him, Solvay decided to rely on two social brokers: one was Baron

---

[48] ACS, 1130–46-1, Dir. commerciale de Milan to Solvay & Cie, 23 Sept. 1926.
[49] ASC-A 1131 Monfalcone, Binder 2, Entrevue avec M. de Harven, 12 May 1925.
[50] ASC-A 1131 Monfalcone, Binder 2, De Harven to Solvay & Cie, 4 July 1927. See also Pizzorni (2006), 53–8; Petri (2004), 253–63.
[51] Romano (1982), 170–5; ASC-A 1131 Monfalcone, Binder 2, De Harven to Solvay & Cie, 4 July 1927; ACS, black binder "Monfalcone," 20.
[52] ACS, RdG, 31 Aug. 1927 & 14 Oct. 1927; ACS, 1133–1-1, Aniene, Historique de la Société, Oct. 1951; Ricci (2008), 31.
[53] ACS, CdG 21 Oct. 1927; ACS, RdG 7 Nov., 9 Nov., and 10 Nov. 1927.

Fassini, of course, but the other was even closer to the minister, Joseph Toeplitz, Sigismond's brother. As Giuseppe Volpi's longtime friend and leading director of the Banca Commerciale di Milano, Joseph Toeplitz could talk favorably about Solvay's industrial presence in Italy.[54] This double intermediation was successful enough to send the discreet *gérant* Robert Gendebien to Italy in December 1927. There, he heard that Baron Fassini had planned a meeting with the minister of communications, Costanzo Ciano, also representative of the province of Livorno. When Gendebien and de Harven opened the minister's door, they were greeted by an astonishing welcome: "I have the pleasure to announce you that the train station of Rosignano will henceforth be named 'Rosignano-Solvay'!" Apparently, Fassini had done a good job. Ciano was adamantly opposed that the development of Adria occur at Rosignano's expense; he could not stand that workers would be laid off from the Rosignano plant.[55]

Gendebien, who had the impression that Adria was not as sacred to the fascist authorities as the *gérants* had initially assumed, met with Minister Volpi twice – on 24 February and 5 March 1928 – to submit various drafts of understanding. His intuition was accurate – a deal could be smoothly concluded after the necessary arrangements with the Istituto di Liquidazioni and the promise to keep the work force. On 3 May 1928, Solvay took over Adria's debt and held 89.81 percent of the shares.[56] When an engineer from Solvay visited the installation, he remarked: "The first impression of an experienced technician walking around the Monfalcone plant is that of an incomplete structure, which had been put on stream before it was ready to operate, and for which the only aim has consisted in producing whatever it gets.... The many problems faced by the plant, which should be studied carefully, will undermine the functioning of the factory, financially speaking, for years to come, and this in spite of the capital and the experience Solvay will ever be able to put in." This was the price paid by Solvay for political stability.

As to the electrolytic unit of Ponte Mammolo, whose takeover had been put on hold because of the Adria case, the whole issue resurfaced only in 1934, once the *gérance* was determined to follow its new electrolytic agenda. In spite of the rather lukewarm conclusions that Robert Hankar had drawn in January 1929 in a report on the prospect of the deal, the *gérants* agreed to resume negotiations with their go-between Baron Fassini.[57] Economic circumstances had changed, however. Mussolini was launching a far-reaching program of autarchic recovery, which put the markets under close scrutiny. The situation

[54] Romano (1982), 17–9, 33–5, 177–9; ACS, RdG, "Visite de M. De Harven," 7 Jan. 1926.

[55] ASC-A 1131 Monfalcone, Binder 3, Pourparlers d'entente avec l'Adria: Voyage de M. Gendebien en Italie, décembre 1927; letter of the Unione Industriale Fascista della Provincia di Livorno to the Prefect of Livorno, 23–27 Dec. 1927; ACS, 1130-46-1, Entretien avec M. le Baron Fassini, 15 Nov. 1927; ACS, RdG, 12 and 23 Dec. 1927.

[56] ASC-O 1131 Monfalcone, Binder 3, "Résumé d'une étude faite sur la Convention à passer avec l'Adria," by G. Piérard, 14 Feb. 1928; ACS, black binder "Monfalcone," 27–30.

[57] ACS, 1133-1-2, Voyage à Rome en janvier 1929. Rapport de M. Robert Hankar, 14 Jan. 1929; ACS, RdG (Appendix A), Note de M. de Harven sur la situation en Italie, 3 July 1930; ACS, RdG, 22 Jan., 11 May, 13 Aug., and 10 Dec. 1929; ACS, RdG, 23 Nov. 1933.

worsened when it came to maneuvering in the highly politicized and formalized web of corporatist groupings. However, Solvay felt the pressure of losing its hand in the production of caustic soda as a result of the deal concluded between Montecatini and IG Farben in the dyestuffs industry in 1931.[58] In April 1935, after having long hesitated to take over the Rumianca electrolysis together with Montecatini, Solvay eventually decided to enter an understanding with the CISA Viscosa holding company. According to the agreement with the Gillet group, Solvay bought out the totality of shares of Aniene. At the special request of the Gillet family, the *gérants* agreed that Baron Fassini would become chairman of the board.[59] This foothold in the electrolytic industry would later be used as leverage for Solvay's expansion in this branch.

By 1935, however, the first impulse remained the causticization process. Van Caubergh moved promptly in this direction. During the first semester of 1936, he forcefully pleaded for an expansion of the soda plant at Rosignano due to the huge demand for caustic soda of the artificial silk industry, a demand that exceeded the production capacity of the Consorzio di Soda e Cloro.[60] He then realized that, for the sake of nationalist tendencies, public authorities were disposed for Solvay to elaborate a joint electrolytic program with Montecatini. That was, for the time being, not a desirable option. Van Caubergh, consequently, advised the *gérants* to opt for an alternative, namely gathering Solvay's electrolytic program in Italy under the banner of Aniene. This could include the building of an electrolytic unit next to the soda plant in Rosignano, as well as in Ferrara.[61] Bold as it was, the strategy proved successful – the authorization was granted in August 1936. The *gérants'* swift reaction in Italy enabled them to narrow down the emerging competition in electrolytic caustic soda and take full profit from the increasing demand for chlorine-based products under the impulsion of the government in view of the war economy.[62]

Into Hostile Camps: The Outbreak of the Spanish Civil War

While Mussolini was actively engaging Italy on the wheels of a "fascist revolution" – "if we can call this perfectly disciplined movement a 'revolution,'" observed the *gérance* in 1923[63] – Spain was undergoing a military dictatorship that favored industrial expansion with the support of the monarchy. The

---

[58] Petri (2006), 107–12; Petri (2004), 266–70; Petri (1998), 231.

[59] ACS, 1106–38-4 A (Folder 1), MM. Gillet to E. Janssen, 26 Oct. 1928; ACS, 1133-1-3 (Folder 1), "Visite de MM. Caubergh et Tremi," 24 Jan. 1935; ACS, 1131-1-3 (Folder 2), Entretien téléphonique MM. Boël-Baron Fassini, 9 Sept. 1935; ACS, 1133-1-1, Aniene, Historique de la Société, Oct. 1951.

[60] ACS, 1130–37-3, "Visite de MM. Van Caubergh et Tremi," 6 April 1936; ACS, RdG 24 Apr. 1936.

[61] ACS, 1130–37-3, "Visite de MM. Van Caubergh et Tremi," 5 June 1936 (including memorandum "Demande d'agrandissement C.S.," 5 June 1936).

[62] ACS, 1001–24-5, "Politique de Solvay & Cie dans le domaine de l'électrolyse," 5 June 1937, 11–2; ACS, 1130–37-3, Section D – Politique industrielle, Produits Chlorés, "Situation en Italie – Discussion du projet gouvernemental de développement des usines électrolytiques" (Note No. 2711), 5 Mar. 1937.

[63] ACS, CdS, 18 Jan. 1923.

development of the Spanish chemical industry, however limited by that time, was blossoming. Yet it relied heavily on foreign capital and, even more directly, on the presence of European multinational firms on its soil – Nobel, Kuhlmann, IG Farben, ICI, Algemene Kunstzijde Unie, Rhône-Poulenc, and Solvay, of course.[64] They, in turn, were largely dependent on the changing conditions of the political climate. And conditions were changing: weakened by the severe impact of the economic crisis, General Primo de Rivera's forced retirement in January 1930 unleashed a period of political uncertainty. The advent of the Second Republic the following year threw the country into the unknown. Solvay's plant at Torrelavega was soon affected. It was the scene of riots and strikes in July and November 1931. These were immediately crushed by the plant manager, Egide Waleffe, who had called for the assistance of the Guardia Civil. When, three years later, another wave of "revolutionary" strikes took place at the plant in the context of the Asturian miners' strike of October 1934 (the so-called Revolution of Asturias), the repercussions, which were initiated and organized by the Guardia Civil, were much harsher. Local authorities selected 221 "agitators," representing almost 25 percent of Torrelavega's work force. They were straight away expelled for their "revolutionary" behavior. Adrien Henrion, who had succeeded Waleffe in 1932, did not react to the purge. Torrelavega was to be very quiet from that day forward.[65]

Apart from these social upheavals, Solvay was concerned – businesswise – with the sudden rise of a competitor in the field of caustic soda. The Sociedad Electro-Química de Flix, which comprised an electrolytic unit founded in 1897 as a subsidiary of Griesheim, turned in 1930 to IG Farben to modernize its installations and significantly expand its production capacity.[66] When René Boël and Philippe Aubertin accidentally heard about the news by discussing with IG Farben's Herman Schmitz in November 1932, the *gérance* replied with a twofold "defensive" strategy: find an agreement with Flix's commercial agent Cros to drastically limit its export volume of caustic soda and develop Solvay's own electrolytic potential.[67] But what should be started first? Coming back from a two-week stay in France and Spain in March 1933, Piérard pointed to the opportunity to "study the Spanish chlorine market and the future possibilities of new outlets" along the lines of the company's general policy for chlorine development in Europe.[68] This gave the *gérance* some food for thought, although chlorine was officially not the priority. After a series of technical and commercial inquiries, the *gérants* came around, at a meeting on 22 November 1933, to the necessity to set up an electrolytic unit adjacent to their soda plant in Torrelavega, rather than elsewhere in Spain. At the same reunion, they insisted that IG Farben be reminded that Solvay "did not seek to wage a battle

[64] For an overview of the Spanish chemical industry in the twentieth century, see Puig (2010) and Puig (2007). I am grateful to Núria Puig for providing me these articles.

[65] Toca (2005), 258–60; Mioche (2009), 8–10.

[66] Puig (2004), 293, 296–8.

[67] ACS, RdG, 8 Dec. 1932; ACS, 1001-24-5, Réunion Technico-Commerciale, 21–22 June 1933; Toca (2005), 205–7.

[68] ACS, 1001-24-2, "Voyage de M. Piérard en France et en Espagne du 3 au 16 mars 1933," by G. Piérard, 28 Mar. 1933, 15.

for chlorine competition in Spain but rather to defend its position in caustic soda."[69] However, during the following months, Solvay constantly referred to its substantial positioning in various national and international chlorine cartels, some of which were with IG Farben, as a means to justify its having received a contingent for the production and sales of chlorine-based products in Spain. Through this pervasive strategy, Solvay was able to win on both sides. When the electrolytic unit of Torrelavega was put into motion in September 1935, Solvay had obtained confirmation that a compromise had been reached under the pressure of IG Farben. Flix agreed to limit its production of caustic soda on the whole Spanish market to a mere 22 percent (with a maximum of ten thousand tons per year) and conceded to Solvay a contingent of chlorine-based products up to three thousand tons per year.[70] This was more than enough for the early start of Torrelavega's unit. Then the civil war broke out.

Between July 1936 and August 1937, Torrelavega was located in the enclave of northern Spain that remained administered by the Republicans. The production had to be put on hold several times because of the isolation of the zone. After the storming of Santander on 26 August 1937 by Franco's troops, the plant resumed its activity and went through the Civil War running a relatively normal regime of production under the ever-closer watch of the nationalist insurgents. The *gérants*' worry, however, lay elsewhere; their eyes converged on Suria. The potash mines of Suria that Solvay controlled almost entirely through Gefucin were located in the Republican province of Barcelona, which saw the most violent confrontation early on. Trying to escape from the uprising of the workers and the assault of anarchist groups in the region, the plant manager, Norbert Fonthier, and two foreign engineers managed to be evacuated to Barcelona, but two other employees were imprisoned and eventually killed. Back in Brussels, Fonthier joined Ernest-John Solvay in exposing the situation of Solvay's plants in Spain to the Belgian minister of foreign affairs, Paul-Henri Spaak.[71] Two other Belgian multinationals with interests in Catalonia – the electricity companies Electrobel and Sofina – shared Solvay's apprehension of being expropriated in application of a decree law issued by the *Generalitat* of Catalonia on 8 August 1936.[72] In the following weeks, and in spite of the energy displayed by Spaak's ministry, the Catalonian authorities delegated a special "interventor" to Suria, whose mission of *intervención* to the *gérants* translated as a pure intrusion of the regime into their business.[73] Measures of general collectivization of the Catalonian industry were also looming.

In view of the ongoing situation, the issue took a more political turn. As soon as August 1936, Sofina's CEO, Henri Speciael, had met Ernest-John Solvay to prepare "a collective action to defend the Belgian interests in Catalonia."[74]

[69] ACS, RdG, 22 Nov. 1933.
[70] ACS, 1121-37-2, CdG, 10 Oct. 1932; Toca (2005), 210–16.
[71] ACS, 1001-29-26, Visite de MM. Solvay et Fonthier au Min. des Aff. Etrangères, 5 Aug. 1936.
[72] Sofina's subsidiary, the Barcelona Traction LPCy, was to be run on a cooperative basis by the workers. ACS, 1001-29-24, 16 Sept. 1936; Ranieri (2005), 85–92.
[73] ACS, 1001-29-26, J. Simon (Gen. Consul of Belgium in Barcelona) to Spaak, 12 Sept. 1936.
[74] ACS, 1001-29-24, 13 and 19 Aug. 1936.

However, by October 1937, the context and the priorities had changed: the Republican army had surrendered in the Basque territory and Franco's advance seemed inexorable. "At Torrelavega," Henrion observed, "nationalist authorities are favorably inclined toward industrial development. But only foreign governments which have recognized Franco's action can take advantage of it" – and this was not the case of France and Belgium.[75] In other terms, the chaotic situation of the regions controlled by the Republicans appeared to be less of a concern to industrialists than the official recognition of the nationalist government of Burgos. As a result, Belgian business leaders gathered into a common lobby group determined to show the Belgian government the "immensity" of the Belgian assets in Spain, as well as the urgency of starting diplomatic relations with Burgos.[76]

The campaign took place on several fronts simultaneously. An official investigation on the Belgian economic interests in Spain was set up, which led to the publication of an influential report in September 1938 – the "Rapport Delcoigne."[77] Fonthier, who had stayed in Burgos and Salamanca as soon as March 1937, wrote a brief note justifying on economic grounds the launch of relationships between Belgium and nationalist Spain. "Countries like England, the Netherlands, Switzerland, and even Czechoslovakia have done so," he went on, "and they cannot be suspected of sympathy for dictatorships."[78] Ernest-John Solvay diffused the note and other brochures to his political entourage, including the Viscount Maurice Lippens, who was a member of the Committee of Foreign Affairs in the Belgian Senate.[79] Louis Solvay was in contact with Marquis de Hoyos, a former board member of Suria, who was well connected with the milieus of Burgos.[80] In the heat of the political climate, the socialist senator Max Buset wrote an article in which he accused Solvay of willingly hindering the functioning of one of its plants located on the Republican side (Suria) while the other, located on the territory gained by the "rebels," was fully on stream. Alerted by this newspaper article, Spaak (then prime minister) asked Ernest-John Solvay for an explanation, which was duly executed in the form of a memorandum describing the situation of Solvay's plants in

---

[75] Mioche (2009), 15–16; ACS, 1001-29-25, Visite de M. Henrion, 27 Apr. 1938. On diplomatic underpinnigs, see Gotovitch (1983).

[76] ACS, RdG 21 Dec. 1937; ACS, 1001-29-25, Communication du M.A.E. – Direction Politique, 4 Dec. 1937; "Enquête sur nos intérêts en Espagne," 6 Dec. 1937; "Situation des intérêts belges en Espagne nationaliste," 1 Mar. 1938.

[77] The civil servant Georges Delcoigne served as head of an "official and provisional" delegation inquiring on "the interests Belgium had to defend in nationalist Spain." See Salmon (1987), 133–4.

[78] ACS, DS 317, "Voyage de M. Fonthier en Espagne blanche (Burgos et Salamanque, 4–13 mars 1937)," RdG 17 Mar. 1937; ACS, 1001-29-25, "Etablissement de relations entre la Belgique et l'Espagne nationaliste," 31 May 1938. The British government only recognized de jure the Franco regime on 27 February 1939.

[79] One of these pamphlets was "Une question à l'ordre du jour: La reconnaissance par la Belgique du Gouvernement National de l'Espagne" written by Viscount Charles Terlinden. ACS, 1001-29-25, E. J. Solvay to M. Lippens, 28 and 31 May 1938.

[80] ACS, 1001-29-25, Hoyos to Fonthier, 13 Aug. 1938.

Spain since the outbreak of the war. [81] This incident did not prohibit Spaak from taking the issue of diplomatic recognition (which made the headline news as "L'affaire de Burgos") before the Belgian Senate on 29 November 1938 – and face important opposition, including in his own political camp, the Socialist Party.[82] After six hours of fierce debate, the final vote eventually gave the majority to the recognition of Burgos – eighty-eight pros, thirteen cons, and fifty abstained (the socialist senators). During his speech, Spaak explicitly exculpated the attitude of the Solvay house and its "potash mining company of Gurlia [sic] in Catalonia."[83]

Nationalist troops marched on Catalonia in January 1939, which opened the way to Franco's final victory on 1 April. It took some time for Suria to resume operations. The plant at Torrelavega, however, was thriving. The project to expand the production capacity of the soda and electrolytic units, which had been considered since 1939, was officially submitted to the Ministry of Trade and Industry in May 1942 and fully accepted in October of that year.[84] The next pending question pertained to the forced nationalization of the plant; it was yet another challenge that Solvay had to face all over Europe during the war.

[81] ACS, 1001–29-25, "Enquête d'abord" by Max Buset (*Le Peuple*, 11 Nov. 1938); ACS, 1001–29-25, Spaak to E.-J. Solvay, 17 Nov. 1938; ACS, 1001–29-25, "Note répondant à la lettre du M.A.E. du 17 novembre 1938," by N. Fonthier, 22 Nov. 1938.

[82] See Saelens (1987).

[83] ACS, 1001–29-25, *Le Peuple*, 30 Nov. 1938; *L'Echo de la Bourse*, 30 Nov. 1938.

[84] ACS, 1121–37-2, "Visite de M. Fonthier," 24 Feb. 1940; "Projet d'augmentation de l'installation électrolytique existante," May 1942; B. Barreda to gérance, 28 Nov. 1942.

Werkszeitung
Deutſche Solvay-Werke A.G., Bernburg

Herausgegeben im Einvernehmen mit dem Dinta
in der Deutſchen Arbeitsfront | 2. Jahrgang | Nr. 8 | 13. April 1935

Zum 120. Geburtstage Bismarcks

„Wenn wir einig bleiben, bilden wir einen harten ſchweren Kloß inmitten Europas,
den niemand anfaßt, ohne ſich die Finger zu zerquetſchen"

(Zum Aufſatz „Zum Gedenken des 1. April 1815" auf Seite 4 der vorliegenden Ausgabe.)

FIGURE 12.1. The DSW company megazine, published by the German Institute for Technical Labor Training (Dinta), was an essential tool for forging the combined feelings of loyalty to the firm and to the German nation through the simultaneous display of different symbols (e.g., Nazi flags, company logo, statue of Bismarck). (Solvay Bernburg Archives.)

12

Facing War Again

The history of chemical companies during World War II has been the subject of many books and articles, especially when it comes to unraveling the experience of the German chemical industry and its involvement with the crimes of the National Socialist regime. For some, World War II was a genuine heir to the legacy of the chemists' war experienced from 1914 to 1918; the use of the Zyklon B pesticide to murder one million Jews in the death camps of Birkenau and Majdanek constituted a major break in the history of humanity. For both sides, however, there was little doubt that science and technology had become potential weapons of mass extermination. Shortly after the war, in the wake of the crime trials of Nuremberg, some studies, many of which were not scholarly, did not resist the temptation to address the events from the standpoint of a judge rather than that of a historian. Industrialists were condemned as early and enthusiast followers of Hitler. Since Peter Hayes and Peter Morris's groundbreaking accounts of the history of IG Farben during the Nazi era, the simplistic and Manichaean interpretations that had emerged during the Cold War have given way to more balanced and nuanced explanations (albeit with many different sensibilities).[1] By drawing a distinction between the political framework provided by Hitler's regime and the nature of managerial decisions taken during that period, they have emphasized the different interests and, sometimes, the divergent cultures between the industrial and financial elite of the 1930s and the Nazi economic policy. Then again, they have also highlighted the multidimensional entanglement of corporate mechanisms in the machinery of the Third Reich – leading sometimes, as the case of Degussa has made clear, to a shift from subtle cooperation to overt complicity.[2]

Unfortunately, the impressive research drive that has shed light on German chemical companies during the war has found few equivalents for European countries subsequently occupied by the Wehrmacht. Despite the important scholarship dedicated to gaining a better grasp of the big picture of economic relations and business-state linkages in the Nazi empire, we still ignore a great

---

[1] Morris (1982); Hayes (2001). The most recent scholarship includes Lindner (2008); Abelshauser et al. (2004); Kobrak (2002), 296–341. Criticisms have focused on apologetic tendencies found in Plumpe (1990). See Hayes (1992) and Plumpe's reply in the same issue.

[2] Hayes (2004). The noteworthy case of the Monowitz factory (in the vicinity of Auschwitz) set up by IG Farben in 1941 has been treated by Wagner (2000) with complementary insights from Schmaltz and Roth (1998).

deal of the wartime organization and business history of chemical enterprises in occupied Europe.[3] This makes the history of Solvay during World War II altogether a timely and a limited enterprise. Because of its ramifications in Germany, the Solvay group might appear a special case in this respect. The important role played by its long-established subsidiary, DSW (see Chapter 2), the commercial and financial agreements it had concluded with IG Farben's forerunners (see Chapter 9), and the commercial ties DSW has developed with German chemical companies through various trusts or *Syndikaten* all tend to indicate a strengthening of Solvay's position in Germany during the interwar period or, more aptly, a reinforcement of Germany in Solvay's international strategy. In spite of some flaws – such as the lagging position of DSW in the production of electrolytic caustic soda (see Chapter 11) – Solvay's overall interests in Germany were far greater than they had been twenty years before. For the company, therefore, World War II could hardly be seen as a mere duplicate of World War I.

12.1 SOCIAL POLICY AND THE NEW ORDER

By the early 1930s, the resentment against the very nature of liberal democracy and laissez-faire capitalism had found new expressions away from political activism. The authoritarian flavor of the new-order ideology had won over many milieus, including industrialists, long before it was implemented, in a radical form, during the Third Reich's expansionist policy. Nowhere was the zeitgeist of the new order so pervasive as in the gradual transformation of labor relations. The adoption of an encompassing set of social regulations inspired by neo-paternalist and Fordist patterns seemed the best answer to prevent the irremediable collapse of the social peace. The threat of communist upheavals was never far away. The extension of the Depression, not the prospect of another war, reinforced this chain of social-oriented initiatives, which focused on improvements in the employment situation and labor stabilization.

The Maison Ernest Solvay

As soon as the new organizational chart was put into motion in November 1931 (see Chapter 10), a fresh impulse was at Solvay in the field of social policy. As head of the Personnel Department, Louis Solvay had insisted to his colleagues that he was given free rein in redesigning the company's social program, a task he conceived of rather broadly. His first action had been to seek advice from former collaborators – René Étienne, Hallam Tuck, Sigismond Toeplitz, and Emil Gielen – before setting forth a plan of action. In a meeting held in Paris in January 1932, Louis Solvay defined three priority measures: initiatives leading to an improvement of the relations between the management and the work force (capital and labor), social measures against unemployment,

---

[3] The most influential syntheses are Milward (1977); Overy (1994); Gall and Pohl (1998); Tooze (2007). An exception to the micro-dimension treatment of the chemical business history during the war is van Zanden, Jonker, Howarth, and Sluyterman (2007).

and the appropriate uses of leisure (e.g., sports, gardening, reading groups).[4] But whatever the directions, he made clear that concrete and specific initiatives, some of them already existing, were far more effective than overarching reforms. For instance, on-the-job apprenticeship had to be generalized to avoid occasional unemployment and wasted time. Programs were to be modeled after the experiments of the Centre de Pré-Apprentissage in Montluçon or the workshop-school programs (*ateliers-écoles*) run by the Chamber of Commerce of Paris. The same rationale went for the female work force. A problem inherited from the war (and a cause of mass unemployment), the issue of female labor needed to be tackled by promoting domestic science and stressing that the genuine role of women was in their household rather than in the plant. Finally, a special emphasis was laid on measures leading to housing ownership.[5]

Overall, the ideas shared by Louis Solvay's think tank aimed at stabilizing workers in a context of social and political upheaval. As such, they echoed the aspiration of the implementation of a classless society, which many national governments were fostering in interwar Europe.[6] With the rapid spreading of the economic crisis, Louis felt that unemployment was the seedbed of organized forms of opposition, which the company could not tolerate. Downsizing was, therefore, the last viable option available. Measures resulting from the studies of the International Labor Organization in Geneva, like the further reduction of work hours (below the eight-hour-day standard) or the introduction of a profit-sharing system, were not considered mature alternatives. Time and again, Louis repeated that the social principles laid by the founding fathers rested on firm and sound foundations; they merely needed to be updated – and grounded on scientific facts. Plant managers were thus asked to send detailed information on various social policy issues they observed on site. The findings were gathered and commented on by Toeplitz, Gielen, and Étienne in a meeting held in Berlin on 5–6 July 1932. Among the conclusions they drew was that the diversity of national frameworks largely outweighed the converging effect of Solvay's social guidelines. Louis's interpretation of the report was unambiguous: "we should have in Brussels a department [service] competent for the study of social issues that should be fully independent from the Technical Direction (Section D)."[7]

But striving for an institutional innovation just a few months after the organizational chart had been painfully adopted was not the most relevant strategy. Louis, who had been closely involved in the previous discussions, proposed a creative solution. He aptly linked the company's program for philanthropy and donations with the social agenda he intended to develop.

---

[4] ACS, Service du Personnel (hereafter SP), Sec. J1 (2.1), Meeting in Paris, 5 Jan. 1932. The psychologist and labor specialist Paul-Auguste Sollier was also invited to give his opinion.

[5] ACS, RdG, 26 Apr. 1932; AHR, Sec. J1 (2.1), Appendix to RdG, 11 Apr. 1932: Memorandum by L. Solvay (29 Mar. 1932).

[6] Lederer (1940); Maier (1975).

[7] AHR, Sec. J1 (2.1), Meeting in Berlin, 5–6 July 1932; ACS, RdG 31 May 1932; ASSR, Brussels SP to C. Van Caubergh, 8 Nov. 1930; ASSR, Notebook S/2, C. Van Caubergh to E. Sougnez (MES), 7 Sept. 1933.

Further, he wished to avoid the division of the winter property owned by Ernest Solvay and his family, which was located a stone's throw from the company's headquarters in Ixelles. The Maison Ernest Solvay (MES), as it was eventually called, combined these objectives in one move. It was launched as a nonprofit organization in October 1932, in the context of a series of commemorations on the tenth anniversary of Ernest Solvay's death.[8] The *gérants* were ex officio members – with Louis as chairman – but the board also included Edmond Solvay, Robert Hankar, Paul Casimir-Lambert, and Baron Emmanuel Janssen, whose experience – and network – as vice chairman of the National Committee for Relief and Food during the war was greatly appreciated. Board meetings of the MES were held monthly, but most routine tasks were undertaken by Louis and his staff exclusively, such as allocating grants and subventions to charity and welfare foundations. Until the outbreak of the war, it inspired or sponsored dozens of institutions (vocational and domestic school at the Couillet plant (École Menagère et d'Apprentissage), libraries and sports facilities, the Solvay Museum, activities (e.g., the seventy-fifth anniversary of Solvay & Cie, jubilee receptions), cultural events, and scientific studies.

By and large, the MES functioned as a semiformal shadow of Solvay & Cie's social policy program. The enthusiasm of its chairman was such that his projects frequently overlapped with, and sometimes curtailed, the action of the *gérance* in this field. The situation was best illustrated during the preparation of an important meeting of plant managers that took place in Brussels on 15–16 October 1936. Commenting on a preliminary note drafted by Louis, René Boël observed that a certain "ambiguity" hovered over the mutual role of the *gérance* and the MES with regard to the orientation and the implementation of the company's social activities. According to Louis, the MES could take direct action with the factories and suggest on-site social experiments.[9] Obviously, his colleagues did not share this view. Shortly after the Brussels meeting, the *gérants* stressed the auxiliary function of the MES as expressed in its bylaws. If it could embark on "theoretical studies... strictly defined, and for specific cases, its findings should never receive a general expression." As a result, they concluded that there was "no room for confusion of any kind," nor "any possibility of misunderstanding" between the *gérance* and the MES in the functioning and objectives of Solvay & Cie's social program.[10]

The reminder was timely, as the role of the MES began to extend the scope of corporate-based social policy – and to make some incursion into the political arena. For most of the *gérants*, this was a line that ought not to be crossed. As

---

[8] The official ceremony included the inauguration of the monument Ernest Solvay, close to the University of Brussels, with a speech by French physicist Paul Langevin, head of the scientific committee of the Solvay Councils of Physics. ACS, DS 193, RdG 5 Oct. 1932; ACS, DS 202, 11 Nov. 1932; AHR, Sec. J1 (1), Inauguration du monument à E. Solvay, Discours de M. Langevin, 16 Oct. 1932.

[9] AHR, Sec. J1 (2.2), Note from L. Solvay, 23 Sept. 1936; AHR, Sec. J1 (2.2), Draft of memo by L. Solvay (with comments from R. Boël), 26 Sept. 1936.

[10] ACS, RdG 5 Nov. 1936, enclosed in ACS, DS 355, "Note concernant le secrétariat particulier du Doyen de la Gérance," by R. Gendebien, 13 Dec. 1941.

soon as December 1933, Edmond Solvay, Baron Janssen, and Paul Casimir-Lambert had warned Louis Solvay that they judged as "too sensitive" his proposal to gather a group of persons discussing about the "recovery of governmental methods" under the aegis of the MES.[11] But this claim found broader expression as the political climate worsened in Belgium in 1936 with the electoral success of the Rexist group, shifting from anticommunist Catholic conservatism to overtly pro-fascist tendencies.[12] In this context, some of the initiatives by the chairman of the MES were perceived as inappropriate by his colleagues. Ernest-John Solvay especially disapproved of the idea to set up a "steering committee studying...a program of modifications that could be brought to the Belgian Constitution" under the banner of the MES.[13] After the war broke out, the debate between Ernest-John and his uncle crystallized about the proper interpretation of Ernest Solvay's political views. Although Louis thought that the MES had to convey moral guidelines that were "in conformity with the legacy of the founding fathers," Ernest-John deemed "impossible to formulate any supposition" on what Ernest and Alfred Solvay would have thought in similar circumstances.[14] The argument went beyond formal rhetoric, though. It culminated with Ernest-John's sudden resignation from the MES in March 1943 – a decision that, contrary to the habits of the family, was made official.[15] What sparked Ernest-John's resolution was that Louis, who made no mystery of his political opinions, had definitively turned the MES into an unofficial political laboratory whose orientation, according to Ernest-John, was running counter to the image of the company. Although technical reasons were brought forward – excessive budget, dysfunctional accounting techniques, mismanagement – it was obvious that the MES was at an ideological standstill shortly after the war. However, the *gérants* waited until Louis's retirement in May 1947 to transfer the MES's activities and funding back in the hands of the company's administration.[16]

Comparing the Italian and German Social Experiments

Before being relegated to the footnotes of history, the MES made a significant contribution to the process of convergence of social policy practices in the plants of the Solvay group. Among the national models of social policy worthy of interest, the Italian and German cases, as seen through the lens of Solvay's works and subsidiaries – Solvay-Rosignano and DSW – aroused many comments. At the request of Brussels, the Rosignano plant manager, Clément Van

[11] ACS, Registre Maison Ernest Solvay (hereafter RMES), 4 Dec. 1933, 10.

[12] Conway (1996), 200–3; Conway (1993).

[13] ACS, DS 307, RdG, 5 Aug. 1936; ACS, RMES, 7 Oct. 1936, 66–70; ACS, DS 310, E.-J. Solvay to L. Solvay, 21 Oct. 1936, and Louis's reply, 24 Oct. 1936. Ernest-John Solvay was himself part of a study program for administrative reorganization, the Centre d'Études pour la Réforme de l'État, headed by civil servant Louis Camu; see Luyten (1988), 626–7.

[14] ACS, RMES, 11 Nov. 1942, 113–15; ACS, DS 361, Note de L. Solvay, 11 Nov. 1942.

[15] ACS, RMES, 15 Mar. 1943, 117; *Moniteur Belge* – Appendix, 20 Mar. 1943, 148, No. 392.

[16] ACS, DS 376, Note de E.-J. Solvay (and comments by R. Gendebien, Pierre Beautier, and Joseph de Dorlodot), 20 Apr. 1945; ACS, DS 391, RdG 7 Jan. 1947.

Caubergh, gave a detailed description of the "corporative and social organization of the Italian economy." He placed particular emphasis on the multilayered levels of labor and management delegations, as well as on the effects that
the twenty-two corporations had on the production and price systems.[17] But
there were other social experiments of interest to collect in the fascist regime,
whose grounding in local communities was one of its hallmarks. At Rosignano, the patterns of Mussolini's alleged social revolution blended with the
company's welfare legacy. By 1934, the plant offered a wide array of state-of-
the-art social actions – working schedule, wages systems, health-care schemes,
leisure activities (dopolavoro), and a corporate housing program for no fewer
than 328 workers' families – all of which matched with, or even outstripped,
the prerequisites of the regime's propaganda machine.[18] In his correspondence
with the official trade union of the province of Livorno (Unione Provinciale
Fascista dei Lavoratori dell'Industria), Van Caubergh had to stress that the
favorable dispositions of the welfare policy of the plant "derived from general
measures adopted by Solvay & Cie" and could not give way to parallel organisms run by the party.[19] The intertwining of business and politics – and the
resolution of conflicts in both milieus – was facilitated by the presence on the
site of notables from local political leagues (Fasci), who subsequently enjoyed
important career advancements – Ulisse Seni (plant manager during the war),
Giorgio Tremi (Van Caubergh's former assistant who became commercial general manager for Italy in 1940), and Giuseppe Dolazza (general manager for
Italy, 1940–1944). Before the war broke out, the plant management attempted
to curb the excessive politicization of the workforce. Already in July 1929, Cyril
Van Caubergh had set forth a memorandum that expressed the limitations of
the company's tolerance to fascist demonstrations: "while we praise those who
take an active part in the various associations of the country – whether it is
exclusively composed of employees or in any another form – we cannot allow
these activities to take place during the working hours."[20]

   In view of the political context, the German case proved even more intrigu-
ing. By April 1929, Paul Masson reported to Brussels the "very satisfying"
impression he received from his visit of the general administration of DSW.
Minor organizational flaws were offset by the "disciplinary spirit of the staff
and, above all, by the value and the personal authority of leaders from the
Vorstand like MM. Eilsberger and Gielen." The organization of labor, he concluded, was favorably influenced by their presence.[21] Then the Depression came
and hit hard the German industry as a whole. After Hitler's election and the
Nazi seizure of power, measures were immediately taken to prevent the increase

[17] ACS, 1340-66-1, C. Van Caubergh to gérance, 28 Aug. 1935. Just in case, Van Caubergh also
   appended to his report the official Contratto Nazionale di Lavoro per gli Operai Addetti alli
   Industrie Chimiche, of June 1929.
[18] ASSR, Seg. C – 4: Istituzioni assistenziali (1934); Celati and Gattini (1998), 30–1.
[19] ASSR, Pers. G 43 b 12, C. Van Caubergh to UPFLI – Livorno, Casse mutue malattie, 9 May
   1935.
[20] Paolini (2007), 21–2; Mioche (2009), 39–40.
[21] ACS, 1151-33-2, Rapport de P. Masson (DSW – Organisation de l'administration centrale),
   16 Apr. 1929.

of the (already-huge) levels of unemployment – shortened working hours (to a maximum limit of forty hours a week), forced retirement after sixty years of age, complementary working programs. They concerned the 3,307 workers and 454 employees at various DSW works.[22] Of course, such policy was expensive and companies had to give in. Like other companies, DSW had to contribute to the various welfare associations set up by the party, the most notorious being the Adolf Hitler Spende der Deutschen Wirtschaft.[23] On 20 January 1934, the proclamation of the Decree on the Organization of National Labor (Gesetz zur Ordnung der Nationalen Arbeit) implemented the authoritarian underpinnings of the *Führerprinzip* in the business community. In a report he submitted to the *gérance*, the chairman of the *Vorstand*, Ernst Eilsberger, bluntly asserted that this piece of legislation, together with the suppression of existing trade unions in favor of the single Deutsche Arbeitsfront (DAF), should be perceived as instruments paving the way to a more profound, "organic transformation" of the German people.[24] Rather than the traditional corporations or units of production, the law recognized only works communities (*Betriebsgemeinschaften*), which were run by the plant leader (*Führer des Betriebes*) in a very hierarchical manner. As a result, nine "acting" *Betriebsführers* were designated at DSW, representing all units of operation.[25] Weimar-era works councils (*Betriebsräte*) were replaced by trustees of labor (*Vertrauensräte*) and by a labor council (*Unternehmensbeirat*). But none of them could interfere with the upper organisms (whereas two representatives of the workers and employees sat in *Aufsichtsrat* according to the previous organizational chart). This institutional machinery – and the "high idealism" it ensued – Eilsberger concluded, was designed to "make the class struggle impossible." In that regard, it was an "immense progress compared with the former organization of the Germany economic life" – and this was an "indisputable truth."[26]

In February 1937, a new set of rules in the plant (*Betriebsordnung*) was suggested by Bernburg. This important document showed the exacerbation of the ideological component at DSW factories in the early stages of the Reich's Four-Year Plan, which started in fall 1936 under Hermann Göring – a period that historian Peter Hayes aptly coined the "nervous years."[27] With the increase of

---

[22] ACS, 1151–37-7, Visite du Vorstand, 11 Sept. 1933 (Appendix: "Measures contributing to stem unemployment," 8 Sept. 1933).

[23] The Adolf Hitler Spende consisted of a "compulsory system of donations that generally amounted to 0.5% of each firm's total wage and salary expenditures" (Hayes 2004, 70). A postwar thesis, conducted by a student from East Germany, estimated at 4,000 *Reichsmarks* the donation made by DSW to the Spende during the last semester of 1933. This was rather modest compared to the 934,000 *Reichsmarks* donated by IG Farben for the years 1933 and 1934. See ADSW, Archiv II, 67, "Zur Politik der Aktionäre der Deutschen Solvay-Werke AG in der Zeit der Faschisierung," by Ingeborg Missbach, 10 May 1967, Anlage 6; Hayes 2001, 96).

[24] ACS, 1340–66-1 (1), Eilsberger to gérance, 5 Sept. 1935; ACS, 1340–66-1 (1), Eilsberger to gérance, 26 Nov. 1935 (Appendix "Nature and duties of the '*Werkscharen der DAF Region Magdeburg-Anhalt*'," dated 25 Sept. 1935). For a description of the law and its effects on IG Farben's constituting companies, see Abelshauser et al. (2004), 272–3; Lindner (2008), 71–6.

[25] ACS, 1340–66-1 (1), Eilsberger to gérance, 26 Nov. 1935 (appendix dated 22 Nov. 1935).

[26] ACS, 1340–66-1 (1), Eilsberger to gérance, 5 Sept. 1935, 29.

[27] Hayes (2001), 163–73.

labor productivity in mind, emphasis was first laid on the long-lasting social character of the company by recalling that it was grounded in the "Solvay social tradition," itself initiated by the "founding father and philanthropist Ernest Solvay." After a gentle reminder of the welfare initiatives that had been made at the occasion of the company's anniversary (e.g., the Ernest and Alfred Solvay Funds, which provided health-care and retirement funds for workers and employees), another defining disposition of the company followed suit – DSW was German in essence. Deutsche Solvay Werke, according to the regulation, "is a *German* joint-stock company [*Aktiengesellschaft*], the whole workforce is German – the *Vorstand*, the managers, the employees, the workers are *German men*. The company is run according to the German spirit. That is why Deutsche Solvay Werke is a German company, although the majority of its shares pertain to Belgian nationals.... Those who belong to Deutsche Solvay Werke can proudly rise up their head as *Germans* and refute with full knowledge of facts the short-sight views which pretend to make us being a foreign company."[28] Eilsberger was thereafter informed that the *Aufsichtsrat*, on which four *gérants* sat, gave his approval to the regulation draft.[29] It was, for the time being, a direct extension of the guidelines of the Nazi regime on the factory floor.[30] But a similar *Gleichschaltung* would soon affect the levels of decision making at DSW.

For the *gérants*, both Italian and German experiments of social policy resorted to an original form of "national mystique." Louis Solvay was wondering how one could convert this reference model and use other "psychological leverages" to "instill a new frame of mind in our French and Belgian factories, a 'Solvay' team spirit."[31] Louis gave this orientation a decisive impetus during the war. A special emphasis in terms of publications concerned the history of the company and the social legacy of Ernest Solvay.[32] But the MES actually promoted the realization of special studies focusing on the "Social Action of Solvay & Cie" (December 1941) and on the "Industrial Relations within the Plant" (February 1942), which exemplified the social role of engineers and physicians and took into account recent findings in industrial psychology.[33] Quite interestingly, this research avenue was taken over by Ernest-John Solvay as soon as he withdrew from the MES. As vice-chairman

---

[28] ACS, 1151–33-1, Visite de MM. Piérard et Masson à Berlin, 5 Mar. 1937 (Appendix *Entwurf der Betriebsordnung*, 16 Feb. 1937; original emphasis).

[29] ACS, 1151–33-1, Voyage à Berlin, Nouveau règlement d'ateliers, 18 Mar. 1937.

[30] In March 1939, a couple of other instructions stemming from the *Vorstand* of DSW concerned the restriction, and eventually suppression, of the use of the French language for commercial purposes (but also for the redaction of the annual report), as well as the generalization of the expression "Heil Hitler" at the end of every correspondence within the Reich (ADSW, Archiv II, Anweisung Nr. 1/39, 14 Mar. 1939; Anweisung Nr. 2/39, 21 Mar. 1939).

[31] AHR, Sec. J1 (2.2), Réunion des directeurs à Bruxelles, 15 Oct. 1936, 1–2.

[32] See Sougnez (1936); AHR, Sec. J1 (1), E. Sougnez, "Historique de la Société: Syllabus d'une conférence aux contremaîtres et employés," 1 Dec. 1942; AHR, Sec. J1 (1), A. Dupont, "Ernest Solvay et ses réalisations sociales à la Société Solvay & Cie," 7 July 1943, as well as the numerous – sometimes published – speeches by René Étienne from 1938 onward.

[33] AHR, Sec. J1 (3.3), RdG 9 Feb. 1942 (Appendix "Action sociale de la Société Solvay & Cie," 17 Dec. 1941); AHR, Sec. J1 (3.3), "Les relations sociales dans l'usine," s.d. [Feb. 1942]. These

of the Belgian Federation of Industrialists (Comité Central Industriel), Ernest-John insisted that the organization set up a special committee dedicated to the development of a social program, a topic that would inevitably emerge after the war. "Industrial leaders should not be later depicted," he claimed, "as a board of industrialists blinded to social issues."[34] Two studies stemming from Solvay's legal and personnel department circulated in the industrialists' federation – *Organization of the Social Function within the Enterprise* (September 1943) and *Social Policy in the Industry* (June 1943). These largely contributed to Ernest-John Solvay's subsequent participation in the ultimate discussions of the Groupe d'Études Sociales, led by industrialist Léon Bekaert, whose concluding report served as blueprint for the postwar social agenda in Belgium.[35]

12.2 THE NATIONAL-SOCIALIST TAKEOVER

Seen from outside Germany, the possibility that one could partly come to terms with Hitler's "organic transformation" of the German society became a bitter illusion when, by 1938, the Nazi conquest of Europe was put into motion. From the Anschluss in March to the occupation of the Sudetenland in October, leading to the dismemberment of the Czechoslovak Republic, the year 1938 witnessed the affirmation of Nazi expansionism at the expense of the Third Reich's eastern borderlands. The repercussions on Solvay were both concrete and immense as its Ebensee and Nestomitz plants were directly concerned by the "events," as Brussels alluded to the political situation euphemistically. The whole configuration of the Solvay-Werke business in Central Eastern Europe (Solvay-Sodabetriebs-Gesellschaft) had to be redesigned, a task that required taking into account the difficult position of its Prague-based partner, Verein Aussig. But it also required handling with utmost care the attitude of DSW in these negotiations. As "greater" Germany was on its way, so was DSW. In a few years' time, a new invigorated generation of men took the upper rein of the company. They were keen to show Brussels that they did not wish to see DSW be treated as a subsidiary anymore.

The Germanization of DSW's Higher Management

On 28 February 1938, Solvay & Cie and DSW organized a ceremony at the occasion of Dr. Ernst Eilbserger's seventieth birthday and thirty years of service at the head of the company. For some years he had devoted some of his time writing the history of DSW and was planning to do some research on Ernest

studies drew on observations in Lamirand (1932) and the research conducted by Alexis Carrel. On Carrel's wartime influence, see Drouard (1995).

[34] ACS, 1340–37-2, CCI, Minutes of the Board Meeting, 6 May 1943. Crucial in that respect was the position held by some members of the Federation of the Chemical Industry in Belgium, of which Ernest-John Solvay was chairman.

[35] ACS, 1340–37-2, E.-J. Solvay to L.-A. Bekaert, 22 Apr. 1944. See also Kurgan-van Hentenryk (1995).

Solvay's philosophy.[36] By the end of 1938, he was expected to step down as chairman of the *Vorstand* and become a retired – albeit acting – "intimate adviser" of the company. Since May 1937, however, the legal counsel of DSW was Graf Rüdiger von der Goltz.[37] The son of a prestigious general who had fought the Red Army in the Baltic Countries until long after the Armistice was signed, Graf von der Goltz junior had inherited his father's penchant for order and authority. Although he and Eilsberger did not belong to the same generation, they both shared the experience of the war (von der Goltz had to endure the amputation of a leg) and a same suspicion vis-à-vis the Weimar Republic. Von der Goltz's influence in the higher echelons of the regime administration was acknowledged, as was his expertise in criminal, rather than corporate, law. At the same time von der Goltz was appointed, in February 1937, Eilsberger suggested choosing Carl Adolf Clemm as member of the *Vorstand* after Karl Hornung's retirement. The director of Kali-Chemie's Commercial Department, Clemm was certainly not an unknown figure in industrial milieus.[38] But it was above all his appointment as leader of the Economic Group for Chemicals (Wirtschaftsgruppe Chemie) that precipitated him at the *Vorstand*.[39] His links with IG Farben and the Nazi corporate machinery made him a valuable asset for DSW.

Considering the political context, Von der Goltz and Clemm were undoubtedly the rising men at DSW. Shortly after his farewell party, Eilsberger reminded the *gérance* that "it was for DSW's best interest to increase the number of German members at the *Aufsichtsrat*." He suggested von der Goltz.[40] During the General Assembly meeting of 19 May 1938, however, the participants renewed the *Aufsichtsrat*'s former composition of four Belgian *gérants* and only one German (E.-J. Solvay, E. Tournay-Solvay, R. Boël, R. Gendebien, and E. Gielen). But the assembly also approved another point at the agenda, whose effect on the company's leadership was perhaps more profound – the conformity of the company's bylaws to the dispositions of the new law on public companies (the *Aktiengesetz*) passed on 30 January 1937. Ironically, the *Aktiengesetz* deprived the General Assembly of the supreme authority it exerted hitherto on the company and entrusted the *Vorstand* with extended power (largely at the expense of the *Aufsichtsrat*). Von der Goltz was the main architect of these modifications, which stirred considerable discussions between

---

[36] Eilsberger (1930a); Eilsberger (1930b). For a short biography, see Eilsberger (1959) and a clipping of the *Deutsche-Bergwerks-Zeitung* (Düsseldorf), 27 Feb. 1938.

[37] ACS, 1151–53-1/4, Projet d'attestation, undated [Nov. 1947]. The document was prepared by the Central Administration of Solvay & Cie in Brussels in view of von der Goltz's rehabilitation after the war.

[38] Eilsberger had long been wary of the head of Kali-Chemie, Theodore Feise, going "hand in hand" with IG Farben's director of the Chemicals Committee, Eduard Weber-Andreä. The appointment of Adolf Clemm was also a maneuver to contain this tandem's growing appetite – and the eventuality of Kali-Chemie's participation in the capital of DSW in "a time when the idea of *Deutschtum* is particularly propagated" (ACS, 1151–40-27, Eilsberger to gérance, 4 Jan. 1936).

[39] ACS, 1340–66-1 (1), Eilsberger to gérance, 5 Sept. 1935, 25; Hayes (2001), 126.

[40] ACS, 1151–53-1/4, Communication téléphonique de M. Eilsberger, 17 May 1938.

Bernburg and Brussels.[41] The reorganization of the higher management took place when the process of legal conformity was nearing completion. On 17 January 1939, the chairman, Ernest-John Solvay, greeted Ernest Eilsberger and Graf von der Goltz as new members of the *Aufsichtsrat*, which was expanded to six members. This brought the *Aufsichtsrat* to quasi parity between Belgians and Germans.[42] Obviously, the *gérance* had deemed it necessary to yield to Eilsberger's request.

This double promotion had an immediate repercussion on the *Vorstand*. The director of the Borth and Wallach mining plants, Aurel Kerstein, was asked to fill the vacuum created by Eilsberger's departure, but most important was Clemm's designation as chairman. Although Ernest-John Solvay had been keen on stressing that the position comprised the same powers as his predecessor, Clemm's thirst was not slaked. Relying on the *Aktiengesetz*, he argued he should obtain the role of "primus inter pares" with casting vote in case of parity.[43] After some hesitation, he was eventually given approval by the Belgian members of the *Aufsichstrat* during a stay in Brussels on 22 November 1939. Clemm's appointment, though decisive for strategic reasons, had produced some turmoil. The DSW plant managers criticized the lack of contacts between them and the *Vorstand*, "even when they came to visit in Bernburg." Clemm was especially in their line of fire; they knew he devoted a substantial part of his time to "other activities."[44] This was also in the mind of the *gérants*: Clemm's former position at Kali-Chemie made the situation very sensitive. By 1939, IG and Solvay (via DSW and Providentia) held 44.66 percent of Kali-Chemie. Suggestions to obtain the majority share came regularly to the fore, but IG Farben was reluctant. At a meeting in Berlin on 6 May 1939, Hermann Schmitz, who had succeeded Carl Bosch as chairman of IG's *Vorstand* in April 1935, told Boël of the "bad impression [of] IG" that could result in increasing their control of Kali-Chemie. After all, the Hannover-based company was, according to Schmitz, "a small independent company, hence very influential in industrial circles and in the Party."[45] For that matter, IG and Solvay were better off keeping a low profile with Kali-Chemie. The same went for Clemm.

The "Aryanization" of Solvay in Central Eastern Europe

With the annexation of Austria to Nazi Germany on 12 March 1938, the Ebenseer Solvay-Werke (ESW) soda ash plant and Hallein electrolytic unit suddenly became German companies. The political fact had still to be converted

---

[41] ACS, 1151-53-7, Meeting with the Vorstand, 9 Dec. 1937; ACS, 1151-53-7, "Gesetz über Aktiengesellschaften und Kommanditgesellschaften auf Aktien vom 30. Januar 1937," Explanations by M. Breue, 20 Apr. 1938; ACS, 1151-53-7, "Règlement d'ordre intérieur du Vorstand," 14 June 1938.

[42] ACS, 1151-53-11, Minutes of the *Aufsichtsrat* meeting, 17 Jan. 1939.

[43] ACS, 1151-53-7, C.A. Clemm to gérance, 19 May 1939 and reply 22 May 1939.

[44] ACS, 1151-53-7, Voyage de M. Masson à Berlin, 4 July 1939; ACS, 1151-53-7, Visite de MM. Clemm and H. Eilsberger, 22 Nov. 1939.

[45] ACS, 1151-37-11, Sitzung des Vorstandes der DSW, 13 Apr. 1939, handwritten note by R. Boël (after 6 May 1939). On H. Schmitz, see Hayes (2001), 25–6.

from an industrial standpoint, which proved less easy than expected. Sent to Vienna on 22 March 1938, P. Vander Eycken and P. Masson felt that the simplest solution was an Anschluss of ESW (and Hallein) to DSW, which was akin to the political situation.[46] ESW, however, was equally controlled by Verein Aussig, which officially only held 49 percent of the company since a 1934 fiscal agreement. After calculation – and notwithstanding Verein's acceptance – the operation would have amounted to having Verein hold between 3 percent and 4 percent of the capital of DSW. For the *gérants*, this was a lesser evil considering the context; they therefore strongly encouraged the selection of this option. But this was overlooking the process of "Aryanization" (*Arisierung*) that defined the economic (and social) principles of the Third Reich from its beginning. Aryanization was a series of laws about the biological distinctions of an "Aryan" and a "non-Aryan," and their outcomes in terms of professional activities. Jews were the main targets – and victims – of this policy. During the early years of the Nazi era, Aryanization had especially concentrated on small and medium-size companies. But by 1938 the regime widened the scope of its purges through the adoption of a series of decrees regulating the Aryan composition of a company's *Aufsichtsrat* and *Vorstand*.[47] In a lengthy note drafted on 11 July 1938, the head of the commercial department of DSW, Carl Breuer, argued that in the case of ESW, the issue of Aryanization, as well as the costs involved in the option of complete takeover of the firm, posed serious difficulties: "as a non-Aryan company and personally responsible of the general partnership of ESW, Aussig is to be considered as a Jewish firm according to the clauses of Decree-Law of 14 June 1938."[48] The delegate of Verein at ESW, Dr. Victor Basch, was the first victim of this purge. He had to be replaced by an "Aryan" on the board.[49]

The situation worsened in the following months as the Nazis marched in the Sudetenland, where the Nestomitzer Solvay-Werke (NSW) plant was located. Besides NSW, which Solvay controlled with Verein Aussig in the same proportion as the Ebensee plant, Solvay also held 15.4 percent in Verein. This participation made Belgium the largest country in terms of foreign direct investment in Czechoslovakia's chemical industry.[50] Conversely, the Germans did not ignore the huge potential of Verein, the fourth-largest chemical concern in Europe and a doorway to a wide array of cartels in Central and Eastern Europe.[51] Therefore, the Munich Agreements, signed on 30 September 1938, which gave the Germans de facto control over Czech territory, were a hard blow to Solvay. Just as they were doing for the Spanish case at the same time (see Chapter 11), the *gérants* mobilized the diplomatic channels to obtain "the complete safeguard of their interests." They reached out to the Belgian minister of foreign affairs, Paul-Henri Spaak, and to the Belgian ambassador in Berlin,

[46] ACS, 1184-37-11, Voyage de Vander Eycken et Masson à Vienne, 22–24 Mar. 1938.
[47] Hayes (1994); Kobrak (2002), 267.
[48] ACS, 1184-37-11, Note to the *Vorstand*, 11 July 1938, 15.
[49] ACS, RdG, 28 Mar. 1938.
[50] Teichova (1974), 279–81.
[51] Hayes (2001), 233–5.

Viscount Jacques Davignon.[52] But this proved completely useless in view of the pace of German expansionism – and the unwillingness of Western powers to contain it.

At the same time, international business adapted to the reorganization of the Czech chemical industry under German banner. At a meeting held in Paris on 12 December 1938, representatives of Solvay and IG Farben confirmed their previous agreements with regard to the repartition of electrolytic caustic soda and chlorine, with a special eye on southeastern Europe. The compromise they reached showed an increase in IG's production quotas largely at the expense of ICI and Verein. "Overall, we can be satisfied with these arrangements," said a relieved Boël.[53] The immense appetite of IG Farben in the region prompted intensified negotiations between DSW and Verein. Without knowing for sure the nature of the takeover (merger or partnership), the first condition posed by DSW was to apply the process of Aryanization on NSW and, to a lesser extent, on Aussig and Falkenau plants. At NSW, Victor Basch was replaced by an "Aryan," the director of the Technical Department at DSW Bernburg, Hans Drechsler, who consequently acted as head of ESW and NSW under the close scrutiny of DSW. Strong pressure was exerted on Jewish personnel: employees and members of the board had to leave the company.[54] Solvay attempted to find other jobs for most of them. Following an agreement reached between Solvay and the Verein as soon as 25 August 1938, the general direction of Solvay-Verein was transferred from Vienna to Prague in connection with a new office to open in Zürich, whereas Drechsler and the daily administration of ESW and NSW plants stayed in Vienna. As a result, some forty employees of Czech nationality moved to the headquarters in Prague, which officially opened its doors on 6 January 1939 and was run by Victor Skala. His compatriot Victor Basch became member of the *Aufsichtsrat*.[55] As to the combine's, Eudore Lefèvre, he moved to the Zürich office around March 1939, where he was the only employee for a long time.[56]

From Zürich, Lefèvre urged Basch to start thinking about the transfer of a series of major industrial interests owned by Solvay (through Gefucin) and Verein Aussig in southeastern Europe. This concerned the artificial fertilizers company Hungaria, the Yugoslavian Works Zorka, and the Marasesti firm based in Bucharest, all of which were held in the overarching portfolio of Verein Aussig (whose 12.83 percent was held by Solvay through Gefucin). Hence, the Gesellschaft für Soda und Chemische Industrie mbH – more frequently called

[52] ACS, 1001–29-13, Gérants to P.-H. Spaak, 14 Oct. 1938.

[53] ACS, 1151–38-46, RdG, 15 Dec. 1938 (Appendix "Réunion du 12 décembre 1938 à Paris").

[54] ACS, 1184–37-11, Voyage de MM. E. Lefèvre et Masson à Berlin, 18–19 Oct. 1938; ACS, 1184–37-11, Visite de MM. Clemm et H. Eilsberger à Bruxelles, 21 Nov. 1938; ACS, Bunker Archives, NSW Prague, D, Administration-Evénements politiques 1938, Nouvelle organisation, "Note betr. Besprechung einer Organisationsfragen von Nestomitz," 6 Oct. 1938; E. Lefèvre to R. Weiss, 10 Oct. 1938.

[55] ACS, 1151–37-11, Minutes of the meeting in Berlin, 29 Nov. 1938. The official name of the Solvay-Verein company in Prague was Solvay-Gesellschaft mbH für Soda-Erzeugnisse.

[56] ACS, Bunker Archives, NSW Prague, U, Nouvelle Société de Prague, various documents, Nov. 1938.–Mar. 1939.

Soud-Industrie – was legally incorporated in Zürich on 7 December 1938 as a partnership company (with an initial capital of CH 20,000), with Lefèvre as the only managing partner.[57] Put briefly, Soud-Industrie functioned as a dummy corporation within Gefucin for the southeastern European assets jointly held (albeit with different proportions) by Solvay and Verein.[58]

Hopes for a renaissance, however, did not survive the changing political situation. German armies entered Prague on 15 March 1939 and transformed the remains of the country into a protectorate of the Reich. The recent Prague office was put in jeopardy. At this stage, the *gérants* saved what they could. First, they authorized stronger "Germanization" (*Eindeutschung*) of the boards (Drechsler joined the *Aufsichtsrat*). Then, and more surprisingly, they obtained from DSW that Solvay (Brussels) took on the direct management of ESW and NSW, which had been transformed into general partnership companies. "It is understood," Ernest-John Solvay and René Boël told their German colleagues in Berlin in May 1939, "that M. Clemm will remain informed of the main issues."[59] But once again, the accommodation was short lived. Less than a year later, the *gérants* entrusted Clemm and Eilsberger with a proxy enabling them to "represent the interests of the Society Solvay & Cie in the business of the Vienna Group, the Ebensee, Nestomitz, and Prague companies." In fact, more than a traditional proxy, the document specified an "unlimited general mandate."[60] Although it only served "in case of a rupture of relations with Belgium," the Brussels administration already knew how to draft these legal forms. The *Generalvollmacht* it had prepared for Clemm in the defense of Solvay's interests in Poland, Zakłady Solvay, on 9 September 1939, served as a blueprint.[61]

12.3 SOLVAY AT WAR: WITHIN OCCUPIED TERRITORIES

Applying the principles of blitzkrieg tactics to Poland, the German army could quietly consider the opening of a western front. The campaign in France and the Low Countries started on 10 May 1940. Although the Netherlands was defeated in roughly four days, it took two weeks more for Belgium to surrender. France followed suit with the signing of the Armistice on 22 June. By early summer 1940, only Great Britain still contested the domination of the Axis

---

[57] ACS, 1187-45-1, Gesellschaft für Soda und Chemische Industrie mbH (Société à Responsabilité Limitée pour la Soude et l'Industrie Chimique), bylaws.

[58] ACS, 1185-37-7 (1), Note by M. Ebrant, 16 June 1945. Soud-Industrie was to be liquidated by Lefèvre on 31 August 1946, with the remaining capital transferred to the Soudière Suisse (also in Gefucin's portfolio). This wartime financial operation, needless to say, was duly referred to by Solvay & Cie in the enduring negotiations with Czechoslovakian, Hungarian, Romanian, and Yugoslavian government officials to obtain a form of compensation after the nationalization process in Eastern Europe after the war.

[59] ACS, 1184-37-12, Conversation avec M. Drechsler à Berlin (with E. Eilsberger, A. Clemm, and H. Eilsberger), 6 May 1939.

[60] ACS, 1151-45-5, Voyage de MM. Masson et Ebrant à Berlin, 4–6 Apr. 1940. A similar "mandate" was given to Ernst Eilsberger and Graf von der Goltz for DSW.

[61] ACS, 1151-45-5.

powers in Europe. For the Germans, the situation posed a real challenge: the spectacular military campaign had to be transformed into a successful political and economic operation. At Solvay, conversely, it entailed engaging in a race against time to safeguard its interests in Continental Europe.

The Politics of Continuity under the System of *Verwaltung*

On 28 May 1940, the day of the capitulation of the Belgian army, a symbolic event occurred at DSW: the General Assembly appointed Ernst Eilsberger chairman of the *Aufsichtsrat*, replacing Ernest-John Solvay.[62] Two months later, they were informed by his son, Helmut Eilsberger, that IG Farben's director of the Chemicals Committee, Eduard Weber-Andreä, had asked Clemm about a possible takeover of DSW in case of a political opportunity.[63] Confronted with these events, the *gérants* present in Brussels – René Boël had dashed to Paris at the invasion of Belgium (see the following section) – adopted a cautious approach. Ernest-John Solvay feared that the loss of DSW entailed a domino effect on Solvay's interests elsewhere in Europe. He was partly relieved by another IG official, Karl von Heider, who stressed that the discussions with Clemm had been largely preemptive. IG merely wished it could somehow help Solvay.[64] This was, after all, in line with the attitude expressed by IG's chairman of the Commercial Committee, Georg von Schnitzler. During his stay in Brussels as co-chair of the German-Belgian Economic Committee on 15–17 June 1940, Schnitzler had met twice with Ernest-John Solvay and Roger Janssen. He had insisted that IG did not intend to take part in the "orgy of plundering"[65] led by Hermann Göring on the Belgian chemical industry (with, perhaps, the notable exception of the dyes branch) and promised to convince other German chemical companies to show some moderation. In other circles, though, Schnitzler was confident that the appropriate moment would come – and, obviously, IG did its best to make that moment come soon enough.[66]

A more official note eventually came from the head of the Management of Enemy Property (Reichskommissar für die Behandlung Feindlichen Vermögens), Friedrich Sperl. When Ernest-John Solvay and Henri Delwart visited him, Sperl immediately told them that Adolf Clemm had been designated *Verwalter* of Solvay's interests in (Greater) Germany. This meant that DSW plants fell under closer scrutiny from the German administration. But the *Verwaltung* system, Sperl went on, also yielded significant advantages: the plants could pursue their normal activity, and they were not, strictly speaking, considered "enemy property." Put briefly, this system enabled DSW to engage in

---

[62] ACS, 1151–33-2, Visite de M. Clemm et Kreshke, 29 June 1940.
[63] ACS, 1151–37-14, Visite de M. Eilsberger, 30 July 1940. This had been denied a month before, see ACS, 1151–37-14, Visite de M. Clemm et Kreshke, 29 June 1940.
[64] ACS, 1151–37-14, Visite de M. von Heider de l'I.G., 14 Aug. 1940.
[65] The expression was coined by John Gillinham and quoted in Hayes (1987), 274.
[66] Nefors (2006), 92–4; Hayes (1987), 276.

a form of collaboration (*Mitarbeit*) rather than confiscation (*Beschlagname*).[67] In a way, the same applied to the Belgian case, where the "politics of continuity" of economic production had prevailed from the beginning. Its main promoter, the head of the Société Générale de Belgique, Alexandre Galopin, with whom Ernest-John Solvay was in close touch, justified it as a means to avoid the starvation of the population and the enforcement of forced labor.[68] Sperl, likewise, wanted to be reassuring. However, his explanations remained unclear from a legal standpoint. Was the *Verwaltung* a form of nationalization in disguise? How could Solvay exert its right as majority shareholder? At approximately the same time, more information was revealed: Eilsberger junior was entrusted with a special mandate (*Sonderbeauftragter*) for the production of soda in French territory. His jurisdiction comprised Solvay's Dombasle and Tavaux soda ash plants, as well as the plants of Marchéville-Daguin and Saint-Gobain's Varangéville. He had received no instruction whatsoever with regard to the salines of Lorraine or to Sarralbe. This series of nominations, rather helpful to Solvay, did not prevent Ernest-John from addressing Helmut Eilsberger with his "dissatisfaction" concerning the "lack of current relations with Bernburg."[69] Clemm and von der Goltz could not be reached. Ernest-John continued to fear that the *Verwaltung* system would not result in preventing other German companies from rushing in on Solvay's interests in Germany, as elsewhere in Europe.

Ernest-John's pessimism was shared by Clemm, who finally came to Brussels on 2–3 October 1940. The appetite of German chemical companies was growing, the *Verwalter* confidentially confirmed. But he was even more worried that rumors of takeover were not expressed "off the record" anymore; they had become public knowledge. Candidates for a – total or partial – takeover of DSW were, according to Clemm, companies including IG, Kali-Chemie, Henkel, Hermann-Göring Werke, and perhaps others. For various reasons, Clemm trusted that many suitors could be eliminated. IG was Solvay's most redoubtable competitor and its only partner in Germany. But IG's 25 percent holding in DSW could be considered an inconvenience in the eyes of the German Ministry of Economic Affairs (Reichswirtschaftsministerium, or RWM), which was apparently eager to turn down IG's greedy pretensions. Kali-Chemie, closely linked to IG, benefited from the same rationale.[70] Henkel and

---

[67] The *Verwaltung* system referred to a special law for German-based industrial properties owned by neutral countries subsequently occupied by the German army – Norway, Belgium, Luxemburg, and the Netherlands. ACS, 1151-37-14, Visite de MM. Solvay et Delwart chez le Dr. Sperl, 12 Sept. 1940.

[68] Nefors (2006), 5–10, 29–38. Since the polemical publication of Gillingham (1977), the scholarship on the Comité Galopin has been huge.

[69] ACS, 1106-37-1, Entretiens à Paris avec M. Philippe Aubertin, 23 Sept. 1940; ACS, 1151-33-3, Visite du Dr. H. Eilsberger, 21 Sept. 1940. H. Eilsberger's official mission was called Sonderbeauftragter für die Soda- und Aetznatronerzeugung im besetzten Gebiet von Frankreich.

[70] As soon as 16 August 1940, Ernest John Solvay had received a visit from Dutch industrialist Alfred Honigmann, who had expressed interest in Solvay's assets in Germany. He was politely turned down, but it later appeared that he was a go-between acting for Kali-Chemie's Theodore Feise.

Hermann-Göring Werke could be contained by Graf von der Goltz, who happened to have good relations with Göring's secretary of state, Erich Neumann.[71] Finally, Clemm suggested that the best option would be to team up with the firm Salzdetfurth, a well-known member of the Kalisyndikat headed by DSW. He praised the loyalty of its general director, Rudolf Stahl.[72] To some extent, Salzdetfurth's choice was the lesser evil for DSW. But Ernest-John Solvay was determined not to give in unless he was forced to. On 11 October, he and Clemm went to see the head of the Chemical Section at the RWM, Dr. Mülert, who also advised Solvay to find a German partner.[73] In view of the threat, the *gérants* elaborated a strategy of containment that highlighted the international dimension of the Solvay group and the potential for the integration of a European syndicate of chemical products, which was at the core of the Reich's "new economic order."[74]

Outline of a Hands-Off Agreement

Recent news from Berlin prevented them from implementing this defensive strategy. On 21 October 1940, von der Goltz came to Brussels and confirmed the rumors he had heard from his political contacts. The Reich was willing to adopt a hands-off policy toward Solvay's interests in Germany. Moreover, the *Reichskommissar* Sperl had suggested that Ernest-John Solvay join Ernst Eilsberger and Graf von der Goltz in a new advisory board (*Beirat*) in charge of assisting the *Verwalter* Clemm on the most essential issues concerning DSW. Finally, the tightening of Clemm's attributions with the *Beirat* was offset by the extension of his jurisdiction over the plants of Ebensee and Nestomitz, Solvay's plants in Solvay-Verein, and in the Ostdeutsche Chemische Werke, the former Zakłady industrial group whose headquarters had been transferred from Warsaw to Krakow, and from there to Poznań.[75] Obviously, the Germans had favored the politics of *Mitarbeit* over *Beschlagname*. This, however, did not prevent the Polish factories of the former Zakłady group to be converted into forced labor camps (as was the case with Montwy) or outlets for nearby concentration camps (as in Podgórze). On a business perspective, the hands-off policy gave way to a compensation designed for IG Farben. Von der Goltz alluded to the interests Solvay had with Verein in southeastern Europe. He pointed to

---

[71] This was a welcome opportunity. In the early months of 1939, the Hermann-Göring Werke had diversely appreciated Solvay's maneuvers to prevent the company from setting up a plant running the Gluud process for gas purification (ACS, 1151-38-42, Conversation téléphonique de M. Boël avec M. Clemm, 28 Feb. 1939).

[72] ACS, 1151-37-14, Conversations avec M. Clemm, 2–3 Oct. 1940.

[73] ACS, 1151-37-14, Minutes of the meeting, 11 Oct. 1940.

[74] ACS, 1151-37-14, "Examen de diverses solutions relatives à notre participation dans les DSW," 14 Oct. 1940.

[75] The gatherings of the *Beirat* took approximately place twice a year. It had been set up by Sperl due to Clemm's health issues but against his will. Therefore, personal difficulties undermined the *Beirat* throughout the war. See ACS, 1151-37-14, RdG 31 Mar. 1942 (Appendix: "Voyage de M. Solvay à Berlin, 23–27 mars 1942"; ACS, 1151-55-2, "Voyage de MM. Solvay, Delwart et Masson à Berlin, 17–18 juin 1943," 23 June 1943).

the artificial fertilizers company Hungaria (of which Solvay held 33.25 percent of the capital through Gefucin), the Yugoslavian Works Zorka (held at 26.42 percent with Verein), and the Marasesti firm based in Bucharest.[76] Leaving these to IG Farben was a way to offset the unsuccessful aims of the concern on DSW – and to divert IG's appetite in these regions, where its interests were frustrated by Verein.[77] This information prompted Ernest-John Solvay to go to Berlin, where he stayed from 22 to 26 November 1940 with Paul Masson. There, he and Clemm met a handful of high civil servants from the RWM who, by and large, confirmed von der Goltz's assertions (the official decision had been taken by the secretary of state of the RWM, Friedrich Landfried, on 12 November 1940). Later, at a meeting with IG's powerful lobbyist and board member, Max Ilgner, Solvay and Clemm were told that a group of German chemical companies formed by IG, Chemische Fabrik von Heyden, and Rütgerswerke wished to reach an "economic collaboration" with Verein with respect to some of the companies it controlled in southeastern Europe. According to Ilgner, the group particularly aimed at the special chemicals, dyes, and pharmaceuticals manufactured by Verein. He appealed to Solvay's favorable influence on Verein, which Ernest-John conceded after he obtained the immediate approval of his Czech partners.[78] The discussions held in Berlin among Solvay, Clemm, and some of IG's main directors (Schmitz, von Schnitzler, and Weber-Andreä) formed the basis of a "protocol" of understanding signed by both parties.[79]

The decision taken by the RWM on 12 November 1940 was a major achievement for Solvay in terms of business-state diplomacy. Looking back at these negotiations in hindsight,[80] it is tempting to emphasize the fruitful intermediation of Graf von der Goltz and Adolf Clemm, in the political and industrial milieus, respectively (Clemm's direction of the WiGru Chemie was certainly not useless). But this is only partly true. A third man played a role that could be truly qualified as capital. Hermann Josef Abs was managing director of the Deutsche Bank, among other influential positions.[81] Abs was appointed member of the

[76] ACS, 1151-37-14, "Résumé des conversations avec le Comte von der Goltz," 21–22 Oct. 1940; ACS, 1151-37-14, "Examen de diverses solutions," 14 Oct. 1940; Teichova (1974), 281.

[77] Hayes (2001), 232–9, 276.

[78] ACS, 1151-37-14, Voyage de MM. Solvay et Masson à Berlin (22–26 Nov. 1940), f. 4: Minutes of the meeting with Dr. Ilgner at Hotel Adlon, Berlin, 22 Nov. 1940; f. 5: Minutes of conversations with MM. Dvoracek and Martinek (Verein), 25–26 Nov. 1940; f. 6: Meeting held at the Ländersbank (Berlin) with H. Schmitz, Schnitzler, and Weber-Andreä, 26 Nov. 1940.

[79] ACS, 1151-37-14, Clemm to E.-J. Solvay, 30 Nov. 1940 (Appendix: Protokol). The document terminates by these lines: "M. Solvay states that he agrees with these efforts in the direction of a European cooperation [i.e., of industrial collaboration between IG and Verein], to which he gives full support inasmuch as he is concerned, adding that it has always been the guideline of Solvay & Cie and that it has always followed it."

[80] ACS, 1151-37-24 (5), "Bericht über Deutsche-Solvay Werke AG, Bernburg," established by the Reichskommissar für die Behandlung feindlichen Vermögens, 25 Feb. 1946 (a copy of this essential thirty-four-page memorandum was held by the British Military Administration and sent to the Belgian Ministry of Foreign Affairs, and then to Solvay & Cie, via the British Embassy in Brussels, on 13 May 1946).

[81] On Abs's multifaceted yet controversial role during the war, see Gall (1999); James (2004); Czichon (1970), 126–7, 130, 139, 142. Czichon's account is polemical (the first edition was

Aufsichtsrat of DSW on 28 May 1940. Less than a month later, he also joined the *Aufsichtsrat* of IG Farben, although he had told Schmitz about him sitting on the supervisory board of the competitor Solvay.[82] By late August 1940, he came to Brussels to persuade Alexandre Galopin to strengthen relations between the Société Générale and the Deutsche Bank (and to override the Dresdner Bank in this respect). Well aware of the substantial interests of the Société Générale, as well as its rival the Banque de Bruxelles, in Czechoslovakia, Romania, and the Balkans, Abs's aim was to develop a large network of financial institutions in southeastern Europe under the domination of Deutsche Bank.[83] This mission coincided with his position at Solvay in many respects. He stopped by at the *gérance* on 22 and 23 August 1940, where he was informed about the threats of absorption of DSW.[84] But the next time he paid the *gérants* a visit was on 4 November 1940. He then laid out the underpinnings of the hands-off policy, which would be officially adopted by the RWM only two weeks later. Abs, needless to say, was well informed and well connected. Moreover, he was well placed to have forged the idea of "trading" interests held by Solvay (with Verein) in southeastern Europe for the preservation of DSW's capital. Before the war broke out, he had been the one exhorting the Creditanstalt, controlled by Deutsche Bank, to sell to Solvay (and Verein) shares in the Yugoslavian Works Zorka, precisely one of the companies in IG's line of fire.[85] The trust that Solvay put in Abs was such that he became member of the *Beirat* on 6 March 1943, a year after Graf von der Goltz was appointed adjunct *Verwalter* (*Verwalterstellvertreter*) to Clemm on 23 April 1942.[86] But his activity for Solvay proved even more instrumental after the war (see Chapter 13).

Labor and Production Trends in German-Dominated Europe

The organizational changes at DSW, and the results achieved with the RWM, had significant repercussions on work-force management and production levels in Solvay plants throughout German-dominated Europe. The decision of *Reichskommissar* Sperl that led to Ernest-John Solvay's designation as member of the *Beirat* on 23 October 1940 allowed the latter to obtain the information he had required about the general course of industrial activities. In view of the difficulties of communication between Brussels and Bernburg (or Berlin), this was not negligible – it gave Solvay an inside view on the wartime development of its German subsidiary. The harnessing of DSW to the war effort yielded profitable results, especially during the last semester of 1940. The inclusion of

---

banned by a judgment of the Stuttgart District Court after Abs complained) but remains good for finding facts.

[82] Gall (1999), 190.

[83] Nefors (2006), 74–5; James (2004), 125–6; Teichova (1974), 343–57.

[84] ACS, 1151-37-14, Visite de M. Abs, 22 Aug. 1940; ACS, 1151-37-14, RdG, 22 Aug. 1940.

[85] James (2004), 125; ACS, 1151-37-14, Visite de M. Abs et Kurzmeyer, 4 Nov. 1940; ACS, 1151-37-14, Voyage de MM. Solvay et Masson à Berlin (22–26 Nov. 1940), f. 5: Minutes of conversations with MM. Dvoracek and Martinek (Verein), 25–26 Nov. 1940.

[86] ACS, 1151-33-4, Meeting of the *Beirat*, Berlin, 24 Mar. 1942; ACS, 1151-33-7, RdG, 31 Mar. 1942.

Eastern provinces in the German Reich offset the relative decline of foreign sales for a while (DSW announced an increase of 5 percent of its overall output in 1940 over 1939).[87] But as soon as 1941, shortages of raw materials and labor difficulties precluded the works to run at full capacity – an experience shared by all Solvay plants in France and Belgium at the time.[88] Besides, the numerous obstacles to the international flow of capital, which were visible since 1938, made it almost impossible to allow expenditures for planned investments. A creative accounting system took place between Solvay and DSW that partly counterbalanced these shortcomings.[89] Last but not least, the use of the *Beirat* was equally essential in providing Ernest-John Solvay with a strategic view, rather than a direct say, of the pursuit of prewar international agreements, particularly sensitive in the electrolytic field – and the pursuit of negotiations with IG Farben concerning respect of the "pool agreement" signed in 1938.[90]

As mentioned, the war had ushered in major changes in the labor situation. The number of mobilized workers at all DSW plants rose from 1,100 in August 1940 to 2,181 in September 1944. Available data show that the workforce grew accordingly throughout the war. From 7,167 workers and employees in January 1939, the highest point was reached, with 9,581, in September 1944. Female workers and German labor conscripts had been requested to fill the gap, but this proved hardly sufficient for the demands of the war economy. Then forced labor came along. A postwar report estimated at 1,200 the total number of prisoners of war and foreign civilians working in the various DSW plants during the war, with a huge turnover due to illness and escapes.[91] In comparison with IG Farben plants, where foreign laborers accounted for a maximum of 25 percent of the total work force by November 1941, the proportion of the foreign work force seems to have been smaller at DSW.[92] But the phenomenon was nonetheless striking. Some of the forced laborers – the bulk of the alleged willing civilian workers – were paid a normal wage; the others received a modest allowance akin to pocket money. Their national origins varied greatly, whether sent to Germany or to Austria. At Hallein, the wartime foreign work force was broken down as follows: 172 prisoners of war (Serbs, Slovenes, and Bosnians); fifty-one foreign civilians (Italians and French); and twenty-seven so-called *Ostarbeiters* (Eastern workers), which referred pejoratively to civilian workers from the German-occupied territories of the Soviet Union.[93]

[87] ACS, 1151-37-14, First meeting of the *Beirat*, Berlin, 23 Nov. 1940.
[88] ACS, 1151-55-2, "Exposé de l'activité générale de la société. Exercice 1942," May 1943.
[89] For instance, in December 1943, DSW reimbursed the loan it had with Solvay & Cie (which was a conversion from the tied-up profits of Solvay & Cie in Germany) through a purchase of IG Farben shares made in January 1942 (ACS, 1001-28-38, "Aperçu relatif à l'activité de Solvay & Cie pendant la période 1940–1944 (résumé fait pour M. Boël) – Allemagne," 9, s.d. [Sept. 1944].
[90] ACS, 1001-25-16, "Conversation à Berlin avec M. Weber-Andreä," 20 Jan. 1942; ACS, 1001-25-16, "Entretien avec M. von Heider de l'I.G.," 19 Nov. 1941.
[91] ACS, 1151-37-24 (5), "Bericht," 27 Feb. 1946, 18–9. On forced labor, see Spoerer and Fleischhacker (2002).
[92] Abelshauser et al. (2004), 311–12.
[93] ACS, 37-1-A; Praml (1998), 11.

Rheinberg's foreign work force comprised about a hundred of prisoners of war, most of them French, Russians, Poles, Ukrainians, and Italians; there were also some twenty women from Ukraine and Poland. Interestingly, the majority of French civilian workers came from Solvay's Dombasle and Tavaux plants. The intermediation of the *Sonderbeauftragter* Helmut Eilsberger seemed to have been critical in reducing their number and orienting their posts.[94]

The Threat of Nationalization in Italy

The German episode had inspired other companies. The Italian chemical concern Montecatini, which was in business with IG Farben in many ways since their joint takeover of the Aziende Chimiche Nazionali Associate in 1931, was certainly one of them.[95] As soon as the war broke out, Montecatini's chairman Guido Donegani made no mystery of his intentions to take advantage of the war to dismember Solvay's Rosignano works. An early adherent to the party, Donegani had all the fascist networks at his disposal to fulfill his ambition. But he needed an industrial ally to eliminate allegations of personal greediness. He thus asked Franco Marinotti, head of SNIA Viscosa, to join him in the plundering. For the manufacturing of its artificial silk products, SNIA Viscosa was absorbing no less than half of Rosignano's caustic soda domestic sales (whereas Montecatini's share amounted to 5 percent).[96] Marinotti thus had some motivation to embark on Donegani's scheme. But he also had good reason to hesitate; he had never had to complain about Solvay's treatment of his company – quite the contrary. Informed by Van Caubergh's alarmist memos, Ernest-John Solvay was asked to go to Italy, where he spent several weeks during the summer of 1941. He discovered that the company's organizational setup there did not help solve these issues. The militarization of Italian plants had led to an important redeployment of Solvay's higher management. Two men who were close to the local fascist regime, Giuseppe Dolazza and Giorgio Tremi, had replaced Van Caubergh as general directors of Solvay Italy. With the support of the *gérance*, Van Caubergh was able to remain in the – previously inexistent – posts of technical adviser and "Solvay's general representative in Italy."[97]

Meanwhile, Ernest-John Solvay's pressure on Marinotti proved fruitful; the leader of SNIA Viscosa secretly promised to retrocede 49 percent of the 50 percent he would receive in the case of nationalization.[98] At the same time, the political context was threatening the deal as a whole. By the spring of 1941, rumors of a huge nationalization plan of foreign companies came to the fore, forcing Ernest-John Solvay to plan a third stay in Italy in less than a semester. War expenses put the Italian economy at strains and the Duce was lacking

---

[94] Rupprecht (2007), 88–90; Ducordeaux et al. (2005), 98–9.

[95] A useful business history is Amatori and Bezza (1990).

[96] Mioche (2009), 38–9.

[97] ACS, 1001–28–38, "Aperçu Boël – Italie," s.d. [Sept. 1944].

[98] ACS, "Voyages de M. Solvay en Italie – 1941," various memos and correspondence. Unless otherwise noted, this section draws on this material.

alternatives. Obviously, Solvay could not rely *orbi et urbi* on the clauses of the hands-off policy crafted by the German RWM. During the first days of his stay (6 November–1 December 1941), Ernest-John came to hear that the nationalization decree was promulgated on 30 September 1941 but did not affect "non-enemy companies." Pragmatic principles had prevailed in Mussolini's reflections: as Italy needed to borrow money from abroad, a nationalization law was not opportune at that moment. Unsurprisingly, this was not to Donegani's liking. The head of Montecatini immediately engaged in a state-of-the-art lobby operation, which amounted to a marathon, considering the fascist bureaucracy. Marinotti told Donegani that he had no intention of teaming up with him, and in a conversation he had with Ernest-John Solvay on 11 November 1941, he assured him that he would steer completely clear of Donegani's maneuvers. Marinotti's flip-flop was also guided by the international ramifications of his company; Saint-Gobain, for instance, had warned about repercussions if SNIA were to take advantage of the nationalization process.

Donegani's reckless behavior prompted Ernest-John Solvay to proceed to a counterlobbying offensive. After a promising meeting with the minister of corporations, Renato Ricci, on 12 November, the upper management of Solvay Italy – Dolazza and Tremi – urged Ernest-John to request a personal hearing with the Duce. Solvay, apparently, hesitated. He eventually met Mussolini on 24 November in the late afternoon at the Palazzo Venezia in Rome. The minutes of the meeting were transcribed by Ernest-John Solvay himself. The Duce gave him his guarantee that this "affair was considered as solved" at Solvay's advantage. After the discussion, which lasted twenty-five minutes, Ernest-John was apparently satisfied: he drank *spumante* at the dinner with Van Caubergh, Tremi, and Dolazza. Ironically, the copy of the Solvay-Montecatini contract of 1934, which proved crucial during the meeting in bringing Mussolini to a favorable decision, had been retrieved by Dolazza only two days before the summit. This amply justifies the usefulness of a well-organized collection of corporate archives.

12.4   SOLVAY AT WAR: IN GREAT BRITAIN AND THE AMERICAS

While Ernest-John Solvay wartime activities took place in European territories under the control of the Axis powers, René Boël devoted a fair amount of his time as *gérant*-in-exile reorganizing Solvay's networks overseas and putting them along the lines set by the Allies. Hence, their wartime experience was unparallel as it can be – and this was about to have direct repercussions with regard to the company's postwar development. But if there was a common point between René Boël and Ernest-John Solvay's respective line of action during the conflict, it was their constant effort to ensure Solvay its prewar autonomy and, at the same time, make sure that the company would not fall in the category of "enemy property." This situation, an apparent paradox, resulted from the company's irremediable intertwining with international politics; this proved no less difficult in the United States than in Germany.

FIGURE 12.2. Rosignano, destroyed by American bombing in June 1940. (Solvay Rosignano Archives.)

Gérant-in-Exile: René Boël in London and Washington

Shortly before the end of the war, as the *gérance* faced an important reorganization, Louis Solvay insisted on discussing directly with René Boël – "the war years have matured him," he said.[99] Considering the latter's individual odyssey through these years, this seems utterly irrefutable.[100] After a three-week stay in the United States, René Boël arrived in Brussels on 10 May 1940 at 2:30 A.M. A couple of hours later, German troops began to invade Belgium. As a military officer, Boël immediately responded to the call to duty of the Belgian army. At the request of the Belgian Ministry of Defense, he was in charge of setting up the liaison between Brussels and the Anglo-French Coordinating Committee, which was headed by an old acquaintance, Solvay's legal counsel in the United States, Jean Monnet.[101] Based in London after the surrender of France, Boël was subsequently asked by the minister of finance of the Belgian government-in-exile, Camille Gutt, to supervise various trade and industrial

[99] ACS, DS 376, "Discussion avec Louis Solvay" by E.-J. Solvay, 30 Mar. 1945.

[100] For the attention of his colleagues of the *gérance*, René Boël reported his wartime activity in three separate notebooks with a series of appendixes. These reports were written at various stages of the war: August 1941, July 1942, and June 1944. Only two of the three notebooks were found in the company's archives.

[101] ACS-O, "Note pour la gérance de la Société Solvay" by René Boël, Box 1, vol. 1 (Apr. 1940–Aug. 1941), Aug. 1941 (hereafter "war notes Boël"), 2–3; Interview with Ida Boël, 27 Nov. 2007.

agreements between the Allies and occupied Belgium.[102] As a result, from the invasion of Belgium until 21 September 1940, his activity for Solvay was almost nonexistent. The only exception was his successful endeavor to avoid Solvay's capital in Great Britain falling under the Trading with the Enemy Act, which would have resulted in the transfer, and freezing, of shares to the custodian of enemy property. In harmony with ICI leaders, Lord McGowan and Jack Nicholson, Boël managed to have ICI officially ensure the control of these assets during the war. Boël's most important financial move, though, had been undertaken back in July 1938. After the Anschluss and the prospect of a political turmoil in or around Switzerland, Boël requested that the bulk of Solvay's ICI shares (approximately £2.6 million) be transferred from Gefucin to Losanac (Montreal) through the Nova Scotia Trust Company. This transfer from Switzerland to Canada, surely decisive in retrospect, also included three hundred thousand shares of Solvay American Corporation (SAC, successor of SAIC), which represented 23 percent of the capital of Allied Chemical held by Solvay (approximately $3.8 million).[103] Taking these financial stakes into account, it is no wonder that Boël asked Camille Gutt for permission to pay his American colleagues a visit, the first one since the invasion of Belgium.

After departing from Lisbon (where he met Solvay's representative and director of Soda Povoa, Clément Dumoulin), René Boël arrived in New York on 11 October 1940. His previous stay had taken place six months earlier (11–27 April 1940) in a context that deserves a little explanation. By late February 1940, Orlando Weber had taken advantage of the "war conditions" in Europe to denounce the allegedly un-American behavior of Solvay's representative at the board of Allied, George Murnane. Through the mouth of Allied's acting chairman, Henry Atherton, Weber had threatened to exclude Murnane from the list of directors to be reelected at the stockholders' meeting scheduled for 29 April 1940.[104] Informed by their legal counsel, John Foster Dulles, the *gérants* feared the prospect of a reproduction of the nightmarish declaration of independence that had taken place during World War I (see Chapter 7). Immediately sent overseas, René Boël was urged by his colleagues to not let such a thing happen. Foster Dulles, in contrast, warned him against undertaking a direct action against Weber or Atherton. The method they agreed on was to form a voting trust within the board of Allied. Through a trust agreement, the group of trustees committed to control the stock of SAC in a direction that could not run counter Solvay's interests. Besides George Murnane, the selected directors were the financiers John C. Traphagen and Thomas Debevoise, both of whom were in line with Solvay's policy, in close touch with the personnel of SAC, and were American citizens.[105] Risky as it was, the strategy paid off: no shareholder opposed the choice of directors. For the second time since the

[102] Jones (1988); ACS-O, war notes Boël, 1:2–5.
[103] At the time, however, the initiative had stirred some complaints from members of the supervisory board (ACS, Viscount Guy de Jonghe Collection, Paul-Casimir Lambert to Conseil de Surveillance, s.d. [Sept. 1938]); ACS, "Répertoire des participations soldées," SAIC.
[104] ACS, 1271-37-14 (12), John Foster Dulles (Sullivan & Cromwell) to gérance, 7 Mar. 1940.
[105] ACS, 1271-37-14 (12), "Voyage aux États-Unis, 11–27 avril 1940" by R. Boël, undated.

events of 1934 and 1935 (see Chapter 9), Weber was defeated by the duo of Boël and Foster Dulles. In addition, the initiative had firmly secured Solvay's foreign capital away from the occupied territories.

Upon his arrival in October 1940, Boël was relieved to learn that the voting trust that he had established was still effective despite Weber's continuous attacks. However, the situation of war, as well as growing nationalism, prevented Boël from playing a major role in Solvay's business in the Americas. Even his friend Foster Dulles had advised him not to give the impression that he was actually running things. As a result, during the whole of his stays in the United States (October 1940–August 1941 and March 1941–July 1942), Boël's activity was torn between two contradictory poles: acting behind the screen and striving for legal recognition of his position as *gérant* of Solvay in territories that were not under German control. The latter issue took up a considerable part of his workload, especially during his second stay in the United States.[106] Underlying Boël's efforts was his intention to supervise the production trends in Solvay's plants located in neutral countries in Europe. He therefore applied an efficient procedure of worldwide circulation of information that included plant managers in Spain (Norbert Fonthier), Portugal (Clément Dumoulin), and Switzerland (Jules Jacob for Zurzach and Eudore Lefèvre for the Zürich-based Solvay-Verein).[107] A third aspect of Boël's manifold activity was to complete the securing of Solvay's financial setup overseas. This mainly involved reinforcing the power of the voting trust and shifting the administration of Solvay's assets from SAC to Losanac under the control of Felix Notebaert. The transfer of financial resources from New York (then New Jersey) to Montreal was not purely coincidental. Boël obviously wanted to regain room for maneuvering, but he also intended to take some distance from the strong antitrust policy adopted by the American government. On 16 March 1944, the public authorities' pressure – nurtured by some competitors – led to a case filed against the constituents of the US Alkali Export Association (Alkasso) under the provisions of the Sherman Antitrust Act.[108] Although Solvay seemed to have been less affected by this complaint than its British partner ICI, the situation called for a subtler repartition of the international alkali export trade.

Mission to Rio: Solvay's Foot in Brazil

In his report to the *gérants*, Boël stated bluntly that "the most important matter in the relations between Solvay and ICI [during the first years of the war] concerned South America."[109] Already in the early 1930s, ICI together with its partner DuPont (with which it launched the joint enterprise Duperial) were already well established in the explosives industry in Argentina and, to a lesser

---

[106] ACS-O, war notes Boël, Box 1, 2:23–38.
[107] ACS-O, war notes Boël, Box 1, 2:47–51; ACS-O, war notes Boël, Box 3, various correspondence.
[108] Glasscock (1969), 52–3.
[109] ACS-O, war notes Boël, Box 1, 1:32.

extent, in Brazil.[110] Shortly after the Depression, the demand for alkali and
chlorine products witnessed particular growth in Brazil under its authoritarian
President Getúlio Vargas. The idea of national production came once again
to the fore. In 1934, ICI engineers started preliminary drillings in Cabo Frio,
about 110 kilometers east of Rio de Janeiro. In September 1938, after lengthy
negotiations with the British, Solvay was able to obtain a share of the Brazilian
pie, which had always exclusively belonged to ICI.[111] A meeting took place
in Paris on 14 March 1940 with Ernest-John Solvay, Philippe Aubertin, and
René Boël, which basically confirmed the building of a soda ash plant and an
electrolytic unit, jointly run – and funded – by ICI, Solvay, and DuPont (via
Duperial Brazil). The outbreak of the war and Duperial's eventual withdrawal
from the arrangement stalled the process for a while, but both Boël and ICI
leaders (Arthur Purvis in particular) were determined to move forward. A
mission to Brazil was planned, which, in view of Boël's agenda, departed at
the end of April 1941. It included Brunner, Mond's vice chairman, J. Lincoln
Steel, and the Belgian engineer Gaston Verhas.[112]

On 26 June 1941, the group met President Vargas, who gave his consent
to carry on the search for rock salt in the region of Cabo Frio. The creation
of two companies was approved: Industrias Chimicas Alcalinas (which subsequently became Industrias Brasileiras Alcalinas, or IBA) and Industrias Chimicas Electro-Chloro (Electro-Chloro), a soda ash plant and electrolytic unit,
respectively.[113] Obstacles came where least expected – in the United States.
Growing concerns about antitrust policies, given the US army's participation
in the war effort, had induced Solvay's American trustees (as well as Foster
Dulles) to hold back from investing in the Brazilian venture. Boël, needless to
say, was stunned. "Solvay & Cie," he observed, "is now stuck in this ridiculous
position: on the one hand, it has promised ICI the sun, moon, and stars in Brazil
(albeit within reasonable boundaries) and has thus received a participation in
the Brazilian business after pleading for a joint project; on the other hand, it
is now in the impossibility to meet its commitments."[114] The situation forced
Boël to transfer a first allowance of $100,000 from his private resources. In the
end, however, he found some consolation in the fact that the little Solvay "had
achieved was still more than what ICI was allowed to do."[115]

Boël's efforts in Brazil paved the way to a redeployment of Solvay's position
in the postwar international trade of alkali and chlorine products. In July 1942,
Boël returned to London to focus on his function of economic adviser to the
Belgian government-in-exile. This opened him up new horizons pertaining to

---

[110] Reader (1975), 219–25.
[111] ACS, RdG 22 Sept. 1938; Glasscock (1969), 26. It also comprised a portion in Electrochlor
Argentina. See ACS, black binder "ICI-Solvay, Argentina," vol. 18.
[112] ACS-O, war notes Boël, "Voyage au Brésil, 3 mai-7 juillet 1941," Box 1, appendix 35, 1–2.
[113] ACS-O, war notes Boël, Box 1, 1:34; ACS-O, war notes Boël, "Voyage au Brésil, 3 mai-7 juillet
1941," Box 1, Appendix 35, 18 bis, 24.
[114] ACS-O, war notes Boël, Box 1, 2:44.
[115] ACS-O, war notes Boël, Box 1, 2:45. Losanac was eventually used as financial vehicle to finance
Solvay's share in Electro-Chloro and to cover research expenditures in Brazil, for a total of
$800,000.

the international public administration (intergovernment monetary and financial negotiations in London, participation in the UN Relief and Rehabilitation Administration in Washington in October 1943, Belgian economic adviser at the Bretton Woods Conference in June 1944).[116] In a way, these activities prefigured the new model of relationships between business and state that would develop after the war.

[116] ACS, DS 366, RdG, 26 Sept. 1944.

FIGURE 13.1. The Solvay Trial at Bernburg, 14 December 1950. (Photographer: Walter Heilig. Bundesarchiv, Berlin.)

13

Solvay's Second Postwar Period

The destruction of the Third Reich, after six years of intense struggle, left Europe in an unprecedented state of desolation and agony. The death of more than forty million soldiers and civilians haunted the atmosphere of the living, and the influx of refugees and expellees rushing westward was a reminder of the scars of the conflict laid bare in Europe. With insidious irony, the immediate postwar era in no way marked a watershed from the previous years. To some extent, the period stretching between 1945 and 1950, labeled the "Brutal Peace" by historian Mark Mazower, witnessed a transition from one war to another – the Cold War.[1] On the political spectrum, Europe witnessed the sudden shift from a liberal antifascist democracy to the traditional model of conservative democracy in the West and the building of communist people's democracies in the East.

Nowhere was the observation more accurate, or the outcomes more visible, than in Germany, which the circumstances of history had transformed into a chaotic political laboratory. In the western territories occupied by the Allied military authorities, industrial firms were pressed to come to terms with the requirements of deconcentration and decartelization that American planners were eager to infuse in corporate milieus, especially outside the United States.[2] As one could have assumed, consistency in the pursuit of this noble dream was far from obvious. There was a huge gap not only between theoretical provisions and their enforcement but also, and more interestingly, between the chosen modus operandi of the Allied military administrations. The situation of IG Farben, whose works were located in the four zones occupied by the Allied powers, is a case in point.[3] What happened to the chemical industry in the Soviet zone, however, is far less elaborated on in the historiography.[4] The fact that Solvay owned fifteen factories and mines in territories occupied by the Russians makes this episode even more fascinating.

At a glance, it would be fair to assume that the parallels between Solvay's respective experiences of the two postwar eras outweigh the differences. In this comparative exercise, however, "to discern parallels is not to claim identities."[5]

[1] Mazower (1999), 215–17.
[2] Berghahn (1985), 84–110.
[3] Stokes (1988).
[4] Karlsch (2000).
[5] Maier (1981), 330.

Therefore, losses of plants, instable market conditions, industrial reorganization, and the increasing intervention of the state in economic affairs could be listed in the category of parallels. Conversely, the major differences between both postwar eras lay in the considerable vagueness vis-à-vis the reordering of the geopolitical arena, on the one hand, and the magnitude of the losses, on the other hand. This chapter intends to shed some light on both these dimensions. The strategies of growth and diversification adopted by the *gérants* approximately at the same time are covered in detail in Chapter 15. The most peculiar aspect of Solvay's second postwar period, one should note, is seeing the company seeking to rapidly shift gears and move ahead in a broader world, but with one foot stuck in the Old World, struggling with its past.

13.1   A DIFFICULT TRANSITION

The View from the *Gérance*

Similar to the political environment, it took some time for Solvay's top management to stabilize. Back in office in September 1944, René Boël kept his colleagues of the *gérance* informed of his activities abroad during the war – and then he took off again. Until the summer of 1945, Boël would frequently assist the Belgian minister of finance Camille Gutt, spending a fair amount of his time between London and Washington. Yet there were urgent matters to tackle in Brussels. Interestingly, another issue preoccupied Ernest-John Solvay more deeply, namely the reorganization of the *gérance* given the planned retirement of Louis Solvay and Émile Tournay. This inevitably stirred a significant number of colorful discussions. Ultimately, it was decided that three new members would step in between March 1945 and May 1947 – Henry Delwart, Jean-Louis Semet, and Pierre Solvay.[6] The change is worth noting for at least two reasons: the newcomers were the first *gérants* born after 1900, and it was the last collective reorganization before Solvay & Cie became a public company in 1967.

As he was in command in Nazi-dominated Europe, Ernest-John Solvay felt responsible in leading Solvay in the difficult transition from war to peace in Belgium. Judicial authorities were paying particular attention to economic collaboration. Like all other Belgian companies, Solvay had to comply with the "Survey for Industrial Activity during the Occupation," prepared by the Ministry of Justice and the Ministry of Economic Affairs. Despite the pressure exerted, the repression eventually concerned only a handful of entrepreneurs who had diverted far from the borders of the "politics of continuity" designed by Alexandre Galopin in 1940.[7] In Italy, legislation set up political cleansing committees (Commissione di Epurazione) in all kinds of companies in July 1944. Plant managers at Monfalcone applied the executive order by distinguishing "political purge," "nonpolitical purge," and "moral purge." As a

---

[6] ACS, DS 369, R. Gendebien and Ph. Aubertin to E. Tournay, 29 Nov. 1944; ACS, DS 372, R. Boël to E.-J. Solvay, 14 Dec. 1944; ACS, DS 376, E.-J. Solvay to L. Solvay, 30 Mar. 1945.
[7] ACS, RdG 15 Feb. 1945; ACS, 1001–4, G. Janson to E.-J. Solvay, 20 Sept. 1945; Luyten (1998), (2010). On the Fabelta-Fibranne case, see ACS, RdG 22 June 1944; Nefors (2006), 273–6; Luyten (1996), 176–7.

result, between July and November 1945, the work force decreased from 714 to 660.[8] Everywhere in Europe, the long-lasting liberation ushered in a period of turmoil and uncertainty.

Ten months elapsed between the first meeting of the entire *gérance* in liberated Belgium (26 September 1944) and the first detailed account of the situation of Solvay's factories in Central and Eastern Europe (27 July 1945). Between these dates – and beyond – the information available was scarce and of poor quality; it naturally gave way to misconceptions. In March 1945, Jean-Louis Semet attempted to draw a distinction between a category of plants "which are or will be occupied by the Allied authorities prior the termination of military operations – Aniene, Rosignano, Aspropyrgos, Polish factories, Linne-Herten, Rheinberg, Borth (Wyhlen, Monfalcone, Ferrare?)" and "the other factories in Germany and Austria," which would be accessible only after the hostilities. For that latter group, "we will have the local personnel and should merely ensure a proper link with the occupying authorities; occasional visits from one of our delegates should suffice."[9] Also in March 1945, Ernest-John Solvay submitted to the head director of the Belgian Ministry of Foreign Affairs, Max Suetens, a memorandum listing Solvay's subsidiaries in Europe. Factories were classified according to a Western-Eastern divide. Bernburg and the German plants located in Saxony belonged to the West, whereas the Austrian factories Ebensee and Hallein were in the East.[10]

Germany, Anno 1945

An important stipulation of the Yalta Conference (February 1945) was the division – and partition – of Germany into four zones of occupation. By April 1945, the big-three powers (the Allies without the French) had further come to the conclusion that Nazi officials should be prosecuted as war criminals and that all Germans should be denazified (and reeducated). But until the Potsdam Agreement (July–August 1945), no consensus had been reached on the final territorial configuration of Germany.[11] Hence, many German regions were liberated without clear insight into their administrative outcome. This was the case of Bernburg, which was liberated by the Third U.S. Armored Division on 16 April 1945. With the exception of the train station bombed on 11 April by the US Air Force, the town and the factory were not damaged. But the situation wreaked havoc in the social fabric.[12] Of a workforce of 3,000 at the start of the war, only 1,600 workers and employees were still active at the Bernburg soda plants (relying mostly on the reserves). In June and July, 300 workers were requested to repair the train tracks and the bridges over the Saale that had

---

[8] ACS, 1137-37-5, Solvay & Cie Direzione Generale per l'Italia – Monfalcone, "Rapport administratif," 12 Dec. 1945, 4–7, 39, 43. On legal documents regarding the *epurazione*, see ACS, 1130–47-18.

[9] ACS, 1151–37-24 (1), "Surveillance technique et administrative des usinées libérées ou conquises par les armées alliées" by J.-L. Semet, 16 Mar. 1945.

[10] ACS, 1151–37-24 (1), "Protection de nos intérêts à l'étranger," Appendix memorandum, 7 Mar. 1945.

[11] Berghahn (1982), 179–80.

[12] Kemper and Lorenz (2008), 34.

been destroyed during the withdrawal of the German army. The lack of coal and transportation impediments prevented Solvay's plants in the region from producing soda ash at a normal capacity (production dropped from 1,200 to 400 tons per day). As a means to lower unemployment, working hours had been reduced to thirty hours per week. Bernburg plant managers even agreed with the nearby Sunlicht Gesellschaft AG to produce soap and cleaning products on the premises.[13] Food supplies and urgent relief were organized by the US military forces, which were rapidly overwhelmed by the needs of the population. On Labor Day (1 May 1945), the head of the Technical Department, Ernst Dörffel, attempted to reassure workers, announcing that "the company Solvay will do whatever it takes to provide for wages and bread."[14]

By mid-June 1945, prior to the Potsdam Conference, news came of the rapid progression of the Russian Army. This prompted the westward escape of several members of the upper management of DSW, including engineers and skilled technicians. The evacuation, however, had not been completely spontaneous. From various sources, it appears that the Counter Intelligence Corps (CIC) – a unit of plainclothes informants within the ranks of the US Army – met on 21 June 1945 with the *Verwalter*, Carl Adolf Clemm, as well as the plant manager of Osternienburg Ludwig Lenoir, *Vorstand* member, to organize their transfer to the West. The following day a convoy containing 40 members of the personnel of DSW and their families (110 people in total) was moving westbound for an unknown destination. For weeks, the underpinnings of this sudden departure remained unanswered. An inside memorandum reported in July that "the largest part of our leading personnel [at DSW] has literally been 'kidnapped' by American CIC officers under mysterious conditions."[15] Only on 14 August did René Boël learn from Helmut Eilsberger (himself in exile in Rheinberg after a passage in Hamburg) that the convoy had crossed Halle and made a final stop in Dornheim, in the vicinity of Darmstadt. Clemm and Le Noir had prepared for the attention of CIC officers a list of engineers and skilled technicians "capable of building a soda plant and an electrolytic unit in Western Germany." This "mysterious transfer" seemingly also included engineers from IG Farben's Bitterfeld plant and academics from the University of Halle; there were 750 persons altogether.[16] Meanwhile, some members of the upper management of DSW declined the American offer: the head of Bernburg's Commercial Department, Otto Bökelmann, decided to stay, whereas another plant manager, Hans Vogl, rushed to Ebensee (although he reached Rheinberg by early August).[17] The Russian Army eventually arrived in the Sachsen-Anhalt in the first week of July 1945. As of 2 July, Bernburg officially fell under the administration of the Soviet zone.

---

[13] ACS, 1151-37-1 (1), C. A. Clemm to P. Masson, 31 May 1945 (appended to "Visite du Lieutenant Bernard" (11 June 1945), 12 June 1945.

[14] Kemper and Lorenz (2008), 34.

[15] ACS, 1151-33-5 (1), "Visites de M. Lalande en Allemagne," 27 July 1945; ACS, 1151-37-7 (1), "Entretien du Lieutenant Serrure avec le Directeur Vogl à l'Usine de Rheinberg en date du 7 août 1945," undated.

[16] ACS, RdG 21 Aug. 1945; ACS, 1151-33-5 (1), K. Honneth [Clemm's secretary] to P. Masson, 28 July 1945.

[17] ACS, 1151-37-7 (1), H. Vogl to gérance, 13 July 1945 and 2 Aug. 1945.

Unsurprisingly, contacts between Brussels and Solvay's German subsidiaries were not facilitated by this confusion. Since the theater of operations and the main centers of decision within the zones of occupation were forbidden to civilians, the *gérants* relied for a while on army officers – some of them working effectively for Solvay – with a pass from the respective Allied military administrations. In May 1945, the Belgian military mission to Germany authorized a Belgian engineer, Lieutenant Bernard, to inquire about the situation at Bernburg. Early in June, Lieutenant R. J. Serrure, an employee at Solvay Brussels, inspected the premises of Rheinberg and Borth-Wallach.[18] A couple of months later, a French army officer and employee at Solvay's Paris headquarters, Lieutenant Charles Lalande, gave the *gérants* an in-depth report on the plants of Wyhlen, Buchenau, and Ebensee. He was at Eisenach when the region became part of the Soviet zone in the first week of July 1945.[19] At the same time, Solvay strove to obtain permanent "liaison officers" whom they could dispatch to their German plants in the Western zone. By July 1945, the objective was only partly fulfilled. The Trade and Industry Division of the Allied Control Council (ACC), which oversaw the administration of Germany's four zones of occupation, only granted the presence of a civil servant who represented the Belgian interests in Germany as a whole. Things were ultimately made easier thanks to René Boël's all-around networks (especially his contact with General Georges Goethals, chief of the Belgian military mission in Berlin) and to the fact that two business acquaintances from ICI had been appointed to the ACC or its military counterpart, the Supreme Headquarters Allied Expeditionary Forces (SHAEF) in Germany.[20] As a result, Major Roger Pourbaix, working at Solvay's Commercial Department and assigned to the Belgian Ministry of Foreign Affairs during wartime, would be assisted by another Solvay employee mobilized by the Belgian Army, Lieutenant R. J. Serrure. Both of them were based in or around the Rheinberg plant, where, everyone assumed, lay the center of gravity of DSW.[21] By December 1945, a liaison officer fully dedicated to the company was sent to Berlin: Robert Audoyer, the son of Solvay's former head of the Central Technical Department, Charles Audoyer.

13.2 FAREWELL TO BERNBURG

Postwar Reorganization, Western Style

Just like before the war, René Boël took command of Solvay's German business. Wearing his uniform, he made his first visit to Rheinberg and Borth sites,

---

[18] ACS, 1151-37-7 (1), "Visites du Ltt Serrure en date du 4 juin," 5 June 1945.

[19] ACS, 1151-37-24 (2), "Visites de Monsieur Lalande en Allemagne (25 juin-20 juillet 1945)," 27 July 1945; ACS, 1151-37-1 (1), Lalande to Aubertin, 8 July 1945.

[20] On General G. Goethals, see Brüll (2009). The chairman of ICI's General Chemicals Division, C. S. Robinson, was ACC's deputy chief of economic division, and E. R. Herbertson, from ICI's Dyestuffs Branch, was responsible for SHAEF's Foodstuffs Department. See ACS, 1151-37-24 (1), "Visite de MM. Masson et Ebrant au Colonel Herbertson," 20 March 1945; note to R. Boël for his stay in London, 16 May 1945; Boël to gérance, 6 June 1945.

[21] Rupprecht (2007), 97; ACS, 1151-37-24 (1), "Visite du Major Pourbaix," 10-13 July 1945.

confirmed as part of the British zone, from 13 to 15 August 1945. The problems he faced were countless. Sure, there was no "Year Zero" in Rheinberg, nor elsewhere in Germany for that matter. The plant had suffered marginal damage and was about to run at a third of its average production capacity (nine hundred tons per day of soda ash, and three hundred tons per day of caustic soda). Financial and commercial impediments represented a heavy blow, but the burden would be overcome over the time. Obviously, Rheinberg and Borth (as well as Wyhlen in the French zone) were not a problem per se. What deeply preoccupied Boël, however, was the potential collapse of Solvay's setting in Germany as a whole. Contrary to the geographical concentration of the chemical industry in Germany, according to which the largest share lay in the British zone,[22] DSW was profoundly rooted in the Eastern territory. According to prewar and wartime figures, the factories that were located in the Soviet zone accounted for roughly 75 percent of DSW's workforce, 55.1 percent of the overall production of soda ash, and 81 percent of caustic soda. There was no electrolysis in the West, or any potassium saltworks, potassium, or lignite mines.[23] Moreover, this industrial architecture was supported by an administration that had been completely disrupted. Clemm's undisputed authority during the war had given way to mistrust within the upper management, as well as between management and workers. The puzzling evacuation of forty members of DSW's upper management from the East inevitably led to a reorganization of the executive staff. But the existence of the so-called Dornheim group also aroused social tensions in Solvay's West German factories. "I have realized that the presence [in Rheinberg] of an excessive number of plant managers represents a nuisance for the factories," remarked R. J. Serrure.[24] These tensions, which were observed at a larger scale in German society, stemmed from the demoralizing effect of Nazism. This was a direct component of Hitler's legacy.[25]

The program of reorganization that Boël had intended to implement thus had to be carried out in close coordination with the guidelines of denazification set forth by the Allies. The matter was tackled while Boël and Pourbaix were visiting Rheinberg. The minutes of the decisions put it straight: "Concerning the former active members of the Nazi Party, general provisions will be adopted as follows: (1) members with more than twenty-five years of service will be retired, (2) members with less than twenty-five years of service will be laid-off with an extra month of wage per year of service, (3) 'dubious' personnel will be put on a provisional leave of absence with two-third of their wage."[26] The latter measure alluded to the members enlisted in the Dornheim group, whose freedom of movement was curtailed by American military authorities as their "evaluation" was pending. Nevertheless, if a political cleansing of "dubious" personnel was deemed a necessary step to move forward, it was not, in the eyes of the gérants, an end in itself. Over time, it appeared obvious that the procedure of denazification with its heavy bureaucratic outlook (a Fragebogen,

[22] Stokes (1988), 70.

[23] ACS, 1151-37-7 (1), "Propriétés en Allemagne," 22 April 1945.

[24] ACS, 1151-37-7 (1), "Note No. 4: Personnel de Bernburg" by R. Serrure, 10 Sept. 1945.

[25] Berghahn (1982), 180-1.

[26] ACS, 1151-37-24 (2), "Voyage de MM. Boël et Pourbaix en Allemagne – 13 au 15 août 1945," 20 Aug. 1945.

or questionnaire, contained no fewer than 131 questions) contrasted with Solvay's eagerness to reconstruct DSW as soon as possible. This methodological contrast took a more personal turn when, in October 1945, Allied authorities announced their intention to appoint special custodians for industrial properties controlled by foreign (Allied) capital in Germany.[27] For Brussels, Carl Clemm, as former *Verwalter*, was the designated candidate for the job. But this choice was contested by the Public Safety Service in the British zone, which pointed to Clemm's appointment as head of Wirtschaftsgruppe Chemie during the war. The situation dragged on for months. It was only in September 1947, as a result of the differing administrative procedures of political cleansing in the three zones of occupation, that Clemm managed to obtain his so-called Persil certificate of denazification. To avoid a potential clash with the representatives of workers and employees (*Betriebsrat*) at the Rheinberg plant, the *gérance* asked him to join the *Aufsichtsrat* of DSW.[28] By that time, a report mentioned that "almost the whole staff [of the Dornheim group] has been taken on again either at the Central Administration or in the factories." In addition, some fifty workers and employees from Solvay's plants in the eastern territories had expressed their wish to be transferred.[29]

In the meantime, Helmut Eilsberger, appointed on 7 February 1946 to the chairmanship of the *Vorstand*, had been selected as head custodian of DSW in the western part of Germany, whereas his colleague at the *Vorstand*, Aurel Kerstein, patiently waited to be denazified. Among Eilsberger's priorities was the necessity to find a creative solution for the administrative transfer of Solvay's activities from east to west. Although Boël had promised in December 1945 that "the head office of DSW will remain in Bernburg," for any change "would be interpreted as an abandonment of Solvay's interests in the Russian zone," the political context forced him to adapt his strategy.[30] Although it was decided to open a provisional office in Rheinberg, the name of Solingen came to the fore as soon as July 1946. Located seventy kilometers south of Rheinberg and close to Düsseldorf, Leverkusen and the other components of IG Farben's Lower Rhine Group, Solingen-Ohligs was in Boël's mind as the possible new site of the central administration of DSW in the western zone. However, after consulting Hermann Abs and Carl Clemm on the matter, it appeared that a more ambitious aim was preferable (essentially on fiscal grounds), that is, the transfer of DSW's general headquarters. The project only materialized on 14 April 1948 after a General Assembly meeting took place, with the official registration on 1 October of that year. By June 1948, almost sixty persons were already employed, many of whom came from the Dornheim

[27] 1151–37-15, "Intérêts belges en Allemagne," 18 Oct. 1945; ACS, 1151–37-24 (1), "Voyage en Allemagne du 20 au 24 octobre" by R. Pourbaix, 27 Oct. 1945.

[28] ACS, 1151–33-5 (1), "Note pour M. Clemm," 18 Oct. 1945; ACS, RdG, 6 Nov. 1945; ACS, 1151–37-24 (1), Serrure to gérance, 12 Dec. 1945; ACS, 1151–37-7 (3), Serrure to gérance, 24 Dec. 1945; ACS, 1151–37-7 (6), "Voyage du Baron Boël et de M. Ebrant en Allemagne," 31 July 1946; ACS, 1151–37-7 (6), "Entrevue avec M. Clemm" by R. Serrure, 16 Feb. 1947; ACS, 1151–37-7 (7), "Courrier rapporté par M. Serrure," 29 April 1947; ACS, 1151–37-7 (7), "Entretien avec M. Serrure" by Ed. Swolfs, 8 Sept. 1947.

[29] ACS, 1151–33-5 (2), "Voyage du Baron Boël (17–20 Nov. 1947)," 25 Nov. 1947.

[30] ACS, 1151–37-24 (4), "Gestion des DSW – 3 décembre 1945," 6 Dec. 1945.

group.[31] A symbolic as well as a pragmatic decision, the transfer also illustrated that the politics of continuity had prevailed in the West. To some extent, this would also be the case in the Soviet zone, although it was a form of continuity very different at first sight. Through its powerful rhetoric, the "official" emphasis was laid on breaking from the past.

Postwar Reorganization, Eastern Style

In sharp contrast with Solvay's plants in the West, Bernburg and the other factories located in the Russian zone obviously whetted the appetite of the occupying authorities. True, two American "scientific consultants" were observed "thoroughly inspecting" the facilities at Rheinberg in August 1945, but this was an exception rather than the norm. Whereas a "team of experts from U.S. industry, as well as their counterparts from other Allied or neutral countries, swarmed over German industrial facilities in the immediate aftermath of the war,"[32] Rheinberg did not endure painstaking inspections. At Bernburg, on the contrary, the swarm of experts was but the prelude to another form of intrusion that would affect many other chemical factories in the region. Shortly after the arrival of the Red Army in July 1945, it was reported that "a great number of Russian officers, chemists especially... are coming every day and asking the most diverse technical questions."[33] The curiosity soon turned into spoliation when, on 17 September, Russian authorities effectively proceeded to the dismantling of Bernburg soda plant in conformity with General Order No. 43 for Reparations adopted by the Soviet Military Administration (SMA) on 28 August. This order, it must be said, had been approved by the American and British Allies at the Potsdam Conference and allowed the Russians access to 15 percent of German industrial equipment and commodities.[34] By early December, Solvay's messenger in Berlin, Robert Audoyer, noted that 30 percent of the site (parts of the soda plant, the cement factory, and the mines of Plömnitz) had already been removed by some four thousand workers and employees, the bulk of which worked at Bernburg. Word spread that the equipment was supposed to form the core of a new plant to be built in or around Sterlitamak, north of Kazakhstan.[35] Similar dismantling operations took place at Theo Goldschmidt AG (Ammendorf plant), Kali-Chemie AG (Bitterfeld), Alexander Wacker GmbH (Mückenberg), and Chemische Fabrik von Heyden AG (Weissig), and many other sites were on the list. In view of the need for chlorine, the third electrolysis of Osternienburg was removed in April 1946, but this was nothing compared to the important dismantling of IG Farben's Bitterfeld at the same time. As to Westeregeln electrolysis plant,

[31] ACS, RdG, 1 Aug. 1946; ACS, 1151–33-5 (2), "Entretien avec M. Serrure le 28 Oct. 1946," 31 Oct. 1946; ACS, 1151–45-8/ACS, 1151–45-2/2, Minutes of the G.A.M. of DSW of 14 April 1948; ACS, 1151–33-5 (2), "Voyage de M. Swolfs à Solingen (8–10 June 1948)," 15 June 1948.

[32] Stokes (1988), 41–2; ACS, 1151–37-7 (1), Note to the gérance, 13 Aug. 1945.

[33] ACS, 1151–33-5 (1), "Extrait d'une lettre de Dr. Dörffel," 12 Aug. 1945.

[34] ACS, 1151–37-24 (1), Gérance to F. Van Langenhove (general director at the Belgian Ministry of Foreign Affairs), 17 Nov. 1945; Kemper and Lorenz (2008), 35.

[35] ACS, 1151–37-24 (1), Audoyer Report, 1 Dec. 1945 and 8 Dec. 1945.

running at extremely low capacity, it was eventually excluded from the reparations list.[36]

Solvay's priority in this turbulent period was to avoid the absence of responsible management. After the evacuation of 22 June 1945, a proxy had been prepared by Clemm whereby he designated Bernburg plant managers Otto Bökelmann and Eric Plünnecke competent for signatures. This informal transfer of authority was acknowledged by Brussels only on 4 January 1946 and formalized by the General Assembly meeting of DSW on 7 February 1946 – Bökelmann became member of the *Vorstand*. This was a fine choice in many respects. Besides being the longtime head of Bernburg's Commercial Department, Otto Bökelmann had never been a member of the Nazi Party. Close to democratic-liberal political groups, he was part of the Purge Committee of the Bernburg Landkreis, a position that provided him with a good knowledge of antifascist milieus.[37] As soon as the measure of sequestration was implemented by the Russians on 17 April 1946 (General Order No. 124), Bökelmann was appointed custodian (*Treuhänder für das Vermögen der alliierten Staaten*) for all DSW sites located in Saxony-Anhalt. However, the modality of application of this procedure in the East differed greatly with what was practiced in the West. Sequestration did not correspond to the protection of industrial properties; confiscation was looming. While René Boël was acting in the upper diplomatic spheres, Otto Bökelmann was mobilizing his local networks. Underlying the latter's argument was the promise, possibly prompted by Boël, that Solvay would not pull out from the eastern territories. The tactics largely paid off: only the potash plant and mines of Solvayhall were transferred to a new Russian-owned company – Sovietische AG für Kali-Dünger (later transferred to the Vereinigung Volkseigener Betriebe [VVB] Kali und Salze). The sequestration under the responsibility of Bökelmann still applied for the remaining plants. This surprising call, which had passed three successive administrative levels, is supposed to have infuriated the Russian authorities.[38] It is in this relatively optimistic atmosphere that Boël and Bökelmann eventually met in Rheinberg in April 1947 and outlined plans for the development of DSW in the East.[39] But this cheerful mood was short lived.

By June 1947, the political context had started to darken. Audoyer begged Brussels to act with more carefulness regarding its strategy in the Russian zone: "the current situation is rather favourable, and one ought not to change it with a brutal action that would inevitably cause unpleasant reactions from the Germans and the Russians."[40] Bökelmann's life was at risk. Perceived as "a man from the West" and suspected to undermine the development of Bernburg, he was at strains not only with the Russians but with some members of the

[36] ACS, 1151-37-24 (5), "Note de M. R. Audoyer: le Chlore en Allemagne," 24 Jan. 1946; ACS, 1151-37-24 (6), Ed. Swolfs to L. Goffin (Belgian Embassy in Washington, DC), 8 July 1946.

[37] ACS, 1151-37-24 (4), Audoyer Report, 20 Jan. 1946, 4.

[38] Kemper and Lorenz (2008), 36; ACS, 1151-37-1 (6), Audoyer Report, 11 Aug. 1946 and 3 Sept. 1946; ACS, 1151-37-24 (6), Ed. Swolfs to L. Goffin, 17 Dec. 1946.

[39] ACS, 1151-37-1 (1) – ACS, 1151-33-5 (2), "Voyage du Baron Boël à Rheinberg (14–16 avril 1947)," 18–20 Apr. 1947.

[40] ACS, 1151-37-7 (7), 3 June 1947.

workers as well. Alternatively, he felt he could not trust his counterparts on the other side of the nascent Iron Curtain. At the *Vorstand*, Helmut Eilsberger was discretely lobbying for the subordination of the Bernburg group to the Solingen administration.[41] Unsurprisingly, Bökelmann took the transfer of DSW's general headquarters from Bernburg to Solingen-Ohligs, for which he was not even consulted, as a broken promise – the last step toward the complete abdication of Solvay from its factories in East Germany. For the *gérance*, however, the measure had merely been adopted in anticipation of the partition of Germany. With the extension of the Marshall Plan aid to West Germany and the refusal of the Russians to implement the currency reform in their zone of occupation, political unification of Germany became an illusion.[42]

The dismantling of Bernburg was completed on 23 April 1948, just nine days after the transfer of DSW's headquarters was approved at the General Assembly meeting.[43] When the official sequestration was terminated in July 1948, the remaining parts of Bernburg, as well as DSW's other factories in the Soviet zone, were handed out to the local authorities of Saxony-Anhalt, acting for the SMA, under the control of another *Treuhänder*, August Kaste, former plant manager of Westeregeln. From a legal standpoint, this meant that the ownership of these sites was restored to Solvay. This was hardly the case, though, for neither the *gérance* nor Solingen had contact with Kaste, whose authority was contested by Bökelmann qua member of the *Vorstand*.[44] This confused organization was put to an end on 19 January 1950 with the official takeover of DSW's eastern sites by the Vereinigung Volkseigener Betriebe (VVB) Dresden-Radebeul, an organizational machinery that stemmed from the recently created German Democratic Republic (GDR). Following his legal intuition, Eilsberger insisted, "[This] does not represent an expropriation yet, but it means a serious impingement upon the property owner's rights."[45] This was quite true: although the operation of "supervision" represented in practice a measure of nationalization, it was not the case on a strictly legal standpoint. The contrast would have important consequences when Solvay S.A. negotiated to get Bernburg back in 1990–91 (see Chapter 20).[46] In the early 1950s, however, the operation of "supervision" merely set the stage to

---

[41] ACS, 1151-37-1 (2), R. Audoyer to Ed. Swolfs, 8 Dec. 1947; ACS, 1151-37-1 (2), R. Pourbaix to Ed. Swolfs, 16 Jan. 1948; ACS, 1151-37-7 (7), 5 Aug. 1947.

[42] ACS, 1151-37-24 (8), "Voyage de M. Swolfs en Allemagne (13–15 juillet 1948)," 19 July 1948.

[43] ACS, 1151-45-8, R. Pourbaix to O. Bökelmann, 3 Aug. 1948 and Bökelmann's reply, 13 Sept. 1948; ACS, 1151-37-1 (2), R. Audoyer to Ed. Swolfs (and appendixes), 3 May 1948; ACS, "East German Files," Box II – Bernburg, Folder 7: "Visites à Bernburg," "Compte-rendu de la visite à Bernburg les 20 et 21.02.1990 (Notice DCT 90.073)," 23 Feb. 1990, Appendix 2A: "Lagesbericht der Zweigniederlassung Sodafabriken Bernburg am 15. Sept. 1948."

[44] ACS, 1151-37-24 (8), "Voyage de M. Swolfs en Allemagne (13–15 juillet 1948)," 19 July 1948; ACS, 1151-37-1 (3), "Voyage de MM. Masson et Swolfs à Düsseldorf 7–9 février 1949)," 14 Feb. 1949; ACS, 1151-33-7, "Visite de M. Pourbaix (3 mars 1949)," 7 March 1949; ACS, 1151-33-7, "Entretien avec M. Pourbaix le 1er août 1949," 3 Aug. 1949; ACS, 1151-37-1 (3), "Voyage en Allemagne du Baron Boël, Pierre Solvay et Ed. Swolfs (22–25 août 1949)," 2 Sept. 1949.

[45] ACS, 1151-37-1 (4), H. Eilsberger to gérance, 2 Feb. 1950.

[46] ACS, "East German Files," Box II – Bernburg, Folder 7: "Visites à Bernburg," "Visite à Bernburg-Stassfurt les 20 et 21.02.1990 (Corporate Planning No. 10681)," 22 Feb. 1990.

the reconstruction of a soda ash plant on the site, a project that had been suggested by the public authorities for some years already. The "new" factory officially went on stream on 13 September 1952, with the first ton of soda ash produced a couple of months later.[47] The initial capacity was planned for 300 tons per day (over time, it increased to 1,500 tons per day). On 5 May 1953, to signify a radically new departure, GDR authorities renamed the factory Volkseigener Betrieb (VEB) Sodawerke Karl Marx.

13.3   THE LIQUIDATION OF IG FARBEN AND ITS CONSEQUENCES

Exchanging IG Farben for Kali-Chemie

Solvay did not wait long to inform the Allied authorities of its interests in IG Farben. After all, IG Farben's assets belonged to Solvay's interests in Germany, and the company felt it was entitled to get them back. Solvay told Belgian authorities that the investment amounted to RM 34.6 million in May 1940 (some 2.72 percent of IG Farben's capital), a figure that was reestimated at RM 38.7 million given Solvay's participation in a series of capital increases in the midst of the war.[48] At the same time, John Foster Dulles was approached to make sure that the message was well received in American planning milieus, which had presumably agreed to break up the powerful chemical conglomerate (only the size of the resulting pieces of the breakup was still unknown).[49] Interestingly, though, Solvay did not immediately state that the investment was part of a larger financial and commercial agreement exchange concluded in 1924 (see Chapter 9). The revelation that IG Farben owned 25 percent of DSW's capital (RM 18.75 million) through its Ammoniakwerk Merseburg GmbH subsidiary came in November 1945. A direct consequence of the confiscation of the IG Farben empire under the supervision of the Allied occupying forces, these interests were threatened with freezing. Because time was of the essence, the *gérance* suggested proceeding to an exchange based on the historical stakes of 1924. Solvay, in other words, accepted to give back RM 22.715 million IG Farben shares in exchange of RM 18.715 million DSW shares.[50] At the height of decartelization, this exchange was turned down by the four-power experts of the IG Farben Control Committee (COIG) on 29 April 1946.[51]

From this date until mid-1948, Solvay kept a low profile as to its interests in IG Farben and instead concentrated its efforts on defending its plants in the East. This was understandable – this period coincided with the trial of

---

[47] Kemper and Lorenz (2008), 38–40.

[48] The bulk of these shares were deposited at the Société de Banque Suisse in Basel, whereas a smaller portion had been saved by Clemm during his evacuation.

[49] ACS, RdG 7, 21 Aug. & 28 Aug. 1945; ACS, 1151-37-24 (1), Boël to F. Van Langenhove, 28 Aug. 1945 (and appendix); ACS, 1151-40-3, Boël to Foster Dulles, 10 Sept. 1945.

[50] ACS, 1151-40-9 (1), Boël to F. Van Langenhove, 20 Nov. 1945; 1151-37-24 (1), Boël to General Goethals, 17 Nov. 1945.

[51] ACS, 1800-40-4, Douglas Fowles (BIFCO) to Walter Schmidt (DSW Counsel), 10 Dec. 1950; ACS, 1151-40-9, "Entretien avec M. Franck," 5 April 1946; ACS, 1151-40-9 (2), General Goethals to Baron van der Straten-Waillet (Belgian minister of foreign trade), 29 July, Appendix COIG/P(47), 11 July 1947.

twenty-four former IG executives. At the request of Hermann Schmitz, former chairman of Farben's board, Solvay gave factual information about the IG officials (Schmitz, Georg von Schnitzler, Max Ilgner, Karl von Heider) that it had business contacts with since the 1924 agreement. Although the trial was perceived as a cutting-edge exercise in the practice of international criminal law (it was part of the four-power trials for war crimes held in Nuremberg under US jurisdiction), its long-awaited verdict stunned observers with the mildness of the punishment.[52] Later in the summer of 1948, the inter-Allied COIG was replaced by two-zone (then three-zone) organizations regarding IG Farben policy. One of them – the IG Farben Dispersal Panel (FARDIP) – was responsible for the executive supervision of the disentanglement (*Entflechtung*) of the chemical combine. After hesitation, it was agreed that it would be fully composed by German prominent industrialists and bankers.[53] An old acquaintance, Hermann Josef Abs, was among them. On December 1948, he was also appointed chairman of the Kreditanstalt für Wiederaufbau, in charge of allocating the Marshall Plan funds in Germany. Abs' positions, therefore, enabled him to embrace the Allies' postwar economic policy in West Germany from multiple perspectives. Solvay, needless to say, was eager to benefit from Abs' advice and assistance for at least two reasons: completing the DSW-IG Farben shares exchange issue and facilitating the progressive purchase of Kali-Chemie shares in possession of IG Farben.[54]

For political and bureaucratic reasons, the question pertaining to the liquidation of IG Farben dragged on for months and years. Meanwhile, René Boël and his specialist for German affairs, Édouard Swolfs (future member of the *Vorstand* of DSW and later of Solvay's Executive Committee), made important moves in the Kali-Chemie issue. Since the end of the war, DSW and Gefucin had owned 22.66 percent of Kali-Chemie. Pursuing a strategy of industrial synergy in the alkali sector in West Germany (with a view to controlling the Heilbronn soda plant) and, incidentally, for fiscal reasons, Boël intended to increase that to 40 percent. In accordance with Abs, the opportunity was seized in July 1949 after Solvay (via DSW) bought an important package of shares. On 31 December 1950, Solvay held 34.08 percent of Kali-Chemie's capital.[55] The ceiling of 40 percent was eventually reached after the takeover of Theo Goldschmidt AG's interests in Kali-Chemie in November 1951, as well as with a series of off-the-radar purchases on the stock market. But in June 1952, in the midst of the breakup negotiations of IG Farben, rumors of sales of the chemical

[52] Stokes (1988), 54–5, 151–6; ACS, 1800–33-2, "Note on Dr. Schmitz," 16 May 1948.

[53] On this, see Kreikamp (1977) and Stokes (1988), 173–9.

[54] ACS, 1151–40-9 (3), "Visite de M. Pourbaix (23 août 1948)," 23 Aug. 1948; ACS, 1151–40-9 (3), "Voyage du Baron Boël et de MM. Guffroy et Swolfs en Allemagne (26–30 septembre 1948)"; ACS, 1151–40-9 (3), Ed. Swolfs to M. Ebrant, 6 Oct. 1948; ACS, 1151–40-9 (3), R. Boël to G. Murnane, 19 Nov. 1948; ACS, 1151–40-9 (3), "Voyage du Baron Boël à Londres (20 novembre 1948) – Conversation avec M. Abs," 23 Nov. 1948.

[55] ACS, "East German Files," Box III – Nationalisations, Folder 5/b, Ed. Swolfs to W. Wendrich, Appendix "Historique de la prise de participation des DSW dans la Kali-Chemie A.G.," 5 Dec. 1972; ACS, 1805–40-2 (2), "Voyage de M. Swolfs en Allemagne (13–15 juillet 1948)," 19 July 1948; ACS, 1805–40-2 (2), "Voyage du Baron Boël et de M. P. Solvay en Allemagne (17–20 décembre 1949)," 24 Dec. 1949.

FIGURE 13.2. The Rheinberg plant of DSW was partly enlarged with help of Marshall Plan aid. (Solvay Rheinberg Archives.)

company's holding of 25 percent in Kali-Chemie came to the fore. Official liquidators of IG Farben were, of course, on their guard and forbade any massive buyout for the sake of decartelization. Abs's intervention was instrumental. He suggested taking the lead of a bank consortium controlled by the Süddeutsche Bank, whose board he was about to chair, which would acquire the majority of IG Farben's holding in Kali-Chemie. In agreement with Abs, DSW could come at a second stage, buying shares regularly from the consortium until late 1955. The strategy proved utterly successful: combined with Gefucin's stock, DSW held 63.56 percent of Kali-Chemie's capital in April 1956.[56]

The deal with Kali-Chemie was completed by the time the negotiations leading to the conclusion of the IG Farben liquidation was decided by executive order on 6 February 1955. Since the refusal of a standard exchange of shares between DSW and IG Farben in 1946, the legal experts of Solvay and DSW had been brainstorming to find a potential breach. The difficulty lay less in the restitution of the historical stock from the 1924 contract than in the subsequent purchases of IG Farben shares that DSW had made between 1924 and 1943. The difference, it is true, was substantial – from RM 22.715 million (1924) to RM 38.7 million since the end of the war.[57] After desperate negotiations with

---

[56] ACS, 1805–37-4, "Visite de MM. Eilsberger et Swolfs (10 juillet 1952)," 14 July 1952; ACS, RdG, 10 July 1952; ACS, 1805–37-4, "Communication téléphonique avec M. Abs," 27 Mar. 1953.

[57] ACS, 1151–49-10, Expert reports of Robert Kirkpatrick, Graf von der Goltz and Walter Schmidt, Aug.–Nov. 1949 (many updates until 1951); ACS, 1151–40-9, "Actions DSW-IG

the three-zone organization supervising the case, the *gérance* reluctantly agreed in December 1951 to proceed to an exchange of shares *ad minima*. Solvay, in other words, could recover the initial 25 percent of DSW's capital (representing RM 18.75 million) in exchange for a bit less than RM 30 million IG shares.[58] The transfer of shares was effective at the beginning of 1952. A portion of Solvay's holding in IG Farben was used to purchase Henkel's interests in Kali-Chemie in conformity with an agreement made in December 1952. The bulk of the remainder (DM 10 million) was exchanged in 1954 for shares of IG's three major successors (also its initial constituents) – BASF, Bayer, and Hoechst. However, the investment did not last long: the *gérance* agreed to divest the IG Farben portfolio between November 1956 and January 1957.[59] This marked an end to an important Solvay chapter.

The Solvay Trials

The exchange of shares between DSW and IG Farben had another – and rather unexpected – consequence in East Germany, which pertained to the general "obsession," the "symbol of evil economic activity" (*Berghahn*), that the giant German chemical company represented for the Allies in the aftermath of the war.[60] On 27 December 1949, while DSW-Solingen was busy increasing its holding in Kali-Chemie, a team of the GDR's Deutsche Wirtschaftskommission launched a series of investigations in the archives room of the administration of Bernburg. Its aim was to find material evidence of Solvay's alleged "hidden ties" with IG Farben, which could have led to the condemnation of Bernburg plant managers as "economic criminals" (*Wirtschaftsverbrechers*) – a crime punishable by five years' imprisonment. On 15 January 1950, five DSW personnel were arrested, and Otto Bökelmann and three other persons were reported missing.[61] In harmony with the *Vorstand*, Bökelmann finally managed to evade arrest and to escape to Frankfurt via West Berlin, just like six of his colleagues.[62] As a result, eight managers and employees of DSW were brought to the Supreme Court of the GDR. The defendants included former *Treuhänder*, August Kaste, and plant manager, Eric Plünnecke, who

Farben: Entretiens du 19 décembre 1949 avec les avocats Comte von der Goltz et Schmidt," 24 Dec. 1949.

[58] ACS, 1151-40-9 (4), "Visite de MM. Eilsberger & Swolfs (27 septembre 1951)," 4 Oct. 1951; ACS, RdG 13 Nov. 1951 and 3 Dec. 1951; ACS, 1151-40-9 (4), "Voyage du Baron Boël et M. Obozinski en Allemagne (15–16 novembre 1951)," 17 Nov. 1951; ACS, 1151-40-9 (4), R. Boël to TRIFCO, 4 Dec. 1951.

[59] ACS, 1800-40-8, "Section B: Note d'information pour la Gérance," 24 Apr. 1953; ACS, 1800-40-8, Service Financier, "Note pour la Gérance," No. 294 (26 Oct. 1956), No. 322 (30 Nov. 1956), and No. 10 (11 Jan. 1957).

[60] Stokes (1988), 37ff.; Berghahn (1985), 86, 92–5.

[61] ACS, 1151-37-1 (4), "Voyage à Berlin (27–29 janvier 1950)" by R. Pourbaix, 3 Feb. 1950 (incl. appendix).

[62] ACS, 1151-33-7, "Communication téléphonique de M. Pourbaix," 1 Feb. 1950; ACS, 1151-33-7, "Voyage de M. Swolfs en Allemagne (13–16 février 1950)," 20 Feb. 1950; ACS, 1151-33-7, "Visite de M. Pourbaix (13 mars 1950)," 16 Mar. 1950; ACS, 1151-37-1 (4), "Visite de M. Pourbaix (9 mai 1950)," 9 May 1950.

had asked the *Vorstand* to be transferred to the West in February 1949. They were accused of sabotaging the GDR's economy, as well as industrial sabotage, mismanagement, misappropriation, and illegal trade. Most of all, they were charged with conspiring with IG Farben. Contrary to the IG Farben trial that took place in Nuremberg three years earlier, the so-called Solvay trial had much in common with the showcase trials in vogue in the GDR in that period.

The trial eventually started on 14 December 1950 – almost a year after the arrest. The courtroom of Bernburg was packed with workers from the soda plant. The international press was invited to attend the event, which rapidly turned into a mockery of justice. The presiding judge, Hilde Benjamin – who happened to be the sister-in-law of the well-known philosopher Walter Benjamin – "did not act in any way as an arbiter between the prosecution and the defense." Deprived of the assistance of their lawyers (and unable to exploit the abundant material they had received from Solingen), defendants were "confronted with questions of the 'have you stopped beating your wife' type, and then directed forcefully to 'answer yes or no.'"[63] Yet unlike similar showcase trials, the audition did not give way to whining pseudoconfessions and breathtaking public repentance. As a matter of fact, at the time of their arrest none of the defendants could ever have been aware of the DSW-IG Farben agreements of 1924, which had been negotiated between the *gérance* and the *Vorstand* with top IG representatives (especially from the Badische). Even at a late stage, Bökelmann did not know about the exchange of shares; he honestly reported that DSW was fully controlled by Belgian capital.[64] During the trial, the DSW administration at Solingen sent documents attesting that the Russian military authorities had been informed of the DSW-IG Farben operation since 1947. But these were discarded by Judge Benjamin. In the end, the prosecution interpreted the defendants' ignorance as the undeniable proof of DSW's subordination to IG Farben. Judge Benjamin sentenced four defendants to fifteen years in prison, and the remainder to penalties varying between two and ten years (Plünnecke's secretary, Ingeborg Köpp, was sent for five years to the work camp of Falkenbach-Himmelsmühle). Families of the convicts were brought to West Germany and put under the financial assistance of DSW.[65]

A second Solvay trial took place in Dessau on 7–8 June 1951. Although it did not receive broad coverage in the media, it led to the indictment of five other DSW personnel in East Germany. Sentences fluctuated between two and eight

[63] ACS, 1151-37-1 (5), Clipping from the *New York Herald Tribune*, 19 Dec. 1950.

[64] ACS, 1151-37-1 (4), "Voyage de M. Swolfs en Allemagne (8 juillet 1950)," 11 July 1950; ACS, 1151-37-1 (5), "Procès contre les fonctionnaires Solvay à Bernburg (Extract of Swedish newspaper *Dagens Nyheter*)," 28 Dec. 1950. Besides A. Kaste and E. Plünnecke, the defendants were Albert Werner, Konrad Blütchen, Willie Rose, Paul Hennings, Ingeborg Köpp, and Max Schneider.

[65] ACS, Bernburg, "Entscheidungen des Obersten Gerichts – Solvay Prozess," *Neue Justiz*, No. 2, Febr. 1951, 78–87; "Sowjetzone: Enteignet den Sodakönig," *Der Spiegel*, No. 28, 13 July 1950, 7–8; ACS, 1151-37-1 (5), "Voyage du Baron Boël en Allemagne (23–25 février 1951)," 27 Feb. 1951.

years in prison, although only one person (Willi Röttgers) was still confined after one year.[66] In January 1956, after lengthy diplomatic pressure, August Kaste was the last convict of the Solvay trials to be released.[67] If he and his other partners in misfortune ever wished to spend some of their leisure time going to the cinema, there was one film they presumably did want to avoid. Showing at movie theaters in GDR since its release in 1953 was the production of Deutsche Film AG titled *Geheimakten Solvay*. This propaganda film was inspired by the first Solvay trial. The weekly magazine *Der Spiegel* reviewed it as a "sabotage tale...drawing upon the same-old routine: directors enslaved to the capital and their American masters versus vigilant party members and industrious skilled workers. Showing only in the East-zone."[68] Nonetheless, beyond their being symbolic operations for the new political regime, the Solvay trials had successfully fulfilled the German Democratic Republic's underlying objective, namely to provide the legitimization for the forced nationalization of DSW that was under way.

13.4 NATIONALIZATIONS IN EASTERN EUROPE: LONG-FOUGHT BATTLES, MODEST RESULTS

Although Germany was, by far, the most important country for Solvay in the heart of Europe, it was not the only one facing profound instability in the aftermath of the war. On a mission to Austria before the Potsdam Conference (July 1945), Lieutenant Charles Lalande reported that Hallein and Ebensee were located in the transitional American zone of occupation, whereas the Vienna office was in the Russian zone. Both plants were in a state of running "in the very next days," with the exception of partial damage to some liquid chlorine mercury cells at Hallein. There was much uncertainty in Czechoslovakia about the fate of the German technical personnel; the plants belonging to Nestomitz Solvay Werke had been ordered nationalized. This concerned Poland as well, where the Zakłady Solvay was taken over by "four different official organizations." As for the Balkans and Romania, information was scarce. The facilities of Lukavac were "partly bombed by Yugoslavian patriots," Ocna Muresului plant was intact, and Turda was "probably destroyed."[69] Between 16 and 28 August 1945, Pierre Solvay spent some time in Austria as part of his military duty in the American army. He carried with him a proxy from the *gérance* giving him "full powers" as "owner of fifty-one percent of the capital of the 'Ebenseer Solvay Werke Kommandit Gesellschaft,' Ebensee." Once he arrived there, though, he heard that Dr. Antonin Srba, the head of Spolek (Aussiger Verein) and Solvay's partner in southeastern Europe, had been appointed governmental trustee for Nestomitz as a prelude to the nationalization of the chemical

---

[66] ACS, 1151–37-1 (6), "Voyage du Baron Boël, de M. P. Solvay et M. Obozinski en Allemagne (22–23 mai 1951)," 31 May 1951; ACS, 1151–37-1 (6), Eilsberger to gérance, 18 June 1951; ACS, 1151–37-1 (7), "Visite de M. Swolfs (2 septembre 1952)," 5 Sept. 1952.

[67] ACS, 1151–37-1 (7), Boël to Spaak, 2 Feb. 1956.

[68] Quoted in Kemper and Lorenz (2008), 37.

[69] ACS, 1151–37-24 (2), "Visites de Monsieur Lalande en Allemagne (25 juin-20 juillet 1945)," 27 July 1945; ACS, 1185–37-4, Gérance to E. Lefèvre, 10 Aug. 1945.

sector.[70] Indeed, Czechoslovakia was the first country to enact a decree on the "nationalization of mining and industrial companies," on 24 October 1945. Sent to Prague in December 1945, Solvay's legal counsel, Robert Kirkpatrick, and the head of Solvay's subsidiaries, Marcel Ebrant, observed that the "drive for nationalization is spontaneous; . . . it is not confined to the communist parties, its most sincere advocates are the social democrats." Their appreciation of Solvay's future in Czechoslovakia was harsh: one could either hope for a measure of exception or, more realistically, prepare for a procedure of (partial) compensation.[71] Severe as it seemed, it was a clear-sighted judgment.

What should Solvay's position be in regard to threats of nationalization? "What counts for us," noted René Boël in January 1947, "is the ownership of our plants[,] and we should strive at keeping this line as much as we can, especially in the field of soda ash."[72] As time went by, however, the company inexorably adapted its hard line of protection in favor of the soft line of compensation. Ultimately, this also affected the Czechoslovak case. Given the scope of the partnership with Spolek (especially the holding in Ebensee plant) and the favorable impression made by the democratic regime, the country had long been handled as an exception by the *gérance* – albeit with some divergence of opinions among *gérants*.[73] But this special treatment was over after the Czech coup of February 1948, which left no other option than a compensation scheme. To some extent, the compensation was "reparations" from the third world war – the Cold War.

The general patterns of Solvay's actions in this respect are summarized in Table 13.1. In spite of the differences that applied from country to country, some converging characteristics can be outlined. First, Solvay joined or took the lead of the various "organizations for the protection of industrial interests" that had been set up, in Belgium as elsewhere, in agreement with the public authorities after the war. Underlying this collective action was the feeling that diplomatic and political milieus, rather than private interests, could successfully yield to compensation. Second, representatives of Solvay were deeply involved in the preliminary negotiations in each organization as to the repartition of the potential compensation, which was based on an estimation of the assets in the foreign country.[74] Third, although one should not overlook the many nuances in this respect, compensation was not proportional to the real worth of the investments. More generally, though, outcomes were not proportional to the tireless efforts that had been put into negotiations. Most of the reparations took place when the company had turned over a new leaf.

---

[70] ACS, Bunker Archives, NSW Prague, Administration, Evénements politiques 1945, E. Lefèvre to gérance, 20 Aug. 1945; ACS, 1185-37-4, "Note pour M. Pierre Solvay," 10 Aug. 1945; ACS, RdG, 6 Sept. 1945.

[71] ACS, Bunker Archives, NSW Prague, Administration, Evénements politiques 1945, "Rapport sur le voyage de MM. Kirkpatrick et Ebrant à Prague (10–21 décembre 1945)," 10 Jan. 1946.

[72] ACS, 1001-37-1, "Réunion du 3 janvier 1947" with R. Boël, H. Delwart, R. Kirkpatrick, G. Janson, M. Ebrant, and Ed. Swolfs, 10 Jan. 1947.

[73] ACS, RdG, 22 May 1947.

[74] For instance, Marcel Ebrant was secretary to the Czech section of the Association des Intérêts Industriels Belges à l'Étranger; Solvay & Cie's economic adviser, Georges Janson, was secretary to the Consortium d'Organismes Belges Créanciers d'Entreprises Belges ou Polonaises Installées en Pologne.

TABLE 13.1. *Nationalized Properties of Solvay and Compensation Schemes in Postwar Central and Eastern Europe*

	Properties/Holdings of Solvay Group	Nationalization Measures	Official Body for Claims and Compensation	Date and Global Terms of Compensation Agreement (if any)	Effective Compensation As % of Estimated Value (for Solvay only)
Czechoslovakia	• 51% of Nestomitz SW • 49% of Ebensee SW • 12.83% in Spolek holding company (former Aussig Verein)	Decree law of 24 October 1945	Committee of Belgian Industrial Interests Abroad (Czech Section)	• Binational agreement of 30 September 1952 (not ratified given Austria's objection) • Binational agreements of 6 July 1964–26 Feb. 1965; fixed-rated cash compensation (complemented with further negotiations between Solvay and the Verein Aussig reached in the mid-1980s)	Undetermined
Poland	89.5% of Zaklady w Polsce: • Montwy soda ash plant • Podgórze soda ash plant • Wapno salt mine • Grodziec coal mines and cement works	Law of 3 January 1946	Consortium for the Defense of Belgian and Luxembourg Properties, Rights, and Interests Nationalized in Poland	Binational agreement of 14 November 1963; fixed-rate cash compensation	Undetermined
Yugoslavia	94.7% of Lukavac soda plant and electrolytic unit (via Gefucin and Soud-Industrie)	Law of 5 December 1946	Committee of Belgian Industrial Interests Abroad (Yugoslavian Section)	Binational agreement of 30 October 1948; fixed-rate cash compensation	85%

Country	Assets	Legislation	Committee	Agreement	%
Romania	51% of Societatea Anonima a Uzinelor Solvay din Romania: • Ocna-Muresului soda ash plant • Turda electrolytic unit	Law of 11 June 1948	Special Committee of Belgian-Luxembourg Interests in Romania	Binational agreement of 13 November 1970; fixed-rate cash compensation	2.6%
Hungary	51% of Hungaria (various chemical products and holding companies) with Spolek (former Aussig Verein)	Law of 29 December 1949	Repartition Committee of Belgian and Luxembourg Industrial Interests in Hungary	Binational agreement of 1 Feb. 1955; fixed-rate cash compensation	16%
German Democratic Republic	• Bernburg soda ash, caustic soda plant • Solvayhall potassium salts plant, potassium mine (Roschwitz), salt mine • Eisenach soda ash plant • Westeregeln electrolytic unit, lignite mine (Caesar) • Osternienburg electrolytic unit, lignite mine (Wilhelm) • Königsaue lignite mine (Georg)	Decree of 6 September 1951	Committee of Belgian Industrial Interests Abroad (German Section)	Contacts for compensation started after official recognition of GDR by Belgium in December 1972; no agreement ever reached	–

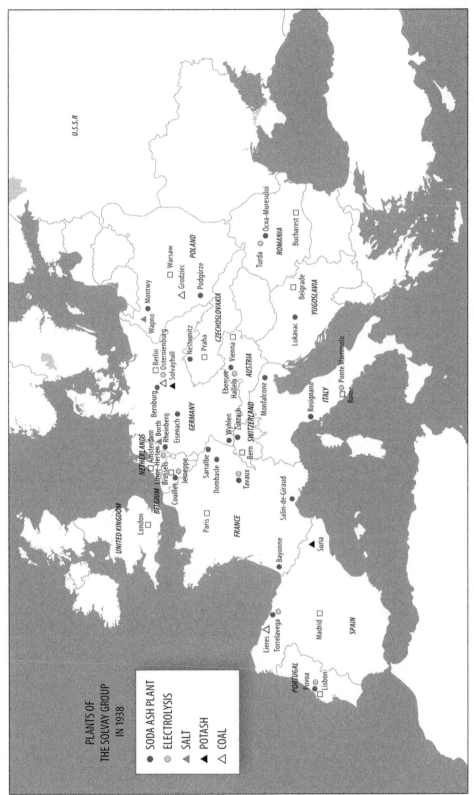

FIGURE 14.1. Map of the Solvay Group plants in 1938.

14

Conclusion of Part 2

The period stretching from 1914 to 1950 is generally associated with two salient characteristics. First, these are years of successive social, political, and economic crises (occasionally combined with glimpses of hope and recovery); second, this is an era profoundly marked by the decline of European societies – or, more aptly said, by the perception of their decline. Up to a certain point, these characteristics match the business history of Solvay. As a company present in all industrialized countries, it is no wonder that Solvay would endure the world's failures and excesses in the first half of the twentieth century. But as noted, this is true only up to a certain point. Picturing the interwar period as a dark zone caught between two shiny, successful, and challenging eras is too simplistic (or plainly too pessimistic). Further, if we can acknowledge that this period was one of a transition between the old and the new, we should certainly not interpret this in a linear sense. It should be taken as a crossroads at which multiple avenues of development are laid out, a situation in which the impression of social and economic collapse could coexist with the prospect of skyrocketing growth.

14.1 BUSINESS AND POLITICS IN THE AGE OF INSTABILITY

After the pioneering years of the 1860s, Solvay experienced forty years of continuous growth coupled with international expansion. The outbreak of World War I marked a complete breakaway from this long history of stable economic development. A rapid glance at the production figures of soda ash seems to confirm the impression of macroeconomic turbulences. The slow growth of the postwar years was followed by almost ten years of uninterrupted production increase. In the plants located in Belgium, France, Spain, and Germany, industrial outputs doubled throughout the 1920s. They tripled in the new successor states of Austria-Hungary, where Solvay had renewed its partnership with the Prague-based Verein Aussig. In Italy, the soda ash factory built in Rosignano during the war was thriving – its production capacity in alkali outweighed that of Torrelavega as soon as 1924. Then came the slump. During the worst year of the Great Depression (1933), levels of production dropped by 25 percent in Dombasle and almost by 50 percent in Bernburg in comparison with the figures of 1929. Although Solvay was hit by the world recession, the industrial impact of the Depression was relatively mild in the chemical sector as compared with others. The recovery was perceptible by

1935, after which production trends soared again until World War II. By then, however, national variations became predominant, mostly because of political reasons. The Torrelavega and Suria plants, for instance, were deeply affected by the Spanish Civil War – albeit for different reasons and in different ways. The war economy, with its focus on strategic products, gave the manufacturing of alkali a strong impetus at least until 1942. But the intensity of the military conflict caused a brutal disruption of the core structure of the economy. The painstaking transition from war to peace notwithstanding, the second postwar period witnessed the start of a state-driven golden age, whose prospects were much brighter for the world's economy.

From this macroeconomic bird's-eye view, it appears that, rather than permanent depression, severe instability had impinged on Solvay's growth during the interwar period. As such, the company was a mirror image of many other businesses, in the chemical industry and others. Yet instability came in many respects. During the interwar period, the course of business development was overshadowed by – or embedded in – the twists and turns of international politics. Political turmoil, in other words, was the other side of economic instability. Solvay was no exception to the rule – quite the contrary.[1] Thirty years after the "socialization" of Lubimoff-Solvay & Cie's two plants in the wake of the Russian Revolution, fifteen of Solvay's factories located to the east of the Iron Curtain were nationalized. As such, the multinational character of Solvay, once an asset and the hallmark of its development, became a burden in the atmosphere of national antagonism, a liability in the face of the collapse of empires. Tensions between business and politics reached a climax during the world wars. The two consecutive invasions and occupations of neutral Belgium by German troops gave way to a transformation of the company's worldwide organization policy. Although Brussels was somewhat isolated from its foreign subsidiaries during World War I, twenty-five years later the special system of *Verwaltung* (sequester) took over Solvay's factories in Nazi-dominated Europe, depriving the *gérance* of the effective supervision of its plants. The fact that members of the *Vorstand* of Deutsche Solvay Werke (DSW) had been appointed to key administrative positions during World War II was instrumental on two grounds: it allowed for intermittent contacts to take place between Brussels and Berlin and, most of all, it enabled DSW to successfully resist takeover schemes instigated by Solvay's main competitors in Germany, including its troubled partner IG Farben. Interestingly, the "hands-off policy"[2] that Ernest-John Solvay was pursuing in occupied Europe with the *Vorstand* of DSW was largely reproduced by his colleague at the *gérance*, René Boël, during his first years in London, New York, and Washington. Indeed, the threat was real to see Belgian capital in Great Britain and the United States considered enemy property and consequently put into protective custody by Allied authorities. Then again, Boël took advantage of relatively greater room to maneuver to sow the seeds of expansion in Brazil, where he trusted that the prospects for growth were promising enough.

[1] See also Kobrak (2002).
[2] The term is coined by Hayes (2001), 276.

14.2 RECASTING INTERNATIONAL INDUSTRIAL RELATIONS

Faced with the outbreak of two world wars in thirty years' time, Solvay's industrial empire has been on the verge of total collapse. In spite of the company's undisputed technical and commercial capabilities, the international political order of 1919 has profoundly changed the economic conditions and the mechanisms of business organization worldwide. The *gérants* all agreed on the main objective, namely the necessity to avoid Solvay petering out in this new global economy. But they largely diverged on the best way to tackle this challenge. For a while, Solvay's strategy had consisted of recovering its industrial power, pursuing its core business, and strengthening its presence in traditional markets. But this nineteenth-century-style industrial program soon reached deadlock. Although harnessing competitors had never been a problem for the group – Solvay had become something of an expert in adjusting marketing and pricing instruments – neutralizing industrial giants was nothing similar. It entailed rethinking the whole set of trade and business techniques. The commercial and financial agreements concluded with BASF and IG Farben's constituents in 1924 were an important step in this direction. The deal included an exchange of capital between DSW and BASF, whose nature would be criticized and exploited by East German officials after 1949. But this was just a part of a wider commercial understanding, whose roots were in the unfounded threat posed by the potentialities of the Haber-Bosch process. Underlying the project, therefore, was Solvay's defensive move to curtail competition in the production of alkali in Germany and Central Europe.

Interestingly, the Badische agreement paved the way to the recasting of Solvay's international agenda. Faced with the prospect of cartelization in the world chemical industry, Solvay fostered market stability and actively sought to set up an overarching international understanding that would include Allied Chemical, Brunner, Mond Co, and IG Farben. As it happens, the operation was implicitly designed to tame Orlando Weber, the autocrat and discrete CEO of the New York–based Allied Chemical & Dye Company, which had been set up in 1920 as a result of the merger of five companies, among which the Solvay Process and the Semet-Solvay Company were important constituents. From a respected industrial actor, Solvay had thus become a minor – albeit the most important, with about 15 percent – stakeholder in the United States' leading chemical group before World War II. To some extent, the Allied episode can be taken as a metaphor of Solvay's international dilemma in the context of interwar chemical cartels – would the company give priority to financial designs or stay firmly committed to its industrial excellence?

This central issue, which took place in the years 1925 and 1926, stirred a fruitful and vigorous confrontation of ideas about the group's long-term worldwide strategy. It undeniably was a key moment in the company's history. The conflicting strategies at stake were broken down into three groups: a challenging (though unorthodox) financial scheme advocated by Emmanuel Janssen; an attitude embodied by Louis Solvay and Émile Tournay-Solvay, which was resolutely averse to risk and to any proposal that might wane Solvay's leadership in the production of alkali; and a third-way alternative suggested by

Ernest-John Solvay, which called for a modest (albeit poorly effective) industrial conglomerate. By and large, however, the outcome of these painstaking
negotiations turned out to be a stalemate for Solvay – and a complete reorga-
nization of the international chemical industry. Indeed, one of the first results
of Orlando Weber's behavior had been to precipitate the merger of Brunner,
Mond with United Alkali and Nobel Industries into a single unit, Imperial
Chemical Industries, whose preferred partner in the United States was DuPont.
The latter company also proved instrumental for IG Farben when it took over
Grasselli Dyestuff in 1928, setting the stage for the creation of American IG
Chemical Corporation a year later. Solvay's ambition for designing its own
international reorganization was put to an end. But it was also the case of its
project for diversification, which Emmanuel Janssen vigorously supported.

14.3 DIVERSIFICATION INTERRUPTED

Solvay, as a result, did not become "a kind of a bank with a 'chemical portfolio,'" as Ernest-John Solvay had put it.[3] After this sudden setback, Emmanuel
Janssen found a meager consolation to his diversification scheme in enlarging
the scope of investments through the company's private financial vehicle –
and Janssen's special brainchild: the Mutuelle Solvay. A crucial stage had
already been achieved in 1921, when, under the impulsion of Janssen, the
Mutuelle made a stunning entry in the flat-glass business through the purchase
of the Libbey- Owens process and its license for the European market, launching the Compagnie Internationale pour la Fabrication Mécanique du Verre
(Mécaniver). More than a mere financial interest, the operation caused some
tensions in the fragile community of glass industry cartels and jeopardized a
handful of local alkali agreements. French glassmakers, in particular, such as
Saint-Gobain, were at odds with the investment, which they felt was a vertical
integration in disguise of Solvay. Tensions were reactivated in 1927, when,
after the disillusion caused by the failure of its international program, Janssen
launched Union Chimique Belge (UCB), a merger of several Belgian chemical
companies, a "little Allied" in itself. A second orientation was taken by the
Mutuelle Solvay in 1928 with an investment in artificial silk industries in
Belgium, Italy, and France (where its ties with the Lyons-based family business
Gillet were reinforced). From a modest family bank, Emmanuel Janssen
had transformed the Mutuelle Solvay into a dynamic holding group with a
diversified portfolio ranging from chemical products (chlorine, nitrogen, and
phosphates) to chemicals for the consumer industries (glass, paper, soap), but
also banks, real estate, and raw materials. Impressive as its development was
throughout the 1920s, the Mutuelle Solvay was severely hit by the financial
crisis. It endured an important restructuration process, mainly through
divestment of stakes and exchange of shares. The Mutuelle was kept under
the close scrutiny of Solvay with a reduced portfolio of chemical interests, and
nonpriority assets were taken over by a new bank set up in 1931 – Société
Belge de Banque. This put an end to the experience of diversification through

[3] ACS, NdG, Note d'Ernest-John Solvay, 27 Apr. 1926.

the Mutuelle. Emmanuel Janssen interpreted this reorganization as a personal denunciation of his role and withdrew from the *gérance* in 1930 in the midst of a managerial crisis that followed Armand Solvay's death the same year. He further concentrated his efforts on the development of UCB, Société Belge de Banque, and Mécaniver, which in 1933 became S.A. Glaces et Verres (Glaver).

In a short span of time, Solvay witnessed the shift from the heroic generation of pioneers to the second and third generations of *gérants*. In terms of managerial style, this meant the substitution of a single and uncontested leader for a more collegial – and thus conflicting – process of decision making. In terms of organizational structure, it consisted in getting the balance right between respecting the traditional corporate mechanisms and adapting those patterns to the newly defined objectives. Overall, if taking over the legacy of Ernest Solvay was not an easy job per se, it proved a task worthy of Sisyphus in these difficult times. In this context, René Boël, who officially became *gérant* in 1931, progressively became the right man at the right place. His ability to play team with his senior brother-in-law, Ernest-John Solvay, and the other young *gérants* (Philippe Aubertin and Robert Gendebien) proved successful in many respects during the 1930s. While Ernest-John was watching over Solvay's interests in the British Imperial Chemical Industries (which accounted for 6 percent of capital), René Boël spent a fair amount of his time regaining Solvay's contested shareholder position in Allied Chemical. There, he acted with the help of a group of corporate lawyers from the Sullivan & Cromwell law firm (especially with John Foster Dulles) and from investment banks (e.g., George Murnane). The strategy largely paid off when, in 1935, Orlando Weber stepped down (i.e., was ousted by a majority group of shareholders) as general manager and became chairman of the board.

Later, Ernest-John Solvay and René Boël's contrasting war experience led to a difference of approach at the head of the group. After the conflict, Boël became a driving force in getting Solvay on the tracks of product diversification. Since his arrival, he had largely been responsible for enabling the Technical Department to inquire into the causes of Solvay's lagging behind the electrolytic process despite its early start. After only a few years, Boël insisted that electrolytic caustic soda was high on the company's agenda. These initiatives turned out to reinvigorate Solvay's focus on chlorine and chlorine derivatives (and on chlorine-based trade international agreements). Although Solvay would tackle a full-fledged diversification policy only after World War II, it is incontestable that the drive for this strategy was rooted in the technical experiments of the 1930s and 1940s.

PART 3

THE ERA OF DIVERSIFICATION AND GLOBALIZATION (1950–2012)

Ernst Homburg

FIGURE 15.1. After 1945, Solvay diversified into plastics. This picture shows autoclaves for the production of PVC at Jemeppe, Belgium, Solvay's first industrial PVC plant. (Solvay Archives.)

15

Growth through Diversification

The Successful Entry into Plastics and Peroxides

Five years after the end of the war, the Solvay management was still strongly involved in a balancing act between looking backward and looking forward. Many of the issues resulting from the war were not yet resolved: the legal status of Solvay's fifteen factories and mines in East Germany and Central Europe, the ownership of the IG Farben shares in the possession of Solvay, and the future of the shares of Deutsche Solvay Werke (DSW) owned by IG Farben (see Chapter 13). These issues demanded a lot of attention from Solvay's leaders. At the same time, they worked hard to recapture Solvay's traditional markets and embarked on new activities in the plastics field. In November 1949 Henri Delwart, *gérant* since 1945, summarized the challenges his company had to meet during the coming twenty years. They were many. Competition would grow more aggressive, and as a result, the margins on the two major products, soda ash and caustic soda, would decrease. To make things worse, the production of caustic soda by means of causticization of soda ash was seriously endangered by the rapid growth of caustic soda produced by electrolysis (see Chapter 11). Moreover, artificial silk produced by the viscose process – the major market of caustic soda – was increasingly being replaced by completely synthetic fibers, which did not need large amounts of caustic soda for their production. As a result of both developments, Delwart predicted that Solvay's causticization plants would have to be closed down. Another major problem was of a financial nature. For its expansion in new directions – both geographically and with respect to its product portfolio – Solvay needed large sums of money, but the export of profits to Belgium was increasingly restricted by foreign governments.[1]

Solvay management's answer to these challenges was twofold. First and foremost, Solvay tried to regain its previously powerful position by continuing its traditional, successful strategies. The second answer was diversification into new product areas such as organic solvents, pesticides, peroxides, and especially plastics. Originally started to defend Solvay's position in the field of caustic soda and electrolysis, these new products increasingly gained momentum of their own. Whereas in 1950 Solvay's product portfolio was confined almost exclusively to soda ash, caustic soda, and inorganic chlorine derivatives, by 1967 nearly half of the company's turnover was realized outside those domains.

[1] ACS, NdG, H. Delwart, "Société Solvay & Cie. – Situation actuelle et perspectives," 2 Nov. 1949.

Moreover, since its beginnings Solvay had served only industrial markets, but by 1967 it started to integrate into consumer products as well. Marketing played a growing role.[2]

These developments took place in a context of almost-uninterrupted economic growth. During the first years after the end of the war, growth rates were still quite low. After the mid-1950s economic growth started to accelerate, though, a trend that continued until the end of the 1960s. During the entire period production and consumption figures for plastics and polymers grew even stronger than the economy as a whole. Up to 1970 plastics remained, in the words of Peter Spitz, the "engine for growth" of the entire petrochemical industry.[3]

The successful engagement of that engine in Solvay's growth trajectory is the main focus of the present chapter. It illustrates the emergence of a new company strategy, namely diversification, which transcended the traditional policy of the two pillars, as René Boël called them: (1) the exchange of technical information between the industrial activities of the group and (2) the conclusion of commercial agreements with the major competitors (see Chapter 6). Finding such a new orientation was far from easy. Some *gérants* said good-bye only reluctantly to the old, well-tested business practices. In the 1950s, two of their colleagues would be the major driving forces of Solvay's transformation: René Boël, *gérant* since 1931, and Henri Delwart. It was Boël who pushed forward Solvay's expansion in Brazil, the United States, and West Germany. Delwart, in his turn, coordinated and stimulated the research activities that were crucial for Solvay's diversification. They were joined late 1955 by Jacques Solvay and five years later by Paul Washer, who would play a role in the backward (Solvay) and forward (Washer) integration of Solvay's production activities. These "integration" activities are discussed in Chapter 16. The present chapter is devoted mainly to the diversification of the product portfolio.[4]

15.1 SOLVAY'S INTERNATIONAL COMEBACK

Before we sketch in detail Solvay's entry in the plastics field, it is important to emphasize that Solvay also regained part of its position in the chemical industry through a strategy that combined cost reduction and cooperation with ICI, with energetic attempts to grow in Brazil, the United States, and West Germany. After great losses in Central and Eastern Europe and the loss of control over its British and American investments, Solvay had largely become a Continental, Western European company, with a far more limited geographical scope than during the nineteenth century. Boël's attempts to grow in Brazil and the United States were a first attempt to reverse that development. Becoming a global company again would occupy Solvay during most of the past sixty years (see Chapters 18 and 20).

[2] "Allocution du Baron Boël . . . 9 juin 1969," *Revue Solvay* (May–June 1969): 11–14.
[3] Spitz (1988), 227–9.
[4] ACS, 1151, interview Count Boël, 16 Jan. 1987.

Immediately after the war, Solvay renewed its close relations with ICI in the field of alkalis and electrolysis (see Chapter 11). On 1 June 1945, a provisional agreement was formulated by ICI with the intention to revitalize mutual relations. "Solvay and ICI," it said, "believing that the pre-war co-operation between them (which has gone on for nearly seventy years) in the technical and commercial development of the alkali business has been of benefit both to the Company and to the industries and communities which it serves, wishes to renew this co-operation." The document confirmed the geographical market divisions that had been agreed on before the war. Solvay would get Continental Europe, as well as the Belgian and French colonies. The United Kingdom, the British Commonwealth, and large parts of Africa and Asia would be reserved for ICI. In nondeveloped markets both companies would cooperate. South America was a matter of discussion.[5]

Around 1950 the close cooperation with ICI, which would last for another three decades, gave Solvay a safe haven for conquesting new alkali markets. This should have compensated for the loss of all its assets behind the Iron Curtain. Three targets were the highest priority: gaining footholds in both Brazil and the United States and regaining a large market share in Germany.

In Brazil, Solvay and ICI created a joint subsidiary, the company Industrias Quimicas Eletro Cloro SA (or Eletro Cloro), which started an electrolysis plant in May 1948 at Elclor, near São Paulo. By the early 1950s René Boël had the firm conviction that the Elclor plant should be greatly expanded to become Solvay's bridgehead for the conquest of the South American market. Apart from ever-larger amounts of caustic soda and chlorine, crop protection agents, PVC, and other organic chlorine products were to be manufactured. With that industrial policy Solvay ran into conflict with ICI. The British firm wanted to focus on Britain and the Commonwealth, and it was not prepared to invest large sums of money in politically unstable Latin American countries.[6]

Apart from these problems with ICI, there also was no unity of vision within Solvay's top management. René Boël and Henri Delwart were in favor of a Brazilian factory with a broad scope that would produce most of Solvay's major products, including organic chemicals. Ernest-John Solvay, in his turn, preferred a focus on alkalis and chlorine. It would take several years before a final consensus was reached. By 1955 ICI decided to grant a PVC license to Eletro Cloro (see Section 15.3), and in the same year, Solvay and ICI came to an agreement with respect to a territorial separation of their interests in Argentina and Brazil. ICI received Argentina, and Solvay, Brazil. The road to the expansion of Solvay's Brazilian business was open. Eletro Cloro started the production of PVC resins (1956), trichloroethylene, high-density polyethylene (HDPE; 1962), corrugated PVC sheets (1964), and peroxides (1974). Solvay's Brazilian subsidiary became an important chemical

---

[5] ACS, 1241–51-1, Proposal for an agreement on alkalis, Winnington, Northwich, 1 June 1945.
[6] [Diafería] (1991), 14; ACS, NdG, R. Boël, "Politique de Solvay & Cie. en Amerique du Sud. Relations avec l'I.C.I.," 5 Oct. 1951.

company with a considerable market share in caustic soda, chlorine products, and PVC.[7]

In the United States Solvay's industrial interest had largely been reduced to a mere financial interest (see Chapter 9). Nevertheless, that interest was substantial. The company owned some 20 percent of the shares of Allied, a company more than four times as large as Solvay. Before the outbreak of World War II, Solvay had created an American trust, the Solvay American Corporation (SAC), and had transferred all its Allied shares to that company. With the considerable dividends of SAC, Solvay was able to finance a large part of its investment in Portugal and Brazil. In 1954 Solvay controlled a financial holding in the United States of more than $134 million, which was about equal to Solvay's total equity. The largest portion of this huge capital was Solvay's stock of Allied shares, with a total value of $93 million. These large financial reserves would play an important role in financing Solvay's growth in the 1950s and 1960s.[8]

Part of that money was also invested in the United States. As is described in Chapter 18, during the 1950s René Boël tried to obtain a controlling interest in Wyandotte Chemicals Corp., a producer of soda ash and a possible springboard for the manufacture of PVC. Because of reluctance from the owners of the US firm and disagreement between the *gérants*, the Wyandotte operation failed in the end. It would take another twenty years before Solvay would invest in the United States on a large scale.

In Germany, Solvay tried to regain in two ways its prewar share of almost 60 percent of the soda ash market, which had dropped to about 40 percent as a consequence of the loss of Bernburg and other East German plants: by a great enlargement of the Rheinberg soda ash factory and by the acquisition of a soda ash plant at Heilbronn. That factory was one of the seventeen sites of Kali-Chemie, in which DSW owned a substantial part of shares (see Chapter 9).[9]

Of these two targets, the enlargement of Rheinberg and the nearby salt mine at Borth was easier to achieve, though costly. Almost immediately after the end of the war, René Boël gave orders to repair and enlarge the plants at Rheinberg. Between 1948 and 1960 production of soda ash at Rheinberg grew from about 200,000 tons to 478,000 tons. There were also investments in new laboratories, the acquisition of a limestone quarry, process automation, a power station, more modern calcination furnaces, and a PVC plant. By 1960

[7] ACS, NdG, H. Delwart, "Accords I.C.I./Solvay. Evolution des problèmes relatifs à l'Amérique (Nord et Sud)," 17 May 1952; ACS-CR, Agreement in regard to the manufacture of vinyl chloride products in Brazil, between ICI, Solvay and Solvic, 1 Apr. 1959; "Connaissez-vous les sociétés filiales? Solvay au Bresil," *Revue du Personnel* (1973) (5): 2–5; interview Robert Friesewinkel, 2 Oct. 2008.

[8] Reader (1975), 49–50; Haynes (1954), 9–11; ACS, black binder "Ibasa"; idem, "Povoa," 5; ACS, 1151, interview Count Boël, 16 Jan. 1987; letter by Robert Friesewinkel to Paul Washer, 13 Dec. 2007; ACS, NdG, R. Boël, "Politique industrielle de Solvay & Cie. aux Etats-Unis," 11 Oct. 1954.

[9] ACS, CdG, 24 Sept. 1958; ACS, 1805-40-2A, Report on a travel of Baron Boël and P. Solvay to Germany, 17–20 Dec. 1949.

Rheinberg was absolutely a stronghold of Solvay within the German industrial landscape.[10]

The acquisition of the majority share of Kali-Chemie, by contrast, proved a complicated affair, given the financial intertwinements of DSW and Kali-Chemie with IG Farben; the divergent views of the Allied occupational powers with respect to the handling of the IG Farben assets; and the competing interests of other business groups, such as Goldschmidt, Flick, and IG Farben's successor Bayer. In 1953 Solvay succeeded in acquiring the majority share of Kali-Chemie (see Chapter 13), and during the following year the Heilbronn plant was integrated into the ICI-Solvay system of benchmarking and exchanging technical information.[11]

As is discussed in Chapter 19, the acquisition of Kali-Chemie would have an important impact on the course of Solvay's history. Solvay decided to buy Kali-Chemie primarily because of its Heilbronn plant. But after it had become the majority shareholder, it had acquired in the same go, "for free," sixteen other factories and mines that made products that were quite foreign to Solvay. In the long run, though, some of these products – pharmaceuticals, barium salts, and (since 1960) fluorine salts – would become important diversifications for Solvay. With about 5,200 workers and employees in 1954, Kali-Chemie was a large acquisition for Solvay. As a result of the consolidation, the overall sales of the Solvay group jumped from BEF 6.7 billion (US$134 million) in 1953 to about BEF 10 billion (US$200 million) in 1954, and Germany became Solvay's largest production center, replacing France.[12]

Looking back on these three major attempts to compensate for the business losses of World War II, we can conclude that the results were mixed. In Germany and Brazil, Solvay succeeded in improving its sales considerably. In the United States, however, the dream to again own a large alkali subsidiary could not be realized. In all three countries it was primarily René Boël who energetically drove the business on. With his large European and transcontinental network, he could easily move in different circles. After the war, he became very active in the European movement and particularly in the European League for Economic Cooperation. This intellectual business pressure group, founded in 1946, strove to foster economic cooperation among Western European countries, "with a view to build prosperity and offer opportunities to create collective wealth in a war torn and fragmented Europe."[13] Boël became its president in 1951 and remained active in that role for no fewer than thirty years. As *gérant* of a company that had factories in many countries, he knew better than anyone else the pros and cons for industry of small internal markets, different legal systems, and different tax regimes. After the establishment of the European Economic Community in 1957, Solvay would

[10] Rupprecht (2007), 106–8.

[11] ACS, CdG, 26 June 1956; ACS, 1151, interview Count Boël, 16 Jan. 1987; idem, "Relations Solvay-IG Farben," 1986.

[12] ACS, CdG, 4 Feb. 1954, 11 Feb. 1960; ARS 1967; ACS, 1805–37-34, "Politique de Solvay à l'égard de la Kali-Chemie," 18 Oct. 1978.

[13] "European League for Economic Cooperation, 60th Anniversary"; see http://www.elec-lece.eu.

still profit for many years from having production plants in many European countries.[14]

15.2 RESEARCH AND DIVERSIFICATION

When PVC production at Solvay started on an industrial scale in 1949, the company had almost fifteen years' experience in the field of organic chlorine chemistry. Without that background it would have been almost impossible to become a successful producer of PVC. Until the mid-1930s Solvay's chemical expertise was totally confined to inorganic and physical chemistry. But in 1935 Solvay started manufacturing its first organic chlorine product: the solvent and degreasing agent trichloroethylene (see Chapter 11). This was the beginning of a new direction, but one that was modest compared to what Solvay's competitors were doing at that time.

Parallel to the manufacture of these products, Solvay started to do research in the field of organic chemistry: on solvents, higher-chlorinated ethanes, tetrachloromethane, hexachlorocyclohexane (HCCH), and chlorinated naph-thalenes and rubber. In 1939 the head of the (research) laboratories, Léon Flamache, put the feedstock problem high on the agenda. For trichloroethy-lene, but also for PVC, acetylene and ethylene were the two most important raw materials. Acetylene could be made from calcium carbide, which was easy to transport but expensive; ethylene could not be transported, which meant that the plant should be situated close to a source of ethylene, such as a coke oven or petroleum refinery. During the following years, the chemists in the research laboratory at Ixelles would study the manufacture of organic chlorine chemicals from acetylene and ethylene, so that Solvay could adapt to changing economic conditions.[15]

Flamache also advocated creating specialized laboratories to study the appli-cation of its products, with a specialized plastics laboratory, for instance, for PVC. With these views, he was ahead of his time, at least inside Solvay. They implied a certain degree of forward integration and active involvement with the problems of the consumers of Solvay's products, and as such, they stood quite squarely in Solvay's strategy, which was formulated around 1930 (see Chapter 10), to keep away from the markets of Solvay's customers.

After the liberation of Belgium in September 1944, it was decided that to defend its position in the alkali field, it was crucial for Solvay to put organic chlorine chemistry at the top of its research agenda. Research in the Cen-tral Laboratory of Solvay at Ixelles was complemented by development work and research executed in the pilot plants and laboratories of the factories at Jemeppe, Zurzach, and Tavaux.[16]

---

[14] Dumoulin and Dutrieue (1993); report of a conversation between Yves Boël and Jean-Marie Solvay, 2 June 2009.
[15] ART, "L'utilisation du chlore en chimie minerale et organique et le développement de son employ," 20 June 1939.
[16] ACS, CdG, 22 Feb. 1945, 22 March 1945, 8 Nov. 1945, 16 May 1946.

The Solvay research effort was growing so quickly during the first post-war period that the Central Laboratory at Ixelles soon became too small. Because of a lack of funds, Flamache decided to give his ambitious research program more focus. This was an important turning point in the almost-unlimited diversification program that Solvay's research organization had taken on board. In October 1947 it was decided to concentrate the expansion program, and most research-and-development activities, on only four products: sodium chlorite, the insecticide HCCH, the weed killer phytohormone 2,4-D, and vinyl chloride plastics. This was indeed the course taken: insecticides, phytohormones, and plastics would become for some years the focal points of research.[17]

By 1950 Solvay's research staff had grown to 150 persons. In September of 1951 the company bought a site at Neder-over-Heembeek (NoH), north of Brussels. This would become the location of Solvay's new central research laboratories. Between 1953 and 1958 laboratory activities were transferred in phases from Ixelles to NoH. The complex was greatly enlarged during the 1960s.[18]

In the 1950s Henri Delwart and his staff formulated a new research program for the Central Laboratory, which was directed at a systematic effort to increase the "valorization" of all by-products of the electrolysis: of hydrogen through research on hydrogen peroxide and sodium perborate; of the amalgam, produced in the mercury cell, through research on uses of sodium; and of chlorine, through research on chlorinated solvents made from acetylene or methane, and on plastics made from acetylene or ethylene (PVC) and propylene (allyl chloride derivatives). This program would steer the research during a large part of the 1950s and give rise to new product diversifications, such as chloromethanes and peroxides.[19]

The first organic chemicals introduced to the market, tri- and perchloroethylene, reached high sales figures and were produced for around fifty years, until they were largely taken out of production for environmental reasons during the early 1990s. Other new products were less successful; they often found a market only during World War II, when competition was less intense and when better alternatives were often lacking. After the war Solvay was probably handicapped by the fact that it did not have a well-functioning marketing organization outside the alkali realm. Moreover, when production of PVC started to become a major outlet for electrolytic chlorine in the 1950s, there were no longer reasons to keep those minor products in production. Chemicals for crop protection are a good example; they are discussed in Chapter 19.

[17] ACS-CR, Contract between L'Immobilière Electrobel and Solvay et Cie., 9 Aug. 1946; ACS, CdG, 30 Oct. 1947.
[18] ACS-CR, "Convention intervenue avec les Bouchonneries Réunies au sujet de l'achat de ses terrains et immeubles de Vilvorde," 4 Sept. 1951; Rapaille (1990), 114–16.
[19] ACS, NdG, H. Delwart, "Politique de Solvay & Cie. dans le domaine des produits nouveaux," 24 Feb. 1955.

15.3   THE WORKHORSE OF THE PLASTICS INDUSTRY: PVC

The fact that several of Solvay's diversifications in organic chemistry failed illustrates how difficult it is for a company to successfully start a new business outside its core area of competence. In the 1940s Solvay's technological leadership in soda ash and causticization was undisputed, but its competences outside that domain were few. A notable research organization was still in its infancy, and a marketing organization was almost nonexistent. Practical experiences with the markets of pesticides and plastics were zero. The failure of Solvay's agricultural business therefore makes even more pronounced the extraordinary achievement of Solvay in acquiring a leading position in PVC within one decade.

That Solvay decided to enter the plastics field, and PVC in particular, after it had decided to embark on organic chlorine chemistry at all, should be no surprise. Since the late 1930s consumption and production of plastics were booming, with annual growth figures of more than 20 percent. During and just after the war, plastics were hyped. Within this new sector, PVC – discovered in 1912, and produced industrially since 1927 – was the market leader. Moreover, the production of PVC consumed large amounts of chlorine. Contemporary observers called "polyvinyl chloride... a large scale, low cost plastic with so many basic applications that it might be considered the workhorse of the thermoplastic industry."[20] This versatility was an additional advantage. By choosing that particular plastic, Solvay avoided becoming dependent on one narrow market segment.[21]

When Solvay negotiated with ICI in the summer of 1945 about licenses on ICI's PVC technology, the topic was not completely new to the Belgian firm. In 1941 the French company Saint-Gobain, a longtime customer, partner, and competitor of Solvay in the alkali field, approached Solvay about cooperating in the production of PVC, and as a result, Solvay in 1943 made plans to construct a pilot plant for vinylchloride monomer (VCM) at Tavaux. Shortly after the war, research on PVC also started in the well-equipped chemical laboratory of the Solvay works at Zurzach, Switzerland, especially investigation of the continuous polymerization process that IG Farben had practiced at its plants at Schkopau and Ludwigshafen.[22]

Learning from ICI

Parallel to the activities going on at Tavaux and Zurzach, Solvay negotiated with ICI. The British company had started research on PVC in 1939, after failed negotiations with IG Farben on the exchanges of licenses in the plastics

---

[20] DeBell, Goggin, and Gloor (1946), 40.

[21] Pistor (1958), 75, 82, 105, 219–20; Freeman and Soete (1997), 121–3.

[22] ACS, NdG, J. L. Semet, "Y a-t-il des obstacles à la conclusion d'un accord avec St. Gobain pour la production de polyvinyles chlorés, et plus tard d'autres produits chlorés secondaires," 10 Mar. 1941; Daviet (1988), 588–9, 607–9; ART, RC/PD, "Programme de recherches du Laboratoire central au cours des prochaines années," 2 June 1942; ACS, CdG, 22 March 1945, 16 May 1946; DeBell, Goggin, and Gloor (1946), 40–1.

field. Two years later, a PVC plant came on stream at Runcorn, in the United Kingdom. The PVC resin was marketed by ICI under the trade name Corvic. After the Japanese had conquered British Malaya, thereby cutting off Britain from its rubber supplies, a larger PVC plant was constructed by ICI at Hillhouse for the British government. As a result, ICI had two well-running PVC plants by the end of the war and experience using Corvic in a number of applications.[23]

René Boël had been kept informed by ICI during his wartime stay in Britain. After the war he strongly emphasized that Solvay should start negotiations on getting full access to ICI's PVC technology. Although it became soon clear also that the German PVC patents could fall into the public domain, Solvay did not want to have only licenses on patents. It wanted a head start in the new field, and therefore increasing its know-how on running plants was essential.[24]

In November 1945 ICI agreed that it would grant Solvay nonexclusive licenses on PVC for Holland, Italy, Belgium, and France. Immediately after the general agreement, without any details on license fees and other legal issues spelled out, the intensive exchange of technical information began. From 28 November to 7 December 1945, a large Solvay delegation visited the PVC installations of ICI at Runcorn and returned home with reports, flow sheets, and technical drawings of both the monomer and the polymer installations. With the help of these and later reports, Solvay could intensify its research at the Central Laboratory at Ixelles and plan the construction of a pilot plant at Jemeppe.[25]

Transfer of technical information on PVC was already in full swing for many months before negotiations on the conditions of the license started in August 1946. It would take until February 1948, though, before an agreement was reached. Mutual trust between the ICI and Solvay was great, because during those months, the exchange of engineers and technical information continued as before.[26]

Playing on Several Chessboards at the Same Time

From 1946 to 1949 research and development on PVC at Solvay took place at Tavaux, Zurzach, Brussels, and Jemeppe. As we have seen, work at Tavaux started during the war. As a result, the developments in France took their own route. In 1948 arrangements had been made with the Société Polyplastics, a subsidiary of the American PVC producer B. F. Goodrich, which had contacted Solvay with plans to construct a PVC factory next door to the Solvay site at Tavaux. For unknown reasons, the PVC plant of Polyplastics at Tavaux never

[23] Reader (1975), 358–9, 361.
[24] ACS-CR, Agreement between Imperial Chemical Industries Limited, Société Solvay et Cie., and Baron René Boël, 25 Feb. 1942.
[25] ART, "I.C.I. – Polychlorure de Vinyle – Fabrication, notes and correspondence," 17 Nov. 1945 to 26 Mar. 1946; ART, "Installation de l'ICI de Weston Point, Runcorn. Voyage en Angleterre du 28.11 au 7.12.45 de MM. Delwart, Flamache, Deprez, Marlier et Klopfenstein."
[26] ART, "I.C.I. – Polychlorure de Vinyle – Fabrication, notes and correspondence," 2 Aug. 1946 to 23 Feb. 1948.

took off. In March 1951 Solvay and ICI decided to include France in the existing general PVC framework agreement.[27]

Work on PVC at Zurzach took the lead during 1946. Early that year René Boël ordered two pilot plants for the production of ethylene – by cracking of oil products – from Wyandotte Chemicals Corp., in the United States (see Chapter 18). They were shipped in 1947 to Jemeppe and Zurzach to be used for the production of PVC. When ICI asked Solvay in February 1947 to start up production of PVC before 1 January 1948, *Direction Générale Technique* (DGT) concluded that only the installations at Zurzach were perhaps ready. The target was not reached, but it was planned to turn the installations into the pilot plant for the entire group. For financial reasons it was decided in 1949 to stop the PVC development work at Zurzach and to use the installations for other purposes.[28]

With two false starts behind it, Jemeppe would become the first Solvay site at which PVC was actually produced on an industrial scale. In Belgium there was also no straight line to the finish. During the first part of 1946, Solvay was approached by the Société Belge de l'Azote et des Produits Chimiques du Marly (SBA) and its subsidiary Société Belge d'Electrochimie (SBE), about developing PVC technology together and starting a joint PVC plant close to the SBE works at Langerbrugge, near Ghent, where it produced calcium carbide, the raw material for acetylene. Already SBA had developed its own PVC process, and it produced the resin on a limited scale. Negotiations went on until December 1947, when Solvay definitely decided in favor of the ICI process; it would become a producer in Belgium. Jemeppe was chosen, which had the advantage that a plant for the production of acetylene from carbide was already available, for the production of tri- and per-chloroethylene. Installations with a capacity of 1,750 tons of PVC per year were constructed that could easily be enlarged to 3,500 tons per year. In the last months of 1949 the VCM and PVC plants at Jemeppe came on stream, supported by experts from ICI. Solvay had become a PVC producer. In hindsight, this was a definitive turning point in the history of the group.[29]

Two Great Problems: Royalty Payments and Product Quality

Apart from acquiring technical mastery of PVC manufacture, commercial aspects also required the company's full attention. In relation to ICI, Solvay wanted to reproduce as much as possible the conditions reigning on the alkali market, namely with Solvay as king on the Continent and ICI as emperor within

[27] ACS, CdG, 30 Aug. 1945, 20 Apr. 1949; ACS, RdG, 8 Nov. 1949; ACS-CR, P.V.C. – France, 19 July 1950; ACS-CR, Imperial Chemical Industries Limited and Solvay & Cie: Agreement adding France to the European countries in which Polyvinyl Chloride is to be manufactured, 17 Mar. 1951.

[28] ACS, CdG, 16 May 1946, 12 Feb. 1948; ACS, RdG, 16 Nov. 1948.

[29] ACS, NdG, H. Delwart, "Chlorure de polyvinyle – Projet d'accord avec la Société Belge d'Electrochimie," 24 June 1946; ACS, CdG, 18 Dec. 1947, 6 Apr. 1950; *Société belge* (1955); ART, "Comte rendu des principales questions traitées au cours de la visite de Mr. Ginns des ICI (19.5 au 27.5.1949)," 15 June 1949; Bolle (1963), 188.

the British Empire. In agreements made in 1947 and 1948, ICI had reserved for itself the right to export its PVC to Europe, as long as Solvay could not satisfy the demand. Solvay, in turn, had the advantage of having good knowledge of the local political and economic conditions in many European countries, and it had electrolysis plants in several of them that produced chlorine, an essential ingredient of PVC. These assets would play a great role in the construction of Solvay's PVC business that, as it were, grew out of Solvay's strong alkali position.

Perhaps to stand stronger with respect to ICI, Solvay's strategy during the first years after the war was to engage itself in local arrangements that were independent of the British giant. In some cases such arrangements were even essential to get permissions from the national governments. The connections with Saint-Gobain and Polyplastics in France and SBA in Belgium have already been mentioned. In Austria Solvay negotiated with the Creditanstalt; in Italy the company cooperated first with Snia Viscosa and later with the Società Anonima Industriale Gomma Sintetica (SAIGS); and in Spain Solvay's national manager, Norbert Fonthier, also preferred developing the market together with local partners. All these initiatives started in 1947, the year in which Solvay also investigated the production of PVC in Brazil.[30]

During those preparations to erect PVC factories in several countries, Solvay encountered major problems with the February 1948 agreement with ICI. Rules imposed by several national governments caused problems regarding the payment of royalties and made it necessary to make specific license contracts for each country. Moreover, in the course of 1948 it became clear that Solvay's potential to develop the PVC market was hindered by the fact that the ICI-Solvay contract was restricted to the mere production of VCM and PVC. Solvay could only make one simple type of PVC at Jemeppe, but in the meantime, ICI had developed a whole array of PVC grades, and the firm was developing the Benelux market to find customers for those grades. Therefore, ICI put pressure on Solvay to include PVC compounds, technical service, and marketing in the contract, for a higher fee, of course. Under these terms, with Solvay selling one grade and ICI the others, customers would be confused, which would make the joint effort vulnerable in light of growing competition.[31]

The Birth of Solvic

By the end of 1948 ICI and Solvay concluded that it was in their common interest to develop a completely different setup, a joint venture instead of a set of licenses. The general framework agreement of 15 October 1949, which specified the arrangements for the Benelux countries, Austria, Italy, and Spain, with Switzerland pending, had the following main features: (1) the establishment of joint ventures between Solvay and ICI, named Solvic, or similar, in the countries mentioned; (2) exclusive licenses and full disclosure of all of ICI's

[30] ACS, black binder "P.V.C. Genèse des Stés. Solvic," 21, 24, 27, 30; ACS, CdG, 30 Oct. 1947, 12 Feb. 1948.
[31] ACS, black binder "P.V.C. Genèse des Stés. Solvic," 27.

PVC know-how, including plastics processing, technical service, and market-ing; (3) the inclusion of copolymers with at least 70 percent vinyl chloride; (4) a duration of thirty years, with the option to prolong; and (5) no payment of any royalties, but instead a donation, for free, to ICI of one-quarter to one-fifth (depending on the country) of the capital shares in the new companies. The contract specified this last arrangement in the following way: up to a specified size of the plant (3,500 tons per year in Belgium, 3,000 tons per year in Italy, 1,200 tons per year in Austria, and 1,000 tons per year in Spain) ICI would get its share in the capital for free; Solvay and the others partners would pay the initial investment. In the case of later plant extensions surpassing those values, ICI would coinvest in relation to the percentage of its share.[32]

It was a brilliant maneuver that removed two great problems in one go. As a result of the new contract, Solvay could reach agreements in Austria and Spain. The faster development of the market, especially in the Benelux countries, guar-anteed greater profits for ICI. Solvay, in turn, had the advantage of remaining in charge on the Continent as majority shareholder, and coinvestments by ICI would help expand the business. Moreover, under the new contract both part-ners would communicate their most recent improvements, which would greatly speed up the learning curve.[33]

Solvic's International Expansion

Shortly after the October 1949 agreement had been concluded, production of PVC came on stream at Jemeppe; PVC plants in other countries would follow. Henri Delwart and Léon Flamache, who had handed over responsibility for Solvay's R&D to Lambert Vanharen and had become general manager of Solvic in Brussels, were the driving forces of that development. They coordinated the global strategy of all the "vic" companies (e.g., Solvic, Halvic). In 1956 Flamache was succeeded by Raoul Berteaux.

We do not discuss the national developments in detail here, but we sum-marize the main data in Table 15.1. In most countries joint ventures were established for production and sales, but not in Brazil and Germany, where the Solvay subsidiaries also became responsible for PVC, with payment of a royalty to Solvic (Belgium) and ICI. For three years Jemeppe was the only PVC plant of Solvic, but then, in 1953, three new plants opened in Italy, France, and Austria. Another three years later Spain and Brazil followed, and two years later Solvic PVC was also produced in Germany. The experience acquired in the existing plants was successfully used in the design and start-up of new ones. Foremen and technicians of Tavaux, for instance, helped in the start-up of the PVC plants at Elclor and Torrelavega. In this way constant learning and improvement

[32] ACS 1241–51-1, "Imperial Chemical Industries Limited and Solvay et Cie.: Agreement in regard to the manufacture of Polyvinyl Chloride in certain European countries," 15 Oct. 1949; ART, "I.C.I. – Polychlorure de Vinyle – Fabrication, notes and correspondence," 10 Dec. 1948 to 5 May 1949; interview Henri Lévy-Morelle, 9 Nov. 2007.

[33] ART, "I.C.I. – Polychlorure de Vinyle – Fabrication," letter D.C. Allen to Solvay & Cie., 2 Aug. 1946.

TABLE 15.1. *The International Development of Solvay's PVC Business, 1949–1959*

Founding Date Joint Venture or Date of License	Country and Area	Operating Company	Partners	Location PVC Plant[a]	Start of Industrial Production and Trademark
26 Oct. 1949	Benelux	Solvic SA, Brussels	Solvay (75%) ICI (25%)	Jemeppe	Oct.–Dec. 1949 Solvic
6 July 1950	Austria	Halvic GmbH, Salzburg	Solvay (51%) Creditanstalt (29%) ICI (20%)	Hallein (PVC)	Nov. 1953 Halvic
19 Oct. 1950	Italy	Solvic SpA, Rosignano, from 1953 Ferrara	Solvay (75%) ICI (25%)	Ferrara (PVC) Rosignano (VCM)	1953 Solvic
7 July 1952	France	Solvic SA (France), Paris	Solvay (75%) ICI (25%)	Tavaux	June–Nov. 1953 Solvic
14 Nov. 1955 + 19 Feb. 1959	Spain	Hispavic SA+ Hispavic Industrial SA, Barcelona	Solvay (36.945%) Cros (36.945%) Azamon (ICI) (21.11%) Thiebaut (5%)	Torrelavega	Mar.–Oct. 1956 Hispavic
6 Apr. 1956	Brazil	Industrias Quimicas Electro Cloro SA, São Paulo	5% royalty to be paid 50–50 to Solvic SA and ICI	Elclor	Apr. 1956 Elvic
15 July 1959	West Germany	Deutsche Solvay-Werke GmbH, Solingen	3% royalty to be paid 50–50 to Solvic SA and ICI	Rheinberg (PVC) Tavaux (VCM)	July 1958 Solvic

[a] If VCM production took place elsewhere, the main VCM supplier is mentioned.
Source: ACS, black binder "P.V.C. Genèse des Stés. Solvic."

took place. On several occasions the start of production anticipated the formal arrangements. Spain was a difficult case because the Franco government opposed foreign influence in the national economy, as well as the transfer of profits to other countries. Negotiations with several Spanish ministries dragged on for almost seven years.[34]

In the second part of 1954, Henri Delwart and René Boël also proposed to the *gérance* to start the production of plastics, notably PVC, in the United States. The American plastics market was developing quickly. More than 50 percent of the global production of plastics was produced there. Therefore, by being present in that country, Solvay would be forced to learn quickly about the sales of plastics in a very competitive market, and it would gain important contacts with customers that were keener than Europeans to absorb innovations. This would give Solvay a great advantage over its European competitors, Delwart and Boël argued. An investment of US$25 million to US$30 million would be needed for the first steps. Later, this bridgehead in PVC could be extended to other processes and products, such as electrolysis, peroxides, solvents, and new co-polymers that were in the development stage at Solvay. As a result of divergent views within the *gérance*, this initiative did not materialize (see Chapter 18). But the example shows clearly Solvay's ambitions to become an important global player in PVC. What would have happened if Solvay had started PVC production in the United States in 1955 is difficult to say. The only thing we can safely conclude is that a decade later it had become almost impossible to start a new PVC plant in the United States. In business timing is crucial. During the 1960s vinyl chloride and PVC started to be produced by petroleum and chemical companies in the United States on such large scale that there was huge overproduction. Most of the later entrants lost a lot of money. Solvay never started PVC production in the United States.[35]

Improving Product Quality and Marketing

To conquer a market, low costs and high product quality are essential parameters. With respect to low production costs, Solvay could build on its general technological expertise, its cooperation with ICI, and its longtime experience with benchmarking. But with respect to product quality and marketing, the situation in the PVC market was very different from Solvay's familiar soda ash market. Instead of a small number of large industrial clients, PVC resins were sold to a great number of small and medium-sized plastics processing firms. Moreover, the versatile workhorse PVC was used in many different applications, such as packaging, pipes, coatings and laminates, construction, music

---

[34] Ducordeaux, Robin, Tétu and Amiot (2005), 145; ACS, black binder "P.V.C. Genèse des Stés. Solvic," 24; ACS-CR, "Convention entre Cros – Solvay & Cie. – M. Thiebaut – Azamon – ICI et Plasvic"; "Convention réglant la fabrication du PVC en Espagne par l'entremise de Plasvic," 22 May 1951; Sánchez Landeras (1998).

[35] ACS, NdG, H. Delwart, "Remarques relatives au projet de participation dans la Durez," 9 Sept. 1954; idem, R. Boël, "Politique de Solvay & Cie. aux Etats-Unis," 10 Feb. 1955.

records, and automobiles, and it was processed by a whole array of different techniques, such as extrusion, calendering, injection molding, and blow molding. To further complicate the situation, mostly additional materials, such as plasticizers, pigments, stabilizers, and fillers, had to be added in varying proportions to satisfy the demands of specific clients. As a result, a great number of PVC grades and compounds (i.e., mixtures of PVC with additives) had to be produced and marketed. This presupposed good knowledge of the requirements of the customers and demanded a completely different approach to the technical service and marketing that were usual at Solvay. Under the leadership of Flamache and Delwart, the Solvic companies took these requirements on board, quite independent of DGT.[36]

Product improvement took place from the start. In the summer of 1950 the Solvic product was already considered of higher quality than the PVC resin of the existing Italian manufacturer Montecatini, "thanks to the value of the ICI process and to our technology."[37] Nevertheless, growing competition in the attractive PVC market demanded further quality improvement. Flamache's earlier proposal to erect specialized plastics laboratories was put into practice. During the 1950s and early 1960s, Solvic founded laboratories and experimental workshops for plastics at Brussels, Tavaux, Milan, Rheinberg, and Barcelona. There, testing methods for PVC resins were improved and applied, new compound formulations were developed, and all kinds of technical advice and support were given to clients and to the sales personnel of Solvic. Parallel to that process, research was done in pilot plants at Jemeppe and in the new development station *fabrication expérimentale* (FEX) at Tavaux. Together, these application laboratories and pilot plants played an invaluable role in the market penetration of Solvic PVC in Europe. By 1956 Solvic already was making dozens of different kinds of PVC.[38]

During the first years of its existence Solvic only made pure PVC resins, so-called rigid PVC, and it succeeded in improving the ICI formulas considerably. Customers who needed different, more flexible types of PVC added plasticizers and other additives themselves. Large plastics-processing firms were well equipped for that. To also serve smaller clients, Solvic decided to start producing PVC compounds, in which the resin was mixed with additives required for certain applications, using technologies developed by the rubber industry. In 1953 a plant to produce compounds, under the trade name Benvic, came on stream at Jemeppe. From 1958 onward, similar Benvic plants were also constructed at Tavaux, Elclor, and elsewhere. Another semimanufactured product was Premix, which was produced at Jemeppe since 1960 and at Ferrara, Rheinberg, and Tavaux a bit later. An energetic publicity effort, with advertisements, publicity films, and presence at fairs and expositions, accompanied the market

---

[36] Buchmann (1944); Kaufman (1969).
[37] ACS, NdG, H. Delwart, "P.V.C. – Italie" and "P.V.C. – France," 19 July 1950; id., H. Delwart, "Politique de Solvay & Cie. dans le domaine des produits nouveaux," 24 Feb. 1955.
[38] ART, PM/GF, "Programme de recherches pour 1964," 27 July 1964; Ducordeaux, et al. (2005), 130, 138–9, 228–9, 279; "Les Matières Plastiques." In *Solvay & Cie* (1958).

TABLE 15.2. *PVC Production and Sales of Solvay's*
Subsidiaries, 1950–1960

Year	Production (tons)	Sales of PVC (BEF million)	Percentage of Total Turnover of the Solvay Group
1950	1,000		
1951	2,500	90	1.3
1952	3,000		
1953	14,000		
1954	17.000		
1955	22,000		
1956	34,000	1,050	8.6
1957	46,000	1,090	8.8
1958	57,000	1,405	11.1
1959	82,000	1,655	12.2
1960	100,000		

Note: Data for 1951, 1953, and 1954 are production capacities.
Source: ACS, 1514-4-1 to 1514-4-6, production and sales of PVC;
Solvay & Cie. Brussels: Solvay & Cie, 1964, 25; AR 1968–1969.

introduction of new PVC grades, compounds, and Premix, especially since the late 1950s, when competition intensified.[39]

Growing to the First Rank

In the 1950s the plastics market expanded greatly. Increasingly, plastics replaced wood, metals, textiles, and natural rubber in numerous consumer goods and applications. Also at Solvic growth of production was impressive (see Table 15.2). Every year the growing demand exceeded expectations. From a mere 1,000 tons in 1950, production grew to about 100,000 tons in 1960, which made Solvay in that year the largest PVC producer in Europe and one of the largest in the world.[40]

These figures leave no doubt that the strategic plan to diversify into PVC had succeeded. There are a few factors that can explain that success. The decision to gain a head start by taking a license on proven technology from ICI certainly was crucial. When Solvay started production in 1949, there were already several European PVC producers, but most of them – apart from the German companies – were still in their infancy. If Solvay would have waited a few years more to first develop its own technology, the situation would have been very different, with higher entry barriers. Moreover, the great rate of expansion of the PVC market during the 1950s gave room for newcomers. Solvay energetically invested in research on all aspects of plastics. It also

[39] ART, Démarrages et Arrêts des Fabrications; idem, Capacité de Production, Solvay & Cie.; ACS, CdG, 15 Feb. 1962; Ducordeaux et al. (2005), 147.
[40] Henson and Whelan (1973), 11; ACS, CdG, 5 June 1957, 15 Feb. 1962; Rupprecht, ed. (2007), 112–13, 126, 138.

introduced marketing organizations and technical-commercial services in the Solvic companies, at arm's length from the alkali business and therefore fully tuned to the new challenges of a complex, differentiated market. Last but not least, Solvay's PVC business followed on its previous multinational experience in alkalis: whereas Solvay's competitors focused almost completely on their home markets, Solvay constructed within a few years a number of plants all over Europe, and even in Brazil. By growing over such a wide front, Solvay could establish itself as the largest European producer. With seven PVC plants in the late 1950s, there were also seven chances to experiment, to fail, and to learn, which led to a cross-fertilization of experiences with the other plants.

But this successful system also had its disadvantages, as when the establishment of the Common Market and the emergence of new, large-scale technologies in the United States intensified competition. By that time Solvay had broadened its plastics basis by starting the production of another bulk plastic, polyethylene, and through a process of forward integration into plastics processing (see Chapter 16).

15.4 BROADENING IN PLASTICS: THE PRODUCTION OF POLYETHYLENE

During the 1940s and 1950s, many producers of plastics resins came to the conclusion that it would be better for their position in the plastics market to produce more than one type of plastic. Solvay thought along similar lines and decided to start producing polyethylene (PE), after investigating polystyrene (PS) and polyethylene, the two most common plastics after PVC, as possible options. For PE only one external raw material was needed, ethylene, whereas for PS also benzene was required. Moreover, Solvay had done some research on the chemistry of ethylene since the late 1930s, because it was also a feedstock option for trichloroethylene and PVC. Nevertheless, the decision to produce PE was far reaching, because until then Solvay had only produced chemicals whose raw material supply it could control. From an early date the company had invested in salt mines, limestone quarries, and coal mines (see Chapter 2). In the case of PE, Solvay did not have its own supply of ethylene, a fact that would have costly consequences.[41]

ICI's Polyethylene and the Belgian Syndicate

Polyethylene was discovered by scientists at ICI in 1933. The new plastic, later called low-density polyethylene (LDPE), was produced at very high pressures, a process that was patented in 1936. Small-scale production at ICI started in 1939. During the war, PE was mainly used as cable insulator in high-frequency radar applications. After the war, ICI tried to monopolize its sophisticated technology as much as possible and refused to grant licenses. After lengthy legal procedures, ICI was forced in the early 1950s to give nonexclusive licenses to US firms. By that time it had been discovered that PE was also an

---

[41] Interview Paul Washer, 29 Nov. 2007; letter Paul Washer to authors, 20 May 2011.

excellent material for the production of plastic films and household products. Demand was booming. The market grew so fast that ICI, with its own plants working at full capacity, decided to also grant a limited number of licenses to European firms; PE became ICI's most profitable product derived from research.[42]

Shortly after the war, several Belgian chemical companies became also highly interested in the production of polyethylene and other products from ethylene. As mentioned already, by June 1946 SBA had approached Solvay to request joining forces in the plastics field. Its research manager, Pierre Schideler, saw a great future in the construction of a large petrochemical complex at Antwerp. He succeeded to get the Société Carbochimique and the Union Chimique Belge (UCB) on board, and during 1946 and 1947 these companies, together with Solvay and SBA, met several times to discuss a collective effort in petrochemicals.[43]

All four companies had different specific interests, and, as a consequence, the joint project only took off slowly. Solvay was reluctant to invest in a petrochemical complex that it did not control itself. It needed its funds badly for its own investment plans. Under pressure from the socialist and technocrat Paul De Groote, then minister of economic coordination and reconstruction, who wanted to support the Antwerp region, the cooperation among the four companies was continued as the Syndicate for Chemical Research on Oil Derivatives, founded in November 1948.[44]

Polyethylene was one of the products on the agenda of the syndicate, and in July 1950 it was decided to ask ICI to grant a license for Belgium. This put Solvay in a difficult position, because the *gérants* preferred to develop ethylene cracking and PE production at Jemeppe. This option was also preferred by ICI, who wanted to grant a PE license for Belgium and Holland to its 25 percent subsidiary Solvic. Solvay installed a cracking pilot plant for ethylene production, purchased from Wyandotte, at Jemeppe and informed the syndicate on 27 December 1950 that the company had decided to go it alone and construct its own polyethylene plant at Jemeppe.[45]

Thereafter, SBA and Carbochimique started a legal procedure against Solvay that lasted at least until 1953. As a consequence, the plans for PE production at Jemeppe were greatly delayed and finally dropped. In the meantime, SBA, Carbochimique, and UCB continued their collaboration. Together with Petrofina and some other companies, they founded Pétrochim in 1954, which constructed a petrochemical complex at Antwerp.[46]

[42] Reader (1975), 318, 323, 349–59, 361, 433, 437, 452, 454; Kennedy (1986), 53–4, 61–71, 76–7, 105–6.

[43] ACS, NdG, H. Delwart, "Chlorure de polyvinyle: Projet d'accord avec la Société Belge d'Electrochimie," 24 June 1946; ACS, CdG, 18 Dec. 1947.

[44] Dumoulin (1997), 132, 176; ACS-CR, "Syndicat pour l'Étude Chimique des Dérivés du Pétrole (S.C.D.P.)," 24 Nov. 1948; ACS, NdG, H. Delwart, "Entretien avec M. de Groote, ancien Ministre de la Coordination Economique et du Reequipement National," 20 Aug. 1951.

[45] ACS-CR, "Compromis d'arbitrage entre la Sté. Carbochimique, la Sté Belge de l'Azote et des Prod. Chim. du Marly, et Solvay & Cie," 12 Nov. 1951.

[46] ACS, RdG, 22 Apr. 1953; Dumoulin (1997), 131–3, 174–8; Mittmann (1974), 255, 263–5.

Phillips's High-Density Polyethylene

When Solvay in 1955 redirected its attention to polyethylene, the international technological and industrial situation had completely changed. By that time ICI had licensed its process to companies in France, Germany, and Italy, which were Solvay's most important markets. Production by Solvay of LDPE was therefore out of the question. Between 1951 and 1953, though, quite unexpectedly, the Phillips Petroleum Company in the United States and Professor Karl Ziegler of the Max-Planck-Institut für Kohlenforschung in Germany had discovered, independently, a harder and more rigid kind of polyethylene – high-density polyethylene (HDPE) – which could be produced at much lower pressures than LDPE with the help of special catalysts. From 1952 onward, Ziegler started to license his process on a large scale to numerous chemical and petroleum companies in Europe, the United States, and Japan. As his process had only been investigated in the laboratory, all technological development still had to be done by the companies that took on the licenses. Phillips Petroleum, however, developed its process industrially and decided to construct two large HDPE plants near two of its refineries in Texas. They were planned to come on stream in late 1956. During the construction of these plants, the Phillips Petroleum Company started to license its process, because "market projections showed demand... would be more than Phillips Petroleum could supply." Accordingly, Phillips Petroleum licensed in 1955 and 1956 its process to companies in Britain, Japan, Germany, and France.[47]

Solvay started to negotiate with Phillips Petroleum as well, after Antonin Šrba of North American Solvay Inc. had informed Solvay's research leader Lambert Vanharen in April 1955 of the possibility of taking out a license on the Phillips process (see Chapter 18). The company succeeded in getting a license for Italy on 17 February 1956, and for Brazil a month later. Licenses for the Benelux countries, Germany, and Spain were investigated by Solvay, but did not result in the end. The fact that, as in the case of PVC, Solvay took a license on more or less proven technology and not a mere laboratory discovery certainly helped the company in getting to the market early. The contract stipulated close technical collaboration between Phillips Petroleum and Solvay in this area for ten years, which was favorable for a beginner, but there was also a price. The initial license fee of US$1,650,000, for Italy alone, was high, higher than the usual fees for the Ziegler process.[48]

The Start of PE Production at Rosignano and Elclor

In 1957 a team of five Belgian and Italian engineers went to the United States to study the production process in the laboratories and factories of Phillips

---

[47] Wertz (1983), 127–32; Martin (2002); Musset (1959).

[48] ACS, 1514-5-11A, letter by Vanharen to North American Solvay Inc., 18 May 1955; id., A. J. Šrba to Solvay Brussels, 12 July 1955; ACS, RdG, 19 July 1955; ACS, "Contrats conclus avec la Phillips Petroleum Cy," Licence Agreement, 17 Feb. 1956; ACS-CR, Solvay-Phillips Petroleum, contracts and letters of 17 Feb. 1956, 29 March 1956; ACS, CdG, 3 March 1956; interview Henri Lévy-Morelle, 9 Nov. 2007; interview Félix Bloyaert, 26 Mar. 2009.

FIGURE 15.2. When Solvay embarked on the production of high-density polyethylene (HDPE), the supply of the raw material ethylene at first was a great problem. At Rosignano special trucks for the transport of liquid ethylene (seven tons), developed by ICI, were used at the end of the 1950s. (Solvay Archives.)

Petroleum. In the meantime, members of DGT discussed with ICI the supply of ethylene to the plant at Rosignano. It was decided that during the first few years ethylene would be procured from Edison, Italy, and transported to the plant in special ethylene tanks under pressure, designed by ICI. Apart from the PE plant, an installation for the production of the chromium oxide catalyst was built at Rosignano, and at Milan a laboratory for product testing and application research on the new plastic. Start-up of the polyethylene plant, in June 1959, went smoothly. This certainly was a great success, because other licensees had encountered serious problems during start-up. Also, product quality was good. It soon appeared that Solvay was the only European producer that had succeeded in producing PE according to the norms set by Phillips Petroleum.[49]

High-density polyethylene, marketed by Solvay under the trade name Eltex, was a relatively new product, with different properties than the older low-density polyethylene. When in 1957 the first producers came to the market, the initial reaction was hesitant. That changed dramatically in 1958 when the hula-hoop rage among American children broke out, which blew over to

[49] ASSR, "Contrat de license exclusive stipulé le 17.2.1956 entre la Phillips Petroleum Company et la Société Solvay & Cie pour la fabrication en Italie de resines de polyolefines," 4 Mar. 1957; ACS, CdG, 19 Sept. 1956, 4 Mar. 1958, 30 Oct. 1959; ACS, "Contrats conclus avec la Phillips Petroleum Cy." Licence Agreement, 31 Aug. 1959, 1 Sept. 1959; ART, "Note pour la Gérance. Examen du programme d'extension du PLT-Rosignano," 16 Oct. 1959.

Europe a bit later. Large orders for HDPE came in from hula-hoop producers. By 1962 the use of the new plastic in the production of bottles was growing spectacularly. Before the Rosignano plant came into production, Solvay had already begun to prepare the Italian and Benelux markets by importing polyethylene made by Phillips Petroleum in the United States. The following year Solvay sold its own product mainly in Italy, the Benelux countries, and Brazil. Exports from Rosignano to the French and German markets were blocked by the exclusive licenses that Phillips Petroleum had granted to other companies. Despite this, production capacity at Rosignano was raised to 4,800 tons per year in 1960 and to 10,000 tons per year three years later.[50]

Elclor would become Solvay's second production location of HDPE. For the production of this new plastic resin in Brazil, Solvay in 1957 decided to establish a separate firm, Petroclor – Indústrias Petroquímicas, which was a joint venture of Eletro Cloro and Solvay. The HDPE plant constructed at Elclor was largely designed with help of the plans and experiences at Rosignano. Because Brazil had no petrochemical industry at that time, Solvay decided to produce ethylene from alcohol, made from sugar cane. In June 1962 the Petroclor plant came on stream.[51]

Research and Innovation

Similar to the case of PVC, also in the field of PE, Solvay decided in favor of a considerable research effort. Henri Delwart and Lambert Vanharen created a few research teams in the Central Laboratory at Neder-over-Heembeek. One of the teams started research on the Ziegler catalyst. Early 1956, Félix Bloyaert, together with his colleagues G. Pirlot and N. Denet, in an attempt to circumvent the Ziegler patents, achieved a real breakthrough by synthesizing a highly active Ziegler-type of catalyst, with three components, colloquially known as the ternary catalyst. By 1959 a well-running process was developed that showed that the ternary catalyst was robust enough to function under practical conditions. It produced a kind of HDPE with different properties from those of the Phillips product. Application on an industrial scale was soon planned, because the license fees to Phillips could be reduced, and the product could be exported to other European countries. The Rosignano plant could become a large-scale unit that would produce polyethylene for all countries of the European Economic Community. The fact that Solvay had taken out patents on the ternary catalyst in all major European countries made such a situation possible.[52]

The industrial installation started production during the second part of 1964. The product was launched simultaneously in Italy, France, the Benelux

---

[50] Wertz (1983), 130–1; Blackford and Kerr (1996), 251–2; ACS, 1051-3-16, "Contrat Solvay & Cie./ Phillips Petroleum pour la production de PLT via catalyseur ternaire"; ACS, CdG, 15 Feb. 1962, 6 March 1963.

[51] ACS-CR, "Contrat Phillips-Solvay conclu pour la bonne exécution du contrat Phillips-Elclor," 29 March 1956; ART, "Ethylène par ethanol," 30 Jan. 1960; ACS, CdG, 5 June 1957, 14 March 1959, 25 Feb. 1962; [Diaféria] (1991), 51.

[52] Interview Félix Bloyaert, 26 Mar. 2009; letter by Félix Bloyaert to the authors, 13 Apr. 2009; ART, "Note pour la Gérance: Examen du programme d'extension du PLT-Rosignano," 16 Oct. 1959.

TABLE 15.3. *HDPE Production by Solvay, 1959–1969 (in tons)*

| Year | Rosignano | | | | Elclor |
	Phillips HDPE	Ternary HDPE	Supported Catalyst HDPE	Total HDPE	Phillips HDPE
1959	1,142			1,142	
1960	3,394			3,394	
1961	4,952			4,952	
1962	6,363			6,363	783
1963	8,473			8,473	1,221
1964	9,017	674		9,691	2,864
1965	7,858	3,114		10,972	3,665
1966	10,004	8,017		18,021	4,330
1967	12,626	15,165		27,791	5,327
1968	13,248	18,840		32,088	?
1969	12,022	21,561	103	33,686	?

Source: ART, "Solvay & Cie. Rapports annuels – Partie technique," No. 1; ART, PDO; ACS, CdG, 15 Feb. 1962.

countries, and Germany. Within a few years the plant was enlarged to more than twenty thousand tons per year, all produced free of royalties, whereas the Phillips Petroleum plant was limited to a level of about twelve thousand tons per year (see Table 15.3). Apart from growing use as plastic resin for bottles, HDPE also was starting to be used as material for dashboards and other automotive parts. Later, automotive would become one of HDPE's most important markets (see Chapter 21).[53]

In the meantime, total staff at Neder-over-Heembeek grew from 820 persons in 1961 to 1,150 in 1965; most of them worked in plastics. In the field of polyolefins (i.e., polyethylene and polypropylene), scientists succeeded in improving the ternary catalyst during the early 1960s by fixing the active ingredients on a so-called support. Looking back on these developments more than forty-five years later, Félix Bloyaert, then head of polyolefins research, remembered:

> We put titanium tetrachloride on [an inert material]. The active catalyst was distributed on a larger surface.... We put the same amount of Ziegler catalyst and of our supported catalyst preparation and discovered that the reaction was much better. It was terrific. We relieved the pressure, opened the vessel and it was completely full of very good white powder. It was a great surprise.[54]

By 1965 the supported catalyst held great promise and was chosen as the preferred catalyst for future extension of Solvay's HDPE production, because the production costs of HDPE were lowered by a factor of three. In 1971 the Phillips Petroleum plant at Rosignano was shut down, and the supported catalyst plant took over production.[55]

[53] ACS, CdG, 21 Sept. 1961, 20 Mar. 1962, 13 June 1963; ART, PM/GF, "Programme de recherches pour 1964," 27 July 1964.
[54] Interview Félix Bloyaert, 26 Mar. 2009; Solvay patent applications of 18 Nov. 1960, 22 Oct. 1962, 25 June 1965, 6 Jan. 1969; Martin (2002), 159, 171, 187nn75–80.
[55] *Solvay & Cie* (1977), 33.

Again, patents first blocked the application of the new discovery. The supported catalyst appeared to be dependent on earlier Ziegler patents. In 1967, Solvay signed a license contract with Ziegler. Two years later, additional licenses were taken out for France and Brazil. Solvay could widely apply its supported catalyst on an industrial scale. After the plant at Rosignano had started production, another HDPE plant with supported catalyst came on stream in October 1970 at Sarralbe, France (see Chapter 16), and in 1972 a similar HDPE plant started production at Elclor. The technology was licensed to other companies and was producing good revenues.[56]

The examples given here clearly show that the research performed at the Central Laboratory, especially in catalysis, led to important industrial applications. Without these innovations Solvay would probably have not been able to keep pace with its competitors. Several of these competing firms tried to strengthen their position in the PE market by extending their product range to polypropylene (PP), a related plastic but one with different properties. Solvay followed the developments in that area closely. Research started in the late 1950s and went on slowly until late 1969, when a true breakthrough was achieved when a new catalyst was found. As is often the case with new discoveries, chance played a large role. The discoverers of the new catalyst, Jean Pierre Hermans, A. Delbouille, and Paul Henrioulle, one Friday were doing experiments with titanium trichloride, one of the components of a new ternary catalyst, and they left the substance in a pot over the weekend. When they returned on Monday, it appeared that the brown titanium trichloride crystals had turned violet. An unknown modification had been discovered. When testing the activity of the new modification, it appeared to be magnificent, to everybody's surprise. Soon Solvay realized that it had found a gold mine. The new catalyst was patented worldwide, and it opened for Solvay the door to polypropylene production. From 1974, a PP plant was constructed at Sarralbe, which started to produce in 1976. Again, large revenues were also received from licensing.[57]

15.5 BECOMING A KEY PLAYER IN PEROXIDES

In a very different area, Solvay's research had good results as well. When Henri Delwart formulated Solvay's research agenda in 1955, one of the priorities was the valorization of hydrogen gas, a by-product of salt electrolysis. The gas could be used for the production of hydrogen peroxide, a bleaching and disinfection agent that could replace the more toxic chlorine in these applications, and a chemical that could be used in the production of perborates, which were in great demand in the detergents industry. Before World War II several processes for the production of hydrogen peroxide had been developed, and they received a great boost during the war when the substance was extensively used as oxygen

---

[56] ACS-CR, Contracts between Prof. Dr. Karl Ziegler and Solvay & Cie, 24 June 1967, 13 Feb. 1969; Martin (2002), 171, 187n81; *Sarralbe* (1986), 28; interview Félix Bloyaert, 26 Mar. 2009; letter by Félix Bloyaert to the authors, 13 Apr. 2009.

[57] Patents 9 Feb. 1959 (NL19590235917), 3 Sept. 1962 (FR PS 1,306,453), and 28 May 1970 (LU19700610007); interview Alfred Hoffait, 14 May 2009.

supplier for the combustion of rocket fuel in German V-1 and V-2 rockets. One of the most successful processes, the anthraquinone process, was developed by H. J. Riedl and G. Pfleiderer during the 1930s and licensed to IG Farben for further industrial development. After the war, the details of that process were diffused by the technical intelligence services of the Allies, and via that route the information also reached Solvay.[58]

Research on the anthraquinone process started in Solvay's Central Laboratory in 1951. Between 1952 and 1954 a pilot plant was constructed at Jemeppe, under the supervision of Daniel Fastrez of DGT, who coordinated development work. As working with hydrogen peroxide is delicate and dangerous, utmost care had to be given to the design of the installations, the purity of the ingredients, and the details of procedures. After the process had been developed successfully, an industrial plant with a capacity of about three thousand tons per year of hydrogen peroxide came on stream at Jemeppe during the autumn of 1958, followed shortly thereafter by similar plants at Tavaux and Rosignano. At all those sites also plants for the production of sodium perborates were constructed. The intermediate anthraquinone needed in those plants was produced at Solvay's site at Linne-Herten.[59]

When the peroxide and perborate plants at Jemeppe started production, these substances were already produced at a site of Kali-Chemie at Bad Hönningen, Germany, where barium peroxide had been produced since 1933. This product was subsequently converted into hydrogen peroxide. Perborates were produced as well. After Solvay had acquired the majority of the shares of Kali-Chemie in 1953, DGT started to investigate with great interest the plants at Bad Hönningen. Although production was running smoothly in 1956, Solvay's anthraquinone process was considered superior, and Kali-Chemie decided to take out a license from Solvay. Between 1957 and June 1959, the production of hydrogen peroxide at Bad Hönningen was converted to the Solvay process.[60]

Within a remarkable short time of two years, Solvay had started four hydrogen peroxide plants in four different countries. The development has some striking similarities with the development of PVC at Solvay. Instead of constructing one large plant for the entire European market, which certainly could have been an option after the conclusion of the Treaty of Rome in 1956, Solvay decided to start with rather small plants on a national basis. Although in the long run that would become a problem (see Chapter 21), in the embryonic phase of a new development this had the advantages of being close to the market and of the cross-fertilization of improvements realized at different sites. Moreover, in the case of a delicate chemical such as hydrogen peroxide, production at a very large scale certainly would have been a dangerous and risky undertaking.

[58] ACS, NdG, H. Delwart, "Politique de Solvay & Cie. dans le domaine des produits nouveaux," 24 Feb. 1952; Davidson, Blockley, and Vigers (1946); "25 ans d'eau oxygénée," *La Revue Solvay* (1983) (3): 18–20.
[59] "Le peroxide d'hydrogène l'épine dorsale de la gamme production d'Interox," *La Revue Solvay* (1983) (1): 12–13; ACS, CdG, 18 Oct. 1957, 18 Sept. 1958, 30 June 1959.
[60] Rüsberg (1949), 64–5; ACS, CdG, 17 Oct. 1956, 18 Oct. 1957, 30 Oct. 1959.

Solvay traveled cautiously along the learning curve and only gradually achieved a scale-up.

Solvay was not the only company embarking on the profitable business of peroxides and ingredients for detergent. Others, such as Solvay's competitor and later partner Laporte, did the same in those years. As a result, when Solvay entered the market in 1959, it was spoiled by overproduction. Use of hydrogen peroxide in missiles grew more slowly than expected, and other producers had already strong positions in perborates. After a difficult first year, Solvay succeeded in greatly enlarging its market share by improving the quality of its products and lowering production costs. In 1959 it achieved a market share of 13 percent in the European Economic Community, but by 1961 this had already grown to 37 percent, which made Solvay one of the largest European producers within only a few years. But this was only the beginning. In 1966 a hydrogen peroxide plant was started at Torrelavega in Spain, and the following year a small plant for pharmaceutical purposes was opened in Portugal. Increased competition in entire Europe forced Solvay to also improve its marketing.[61]

In the meantime, Solvay had started talks with the British company Laporte, partly to investigate collaboration in peroxides but also because Solvay was interested in Laporte's process for producing titanium dioxide. Negotiations on the latter topic failed in the end, but an agreement on peroxides was reached in 1970. Solvay and Laporte decided to create a joint venture, Interox, in 1971. Solvay introduced seven plants to the joint venture, in Belgium, the Netherlands, France, Italy, Germany, Spain, and Portugal. Laporte, in turn, transferred two plants in the United Kingdom to Interox, as well as plants in Germany and Australia, and minority interests in firms in Japan, India, South Africa, France, and Spain. It was a great move, creating in one stroke the largest global player in the peroxides business. Solvay and Laporte immediately started to further invest in the growth of Interox. During the 1970s, new plants were created in Finland, Brazil, Yugoslavia, and – at the end of the decade – in the United States. Interox kept its leading global position in this way. For Solvay, peroxides were one of its most profitable businesses. It replaced chlorine for environmental reasons as the main bleaching agent in the paper and pulp industries, which constituted a huge market (see Chapters 18 and 21).[62]

15.6 CHANGE AND CONTINUITY

In many respects in 1967 Solvay (see Chapter 17) was a very different company from in 1950. In response to the threats sketched by Henri Delwart in his note

[61] ACS, CdG, 12 Feb. 1959, 21 Sept. 1961, 15 Feb. 1962; "Réunion Oxy," *Revue Solvay* (March–April 1969): 15.

[62] ACS, RdG, 15 May 1966; Sánchez Landeras (1998), 186; ACS-CR, Laporte/ Solvay: Declaration of Intent, 12 March 1970; idem, Agreement between Laporte Industries (Holdings) Limited, London, and Solvay & Cie. SA, Brussels, 30 June 1970; AR 1970: 22–3; "Parlons produits: Les peroxydes," *Revue du Personnel* (Dec. 1971–Jan. 1972): 5–9; "Laporte Industries (Holdings) Ltd," *La Revue Solvay* (Feb.–Mar. 1975): 3–5.

TABLE 15.4. *Sales of Different Product Groups, as Percentages of Total Sales of the Solvay Group*

Year	Soda Ash and Caustic Soda	Chlorine and Chlorine Products	Plastic Resins and Compounds	Plastic Products	Peroxides	Other Products
1951	81	8	1	0	0	10
1967	30	9	19	15	4	23

Note: Total sales grew from BEF 5,000 million (US$100 million) in 1950 to approximately BEF 29,000 million (US$580 million) in 1967.

Source: ACS, CdG, 11 Feb. 1960; AR 1967.

of November 1949, Solvay had embarked on a threefold strategy: strengthening the existing alkali business, diversifying into plastics and peroxides, and integrating forward and backward into final products and raw materials (see Chapter 16). Here we have mainly focused on the second element. The results of that diversification strategy certainly were remarkable. Whereas in 1951 almost 90 percent of Solvay's sales were in alkalis and chlorine, in 1967 this had fallen to less than 40 percent (see Table 15.4). Moreover, the 10 percent of other products in 1951 (e.g., salt, potassium salts, calcium chloride) were closely related to the alkali business, but in 1967 this group included new product areas such as pharmaceuticals, barium salts, and fluorine products (all products of Kali-Chemie) that potentially held great promise for the future. The most spectacular change, though, was the growth of Solvay's plastics resins and plastic products (see Chapter 16) businesses, together from almost zero to more than one-third of total sales.

The table, which shows only the sales of marketed products, camouflages the enormous growth of chlorine production at Solvay. In fact, chlorine production grew more than tenfold between 1950 and 1967, from 66,000 tons to more than 680,000 tons, and inevitably, because in a salt-electrolysis chlorine and caustic soda are produced at the same time, caustic soda production also grew, from about 75,000 tons to 770,000 tons. There is some irony in this development, at first glance at least. Solvay invested in electrolysis and chlorine products, such as plastics, to defend its caustic soda market. But by so doing, it at the same time undermined its own causticization plants. Production of these plants went down from about 690,000 tons in the peak year 1951 to 240,000 tons in 1967. Between 1952 (Monfalcone) and 1977 (Ebensee), Solvay closed down all its causticization plants, except Povoa, that until Portugal's EU membership in 1986 could work with profit as a result of Solvay's absolute monopoly on the protected Portuguese market.[63]

But the irony is only superficial. The decline of causticization and the rise of electrolytic caustic soda was part of a global development that was larger than Solvay. Whereas before World War II there was an oversupply of chlorine, during the 1960s the roles were completely reversed, largely as a result of the growth of the plastics industry. Chlorine was in great demand, and caustic soda

[63] ART, PDO.

was sold at a loss. If Solvay would not have taken part in this development, its situation would have been worse. In that case, Solvay would have become a soda ash producer of limited scope, in a market that would increasingly have been threatened by caustic soda produced by electrolysis.

To protect its traditional markets, Solvay followed a strategy of cost reduction via scaling up. Large soda ash plants, such as Dombasle, Rosignano, Rheinberg, and Torrelavega, became even larger; small plants, such as Wyhlen (1959), Giraud (1961), Bayonne (1965), and Monfalcone (1969), were closed down, unless local conditions still made small plants profitable for a while, as in the case of Povoa, Zurzach, and Ebensee, all situated in countries that were not part of the European Economic Community. The fact that Solvay closed down three soda ash plants and seven causticization plants between 1950 and 1967 was quite unusual for the company and illustrates the growing role of competition, predicted by Delwart in 1949, and the increasing role of the European Common Market.[64]

Next to scaling up and selective closure of plants, a third strategy to defend the caustic soda position was innovation. After about 1960 Solvay worked hard on the development of a new way of chlorine production, without producing caustic soda at the same time. The answer was finally found in the construction of a new type of electrolysis installation, with diaphragm cells instead of the common Solvay mercury cells, connected to soda ash works. The caustic lye produced in the diaphragm cells was transported to the soda ash plant and was there carbonated to soda ash. The first installation of this new type came on stream at Dombasle in 1965. Four years later, similar electrolysis plants started production at Rheinberg and Jemeppe. In the case of Jemeppe, a pipeline of twenty kilometers was constructed to connect the new electrolysis unit with the soda ash plant at Couillet.[65]

By a combination of offensive (plastics) and defensive (alkalis) strategies, Solvay succeeded well between 1950 and 1967 to remain the most important player on the Continental alkalis market and to move to the first rank in PVC. The period clearly was a transitional one, characterized also by tensions between the *gérants* that saw Solvay still primarily as an alkali firm, and those who wanted to place the company on a far-broader product basis. Partly as a result of those tensions, many characteristics of the company were still very similar to its situation in 1950, despite all the drastic changes: Solvay was still largely a European company (Brazil contributed less than 4 percent to production); engineers still dominated the company culture; the financial accounting system was still far from perfect because of the priority given to technical accounting; and Solvay's market orientation, though greatly improved, was still very modest compared to that of other companies. A transformation of the company had started; its realization was incomplete (see Chapter 17).

[64] ART, PDO.
[65] ART, PDO; ACS-CR, "Arrêté ministeriel relative à une permission de transport de saumure et de lessive caustique par canalisations entre Couillet et Jemeppe-sur-Sambre, accordée à Solvay et Cie," 7 Oct. 1968; Mittmann (1974), 141–2.

FIGURE 16.1. For the production of ethylene (for HDPE) and acetylene (for PVC) a cracker was constructed at Rosignano; this photo is from the 1960s. (Solvay Archives.)

Enlarging Scale and Scope

Backward and Forward Integration in the 1960s and 1970s

The 1960s were a watershed in the evolution of the European chemical industry. As a result of a combination of political, economic, and technological influences, the entire industry went through a process of unprecedented scaling up, with severe consequences for capital intensity and profitability. Competition grew to levels previously unknown. To stand stronger in that competitive war, companies integrated backward as well as forward. They tried to secure in this way their feedstock supply and the sales of their products. Solvay was no exception.[1]

In the field of plastics it all started in the United States in the 1950s. Attracted by the huge profits of an exponentially growing market, oil companies – used to large-scale operations – had stepped in. As long as the market was growing faster than the increase of capacity all went well, but during the late 1950s the first signs of overcapacity appeared. In the field of PVC the firm Dow Chemical produced a shock wave through the industry when it announced in 1955 that it had the ambition to become a giant supplier of vinyl chloride, which it would sell to other PVC manufacturers. Several plastics-processing companies started to integrate backward, buying vinyl chloride monomer from Dow, and as a result the number of American PVC producers grew from nine in 1955 to twenty in 1958. Prices of PVC sank from US$0.35 per pound in 1955 to US$0.18 in 1960. "The crying towels were out all over the place," one of the producers said.[2]

The dominant answer of the American manufacturers to such price erosions was reduction of the unit costs by scaling up. The large-scale PE plants constructed during the 1950s needed increasing amounts of ethylene. To fulfill that need, naphtha steam crackers of growing capacity were developed. Between 1960 and 1964 several engineering contractors succeeded in improving the furnaces and other parts of these steam crackers to such a degree that a new generation of crackers emerged. Whereas in the United States in 1955 capacities of 20,000 tons of ethylene per year had been usual, in 1965 crackers of 100,000 tons per year came on stream, and only five years later capacities of 300,000 to 450,000 tons per year had become the norm. It was a revolution,

---

[1] "Allocution du Baron Boël ... 9 juin 1969," *Revue Solvay* (May–June 1969): 11–14.
[2] Spitz (1988), 395–7, 399, 401–2, 407; Blackford and Kerr (1996), 236–41, 251–2, 254.

and it affected almost the entire petrochemical industry. It also brought the petroleum industry and the chemical industry in close mutual contact.[3]

The lower prices of ethylene from naphtha had a large impact on the production of feedstocks for plastics from other sources. Production of ethylene from sugarcane for instance, as practiced by Solvay in Brazil, soon became uncompetitive. Making acetylene from the nonpetroleum feedstock carbide suffered the same fate. Until the late 1950s, most producers of PVC made their monomer from acetylene, because it could quite simply be produced from carbide, which was easy to transport, whereas the alternative process starting from ethylene had several disadvantages. But when, after 1958, competition intensified and PVC prices dropped, many producers saw no other alternative than turning to the ethylene process. Between 1960 and 1964 several manufacturers (e.g., Dow, Goodrich, Stauffer), seemingly independent of one another, found an improved production process of vinyl chloride monomer (VCM) starting from ethylene: the so-called oxychlorination process. This new process revolutionized the industry, helped by the fact that ethylene prices were falling permanently. Within a few years, all manufacturers in the United States adopted the oxychlorination process, and at the same time the size of VCM plants grew in a few years from about 45,000 to 90,000 tons per year to 270,000 to 360,000 tons per year. These were the days that the sky seemed to be the limit, but reality was harsh. Many firms lost a lot of money because of overproduction.[4]

These American developments did not fail to have an impact on the European chemical industry. Although the economic historian Raymond Stokes is right in stating that it took the European firms several years of uncertainty before they could decide to shift from acetylene to ethylene, there was a turning point around 1963–4. Since the establishment of the European Economic Community in 1957 and the progressive reduction of trade barriers, several American chemical and petroleum companies decided to construct large-scale chemical plants and refineries in Europe to serve the entire Common Market of the then-six member states. As a result of those investments and because of American imports, competition strongly intensified, with price erosion of many basic chemicals as a result. During the 1960s, therefore, European chemical companies increasingly faced the same devil's dilemma as their American counterparts: if they would not join the collective "rage" of plant enlargement, they would be forced out of business by low-cost competitors; but if they would enlarge their installations, overproduction would almost certainly be the result, and profits would go down to zero, or worse. This is, briefly stated, the trap in which parts of the European chemical industry started to be caught up in during the 1960s, by a combination of political (Common Market), economic (intensified competition), and technological (e.g., engineering improvements in crackers, VCM plants) factors.[5]

[3] Spitz (1988), 437–61; Reuben and Burstall (1973), 170–3, 197.
[4] Spitz (1988), 390–417.
[5] "ECN 25th" (1987), 31–3; Stokes (1994), 195–6, 241; Homburg (2004), 191–206; Jones and Miskell (2005).

16.1 SOLVAY'S INCREASED DEPENDENCE ON OIL

Solvay was affected by these developments in a special way. For decades one of the great assets of the company had been its ability to integrate its establishments in a superb manner in any European country, facilitated by the fact, according to *gérant* Paul Washer, that Belgium was a small country and that Solvay was a family firm.[6] The start of the Common Market and the advance of large-scale, low-cost producers in Europe suddenly turned this asset of being locally embedded into a disadvantage: Solvay's plants in some countries were producing at too small a scale in comparison with some of their competitors (see Chapter 21).

The Unhappy Story of the Rosignano Cracker

The issue of feedstocks for plastics naturally occupied the *gérance* from an early date. Already in 1955 the head of DGT, Charles Guffroy, initiated studies to install a cracker at Tavaux, and a few years later Solvay intended to develop Tavaux into a center of chlorine petrochemistry. There were plans to construct a refinery in Burgundy, to which Tavaux would be connected via a short pipeline. A cracker and a polyethylene plant were planned to come on stream by 1963. None of these plans was realized, though.[7]

As a result, Solvay's large complex at Rosignano would become the company's first petrochemical site. There certainly was a need for it to do so. The Italian PVC market and the PVC plant at Ferrara were expanding greatly, and Rosignano had to supply the Ferrara plant with growing amounts of VCM. Moreover, since 1959 the HDPE plant was in production, but the solution for supplying ethylene, in tanks under pressure (see Chapter 15), was cumbersome. If production were to grow, it definitely would be cheaper to construct a cracker on the Rosignano site. Searching for a solution, DGT's attention was caught by a technology offered by the Italian firm Montecatini, which had developed a light-naphtha cracker on a pilot-plant scale at Novara that could produce both acetylene and ethylene. For Solvay this seemed a wonderful solution, because both the VCM plant and the HDPE installations could be supplied with acetylene and ethylene, respectively.[8]

After a first visit to Montecatini, in February 1960, concrete plans were made for a cracker that could produce 20,000 tons per year of acetylene and 30,000 to 45,000 tons per year of ethylene. It was a large cracker, certainly not much smaller than steam crackers constructed in those days. Although Montecatini only had experience with furnaces that produced 7,500 tons per year of acetylene, Guffroy convinced the *gérants* to take the license, just

---

[6] Washer (2007).

[7] ACS, CdG, 9 June 1955, 4 Mar. 1958, 30 Oct. 1959; Ducordeaux, Robin, Tétu, and Amiot (2005), 148, 150, 279; Barré (1961).

[8] ART, "Cracking Montecatini pour production Acétylène, Ethylène, Méthane à partir d'essence légère" (1960); [Bertoni, Foschi, Guerra, and Zannoni] (2006), 84–5, 87.

before his retirement on 1 May 1961, because he argued, "Solvay will make it work!"[9]

Construction took far longer than expected, though, and many technological problems had to be solved. All the time new cost estimates were made, and the latest estimate was always higher than the previous one. When the cracker finally came on stream in 1965, the capacity of the installation was below the level of a profitable exploitation. During the first years of production, losses were therefore huge. The entire design appeared to be a technological failure, which led to litigation with Montecatini. In 1970 again, large new investments were needed to improve the plant. The plant finally started to function properly, due to the skills of DGT, but by that time the cracker was clearly obsolete in economic terms. Its capacity was too small, and therefore the production cost of its ethylene too high. In the second half of the 1970s it was decided to shut the Rosignano cracker down and to supply the site by shipping cheap ethylene from steam crackers in tankers to the port of Vada, near Rosignano. This maritime transport of ethylene was a novel development at the time. In 1979 the pipeline between Vada and Rosignano and the landing facilities for tankers were ready. The Montecatini cracker was finally shut down. Over almost twenty years, enormous sums of money had been lost.[10]

Looking in hindsight at the gloomy development of the Rosignano cracker, one can conclude that, above all, the timing was particularly unfortunate. When in early 1961 the decision was made, it still was quite a sensible one. But between 1960 and 1964 the revolution in furnace design of world-size steam crackers meant that when the Rosignano cracker came on stream in 1965, several of Solvay's competitors could get their ethylene at far lower costs. Moreover, the development of oxychlorination meant that by 1965, both PVC and HDPE could be made from ethylene at competitive cost prices: the rationale for the Montecatini cracker had evaporated.

Solvay followed the development of steam crackers with great interest. In April 1963 Luciano Balducci, who coordinated the construction of the Rosignano cracker, visited ICI's three steam crackers at Wilton, to be informed about ICI's plans to replace those recently constructed crackers by one single ethylene plant of two hundred thousand tons per year. Other companies made similar brave decisions. Hoechst, for instance, had invested no less than DM 260 million in the development of its high-temperature pyrolysis process before its first plant came on stream in 1960. But already the following year, the board of Hoechst decided to close down that plant and procure its ethylene from large-scale cracking facilities that were being built.[11]

---

[9] ART, "Données complémentaires sur cracking Montecatini." (1961); interview Paul Washer, 29 Nov. 2007; letter Paul Washer to the authors, 9 Jan. 2008.

[10] ART, "Estimation prealable des depenses annuelles pour cracking de Rosignano," 18 Apr. 1963; id., "Programme de l'installation cracking de Rosignano," 15 Jan. 1964; id., "Situation actuelle et perspectives du cracking de Rosignano," 5 Feb. 1970; Solvay & Cie. (1977), 42; interview Paul Washer, 29 Nov. 2007; letter Paul Washer to the authors, 12 July 2009.

[11] ART, "Steam-Crackings éthyléniques. Visite à l'ICI-Wilton le 8.4.1963"; ACS, CdG, 13 June 1963; Stokes (1994), 169, 190–3, 240–1.

The illuminating examples of ICI and Hoechst show that the crucial issue is not the decision to construct an acetylene-ethylene cracker at Rosignano but the fact that Solvay did not cancel the whole project in 1964 or 1965 and participate in a steam cracker instead. Opposing views within the *gérance*, together with the position taken by the powerful DGT, provide the answer. For DGT, the whole issue of the Rosignano cracker had turned into a matter of prestige. Solvay's technology department had always excelled in its ability to improve and optimize any chemical process. It had maintained technological leadership in soda ash and electrolysis for many decades; it had brought Solvay's PVC, HDPE, and peroxides technology to first rank; and it had therefore cultivated an esprit de corps that DGT could make everything work. As a result of this attitude, supported by some members of the *gérance*, only after DGT had succeeded in solving the technological problems could Solvay management admit that it had found in this field its economic Waterloo at Rosignano. When that hurdle was overcome, new plans for the ethylene supply to the Italian complex could take shape.[12]

The New VCM Plant at Tavaux

During the construction of the Rosignano cracker, Solvay was struggling also in more general terms with it hydrocarbon supply. During 1961 and 1962, Henri Delwart, Jacques Solvay, and Paul Washer negotiated with Mobil Oil to create two petrochemical and plastics joint ventures in Europe and the United States. But in the spring of 1962 Solvay decided that the risks of cooperation with a firm far larger and richer than Solvay were too great.[13]

In June 1963 research leader Lambert Vanharen presented an overview of the hydrocarbon feedstock supply to the Solvay plants and pointed to serious bottlenecks in the supply to Tavaux, Jemeppe, and Rheinberg. Especially with respect to the largest Solvic PVC plant, at Tavaux, the conclusion could not be avoided that a large new monomer plant should be constructed, together with an ethylene steam cracker. Both ICI and Solvay studied the construction of a steam cracker that could supply 100,000–150,000 tons per year of ethylene, which would possibly also feed a joint ICI-Solvay polyethylene plant at the site. At the same time Solvay investigated the options for the construction of a cracker and negotiated licenses for the oxychlorination process. The strategic vision of Solvay's management was clear: Tavaux would develop into a first class, large-scale complex of ethylene, VCM, and PVC manufacturing.[14]

On 21 June 1963, Solvay, ICI, and Solvic signed an agreement with the American Ethyl Corporation, a major supplier of VCM to the American market. Solvay, ICI, and Solvic agreed to share their know-how in the field of

---

[12] ACS, NdG, P. Washer, "Remarques sur le plan financier 1963–1967," 10 Feb. 1964.
[13] ACS, NdG, J. Solvay, "Joint venture pour la fabrication de matières plastiques," 11 Dec. 1961; id., [Washer], "Negotiations avec la Mobil," 8 Jan. 1962; Washer (2007); letter Paul Washer to the authors, 9 Jan. 2008; letter Paul Washer to the authors, 12 July 2009.
[14] ACS, CdG, 13 June 1963.

PVC, in return for Ethyl's know-how with respect to the production of the monomer.[15]

A few months later, Maurice Petit, an engineer from Tavaux who would become the project manager of the new VCM plant, was sent to Ethyl Corporation to study the new process. After his return, he was engaged for one year at DGT in Brussels to coordinate the engineering of the plant. At the same time Jacques Viriot and Maurice Forêt successfully studied the new process on pilot-plant scale at the *fabrications expérimentales* (FEX) at Tavaux. On the basis of this work at Tavaux and Brussels, in May 1965 the final decision was made to construct a new VCM complex at Tavaux.[16]

In the meantime, the decision to construct an ethylene steam cracker at Tavaux had been abandoned. During those very years, the capacity of steam crackers was a fast-moving target. Capacities of 100,000 tons per year that had been viewed as profitable in one year were considered unprofitable the next year, because of the rapid scaling-up that took place, with lower production costs as a result. Solvay therefore decided not to go it alone but to participate in a large, collective cracker at Feyzin, south of Lyons, together with the Société Nationales des Petroles d'Aquitaine, Progil, and Ugine. An ethylene pipeline of more than 180 kilometers was constructed between Feyzin and Tavaux, to supply the new VCM plant. Early in 1967 the Feyzin cracker came on stream, and in March 1967 the first ethylene arrived at Tavaux. After the Rosignano cracker, Solvay had set a second step in the field of petrochemicals. In 1970 the production capacity of the new VCM plant was enlarged to 185,000 tons per year. For that quantity, about 83,000 tons of ethylene are required, a figure certainly too low to justify the construction of a separate cracker at Tavaux. The decision to integrate backward in cooperation with other companies was a wise one.[17]

Spreading the New VCM Concept

When the decision to construct the Tavaux VCM plant was made in 1965, there was little doubt that in due course all the other VCM production sites of Solvay would be restructured from acetylene to ethylene feedstock. The investments were high, but they were absolutely necessary. In 1967, Solvay's PVC business was in danger of becoming loss making, unless it would produce VCM by oxychlorination.[18]

Jemeppe became the first production site to follow the Tavaux example. In the summer of 1969 the new VCM plant at Jemeppe came on stream. Ethylene was supplied by Dow Chemical, which had constructed a naphtha

[15] ACS-CR, "Solvay et Cie. – and – Imperial Chemical Industries Limited – and – Solvic S.A. – and Ethyl Corporation: Agreement relating to vinyl chloride monomer, polymers, copolymers and compounds," 21 June 1963.

[16] Ducordeaux et al. (2005), 182–3, 215, 229; interview Jacques Viriot, 10 Aug. 2009.

[17] ACS, NdG, J. Solvay, "Comparaison des prix de vente rentables du monomère." 31 Jan. 1966; ACS, RdG, 17 June 1965; Aftalion (2001), 286, 296, 305; Ducordeaux et al. (2005), 124, 182–3, 185–6, 280.

[18] ACS, NdG, P. Washer, "Rentabilité par groupes de produits," 31 July 1967.

cracker of four hundred thousand tons per year at its petrochemical complex at Terneuzen, in the Netherlands. Dow also constructed a pipeline from Terneuzen to a newly acquired Solvay site at Antwerp, and Solvay constructed an ethylene pipeline between its sites at Antwerp and Jemeppe. In 1972 the extended pipeline network of the Aethylen Rohrleitungs-Gesellschaft (ARG), a joint venture founded in 1969 among BP, DSM, and four German companies, was connected to Solvay's Antwerp site. The large crackers in Germany, Belgium, and the Netherlands became interconnected via that network, so that in case of fluctuations in production or demand, the other crackers could take over and guarantee the supply of feedstock to the connected chemical plants.[19]

In Spain, Solvay decided to construct its new VCM plant not at Torrelavega, where the supply of ethylene was poor, but at a site at Martorell, near Barcelona. A joint venture, Vinichlor, was created together with Péchiney and Saint-Gobain, Dow, and a Spanish company, which erected a large VCM plant on the site between 1970 and 1972. The product was partly transported to the Hispavic PVC factory at Torrelavega, where the old VCM plant was closed, and partly used in a new PVC factory that Hispavic constructed on the Martorell site.[20]

After Rheinberg was connected to the ARG ethylene network and a VCM plant producing two hundred thousand tons per year had come on stream in 1974, all Solvay VCM and PVC sites had been converted to oxychlorination, except for Hallein, Rosignano, and (partly) Elclor. In 1969, the acetylene VCM plant at Hallein closed down, and from that date the Halvic plant bought its VCM from the nearby factory of Wacker at Burghausen, Bavaria. The VCM plant at Rosignano closed, together with the cracker, in 1979. In the competitive world of PVC, only large and integrated electrolysis-VCM-PVC complexes would have a future (see Chapter 21). European integration and technological scaling up had their consequences.[21]

Large-Scale Production of Polyolefins

Because of the importance of ethylene as a feedstock, some of the *gérants* of Solvay had contemplated constructing the HDPE plants on new sites close to petroleum refineries. But Charles Guffroy and his successor Albert Bietlot were strongly in favor of constructing the HDPE plants on traditional Solvay sites; not only because of the availability of general utilities and workshops but also for social reasons. In their view, because of the inevitable decline of

[19] ACS-CR, "Contrats ethylene/ chlore/ lessive caustique conclus avec la Dow Chemical Nederland." 22 May 1967; id., letter Solvay to Dow Chemical International, Zürich, 2 June 1967; Mittmann (1974), 35–6, 43, 75–7, 79–85, 132–6, 142–4, 250–1, 260, 272, 277, 285, 295, 301; "ECN 25th" (1987), 32.

[20] ACS, NdG, P. Washer, "Hispavic – Situation d'avenir," 9 May 1966; ART [Berhaut-Steel], several notes on the C2H4 pipeline from Tarragona to Martorell, 1975.

[21] Rupprecht (2007), 136, 142, 145; ART, Démarrages et Arrêts des Fabrications; *Solvay Revue*. 35 (May 1983), 31, 34.

caustic soda, it was important to start alternative productions on Solvay sites to guarantee employment for personnel who could become redundant.[22]

With a total capacity of about 37,500 tons per year in 1970, the HDPE plants at Rosignano were only of modest size. By 1965 the Solvay leaders were strongly aware that their polyethylene business would be in trouble if they did not hurry to scale up. The quality of Solvay's PE was at least as good as that of the competition, but the scale of production was too low. Hoechst, for instance, had just constructed a HDPE plant producing one hundred thousand tons per year. Good locations for large-scale production would be Antwerp or the Rhine region, but within Solvay there was also a long-lasting commitment to France. During the previous years, Tavaux had been considered several times as a possible location for a French PE plant.[23]

On 10 October 1970 Solvay would indeed start producing HDPE in France, though not at Tavaux, but at Sarralbe. In this decision the problematic future of Sarralbe's soda ash plant played a large role. Early in 1968 the steam cracker of CdF-Chimie at Carling came on stream, situated only thirty kilometers from Sarralbe. Albert Bietlot, a social-minded leader who had become a member of the Executive Committee on 1 January 1968 (see Chapter 17), saw this as an excellent opportunity to save Solvay's factory at Sarralbe. With the large soda ash works at Dombasle nearby, it was obvious that sooner or later Solvay would concentrate all its soda ash production in the north of France at Dombasle and shut down the Sarralbe plant. Growing environmental concerns aggravated the situation. The Sarralbe works discharged considerable amounts of salty effluents into the Sarre River, a situation that was monitored critically by the local authorities. Therefore, Bietlot argued, Sarralbe should be converted into a petrochemical plant, so that employment of the workers of the soda ash plant would be guaranteed after its closure. In 1969 construction of the HDPE plant started at a newly acquired area at Sarralbe, close to the soda ash factory. A pipeline between Carling and Sarralbe, realized in 1970, supplied the necessary feedstock to the new installations. After the plant came on stream, it was soon enlarged to one hundred thousand tons per year.[24]

Sarralbe became an even-larger petrochemical complex after the decision was made to also construct a polypropylene (PP) plant at the site, to exploit the high-yield suspension polymerization process discovered by scientists of the Central Laboratory at Neder-over-Heembeek (see Chapter 15). Naphtha-fed steam crackers not only produce ethylene but also considerable amounts of propylene. Therefore, the necessary raw material was available at nearby Carling. A project team, which included future plant manager Alfred Hoffait, started in 1972 with the design of the new plant. Construction started in 1974, and two years later the first Solvay PP was successfully produced. The product was received well by customers. Although overcapacity within the

---

[22] Washer (2007); letter Paul Washer to the authors, 9 Jan. 2008.

[23] ACS, 1051-3-16, "Contrat Solvay & Cie./ Phillips Petroleum pour la production de PLT via catalyseur ternaire."

[24] Mittmann (1974), 147–8, 150–2, 155; *Sarralbe* (1986), 22, 28; "L'usine de Sarralbe." *La Revue Solvay* (1983) (2): 4.

sector permanently lurked around the corner, scaling up was considered the best way out. Therefore, production capacity was doubled to one hundred thousand tons per year by 1981. During all those years, the closure of the soda ash plant had been delayed at several occasions. But its time had come. During 1983 and 1984, after almost a century of production, the soda ash plant was finally shut down in phases.[25]

Despite the great development of the production of polyolefins at Sarralbe, one should not ignore the disadvantages of the location. Sarralbe was quite far from the great petroleum and petrochemical production centers of northwestern Europe and from seaports, for exporting. Moreover, the site was not part of an interconnected network of pipelines and crackers but was completely dependent on the Carling cracker. That disadvantage became clear during the mid-1980s, when CdF-Chimie suddenly threatened not to renew the supply contract. Only after intense political lobbying and public protests was a new agreement concluded. Sarralbe's polyolefin production had been saved, but the episode made abundantly clear that the location and Solvay's position on the ethylene market were both vulnerable (see Chapter 20).[26]

Three years after the start-up of the HDPE plant at Sarralbe, Solvay was able to acquire a far-larger HDPE plant at Deer Park, Texas, from Celanese. A few years later Solvay also constructed a PP plant at that site (see Chapter 18). In the early 1990s HDPE and PP plants were also erected at Solvay's site at Antwerp, well situated amid petrochemical complexes that could guarantee a good supply of ethylene and propylene. In those years Solvay advanced to the first place, globally, with respect to its total HDPE capacity, despite being ranked fifth in Europe. In PP Solvay was much smaller, though, ranked eighth, both globally and in Europe, during the early 1990s (see Chapter 22).

16.2 CLEAN AUTOCLAVES BUT AN INJURED IMAGE

Issues related to practices at the shop-floor level and to the public image of plastics have remained in the background. Though important, they did not play a great role in strategic discussions at the top level of the company. During the 1970s that situation changed, especially with respect to PVC. Around 1970 new facts were discovered relating to the health of workers who cleaned the autoclaves, and then the issue reached the public domain. Intense debates among industry, politics, the press, and the public at large took place that did not fail to have an influence on the public image of the PVC industry.[27]

Cleaning Autoclaves

Like most other PVC producers, Solvay polymerized its VCM to PVC by means of batch processes in autoclaves, reaction vessels in which the polymerization reaction could be executed under high pressure. After each batch, the autoclave

[25] *Sarralbe* (1986), 22, 26, 28, 35; ART, Démarrages et Arrêts des Fabrications; ARS 1974–1977.
[26] Ducordeaux et al. (2005), 224–6; "Solvay en France," (1988); interview Paul Washer, 29 Nov. 2007.
[27] Levinson (1975); Brown (1979); Westermann (2007), 237–314.

had to be cleaned. During the 1950s and 1960s, one or two workers entered the reactor to remove the skin of polymer that remained on the reactor walls and mixer blades by manual scraping with putty knives. They were often in the reactor for about fifteen to twenty minutes, in an atmosphere with a relatively high concentration of the gaseous monomer vinyl chloride. Although the sweet, apple smell of VCM was not extremely nasty, the job of cleaning the autoclaves was not a pleasant one. It was usually reserved for new employees (usually young men) who would be transferred to other jobs when they gained seniority.[28]

Incidental reports in the medical literature on cases of occupational illness among PVC workers were mostly related to accidents and acute toxicity. There was much uncertainty about the chronic effects of VCM and other chemicals used in PVC manufacture. In the course of the 1960s, when the scale of production grew, a specific clinical syndrome was encountered a number of times. Some workers complained about severe pain in their fingers. Often bone changes, shortened fingers, and clubbed fingers were diagnosed by doctors. The syndrome was called acroosteolysis. Of 218 autoclave cleaners at Solvay, eleven cases were reported up until 1966. But at first the specific cause remained uncertain. Solvay almost immediately ordered the use of gloves among the autoclave cleaners. But at that time, no fundamental changes were made to the production installations by any of the producers. This would all change after a medical doctor working for Solvay published his results in 1970.[29]

In 1970 the Italian physician Pier Luigi Viola presented a paper on the occurrence of cancer in rats that had been exposed to very high doses of vinyl chloride. This was the first public announcement of a link between VCM and cancer. Viola was director of the Ospedale Aziendale, founded by Solvay at Rosignano, and was connected as medical doctor to the Solvay plant. To study the relation between VCM inhalation and acroosteolysis, in the late 1960s he had started an experimental study on rats in the cellars of the hospital. During those studies, he found that the rats developed cancers in several parts of their bodies. These results induced Professor Cesare Maltoni of Bologna University to include workers in VCM and PVC production facilities in his studies on the effects of chemicals on the respiratory tracts of Italian workers. Hearing about this, Montedison contacted Maltoni and suggested that the entire investigation be extended to the experimental study of the biological effects of VCM on animals. In 1971 Solvay, ICI and Rhône-Progil decided to join the initiative. They founded the European Cooperative Group, which from 1971 to 1973 sponsored Maltoni and his team in their study of the health effects of VCM. Maltoni found that a specific cancer, angiosarcoma of the liver, was the most typical effect of VCM, not only at the very high doses studied by Viola but also at exposures of 250 parts per million or lower. In 1972 these results were communicated to American manufacturers, who started their own studies.[30]

[28] Cook, Giever, Dinman, and Magnuson (1971).
[29] Brown (1979), 128–30; ART-HSE, Minutes of the "Hand Disease Medical Meeting" held at Terrace Hilton Hotel in Cincinnati, 6–7 June 1966; Cordier, Fievez, Lefèvre, and Sevrin (1966); Cook et al. (1971).
[30] Viola (1970); Brown (1979), 131; Maltoni and Lefemine (1974), 387–8.

The Press, the Public, and Politics: Anxiety about VCM

Parallel to the research going on in Europe and the United States, a local department of the German Communist Party started to campaign against the PVC works of Dynamit Nobel at Troisdorf, near Cologne, where several cases of illness had been discovered. The sensitive issue reached the public after the influential and widely read weekly *Der Spiegel* in December 1973 published an article on the "Gefährlicher Kunststoff" (dangerous plastic) PVC. Two weeks later Germany's most prestigious newspaper, the *Frankfurter Allgemeine Zeitung*, published an article on liver damage caused by PVC manufacture. Several political parties took the issue on board.[31]

On 22 January 1974, when the public debates in Germany were approaching the boiling point, a "publicity bomb" exploded in the United States. That day, the large PVC manufacturer B. F. Goodrich informed the health authorities, their own workers, and the public at large that three workers had died between September 1971 and December 1973 of angiosarcoma of the liver. The US public authorities, who had been quite passive to that point, responded immediately and organized the Informal Fact-Finding Hearing on Possible Hazards of Vinyl Chloride Manufacture and Use on 15 February 1974, at which Maltoni presented his results. Already on 5 April 1974 the American authorities issued an emergency standard that required producers to reduce VCM exposures to below fifty parts per million.[32]

The issue was widely discussed during 1974. In the United States the participants in public hearings were polarized in two camps: the industry opposed the new standards, and the other groups, such as trade unions, environmentalists, and government experts, supported them. The controversy focused on finding a safe exposure level and economic feasibility. Despite all the controversy, the American occupational health authorities officially issued a permanent standard of one part per million averaged over an eight-hour period, with a ceiling of five parts per million averaged over a fifteen-minute period, which became effective on 1 January 1975. Between 1974 and 1980 similar standards came into force in Canada, Japan, and several European countries. Almost all PVC producers succeeded in improving their production processes in such a way that VCM exposure was greatly reduced.[33]

Solvay's Response

At Solvay, the first signs of what would later be recognized as acroosteolysis had been discovered in Jemeppe in 1962. The Belgian physician and toxicologist Marcel Lefèvre, who worked for Solvay, immediately took up the issue. During the following few years, he coordinated with the medical officers working for other PVC plants of Solvay, and they started an extensive investigation into the causes of the new disease. In 1966 he also participated in a meeting with other manufacturers, devoted to the mysterious "hand disease." As mentioned already, research into these occupation health issues continued at Solvay for

---

[31] Westermann (2007), 244–56.
[32] Creech and Johnson (1974); Brown (1979), 125–6, 128–9, 131–2.
[33] [le Ricousse] (1980).

several years; Viola's research is an example, as is the support given to Maltoni. All this was rather confidential, though. Public statements were not made, so as not to disquiet the workers or customers. After B. F. Goodrich made the information public, Solvay could not stay behind.[34] Early in 1974, the company publicly clarified its position for the first time in its 1973 annual report:

> The press has recently reported cases of serious affections among workers employed in polymerisation units outside our Group. These diseases could be caused by vinyl chloride monomer. The problem of the toxicity of vinyl chloride has been studied for many years by our own research teams and also in specialized laboratories, in collaboration with other PVC producers. These studies, which have our continuing attention, lead us to consider that working conditions which have been gradually adapted at our polymerisation units have reached the required safety level.[35]

Despite Solvay's longtime occupation with the subject, there was still much to be done in light of the ever-lower safety levels. Later evaluations showed that as a result of high VCM exposures, there were 230 victims of VCM angiosarcoma worldwide, 7 of whom were in Tavaux. In early 1974 those facts were not yet known.[36]

As soon as the full extent of the dangers became clear during the first months of 1974, the managers of the PVC plants were alarmed by DCT (formerly DGT). Paul Métaizeau, plant manager of Tavaux, immediately set aside a budget for instruments to monitor the atmospheric concentration of VCM in the polymerization rooms. Because of the low permitted concentrations, sophisticated laboratory instruments – chromatographs – were installed in industrial practice. At the same time Solvay contacted its competitors to collectively investigate improved cleaning methods. A great leap forward was made in 1976, when PVC started to be purified before drying and when so-called vapor strippers were installed that subjected the slurries to a second purification. Between 1974 and 1978 the work environment in the polymerization rooms was greatly improved. Concentrations of VCM dropped from 150 to 300 parts per million before 1974 to 0.1 part per million by 1990. No cases of angiosarcoma have been reported among workers who were employed under the new conditions. Within a few years Solvay had successfully responded to new insights and new legal requirements.[37]

The Injured Image

Although the problem of the cleaning of the autoclaves was successfully solved, the whole debate over the carcinogenicity of VCM had important side effects

---

[34] ART-HSE, Dr. M.-J. Lefèvre, "Informations relatives aux cas pathologiques décelés par l'IMTR (des cas d'acroostéolyse)," 13 Feb. 1964; id., "Réunion des médecins du travail Solvay à Bruxelles le 26 février 1964 – Exposé du Dr J-M. Cordier"; id., Minutes of the "Hand Disease Medical Meeting" held at Terrace Hilton Hotel in Cincinnati, 6–7 June 1966.

[35] ARS 1973, 22.

[36] Ducordeaux et al. (2005), 163, 191, 196.

[37] Ducordeaux et al. (2005), 163, 191, 196–7, 280–1; ARS 1975: 23; ARS 1976: 26–7.

that would continue to bother the industry for several decades. In the press, as well as in public debate, there was not always a clear distinction made between VCM and PVC, or between the manufacture of PVC and plastics products made from PVC. As a result, the dark shadow of the VCM episode was cast over the PVC industry and the plastics industry in general.[38]

The public debates gradually transformed from a discussion of occupational diseases to debates on the environmental hazards of the PVC industry. In 1976 the discussion, for instance, shifted to the issue of VCM residues in plastic foils for foodstuffs. Suddenly, VCM, and by implication PVC, was a problem not only for workers but also for society at large. Later, the environmental movement started to attack the waste management of the PVC and chlorine industry as a whole. In the 1970s the PVC industry acquired a negative image, in some circles at least, and it took until the late 1990s before that picture changed (see Chapter 21).[39]

16.3 FORWARD INTEGRATION INTO MAKING PLASTIC PRODUCTS

Although these image problems induced some consumers to turn away from plastics and buy natural materials instead (e.g., wooden children's toys), the plastics markets continued to grow uninterruptedly during the 1970s. Competition was growing, though, and profit margins in plastic resins production declined. To defend its position in PVC, and to learn more about the versatile plastics markets, Solvay decided to integrate downstream into the manufacturing of plastic products.

As is often the case in business, the first steps in the new domain of plastics processing were made by Solvay before any explicit long-term strategy was formulated. The first manufacturer of plastic products acquired by Solvay was Hedwin Corp., of Baltimore, United States, which was taken over in 1958 to have an observation post on the advanced American plastics market. Hedwin was a rather small company that had specialized in the production of packaging for industry.

The following year Solvay took over two more companies, the packaging firm Nest-Pack in Bologna, Italy, and Plasticos Plavinil in Brazil, a large company that was engaged in calendering. Both companies were important customers of Solvic and Elclor, respectively, and both were in financial trouble. Solvay's decision to participate financially was clearly an ad hoc decision, taken to avoid the two companies turning into competitors for financial support. The first aim of the acquisitions was therefore to guarantee captive use of Solvic's PVC. In the case of Nest-Pack, owned by members of the Martelli family, Solvay took over 55 percent of shares and committed itself to an investment program. Solvic took the opportunity to run Nest-Pack as a pilot enterprise,

---

[38] "Tod im Plastik." *Der Spiegel* (1974) (27); "Werden wir auf Kunststoffe verzichten müssen?" *Die Zeit*, 28 June 1974, 37; M. Tushen, "Disaster in Plastic," *Health/PAC Bulletin* 71 (1976): 1–16.

[39] Westermann (2007), 288–310.

which would help Solvic study new applications in the packaging sector. Learning more about the PVC market and improvement of PVC grades for packaging were therefore secondary aims of the acquisition.[40]

Plasticos Plavinil, founded in 1946, was one of the largest producers of PVC products in Latin America. Since 1957 it had been the most important client of Solvay's subsidiary Eletro Cloro, and already by 1959 Plavinil had large debts to that company, which it was unable to pay. To arrive at a solution, Eletro Cloro signed an agreement with important Plavinil shareholders in September 1959, and it took over 50 percent of its shares. With about one thousand employees in 1973, Plavinil was an important actor in Solvay's South American market.[41]

At about the same time, Raoul Berteaux and his coworkers at Solvay's newly created Plastics Department at Brussels (see Chapter 17) came to the conclusion that there was a bright future for PVC in housing and construction. To develop that market, Solvay decided to start making corrugated PVC sheets itself. Taking that step was far from obvious. Ever since the discussions between Emmanuel Janssen and other *gérants* in the 1920s, the principle not to intervene in the business of its customers had become a cornerstone of Solvay's company strategy (see Chapter 10). After lengthy discussions, an exception was made, but with strict conditions. A strategy was formulated for the new field in 1960 that rested on two pillars: (1) the decision not to hurt Solvay's major customers, who were mainly in the domains of calendering, extrusion, and injection, and therefore to concentrate on the application of plastics in the field of construction and packaging, and (2) the use of these plastics-processing activities primarily as observation posts and as a means to learn more about the technologies used by Solvay's customers. Moreover, contrary to all other internal deliveries within the Solvay Group, PVC was sold at market prices, not against cost prices, to the processing subsidiaries.[42]

On the basis of the formulated strategy, production of corrugated PVC sheets could start. After experiments had been done at the experimental plastics workshop at Tavaux, Solvay took a license on a manufacturing process developed by Roberto Colombo at Turin. In 1959 a Colombo pilot plant was constructed at Tavaux. The following year Solvay established three large-scale production units at Tavaux, Jemeppe, and Bochum in Germany, with a total capacity of one million square meters per year. Sales grew quickly. By 1962 about four thousand tons of PVC were processed in these installations. Similar but smaller installations for the production of corrugated sheets were constructed at Torrelavega, at Elclor, and in Portugal.[43]

---

[40] ACS, binder Handwritten history of the Processing Sector 1958–1979 (July 1979).

[41] ACS-CR, "Accord entre la CIA Fomento Industria Plastica et Elclor: Prise de participation dans Plavinil," 4 Sept. 1959; ACS, binder Handwritten history of the Processing Sector 1958–1979 (July 1979).

[42] ACS, RdG, 12 Jan. 1960; Washer (2007); interview Paul Washer, 29 Nov. 2007; ACS, binder Handwritten history of the Processing Sector 1958–1979 (July 1979); Paul Washer, "Memo to the historians – The TR adventure," 20 May 2011.

[43] Ducordeaux et al. (2005), 165–6, 280; ACS, binder Handwritten history of the Processing Sector 1958–1979 (July 1979); ACS, CdG, 15 Feb. 1962.

International Expansion in All Domains of Plastic Processing

In December 1960 plastic processing received recognition at the top level of the company. That month, Paul Washer was added to the *gérance*, with a specific responsibility for the processing sector. Under his leadership plastic processing would grow out to one of the five main activities of the Solvay Group in the 1960s and 1970s (see Table 15.4).

From 1962, Washer and Berteaux started a vigorous acquisition strategy, which would become the major engine of growth of Solvay's processing sector. In 1962 Solvay took a 33 percent share of the Spanish calendering firm Manhusa, as well as a 49 percent interest in the cable manufacturer Saenger in Spain. In Germany the firm 1001 Plastik was acquired, and in the United States Hedwin bought the Baldwin company, a producer of plastic pipes. On several occasions these acquisitions were kept secret, to avoid a negative response among Solvay's customers. In January 1963 again a calendering firm was acquired, the Italian company Filatura Corti Fratelli (FCF), which brought Solvay its first involvement in the calendering of rigid PVC.[44]

By that time, as result for increased competition in the field of plastics resins and the continuous lowering of resin prices, several competitors, such as DuPont, ICI, and Phillips Petroleum, also decided to integrate vertically into the plastics-processing field. Solvay therefore decided to enlarge its involvement in that field. In 1963 a new strategy for plastics processing was formulated that explicitly stated that Solvay had the intention to grow considerably in that new area. From now on, the company would also occupy itself with calendering, extrusion, and injection, next to the existing activities in the use of rigid PVC in construction, and with the production of bags and bottles. By 1 January 1963 Solvay had invested BEF 450 million (US$9 million) in the sector, and investments of BEF 2,500 million (US$50 million) until 1967 were planned.[45]

Table 16.1 clearly shows that Solvay invested vigorously in plastics processing. Within only five years, from 1958 to 1962, the company succeeded in establishing bridgeheads in seven different countries and in the Benelux. Moreover, Solvay spread its activities over all important sectors of the processing field: packaging since 1958, calendering and coatings since 1959, and housing and construction since 1960. Between 1958 and 1970 more than forty factories were acquired or constructed in these fields. Because of the existing relationships between firms acquired and their customers, and in particular because of the fact that plastic resins were also largely sold to other clients, it was Solvay's policy not to use the brand name Solvay for finished plastic products.[46]

Not all acquisitions proved a success. In the United States the piping firm Baldwin, acquired in 1962, was sold again in 1965. Large sums were also lost in the case of the Vypak Corporation, which was established in

---

[44] ACS, binder Handwritten history of the Processing Sector 1958–1979 (July 1979).
[45] ACS, binder Handwritten history of the Processing Sector 1958–1979 (July 1979); [Wertz] (1983), 132–3; ACS, CdG, 6 March 1963, 13 June 1963.
[46] Paul Washer, "Memo to the historians – The TR adventure," 20 May 2011.

TABLE 16.1. *Start of Plastics Processing by Solvay in Different Countries, 1958–1970*

Country	TrC (calendering and coating)	TrB (building and construction)	TrE (packaging)
United States		1962	1958
Italy	1963		1959
Brazil	1959	1964	
Germany	1968	1960	1962
Benelux	1967	1960	1969
France	1964	1960	1963
Portugal		1962	
Spain	1962	1962	1964

Source: ACS, binder Handwritten history of the Processing Sector 1958–1979 (July 1979).

November 1964 as a joint venture among Ethyl Corporation, Solvay, and Hedwin.[47]

One of the most important acquisitions in plastics processing during the 1960s was the Établissements Maréchal, which Solvay bought from Rhône-Poulenc in December 1964. Maréchal, already founded in the nineteenth century, was one of the most important French calendering firms. It owned four factories: the mother plant of the company at Vénissieux, near Lyons, and establishments at Croissy, Thaon-les-Vosges, and Wallignies. After acquiring the firm, Solvay first started a rationalization program, to raise Maréchal's profitability, and it closed the factory at Wallignies. Soon thereafter it was decided to develop Maréchal into the major coordination center of Solvay's European activities in the field of calendering and coatings, under the leadership of Jacques Viriot, the former head of research and development at Tavaux. Later acquisitions in this field, such as Hules de Gava in Spain, Weesp Plastics in Holland, and Griffine and Dawant in France, were closely linked via technical and management contracts to Maréchal or were integrated into it in the 1970s.[48]

The Development of the PVC Bottle

The invention of plastic bottles for mineral waters was perhaps one of the greatest contributions of Solvay to the plastics products market. Solvay was the first producer of those bottles, and today no one can deny that the use of plastic bottles for mineral water is gigantic, indeed. The initial response among Solvay's top people was hesitant, though. When Paul Washer showed one of the Solvay PVC bottles at a board meeting of Solvay in the 1960s, another

---

[47] ACS, binder Handwritten history of the Processing Sector 1958–1979 (July 1979); ACS, NdG, P. Washer, "Vente de Vypak," 30 Nov. 1966.

[48] ACS, black binder "La Transformation"; "Activités calandrage et enduction." *La Revue Solvay* (1975) (2): 6–11; Cayez (1988), 224, 249; ACS, NdG, P. Washer, "Calandrage – Politique en vue d'accoitre la rentabilité," 15 Feb. 1967; "Solvay en France" (1988).

board member, Roger Janssen, said that the new bottles would never succeed because they were too ugly. In response, Washer threw an empty bottle at him, and Janssen changed his opinion when he discovered how incredibly light it was.[49]

Already at the end of the 1950s polyethylene was used in America for the blowing of bottles, but not for mineral waters. Early in 1962 Raoul Berteaux reported that the use of HDPE for the blowing of bottles was growing in a spectacular way in the United States, but it was almost unknown in Europe. He proposed that Solvay explore the European market by installing bottle-blowing machines with certain clients. Jean Sikner, head of the plastics workshop at Tavaux, thereupon decided to experiment with PVC instead of HDPE. The same year his team succeeded in producing the first PVC bottle.[50]

To develop production on an industrial scale, Sikner contacted a producer of injection and glass-blowing machines at Berlin, and testing went on in the facilities of that producer. Experiments were stopped, though, after it appeared that the stabilizer used in the PVC mixture gave a nasty smell to the content of the bottle. For the immediate future, finding nontoxic, odorless additives for PVC applications became a research topic of great importance. At Tavaux, Jean Sikner and his team concentrated on research on such additives for blow extrusion that could be used in packaging applications for foodstuffs, and at Rheinberg a research team focused on similar additives for premix applications. By 1963 Sikner succeeded in finding a stabilizer that was good enough for foodstuffs applications, as well as a co-polymer that made the bottles better shock proof. These advances were welcome, because the French company Lesieur, which was selling sunflower oil in glass bottles, had asked for Solvay's help in shifting from glass to plastic bottles. One of Lesieur's engineers had developed a blowing machine that could produce 1,200 bottles per hour. With that equipment, Solvay's first commercial production of bottles came on stream.[51]

Impressed by the developments in the United States, Sikner, Solvic, and persons at Solvay's plastics department became great promoters of the plastic bottle. In August 1963 the French headquarters of the Solvay Group (DNF) created a separate company for the production of plastic packaging and construction applications, the Société Bourguignonne d'Application Plastiques (BAP). In 1964 a factory was constructed at Chevigny-Saint-Sauveur, close to Dijon, which started the production of plastic bags the same year. In late 1964 and early 1965 the production of corrugated PVC sheets was moved from Tavaux to Chevigny. After the production of bottles for Lesieur had proved successful, DNF also transferred that production to Chevigny, using bottle-blowing machines that had been improved by Solvay engineers. Demand for the new PVC application rose quickly. In 1967 the bottles production line of BAP had

---

[49] Interview Paul Washer, 29 Nov. 2007.
[50] "Les Matières Plastiques," in *Solvay & Cie* (1958); ACS, CdG, 15 Feb. 1962; Ducordeaux et al. (2005), 171, 280.
[51] Ducordeaux et al. (2005), 171, 280; ART, PM/GF, "Programme de recherches pour 1964," 27 July 1964.

FIGURE 16.2. Soon after the start of Solvay's processing sector, bottles made from PVC by Solvic became a major product. In the 1960s the company tried to launch, unsuccessfully, the use of PVC bottles for beer. (Solvay Archives.)

to be enlarged, and in the year 1968 the factory at Chevigny already produced one hundred million bottles. Within only five years the innovation of the PVC bottle had become a great success.[52]

Anticipating growing demand, Solvay decided in 1963 and 1964 to also start producing plastic bottles in Italy and Spain. Three companies were founded with that aim, together with local partners. In 1969 BAP erected a second French bottle factory at Grenay, near Lyons.[53]

A major breakthrough occurred in April 1968 when the Vittel company, a large French producer of mineral water, received permission from the French government to sell its water in PVC bottles instead of glass. The same year Vittel entered the market with a restyled plastic bottle of greater elegance that contributed to the successful marketing of mineral waters in plastic bottles. The example was soon followed by Evian, one of Vittel's competitors. Already in 1969, Solvay estimated that 175,000 tons of PVC would be needed in 1970 for plastic bottles alone if all producers of mineral waters would shift on a large scale from glass to plastics. It was a gigantic potential market. Solvic therefore forced Solvay's processing department to sell its know-how

[52] ACS, CdG, 13 June 1963; ACS, black binder "La Transformation"; ACS, binder Handwritten history of the Processing Sector 1958–1979 (July 1979).
[53] ACS, binder Handwritten history of the Processing Sector 1958–1979 (July 1979).

in making PVC bottles to other bottle makers, such as Sidel, to enlarge PVC consumption.[54]

The growing public concern, during the mid-1970s, about the dangers of vinyl chloride did not fail to have an impact on the future of the PVC bottle. As a result of fears among the public and official authorities that small traces of carcinogenic VCM might be present in the PVC used for bottles for mineral water, several producers of mineral waters started to use bottles made of PET (polyethylene terephtalate). For non-foodstuff applications and for sunflower oil, BAP continued to use PVC as before. In 1981 it consumed more than thirty thousand tons of PVC, which made the company then the largest captive user of PVC inside the Solvay Group. In 1987, when BAP was still producing 250 million bottles each year, its largest customer, Lesieur, contemplated shifting to the use of PET as well, Solvay quickly decided to sell BAP to the French company Carnaud. It was just in time. Shortly thereafter, the market of PVC bottles collapsed.[55]

Management and Rationalization of the Plastics-Processing Sector

Within the Solvay organization the processing sector was quite an anomaly. Traditionally, DGT had exercised a strict control over the soda ash plants and electrolysis installations via a sophisticated system of reporting and benchmarking. When Solvay started the production of PVC, that part of the business had been more or less set aside within the Solvic organization. The processing sector was kept at an even-greater distance from the "ordinary" Solvay business, as is clearly illustrated by the fact that PVC was delivered at market prices to the processing subsidiaries of the company. The numerous acquired companies at first kept a large degree of independence with respect to their management, production, and sales, although, according to former Executive Committee member Albert Rampelberg, Solvay later imposed too much bureaucracy on these small units.[56]

After taking over a processing firm, Solvay's recipe was largely the same in all cases. Following the acquisition, drastic rationalizations were carried through: the closing of old plants; modernization of installations; construction of new, large centralized factories; and the swapping of product portfolios between factories, so that production of one type of product was concentrated at one location. Between 1965 and 1968 gradually a clustering of activities within the processing sector was introduced, which resulted in three major groups of companies: TrC (calendering and coating), managed by Viriot; TrB (construction), managed by Désiré Gauthier; and TrE (packaging), managed by Jean Milleroux. Within these clusters growth strategies and rationalization

---

[54] Ducordeaux et al. (2005), 185; interview Paul Washer, 29 Nov. 2007; Paul Washer, "Memo to the historians – The TR adventure," 20 May 2011.

[55] ACS, [Rampelberg], "La Transformation: Ses charactéristiques – Ses problèmes – Son apport," 9 June 1982; ACS, MoE, 20 Jan. 1987, 15 Dec. 1987; PR, 20 June 1988: The Solvay Group – Development of PVC packaging in France. Solvay and Carnaud intend to unite their efforts; interview Aloïs Michielsen, 21 Apr. 2011.

[56] ACS, RdG, 12 Jan. 1960; Washer (2007); interview Albert Rampelberg, 4 Apr. 2008.

programs were formulated, although they would not be totally implemented until the end of the 1970s. By this organizational move, for the first time a kind of product organization was introduced to Solvay, largely outside the control of DGT and the country organizations. In the case of the Sociedad General de Hules, for instance, Washer explicitly ordered, with the support of Boël, that Maréchal should define the strategy and supervise the management of that company, not the general management for Spain, which had been the practice within Solvay to that point.[57]

There was one unusual spin-off of the processing sector that had not been intended when Solvay entered this field: namely the all-round management training the sector offered. Because of the relative autonomy and the rather small size of most of the processing subsidiaries, Solvay engineers were frequently appointed at a young age to management functions at the top of those firms. As chief executives of those companies they were responsible not only for the technical side of the business but also for the sales, personnel, profits, and the balance sheet. In this way, they got the opportunity to develop general management skills, which were hard to acquire at other positions within Solvay. According to Aloïs Michielsen, later CEO of Solvay, the processing sector functioned as a kind of "internal business school" of Solvay.[58] It is striking, indeed, that several members of the Executive Committee worked part of their careers in managerial roles in the processing sector.[59]

As a result of the large investments in this sector after 1962, by 1967 plastics products accounted for 15 percent of total sales of the Solvay Group, as compared to 30 percent for alkalis and 19 percent for PVC and HDPE (see Table 15.4). It was a considerable change of portfolio for the company, and within only five years. During the 1970s, the processing sector would continue to grow. Major acquisitions were those of Alkor (1978) and Draka-Polva (1 January 1979). Both companies also owned international subsidiaries, so these acquisitions strengthened Solvay's position in the processing field in large parts of Europe. Solvay also constructed new processing plants. Sometimes, as in the case of Pontemammolo in 1969 and Monfalcone in 1970, this happened partly for social reasons, following the closure of electrolysis and soda ash plants on those sites. As a result of these investments, Solvay's processing sector employed more than twelve thousand persons in 1981. Then the captive use of Solvay's plastics by the sector was more than 120,000 tons of PVC, 7,000 tons of HDPE, and 3,000 tons of PP.[60]

At the end of the period discussed here, one market segment gained importance for the processing sector of Solvay: the car industry. Already during the 1960s several subsidiaries made parts for automobile interiors. In 1969 the

[57] ACS, NdG, P. Washer, "Organisation du Department Transformation," 7 May 1968.

[58] Interview Aloïs Michielsen, 16 Apr. 2008.

[59] Examples, next to Michielsen, are Victor Dierinckx, Christian Jourquin, and Jacques van Rijckevorsel.

[60] ARS 1967; ACS, binder Handwritten history of the Processing Sector 1958–1979 (July 1979); ACS-CR, letter Direction Nationale Benelux, Solvay, to NKF Groep BV, Rijswijk, 21 Dec. 1978; ARS 1980: 31; ACS, [Rampelberg], "La Transformation: Ses charactéristiques – Ses problèmes – Son apport," 9 June 1982.

French company Dawant was acquired with the special aim of strengthening Solvay's sales to the car industry. Five years later the plastics products for automobiles were grouped together in a separate automobile department. During those years Solvay's attention moved gradually from the interior to the technical parts of cars, and, as described in Chapter 21, in the 1980s especially to fuel tanks. During the following decades Solvay would become one of the leading producers in that field.[61]

16.4 GROWTH IN PLASTICS AND ITS CONSEQUENCES

If one summarizes Solvay's development in plastics between 1945 and 1980 – the entry into the business, its scaling up, the backward integration into crackers (e.g., Rosignano, Feyzin), and the forward integration into plastics products – one can only conclude that impact on the company has been tremendous. Immediately after World War II, plastics was only a research issue at Solvay, without any sales; around 1980, in contrast, plastic resins (PVC, HDPE, PP) accounted for 25–28 percent of total sales, and the processing of plastics for 19–21 percent of sales. That means that, taken together, plastics sales were almost half of Solvay's entire business. This shows how revolutionary the entry into plastics was.

That entry also had great consequences. Solvay became dependent on petrochemical feedstock, but its bargaining power in the ethylene and naphtha markets was only modest. This would remain a great problem for Solvay in the years to come. It would also make Solvay's plastics business highly cyclical (see Chapter 20).

Also, financing became a problem of growing importance. As shown already, competition in the field of petrochemicals demanded investment in production units of an ever-larger scale. To stay in the business, Solvay could not avoid taking part. But the financial burdens were enormous, more than a limited partnership could bear. During the 1960s, Solvay's *gérants* became increasingly aware that Solvay was in need of large bank credits for the realization of its industrial strategy. That could be achieved, as we discuss in Chapter 17, only by transforming Solvay & Cie into a joint-stock company. Solvay's product differentiation and integration were the first, incomplete, steps in Solvay's turnaround. They were followed by changes that were at least as drastic, in the field company governance, management, and organization.

[61] ACS, binder Handwritten history of the Processing Sector 1958–1979 (July 1979); "Solvay en France" (1988); ARS 1979.

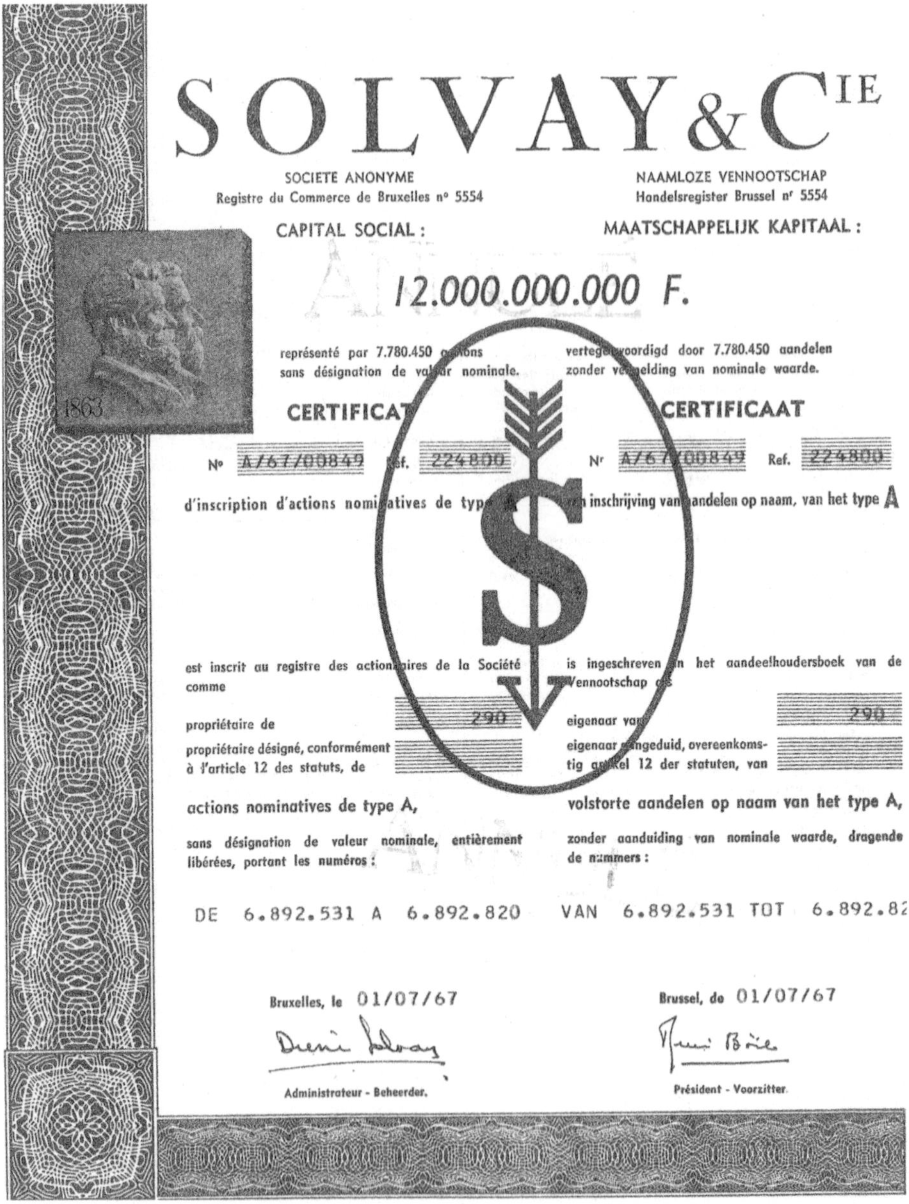

SOLVAY & CIE

SOCIETE ANONYME
Registre du Commerce de Bruxelles n° 5554

NAAMLOZE VENNOOTSCHAP
Handelsregister Brussel nr 5554

CAPITAL SOCIAL : MAATSCHAPPELIJK KAPITAAL :

12.000.000.000 F.

représenté par 7.780.450 actions sans désignation de valeur nominale.

vertegenwoordigd door 7.780.450 aandelen zonder vermelding van nominale waarde.

1863

CERTIFICAT CERTIFICAAT

N° A/67/00849 Ref. 224800 Nr A/67/00849 Ref. 224800

d'inscription d'actions nominatives de type A

van inschrijving van aandelen op naam, van het type A

est inscrit au registre des actionnaires de la Société comme

is ingeschreven in het aandeelhoudersboek van de Vennootschap als

propriétaire de 290

eigenaar van 290

propriétaire désigné, conformément à l'article 12 des statuts, de

eigenaar aangeduid, overeenkomstig artikel 12 der statuten, van

actions nominatives de type A,

volstorte aandelen op naam van het type A,

sans désignation de valeur nominale, entièrement libérées, portant les numéros :

zonder aanduiding van nominale waarde, dragende de nummers :

DE 6.892.531 A 6.892.820 VAN 6.892.531 TOT 6.892.82

Bruxelles, le 01/07/67 Brussel, de 01/07/67

Administrateur - Beheerder. Président - Voorzitter.

FIGURE 17.1. A share of the new public company Solvay & Cie SA (1967). (Solvay Archives.)

Solvay Goes Public

Financial and Organizational Limits of a Family Firm

Solvay's spectacular transformation from an alkali enterprise into a much-broader chemical company with a strong business in plastics was a great effort. From the start, the *gérance* was well aware of the financial consequences. Already in 1949, when the PVC business took off, there were great worries about whether Solvay would be able to get enough capital for its expansion. In those days the consequences of the war losses, the limitations in the transfer of capital from one country to another, and the recent introduction of a Belgian tax on capital were strongly felt. In April 1949 the *gérants* discussed the question of whether it would be better to change Solvay into a joint-stock company, which would give the company better access to capital markets. The dangers of a possible unfriendly takeover were considered too great, though. Moreover, with assets in Belgium, France, Spain, and Italy the change of legal status would have unpleasant consequences for taxation in those countries, while at the same time the property rights on mining concessions could have become a problem. All *gérants*, therefore, had the firm conviction that Solvay's independent legal status as a family firm was one of its greatest assets. In the following years, it was mainly Ernest-John Solvay, the chairman of the *gérance*, who warned time and again that the diversification into electrolysis and PVC was too costly and not profitable. He was strongly convinced that soda ash should remain Solvay's core and that in other areas only investments with high, and proven, profitability should be considered.[1]

Over the following two decades, the issue of changing Solvay into, a joint-stock company frequently returned to the agenda. But only when René Boël succeeded Ernest-John Solvay as chairman of the *gérance* on 1 January 1964 did the issue become the highest priority. By then, increased competition and scaling up in petrochemicals demanded large financial means to stay in the race. The issue of changing the family partnership into a joint-stock company could not be delayed any further.

In this chapter we investigate the reasons for changing Solvay into a joint-stock company, the nature of that change, the way Boël succeeded in largely preserving the family character of the company, the precautions taken against unfriendly takeover, and the consequences of this important change. Parallel to the far-reaching modification of Solvay's legal status, René Boël and his future

---

[1] ACS, RdG, 23 Mar. 1949, 20 Apr. 1949.

TABLE 17.1. *Investments, Profits, and Sales at Solvay, 1955–1967*
(in million BEF)

Year	Investment Budget at the Start of the Year (excl. KC and Brazil)	Net Result (before taxes)	Cash Flow	Sales	Investment as % of Sales
1955	1,200			11,000	10.9
1956	1,900	1,000	2,000	12,140	15.7
1957	2,300			12,345	18.6
1958	2,300		2,157	12,700	18.1
1959	1,600	1,320	2,476	13,620	11.7
1960	2,200	1,613	3,160	16,000	13.8
1961	3,100	1,568	3,161	17,300	17.9
1962	3,500	2,008	3,926	18,000	19.4
1963	4,200	1,818	4,235	20,000	21.0
1964	5,000	2,128	4,736	23,700	21.1
1965	5,600	1,470	4,360	26,300	21.3
1966	5,100	1,882	5,099	28,467	17.9
1967	3,200	1,342	4,961	29,234	10.9

Notes: It appeared to be difficult to construct a uniform series of investments. Often, Brazil and Kali-Chemie were not included, sometimes only Brazil, and occasionally both. The longest uniform series could be obtained by not including KC and Brazil. The budgets of 1964, 1965, and 1967 have been calculated by dividing the expenditures by 0.8 (usually about 80 percent of the budget was spent in the financial year).

Source: ACS, CdG, 24 Feb. 1955, 3 Mar. 1956, 7 Mar. 1957, 4 Mar. 1958, 14 Mar. 1959, 8 Mar. 1960, 9 Mar. 1961, 20 Mar. 1962, 28 Feb. 1963, 25 Mar. 1966, 16 Jan. 1967.

successor, Jacques Solvay, decided to also deeply alter the internal organization. It would take several years before the existing functional organization, with the technology department in a central role, would change into a more balanced matrix organization, in which next to the functional departments (e.g., technology, finance, personnel, sales), the product groups and the country organizations would also play a role (see Section 17.3).

17.1 DIVERSIFICATION AND ITS FINANCIAL CONSEQUENCES

After the pessimism of the immediate postwar years, during the 1950s a feeling of optimism and confidence in growth took possession of the Solvay leaders. The company started to invest heavily in the growth of its plastics and alkali businesses, as well as in research. The percentage of sales used for investments grew strongly from 11 percent in 1955 to almost 19 percent in 1957 (see Table 17.1).[2]

In those days, the investments were proposed and controlled almost completely by DGT, Solvay's General Department of Technology, headed by Charles Guffroy. The Financial Department merely had the role, in this area at

[2] ACS, CdG, 24 Feb. 1955, 3 Mar. 1956.

least, to search for ways to finance the wishes of the engineers. In view of the growing financial demands, in 1956 the Financial Department was asked to make a five-year plan for 1956–1960, to investigate the financial implications of the investment plans and the provision of funds. The prospects were positive. Solvay had BEF 1 billion (US$20 million) in its treasury, and at the end of those years, that would be still the same, despite the large investments planned.[3]

Reality turned out to be different, though. In February 1959 it became apparent that as a result of price drops in PVC, lower profits, higher depreciation, and larger overheads, the treasury reserve of BEF 1 billion had almost evaporated. Only by selling its IG Farben shares and other investments had Solvay been able to finance its investments during the previous year. New calculations showed that to continue its expansion strategy, Solvay would be forced to turn to external funding at the end of 1959, for one of the first times in its history. The *gérants* responded immediately and adequately to this alarming news. They lowered the investment budgets in the 1959–1963 financial plan and kept the maintenance costs of factories to a minimum. When in 1960 the business outlook improved, it soon seemed as if Solvay could continue its diversification policy without great hindrances. The year 1960 broke all recent records.[4]

To be able to access external loans in the future more easily, the *gérants* decided that it would be important to strengthen Solvay's equity. A new Belgian tax law of 15 July 1959, which freed companies from paying tax on the growth of equity as a result of mergers, paved the way for a most remarkable step, namely the absorption of North American Solvay Inc. (NAS) by Solvay (see Chapter 18). This merger was the brilliant idea of François Bilteryst, a manager in Solvay's Financial Department. He devised a plan in which the assets of NAS – amounting to about BEF 10 billion (US$200 million), mainly in the form of shares of Allied Chemicals – could strengthen Solvay's financial position while at the same time all was recorded on the books in such a way that taxation could be avoided. The social capital of Solvay was raised from BEF 4 billion to 8 billion (from US$80 million to US$160 million). On the new balance sheet the increase of about BEF 10 billion in the form of (Allied) participations was compensated by a BEF 4 billion increase of the social capital and nearly BEF 6 billion "bonuses of the merger." With this enlargement of Solvay's equity, it would be easier for the company to attract external funding. In November the general assembly of Solvay agreed with the operation, and on 15 December the merger was concluded in the presence of two Belgian notaries. All became effective as of 31 December 1961. In a more distant future the large package of Allied shares would play an important role in the financing of Solvay's industrial expansion (see Chapter 18).[5]

---

[3] ACS, CdG, 3 Mar. 1956, 5 June 1957.

[4] ACS, CdG, 12 Feb. 1959, 14 Mar. 1959, 30 Oct. 1959, 29 Mar. 1960, 17 May 1962; ACS, 1151, on the selling of the IG Farben shares; fax Robert Friesewinkel to the authors, 2 Nov. 2010.

[5] On 31 March 1957 North American Solvay Inc. absorbed the Solvay American Corporation by merger. Since that date, all of Solvay's Allied shares were owned by NAS. ACS, 1293-2-1; ACS, CdG, 21 Sept. 1961; ACS, black binder "Relevé des notes juridiques," Henry Lévy-Morelle, "North American Solvay Inc. – Avis du Conseil de Surveillance sur l'opération N.A.S"; ACS,

The New Insights of Henri Delwart and Paul Washer

At the start of the 1960s, the *gérance* increasingly became aware that the plastics business had introduced Solvay into a "game" that was not familiar to the company. In alkalis Solvay was one of the largest companies in the world. It operated from a position of strength and had dominant positions in many national markets. In plastics, however, Solvay confronted large and aggressive competitors with deep pockets, such as the IG Farben successors, BASF, Bayer, and Hoechst, as well as American and European oil companies.

The consequences of that new situation for Solvay were first formulated explicitly in early 1962 in two notes by Henri Delwart and Paul Washer, written in the context of a possible cooperation with Mobil Oil (see Chapter 16). Delwart argued that science and technology were developing at an accelerated speed, which caused rapid changes in society. The creation of the European Common Market only reinforced that process. To survive increased competition and to stay at the "front of progress," high investments in research and development (R&D) were essential; they had to be financed by rapidly growing sales in a broadening range of markets. In the case of Solvay, it had been calculated that the profits of the alkali business would seriously decline by 1970, and even more so thereafter. In the meantime, BASF, Hoechst, and Bayer would double their profits if they were able to continue to grow at their present rate. Under these circumstances Solvay had no other choice than to reorient itself to new growth areas, such as plastics, whose businesses were developing more rapidly than the alkali business. But in these new competitive areas Solvay could operate successfully only if it would produce and sell at a scale that matched the scale of the competitors. To achieve that goal, Solvay would need to invest far greater sums than previously, both in R&D and in production capacity. It would also be present in the fast-growing American market, to reach the sales levels that could justify the high overhead costs in R&D. The legal form of Solvay as a limited partnership made these strategic demands a rosy dream, though. The required sums could not be generated by self-financing, and banks would never give the large sums needed to a limited partnership.[6]

In a nutshell, Delwart put all issues on the agenda that would occupy the *gérance* during the following years: growing competition; the role of the European Economic Community; expansion of the R&D facilities; the importance of entering the United States; growing capital requirements; and last but not least, the need to restructure the legal form of the company. Two weeks later Paul Washer largely underlined the same issues. He specifically pointed to the consequences of the Common Market. Solvay always had the advantage that it had production units in many countries, but that competitive advantage had ceased to exist. Competitors in plastics were constructing large-scale plants

---

AG, 12 June 1962; ACS, 1001–1-7, letters 1 Sept. 1961; ACS, RdG, 15 Dec. 1961; "Solvay & Cie., société en commanite simple, à Ixelles. Fusion. – Augmentation de capital: Modification aux statuts," *Bijlage tot het Belgisch Staatsblad – Annexe au Moniteur Belge* (8 Jan. 1962), 411; interview Robert Friesewinkel, 2 Oct. 2008; letter Robert Friesewinkel to Paul Washer, 13 Dec. 2007; interview Henri Lévy-Morelle, 9 Nov. 2007.

[6] ACS, NdG, H. Delwart, "Le progress techniques et la gestion des entreprises: Cas de Solvay & Cie," 28 Feb. 1962; Sermon (1960).

to serve the entire Common Market, with lower production costs per ton of product. In his view, Solvay could compensate for its disadvantages only by enlarging its sales to other continents; by diversifying into plastics processing; by collaborating with other partners in R&D; by licensing its know-how outside Europe; and by creating joint ventures in plastics in Europe with companies such as Mobil Oil, which could supply funds for investments.[7]

Finding Funds for Accelerated Growth

Although the creation of the joint venture with Mobil fell short, the idea that higher levels of investment were needed for Solvay's survival was embraced by the *gérance*. When during the early 1960s the investment level rose again to 20 percent of sales or more (see Table 17.1), this meant that additional financial resources had to be found to realize that investment rate. Solvay tried to get loans from domestic and foreign banks. With the capital enlarged by the merger with NAS, and the Allied shares as a possible security, it succeeded in getting loans from the Belgian Société Nationale de Crédit à l'Industrie, the Italian bank Mediobanca, and the American First National City Bank. Later, the company also succeeded in obtaining a large loan of BEF 1 billion from the Société Générale de Banque.[8]

In 1961 Solvay also decided to sell large parts of its holding of ICI shares, to finance its expansion projects. In that year Solvay still held about 3 percent of the total share capital of ICI, some eight million shares. During the following years, the British banking house Schröder sold about one million of those shares each year on the stock market, called "the Solvay tap" by the *Financial Times*. Selling shares of Allied Chemical was not considered at that time, as a result of Solvay's policy to spread its risks over two continents in view of the Cold War.[9]

Each year a growing financial gap had to be bridged. The large costs of the crackers at Feyzin and Rosignano made it almost inevitable, according to Paul Washer, that Solvay would become a joint-stock company. By June 1965 the problems of the group with respect to the financing of investments had become so serious that the *gérants* decided to limit the total investments of the group to a well-defined maximum each year. According to forecasts made during that summer, Solvay needed loans of a total of BEF 9 billion for the period 1966–1969 alone. As it was doubtful whether the company would succeed in getting these loans, reducing the future investment budgets seemed the only way out. Early in 1966 the *gérants* even decided to cut the running investment budget by BEF 1 billion to reduce the debt ratio of the company (see Table 17.1).[10]

---

[7] ACS, NdG, P. Washer, "Matières plastiques – politique industrielle," 12 Mar. 1962; interview Paul Washer, 29 Nov. 2007.

[8] ACS, NdG, P. Washer, "Remarques sur le plan financier 1963–1967," 10 Feb. 1964; id., P. Washer, "Financement exterieur necessaire en cas de poursuite des investissements au rhytme actuel," 7 May 1965; ACS, CdG, 17 May 1962; ACS, RdG, 25 Apr. 1966.

[9] ACS, RdG, 6 June 1961, 15 Jan. 1963, 25 Aug. 1964, 29 Sept. 1964, 24 Feb. 1965, 26 Jan. 1966, 15 July 1966; Haber (1971), 351; ACS, 1290-37-7 /1; letter Robert Friesewinkel to Paul Washer, 13 Dec. 2007.

[10] ACS, NdG, P. Washer, "Financement exterieur necessaire en cas de poursuite des investissements au rhytme actuel," 7 May 1965; id., P. Washer, "Problème des effectifs," 27 Aug. 1964; id.,

At the same time the *gérants* decided to reduce the personnel numbers and freeze all new engagements. Solvay started to analyze in detail the too-high personnel figures of its French and Italian plants at Sarralbe, Monfalcone, Ferrara, Rosignano, Dombasle, and Giraud, and it embarked on a comparative study of personnel figures of "friendly" enterprises in Britain and the United States: ICI, Allied, Dow, and Ethyl. In November 1966 the *gérants* decided to prolong the freezing of the engagement of new personnel and to initiate an in-depth study of the personnel costs at the Central Administration and in the national organizations, to cut away all duplication. This would be the prelude to larger organizational changes to come (see Section 17.3). Personnel figures of the Solvay Group were reduced from 40,400 at the start of 1966 to 39,500 at the end of 1967, despite production growth. Also several plants were shut down or sold: the soda ash works at Bayonne (1965) and Monfalcone (1969); the causticization plants at Zurzach (1965), Dombasle (1967), and Rosignano (1969); and the electrolysis works at Aspropyrgos (1967), Pontemammolo (1969), and Baba Ali (1971).[11]

Despite all these drastic measures, Solvay would not be able to find the necessary finances for its ambitious expansion programs, as long as it would remain a limited partnership, and in 1965 the *gérants* came to the conclusion that the option of transforming Solvay into a joint-stock company should be studied seriously.

17.2   THE TRANSFORMATION INTO A JOINT-STOCK COMPANY (1967)

On 26 and 27 November 1964 René Boël and Jacques Solvay traveled to Frankfurt to attend a meeting of the Supervisory Board of DSW. They used the occasion to have a confidential meeting with Hermann Abs, the leader (*Vorstandssprecher*) of Deutsche Bank and one of the most influential bankers of Europe. Solvay and Abs had a long-standing relationship that dated back to the beginning of World War II (see Chapter 12). After the war, Abs had become a board member of DSW, and since 1953, he was chairman of both DSW and Kali-Chemie. As such he stood in regular contact with René Boël especially. He also cooperated closely with Boël in the European League for Economic Cooperation, of which he headed the German section. As a result, there was a great degree of trust between Abs and the *gérants* of Solvay.[12]

René Boël and Jacques Solvay asked Abs's advice on Solvay's financial problems in realizing its ambitious investment program. They offered Abs all relevant financial figures; this almost certainly was the first time that the company disclosed its figures to someone who was not a member of the shareholding families. Abs accepted the mission. He was left completely free with respect to

P. Washer, "Essais de classification prioritaire des fabrications," 27 Apr. 1965; ACS, RdG, 12 Jan. 1965, 10 Sept. 1965; ACS, MoE, 24 Apr. 1968; interview Paul Washer 29 Nov. 1967.
[11] ACS, RdG, 15 and 16 Feb. 1966, 7 June 1966, 8 Nov. 1966; ACS, CdG, 24 June 1965, 16 Jan. 1967, 8 June 1967; ACS, NdG, P. Washer, "Instructions pour les directeurs generaux," 28 Feb. 1966; id., P. Washer, "Evolution de la rentabilité pendant la periode 1956–1966," 4 Aug. 1967; id., P. Washer, "Politique d'investissements," 28 Mar. 1968; ACS, MoE, 24 Apr. 1968.
[12] ACS, RdG, 25 Nov. 1964, 2 Dec. 1964.

his conclusions, with one important exception: Solvay wanted to stay independent and not become part of another chemical company. During 1965 Boël, Solvay, and Abs met several times. In the course of these conversations the idea to transform Solvay into a joint-stock company gradually took shape, and the German banker was asked to give advice on placing Solvay shares on different European stock markets.[13]

Earlier Views within Solvay on Becoming a Joint-Stock Company

When the *gérants* started to consider the transformation of Solvay into a joint-stock company in 1964–1965, this certainly was not the first time they had done so. From the 1880s, the *gérance* had contemplated on several occasions turning the company into a joint-stock company (see Chapters 3 and 10). On all occasions, though – when this "sea-serpent," according to Henri Lévy-Morelle, popped up again – the final answer had been negative.[14] The most important argument was Solvay's strong determination to stay independent, at all costs. Solvay was a family firm at many levels of the organization: on the level of the associates and *gérants* but also on the level of the employees. Often, the children of Solvay employees entered the employ of the company as well. There was a strong feeling of belonging to one big family. When, for instance, Louis Solvay and Émile Tournay left the *gérance* in 1947, Ernest-John Solvay held a speech in which he movingly spoke about "our dear old family business," with all its team spirit and camaraderie. And when in 1966 his son Jacques Solvay analyzed the pros and cons of becoming a joint-stock company, he wrote that an unfriendly takeover would perhaps not be a great problem for the shareholders, because of the possible financial benefits, but for "the staff members and executives of the enterprise, I would consider it an unacceptable event."[15] Several studies were therefore undertaken to find protective arrangements against hostile takeover in the case of a joint-stock company, and conversations took place with the members of the Commission Bancaire, Eugène de Barsy, and Maurice Hermans, but each possible solution often generated its own specific problems. The obligation of joint-stock companies to annually publish financial figures and balance sheets did not greatly attract the *gérance* either. Solvay had a long tradition of secrecy, which was much cherished by all those involved.[16]

A second argument against going public had been taxation. Solvay was a Belgian limited partnership with factories and offices in four different nations: Belgium, France, Spain, and Italy. There was different legislation in each

[13] ACS, RdG, 25 Nov. 1964, 12 Jan. 1965, 24 Feb. 1965; ACS, 1001–45-1, conversation by Baron Boël and J. Solvay with Mr. Abs on 29 June 1965, and letter Hermann J. Abs to Solvay & Cie, 27 Dec. 1965.

[14] Interview Henri Lévy-Morelle, 9 Nov. 2007.

[15] J. Solvay, "Transformation de la Société," 9 Aug. 1968.

[16] ACS, black binder "Relevé des notes juridiques," Vander Eycken, "Y aurait-il des difficultés à transformer actuellement notre Société en société anonyme," 14 Apr. 1928 (RNJ); ACS, 1004–1-6, E.-J. Solvay, "Démission de M. Louis Solvay et de M. Tournay de leurs functions de gérants de la société Solvay & Cie," 5 May 1947; ACS, NdG; ACS, RdG, 20 Apr. 1949; interview Pierre Casimir-Lambert, 22 June 2009.

country with respect to the taxation on capital enlargements and dividends. This made Solvay's situation complicated. On several occasions the creation of separate joint-stock companies in France, Spain, and Italy had been considered, analogous to DSW in Germany, which would have made Solvay a kind of holding company. But in the end the danger of losing control over the industrial activities and over Solvay's unique technology was considered too great.[17]

A last factor was the issue of concessions right, in the field of mining especially. The limited partnership Solvay & Cie was the owner of these concession rights in the four countries mentioned. In the case of the creation of new, separate public companies it was far from evident that the governments involved would grant the (free) transfer of these old rights to the new legal entities.

For all those reasons, Ernest-John Solvay drew the conclusion around 1950 that the transformation into a joint-stock company was interesting from the point of view of attracting finances but that it was not the right moment, and the step was too radical. Perhaps, he remarked, twenty-five years later the issue could be investigated again. The transformation of Solvay into a joint-stock company was therefore not put on the agenda as long as he was chairman of the *gérance*. When on 1 January 1964 René Boël succeeded him, the debate on the legal status of Solvay could be reopened.[18]

Changing Belgian Company Law

On 14 April 1965 a new Belgian tax law was enacted that abolished all taxation in the case of the change in legal status of a company. That, naturally, was a positive event for Solvay, given its intentions in that direction. Solvay discovered soon, though, that the situation in the field of company law was quite different and almost contrary to that of the tax law. On 26 May 1965, Solvay's legal counsel Henry Lévy-Morelle asked for advice from Henri Simont, an influential barrister at the Court of Appeal in Brussels, where he had done an internship. Simont made clear that earlier judgments by the Court of Appeal implied that the legal transformation of a company required the creation of a new legal entity and dissolution of the old one. This had serious consequences for Solvay, because it threatened, among other things, Solvay's concession rights and licenses in Belgium, France, Italy, and Spain.[19]

At a meeting of the *gérance* in September 1965 the latest state of affairs with respect to the change of legal status of Solvay was reviewed in great depth, building on the advice of Abs, the inquiries by Lévy-Morelle, and studies by Solvay's Financial Department. It was concluded that, for the financial future of the company, a change of legal structure was inevitable, but also that Belgian company law in fact blocked that option in practice. The *gérants* therefore

---

[17] ACS, RdG, 20 Apr. 1949, 1 Feb. 1951; ACS, black binder "Relevé des notes juridiques," Kirkpatrick, "Conversion d'une société de personnes en société anonyme," 27 Apr. 1949.

[18] ACS, RdG, 20 Apr. 1949, 10 Sept. 1965; interview Henri Lévy-Morelle, 9 Nov. 2007; interview Paul Washer, 29 Nov. 1967; interview Robert Friesewinkel, 2 Oct. 2008.

[19] ACS, 1001-1-7, "Examen du Projet de loi no. 92 du point de vue exclusif de Solvay & Cie," 23 Feb. 1965; ACS, black binder "Relevé des notes juridiques," H. Lévy-Morelle, report meeting with Mr. Simont on 26 May 1965; ACS, RdG, 10 Sept. 1965; interview Henri Lévy-Morelle on 9 Nov. 2007.

FIGURE 17.2. The Solvay *gérants* on the occasion of the opening of a new company restaurant at the company's headquarters (1960). (*Left to right*) René Boël, Ernest-John Solvay, Robert Hankar (*gérant* of the Mutuelle Solvay), Jacques Solvay, Pierre Solvay, and Henri Delwart. (Solvay Archives.)

decided that Solvay should take the initiative to change the country's law. The only way to speed up the usually slow procedures at the Ministry of Justice and inside the parliamentary commissions would be a direct intervention at the level of the minister by the Commission Bancaire, an influential body created in 1935 to regulate all major issues concerning banks, insurance companies, and financial markets. Therefore, it was concluded, Solvay would contact the Commission Bancaire and put the issue on the table.[20]

Soon thereafter, René Boël and Henry Delwart made an appointment with the chairman of the Commission Bancaire, Eugène de Barsy. They successfully made clear that for multinational companies such as Solvay, a change in Belgian company law was of decisive importance. This conversation paved the way for more detailed deliberations on the text of a bill between Solvay's legal counsel Lévy-Morelle and staff members of the commission. Things went quite smoothly, because already on 23 December 1965 the Commission Bancaire sent the draft text of a new company act to the Belgian minister of justice, Pierre Wigny.[21]

[20] ACS, RdG, 10 Sept. 1965, 14 Sept. 1965. On the Commission Bancaire, see Bruyneel (1978).
[21] ACS, black binder "Relevé des notes juridiques," H. Lévy-Morelle, reports meeting with Messrs. Gelders and Lebrun on 6 Oct. 1965; ACS, CdS, 16 Dec. 1965; ACS, 1001-45-2, letter Henri Simont to Solvay & Cie, 21 Dec. 1965, and letter of the Commission Bancaire to Minister P. Wigny, 23 Dec. 1965; interview Henri Lévy-Morelle, 9 Nov. 2007; interview Jacques Solvay, 27 Nov. 2007.

After that date, René Boël was in close contact with the minister and received advice how to lobby Parliament for the act. In May 1966 the minister sent the bill, with his personal introduction, to the commission on legal matters of the Chamber of Representatives, and in July of that year the bill was sent to the Senate. On 23 February 1967 the bill, after having been accepted by both the Chamber and the Senate, finally reached the status of a law. Article 167 of this new act on commercial companies solved the issue of the transformation of the legal status of firms in a satisfactory manner. Although the issue of changing the law was probably "in the air," and other multinationals must also have felt the same problem, it certainly was remarkable that Solvay had such a great influence on the adoption of a law. The last big hurdle in Solvay's way to becoming a joint-stock company had been removed.[22]

Preserving Control by "the Families"

During the year and a half that the bill was being prepared by the Commission Bancaire and finding its way through Parliament, the Financial and Legal Departments of Solvay were occupied with devising a structure for the new legal entity that would guarantee a solid protection against unfriendly takeover. On the one hand, the structure and statutes of the new company needed to be such that the continuity of Solvay's management and strategy would be guaranteed. On the other hand, the change in legal status was to help Solvay gain the same access to the financial markets of the European stock exchanges, under the same favorable conditions, as the company's competitors had. Companies such as Hoechst, Bayer, and BASF were doubling their social capital every ten years, and Solvay had been unable to compete with them on that front.[23]

There certainly was some tension between these two criteria. If almost all shares of the company were to stay in the hands of the shareholding families without really being negotiable, the small portion of shares on the stock market would lose much of its attraction. This would have consequences for Solvay to access funds under favorable conditions. In contrast, if Solvay were to try to double its social capital every ten years, this would soon exceed the financial strength of its traditional shareholders. A larger influence of third parties would then become inevitable. Solvay was therefore struggling with questions such as the following: What types of shares should we create? What portion of our social capital should be freely transferable on the stock markets? Should we create profit shares that give extra protection?[24]

[22] ACS, RdG, 10 May 1966, 21 Mar. 1967; ACS, NdG, R. Boël, "Conversation avec M. de Barsy le mercredi 28 septembre 1966"; ACS, black binder "Relevé des notes juridiques," H. Lévy-Morelle, " Transformation de la Société Solvay & Cie. en société anonyme: Projet de loi sur la transformation des sociétés commerciales," 19 Jan. 1967; interview Henri Lévy-Morelle, 9 Nov. 2007.

[23] ACS, NdG, J. Solvay, "Transformation de la Société," 9 Aug. 1966; ACS, 1001–45-2, speech René Boël to the Solvay staff, 3 Mar. 1967.

[24] ACS, RdG, 24 Feb. 1965, 15 July 1966; ACS, 1001–45-1, conversation by Baron Boël and J. Solvay with Mr. Abs on 29 June 1965; ACS, NdG, J. Solvay, "Transformation de la Société," 9 Aug. 1966; ACS, black binder "Relevé des notes juridiques," H. Lévy-Morelle, report meeting with Mr. Simont on 18 Aug. 1966; interview Henri Lévy-Morelle, 9 Nov. 2007.

René Boël and Paul Washer discussed these issues in September 1966 extensively with Eugène de Barsy of the Commission Bancaire, who was fully aware of the danger that wealthy oil companies would play a growing role inside the chemical industry and was in favor of registered shares. The idea of profit shares with voting rights was not very well received by him, though. He thought it was a kind of "trick" that one should not use. As an alternative, he sketched a structure with three types of shares: (1) registered shares, paid up to 25 percent, created by a distribution to associates (the fact that these shares were only partly paid up would give an extra degree of protection); (2) registered shares, which would be transferable only to cousins to the fourth degree; and (3) shares to bearer. To protect the company against a takeover, the first two types of shares would constitute a majority, but that majority should not be too large. Within about three years, de Barsy argued, the shares to bearer would account for about 40 percent of the stock, to make Solvay shares financially attractive. Also, Abs had emphasized that Solvay should bring at least 20 percent of its shares to the stock exchange from the start.[25]

In the following months, Solvay drafted its new statutes along these lines, in close collaboration with the Commission Bancaire. In February 1967, when it had become clear that the new law on commercial companies would almost certainly be accepted by Parliament, the *gérants* unanimously decided to change the limited partnership to a public joint-stock company. It was also decided that the extraordinary general assembly would be held on 12 June and that the joint-stock company would start as of 1 July 1967.[26]

The Crucial Date: 12 June 1967

Until February 1967 only a few people inside Solvay were informed about the transformation into a joint-stock company. Everything had been handled with great confidentiality. When the decision had been made to inform personnel, families of associates, members of the supervisory board, and the financial world and public at large, Solvay's modest public relations service was enlarged, and for the first time in its history the publication of press releases was considered. For the other constituencies the members of the *gérance* personally took the lead in creating a basis for the acceptance of the legal transformation by the families and the personnel. On 20 February the Conseil de Surveillance was informed, and later that day René Boël and Pierre Solvay held a meeting with representatives of the families that held the "parts" of the limited partnership (see Table 17.2). On 3 March René Boël held a personal speech to the Solvay staff of the Central Office at Brussels, in which he informed the personnel for the first time and asked them to keep the same team spirit as before. A week later a press release informed the public at large.[27]

---

[25] ACS, NdG, R. Boël, "Conversation avec M. de Barsy le mercredi 28 septembre 1966"; id., P. Washer, report of meeting of Mr. de Barsy with the *Gérance* on 28 Sept. 1966; ACS, RdG, 11 Oct. 1966; letter Robert Friesewinkel to Paul Washer, 13 Dec. 2007.

[26] ACS, RdG, 7 Feb. 1967.

[27] ACS, RdG, 24 Jan. 1967, 21 Feb. 1967, 7 Mar. 1967; ACS, 1001–45-2, speech René Boël to Solvay staff, 3 Mar. 1967.

TABLE 17.2. *Shares of Solvay & Cie Held by the Different Family Groups (1 July 1967)*

Family Group (and descendants of)	Share in the Social Capital (%)
Ernest Solvay	30.0
Alfred Solvay	17.5
Alexandre Solvay (excl. descendants of Ernest and Alfred)	8.5
Guillaume Nélis	7.5
Léonard Pirmez	14.0
Hyacinte Pirmez (excl. descendants of Léonard)	7.0
Valentin Lambert	6.0
Gustave Sabatier	2.5
Prosper Hanrez	2.0
Total	95.0

Note: The remaining 5 percent was held by the Mutuelle Solvay and dispersed among many families related to the old associates.

Sources: Pierre Casimir-Lambert, *Aperçus historiques sur Solvay & Cie* (typescript, Summer 1967), pp. 19–21; Robert Friesewinkel, "Aperçu des tâches incombant aux services financier de Solvay Bruxelles entre 1950 et 1967... Services 'Fiscalité' et 'Actionnaire'" (typescript, 2008); annex to the *Belgisch Staatsblad/Moniteur belge* (24 June 1967), 12473–502.

After in April 1967 Solvay's social capital had been enlarged from BEF 8 billion to 10 billion, by the creation of new parts, paid up at only 20 percent, the crucial decision to change the limited partnership Solvay & Cie into the joint-stock company Solvay & Cie SA was made at an extraordinary general assembly on 12 June 1967. Support was unanimous. After more than eighty years of discussion, Solvay finally had become a joint-stock company; the "sea-serpent" had disappeared.[28] By accepting the new statutes, the general assembly created three types of shares: so-called A shares to bearer, negotiable at the stock exchange (20 percent of total shares); registered B shares, which could only be sold to physical persons (60 percent of total shares); and C shares (20 percent of total shares), which were also registered, but only paid up 20 percent.[29]

By this procedure the continuity of management and control was firmly ensured. With 80 percent of all shares (B and C) registered in the names of the previous associates, and transferable under only certain conditions, the desired protection of Solvay against hostile takeover was guaranteed, at least for the time being. In many respects the transition from a limited partnership to a joint-stock company was for Solvay a gradual process. The family culture of the company largely stayed alive, and the strategy of the company did not change. Nevertheless, those immediately involved perceived the move as no less than a revolution. One of the significant visible changes, in the early years, was the

---

[28] Interview Henri Lévy-Morelle, 9 Nov. 2007.
[29] ACS, AG, 27 Apr. 1967 and 12 June 1967; ACS, RdG, 7 Feb. 1967, 5 Apr. 1967, 9 May 1967, 30 May 1967; ACS, 1001–45-2, communications by the Gérance to the families of associates, and to the personnel, respectively 30 May and 30 Nov. 1967; ACS, 1001–1-7, note on capital extensions 1961–1967.

obligation to publish annual financial figures. Solvay performed this task seriously. Already in 1969 the company won a Belgian prize for the best annual report.[30]

The Board of Directors and the Supervisory Board

At the level of the governance and management bodies, the transition was quite gradual as well. At first, the Solvay board of directors was fully identical to the team of the five former *gérants*: Boël, Delwart, Pierre Solvay, Jacques Solvay, and Washer. The same was the case on the level of the supervisory bodies: the seven members of the Conseil de Surveillance of the limited partnership all became members of the Collège des Commissaires of the joint-stock company. Nevertheless, in statutes, and soon in practice, the strict separation between the *gérants* of the Solvay family (including their descendants, such as the Janssens, Boëls, Delwarts, and Washers) and the families of the silent partners, the *commanditaires* (e.g., the Pirmezes, Nélises, and Lamberts), partly disappeared. Members of the Pirmez, Nélis, and Lambert families could now sit on the board of directors. Leading members of the Conseil de Surveillance, in particular the chairman Baron Léon Coppens d'Eeckenbrugge, together with Valentin Casimir-Lambert, had discussed these issues several times with René Boël. A gentlemen's agreement was reached that between 1967 and 1973 the board of directors would gradually arrive at a more balanced composition, which would also include former silent partners, external directors, and directors promoted from the levels of Solvay's higher management.[31]

In the statutes a distinction was made between ordinary board members and board members responsible for daily management. Initially, as only the five former *gérants* belonged to the board, all members were in the second category. At the advice of the American consultant Dick Paget (see Section 17.3), the phrase "board members responsible for daily management" was soon abolished, and by 1 January 1968 it was replaced by the Executive Committee. In Paget's view, the daily management should be delegated to the higher management levels of the staff, whereas the board of directors should concentrate on issues of strategic importance. In practice, it would take quite some time, though, before a clear separation of roles would take shape within Solvay (see Chapter 22).

On 1 January 1968 two new members entered both the Executive Committee and the board: Albert Bietlot and Édouard Swolfs. Both were highly respected members of Solvay's managerial staff who had made their careers during decades in the company. Bietlot, a son of a Solvay worker, had started from a modest function within the technical staff and had passed through all the ranks until he had become chief executive of technology. Swolfs, in his turn, had worked more on the commercial side of the company and had

[30] ACS, 1001–29-6, speech Baron Boël, 11 Feb. 1970; interview Henri Lévy-Morelle, 9 Nov. 2007; interview Jacques Solvay, 27 Nov. 2007.

[31] ACS, RdG, 21 Feb. 1967, 7 Mar. 1967, 30 May 1967, 5 Mar. 1968; ACS, 1001–45-2, communications by the *gérance* to the families of associates on 30 May 1967; Casimir-Lambert (1967), 19 –21; interview Henri Lévy-Morelle, 9 Nov. 2007; letter Pierre Casimir-Lambert to authors, 29 Apr. 2009; interview Pierre Casimir-Lambert, 22 June 2009.

served as managing director of DSW for about fifteen years. Their appointment to the highest positions in the company was not unique (Hanrez had been appointed in 1880, and Hannon in 1907), but it certainly was a great step in the development of Solvay after World War II. According to Jacques Solvay, their technical, moral, and managerial qualities had been of such a high standard that the leading families used the opportunity of the "transformation" to give them a larger role.[32]

Half a year later, the general assembly appointed five new directors, three of which were from the Solvay family (Roger Janssen, Pierre de Laguiche, Jean-Louis Semet) and two others who belonged to the families of the silent partners (Hugues le Hardy de Beaulieu and Valentin Casimir-Lambert). They all were not members of the Executive Committee, so for the first time the board of directors and the Executive Committee did not fully overlap.[33]

In 1970 a next step was made when two external board members were appointed: the banker Wilfried Guth, who had succeeded Hermann Abs as leader of Deutsche Bank, and the former European commissioner for industry Guido Colonna di Paliano. Gradually, by the mid-1970s, a kind of equilibrium was reached in which the board of directors was composed of four descendants of Ernest Solvay, two descendants of Alfred Solvay, two descendants of the *commanditaires*, two external directors, and about four former staff members of Solvay. These last ones always were also members of the Executive Committee.[34]

Parallel to this development in which the board of directors became a mixed managerial and supervisory board according to the Anglo-American model, the role of the Collège des Commissaires became increasingly marginalized. In 1986, as a result of changes in company law, it was decided to abolish the Collège des Commissaires and include some of its members on the board of directors of Solvac, a holding company created in 1983.[35]

Introducing the Solvay Share at the Stock Exchange

Despite the creation of A shares, when Solvay started its life as a joint-stock company in July 1967, all its shares still were in the hands of the founding families (see Table 17.2). As the entire operation took place to improve Solvay's financial situation, it was important to soon have an extra release of A shares at the stock exchange. Therefore in June 1967 a syndicate of four banks was formed, of which the Belgian Société Générale de Banque (SGB), of which the Solvays, Janssens, and Boëls were major shareholders, took on the coordination. Deutsche Bank, Credit Suisse, and Lazard Frères joined SGB.[36]

It was decided to raise Solvay's social capital from BEF 10 billion to 12 billion (US$240 million), with the release of 850,000 new A shares. They

[32] ACS, 1001-45-2, "La Transformation de Solvay & Cie. en Société Anonyme," 30 Nov. 1967; interview Henri Lévy-Morelle, 9 Nov. 2007; interview Jacques Solvay, 27 Nov. 2007.

[33] ACS, MoE, 6 June 1968; ARS 1967–1969.

[34] ARS, 1967–1980; interview Daniel Janssen, 23 Jan. 2008.

[35] ACS, MoE, 21 May 1968; ARS, 1986; interview Henri Lévy-Morelle, 9 Nov. 2007; interview Daniel Janssen, 23 Jan. 2008.

[36] ACS, MoE, 4 July 1967, 25 July 1967.

were introduced on 27 November 1967 at the Brussels Stock Exchange at a price of BEF 2,900 per share. The introduction was successful; the price immediately climbed to BEF 3,080. The Solvay shares were also placed at the stock exchanges of Antwerp and Paris, and a bit later of Zurich.[37]

After the public release of November 1967, about 29 percent of shares were A shares, 53 percent were B shares, and 18 percent were C shares. Solvay had committed to the Commission Bancaire that it would accompany every large release with a step-by-step payment of C shares. The company therefore decided in 1970 to raise the payment of C shares from 20 percent to 40 percent. This injected BEF 400 million (US$8 million) into the company.[38]

Soon after the introduction of the A shares at the stock exchange, the company's quotation went down. Compared to the average of all the other quotations at the Brussels Stock Exchange, the value of Solvay shares went down to about 50 percent of the average value in 1973. It then improved a bit but hovered around 70 percent of the average value until the early 1980s. Moreover, the fact that the majority of the shares, namely the B and C shares, were not very mobile also played a role. Whatever the cause, the result of the sorry fate of Solvay shares on the stock exchanges was that it became almost impossible to hold a second large release. The Executive Committee was well aware that Solvay should first improve its profitability to have a better stock quotation, but the results were too modest. Until 1987 Solvay's social capital remained at BEF 12 billion. In light of the target to double social capital every ten years, following the example of the German companies, one is tempted to conclude that the entire operation to transform the partnership into a joint-stock company had totally failed. That would not be a fair conclusion, though. From about 1970 almost the entire chemical industry went into decline, and Solvay was no exception. But one could say that the transition came too late. Changing the Belgian law caused a two-year delay, which meant that Solvay could profit less from the booming 1960s.[39]

The Creation of Solvac (1983)

Despite attempts to improve the situation, both the mobility and the quotation of Solvay shares remained low during the 1970s. Increasingly, the company perceived this as a problem. Two main causes were at the heart of it: (1) the low number of A shares compared to B shares, which made Solvay shares not attractive to large institutional investors and (2) the fact that a new

[37] ACS, MoE, 12 Sept. 1967, 3 Oct. 1967, 24 Oct. 1967, 5 Dec. 1967; ACS, NdG, R. Boël, "Visite du Baron L. Coppens d'Eeckenbrugge et de M. V. Casimir-Lambert le lundi 2 Octrobre 1967"; ACS, 1001-28-37, letter R. Boël to P.E. Janssen of the Société Générale de Banque, 24 Oct. 1967; letter Robert Friesewinkel to Paul Washer, 13 Dec. 2007; interview Robert Friesewinkel, 2 Oct. 2008; *Recueil Financier*, cited by the Studiecentrum voor Onderneming en Beurs (SCOB) database of the University of Antwerp. We thank Frans Buelens of SCOB for his collaboration.

[38] ACS, 1001-1-7, meeting R. Boël with Messrs. Rostenne and P.E. Janssen, 30 Jan. 1969; ACS, 1004-2-1, letter Société Générale de Banque to Solvay & Cie, 3 Feb. 1970; ACS, MoE, 20 Feb. 1969; ACS, MoB, 21 Apr. 1969, 26 May 1970; ACS, AG, 8 June 1970; interview Henri Lévy-Morelle, 9 Nov. 2007; letter Robert Friesewinkel to Paul Washer, 13 Dec. 2007.

[39] SCOB database of the University of Antwerp; ACS, NdG, P. Washer, "Politiques d'investissements," 21 Feb. 1968; interview Robert Friesewinkel, 2 Oct. 2008.

release of A shares would require the owners of C shares to raise money for an additional payment of their shares. For several owners of C shares this would be a high financial burden. In the early 1980s Executive Committee member Paul Washer, together with board member Yves Boël and the head of Solvay's Financial Department, Robert Friesewinkel, tried to solve the problem of the C shares. Finally, after consulting the Commission Bancaire and receiving advice from the lawyer Lucien Simont, son of Henri Simont, the answer was found in the creation of a holding company for the C shares, which would be named Solvac. A crucial element in finding this solution was a royal decree, of 9 March 1982, that created the possibility of special "shares with tax benefits" to stimulate venture capital. With this instrument it was possible to propose to the holders of C-shares that they bring their 40 percent paid-up C shares plus a minor cash contribution into Solvac, in exchange for fully-paid-up Solvac shares, which were more marketable and entitled to much more favorable tax treatment, with respect to both income taxation and inheritance duties. Holders of C shares would thus be relieved from their 60 percent liability while enjoying significantly improved net income.[40]

Creating Solvac was a risky operation. In advance it was far from certain whether holders of C shares would indeed offer their shares to the newly created company. When Solvac was established on 24 January 1983, the response of the shareholders was beyond expectations, though. More than 1.3 million C shares were offered, which represented 16.9 percent of the voting rights of Solvay. On 5 April 1983 the Solvac share was introduced at the Brussels Stock Exchange. In November 1983 the planned capital enlargement took place, and by then the remaining holders of C shares had offered their shares to Solvac. The participation of Solvac in Solvay thereby increased to 23.4 percent. Solvac shares were all registered and reserved to physical persons. In that way, the danger was avoided that institutional investors or other companies would succeed in controlling Solvay via Solvac.[41]

After full payment of the C shares, there was no longer a need to distinguish B and C shares, and as a result, both shares were amalgamated. Moreover, during the creation of Solvac it was realized that Solvac could serve as an excellent means to protect the interests of Solvay's traditional shareholders (see Chapter 22). In the course of 1984 the B shares were also amalgamated with the A shares. Since April 1984 only one type of Solvay share exists, nonregistered and freely transferable. Solvac became the platform on which the different family groups reflected together on the future of Solvay and the safeguarding of their interests.

The whole operation had a positive effect on the Solvay quotation. Between 1982 and 1987 the value of the Solvay share skyrocketed, growing much faster

---

[40] Interview Henri Lévy-Morelle, 9 Nov. 2007; letter Yves Boël to Daniel Janssen, 22 Nov. 2007; interview Paul Washer, 29 Nov. 2007; letter Robert Friesewinkel to Paul Washer, 13 Dec. 2007; interview Robert Friesewinkel, 2 Oct. 2008; fax received from Robert Friesewinkel, 2 Nov. 2010.

[41] Letter Robert Friesewinkel to Paul Washer, 13 Dec. 2007; interview Pierre Casimir-Lambert, 22 June 2009; ARS, 1982–1984; database Guy Fautré; SCOB database of the University of Antwerp, http://www.solvac.be/informationsactionnaires/historique/0,,63746–3-0,00.htm.

than the average share value at the Brussels Stock Exchange. In 1988 the social capital of Solvay increased from BEF 12 billion to almost BEF 32 billion (US$870 million), by putting in the reserves. There also was a small release of new shares, on the occasion of the 125th anniversary of the company, to give Solvay's personnel the opportunity to become shareholders.[42]

17.3 MODERNIZING MANAGEMENT AND ACCOUNTING

In response to the financing problem of the 1960s, the *gérants* of Solvay decided to move in two directions. On the one hand, they explored, as we have seen, the possibilities of getting better access to capital markets by transforming their firm into a joint-stock company. On the other hand, they became increasingly aware that reducing the cost prices of the Solvay products was of vital importance. Compared to several competitors, Solvay had too many employees as a result of an organization that had grown increasingly complex. Moreover, the existing bookkeeping practice of the company was not well suited to answer the question of where the profits and losses were made. As a result, in the late 1960s changing the organization, management, and accounting practices of the company moved to a high place on the agenda.

The Evolution of the Solvay Organization

Originally, Solvay had a functional, highly centralized organization. In the 1880s and 1890s separate services for the technological, commercial, and financial tasks were created, next to the General Secretary's Office, which handled the correspondence of the *gérance*. In the course of time, a country organization developed: first in France and Germany, then in Austria, Poland, Switzerland, Italy, Spain, and other countries. From the 1920s, a greater need for national coordination was felt. Two major reasons seem to have played a role. The first was political. When in the 1930s the (fascist) governments of Italy and Spain followed an increasingly nationalistic course, local presence and good contacts with authorities became of growing importance (see Chapter 11). A second reason was the expansion of the Solvay group. When the company created more than one production center in a country, a need for coordination in the fields of sales, procurement, and recruitment emerged. On 1 January 1951 the existing commercial office at Paris was changed into the General Office for France (DGF, Direction Générale pour la France). In 1958 the General Office for the Benelux was created.[43]

After World War II, the role and size of these national organizations grew considerably. In 1967 there were 680 persons employed at Solvay's central

---

[42] Interview Daniel Janssen, 16 Oct. 2007; interview Henri Lévy-Morelle, 9 Nov. 2007; interview Paul Washer, 29 Nov. 2007; interview Pierre Casimir-Lambert, 22 June 2009; SCOB database of the University of Antwerp.

[43] See Chapters 2, 3, and 10; ACS, 1001–28-37, "Organisation de la Société Solvay & Cie," 9 Mar. 1944; ACS, RdG, 3 Sept. 1958; PPSF, Cresap,McCormick and Paget, "Solvay & Cie. Study of Organization," 20 June 1967.

headquarters at Brussels, but more than 400 persons at DGF in Paris alone. The central offices of the national organizations of Italy, Brazil, Germany, the Benelux countries, and Spain all had between 150 and 250 staff. Only the offices in Vienna, Lisbon, and Zurzach (Switzerland) were much smaller, with between 35 and 65 staff.[44]

Next to these functional and national organizations, a third organizational layer gradually developed from the late 1950s, namely a product organization. It originated in the PVC business of Solvay, which was set up in the form of the Solvic companies, outside the Solvay organization. When Solvay also started with the production of polyethylene (HDPE), it was decided to erect at Solvay's central administration the Plastics Department (DMP, Direction des Matières Plastiques), headed by Flamache's successor Raoul Berteaux, which started on 1 January 1959. This department coordinated PVC and HDPE activities, both commercially and technically. The Commercial Department (DGC) of Solvay focused completely on alkalis and other chemical products and left the entire plastics field to DMP. To a lesser extent, this was also true for DGT.[45]

In the course of 1962 and 1963 all products outside the plastics business started to be grouped together as "traditional products." When René Boël succeeded Ernest-John Solvay as chairman of the *gérance* on 1 January 1964, he created divisions for plastics and traditional products. The latter was renamed the Chemical Products Division (DPC), headed by Bietlot, at the start of 1965; the Plastics Division (DMP) continued under Berteaux.[46]

These organizational units were not similar to divisions of large American and European multidivisional corporations. They were not autonomous, did not have operational responsibilities, and did not they have their own balance sheets and profit and loss accounts. They were mere staff services, or knowledge centers, that focused on certain product groups but had to cooperate with the other functional services and with the country groups on all kinds of issues. In the three-layered Solvay organization, the country organizations were the most important places where authority rested and value was created.[47]

Duplication and Other Problems

The evolution of that three-layered organization created several problems. It was not always clear who was responsible for what. In the company culture of Solvay there was an aversion to putting responsibilities explicitly on paper. Personal contacts throughout the organization should, ideally, solve problems when they arose. This was not always successful. Already in 1955 Jacques Solvay noted that the country organizations could not operate as flexibly and

---

[44] ACS, CdG, 8 June 1967; PPSF, Cresap, McCormick, and Paget, "Solvay & Cie. Study of Organization," 20 June 1967.

[45] ACS, RdG, 4 Nov. 1956; ACS, 1130–37-8, letter DGI, Milan, 15 Dec. 1958; id., meeting Boël and Delwart with the Direction des Matières Plastiques (DMP), 7 Dec. 1959; interview Auguste Gosselin, 3 Nov. 2009.

[46] ACS, CdG, 20 Mar. 1962, 28 Feb. 1963, 26 Feb. 1964, 29 May 1964; ACS, 1001–28-29, note by R. Boël on the internal regulations, 18 Jan. 1963; ACS, RdG, 15 July 1963.

[47] Chandler (1962); ACS, 1001–28-37, "Organisation de la Société – Terminologie," 12 Nov. 1958.

on alert as needed, because of the dominant role of DGT. Moreover, for all new projects national chief executives had to address four different functional departments – technical, commercial, personnel, and financial – which resulted in delays and lack of coordination. He therefore proposed giving national country headquarters more autonomy.[48]

During the following decade, that was exactly what happened. Between 1956 and 1964 the national headquarters doubled in size. At the same time, though, the Central Administration in Brussels grew strongly as well. By 1964 it had become increasingly clear that Solvay had high and growing personnel costs, as well as much duplication in its organization. In a meeting of the management team (Conseil de Gérance) in June 1964, Paul Robert, head of the Personnel Department, showed the urgency of the situation. The same, often-detailed documents were sent by factories to both organizations. There was a growing stream of paper that had to be processed at all three levels, but it was often not clear which information was really needed at a certain managerial level. Therefore, Robert had set up a small task force to try to redefine the tasks of the Central Administration and the national organizations.[49]

Solvay was not unique with respect to organization problems like these. Other chemical companies also struggled with their organizations and had hired management consultants. For instance, ICI had hired McKinsey in 1966, and Solvay was interested in learning more about ICI's experiences. In June of the same year, Jacques Solvay became a board member of Allied Chemical (see Chapter 18). During one of his first board meetings, he learned that Allied was involved in restructuring its organization and had hired the management consulting firm of Cresap, McCormick, and Paget. He contacted one of the partners of the firm, Dick Paget, immediately and had several conversations with him. In November 1966 Jacques Solvay concluded that Paget should be invited to analyze and improve Solvay's organization, paying special attention to issues of centralization and decentralization, to the division of labor between the Central Administration and the national organizations, and to the reduction of personnel in the factories.[50]

Dick Paget's Proposals

In January 1967 Dick Paget visited the Solvay headquarters at Brussels for three days, where he spoke to several executives. During the following few months, he and his team investigated the situation in depth, and on 20 June Paget reported his recommendations to René Boël. His report gave a unique picture of Solvay in the mid-1960s.[51]

According to Paget, the legal form of the limited partnership had led to an unusually great concentration of policy and planning functions, and some

---

[48] PPSF, J. Solvay, "Evolution des tendencies dans l'organisation de Solvay & Cie: Organisation actuelle," 5 Apr. 1955.

[49] ACS, CdG, 12 June 1964.

[50] ACS, RdG, 10 May 1966, 20 Dec. 1966, 10 Jan. 1967; ACS, NdG, J. Solvay, "Conversation avec Dick Paget," 30 Nov. 1966.

[51] ACS, RdG, 17 Jan. 1967, 10 Apr. 1967, 23 May 1967; PPSF, Cresap,McCormick and Paget, "Solvay & Cie: Study of Organization," 20 June 1967 (also ACS, 1001–37-4).

executive functions, in the *gérance*. Financial data had been hidden not only to outsiders but also to most department executives. The large Central Administration had been created to process a great amount of information for the *gérants*, but the departments were functionally separated, and only at the top of the organization did all the information come together. The broadness of the range of problems with which the *gérance* concerned itself was much too large. Also, the absence of the delegation of authority over expenditures to line or staff executives, which was caused by the unlimited financial liability of the *gérants* in the limited partnership, was unusual in companies of Solvay's size. Therefore, Paget argued, the transformation to a joint-stock company was an excellent moment to change these practices radically and to introduce a greater delegation of authority.

The delegation that had taken place thus far was mainly to the level of the national organizations. That had been a rational move when Solvay was almost exclusively a one-product organization, producing mainly soda ash, but the company had since diversified, and as a result, the present organization did not fit the needs of a multiproduct company.

The third and last major problem mentioned by Paget was the rather poor financial performance of the group. Operating profits between 1962 and 1965 had slightly declined, but net profit after taxes, as a percentage of sales, fell by a third in four years (from 5.4 percent to 1.8 percent). Given increased competition, ongoing European unification, and the growing need to innovate, to create new products with higher margins, it was of the utmost importance for Solvay to reduce its costs, make its organization more efficient, and manage its business in such a way that its financial performance would improve.[52]

To overcome these three fundamental problems, Paget came up with a number of recommendations. First, he argued that the product organization should be improved and that product managers should be appointed, a function that did not exist at Solvay at that time. Second, all service functions should be unified in separate departments that should supply the product groups with their services. At present the two product divisions, DPC and DMP, had created their own manufacturing, engineering, commercial, and research staffs, which had caused a lot of duplication. In the third place, the tasks of the national chief executives should be more clearly defined in relation to the tasks at the Central Administration. A number of their present tasks could better be delegated to the product managers, Paget thought.

With this advice, Paget proposed changing the three-level organization into a true matrix organization, with clearly defined tasks for all organizational units and specified mutual relations. In his view, three organizational groups should be created, each one under one executive director: one for product management, one as a coordinator of national managements, and one for supporting services. In addition to these fundamental changes in the organization as a whole, Paget also thought that the collegial way of decision making inside the *gérance* was inefficient, because it produced a situation in which all members studied many documents. He proposed appointing a chief executive officer and

[52] PPSF, Cresap, McCormick, and Paget, "Solvay & Cie. Study of Organization," 20 June 1967.

giving other executive directors well-defined tasks, such as to head one of the three organizational groups. He felt that the Research Department should be reorganized as well and put under a single leadership. Inside the research organization, special departments for new products and new processes would be created to initiate research relevant to the long-term future of Solvay.

On top of these changes, a far better management and accounting system would be developed to give better insights into sales, costs, expenses, and profits of each responsible unit. In the existing Solvay accounting system, which was more geared toward issues of taxation, this was completely impossible.

Changing the Organization

Despite some divergent views among the *gérants*, most of Paget's proposals were embraced and implemented as of 1 January 1968. The most visible of these changes was the elaboration and improvement of the products organization. A separation into just two divisions clearly was too crude, whereas a subdivision into eight, or even thirteen, product groups would also be unbalanced, because of the great differences in size among the groups. As a result of studies that considered many alternatives, a division into four different product groups was developed during the second half of 1967, each with maximum internal coherence and minimal relations with other groups:

1. Alkalis and chlorine (A), which included the soda ash and electrolysis plants
2. Derivatives (D), which included the salt and potassium mines, and non-alkali sodium, calcium, and potassium products
3. Peroxides (O), which included hydrogen peroxide, perborates, and chlorates
4. Petrochemicals (P), which included cracking and its products, PVC, and polyolefins

These four product groups were created as of 1 January 1968 and put collectively, as proposed by Paget, under one executive director, Albert Bietlot, who had been promoted to the board of directors on the same date. Plastics processing continued as a separated production group, under Washer.[53]

As proposed by Paget, all the national organizations were placed under one executive director, Édouard Swolfs, who, like Bietlot, had been appointed at the start of 1968. With respect to the supporting services, though, most stayed at it was: René Boël was responsible for the Central Secretary's Office and the Financial and Legal Departments, Pierre Solvay remained responsible for Personnel, and Henri Delwart for Research and Development. Only under Jacques Solvay did a reshuffling of tasks take place. He headed a new domain, Logistics,

---

[53] ACS, RdG, 20 June 1966; ACS, MoE, 15 Nov. 1967, 12 Dec. 1967; PPSF, "Unités de Production," 1 Jan. 1967 (two tables); id., Solvay & Cie, Structure at 1 Jan. 1968; id., Organigramme Solvay & Cie, 25 Mar. 1968; ACS, NdG, P. Washer, "Organisation du Department Transformation," 7 May 1968; interview Robert Friesewinkel, 2 Oct. 2008.

in which the Technical and Commercial Departments were grouped together, following Paget's advice to separate product management tasks from services. In Paget's view, Bietlot, Swolfs, and Jacques Solvay were the three crucial executive directors – heading Products, Countries, and Services, respectively – who should closely cooperate.

Paget carefully coached the implementation of the new organization. Monitoring the implementation during the summer of 1968, he noticed the embryonic state of the marketing activities of the company, a field in which indeed Solvay's track record was poor; the little progress made with the management control system; the fact that long-range planning, under Berteaux, and new product development, under Bloyaert, were in their infancy; and the great distaste inside the company for putting the duties and responsibilities of the organizational units on paper.[54]

The new organization introduced in January 1968 was just the first step in a longer process of organizational change. The management consulting firm of Cresap, McCormick, and Paget stayed involved in the introduction of subsequent adaptations. A target date was set for 14 June 1971, when Jacques Solvay succeeded René Boël as chairman of the board. As chairman, he would be freed of all operational responsibilities to fully concentrate on strategy and long-range planning. As a result, in 1970 and 1971 a reshuffling of the other directors' responsibilities took place. The more strategic role of chairman certainly was a novel step. Corporate Planning, which reported directly to the chairman, was tasked with integrating planning efforts of the other departments. Moreover, Jacques Solvay took over from Swolfs the responsibility of the country organizations, which symbolized his role as head of the group's international activities.[55]

On 1 January 1972 the differences among national organizations, functional services, and product organization received a stronger emphasis with the introduction of new names, as well as greater independence and higher status for the product groups. Until then the nine country organizations on the one hand and some department on the other had both been given the status of "General Directorates" (Directions Générale), thereby blurring the fundamental difference between the two groups. At the start of 1972 the central offices of the national organizations were renamed national directorates, and the services and product groups in Brussels became central directorates. The four product groups, which had functioned as sections of a broader product group under Bietlot, all became independent central directorates. Also the research organization was reorganized, and for the first time centralized and unified as one central directorate, under a new director, Jacques Viriot, who succeeded Henri Delwart. The Solvay organization would largely continue in this way until the 1990s (see Chapter 21).[56]

[54] PPSF, letter from Cresap, McCormick, and Paget, 3 July 1968.
[55] PPSF, letter Richard M. Paget to Baron Boël, 21 Nov. 1969; ACS, MoE, 2 Dec. 1969; PPSF, Direction "Corporate Planning, 19 Feb. 1970; interview Paul Washer, 29 Nov. 2007.
[56] PPSF, "Organisation," 18 Oct. 1971; interview Félix Bloyaert, 26 Mar. 2009.

The Difficult Change in Management and Accounting Practices

Although not all of Paget's proposals had been accepted, changing organizational structures proved far easier than changing the complicated accounting system and the usual management practices. Before 1967, Solvay never had implemented consolidated bookkeeping but always had produced separate balance sheets and profit and loss accounts for the different subsidiaries. Its financial department had a good record "optimizing" tax payments in the four countries where the mother company was operating but had little experience in evaluating the financial performance of individual products. All calculations with respect to products were in fact delegated to DGT and its successor departments. Over a century the technology department had developed a very sophisticated system of technical bookkeeping, and in the 1960s and 1970s, Albert Bietlot was the only person inside Solvay who really understood the translation of the technical accounting into commercial and financial accounting. Like Guffroy before him, Bietlot was, according several observers, the "true boss" of Solvay during his time as head of DGT and, later, executive director. He received full support from Jacques Solvay.[57]

Under these circumstances, changing management practices was no easy affair. Nevertheless, improvement of the practices was badly needed. Return on investment had been going down for years, and therefore, apart from crude cost cutting, a selective investment policy directed to products of high return on investments was required. That could only be done, however, if management had the proper accounting tools. Therefore, introducing a managerial accounting system was a necessity. Resistance was great, though, and it is tempting so see that as an example of Jan Romein's law of the handicap of a head start. Because Solvay was one of the first chemical companies that developed a sophisticated system of technical control, which had proved successful, it was difficult for the company to accept, under changed conditions, other options.[58]

Some progress was made, though. On the advice of Paget from 7 to 27 September 1969 a group of nine Solvay executives was sent to the United States, where they visited about nine different chemical and petrochemical plants and refineries (e.g., Dow, Ethyl, Allied), to study American accounting methods and administrative organization; however, it was not until the mid-1980s that a true managerial accounting system would be introduced (see Chapter 21).[59]

[57] Interview Paul Washer, 29 Nov. 2007; interview Robert Frieswinkel, 2 Oct. 2008.
[58] ACS, NdG, P. Washer, "Resultats par produits," 23 Apr. 1964; id., "Suggestions pour un programme de réforme interne de Solvay & Cie. en vue d'augmenter la rentabilité des capitaux investis," 12 July 1966; id., P. Washer, "Politiques d'investissements," 21 Feb. 1968; ACS, RdG, 8 Nov. 1966; PPSF, (3 July 1968) letter from Cresap, McCormick and Paget, 3 July 1968; http://en.wikipedia.org/wiki/Jan_Romein.
[59] ACS, PD Désiré Lega; interview Robert Friesewinkel, 2 Oct. 2008; interview Paul Washer, 29 Nov. 2007; oral communication Daniel Janssen, 2 Feb. 2010; letter Paul Washer to the authors, 20 May 2011.

FIGURE 18.1. The polyolefins plant at Deer Park, Texas. (Solvay Archives).

18

The Long and Winding Road to Deer Park

Solvay's Return to the United States

Since the end of World War II, the idea to again become active industrially in the United States was a cornerstone of Solvay's company strategy. Next to diversification into plastics and other new products, the enlargement of geographical scope was a goal embraced by all the *gérants*, though to varying degrees, and the large and dynamic American market was one of the most obvious candidates for such expansion. There were several reasons for such a policy. First, the immense loss of Solvay's activities in Eastern Europe generated a desire to find compensation elsewhere. Second, when research costs continued to rise over the course of the 1950s and 1960s, there was a growing need for larger sales by entering new markets, to generate higher revenues to finance research. A third important reason, shared by many European business leaders, was the strong conviction that the United States was the place where it all was happening. One simply had to be there to take part in the latest technological, scientific, and commercial developments. During the Cold War, a fourth important reason was added to these arguments: the company and shareholders realized the possibility of a Soviet attack on Western Europe and therefore wanted a substantial part of their assets to be in North America. During the 1970s, when the fear of a Soviet attack had largely passed, the growing influence of left-oriented parties in Western Europe favored investments in the United States. Last but not least, there were emotions concerning the history of the company – feelings of resentment almost – that told Solvay leaders that the glorious start of their company in the United States should get a follow-up.

By 1954, Solvay controlled a financial holding in the United States with a market value of more than US$130 million, mainly consisting of Allied shares (see Chapter 15). The remaining US$40 million was in stock holdings in Wyandotte Chemicals Corporation (see Section 18.1) and the Libbey-Owens-Ford Glass Company, as well as government bonds and some smaller shareholdings.[1]

Evaluating the situation of Solvay in the United States, Ernest-John Solvay wrote in December of that year:

> The formation of Allied has not strengthened the industrial position of Solvay & Cie, it has weakened it.

---

[1] ACS, NdG, R. Boël, "Politique industrielle de Solvay & Cie. aux États-Unis," 11 Oct. 1954; ACS, CdG, 24 Sept. 1954; Metzner (1955), 2:363–71.

From a financial point of view, on the other hand, we have not complained. Allied has been an excellent investment and so to speak the source of the financial power of the N.A.S. The N.A.S. has a value of more than 30 percent of the total assets of Solvay & Cie; its assets have been well managed and are an extremely valuable financial potential, which, if used wisely, provides us with great opportunities for new businesses.[2]

On the need to start new business in the United States all *gérants* agreed. But on the products that Solvay should manufacture in America and the risks it could take, there was less agreement. René Boël was the greatest driving force inside the *gérance* with respect to setting up new Solvay business in the United States. Before and during World War II, he visited the United States many times. He came to love the country; he developed close friendships with his American business contacts, such as John Foster Dulles and George Murnane; and he became enthusiastic about the American way of doing business. He therefore explored, between 1945 and 1955, numerous business options, in particular with respect to "Wyandotte," but in the end none of these attempts bore fruit, as is described herein.[3]

It would be Jacques Solvay who in 1974 finally would succeed in taking over a major American chemical activity: the high-density polyethylene (HDPE) business of Celanese, with large production facilities at Deer Park, Texas. That acquisition would prove a major step in the globalization of Solvay. With the Deer Park HDPE production facilities as a bridgehead, Solvay was able to establish a fast-growing and highly diversified chemical business in the United States.

18.1 OPERATION WYANDOTTE

Wyandotte Chemicals Corporation was founded in 1893 by members of the Ford family – not direct relatives of the car manufacturers of Dearborn – as the Michigan Alkali Company, in the city of Wyandotte, near Detroit. From 1937, Solvay's relation with Michigan Alkali intensified when the American company decided to construct an electrolysis plant next to its soda ash plant and approached Solvay for a license on its mercury cell. In 1943, the Michigan Alkali Company changed its name to Wyandotte Chemicals Corporation (WCC).[4]

After World War II, the contacts between Solvay and WCC were resumed: WCC had plans to enter the field of organic chlorine chemistry and constructed a pilot plant to produce ethylene and propylene by means of cracking. This interested Solvay greatly because of its plans with respect to PVC and other organic chemicals. In early April 1946 René Boël traveled to Detroit and agreed

---

[2] ACS, NdG, E.-J. Solvay, "Considerations sur la politique de Solvay & Cie," 21 Dec. 1954. The low value of 30 percent results from the book value of the shares; the market value of US assets was much higher.

[3] See Chapter 12. Interview the late Countess Mathilda Boël, 27 Nov. 2007; conversation between Jean-Marie Solvay and Yves Boël, 2 June 2009.

[4] See Chapters 3, 9, and 11. For the history of Wyandotte Chemicals Corporation and other industrial ventures of the Ford family, see Pound (1940); Aiken (1957).

with the Ford family to enlarge the existing technical cooperation to cracking and some other areas of organic chemistry. Two cracking pilot plants were ordered by Boël and shipped from Wyandotte to Jemeppe and Zurzach in the course of the following year (see Chapter 15).[5]

Boël also discussed with the Ford family the option of a more intense cooperation. The Fords, like Solvay, wanted eagerly to enter the booming field of organic chlorine chemistry, but they lacked the financial means for an expansion program, as well as much of the know-how needed. On both fronts, Solvay could help. For Boël the contacts with Wyandotte offered an excellent opportunity to get a strong industrial foothold in the United States. The company produced soda ash, caustic soda, and chlorine, Solvay's key products, and it was willing to start the production of PVC in the future. A more ideal candidate for a (partial) takeover could hardly be imagined.[6]

Nevertheless, it would take two years before contracts between Solvay and Wyandotte could be finalized, resulting in Solvay taking a 24.99 percent interest in WCC. It took so long because Solvay wanted to avoid problems with the US antitrust Sherman Act, given its 20 percent interest in alkali producer Allied and the planned 25 percent interest in WCC. Moreover, in Europe the *gérance* confronted "the almost unanimous wish of the associates [to] monetize their parts more easily." A possible solution for that problem, which would leave the private partnership intact, was transferring Allied shares, disposable on the stock market, to the associates of Solvay, in exchange for their "parts" in Solvay (the capital of the private firm Solvay & Cie was divided into so-called "parts," that were held by family members. These were different from shares that could be traded). Boël and George Murnane thereupon got the brilliant idea to kill two birds with one stone. By combining the Wyandotte operation with the transfer of Allied shares to Solvay part-holders, Solvay could avoid violating the Sherman Act, and at the same time its associates would receive dividends in dollars. An ingenious operation was executed, too complex and detailed to sketch here, in which a new public investment company, the Solvay American Corporation (TSAC), was created; the Solvay American Company (SAC) was renamed North American Solvay Inc. (NAS). There was a public release of preference shares of TSAC to finance the acquisition of Wyandotte shares, for about US$17 million. These preference shares were convertible into Allied shares on request. In the course of the 1950s almost 11 percent of the Solvay "parts" were exchanged for Allied shares.[7]

The final transaction was concluded in April 1948, when the general assembly of WCC accepted the agreement. Solvay received the right to nominate three of twelve members of WCC's board of directors. Soon thereafter, George

[5] ART, Wyandotte, letter of 28 Jan. 1946; ART, Zurzach-Cracking, letters of 18 Feb., 9 Apr., and 24 Apr. 1946; ACS, 1291–37-1, Forsyth to Boël, 26 Apr. 1948.

[6] ACS, 1291–37-1, René Boël, to George Murnane, 11 June 1946.

[7] ACS, 1291–37-2, "I. Echange parts Solvay contre Allied. II. Participation dans Wyandotte," 12 Apr. 1948; ACS, Baron Boël, Wyandotte files, Annual Meeting WCC, 4 May 1948; id., Solvay "W" book, Aug.-Sept. 1947; ACS 1291–37-1, letters and memoranda 1946–1947; letter by Robert Friesewinkel to Paul Washer, 13 Dec. 2007; fax from Robert Friesewinkel to the authors, 2 Nov. 2010.

Murnane, René Boël, and Eli W. Debevoise entered the family business of the Fords as directors of WCC; the other nine directors were all members of the family. Solvay received preferred stock with voting rights, but only for seven years. During those years, trust would grow between the Solvay family and the Ford family. Before 31 October 1955 Solvay was to decide whether it would convert its shares into common stock or into preference shares with a guaranteed dividend of 4 percent, but without voting rights.[8]

Five years later, in April 1953, Boël started negotiations with the Ford family about enlarging Solvay's stake in the American company, because it could only function as Solvay's dreamed-of bridgehead in the United States when Solvay held the majority. He proposed an extension of the capital of WCC, so that Solvay could enlarge its interest to 50 percent or 51 percent. With the extra money WCC could then embark on an ambitious extension program based on new Solvay technology. Divergent views between different branches of the Ford family made negotiations, largely through Murnane, very difficult. They took many months. In a final attempt to force a breakthrough, René Boël and Ernest-John Solvay went to Wyandotte in February 1954, but no agreement could be reached, because one branch of the Ford family had great trouble over losing control of their family firm, a viewpoint that Solvay leaders surely could easily imagine.[9]

At a meeting of the *gérance* on 9 April 1954, Ernest-John Solvay concluded that Solvay should wait and not raise its offer. The dangers of doing business in the United States were in his view too large, and the position of foreign shareholders in that country was often too weak, as the experiences with Allied Chemical had shown. These conclusions by the chairman of the *gérance* in fact meant that Operation Wyandotte was over. As a result, in October 1955 the shares were converted into preferred shares without voting rights, and Boël and Debevoise stepped down as members of the board. In 1961, when the quotation was relatively high, Solvay sold its last shares of WCC. An involvement of more than fifteen years had come to an end.[10]

In evaluating why Operation Wyandotte failed, one must conclude that it did so for a number of reasons. As a family firm, WCC was very similar to Solvay;

[8] ACS, 1291-37-1, letter Boël to *gérance*, 12 Sept. 1947; id., Draft Agreement between Wyandotte Chemicals Corporation and American Chemicals Inc., 6 Oct. 1947; id., letter Forsyth to Boël, 26 Apr. 1948; ART, Wyandotte, travel report R. Boël to Detroit, 7–8 Apr. 1948; ACS, 1291-37-2, "I. Echange parts Solvay contre Allied. II. Participation dans Wyandotte," 12 Apr. 1948; ACS, CdG, 22 Apr. 1948; ACS, Baron Boël, Wyandotte files, historical overview, 13 Oct. 1953.

[9] ACS, Baron Boël, Wyandotte files, historical overview, 13 Oct. 1953, with handwritten additions; ACS, RdG, 30 Apr., 12 May, 2 and 23 June, 4 Aug., 27 Oct., and 8 Dec. 1953, 6 and 27 Jan., 12 Feb., and 13 Oct. 1954; ACS, Baron Boël, Wyandotte files, Board Meeting of WCC, 25 Feb. 1954; letter by Robert Friesewinkel to Paul Washer, 13 Dec. 2007; interview Jacques Solvay, 16 Jan. 2008.

[10] The preferred shares, which Solvay had acquired for US$13.5 million, were sold for US$11 million, for a loss of US$2.5 million. But this was partly compensated for by a profit on the selling of the ordinary shares of Wyandotte. See ACS, RdG, 28 Nov. 1946, 23 Mar., 9 and 15 Apr., 5 and 25 May, 25 June 1954, 19 July, 14 Oct. 1955, 7 July and 23 Aug. 1961; ACS, Baron Boël, Wyandotte files, Board Meeting WCC, 27 Oct. 1955; ACS, 1293-2-1, Board meeting of NAS, 18 Mar. 1957; ACS, 1291-33-1, meeting on dissolution of NAS, 22 Nov. 1961.

many family members involved had problems with giving up their control of the business. No doubt, these hesitations among a large minority of the Fords to give up the family character of their business were a major cause of the failure of Operation Wyandotte.

But there is also a Solvay side to this. There was no strong unity of vision among the *gérants* with respect to the investment. Working on the issue during the autumn of 1953, Murnane complained several times to Boël that he found Solvay's American projects vague and not fixed enough. René Boël and Henri Delwart were strongly in favor of starting industrial production in the United States, using the latest Solvay's technology, but Ernest-John Solvay, who had witnessed all stages of the problematic Allied-Solvay relations since his entry into the firm in 1921, was more cautious. He had a deep mistrust of the American business environment, and he held different views on the application of Solvay's latest technologies in the United States. When it appeared that DGT was not enthusiastic either about the acquisition of Wyandotte, it proved impossible to formulate a coherent development plan for the future of WWC. When Boël looked back to the Wyandotte affair in January 1987, he still deplored that, because of a "unfortunate misunderstanding on the part of the top management [*gérance*], and the strong determination by technical services inside Solvay's central office not to realize the project," the acquisition of a majority interest in Wyandotte had failed, with the unhappy consequence that it would take another twenty years before Solvay would make a real comeback in the United States. Obviously, the divergent views within the *gérance* had been better remembered by Boël than the refusal by the Ford family to give a majority of shares to Solvay.[11]

18.2 OPPOSING VIEWS

That the strategic visions of René Boël and Ernest-John Solvay with respect to Solvay's operations in the United States differed so greatly came only fully to the fore during the year after the Wyandotte debacle. Already in early 1952 Boël had formed a small team of competent chemists and engineers inside North American Solvay – Carl DeLong; Alexis Basilevsky; Rudolf Knoepfel; and especially Antonin Šrba, a former managing director of Verein Aussig – who helped him with the development of technical projects and business plans for the United States and who greatly assisted in building up the Solvay business in Brazil, Boël's other darling. Between 1952 and 1954 that team developed several proposals, including detailed plans for a complex working in the areas of PVC, tetraethyl lead, solvents, and electrolysis in California.[12]

Ernest-John Solvay was not very happy with all these "dispersed and confusing studies undertaken by NAS," as he thought they did not "correspond to

[11] ACS, Baron Boël, Wyandotte files, historical overview, 13 Oct. 1953; ACS, 1151, "Politique industrielle du Groupe Solvay," interview Count Boël, 16 Jan. 1987.
[12] ACS, 1291-33-1, travel R. Boël to the United States, 27 Dec. 1951–14 Jan. 1952; ACS, 1291-37-4, NAS, Meeting, 25 Apr. 1952; ACS, 1291, returned documents, meeting 5 Oct. 1953; ACS, NdG, R. Boël, "Politique industrielle de Solvay & Cie. aux États-Unis," 11 Oct. 1954.

a coherent industrial view."[13] Shortly after the tense Wyandotte meeting of the *gérance* on 9 March 1954, René Boël informed Šrba that the policy with respect to the United States had changed completely and that NAS should immediately stop all projects. That this was a dramatic turn of events, indeed, is clearly illustrated by Šrba's response. On 21 April 1954 he returned all correspondence on the NAS projects to Brussels, with a short note saying that given the changes of policy, the documents were not relevant to NAS anymore.[14]

Despite this, North American Solvay informed the *gérance* in August 1954 about the possibility of taking a dominant interest in the company Durez Plastics & Chemicals Inc., of Tonawanda, New York, which controlled about one-third of the US market for phenol resins and had been followed with much attention by Šrba and Boël since at least 1952. This message sparked the tinder. All accumulated frustrations between Ernest-John Solvay and René Boël on the course to be taken with respect to the United States culminated in a conflict on the Durez Plastics issue, which went on for many weeks.[15]

According to Boël and Delwart, Solvay, just like other large European producers, should have a subsidiary in the United States to exploit the processes developed by Solvay's Development Department. Starting production of PVC in the United States was to be the spearhead of Solvay's industrial policy (see Chapter 15). One way of getting a head start was to acquire an American company, and Durez seemed an interesting candidate.[16]

In at least two important respects, the viewpoint of Ernest-John Solvay differed greatly. First, as we have seen, he generally had a less positive opinion about the American business environment, and the failure of the Wyandotte operation had only reinforced that view. Second, he thought that Solvay should build on its technological strengths in soda ash production and electrolysis, and not diversify too much in other, risky directions. Even Solvay's PVC technology, in his view, was not well developed enough to introduce it to the aggressive American market. On top of these two crucial policy differences, there were also differences in personality and in management style. Commenting in September 1954 on another plan coming from the Research and Development Department, Ernest-John Solvay remarked that he did "not need hypotheses, but figures: on tons, fixed assets, cost prices, construction time, profitability" – an illuminating remark, which reveals a lot about how he perceived the ambitious projects of his colleagues.[17]

During a meeting of the *gérance* on 13 October 1954, the two opposing strategic views clashed. All colleagues – Henri Delwart, Pierre Solvay, and Philippe Aubertin – with the exception of Ernest-John Solvay, agreed with a note written about Durez by Boël. In an emotional speech Ernst-John Solvay

---

[13] ACS, RdG, 20 July 1954.

[14] ACS, 1291, returned documents, 21 Apr. 1954; ACS, RdG, 13 Oct. 1954.

[15] ACS, 1291-37-4, NAS meetings, 24 June and 16 July 1952; ACS, RdG, 24 Aug. and 15 Sept. 1954; Haynes (1954), 138.

[16] ACS, NdG, H. Delwart, "Remarques relative au projet de participation dans la Durez," 9 Sept. 1954; id., R. Boël, "Politique industrielle de Solvay & Cie. aux États-Unis," 11 Oct. 1954; id., H. Delwart, "Politique de Solvay & Cie. aux États-Unis," 24 Feb. 1955.

[17] ACS, RdG, 24 Aug., 15 Sept., 13 Oct. 1954; ACS, CdG, 24 Sept. 1954.

argued that it was premature to introduce Solvay's new processes to the United States, and Durez Plastics in particular did not have good synergy with the rest of Solvay. Moreover, it would be far too expensive and therefore not worth being studied at all. "These are nice dreams," he exclaimed, "but they are not objective at all!" After insisting that his colleagues think it all over again, and take responsibility, he demonstratively left the room – a rare event in the history of Solvay.[18]

The meeting was a turning point in Solvay's strategy with respect to the United States. For Ernest-John Solvay the cup was full – a new approach regarding the US issues was needed. And he was right. Lambert Vanharen, head of Solvay's research and development, who was sent to the United States to investigate the potential of Durez Plastics, came to the conclusion that Durez did not show sufficient technical advantages to justify Solvay's participation in that company. Until March 1955 the exchange of views with respect to Solvay's American strategy continued, but no new viewpoints were developed, and new attractive options did not emerge. With a few minor exceptions, Solvay's activity in the United States came to a standstill. René Boël increasingly turned his attention to Brazil and, later, to the transformation of Solvay into a joint-stock company.[19]

During the following years, the technical team of NAS was dismantled in steps, but what remained was not totally unimportant. For a while NAS kept its role as a window onto developments in the United States. When on 27 April 1955 a note on the Phillips polyethylene process, and the possibility of licenses, appeared in *Journal of Commerce*, Antonin Šrba mailed the article to Solvay in Brussels that day. As a result, Solvay was among the first European companies to contact Phillips for more information and for licenses, and therefore was able to obtain options on licenses for Italy, Spain, the Benelux countries, and Brazil. Also during the months that followed, Šrba played a crucial role in negotiations between Solvay and Phillips, as well as in studies of the HDPE market. As such, he, too, stood at the base of one of Solvay's new activities. After the Solvay company had acquired the plastics-processing company Hedwin in Baltimore (see Chapter 16), Šrba was made managing director of that small firm.[20]

During the early 1960s, Solvay occasionally entered into talks and negotiations with American companies, in line with the decision of 1955 that it could explore opportunities concerning PVC and plastics. Within that framework, it made contact with Allied, Spencer, and Mobil Chemical (see Chapter 16). During a meeting to prepare negotiations that the young *gérants* Jacques Solvay

---

[18] ACS, RdG, 13 Oct. 1954, with appendix.

[19] ACS, RdG, 1 Mar. 1955; ACS, NdG, E.-J. Solvay, "Considerations sur la politique de Solvay & Cie," 21 Dec. 1954; id., R. Boël, "Politique de Solvay & Cie. aux États-Unis," 10 Feb. 1955; id., E.-J. Solvay, "Voyage aux États-Unis (fin mars-début avril 1955)," 12 Apr. 1955; interview Whitson Sadler and René Degrève, 12 May 2010.

[20] ACS, NdG, E.-J. Solvay, "Voyage aux États-Unis (fin mars-début avril 1955)," 12 Apr. 1955; ACS, black binder "Amerique," "Hedwin Corporation: Historique de l'acquisition de cette société," 15 Dec. 1983; ACS, 1514-5-11, letter A. J. Šrba to Solvay & Cie, 17 Feb. 1956; id., letter by Vanharen to North American Solvay, 18 May 1955; id., letter A. J. Šrba to Solvay & Cie, 12 July 1955; ACS, 1291-37-5, letter DGI to Rosignano, 7 March 1957.

and Paul Washer would have with Mobil Chemical in London, Ernest-John Solvay gave a wonderful illustration of how strongly the history of Solvay was always present inside the company. He warned them that in case of cooperation, it should be a *mariage de raison*, not a *mariage d'amour*. "The experiences that we have in our relations with Americans are not encouraging." On several occasions Americans appeared to be the worst partners Solvay ever had. The Hazards profited from World War I, according to Ernest-John, and behaved very "ungentlemanlike." And when Weber took over Allied, he appeared to be the worst of our "friends." Therefore, Ernest-John Solvay thought, it would not be possible to find loyal friends among future American partners. The best one could hope for was to cooperate on well-defined goals for a limited period of time. Nevertheless, he wished his young colleagues "good luck" with their conversations in London.[21]

18.3 MAKING A NEW START

After the celebrations of the hundredth anniversary of Solvay, Ernest-John Solvay retired as chairman of the *gérance* and was succeeded by René Boël on 1 January 1964. With respect to the United States, a new start could be made, and it was. During the following two decades, it was Ernest-John's son, Jacques Solvay, who would become the major driving force behind Solvay's reentry to America.

From April 1947 to February 1950, after his graduation as electrical and mechanical engineer from the Free University of Brussels, Jacques Solvay had worked as an engineer for General Electric in Bloomfield, New Jersey. During those years, he started to feel at home in the United States. He was fascinated by the country, and he had met his future wife, Marie Claude Boulin, who was French but had lived in New York since her early childhood. In 1950 the young couple returned to Europe, where Jacques started working for Solvay in many different plants and departments, to prepare himself for the position of *gérant*, which he became on 16 December 1955, at the age of thirty-five.[22]

These private circumstances help us understand why Jacques Solvay's attitude toward the United States differed from that of his father. His personal experiences had been positive, and unlike his father, he did not carry the burden of unpleasant experiences with persons and companies such as the Hazards, Allied, and Wyandotte.

A new start was made in the mid-1960s when Solvay entered into a rapprochement with Allied. During the preceding decade, Solvay's interest in Allied Chemical had gone down from about 22 percent to about 10 percent for a number of reasons, one of which was the conversion of TSAC preferred shares into Allied shares. Nevertheless, a shareholding of 10 percent in a company as large as Allied was still substantial. Over the course of the 1960s, René Boël thought

---

[21] ACS, RdG, 15 Dec. 1961.
[22] Interview Jacques Solvay, 16 Jan. 2008; *Jacques Solvay Hommage*, special issue 1920–2010; interview Whitson Sadler and René Degrève, 12 May 2010.

that the time had come to try again to get Solvay representation onto the board of Allied.[23]

In April 1965 Jacques Solvay, Paul Washer, and a number of senior Solvay executives visited Allied Chemical in New York. A start had been made. Boël, discussing the issue with Chester Brown, Allied's CEO, at first aimed to get two of his American confidants on the board, one from Lazard Frères & Co. and one from Sullivan & Cromwell. But André Meyer, CEO of Lazard Frères & Co., advised him that industrial experience on the board was indispensable. Chester Brown agreed, and on 25 June 1966 Jacques Solvay entered the board of Allied Chemical. A year later, André Meyer joined him. Boël's aim was fulfilled: Solvay had its two board members.[24]

For Jacques Solvay a period of close contact with the United States started. The board meetings of Allied took place almost every month, and on the margins of those meetings, Jacques Solvay gradually developed his American network. He bought a summer house on the coast of Massachusetts; he met frequently with André Meyer, George Murnane Jr., Frank Pizzitola, and other partners of Lazard Frères & Co., as well as with the consultant Dick Paget and top executives of Allied, such as the future CEO Jack Connor. He was invited to the Conference Board, and later to the meetings of the American Enterprise Institute (AEI) organized at Beaver Creek, Colorado, by President Gerald Ford. Several of his American contacts became his close friends.[25]

On 14 June 1971 Jacques Solvay succeeded René Boël as chairman of the board of directors of Solvay and as chairman of the Executive Committee. During an informal meeting with Paul Washer in Lisbon from 24–26 July 1971, devoted to the mid- and long-term strategy of the company, Jacques Solvay explicitly stated that he wanted to realize an industrial position of Solvay in the United States and that he was considering selling Solvay's Allied shares for that purpose.[26]

Although it would take several years before Solvay would sell those shares, Allied Chemical would become the first serious partner in Solvay's attempts to start industrial production in the United States. The key asset in these talks, as well as in most of the subsequent actions, were Solvay's patents on highly active catalysts for the production of the high-density polyethylene (HDPE) and polypropylene (PP) (see Chapter 16). During 1972 and 1973, negotiations took place to create a 50–50 joint venture in HDPE in the United States, which would produce at Allied's site at Baton Rouge, Louisiana. Early in 1973, one

[23] ACS, 1271-65-1, "Allied Chemical Corporation," 6 July 1970; letter by Robert Friesewinkel to Paul Washer, 13 Dec. 2007; personal communication by Robert Frieswinkel, 2 Nov. 2010.

[24] MES, *To record a pleasant visit – April 15, 1965. Allied Chemical Corporation, New York, N.Y.* (photo album); *Jacques Solvay Hommage*, special issue 1920–2010; ACS, RdG, 11 May, 9 Nov. and 21 Dec. 1965, 13 Jan., 1 Feb., 10 May, and 7 July 1966 ; ACS, 1293-1-3, letter René Boël to Chester Brown, president of Allied, 24 May 1966; id., travel of H. Lévy-Morelle to New York, 4–9 Feb. 1967. On André Meyer, see Reich (1983), esp. 214–17.

[25] ACS, RdG, 5 and 26 July, 6 Sept., 3 and 30 Nov. 1966, 31 Jan., 10 Mar., 10 Apr., 30 May, 8 Aug. 1967; PPSF, Allied file, letter John S. Gates to Jacques Solvay, 2 Dec. 1966 and 14 Mar. 1967; interviews with Jacques Solvay, 27 Nov. 2007 and 16 Jan. 2008.

[26] PPSF, Org 70-71, meeting Jacques Solvay and Paul Washer in Lisbon, 24–26 July 1971.

of Solvay's plastics experts, Luciano Balducci, of Rosignano, was sent for six months to Allied to study the Baton Rouge plant and the US polyethylene market in detail. In the summer of 1973 these talks and investigations resulted in a draft agreement on a 50–50 joint venture. But during the following weeks it appeared that there were conflicting views on the financial side of the deal. On top of the licenses on Solvay's technology, Allied requested from Solvay a payment of US$26.8 million. Solvay thought that US$17 million was a more reasonable price. A proposal by Jacques Solvay to agree at a price halfway between the two amounts was not accepted by Jack Connor. In September 1973 Allied stopped all negotiations. Looking with historical distance at the issue, with Solvay's strong desire to produce in the United States in mind, one can only be surprised at that outcome, given the rather small difference between the two prices, in the light of the far higher price that Solvay later paid to Celanese.[27]

Over the following months, Solvay energetically tried a whole array of options. It negotiated with US Steel on a 50–50 joint venture in polyolefins; with Hercules on technical cooperation on polypropylene; with Gulf and with American Petrofina, and its subsidiary Cosden, on licenses and industrial cooperation; and with Olin Corporation on a joint venture with Solvay in the field of electrolysis. In almost all these negotiations, Jacques Solvay cooperated closely with his usual American consultants, George Kern of Sullivan & Cromwell, and André Meyer and Frank Pizzitola of Lazard Frères & Co.[28]

With the exception of a technical agreement with Hercules on polypropylene, concluded in February 1974, most of the talks did not have a positive outcome. But in June 1974 – when negotiations with US Steel and Olin were still going on – Frank Pizzitola, who had worked for Celanese some years before, informed Solvay that his former employer had plans to sell its HDPE business. Already at the end of the same month, Jacques Solvay had a talk with Robert L. Mitchell, Celanese's group vice president of chemicals, plastics, and coatings. As would become clear shortly, that proved a crucial step: finally Solvay could get its large production site in the United States.[29]

18.4 THE ACQUISITION OF DEER PARK

Celanese Corporation of America – there was also a British Celanese – had been founded as a coatings and synthetic fibers business in 1918, first under a different name, by members of the Alsatian Swiss Dreyfus family. During World War II the company diversified into plastics, and in the 1950s it took, just like Solvay, a license on the Phillips solution process for the production of HDPE. Construction of the polyethylene plant, situated at Deer Park, forty kilometers from Houston, started in 1956, and already by the following year the

[27] *The Solvay Story* (1964); ACS, MoE, 7 Mar. 1972, 18 Apr. 1972, 3 Oct. 1972, 6 Feb. 1973, 15 May 1973, 10 July 1973, 30 July 1973, 21 Sept. 1973; AHR, PD Balducci.
[28] ACS, MoB, 26 Nov. 1973; ACS, MoE, 22 Jan. 1974, 19 Feb. 1974, 2 Apr. 1974, 3 May 1974, 2 July 1974; ACS-CR, agreement Solvay-Hercules, 11 Feb. 1974; PR, 2 Apr. 1974.
[29] ACS, MoE, 24 June 1974; interview Whitson Sadler and René Degrève, 12 May 2010.

first Celanese's HPDE came on the market. During the 1960s, the production facilities were greatly enlarged. When Solvay started negotiations with the American company, the total capacity of the Deer Park plant, which employed about three hundred people on eighty-four hectares, was about two hundred thousand tons, making it one of the biggest HDPE plants in the United States.[30]

In complete contrast to the laborious previous negotiations with Wyandotte and Allied, the talks with Celanese went very smoothly. It was soon clear that Bob Mitchell definitely wanted to sell the polyethylene business. From 23–25 July a Solvay delegation visited the Deer Park plant. Apart from Jacques Solvay, who headed the team, the delegation members were Claude Loutrel, director of Solvay since June 1974, who was liberated from his tasks in Italy to support Jacques Solvay in the negotiations; Jacques Pinta, head of Solvay's plastics business; and two specialists of Solvay's polyethylene technology, J. Stevens and J. Hélin. Their first impression was favorable, although the plant looked a bit like a "Phillips museum," because, unlike in Rosignano, Elclor, and Sarralbe, no newly developed technologies had been added.[31] Nevertheless, the expectation was that the plants could become quite profitable after Solvay's own PE process was implemented. Negotiations started, and on 17 September 1974 Jacques Solvay could tell his colleagues that an agreement had been reached. This was a great and long-awaited event.[32]

Originally, Celanese had asked for a sum of US$90 million for its polyethylene business, which included not only the Deer Park plant but also marketing and sales teams, distribution facilities, and a research team on polyolefins in Celanese's central research laboratory in Summit, New Jersey. But Jacques Solvay, assisted by Frank Pizzitola and his team from Lazard, succeeded in getting the price down to US$70 million, to which a working capital of US$10 million to US$15 million should be added. The total sum required was therefore about US$80 million to US$85 million. On 23 September, Solvay's board of directors agreed with these results, and two days later the board of Celanese did the same. On 25 September 1975, Jacques Solvay flew to the United States to inform employees of Celanese in New Jersey and Texas himself. He also flew by helicopter to his friend Jack Connor, Allied CEO, to tell him personally about Solvay's latest acquisition, and to Dick Paget, who was going to advise Solvay on organizational matters and on the integration of Celanese's personnel into the Solvay work force.[33]

It was decided that Solvay would take over all personnel of Celanese's HDPE business. Len Emge, the plant manager, would keep his position and remain a member of the Operating Committee. Most important, the Lazard bank succeeded in obtaining large long-term loans from US credit suppliers: US$40 million from the insurance company Prudential and US$20 million from New York Life. These loans were needed because the low price of Allied shares

[30] Haynes (1954), 72–4; Soltex (1977), 1–2; PR, 25 Sept. 1974.

[31] ACS, MoE, 30 July 1974.

[32] ACS, MoE, 2 July 1974, 17 Sept. 1974; interview Jacques Solvay, 27 Nov. 2007.

[33] ACS, MoB, 23 Sept. 1974; PR, 25 Sept. 1974; interview Whitson Sadler and René Degrève, 12 May 2010.

excluded the selling of those shares as a means of (partly) financing of the deal. The remaining US$25 million, needed to fund the equity of Solvay's new American subsidiary Soltex Polymer Corporation, established on 15 November, was supplied by a loan from the Société Générale de Banque. With an interest rate of more than 10 percent, capital costs were high. These were the years of the first oil crisis and of huge inflation. On 19 November 1974 the final contracts and agreements among Solvay, Soltex, and Celanese were signed. From that day, Soltex Polymer Corporation was the owner of Celanese's HDPE business, and it took over all operational responsibilities. After a long and winding journey of almost fifty-five years, Solvay had finally succeeded in acquiring again a large industrial business in the United States. Moreover, the business was not a joint venture but was wholly owned, which provided far better opportunities for expansion and diversification. As a result, still today Jacques Solvay is remembered inside the company as the man "who brought Solvay back to the United States."[34]

One of the immediate consequences of the deal with Celanese was that Solvay's close relation with Allied changed. The acquisition of the Deer Park plant turned both companies into competitors on the American HDPE market, and therefore a Solvay executive sitting on Allied's board would violate US antitrust laws. For that reason, Jacques Solvay informed Jack Connor immediately in September 1974. A few days after 19 November, he indeed stepped down as board member of Allied. Frank Pizzitola, who had succeeded André Meyer, stayed on the Allied board and could give Solvay, as a major shareholder of Allied, some information, as long as polyethylene was not discussed. As a friend, Jacques Solvay also stayed in touch with Jack Connor. Selling Allied shares only became more important. Solvay badly needed the money that was locked up in the shares. When from 1975 large funds were needed for the construction of a cracker (see below), while the Allied share price finally was going up, Jacques Solvay asked Whitson Sadler and Frank Pizzitola of Lazard to develop a program to sell the shares. It was not easy, but in 1977 Pizzitola discovered that Bill Miller, CEO of Textron Inc., was aiming to enlarge Textron's shareholding in Allied to 21 percent. Soon a deal could be made. In May 1977 Solvay and Textron agreed that within two and a half years, depending on the quotation on the stock exchange, Solvay would sell its entire block of 10 percent to Textron. During 1977 and 1978, indeed half of the shares were sold, but then the quotation went down. It would take until 1985 before Solvay sold its last Allied shares. Only then did a (financial) relationship that existed for more than one hundred years come to its end.[35]

[34] PPSF, USA Contacts Divers, handwritten diary of Jacques Solvay, 25 Sept.–19 Oct. 1974; ACS, MoE, 17 Oct. 1974, 18 Nov. 1974; ACS, MoB, 25 Nov. 1974; *The Solvay Review* (1985) (1): 1, 5; Rapaille (1990), 123; *Solvay* (1988), 17; *Jacques Solvay Hommage*, special issue 1920–2010; interview Whitson Sadler and René Degrève, 12 May 2010.

[35] ACS, MoE, 1 Oct. 1974, 3 Dec. 1974, 17 Sept. 1975; PPSF, USA Contacts Divers, letter Frank J. Pizzitola to Jacques Solvay, 6 July 1976; *Soltex* (1977), 20; PPSF, box Pizzi, notes on phone call of Jacques Solvay with Frank Pizzitola, 24 Mar. 1977; ACS-CR, agreement between Solvay and Textron, 27 May 1977 (12 Oct. 1984); Coenjaers and Legrand (1984), 30.

18.5 PRODUCING POLYOLEFINS IN AMERICA

When Soltex Polymer Corporation started doing business in November 1974, Solvay appointed its own people to key positions. Three of the six board members of Soltex came from Solvay: Jacques Solvay, as chairman; Claude Loutrel, as president and CEO; and Rudolf Knoepfel, as director. The three external directors were Whitson Sadler, from Lazard; George Kern, from Sullivan & Cromwell; and John McCabe, from Cresap, McCormick, & Paget – so Solvay's US advisers were all represented on the board. During the first five years of the company, Loutrel, who had become a member of Solvay's Executive Committee on 1 January 1975, flew at least once a month to Texas to chair a meeting of Soltex's Executive Committee or to attend a board meeting. In the day-to-day management he was joined by two former Solvay employees: the polyolefins expert Michel Osterrieth, appointed executive vice president, and René Degrève, former head of Solvay's financial reporting, who became secretary and treasurer. Plant manager Len Emge became vice president of operations. It was this team that built up the Soltex operations in the United States, assisted by the vice president of marketing Maurice Fitzgerald and the three external directors. Jacques Solvay was closely involved as well. He was the driving force in the strategic development of the company, chaired all board meetings, and often joined Loutrel on his journeys to the United States.[36]

One of the most urgent issues that occupied the Soltex leadership was the supply of ethylene to the plant. Already in July 1974, during the start of the negotiations, it had become clear that Celanese had supply contracts for only the following two years, and these contracts guaranteed at best a production level of about 50 percent of full capacity. The rest of the required feedstock had to be purchased on the market. In the wake of the 1973 oil crisis, ethylene prices were high and future prospects were uncertain. It was therefore difficult, if not impossible, to conclude favorable long-term contracts. Because of shortages in ethylene supply, during the first months of its existence, Soltex was unable to produce enough HDPE to fulfill the demands of its customers. The old Phillips plant was stopped in May 1975 and mothballed. In the meantime, Claude Loutrel and his coworkers negotiated with oil companies such as Petrofina, Arco, Phillips, and Shell. Parallel to that, Whitson Sadler at Lazard undertook a study of the US ethane market, as an alternative way to get feedstock, by transforming ethane into ethylene. By the summer of 1975, neither of the two approaches had produced lasting results.[37]

Therefore, it was of great interest when Pizzitola and Sadler in July 1975 sketched a third option. They had been informed that Champlin Petroleum, a subsidiary of the Union Pacific railway company, was investigating the

---

[36] ACS, 1294-53-2, Board meetings Soltex, 15 Nov. 1974–29 Oct. 1980; id., meeting Executive Committee Soltex, 12 Dec. 1974; ACS, MoB, 25 Nov. 1974; *Soltex* (1977); AHR, PD Osterrieth; id., PD Degrève; interview Claude Loutrel, 31 Jan. 2008; interview René Degrève, 2 Dec. 2008.

[37] ACS, MoE, 16 July 1974, 1 Oct. 1974, 17 Dec. 1974, 21 Jan. 1975, 17 Mar. 1975, 1 July 1975; ACS, 1294-53-2, Board Minutes Soltex, 20 May 1976; interview Whitson Sadler and René Degrève, 12 May 2010.

construction of a steam cracker, close to its refinery at Corpus Christi, Texas, and was looking for partners. The members of the Executive Committee saw this as an excellent opportunity. Assuming participation of 20–25 percent, which would cost about US$100 million, they believed that Soltex could be supplied with about 40–50 percent of the cracking products (ethylene and propylene). This would make it possible to greatly extend the Deer Park plant, with the construction of a PP plant and enlargement of the HDPE plant.[38]

Jacques Solvay and Claude Loutrel started negotiations with Champlin and Union Pacific, and soon a third partner was found as well: Solvay's "good old friend" ICI, which had much know-how on the cracking process. In November 1975 agreement on the principles was reached, and a year later the final agreement about the establishment of the cracker was signed. Together, ICI United States, Champlin Petroleum, and Soltex Polymer Corporation founded the Corpus Christi Petrochemical Company (CCPC), in which Soltex would take an interest of 25 percent and the other two partners 37.5 percent each. The size of the steam cracker would be enormous, because it was designed to produce about 540,000 tons of ethylene and 250,000 tons of propylene per year. Total investment was estimated at US$600 million. Apart from the cracker, a network of pipelines for naphtha, ethylene, and propylene would have to be constructed as well, to connect the cracker to the Champlin refinery and to the production sites of ICI and Soltex. Via a pipeline the steam cracker would also be connected to the Gulf Coast ethylene grid. Construction began in 1977, and after some delays and financial losses, the Corpus Christi cracker came on stream in 1980. Soltex had its own supply of olefins.[39]

Because of difficult economic circumstances in 1975, Soltex could only gradually realize the conversion to Solvay technology and the expansion programs that had been originally planned. In the second part of 1975 a technical streamlining (" debottlenecking") of the HDPE plant took place, as well as the partial introduction of the Solvay PE process, with the active supported catalyst. The Phillips process remained in operation, though, because it produced a kind of HDPE that was excellently suited for blow-molding applications, such as milk bottles.[40]

Early in 1975 the marketing department was transferred from the Celanese office in Newark to Texas, to better coordinate production and marketing. It was also decided to acquire and upgrade an office building in nearby Houston, to which the administrative and marketing departments from Deer Park would be moved, as well as the laboratory and the technical sales force from Summit,

[38] ACS, MoE, 29 July 1975.
[39] ACS, MoE, 17 Sept. 1975, 18 Nov. 1975, 16 Dec. 1975; PPSF, USA Contacts-Divers, letter James H. Evans, President Union Pacific Corporation, to Jacques Solvay, 30 June 1976; ACS-CR, Ethylene Complex Partnership Agreement, 15 Nov. 1976; PR, "Participation of the Solvay Group in an important ethylene production complex in the U.S.A.," 30 Nov. 1976; ACS, 1294-53-2, Board Minutes Soltex, 25 Jan. 1979; *The Solvay Review* (1985) (1): 13; interview Whitson Sadler and René Degrève, 12 May 2010.
[40] ACS, MoE, 3 Dec. 1974, 6 May 1975; ACS, 1294-23-1, PE-HD-USA. Soltex-Solvay research coordination meeting, Houston, Jan. 26–27, 1977; id., "PE-HD-USA: Amélioration de la qualité des resins fabriquées à Deer Park," 15 June 1977; *Timeline Poster* (2000).

TABLE 18.1. *Production and Sales of High-Density Polyethylene and of Polypropylene by Soltex Polymer Corporation, 1975–1999 (in 1,000 tons)*

Year	Production HDPE	Sales HDPE	Production PP	Sales PP
1975	n.a.	125	–	–
1980	255	247	47	45
1985	409	408	102	106
1990	569	553	197	192
1995	651	640	213	214
1999	821	816	371	381

Note: n.a. = not available.

Sources: ART, PDO; *Timeline Poster* (2000).

New Jersey. On 24 August 1976 the new Soltex headquarters in Houston were officially inaugurated.[41]

In 1977 production and sales figures for the first time surpassed the original (1974) capacity of two hundred thousand tons. Many subsequent expansions would follow (see Table 18.1), but other producers increased their capacities as well. For many years Soltex's market share of the US HDPE market stayed around 13 percent, which still made it one of the largest US producers. Soltex had a strong position in the food market especially (e.g., HDPE milk bottles), with a market share of about 33 percent.[42]

In 1975, two American engineers were sent to Sarralbe to get experience with the construction and start-up of the polypropylene plant, and to apply that knowledge later in the United States. The next year Solvay decided to construct a PP plant at Deer Park; planning for it would come on stream in 1979 when the Corpus Christi cracker would start with its propylene deliveries. With a total budget of US$70 million, the investment came close to the sum for which Solvay had purchased the entire Deer Park plant; but in those years of high inflation, the dollar of 1977–1979 differed quite considerably from that of 1974. During the construction of the plant, Soltex started the market development of its product, using polypropylene made at Sarralbe or by Hercules, the US market leader with which Solvay had arranged cross-licensing and technical cooperation. The plant started up in October 1978, earlier than planned. But soon dark clouds appeared. Several other companies had also entered the market. Between 1976 and 1980, the capacity of the US polypropylene industry grew from 1.35 million to 2.25 million tons. That rapid growth in a short time led to great overcapacity in the industry. On top of that, Soltex had serious manufacturing problems that were difficult for local technical staff to resolve. Several experts from Brussels, such as Auguste Gosselin, who in 1979 succeeded Jacques Pinta as head of plastics, went several times to Deer

[41] ACS, 1294-53-2, Board Minutes Soltex, 5 Feb. 1975; ACS, MoE, 29 July 1975; PPSF, USA Contacts Divers, letter Rudolf W. Knoepfel to Jacques Solvay, 12 Aug. 1976.

[42] ACS, 1294-53-2, Board Minutes Soltex, 30 May 1975; ACS, MoE, 3 June 1975, 18 Nov. 1975; *Soltex* (1977), 2; *The Solvay Review* (1985) (1): 2; Vanden Driessche (1985); "A Look at David Birney," *Today Solvay America* 1 (3) (Sept. 1989): 3.

Park to help tackle the problems. To make matters worse, by 1980, when the PP manufacture at Deer Park was still not running smoothly, the entire plastics industry was hit hard in the wake of the second oil shock, of 1979–1980, and Soltex in particular by the losses of the CCPC cracker (see Chapter 20). In 1981 Soltex decided to shut down one of the two PP production lines because of the crisis. Suddenly, the yield went up; the remaining production line performed far better. So, by accident, the cause of the trouble was found: a flaw in the design that caused a lack of compression when both lines were in operation. When after mid-1982 the economic situation improved, the PP plant had been reconstructed and showed an excellent performance. The year 1983 was a wonderful one for the industry. Sales of PP grew quickly (see Table 18.1), as did profits. Soltex succeeded in raising its market share in PP from 2.3 percent in 1980 to about 5 percent at the end of the 1980s.[43]

After the second oil shock, manufacturing and sales of HDPE and PP continued to grow at Soltex (see Table 18.1), although the cyclic character of the polyolefins business increasingly started to worry Solvay's leaders. To reduce risks and improve profits, Soltex management worked hard to broaden and upgrade the product range. As a result, along with the dominant product range for blow molding, HDPE varieties for injection and extrusion applications were developed. By combining the Phillips and Solvay technologies, Soltex succeeded in arriving at "one of the widest product lines in the United States, with some 100 resins covering all major HDPE applications," according to the company magazine.[44] Premium resins for special applications were developed as well. At the end of 1989 the new Technical Center, where one hundred people worked, opened its doors, to facilitate technical support, quality services, and product development. "We cannot just compete in the commodity resin sector against major oil companies," David Birney, then executive vice president and general manager of polymers, said. "Our future lies in developing a technically sophisticated product mix."[45]

Along with these innovations, costs had to be cut. One of the largest "bleeders" in the Solvay group was the Corpus Christi Petrochemicals Company, which had suffered huge losses each year since it started operations in 1980, also as a result of high feedstock prices. When technical improvements and a conversion to gaseous feedstock did not have the required results, in 1983 Solvay's leadership started considering the option that Soltex try to sell its interest in CCPC. During the years of crisis, though, it was almost impossible to sell Solvay's share in CCPC for a reasonable price. A few years later times were more favorable, and the ethylene market was turning around. When Daniel Janssen became chairman of Solvay's Executive Committee in June 1986, he soon called the CEO of Solvay America, Whitson Sadler, and asked him to sell

[43] ACS, MoE, 18 Nov. 1974, 7 Jan. 1975; 75); ACS, 1294-53-2, Board Minutes Soltex, 20 May 1976, 30 Mar. 1977, 16 Feb. 1978, 23 Jan. 1980; PR, Construction of a polypropylene unit at Deer Park, 24 May 1977; Dyer and Sicilia (1990), 393–4; interview Auguste Gosselin, 27 Nov. 2009; interview Whitson Sadler and René Degrève, 12 May 2010.

[44] *The Solvay Review* (1985) (1).

[45] *Today Solvay America* 1 (3) (Sept. 1989).

CCPC as rapidly as possible. Sadler was to seize the opportunity of the changed market conditions to secure the necessary long-term contracts for ethylene and propylene.[46]

Champlin, ICI, and Solvay America prepared a descriptive memorandum for Occidental Petroleum, thinking it was a logical buyer for the cracker. But another party would make the deal: Gordon Cain of the Sterling Group, in Houston. Cain and Sadler came to the agreement that Cain, in addition to buying the shares of ICI and Champlin, would buy Soltex's share in CCPC for US$75 million – a write-down of US$86 million was recorded in 1986 when the transaction was imminent to bring the value of Soltex's share in CCPC to US$75 million after early repayment of CCPC debt – but that Soltex then would buy back 40 percent of the cracker for a US$25 million investment to give Cain an industrial partner that would help the financing of the deal. This created a difficult and tense situation, because Daniel Janssen, then Solvay's CEO, wanted to get out of cracking completely. Talking about the issue with Jacques Solvay, then chairman of the board, Sadler recalled that he was told that a US$25 million investment was out of the question and that the maximum Jacques Solvay could get approved by the board was US$15 million, for which Soltex would get preferred shares and an ownership of 25 percent of the cracker. The board of Solvay agreed with this, as did Cain. In February 1987 the intention to come to a deal was announced. Half a year later, in July, the deal was made, also with ICI and Champlin, which sold all their assets. Gordon Cain made a good business out of this. He merged CCPC with some of his other businesses into Cain Chemical Inc. and sold that company, including its 75 percent interest in CCPC, early in May 1988 to Occidental Petroleum for US$2 billion. Occidental wanted also to buy the preferred stock owned by Soltex. A tense negotiation took place. Roger Hirl and Dr. Dale R. Laurence of Occidental asked Sadler to name a price – if acceptable to Occidental a deal would be closed, and if not, Soltex would continue to own 25 percent of the cracker. Sadler asked US$115 million, and Occidental immediately agreed. On 2 June 1988 the deal was announced. Within a year, Soltex had made a handsome profit on this deal of US$100 million, which was a welcome partial compensation of the gigantic losses suffered during the previous years. Finally, Soltex was completely out of the unlucky cracker business. Ethylene supply was guaranteed by several supply contracts with oil companies, such as Texaco.[47]

During the 1990s, the Deer Park polyolefins HDPE and PP received awards for their excellent quality, and the company was ranked first in overall customer satisfaction. But the competition from large oil companies, which had moved into polyolefins on a huge scale, was increasingly felt. As is discussed at length in Chapter 22, in 2001 Solvay sold its PP activities to BP and received

---

[46] Personal communication by Daniel Janssen, 19 Apr. 2010; phone call with Claude Loutrel, 14 Sept. 2011.

[47] Coenjaers and Legrand (1984); *The Solvay Review* (1985) (1): 3, 13–14; PR, Sale of Corpus Christi Steam Cracker, Solvay, 28 Feb. 1987; PR, Sale by Solvay America Inc. of its preferred stock of CCPC Chemical Inc., 2 June 1988; interview Whitson Sadler and René Degrève, 12 May 2010.

the Engineering Plastics business of BP-Amoco (e.g., polysulfones, originally developed by Union Carbide) in return. This was a major reinforcement of Solvay's specialty polymers business. Four years later Solvay also sold all its HDPE activities to BP, after having run them since 2001 in the form of a Solvay-BP joint venture. The product that had formed the basis of Soltex at its start in 1974 was divested. Solvay America would continue in a strongly altered form.[48]

18.6 TOWARD A DIVERSIFIED SOLVAY AMERICA

Already in the 1950s, René Boël and Henri Delwart had defended the view that the acquisition of a "monoproduct" business should serve as a springboard for the establishment of more diversified industrial activities in the United States. Jacques Solvay fully agreed; therefore, from the moment that Soltex was established, he thought about the possibilities of enlarging the Soltex product portfolio and acquiring other American companies. One of the earliest options considered in December 1974 was the construction at Deer Park of a polyacrylonitril (PAN) plant, a plastic with properties different from HDPE. But after investigations, and contacts with Monsanto and Continental Can, it was decided two years later not to go that way.[49]

In the summer of 1975 Frank Pizzitola and Jacques Solvay made plans on enlarging Solvay's scope in the United States outside the plastics domain; and the following year it was decided to put Solvay's American business on a track of expansion and diversification. To drive that new mission of Soltex forward, a new leader would be found. Michel Osterrieth, executive vice president of Soltex, was an expert in the field of polyolefins, but he was not the right man to lead the new diversification program. Jacques Solvay held the view that the new leader preferably should be an American, with better insights into the US legal system, and more deeply embedded in American business life. Therefore, during a flight from Houston to New York, Solvay asked Whitson Sadler – who had been an external board member of Soltex since November 1974 – whether "he wanted to be a banker the rest of his life." "Not if you let me run your US operation," Sadler replied. Instead of being a partner at Lazard, he wanted to run a business himself. Sadler was appointed, and over the following twenty-five years of his career with Solvay America, he would greatly expand the business, fully supported by the Solvay leadership, which was strongly in favor of considerably enlarging Solvay's business in the United States.[50]

Whitson Sadler studied economics and finance, and some chemistry and history, at University of the South, Sewanee, Tennessee, and at Harvard, and was computer systems project leader in the US Navy. He joined Lazard Frères

[48] *Timeline Poster* (2000).
[49] ACS, MoE, 3 Dec. 1974, 29 July 1975; extracts from Soltex Board meetings, received from René Degrève, May 2010.
[50] ACS, MoE, 17 Sept. 1975; *The Solvay Review* (1985) (1): 2; Ainsworth (1992): 17; Jackson (2000): 10; interview Jacques Solvay, 27 Nov. 2007; interview Whitson Sadler and René Degrève, 12 May 2010.

& Co. in 1970 and was promoted to general partner in 1975, working in the corporate finance section of that bank. On 1 January 1977 he started working for Solvay, as vice chairman of Soltex Polymer Corporation in Houston. During the following three years, the top management of Soltex was restructured step by step. In February 1978, Sadler replaced Loutrel as CEO, and Osterrieth replaced Loutrel as president. Claude Loutrel remained chairman of the Executive Committee of Soltex. At the end of 1979, when Osterrieth became head of Salsbury, Sadler became president and CEO, and Loutrel replaced him as vice chairman. Loutrel's five years of day-to-day management of the company had ended; an American was leading Solvay's business in the United States. Together with René Degrève, the newly appointed lawyer Ed Buckingham, and others from the management team, Sadler would come to expand "Solvay's investment to create a North American presence for Solvay in all four of its...global sectors of activity: chemicals, pharmaceuticals, plastics and processing."[51]

The first two construction projects – a peroxides plant and a plant for the production of synthetic pulp – would be realized at Deer Park. In 1978 Solvay announced that it would create a subsidiary, Interox America, together with the British firm Laporte, Solvay's partner in peroxides since 1970. Interox America constructed plants for the manufacture of hydrogen peroxide and sodium percarbonate on the Deer Park site of Soltex. The peroxides plant started up in November 1979 – this was Soltex's first step outside the plastics realm. Within a few years, Interox America succeeded in conquering 20 percent of the US market by focusing on highly pure grades. Its successful head of marketing, the Englishman David Birney, from Laporte, in 2001 would advance to the highest company position in North America when he succeeded Whitson Sadler as Solvay's chief executive of the North American Free Trade Agreement (NAFTA) region. A second plant, at Longview, Washington, was inaugurated in 1989 by Jacques Solvay.[52]

The plant for the production of synthetic pulp for the paper industry, made from polypropylene, was the result of a project with Hercules, incorporated as the joint venture Lextar. It came on stream in 1981, managed by Len Emge, who had been replaced as Deer Park plant manager by John Merian. A similar plant was erected in Europe, at Solvay's Rosignano site. Solvay's unsuccessful interest in this business was not long lived. In November 1981 Solvay sold its share in Lextar to Hercules.[53]

[51] ACS, 1294–53-2, Board Minutes Soltex, 26 Jan. 1977, 16 Feb. 1978, 8 Nov. 1979; interview Claude Loutrel, 31 Jan. 2008; interview René Degrève, 2 Dec. 2008; interview Whitson Sadler and René Degrève, 12 May 2010.

[52] ACS, MoE, 4 Nov. 1975, 16 Dec. 1975; PR, Interox announces new manufacture of hydrogen peroxide and sodium percarbonate in the USA, 30 Mar. 1978; ACS, 1294–53-2, Board Minutes Soltex, 25 Jan. 1979, 23 Jan. 1980; *The Solvay Review* (1985) (1): 4, 7–8; Vanden Driessche (1985); Rapaille (1990), 123; *Solvay* (1988), 17; Ainsworth (1992).

[53] ACS, MoE, 4 Nov. 1975; ACS, 1294–53-2, Board Minutes Soltex, 30 Nov. 1976, 23 Jan. 1980; PR, Solvay-Hercules joint venture in the field of synthetic pulp, 8 Feb. 1979; PR, Construction of a Pulpex production unit by Lextar (Solvay-Hercules) at Deer Park, 29 Nov. 1979; PR, Solvay sells to Hercules its interests in Lextar, 30 Nov. 1981.

Gradually, Soltex Polymer Corporation was transformed from a manufacturing company of polyolefins to the coordination center of Solvay's businesses in the United States. In April 1979, for instance, Solvay's shareholding in Hedwin was transferred to Soltex. Later that year, a larger step was taken when Soltex acquired Salsbury Laboratories, a major producer of poultry vaccines. It was Solvay's first large acquisition in the domain of the life sciences (see Chapter 19). Whitson Sadler recalled that during a trip to Corpus Christi, Jacques Solvay had told him that Solvay had decided to grow in the field of biochemistry. Sadler thereupon phoned his former colleague at Lazard, Frank Pizzitola, who happened to know that the owners of the Salsbury Laboratory wanted to sell the company. The deal, which closed on 30 September 1979, was a major watershed in the history of Solvay. Michel Osterrieth was appointed president and CEO of the new acquisition.[54]

Other acquisitions would follow, such as the plastics-processing firm Wall Trends in December 1981 and TH Agriculture & Nutrition Company Inc. in 1984. By that time, Solvay had considerable business in America. Sales had risen from US$100 million in 1977 to US$500 million (excluding CCPC and Interox), part of which clearly came from outside plastics. Then, about 12.5–14 percent of Solvay's total sales were realized in the United States. More important, Jacques Solvay and Whitson Sadler had the firm intention to make more acquisitions in the realm of animal and human health. Therefore, it was increasingly perceived as an anomaly that all these diverse activities operated under the umbrella of a polymer corporation, Soltex. In 1984 the decision was taken to create an American holding company under which the other companies would fall. On 19 October 1984, TSAC was renamed Solvay America Inc., which would become that holding company. The traditional activities of TSAC were continued by another company, Solvay Technologies, managed by Michel Osterrieth, who succeeded Rudolf Knoepfel in that position. In November 1984, the creation of Solvay America was publicly announced. Solvay could then operate in the United States as one single entity, recruit senior staff, and profit from Solvay's reputation of technical excellence. Sadler became president and CEO of Solvay America, and Jacques Solvay its chairman.[55]

Solvay America also succeeded in getting its brand name Solvay back in the United States; Allied had owned the name since 1920. Allied had gone out of chemistry almost completely, certainly after its merger with Signal in 1985, and so did not use the name anymore. Its Syracuse plant had been closed down in the early 1980s and demolished in 1985. After lengthy negotiations, Solvay America in 1989 finally bought the brand name for US$500,000. According to Whit Sadler, this was a bargain, given the fact that Bayer around that time paid US$25 million to get its name back in the United States. The

---

[54] *The Solvay Review* (1985) (1): 2, 9–10; Ainsworth (1992): 19; extracts from Soltex Board meetings, received from René Degrève, May 2010; interview Jacques Solvay, 27 Nov. 2007; interview Whitson Sadler and René Degrève, 12 May 2010; AHR, PD Osterrieth.

[55] *The Solvay Review* (1985) (1): 1–2, 11, 15; Vanden Driessche (1985); *Jacques Solvay Hommage, Special Issue 1920–2010*: 9; extracts from Soltex Board meetings, received from René Degrève, May 2010; interview Whitson Sadler and René Degrève, 12 May 2010.

FIGURE 18.2. A transport vehicle in the trona (natural soda ash) mines in Wyoming, United States. (Solvay Archives).

following year the Soltex Polymer Corporation was renamed Solvay Polymer Corporation.[56]

In the meantime, Solvay America continued to grow in the life sciences (see Chapter 19). In 1985 the animal health division of E. R. Squibb & Sons was acquired, and the following year Daniel Janssen, who had become part of the Executive Committee of Solvay in 1984, succeeded in purchasing the pharmaceutical company Reid-Rowell, in Marietta, Georgia, for US$117.5 million (see Chapter 18). Several smaller companies were also acquired and incorporated as Kalipharma, Kali-Duphar, D&S Plastics, Solkatronics Chemicals, Solvay Construction Materials, and so on. Moreover, the company also started to extend its activities into Canada and Mexico.[57]

Another jewel in the crown of Solvay America was realized with the purchase from Tenneco Minerals of the world's most productive natural soda ash (trona) facility, at Green River, Wyoming, for US$500 million in May 1992. With a capacity of 1.8 million tons, the production facilities of Tenneco were twice as large as Solvay's then largest soda ash plant, Rosignano. Already in 1972 Jacques Solvay had tried to acquire the natural soda activities of Kerr McGee at Searles Lake, California, but that attempt fell through. The great push, Sadler said, came from Daniel Janssen. He argued that, for Solvay to keep its worldwide leadership in soda ash, it would be essential to be on the

[56] *An inside look* (1981); [Jim Naughton], *Solvay, can it survice the silence?*, Special Section of *The Post-Standard* (n.d. [1986]); interview Whitson Sadler and René Degrève, 12 May 2010.

[57] PR, "Reprise par Solvay de la division santé animale de Squibb aux États-Unis," 9 May 1985; PR, Acquisition of Reid-Rowell by Solvay, 24 Feb., 1986; *Today Solvay America* 1 (3) (Sept. 1989): 4–5; Ainsworth (1992); interview Whitson Sadler and René Degrève, 12 May 2010.

TABLE 18.2. *Solvay America's Organization and Product Mix in 1992*

Solvay America				
Plastics	Health	Peroxygens	Plastics Processing	Alkalis
Solvay Polymers (Houston)	Solvay Animal Health (Minneapolis) (incl. Canada + Mexico)	Interox America (Houston, TX)	Solvay Automotive (Troy, MI) (incl. Canada + Mexico)	Solvay Minerals (Houston) (incl. 80% soda ash with Asahi Glass)
D&S Plastics (Detroit) (50/50 with Dexter)	Solvay Pharmaceuticals (Marietta, GA)		Hedwin Corp. (Baltimore, MD)	Solvay Performance Chemicals (Greenwich, CT)
	Solvay Enzymes (Elkhart, IN)		Solvay Industrial Films (Baltimore, MD)	Solkatronic Chemicals (Fairfield, NJ)
	Kingswood (Ontario)		Wall Trends (Avenel, NJ)	Sales y Óxidos (Monterrey, Mexico)

Source: Ainsworth (1992).

(heavily protected) American market, and this would only be possible if production facilities could be acquired. In negotiations with Tenneco, Lazard Frères & Co. again played a role. But that company had greatly changed during the 1980s, and its role was less positive for Solvay than it had been in the past. The bank tried to raise the price of the deal by playing off Solvay against another bidder. Finally, Sadler offered a price of US$500 million dollars for an 80 percent share in the newly founded company Solvay Minerals, and the Japanese Asahi Glass Company would maintain its 20 percent. With this expensive, but important deal – which would raise Solvay's worldwide soda ash capacity to more than six million tons, well ahead of the next-largest producer, FMC (Food Machinery and Chemical Corporation) – Solvay's fifty-year close relation with Lazard deteriorated.[58]

After the acquisition of the Green River plant, the Solvay America portfolio was almost as broad as Solvay's product range worldwide (see Table 18.2). There was no doubt that Solvay had realized its industrial ambitions

[58] ACS, MoE, 22 Aug. 1972, 12 Sept. 1972, 5 Dec. 1972, 4 Nov. 1975; Ainsworth (1992); Cohan (2007); *Timeline Poster* (2000); interview Daniel Janssen, 13 Nov. 2007; interview Whitson Sadler and René Degrève, 12 May 2010; http://www.fmc.com/AboutFMC/CorporateOverview/FMCHistory.aspx?PageContentID=7.

in America. In 2000 sales of Solvay America amounted to US$2.25 billion, and the number of employees was almost five thousand. The old dreams of René Boël had more than come true. But after the sales of animal health and enzymes activities to American Home Products, in 1996 (see Chapter 19), and of the polyolefin activities to BP (see Chapter 22), Solvay's position changed again.[59]

---

[59] Jackson (2000).

FIGURE 19.1. Research on fermentation in the Solvay laboratories in the 1980s. (Solvay Archives.)

19

From Bulk to Brains

Solvay's Entry into Pharmacy and the Life Sciences

Until the late 1970s Solvay could be characterized technologically by almost organic growth and a high degree of process integration. Electrolysis had grown out of the alkali manufacture; the two by-products of the electrolytic production of caustic soda, chlorine and hydrogen, had resulted in the production of PVC and peroxides; and finally, the company had started to produce polyethylene and had integrated forward into plastics processing to protect its leading position in PVC. At the end of the 1960s this had resulted in a company strategy focusing on six "main lines of strength," as they were called – alkalis, salt, chlorine and derivatives, peroxides, plastics, and plastics processing – together embracing more than 85 percent of Solvay's production.[1]

At the end of the 1970s that coherent industrial structure was quite suddenly supplemented by new activities in the field of the life sciences. In July 1978 Jacques Solvay and Jacques Viriot, the Executive Committee member responsible for research and development, sketched a number of ideas with respect to Solvay's prospects in fields that depended more on "brains" than on manual labor: active ingredients for pharmaceuticals made by organic synthesis, biotechnological products such as enzymes, organic pesticides, nutritional products, and new types of biological medicines. A small producer of biological pesticides, called Biochem, was taken over, the pharmaceutical activities of Solvay's subsidiary Kali-Chemie (see Section 19.2) were strengthened, and Kali-Chemie embarked on several activities in the field of biotechnology. In December 1978 Solvay started talks with the American veterinary company Salsbury Laboratories, which was taken over in October 1979. A few months later the Dutch company Philips-Duphar, active in the fields of pharmacy, veterinary medicine, vitamins, and pesticides, was acquired. Within two years Solvay had diversified into an almost totally new area. In 1980, tiny medical tablets figured prominently on the cover of the annual report, whereas a year before the huge ethylene pier near Rosignano had been the "flag." A revolution obviously had taken place.[2]

---

[1] "Allocution du Baron Boël . . . 9 juin 1969," *Revue Solvay* (May–June 1969): 11–14; "Allocution de M. Jacques Solvay . . . 12 juin 1973," *Revue Solvay* (June–July 1973): 2–5; ACS, file De Bois, seminar, 2–6 June 1975.

[2] ACS, MoE, 27 July 1978, 19 Dec. 1978, 27 Mar. 1979; ACS, MoB, 25 Sept. 1978.

19.1 THE FIRST OIL SHOCK AND THE CRISIS OF THE 1970s

To understand the revolution, it is important to describe the economic crisis of the 1970s that hit the chemical industry hard. The economic climate started to deteriorate in the late 1960s, but it was aggravated dramatically by the first oil shock of 1973. Together, these developments brought the chemical industry and the rest of the Western economy in a deep crisis. The reasons for that change, after two postwar decades of uninterrupted growth, are complex and diverse. The flattening off of demand and saturation of markets were part of it, as was the hugely increased labor costs in the West during the 1960s, which partly led to high inflation. A growing role of the state in many segments of society, leading to ever-higher taxation, was another factor. Innovation slowed. Competition by low-wage third-world countries endangered entire European industrial sectors, such as the textile industries, also influencing the sales potential of other industrial branches in Europe. Monetary phenomena, in particular the dollar crisis of August 1971, when the United States decided to break away from the Bretton Woods agreement and the gold standard, produced uncertainty about currency exchange rates. It also led indirectly to decisions by the member countries of the Organization of the Petroleum Exporting Countries (OPEC) to drastically raise the price of crude oil in the autumn of 1973. As a result of these changes in the economic environment, companies were squeezed between higher cost prices of their products – as a result of higher labor cost, higher raw material prices, and higher taxation – and lower market prices, due to overcapacities and intense competition.[3]

For Jacques Solvay and other leaders of chemical enterprises, those times were perceived as an age of discontinuity (Drucker) and uncertainty (Galbraith). Would the oil prices stay high or go down? Would the OPEC countries put their money in European and US bank accounts or invest it in competitive petrochemical complexes? How would the exchange rates between different currencies develop? This all culminated in one of the most frequently asked questions during the early 1970s: is this a usual but deeper, cyclic business depression or a more permanent crisis of a structural nature?[4]

During the first years of the 1970s, the Executive Committee assumed that the crisis was cyclic and temporary. Therefore, money available for investments was used for capacity extensions and improvements in Solvay's strongholds (e.g., soda ash, VC-PVC, HDPE), to be a strong and low-cost producer when the crisis would be over, and all plants could again work at full capacity. As a result, Solvay's debts as related to its own capital and reserves grew from about 20 percent in 1969 to almost 36 percent in 1972. Thereafter, investments in rationalization had priority over capacity enlargement, because overcapacities

---

[3] Frieden (2006), 363–91; Eichengreen (2007), 252–93; Castel (2005), 211–31; "Allocution de M. Jacques Solvay . . . 12 juin 1972," *Revue Solvay* (June–July 1972): 13–16; Paul Washer, "L'espoir après la décadence?" *Revue Solvay* (1981) (2): 3–4.

[4] Drucker (1969); Galbraith (1977); Spitz (1988), 462–506. Jacques Solvay studied the works of Peter Drucker extensively in Sept. 1971, after he had become chairman of Solvay. See PPSF, file Organisation 1970–71.

persisted in most key products. The debt ratio went down again, but the focus on the six main lines did not really change.[5]

By 1975 it had become clear that the crisis was not of a temporary nature but was structural. Profitability stayed at an unusual low level, year after year. The cash flow that had been about 14–15 percent of the sales during the first half of the 1970s went down to 10–11 percent in the second half of that decade. This was not typical for Solvay; it was a phenomenon that hit the entire chemical industry (see Table 19.1). By contrast, as noted in Solvay's annual report in 1975, the pharmaceutical industry "cushioned against short-term trends, remained largely unaffected" by the crisis.[6]

It was in that context that Solvay started to think about alternatives and about steering the company away from the dominant influence of petrochemicals. During a board meeting in July 1974 it was suggested, for the first time, to partially reorient the research to new domains. But what domains should be chosen, and how should the expertise for those domains be acquired? For a while uncertainty prevailed. Changing a successful business strategy is a risky affair. In many of the possible new markets there were strong competitors. Moreover, the organizational structure of Solvay, with a dominant influence of the national organizations experienced in selling the traditional products, was not very well suited to the introduction of completely new consumer products. By 1977 a new direction had been chosen. In the first place this happened because the company wanted more noncyclical products and higher value-added. Second, there was the problem of high oil prices. Biotechnology and biochemistry held the promise of using plant materials as sources of chemical feedstock. There also was the prospect that these fields would lead to what the Solvay 1976 annual report called a "second generation of synthesis processes centered on the use of near normal temperatures and of low or zero pressures," which would lower energy consumption and therefore help reduce dependence on oil supplies. In the third and last place, there was the general idea that biochemistry would lead to a new wave of scientific and technical innovations. Solvay would not stay along the sideline; it just had to be informed about what was going on.[7]

Solvay certainly was not unique in making such a strategic shift toward the life sciences. It was part of a trend. During the second part of the 1970s, or even earlier, many major chemical companies in the United States, Japan, and Europe diversified into pharmaceuticals, agricultural chemicals, chemical specialties, and biological products (see Chapter 20). Compared to several of these companies, Solvay had one advantage: it had a subsidiary that had been

[5] "New Look" (1971); ACS, MoE, 28 Mar. 1972, 4 Dec. 1973; "M. Solvay face à la presse," *Revue Solvay* (Dec. 73–Jan. 74); "Allocution de monsieur Jacques Solvay . . . 10 juin 1974," *Revue Solvay* (June–July 1974): 3–6.

[6] "Allocution de monsieur Jacques Solvay . . . 9 juin 1975," *Revue Solvay* (June–July 1975): 3–5; ARS 1975: 11.

[7] ACS, MoB, 8 July 1974, 25 Sept. 1978; PPSF, Box 1972–80, "Problèmes à long terme," 16 Feb. 1976; id., "Politique du Groupe," 12 Mar. 1976; ARS 1976: 14, 33, 36; ARS 1977: 28, 32; ARS 1978: 9, 35; "Allocution de monsieur Solvay . . . 13 juin 1977," *Revue Solvay* (June–July 1977): 2–5; ACS, MoE, 17 June 1977; interview Claude Loutrel, 31 Jan. 2008.

TABLE 19.1. *Business Development of the Solvay Group and the Belgian Chemical Industry, 1969–1980*

Year	Annual Growth of Sales (%)	Annual Growth of Net Profit (%)	Annual Growth of Cash Flow (%)	Cash Flow as % of Sales	Debt Ratio (%)	Net Profit as % of Sales	Net Profit as % of Sales (average of 78 Belgian chemical firms)
1969	15.3	82.1	25.5	18.1	19.8	8.2	
1970	11.3	-33.0	-8.7	14.8	23.0	4.9	
1971	7.6	-6.1	1.9	14.0	33.7	4.3	
1972	15.0	15.6	13.2	13.8	35.6	4.3	
1973	22.7	41.6	31.1	14.8	32.5	5.0	4.47
1974	22.9	17.4	24.2	14.9	30.6	3.8	4.42
1975	2.4	-58.7	-30.1	10.2	35.1	1.5	0.68
1976	9.4	298.5	43.3	13.3	31.9	5.6	0.99
1977	5.7	-45.5	-16.5	10.5	34.0	2.9	0.30
1978	5.0	21.8	7.9	11.0	35.8	3.4	0.55
1979	27.2	44.3	28.7	11.1	36.3	3.9	1.16
1980	14.4	-61.5	-19.2	7.5	40.2	1.4	0.34

Sources: Columns 2–7 are calculated on the basis of ARS, 1969–1980; column 8, on the basis of "Notre nouvel atout: Les biotechnologies," *Revue Solvay* (1981) (2): 5–8.

making pharmaceuticals for years and that had made a start in biotechnology: Kali-Chemie. For a long time Solvay's top management had hardly paid any attention to these production lines. "When Baron Boël returned from Germany he took pills with him that he showed, as a joke, in the *gérance*," said Paul Washer. "That was all what was discussed about these pharma activities." They had suddenly become relevant.[8]

19.2 KALI-CHEMIE AND ITS PHARMACEUTICAL ACTIVITIES

Solvay had acquired a majority interest in Kali-Chemie in the 1950s as part of its strategy to regain market share in the West German soda ash market (see Chapter 15). The acquisition is a nice example of the role of unintended consequences in history. Solvay decided to buy Kali-Chemie foremost because of its Heilbronn soda ash factory. But after it had become the majority shareholder, it had acquired, in the same go – unintentionally more or less – sixteen other factories and mines (see Chapter 15), including pharmaceutical activities. The German company, with headquarters in Hanover, was managed by Solvay at double arm's length. The majority of the shares were not directly held by Solvay but by DSW, a company that stood apart from Brussels as well, because of its long German tradition and the fact that part of the DSW shares were owned directly by Solvay family shareholders, not by the company. In the 1950s and 1960s the two leaders of DSW, Helmut Eilsberger and Édouard Swolfs, were on the supervisory board of Kali-Chemie, along with a banker – Hermann Abs, later succeeded by Wilfred Guth – and a lawyer. German law carefully guarded the rights of minor shareholders, and the two last mentioned board members protected their interests. As a result, the influence exercised by the Executive Committee on the business of Kali-Chemie was rather small. Swolfs saw Kali-Chemie as his personal domain, which he managed quite independently, together with the three members of the *Vorstand* (executive board) of Kali-Chemie. After Swolfs entered the board of directors and the Executive Committee of Solvay, in January 1968, he stayed on the supervisory board of Kali-Chemie. Now there was a direct link between Brussels and Hanover, but it was still mediated by Swolfs and hardly subject of much discussion among members of the Solvay top management.[9]

When Cyril Van Lierde, from Solvay Italy, was appointed as the first non-German member of the *Vorstand* of Kali-Chemie, in 1975, Wilfred Guth told him, "Forget from now on that you are a Solvay man." Moreover, Swolfs gave him no specific mission other than trying to gain the confidence of his German colleagues. As a result, the *Vorstand* of Kali-Chemie was quite free in choosing its own business strategy.[10]

[8] Bud (1993), 141–62; Chandler (2005), 27–30; interview Paul Washer, 29 Nov. 2007; letter Paul Washer to authors, 11 July 2011.

[9] ACS, file Kali-Chemie, "Politique de Solvay à l'égard de la Kali-Chemie," 18 Oct. 1978; interview Paul Washer, 29 Nov. 2007; interview Albert Rampelberg, 4 Apr. 2008.

[10] AHR, PD Van Lierde, letter Swolfs to Guth, May 1973; ACS, MoE, 3 Dec. 1974; interview Cyril Van Lierde, 13 Oct. 2008.

Almost by accident, Solvay gained greater control over Kali-Chemie (KC), with a catastrophe that took place in a potassium mine of Kali-Chemie in Ronnenberg in 1975. For years there had been water leaks in the Ronnenberg mine, but the mining engineers thought the problems were manageable. In 1975 the situation suddenly deteriorated, and by the end of June 1975 it had gone out of control. The mine had to be given up, and major damages, costing more than DM 20 million (US$8 million), also to third parties, resulted. It was big news in the German press and the price of the KC share at the stock exchange fell greatly. Albert Rampelberg, who had succeeded Swolfs as top executive of DSW, used the opportunity immediately by buying at the stock market as many shares as DSW could get. In this way, DSW was able to raise its shareholding in Kali-Chemie between 1976 and 1978 from about 65 percent to more than 78 percent. That made it possible for DSW to gradually enlarge its control over Kali-Chemie and finally merge with that company into one German organization in 1989 (see Chapter 20).[11]

The Growth of Pharmacy at Kali-Chemie

Production and marketing of pharmaceuticals at Kali-Chemie had started in 1900 when the Chemische Fabrik Rhenania, one of the predecessors of KC, introduced the pancreatic enzymes extract Pankreon to the market. It was soon produced in growing quantities in a plant at Altona, near Hamburg. After Kali-Chemie had been formed in 1928, the company took over a few small pharmaceutical companies in the mid-1930s. At the end of the 1950s it was decided to concentrate all pharmaceutical production at Neustadt am Rübenberge, not far from Hanover. At that time the production of pharmaceuticals accounted for about 5 percent of Kali-Chemie's total sales. But after the construction of the new plant, that figure would rise quickly.[12]

Around that time, the profits of the important fertilizer division of Kali-Chemie started to erode, given growing competition on the European market. To counter that negative tendency, the *Vorstand* of Kali-Chemie decided on its own for an offensive strategy of diversification: a joint venture with an American producer of catalysts was concluded (1959); a fluorine mine at Bad Wimpfen, Germany, was bought (1960); and a license agreement with Allied Chemical was made for the production of chlorofluorocarbon compounds (1961) (see Chapter 21). A vigorous expansion strategy for Kali-Chemie's pharmaceutical sector was part of the same policy. Almost every few years a new product was introduced: Presomen in 1962, Paspertin in 1965, Pankreoflat in 1966, and Valmane in 1968, to name a few of the most important ones. A modern pharmaceutical research laboratory was opened at Hanover in 1966.

[11] ACS, MoE, 6 Nov. 1974, 22 Apr., 21 Oct. 1975, 4 Oct. 1977; ACS, MoB, 7 July 1975; ACS, 1805-37-34, Kali-Chemie, meeting 24 Oct. 1978; interview Albert Rampelberg, 4 Apr. 2008.
[12] Rüsberg (1949), 72-3, 84; ASD, Prüfungsbericht KC 1959; id. 1960; Kuhlmann and Rudmann (2000).

Sales of pharmaceuticals tripled during the 1960s to about 13 percent of total sales of Kali-Chemie.[13]

Despite the great successes in pharmacy, obtaining a stronger market position was difficult, given increased competition and changing regulations. Late in 1961 it was discovered in Germany that the drug thalidomide (Softenon), introduced to the market only three years earlier, had disastrous side effects. From 1962, therefore, most countries, with the Food and Drug Administration (FDA) in the United States in a leading role, considerably sharpened the required testing procedures for drug safety. In the following years and decades these registration procedures would only continue to grow in extension and complexity. As a result, the research, testing, and registration costs of the drug companies grew tremendously. Moreover, because of longer development times, the ever-greater R&D costs had to be earned back within a shrinking number of years. That had two major consequences. First, a pharmaceutical company would introduce its new product to as many different markets as possible, to have the highest possible revenues in a short time. Second, a company would have a certain minimal size, or "critical mass," to generate enough sales to be able to bear the high R&D-costs necessary to introduce a new pharmaceutical product every few years.[14]

When the leaders of Kali-Chemie's pharmaceutical division, Kurt Ihbe, Fritz-Jürgen Roth, and Siegfried Funke, realized the new situation, they decided to complement the enhanced research effort by an aggressive international acquisition strategy, to achieve both critical mass and a larger market. In 1967 and 1968 the Neustadt plant was greatly enlarged to better serve the export markets. In 1969 Kali-Chemie succeeded in obtaining a minority interest in the Laboratorios Kriya, in Mexico City. This would be the first of a long list of foreign subsidiaries. In March 1969, the Portuguese company Quimifar was taken over. At the same time, Kali-Chemie was also active on the Spanish pharmaceutical market, via its subsidiary Kali-Chemie Iberia. In June 1970 a separate Spanish pharmaceutical firm was established, Kalifarma, based in Barcelona.[15]

The most important acquisition in those years was the Laboratoires de Thérapeutique Moderne Latéma, of Paris, a company with a sales figure of about 60 percent of the pharmaceutical sales of Kali-Chemie itself. Because of the size of the deal, leaders of Solvay – in particular Swolfs, Delwart, and Boël – were involved in the negotiations, which led to an agreement in July 1969. The company had production facilities at Suresnes, near Paris. Moreover, it had a research laboratory with a pipeline with new developments, an interesting portfolio of patents and trademarks, a Belgian sales subsidiary, and important export activity (e.g., Algeria, Japan). The acquisition also enriched Kali-Chemie

[13] ASD, Prüfberichte KC, 1959–1970.
[14] Silverman and Lee (1974), 94–8; Friedrich, Hehn, and Rosenbrock (1977), 191–2; Le Fanu (1999), 211–20; ASD, Prüfberichte KC, 1966–1972; ARS 1978: 34.
[15] ASD, KC Prüfbericht P1968: 14–15; id., P1969: 13–14, 19–26; id., P1970: 55–7; id., P1973: 79–80; ACS, MoE, 17 June 1968, 3 Dec. 1968; "Kali-Chemie A.G. – Nouvelles activités," *Revue Solvay* (July–Aug. 1969): 20.

with new therapeutic domains – painkillers, tranquilizers, and multivitamin preparations – as well as with new gastroenterological drugs, which was its own core business.[16]

With activities in Germany, France, Belgium, Spain, Portugal, and Mexico, Kali-Chemie had succeeded in internationalizing its pharmacy business in fewer than two years. To put all national subsidiaries on the same footing, the German activities were consolidated on 1 October 1972 as Kali-Chemie Pharma GmbH (KCP). This counted with about 680 employees, 290 at Hanover (in management, administration, and research) and about 390 at Neustadt. Total sales in pharmacy in the meantime had grown to about DM 100 million (US$33 million), of which about DM 60 million was from KCP and the rest mainly from Latéma. Two years later, total personnel were about 1,380, with 710 in Germany and 670 abroad.[17]

Despite the spectacular growth that had been achieved in just a few years, it was clear to Roth and his colleagues that Kali-Chemie Pharma still did not have enough critical mass. Therefore, further acquisitions were needed, or even a merger with another pharmaceutical company of equal size. In the autumn of 1974, the members of the Executive Committee of Solvay were contemplating a multiportfolio swap among Solvay, UCB (Union Chimique Belge), Kali-Chemie and Laporte, with the option of uniting the pharmaceutical activities of Kali-Chemie and UCB. These studies were extremely confidential, and one can doubt whether Fritz-Jürgen Roth knew about them. At the same time, he was negotiating with the German firm Degussa about a 50–50 joint venture in pharmacy. The negotiations went on until the end of 1975, but finally the supervisory board of Degussa did not agree. Also the portfolio swap with UCB and the other firms did not take place. If one of these two operations would have succeeded, Solvay would have had no in-house pharmaceutical activity when it decided to change its strategy. This would have made the history of Solvay a different one, Cyril Van Lierde concluded. At that time, half of the members of the Executive Committee still had great doubts whether pharmacy should have a place inside Solvay at all.[18]

Parallel to the talks with Degussa, Roth also tried to find new acquisitions. In the second part of 1975 he negotiated with the German firm Gebrüder Giulini and the French company Laboratoires Sarbach. Then he fell seriously ill, and the negotiations were successfully concluded by Van Lierde, who from

---

[16] ASD, KC Prüfbericht P1969: 13–19, 68; id., P1970: 51–3; id., P1971: 58–62; ACS, MoE, 18 Apr. 1969; PR, 24 July 1969: La Société Solvay investit dans l'industrie du médicament; "Connaissez-vous les sociétés filiales? La Kali-Chemie AG, un groupe d'entreprises au sein du Groupe Solvay," *Revue du Personnel* (Aug.–Sept. 1970): 8–12.

[17] ASD, KC Prüfbericht P1972: 6, 8, 62–5; id., 1973, Anhang: 53–4; ARS 1972: 27; ACS, 1004-2-1, letter Jacques Solvay to P. Casimir-Lambert, 3 May 1974; ACS, Programme d'assainissement 1974, "Quelques élément d'information sur les sociétés Laporte, Kali-Chemie et UCB," 25 Nov. 1974.

[18] ACS, MoE, 30 July, 1 Oct. and 6 Nov. 1974, 22 Apr., 21 Oct. and 2 Dec. 1975; ACS, Programme d'assainissement 1974, files on the joint restructuring the Solvay Group, UCB, Laporte and Kali-Chemie," Nov. 1974; PPSF, Box 1972–80, "Problèmes à long terme," 16 Feb. 1976; interview Paul Washer, 29 Nov. 2007; interview Cyril Van Lierde, 13 Oct. 2008; interview Claude Loutrel, 31 Jan. 2008; interview Albert Rampelberg, 4 Apr. 2008.

that point would lead the pharmaceutical business of Kali-Chemie. Again, these were large acquisitions, aimed to "extend the range of [Kali-Chemie's] specialties and to increase the potential of its research services."[19] The pharmaceutical sector of Giulini, including its over-the-counter-subsidiary Lyssia, was acquired for DM 55 million (US$22 million) and Sarbach for FF 63 million (US$14.5 million). Kali-Chemie could finance these transactions itself, by which the sales of the pharmaceutical activities of Kali-Chemie grew by 65 percent. The personnel of the pharmacy sector grew from 1,415 to almost 2,400. Guilini, based at Ludwigshafen, was mainly active on the market of cardiovascular drugs. Shortly after the acquisition, which formally took place as of 1 January 1976, production was transferred to Neustadt and research and marketing to Hanover. The subsidiary Lyssia, located at Wiesbaden, was a successful producer and distributor of over-the-counter drugs and cosmetics. Laboratoires Sarbach, in turn, at Châtillon-sur-Chalaronne, near Lyons, and taken over as of 1 February 1976, was a producer of antibiotics and immunological medicines, such as vaccines. After the takeover, the French subsidiaries of Kali-Chemie were reorganized. The production of both Latéma and Sarbach was concentrated at Châtillon.[20]

Kali-Chemie had succeeded in this way to considerably enlarge its pharmaceutical activities, but the fierce competition in that market meant that the required critical mass of companies was increasing all the time. The company therefore energetically continued its policy of exogenous growth by acquisition. In 1977 a sales organization, Kali-Chemie Pharma GmbH, was established in Vienna, and two small pharmaceutical companies were taken over in Belgium. A year later, the producer of active ingredients Bonnet-Boyer at Nucourt in France was bought, as well as the company Nezel in Spain. The most important goal, though, was to obtain footholds in the largest pharmaceutical markets of the world: the United States and Japan. From 1977, Kali-Chemie was actively searching for an acquisition or participation in the United States. After two previous attempts had failed – partly because the Executive Committee of Solvay was unwilling to finance the deals, which they considered too large – Kali-Chemie finally succeeded in 1979 in buying the shares of Purepac Laboratories Corporation in Elizabeth, New Jersy, a producer of generic medicines (i.e., drugs that are no longer protected by a patent). With 305 employees and sales of about US$18 million, it was a rather small company, but Kali-Chemie had its much-wanted foothold in the United States. The same year, a company was also created in Tokyo, Kali-Chemie Far East.[21]

[19] ARS 1975: 26.

[20] ACS, MoE, 21 Oct., 2 Dec. 1975; ASD, KC Prüfbericht P1975: 7–9; id., P1976: 42–3; id., P1979: 6; ARS 1976: 14, 32–3; "Allocution de monsieur Jacques Solvay...14 juin 1976," *Revue Solvay* (June–July 1976): 2–5; ACS, 1010–10, Kali-Chemie: Report by the Vorstand, 16 Mar. 1979; "Lyssia, usine chimico-pharmaceutique à Wiesbaden (RFA)," *Revue Solvay* (1980) (1): 5–6; interview Cyril Van Lierde, 13 Oct. 2008. Roth died 5 Jan. 1977.

[21] ASD, KC Prüfbericht P1977: 34; id., P1978: 5–6; id., P1979: 5–6; ARS 1977: 28; ARS 1978: 29, 34; ACS, MoE, 4 Oct., 3 Nov., 15 Nov., 6 Dec. 1977, 19 Sept. 1978, 2 Feb., 19 June 1979; ACS, MoB, 9 July 1979; Kurt Reimann, "Kali-Chemie sur la voie de nouveaux marchés en pharmacie: Purepac Laboratories Corporation," *Revue Solvay* (1980) (2): 14–15.

At the moment that Solvay decided to enter pharmacy and the life sciences on a large scale, Kali-Chemie had succeeded in developing its pharmaceutical sector in about ten years in an extraordinary way through repeated acquisitions. Sales had grown between 1969 and 1978 more than sevenfold. With a sales figure of more than DM 300 million in 1978 – which then was about 28 percent of total sales of Kali-Chemie and 4.5 percent of sales of Solvay – and with a presence in many different countries, a medium-sized pharmaceutical company of good standing had been created. The ultimate target of a market share of 1 percent in countries where Kali-Chemie was active was mostly not reached, though. In Germany, Austria, and France that goal had been achieved; in Turkey (0.9 percent) and Portugal (0.8 percent) it was close to 1 percent; but in other European countries a lot remained to be done, and more so in the United States and Japan.[22]

19.3   THE GREAT LEAP FORWARD (1979–1980)

In March 1979 during a speech at a business management conference, Jacques Solvay reflected on the situation of the pharmaceutical division of Kali-Chemie. Using the conceptual framework of the Boston Consulting Group, he argued that for a balanced portfolio of products in all phases of their life cycle, Kali-Chemie should annually spend DM 50 million on research. Assuming that 10 percent of sales would go to research, this meant that a sales figure of DM 500 million should be realized to survive in the long run. But sales only were DM 300 million, he said, so the pharmaceutical activities were below the "critical mass."[23]

About a year later a pharmaceutical company – Philips-Duphar – was purchased that helped Solvay's pharmaceutical business to just reach that critical mass. Also, a veterinary company – Salsbury Laboratories – was acquired that had specialized in poultry vaccines, in which it had achieved a leading global position. A new episode of Solvay's history began.

Salsbury Laboratories

Salsbury Laboratories was founded by Joseph E. Salsbury (1887–1967), an English immigrant and veterinarian, in Charles City, Iowa, in 1926. He started by making health-care products for poultry. After World War II he added production lines for larger animals, especially pets, and for fine chemicals. In the 1970s the plant at Charles City basically had three production units: a biological department for the production of poultry vaccines and other animal vaccines; a pharmaceutical department, in which active ingredients for veterinary medicines were mixed, also with fodder; and a chemical department in which some of the active ingredients were synthesized. In the United States and in some other countries, Salsbury occupied a top position in the market for

---

[22] ACS, 1010–10, Kali-Chemie: Report by the Vorstand, 16 Mar. 1979.
[23] PPSF, Box 1972–80: J. Solvay, "Nécessité et confiance dans le succès de l'initiative industrielle future," Speech, Mar. 1979.

poultry vaccines. It had foreign production centers in Mexico and Brazil, and smaller ones in Spain and Argentina. In addition, there were sales subsidiaries and mixing installations in Canada, England, France, and Germany.[24]

That Solvay bought Salsbury Laboratories was largely due to initiatives by Jacques Solvay. Together with the decision to acquire Biochem, the company had decided to grow in the field of biochemistry, preferably in America. Whitson Sadler recalled that during a trip to Corpus Christi, Texas, in 1978, Jacques Solvay spoke with him about these issues, and the idea was born to ask Frank Pizzitola of Lazard to look around for options. It also could have been helpful for Kali-Chemie, which was searching for an American subsidiary. The first serious option proposed by Pizzitola was Salsbury. In December 1978 Georges Vanden Berghen, head of Solvay's Corporate Planning Department, and Cyril Van Lierde, boss of Kali-Chemie, traveled to Charles City to visit the company. They concluded that although it was not the pharmaceutical company Van Lierde was looking for, it might be an interesting acquisition for Solvay. Therefore, on 12 January 1979 Jacques Solvay, Jacques Viriot, and Claude Loutrel visited Salsbury. They concluded that the company might become a good springboard for future US activities of the group in the domains of biochemistry, agrochemistry, and special chemicals.[25]

The negotiations – conducted mainly by Sadler and Pizzitola, and assisted by Loutrel and George Kern – were dominated by environmental issues. In 1977 the Environmental Protection Agency (EPA) had discovered that two landfill sites near Charles City were heavily polluted by toxic waste produced by Salsbury's chemical department. One of the sites had been used as a dump from 1949 to 1953, and the other from 1953 to 1977. Therefore, parallel to the negotiations, talks with the EPA had to take place. Although it appeared that the situation was less serious than first thought, great risks remained. Finally, an agreement was reached that in the future, John G. Salsbury, the son of the founder, would pay half the costs of the cleanup operations, up to a certain amount. From the total price of the acquisition of US$45 million, US$17 million was put in a reserve fund, dedicated to possible environmental costs. On that basis a purchase and sales agreement between Soltex and Salsbury was signed on 10 October 1979.[26]

Philips-Duphar

Philips-Duphar (Dutch Pharmaceuticals) was founded in 1930 by the large Dutch multinational Philips and the chocolate manufacturer Van Houten. In the years before, scientists at the Physics Laboratory of Philips had discovered

[24] ARS 1979: 36; "Salsbury Laboratories." *Revue Solvay*, (1980) (2): 6–10; "Le Groupe Solvay et la santé animale," *Revue Solvay* (1983) (2): 12–15.

[25] ACS, MoE, 19 Dec. 1978, 2 Feb. 1979; ACS, MoB, 22 Jan. 1979; interview Jacques Solvay, 27 Nov. 2007; interview Whitson Sadler and René Degrève, 12 May 2010.

[26] ACS, MoE, 27 Mar., 19 June 1979; ACS, MoB, 26 Nov. 1979; Web sites EPA, Region 7: http://epa.gov/Region7/factsheets/2005/fs_5yr_review_shaw_ave_superfund_site_charles_city_ ia0305.htm; http://epa.gov/Region7/factsheets/2005/fs_5yr_rev_labounty_sprfnd_charles_city_ ia1105.htm.

how human skin produced vitamin D under the influence of ultraviolet light. On the basis of that discovery, a photosynthetic pathway was designed for the artificial production of vitamin D. Philips-Duphar was established for that purpose. Van Houten was involved to give the vitamin pills a better taste; it also supplied the first production site near its factory at Weesp, not far from Amsterdam. During and after World War II small companies were acquired that produced pharmaceuticals (1941), and pesticides (1946). At the same time, supported by Philips, an ambitious research effort was set up. Through its own research and a number of licenses, Philips-Duphar was able to diversify from vitamins and pesticides to other classes of drugs and therapeutic domains: cardiovascular drugs (1946), vaccines (1950), sex hormones (1960), gastroen-terological medicines (1965), central nervous system drugs (1970), and trau-matology (1974). By 1980 this had resulted in a company structure with four divisions: pharmaceuticals, veterinary products, phytopharmacy (crop protec-tion), and biochemicals (vitamins and fine chemicals). Management, research, and production were highly concentrated in the Netherlands, but sales sub-sidiaries and formulation plants were set up in other countries as well; and there had been a research center for clinical trials in the United States since 1970. By contrast to Kali-Chemie, which grew via acquisitions, the growth of Philips-Duphar had been mainly endogenous. At Kali-Chemie 9–10 percent of sales revenues were spent on research, but at Philips-Duphar this was almost 24 percent.[27]

After negative financial results in several of its other divisions in 1971, Philips decided to divest Philips-Duphar. It was not considered a core business of the lighting and electronics multinational. Moreover, Philips-Duphar was lacking critical mass and therefore interested in finding a partner. Starting in 1972, several negotiations took place, but they all failed, not least because the labor unions and the Company Council did not approve of the deals. It was in that context that Solvay came into the picture.

Between about May 1977 and August 1978, Solvay had been negotiating with Philips and its subsidiary Nederlandse Kabelfabriek (NKF) about the acquisition of the Draka-Polva group of plastics-processing companies (see Chapter 16). During the talks, NKF's CEO C. B. van de Panne had been impressed by the way Solvay handled the social side of the deal. On 1 January 1979 Draka-Polva became part of Solvay. A little later, van de Panne phoned Albert Rampelberg, who had been part of Solvay's negotiation team, telling him that Philips-Duphar was for sale and that he thought that Solvay would be able to handle the difficult relations with the trade unions and the Company Council. It was an opportunity that came at the right moment in Solvay's history. Negotiations started in March 1979.[28]

---

[27] "Duphar: 2500 nouveaux collègues," *Revue Solvay* (1980) (2): 10–13; Sprenger (1992); Urban (2005).

[28] ACS, CdL, "Negotiations Duphar – Salsbury," 22 June 1982; interview Albert Rampelberg, 4 Apr. 2008; interview Cyril Van Lierde, 13 Oct. 2008; interview Christian Jourquin, 27 Sept. 2010; interview Paul Washer, 29 Nov. 2007; Sprenger (1992), 109; ACS, MoE, 27 Mar., 5 June 1979.

FIGURE 19.2. Aerial view of the site of Duphar at Weesp, the Netherlands. (Solvay Archives.)

It soon became clear that Philips-Duphar was an attractive acquisition for Solvay. There were interesting complements with both Kali-Chemie and Salsbury, geographically and in terms of product, so through this takeover Solvay could strengthen its human health and animal health activities at the same time. Moreover, there were interesting drugs in the pipeline, such as the antidepressant fluvoxamine. Because Solvay was the only party at the negotiation table and given the labor guarantees Solvay offered, it could arrive at a price of Dfl 225 million (US$113 million), a bargain for a company with annual sales figures of about Dfl 400 million and a head count of 2,250. In exchange for the low price, Solvay promised to respect the integrity of the Duphar group and not merge it at short notice with Kali-Chemie. Therefore, Solvay, not Kali-Chemie, would do the takeover. Solvay also promised not to collectively dismiss sections of the personnel for a period of three years.

On the basis of these principles, Philips, Philips-Duphar, and Solvay signed an agreement in January 1980. Three months later, Solvay and Philips-Duphar submitted a lengthy document to the Company Council and the unions. During a long meeting in a nearby castle, Albert Rampelberg and his Solvay colleagues were able to convince their counterparts that a takeover would also be good for Duphar. On 25 June the Company Council gave positive advice on the takeover bid, and as a result, Philips-Duphar became part of Solvay as of 1 July 1980, under the new name Duphar. After eight years of fruitless attempts,

TABLE 19.2. *Solvay's Life Sciences and Special Chemicals Portfolio after the Acquisition of Salsbury and Duphar*

Activity	Solvay	Kali-Chemie	Salsbury	Duphar
Pharmaceuticals		X		X
Veterinary products			X	X
Biochemistry: enzymes, food, proteins, etc.	NoH Soda Povoa	X		
Agrochemistry, agrobiology, crop protection	Biochem			X
Fine chemicals	NoH Jemeppe, etc.	X	X	X

Note: See also ARS 1980: 9; "Notre nouvel atout: Les biotechnologies," *Revue Solvay* (1981) (2): 5–8.

Philips had finally succeeded in divesting its pharmaceutical business. Solvay also bought all the shares of the British fine chemicals producer Peboc, which owned know-how on vitamin D3, an important product for Duphar.[29]

In the new top management, Solvay included the previous managing director of research and production Herman Geuens, a medical doctor of Belgian stock, born in Antwerp and educated at Louvain. He would become the new CEO and was seconded by the young commercial engineer (from the Brussels business school) Christian Jourquin, who was transferred from Brussels to the Duphar central office at Amsterdam.[30]

19.4 CONSOLIDATING NEW BUSINESSES IN TIMES OF CRISIS

In a short period of time Solvay had started many activities in a totally new field. It was time to consolidate and organize that seventh main line of strength. Even the statutes of Solvay were adapted in 1981 to the new situation. Consolidating these activities was complex, though. First, many of the activities in human and animal health were managed at a global scale, whereas Solvay was built on the pillars of national organizations. Second, the diversity in the group of the newly acquired products of soft chemistry was great. Both technically and commercially, there were great differences among pharmaceuticals for human use, products for the veterinary markets, fine chemicals, biological and chemical pesticides, and biotechnological products such as enzymes and proteins (see Table 19.2). Third, a severe economic crisis broke out that severely limited the possibilities of expansion in the new sector.[31]

---

[29] ACS, MoB, 5 June 1980; ACS, MoE, 3 June 1980, 15 Sept. 1981; PR, 24 Jan. 1980: Reprise possible de Philips-Duphar par le Groupe Solvay; PR, 1 July 1980: Takeover of Philips-Duphar signed; interview Albert Rampelberg, 4 Apr. 2008; interview Christian Jourquin, 27 Sept. 2010.

[30] AHR, PD Geuens; interview Albert Rampelberg, 4 Apr. 2008; interview Christian Jourquin, 27 Sept. 2010.

[31] R. Charton, "Solvay se présente...," *Revue Solvay* (1980) (2): 2–5; ACS, MoB, 25 May 1981.

How to organize that diversity? The four product departments at the Central Administration in Brussels lacked the know-how and commercial spirit to do it. They were thinking in terms of thousands of tons, megawatts, and engineering perfection, not in terms of kilograms, soft reaction conditions, and product life cycles. Therefore, Solvay created a new central department, Specialties, early in 1979, headed by Luciano Balducci, who after a career at Rosignano had headed the commercial department in Italy under difficult circumstances. In the beginning, the Specialties Department included all products mentioned here, except pharmaceuticals, as well as special polymers for high-tech markets. It was in fact a department for new business development, similar to those created by other companies at that time. Managing all those product groups in detail by a single staff organization was difficult, though, and therefore most of the work was delegated to the local competence centers of the various subsidiaries. Balducci's role was mainly one of monitoring, gathering new ideas, and offering incentives. In the field of animal health, Balducci chaired the International Veterinary Committee, which coordinated the strategies of Salsbury and Duphar. The similar International Pharma Committee was established to coordinate the policies of Kali-Chemie and Duphar, first chaired by Van Lierde and then by Geuens. At the start of 1982 the Pharmaceuticals Department was created as part of the Central Administration, headed by Geuens.[32]

One of the most controversial issues concerning the new products was their relation to the national managements of Solvay. The national chief executives and several members of the Executive Committee were in favor of organizing the operational activities in the life sciences on a national basis. But those more closely involved in the pharmaceutical business – Albert Rampelberg, Cyril Van Lierde, and Christian Jourquin – were strongly opposed. They started a crusade to prevent that kind of integration. "When you buy an activity," Jourquin argued, "the risk is that you love it so much that you strangle it. . . . The great danger about the integration was that if you integrate activities you don't know on a country-by-country basis, and put them in the Solvay organization, you destroy the business." It took two years of conflict with national managers before, gradually, in 1981 and 1982 a separate organization for pharmaceuticals was created.[33]

In 1981 the Solvay Group for the first time since World War II closed the accounting year with losses (see Chapter 20). These were not the best times for the development of the new life sciences business. Solvay simply had no cash for expansion. Crop protection, which had been Duphar's largest division by far during the mid-1970s, was losing money, too. The Executive Committee therefore decided soon that crop protection should be divested. Although it took quite some time before that intention materialized, the decision shows the

[32] ACS, MoE, 27 Mar. 1979, 2 June 1981; ARS 1980: 38–41; "Notre nouvel atout: Les biotechnologies," *Revue Solvay* (1981) (2): 5–8; ACS, 1001-26-1, "Problèmes à long terme," 15 Feb. 1982; Chandler (2005), 59–62, 90–1; AHR, PD Geuens.

[33] ACS, 1072-2-1, "Organisation de nos activités allemandes et pharmaceutiques," 13 June 1980; ACS, 1072-2-1, report meeting General Managers at Châtillon, 18–19 May 1981; interview Albert Rampelberg, 4 Apr. 2008; interview Christian Jourquin, 27 Sept. 2010.

limitations imposed by the economic situation. At NoH also the construction of a fermentation pilot plant was postponed.[34]

Another issue that occupied the Solvay leadership was finding a successor to Jacques Solvay, who was approaching the age limit. After the transformation of Solvay into a joint-stock company, the number of positions of the founding families in the Executive Committee had steadily declined, until after 1972 only Jacques Solvay and Paul Washer were left (see Chapters 18 and 22). As there was a still certain preference that the chairman of the Executive Committee would be a descendant of Ernest or Alfred Solvay, several options were considered, including the engagement of a highly competent member of the family from outside the company. Jacques Solvay chose that last-mentioned option and decided to ask Daniel Janssen, grandson of former *gérant* Emmanuel Janssen and a nephew of René Boël. Janssen had since 1975 been CEO of the chemical and pharmaceutical company UCB, created by his grandfather. He had studied engineering and nuclear physics at the Université Libre de Bruxelles and business administration at Harvard University. With his engineering background and his extensive international network in business circles, he seemed an excellent candidate to chair the Solvay Executive Committee, but it was not an easy decision for him: UCB was his family business, which he had helped flourish. He had not planned to leave that company. But when Jacques Solvay asked him specifically to lead the continued move of Solvay to pharmaceuticals, a sector that Janssen knew well, and to improve the growth figures of the company, he accepted the challenge to make this mission a success. It was agreed that he would not break totally with his family business: as vice president of the board of directors of UCB, he continued to stay in touch with his previous firm.[35]

In June 1984, Daniel Janssen was elected to the board of directors of Solvay and became member of the Executive Committee, replacing Viriot. On 2 June 1986, he succeeded Jacques Solvay as chairman of the Executive Committee. As responsible member for pharmaceutical and specialties in the Executive Committee, he would contribute to the subsequent development of the life sciences sector.

19.5 VETERINARY MEDICINES AND OTHER SPECIALTIES

The Specialties Department, created early 1979, was a successor to the New Products Development Department of the research organization of Solvay, under Félix Bloyaert. Small batches made in pilot plants were sold by that department to customers, but the research organization was not the best place for commercialization. From 1979, therefore, Balducci took responsibility for the commercial development of new products with high value-added, such as

[34] Sprenger (1992), 98, 122; ACS, 1020–10, "Plan Financier," 16 Mar. 1982; ACS, MoE, 28 June 1982; ACS, 1020–10, meeting Executive Committee with Geuens, 20 Apr. 1982; ACS, 1020–10, Félix Bloyaert, "Note à monsieur Solvay," 20 Oct. 1981.
[35] Interview Paul Washer, 29 Nov. 2007; interview Albert Rampelberg, 4 Apr. 2008; interviews Daniel Janssen, 16 Oct. and 13 Nov. 2007.

special polymers, fine chemicals, biological and other pesticides, and veterinary products, in close collaboration with the research department.[36]

In June 1983, Balducci was promoted to general manager for Italy; he was succeeded by Alfred Hoffait, a previous collaborator of both Bloyaert and Balducci. The following year, Daniel Janssen took over the final responsibility for this area from Viriot. When Janssen became president of Solvay in 1986, he split the Specialties Department into a department devoted to Animal Health Products and another, integrated into the Plastics Department, devoted to special polymers activities. In this section, we briefly describe some major developments related to Solvay's specialties, except for the technopolymers and special polymers, which are discussed in Chapter 21.[37]

Crop Protection

Of all the specialties of the 1980s, those serving the protection of crops had the longest history at Solvay, though an interrupted one. Shortly after World War II, Solvay had entered the field mainly to help ICI expand on the Continental market. In October 1947 the expectations were high (see Chapter 15). Together with ICI's subsidiary Plant Protection Ltd., Solvay in 1947–1948 founded three 50–50 joint ventures for the sales of insecticides and weed killers: one in the Benelux countries (Selchim), one in France (Sopra), and one in Italy (Solplant). The active ingredients, such as the insecticides HCCH and Isogam, were produced in Solvay's plants at Zurzach, Linne-Herten, Tavaux, Ferrara, and Elclor, and the phytohormones MCPA, or methoxone, and 2,4-D, or chloroxone, at Giraud. That site would become the central production location for the weed killers. Situated at an isolated spot in Camargue, in the south of France, Giraud was an excellent place – it was thought at that time – for the production of toxic and unpleasantly smelling chemicals. Solvay could discharge its noxious effluents directly into the Rhône River, close to the sea; at Tavaux, which also was considered as a location, there were no good options to get rid of those unpleasant by-products.[38]

There were many strong competitors, though, and the farmers were not very familiar with the use of insecticides and weed killers. Entering the market profitably would be difficult. Large sums had to be spent on advertisement. In the European market there were losses in several years. Only in Brazil did demand strongly exceed the expectations. Between 1953 and 1955 Solvay's European plants of HCCH and isogam were shut down, also because of technical difficulties, and the plant at Elclor followed a few years later. In 1961 production of phytohormones at Giraud was stopped. So insecticides and herbicides never became the new outlet for chlorine that Solvay had hoped for in 1947. Solvay decided to sell its shares in the French and Italian companies in 1967 to ICI.

[36] ACS, MoE, 28 Mar. 1972, 20 Mar. 1973; ARS 1978: 8, 35; ARS 1979: 12–15; ACS, 1020–10, Report by Mr. Bloyaert, 15 Jan. 1979; interview Alfred Hoffait, 24 May 2009.

[37] Interview Alfred Hoffait, 24 May 2009; e-mail from Alfred Hoffait to authors, 11 Jan. 2011.

[38] Kennedy (1986), 149; ACS, CdG, 6 Nov. 1947, 7 Sept. 1948, 19 Oct. 1950, 25 June 1953; Daumalin, Lambert, and Mioche (2007).

In April 1969 the remaining phytochemical activities of Selchim were sold to that company. This was the end of Solvay's involvement in this sector, until crop protection reappeared when Solvay took over Biochem in 1978.[39]

In the 1980s, crop protection at Solvay rested on two legs: Biochem's biological insecticides and the chemical products of the far-larger Crop Protection Division of Duphar. Gradually, both activities were integrated into one organization, which could also offer mixed or alternate chemico-biological treatments of plants and insects, a process that was concluded in 1986. Biochem's products Bactospeine and Bactimos were strongly advertised as biological, environmentally friendly products to fight unwanted insects. Duphar's showpiece Dimilin was highly selective, so its environmental friendliness was a leading edge as well.[40]

Unfortunately, the positive qualities of some of the products did not apply to the production processes that had been applied in the past. Philips-Duphar's pesticides factory in the docks area west of Amsterdam, erected in 1955, had produced several tons of highly toxic waste during the 1950s and 1960s. Between 1960 and 1969, about two thousand tons of such waste had been dumped in the landfill Volgermeerpolder, north of the Dutch capital, with the consent of the municipality. In March 1980 someone by accident found drums with toxic waste and informed the press. Investigations started. On 1 July, the very day that Solvay acquired Duphar, drums with Lindane (HCCH of Duphar) were found, which led to the establishment of a citizens' committee to fight the pollution. In August 1980 that committee announced the presence of dioxins. When that word, widely known as a result of the Seveso disaster in Italy four years earlier, appeared in the press, alarm bells started ringing. The Executive Committee immediately discussed the issue, on 8 September 1980.[41]

Although the pollution had not been caused when Solvay had authority over the production, the company had a great problem. Duphar was constantly attacked by well-organized protest groups, by the press, and by authorities who wanted to let Duphar pay for the huge, inevitable cleanup operation. The damage to Duphar's reputation was great, and some veterinary doctors boycotted the products. It also became difficult to hire qualified personnel. On 1 September 1983 the Dutch state summoned Duphar to court, and in early 1988 it put in a claim of Dfl 70 million against Duphar for the cleanup of the polder, arguing that the company knew in the 1960s that its waste was highly toxic. Duphar responded that the dioxin concentrations measured could not be detected with the instruments of that period. For some years, Christian Jourquin, who had succeeded Geuens as general manager of Duphar, had to

[39] Reader (1975), 456, 458; ACS, 1114-53 – 1114-55, Sopra, annual reports, notes and correspondence, 1948–1967; ACS, CdG, 12 Feb. 1948, 20 Apr. 1949; Daumalin, Lambert and Mioche (2007); ACS, MoE, 15 Oct. 1968, 1 Apr. 1969; letter Paul Washer to authors, 11 July 2011.

[40] ARS 1981, 27–9; ARS 1986, 35; "Biochem: La biotechnologie au service de l'agriculture mondiale," *Revue Solvay* (1984) (1).

[41] Buijs, Kaars and Trommelen (2005), 57–94; "Address by Mr. Jourquin ... at the conference on the Rhine, Strasbourg, Mar. 3–4, 1988," *Solvay Revue*, (1988) (2): 20–4; ACS, MoE, 8 Sept. 1980.

spend 50 percent of his time on this affair. Duphar handled the issue seriously and on several fronts. It started to communicate far more openly with citizens and authorities, more than was usual among chemical companies. Gradually, Duphar's reputation improved. Although in May 1989 Duphar was condemned in court to pay the sanitation costs, the company won its case in higher courts in 1992 and 1994.[42]

The crop protection activities not only caused a bad reputation; they were also losing money. Selling the activity was not easy, though. Rhône-Poulenc and Uniroyal were approached, but they were not interested. The division was top heavy, with too-small legs under a large research head. The research was strongly integrated with the organic chemical research for pharmaceuticals. As a result, there was no consensus on the issue. In 1991, the Executive Committee redefined Solvay's strategy (see Chapter 21) and decided to definitely sell the crop protection activities. Duphar's Vitamins and Chemicals Division was merged with the Crop Protection Division into the new Bio and Pharma Intermediates Division, and the crop protection activities were put up for sale. That same year, Solvay succeeded in selling its biological insecticides (Biochem) to Novo Nordisk. Duphar's pesticides research site was sold in 1993. Without the top-heavy research head, it was easier to sell the remaining activities. After long negotiations, Solvay finally succeeded in selling the crop protection activities to the American company Uniroyal in 1995.[43]

Fine Chemicals and Vitamins

Fine chemicals are chemical substances produced in relatively small quantities. They are used as intermediates for organic synthesis of pharmaceuticals, cosmetics, and other final products or as additives to certain plastics. Around 1970 Solvay and its 50 percent subsidiary Interox were making several of those products for other Solvay subsidiaries, but only as a result of the oil crisis was the idea born to make a business out of them. In 1975 it was proposed to rationalize production by concentrating the manufacture of a large number of substances on one Solvay site, for instance at Bayonne or at Giraud, and to construct there modern, flexible, multipurpose installations in which the chemicals could be made at low cost.[44]

In the meantime, Kali-Chemie had acquired the fine chemicals producers Syntha, at Froissy, near Beauvais (1972), and Boyer at Nucourt (1978). At

---

[42] Interview Christian Jourquin, 27 Sept. 2010; Buijs, Kaars and Trommelen (2005), 87–94; ACS, MoE, 28 July 1987, 2 July 1991, 23 Dec. 1992; ACS-CR, Settlement Agreement between Philips and Solvay, 27 and 29 Nov. 1995.

[43] ACS, 1020–10, meeting Executive Committee with Geuens, 20 Apr. 1982; ACS, MoE, 28 June 1982, 29 May 1991, 23 Dec. 1992, 25 Oct. 1994, 16 May 1995; ARS 1987: 40–1; Christine Simon, "Le credo de Solvay: La diversification dans l'innovation," *Le Soir* (24 June 1988): 16; interview Christian Jourquin, 27 Sept. 2010; Urban (2005); ACS-CR, agreements between Novo Nordisk, Duphar and Solvay, 19 June 1991.

[44] ACS, 1001–17–1, "Remarques sur la note CP 75.014 – Exposé du 17.2.1975 au Comité Exécutif"; ACS, 1001–17–1, "Lignes directrices du Plan 1976–1978"; ACS, MoE, 7 and 17 June 1977.

both locations Kali-Chemie was struggling with environmental problems, and therefore it was decided to merge Syntha and Boyer, in the form of a 50–50 joint venture between Solvay and Kali-Chemie, and to move their production, and that of some Solvay products, to Giraud, which again was considered a good location for the production of ugly smelling or otherwise unpleasant chemicals. In 1981 the new multipurpose installations at Giraud went on stream.[45]

After the acquisition of Salsbury (1979), Duphar (1980), and Peboc (1980), the range of fine chemicals at Solvay was further enlarged, and vitamins were added. To rationalize and optimize production, and especially to improve commercialization, an inventory of the products was made. It appeared that about four hundred different products were made in fifteen plants of Salsbury, Duphar, Peboc, Kali-Chemie, Syntha, Solvay, and Interox. In 1984 the vitamins business grew with the acquisition of the Nutrition and Health Division of Thompson-Hayword Agriculture and Nutrition Company (THAN), which continued as Duphar Nutrition.[46]

The dream of the 1970s of the bright future of fine chemicals did not come true, though. There were hundreds of small and large companies in Europe that were making these products, and Solvay did not own a unique technology to strengthen its position. As a result of the losses in this sector, by 1991 the Executive Committee decided to merge parts of the sector with the production of pharmaceuticals or to sell them. The problematic Fine Chemicals Department of Salsbury, which was frequently losing money and continued to be associated with pollution affairs, was divested, as was Duphar Nutrition. Syntha was absorbed into LTM (Latéma); the activities at Duphar were concentrated in the Bio and Pharma Intermediates Division, mentioned earlier; and Peboc was sold in 1995 to Eastman Chemical. Twelve years later, in 2007, Solvay Pharmaceuticals sold its remaining activities in fine chemicals and vitamins to Dishman Pharmaceutical and Chemicals, in India.[47]

Biotechnology: Enzymes and Proteins

Although biotechnology had already been pioneered by companies in Britain, the United States, and some other countries, it was in 1970 in Japan and Germany that this new field became for the first time a policy category, which meant that the field was stimulated largely by states and by national employers' organizations. The search for more environmentally friendly technologies played a major role in that respect.[48]

[45] ACS, MoE, 6 Dec. 1977, 2 Feb., 2 July 1979; ACS, 1010-10, Kali-Chemie: Report by the Vorstand, 16 Mar. 1979; ACS, MoB, 24 Mar. 1980.

[46] ACS, 1020-10, "Situation dans le domaine PrS," 23 Oct. 1981; "La face cachée du Groupe Solvay: La Chimie fine," *Revue Solvay* (1983) (1): 16–17; ACS, MoE, 7 Feb. 1984.

[47] Interview Alfred Hoffait, 24 May 2009; ACS, MoE, 7 Feb. 1984, 21 Oct. 1986, 21 Feb. 1989, 30 Apr. 1991, 10 May 1994; ACS-CR, agreement Eastman Chemical (UK) – Solvay Duphar – Peboc, 8 Sept. 1995; ARS 1995: 39; "Dishman acquires Solvay's fine chemicals," *Economic Times*, 9 July 2007.

[48] Bud (1993), 141–62; "ECN 25th" (1987), 49.

The forward-looking management of Kali-Chemie had decided some ten years earlier than Solvay to become part of that new development. In November 1968, Kali-Chemie concluded an agreement with Nagase & Co. Ltd., from Osaka, Japan, to construct a fermentation plant for the production of enzymes for detergents, to be built at its Nienburg site. It came on stream at the end of 1969. The *Revue Solvay* rejoiced that "a decisive step was taken in the field of biochemistry, which has great potential for future."[49] The start of the business was difficult, though, as a result of technical problems in the unknown field and strong competition in the detergents market. Therefore, Kali-Chemie decided to widen the scope of its enzymes business by starting the production of enzymes for the food and beverages industries. An agreement with the American firm Miles Laboratories was made, and the joint venture Miles Kali-Chemie was established in 1972. In the late 1970s Miles Laboratories was taken over by the German chemical giant Bayer, but the cooperation with Kali-Chemie continued.[50]

Although the technological difficulties with the fermentation plant continued at least until 1975 and Miles Kali-Chemie was losing money every year, Kali-Chemie remained confident that the field was important for the future. In 1978 it decided to further enlarge its bio-related activities with the construction of a pilot plant for fish breeding at Nienburg; the fish would be fed waste proteins from the food industries. The joint venture Aqua-Farming was set up for that purpose, together with the company Gebrüder Sulzer of Wintherthur. The same year, Kali-Chemie took a financial interest in Dansk Proteins, a large company owned by Danish milk producers, to produce proteins by ultrafiltration from whey, a by-product of cheese making. The company also established a joint venture with Dansk Proteins, called Biogena, which would valorize the lactose present in the filtrate for uses in the food industries. Plants for these two processes were constructed in Denmark.[51]

Fish breeding was scaled up with the establishment of Fischland, a joint venture between Kali-Chemie and Nordfleisch that in 1980 established a large fish farm for rainbow trout next to a Nordfleisch factory near Hamburg, to use warm waste water and protein waste of the plant. It was advertised as a solution to the world shortage of proteins, and the company started selling its trout at the end of 1982. Solvay acted along similar lines by starting in the salt marshes of Soda Povoa, Portugal, breeding trials for mini-shrimp, also rich in protein. But fish breeding was not really Solvay's business, and in 1983 there came an end to the loss-making excursion into this domain.[52]

[49] "Kali-Chemie A.G. – Nouvelles activités," *Revue Solvay* (July–Aug. 1969): 20.
[50] ASD, KC Prüfbericht P1968: 13; id., 1971: 17; id., 1972: 20, 55–8; id., 1974: 51–2; ARS 1968: 22–3; ARS 1970: 27; ARS 1972: 27.
[51] ASD, KC Prüfbericht P1978: 5; ACS, 1010–10, Kali-Chemie. Report by the Vorstand, 16 Mar. 1979; ACS, MoE, 5 Feb. 1980; "Kali-Chemie et les laiteries danoises: Danmark Proteins A/S," *Revue Solvay* (1980) (1): 7; ARS 1984: 35; ARS 1985: 38.
[52] ASD, KC Prüfbericht P1980; id., P1983: 6; ARS 1981: 29; ARS 1982: 32; "Notre nouvel atout: Les biotechnologies," *Revue Solvay* (1981) (2): 5–8; interview Christian Jourquin, 27 Sept. 2010.

From 1975, Solvay entered the field of biochemistry and biotechnology by setting up a research group on enzyme catalysis at NoH. This was a sensible choice, given Solvay's expertise in catalysis in general. By 1979 the new line of development became more concrete when Solvay cooperated with the large sugar factory at Tienen, Belgium, to develop a biotechnological process. Plans were made to let the biochemical research effort at NoH grow from twelve full-time equivalents in 1979 to fifty-five in 1990. In 1980 also Kali-Chemie entered the domain of sugar by-products by starting the joint venture Aminopepta-Chemie with a German beet sugar producer, to develop a process for the production of amino acids from the wastes of sugar factories.[53]

The crisis of 1981 set an abrupt end to this extraordinary burst of new ventures between 1978 and 1980. Miles Kali-Chemie and Dansk Proteins/Biogena continued to develop and expand production and sales, but for a while no new activities were undertaken. In 1986 the fermentation pilot plant at NoH, whose construction had been postponed because of the crisis, came on stream. The following year, a cooperation of several years between Solvay's research department and Professor Marc Anteunis of the University of Ghent culminated in the establishment of the company Peptisyntha & Cie, which would run a pilot plant at NoH to produce peptides, which are fragments of proteins, according to a process invented by Anteunis. In 1989 commercialization started successfully.[54]

Peptisyntha would be the only activity in the field of enzymes, proteins, and peptides that would survive inside the Solvay group to the twenty-first century. In 1994 Kali-Chemie sold its interest in Dansk Protein, including Biogena. And although the enzymes business for a while would expand greatly in the United States, Argentina, and Japan, when in 1990 Solvay took over industrial enzymes activities from Miles, it was decided later in the 1990s to divest those activities. The result had been disappointing for several years, and because of large-scale market concentration, Solvay's position had changed within a short time from an important producer in the world enzyme market to a relatively minor participant. In 1996 Solvay Enzymes was sold to Genencor International.[55]

Animal Health

Veterinary medicine was a much larger field for Solvay than enzymes or fine chemicals. Especially in the field of vaccines, for poultry and pets in particular,

[53] ACS, MoE, 4 Nov. 1975, 27 Mar. 1979, 1 June 1982, 18 Apr. 1984; ACS, 1020–10, Report by Mr. Bloyaert, 15 Jan. 1979; ASD, KC Prüfbericht P1983: 6; R. Charton. "Solvay se présente...," *Revue Solvay* (1980) (2): 2–5; ACS, 1095-1-1, "Evolution du Laboratoire Central pendant la décennie 1980–1990," 3 Sept. 1980.

[54] ARS 1984: 35; ARS 1986: 36; ARS 1988: 47; "Inauguration de la nouvelle unité de Fermentation à NOH," *Revue Solvay* (1986) (3): 35–6; "Peptisyntha: Une équipe pour la chimie de pointe," *Revue Solvay* (1987) (1): 12–14.

[55] ACS, MoE, 21 Sept., 26 Sept., 7 Nov. 1989, 23 Jan., 15 May, 6 Nov., 20 Nov. 1990, 10 June, 28 June 1994, 7 Nov. 1995, 2 Feb., 14 May 1996; ARS 1990; ARS 1991: 32; ARS 1994: 33; ARS 1995: 39; ARS 1996: 33; ACS-CR, several contracts among Genencor International, Solvay, and Solvay Enzymes, Mar.–Sept. 1996.

Salsbury Laboratories and Duphar were strong players in America and Europe. The first important challenge, therefore, was to coordinate and integrate the national activities of both companies as much as possible. In broad outline, the result was that Salsbury's European subsidiaries were integrated into the Duphar organization, whereas Salsbury led on the American continent and in Africa. In addition, there were exports to some eighty countries, especially to the Far East (see Chapter 20). In 1983 total sales reached US$100 million. Research at Charles City (Salsbury) and Weesp (Duphar) led to several new products, including a vaccine for young pigs called Ecobac, which was one of the first products inside the Solvay group made by genetic engineering.[56]

The importance of the American veterinary market and the importance of the United States for Solvay in general meant that US expansion was a prime target. In 1984 Michel Osterrieth was succeeded by Miles D. Freitag as CEO of Salsbury. Osterrieth got the special task to investigate, together with Hoffait, a strategic acquisition in the United States. At that time, Daniel Janssen entered the Executive Committee, with animal health as one of his fields of activity. When it appeared that the large American company E. R. Squibb & Sons was willing to sell its animal health division to Solvay, Janssen in January 1985 traveled to the United States to start negotiations. A few months later, an agreement was reached. Solvay Veterinary Inc., a subsidiary of Salsbury founded for that purpose, acquired the Squibb activities for about US$25 million. In this way Salsbury got the ownership of a sales organization of fifty persons for ethical products in the United States that greatly improved its market penetration among veterinarians. Squibb would continue to produce those pharmaceutical products for animals for which Solvay and Salsbury would have the exclusive rights to US sales.[57]

In 1986 Hoffait was succeeded by the medical doctor Christian De Sloover as head of the Animal Health Department. In those years the Asian market grew in importance, and the company became, under De Sloover, more active in Southeast Asia and Japan (see Chapter 20). Production in Asia started in 1988, when Solvay founded a joint venture in India together with the local company Biological E. Ltd. It also started selling veterinary medicines in Thailand that year.[58]

Despite that continued international expansion, in most years profits were rather poor. Solvay was strong in prevention (vaccines) but not in therapeutic areas. In mid-1995 it became obvious to the Executive Committee that human pharmacy had more growth potential for Solvay, and the company decided to sell the animal health sector. A buyer was found: American Home Products Corporation, a large producer of pharmaceuticals and veterinary medicines. After 1996 all veterinary activities were handed over to the American company,

---

[56] ARS 1980: 39; ARS 1982: 30; ARS 1983: 32; ACS, MoE, 2 June 1981; "Le Groupe Solvay et la santé animale," *Revue Solvay* (1983) (2): 12–15; "L'institut bactériologie de Tours (I.B.T.)," *Revue Solvay* (1983) (3): 11.

[57] ACS, MoE, 25 May 1984, 2 Apr., 5 May 1985; PR, 9 May 1985.

[58] PR, 15 Apr. 1988, "The Solvay Group and Biological E. Ltd. set up a joint venture in India in the animal health sector"; ACS, MoE, 21 June 1988.

for the handsome sum of US$400 million, which was reinvested in human pharmaceuticals.[59]

19.6 GROWING IN PHARMACEUTICALS

The development of Solvay's life-science businesses started around 1980 as a major reorientation of the company toward the life sciences, but at the end of the 1990s only human pharmaceuticals were left.

After the acquisition of Duphar, one of the major challenges was the coordination and gradual integration of the pharmaceutical activities of Duphar and Kali-Chemie. There was a considerable difference in size. In 1980 Kali-Chemie employed some 3,000 persons in its pharmaceutical plants, services, and subsidiaries. Duphar had a total head count of about 2,300, but only about 50 percent of them worked in the Pharmaceutical Division. In 1981 all Solvay's pharmaceutical activities together employed about 4,200 persons, 8 percent of the total personnel of the group. Most of them were employed in France (1,230), followed by Germany (1,040), the Netherlands (710), the United States (390), and Spain (380). Also in terms of sales, Kali-Chemie was more than two times as large as Duphar. Of the total pharmaceutical sales of BEF 9.7 billion in 1980 (US$320 million), no less than BEF 6.7 billion was generated by Kali-Chemie.[60]

The Solvay leadership chose not to emphasize these differences but to focus on the complementarities. Kali-Chemie was more sales and marketing oriented; Duphar was more research oriented. Also geographically, Kali-Chemie and Duphar supplemented each other in an interesting way. Duphar was strong in the Netherlands, Belgium, and the United Kingdom; Kali-Chemie in Austria, Germany, France, and on the Iberian Peninsula. Together they succeeded in achieving a market share of more than 1 percent in several countries, which had always been a goal of Kali-Chemie (see Table 19.3). In comparison to Solvay's other product groups these market shares look tiny, but the pharmaceutical market was totally different from the chemical market and extremely competitive. Even the largest pharmaceutical producer at that time, Hoechst, had a global market share of only 3.35 percent (Solvay's was 0.55 percent). Moreover, Solvay decided to focus on certain niche markets in which it could obtain a dominant position.

There were also synergies in the therapeutic domain, despite the fact that the companies' product portfolios were quite different. Kali-Chemie had mainly grown via acquisitions, and as a result it produced no fewer than two hundred different products. The eleven most successful ones generated 65 percent of total sales. Duphar, by contrast, had grown mainly endogenously, on the basis of licenses and of its own inventions. Its eight most successful products

[59] ACS, MoE, 21 June 1988, 29 Aug. 1995, 15 Sept., 15 Dec. 1998; ACS-CR, contracts between American Home Products/Fort Dodge and Solvay, 31 Oct. 1996–19 Mar. 1998; interview Christian Jourquin, 27 Sept. 2010; interview Alfred Hoffait, 24 May 2009; interview Daniel Janssen, 13 Nov. 2007.

[60] ACS, 1072–2-1, "La pharmacie," 26 Aug. 1981.

TABLE 19.3. *Market Shares of Kali-Chemie and Duphar-Pharma in 1980 (%)*

Country	Duphar	KC	Total
Netherlands	2.14	0.29	2.43
Austria	0.33	1.51	1.84
Federal Republic of Germany (FRG)	0.22	1.50	1.72
Belgium	1.13	0.52	1.65
France	0.38	1.00	1.38
United Kingdom	1.21	0.0	1.21
Spain	0.37	0.80	1.17
Portugal	0.34	0.81	1.15
United States	0.0	0.17	0.17

Source: ACS, 1072-2-1, "La pharmacie," 26 Aug. 1981.

generated 96 percent of sales. Duphar focused on just five market segments. Kali-Chemie was more diversified. There were three therapeutic domains in which both companies were active: drugs for the cardiovascular system, gastroenterology, and immunological medicines. In addition, Duphar had a drug for the central nervous system (fluvoxamine) in the pipe-line, so soon there would be four domains of overlap. In these four domains (see Table 19.4) Duphar generated 75 percent of its sales and Kali-Chemie only 45 percent. In those areas coordination was needed, especially to avoid duplication.[61]

In the first meeting of the general managers of the pharmaceutical sectors of Duphar and Kali-Chemie, held in May 1981 at Châtillon, important targets were defined: the improvement of the position of the company on the two largest pharmaceutical markets in the world, the United States and Japan; the acquisition of an ethical company in the United States, next to Kalipharma Inc. (formerly Purepac); integration of the units for the development of ethical drugs of Duphar and Kali-Chemie in the United States; and finally, a better coordination of research at Duphar and Kali-Chemie. These targets, and a few others, would occupy Solvay for the years to come.[62]

In the meantime, some important products were launched. Kali-Chemie introduced its new pancreatic enzyme Kreon in 1982 to the German market. During the following years it was introduced in other countries as well. It would become an important product for Solvay (see Chapter 22). Duphar, in turn, had high expectations with respect to its antidepressant fluvoxamine. It was introduced in September 1983 to the Swiss market, in 1984 in Germany, and over the following years very successfully to other European markets. In 1982 Duphar had granted an option for the US market to the pharmaceutical giant

[61] ACS, 1072-2-1, "La pharmacie," 26 Aug. 1981; ACS, 1020–10, meeting Executive Committee with Geuens, 20 Apr. 1982.

[62] ACS, 1072-2-1, report meeting general managers at Châtillon, 18–19 May 1981; ARS 1982: 28–9; ACS, 1020–10, meeting Executive Committee with Geuens, 20 Apr. 1982; ACS, MoE, 1 June 1982; "Dans le monde entier Solvay aide à guérir," *Revue Solvay* (1983) (1): 8–11; "Les Kali-Duphar Laboratories Inc.," *Revue Solvay* (1983) (1): 15; interview Daniel Janssen, 13 Nov. 2007.

TABLE 19.4. *Product Synergy between Kali-Chemie and Duphar (1980)*

Therapeutical Category	Kali-Chemie	Duphar
Cardiovascular system	Digi-Pulsnorma (2%)	Serc/Betaserc (19%)
	Neo-Gilurythmal (6%)	Duvadilan (14%)
	Orthoheptamin	
Immunology	IRS 19 (2%)	Influvac (8%)
	Imudon	
Gastroenterology	Paspertin (11%)	Duspatalin (18%)
	Pankreon (8%)	Duphalac (16%)
	Pankreoflat (6%)	
	Acidrine (3%)	
	Dicetel (2%)	
Central nervous system	Baldrian (5%)	Introduction 1983
	Valmane	(fluvoxamine =
		Luvox)

Note: Percentages refer to the share of sales of Kali-Chemie and Duphar, respectively.
Source: ACS, 1072-2-1, "La pharmacie," 26 Aug. 1981.

Merck, Sharp, & Dohme (MSD). When MSD in 1985 returned the option, a new situation emerged. The way was free for Solvay to introduce the important product fluvoxamine to the American market. That was a wonderful option, because of the enormous growth potential of the new Duphar drug (see Chapter 22).[63]

Late in 1985, Frank Pizzitola of Lazard came up with the small (380 employees) but quickly growing company Reid-Rowell, based in Marietta, Georgia, near Atlanta, that a few months earlier just had been formed by a combination of the firms Reid-Providence and Rowell Laboratories. Both companies had already been approached without success by Van Lierde in 1981. The Solvay negotiators, Rampelberg, Janssen, and Geuens, supported by Pizzitola, had more success. In February 1986 an agreement was reached, although for a high price of US$117.5 million, about 1.5 times the intrinsic value of the company. Solvay was willing to pay that price because of the high expectation for growth in pharmacy and its importance for the company in general, and because of the importance of the American market in particular. To enter that market, Janssen and Rampelberg argued, a sacrifice had to be made. Kali-Chemie and Duphar took on the debts and welcomed the new opportunity.[64]

With the help of Solvay, Reid-Rowell was able to grow quickly. But a major reason for the acquisition, the launching of fluvoxamine on the American market, with the US trade name Luvox, was troublesome. By 1992 its registration

[63] ACS, 1072-2-1, "Commentaires sur les activités Pharmacie," 16 Sept. 1982; ARS 1982: 28–9; ARS 1984: 30–1; ARS 1985: 32–3; ACS, MoE, 2 July 1985; interview Daniel Janssen, 13 Nov. 2007; interview Christian Jourquin, 27 Sept. 2010.

[64] ACS, MoE, 2 Dec. 1985; PR, 24 Feb. 1986: "Acquisition of Reid-Rowell by Solvay"; "Acquisition of Reid-Rowell opens the American Market for the Products of Kali-Chemie and Duphar," *Solvay Review* (1986) (2): 20–1; Moorman (1987); interview Daniel Janssen, 13 Nov. 2007; interview Albert Rampelberg, 4 Apr. 2008; interview Whitson Sadler and René Degrève, 12 May 2010; interview Christian Jourquin, 27 Sept. 2010.

had still not been granted by the FDA. In the same time, Solvay's competitor Eli Lilly asked for a registration of its product Prozac, a direct competitor of Luvox. The FDA preferred Prozac, and as a result, the registration of Luvox was delayed time and again, despite the fact that Solvay joined forces with the large company Upjohn to improve its position in the United States (see Chapter 22).[65]

This example shows the difficulties innovative pharmaceutical companies faced. Despite the successful acquisition, also in 1986, of the Italian company Unione Chimica Medicamenti, which gave Solvay access to the large Italian market, reaching the target set in 1981 of gaining 1 percent of the world market was not easy. Governments and health authorities tried to keep drug prices down. Drug registration grew increasingly costly and complex, which made it difficult to innovate. After the successful products of the 1980s, Solvay Pharmaceuticals, the name that replaced Duphar and Kali-Chemie in this sector in 1991, introduced several new medicines to the market, but there was no blockbuster among them that could boost the growth of the company. In the 1990s the Executive Committee decided to completely focus on pharmaceuticals and to sell the crop protection, enzyme, and animal health activities. All money gained in this way was reinvested in the human health sector. As is described in Chapter 22, strategic alliances with other companies and acquisition would be increasingly necessary to compensate for the reduced innovation performance of Solvay's pharmaceutical R&D.[66]

---

[65] Ainsworth (1992), 17–20; interview Daniel Janssen, 13 Nov. 2007; interview Albert Rampelberg, 4 Apr. 2008; interview Whitson Sadler and René Degrève, 12 May 2010; interview Christian Jourquin, 27 Sept. 2010.

[66] ACS, MoE, 19 Nov., 3 Dec. 1985; PR, 12 June 1986; ARS 1990: 32; interview Daniel Janssen, 13 Nov. 2007; interview Albert Rampelberg, 4 Apr. 2008; interview Christian Jourquin, 27 Sept. 2010.

FIGURE 20.1. Construction of the peroxides plant at Map Tha Put in Thailand, at the end of the 1980s. (Solvay Archives.)

20

Solvay in the Age of Globalization

Five years after the first oil shock, a second began. In a short time, prices doubled from US$40 to US$80 per barrel. The year 1979 was still a good one for the chemical industry, but at the end of it the prices of petrochemical feedstocks started to rise. At the same time, high inflation, high interest rates, and rising energy costs led to a stagnation of demand in economic sectors such as the car industry and construction. These were important markets for plastics, and as a result, market prices of plastics started to fall to below the production costs, aggravated by too-optimistic capacity enlargements that had taken place during the previous years. Squeezed between rising cost prices and falling sales prices, many chemical companies were in the red in 1980, 1981, and 1982. Also in 1981 the Solvay group suffered the first consolidated loss in its history.[1]

The situation of the industry was so serious that almost all chemical companies had to recalibrate their policies. For instance, BASF and DuPont decided to integrate backward into oil and gas, to improve their control over feedstocks. Most firms, though, tried to move out of bulk chemicals as much as possible and to diversify selectively into product sectors with higher value-added. Rhône-Poulenc, for instance, decided after heavy losses to restructure its fibers business greatly; to divest most of its bulk plastics; and to focus on pharmaceuticals, agricultural chemicals, and other product lines that promised high revenues. Parallel to these changes in company strategy, the plastics and fiber manufacturers reduced overcapacities by closing down old and unprofitable plants.[2]

When after 1983 the chemical economy improved, there were still reasons to reposition corporate strategy. The years of uninterrupted growth (1955–1970) were definitely over. Only three growth strategies remained: geographical expansion, a focus on special products with high earnings but often modest sales, and concentration on distinguished fields of strength with substantial turnover. Almost all companies embarked on the first strategy, and most of them, including Solvay, combined elements of the second and third avenues of growth. As result of these changes in product portfolios – reinforced by the growing role of leveraged buyouts, shareholder value, and corporate raiders – the landscape of the chemical industry greatly changed. Some chemical

[1] "ECN 25th" (1987), 49; Frieden (2006), 363–91; Schröter (2007).
[2] Bower (1986); *Innovating* (1995), 106–9.

companies of great historical renown were broken up into separate, more focused companies, or even disappeared completely: Allied Chemical in 1985, Hoechst in 1999, Union Carbide in 2002, and ICI in 2008.[3]

In this changing landscape Solvay had to find its own way. In this chapter we will see how the company responded to the crisis of the early 1980s, apart from the continued effort to grow in the life sciences (see Chapter 19). One of those responses was the decision to enlarge Solvay's geographical diversification, not only by investing more strongly in the United States but also by establishing offices and production plants in Asia.

20.1   SHAKEN BY THE OIL SHOCK

In 1979, plastic resins accounted for 28 percent of Solvay's sales, and the processing of plastics for 21 percent. It is therefore no surprise that Solvay was hit hard when in 1980 the plastics crisis started. In March 1980 the first signs of a coming crash announced themselves, but only in November 1980 did it become obvious that the results were going down dramatically. Paul Washer, then responsible for finance, and Jacques Solvay had a lunch meeting on 11 December to discuss the situation. Five days later, Jacques Solvay informed the other members of the Executive Committee that the financial results of the company gave cause for great concern. The debt ratio would grow to more than 40 percent, which had been the ceiling the company had always obeyed. He announced an embargo on all acquisitions, on all investments in nonessential or unprofitable businesses, and on hiring of new personnel. In a meeting at Brussels on 2 February 1981, all the national and central top-executives were informed. In almost all countries the company was losing money; costs had to be cut wherever possible.[4]

Over the course of 1981, it became clear that large losses were being incurred in polyolefins and especially PVC. Solvay's plastics-processing activities were hit as well. On top of that, the Corpus Christi cracker, which had just been started up, could not work at full capacity and proved a major bleeder. There was an ongoing cash drain in the United States. Every month Washer's Financial Department had to supply BEF 175 million (US$4.7 million) to Soltex, to settle losses. At the same time, the total losses on PVC in Europe were even higher. Together, the industrial losses on plastics, plastics processing, and the Corpus Christi cracker amounted to more than BEF 7 billion (US$190 million) (see Table 20.2). Because of the profits earned in alkalis, peroxides, and pharmaceuticals, though, there was a total net industrial loss of "only" BEF 1,850 million. After taxes and the results of financial activities, this figure was further reduced to a consolidated net loss of BEF 752 million in 1981.[5]

[3] Schröter (2007), 66–79.

[4] PPJF, Déjeuner Washer (handwritten) notes and letters from Paul Washer to Jacques Solvay, 18 Mar. 1980, 12 Nov. 1980, 4 Dec. 1980, 10 Dec. 1980; ARS 1979: 8–9; ACS, MoE, 16 Dec. 1980; ACS, 1020-10, meeting national and central general managers in Brussels, 2 Feb. 1981; ACS, MoB, 23 Mar. 1981.

[5] PPJF, "Politique de sauvegarde," 1 Apr. 1981; PR's on results Solvay Group, 23 Apr. 1981, 30 Sept. 1981, 17 Apr. 1982; ACS, 1020-10, "Plan Financier. Exposé du 16 mars 1982."

A serious situation demands drastic measures. In 1981 and 1982 Jacques Solvay was actively involved in talks and negotiations with other European manufacturers of PVC and polyolefins to reduce production capacities. As president of the Conseil Européen des Fédérations de l'Industrie Chimique (CEFIC), from 1980 to 1982, as well as of the more informal Club de l'Industrie Chimique, Jacques Solvay naturally was a key player. Together with a top manager of Rhône-Poulenc, he contacted Étienne Davignon, brother-in-law of Pol Boël and then commissioner for industry of the European Commission, about permission to erect a temporary "crisis cartel" to solve the tremendous problems of the European plastics sector. Although in the end no crisis cartels in plastics were formed, given conflicting views inside the European Commission, all producers cut their capacities by 20 percent or more. Solvay suspended a major PVC production line at Tavaux from 1981 to 1984, and in 1983 it permanently closed down its PVC plant at Torrelavega. In the United States one of the two production lines for polypropylene was stopped (see Chapter 18). At the same time, Jacques Solvay and other plastic manufacturers negotiated the reduction of feedstock prices. Moreover, together with Claude Loutrel, he negotiated with Union Oil and ICI, Solvay's partners in CCPC, the ethylene and propylene sales prices of the Corpus Christi cracker and divestment of the cracker altogether. Agreement with the other partners could not be reached, though. For his achievements for the European chemical industry, Jacques Solvay received the Centenary Medal of the British Society of Chemical Industry in 1984.[6]

Solvay also closed down the fertilizer plant of Kali-Chemie in Brunsbüttelkoog, Germany, and sold the remaining potassium and fertilizer activities to Kali und Salz AG and to Superfos A/S of Denmark. Shortly thereafter, the potassium activities at Suria in Spain were divested. The same happened to Solvay's interest in the synthetic paper-pulp activities at Rosignano and Deer Park, which were sold to Hercules in November 1981. During the following years a calendering plant was closed in the Netherlands, as were the soda ash plant at Sarralbe and the installations for diaphragm electrolysis at Rosignano and Jemeppe. At all sites great efforts were made to achieve energy savings and reduce personnel costs, which led at the Belgium plants at Couillet and Jemeppe in 1983 to social conflicts and strikes. Finally, in 1985, Solvay succeeded in selling its (polyurethane) foam activities to British Vita.[7]

Despite all these changes in its portfolio, Solvay's cash flow and profits were unusually low during the entire first half of the 1980s. In 1983, the debt ratio

---

[6] ACS, 1001–26-1, "Politique générale," 3 Apr. 1981; ACS, MoB, 23 Nov. 1981, 22 Mar. 1982, 19 Apr. 1982; ACS, MoE, 16 Mar. 1982, 26 July 1982, 19 Oct. 1982; ACS, CdL, "Mémorandum sur notre développement aux USA dans les domains des Polyoléfines (Soltex Polymer Corp.) et du Steam Cracking (CCPC, Corpus Christi Petrochemical Cy)," 15 Feb. 1982; Jacques Solvay. "The Chemical Industry in the EEC." *Revue Solvay*, (1984) (1): 8–18; "ECN 25th" (1987): 52; Bower (1986), 30–1, 46, 61, 181.

[7] ACS, MoE, 28 July 1981, 5 Apr. 1982, 18 June 1985; ACS, MoB, 23 Nov. 1981, 22 Nov. 1982, 1 July 1985; PR, 25 Mar. 1983, "Conflit social à Couillet"; PR, 7 Oct. 1983, "Solvay: Grève sauvage à Jemeppe-sur-Sambre"; "ECN 25th" (1987), 52; interview Olivier Monfort, 21 Apr. 2011.

grew to more than 44 percent (see Table 20.1). For many other companies, that debt ratio would not have been reason for great worry – at BASF, Bayer, Hoechst, and Rhône-Poulenc debt ratios of 50–60 percent were not unusual – but for a family firm like Solvay such ratios were out of the question. However, there were divergent opinions inside the Executive Committee about the future strategy and measures to reduce the debts. Paul Washer held the view that far more product groups should be divested, polyolefins in the first place, and that more radical cuts in personnel were required: about 10 percent of the employees, or some five thousand people. For Jacques Solvay reducing total staff by five thousand seemed unrealistic, not to mention the resistance the company would encounter from trade unions and governments.[8]

When, in September 1981, Solvay indicated that it might close the year with a loss, that was a great psychological shock for the family shareholders. The Solvay quotation at the Brussels Stock Exchange dropped instantly and arrived at an all-time-low of 1,675 in November 1981. That month the Board of Directors of Solvay was informed that due to cash drains in the USA (CCPC) and Solvic (PVC), the debts of the company had grown within ten months from BEF 25.4 billion to 30.4 billion (US$800 million). The Executive Committee announced that it would start an ongoing reorganization. Despite that, the Board decided to investigate in depth the causes of the losses and the means to recover, not in the last place because of the diverging views between Jacques Solvay and Paul Washer. In the following months the idea took shape to establish a small Liaison Committee of Board members to perform that task.[9]

The Liaison Committee

In March 1982 the Liaison Committee was inaugurated, with Jacques Solvay, Yves Boël, Paul-Emmanuel Janssen, Pierre Casimir-Lambert and Albert Bietlot as members, and another, varying, Executive Committee member that would be present depending on the topic of the meeting. The tasks given to the committee were threefold: (1) to investigate the causes of the great losses and to examine the measures taken by the Executive Committee; (2) to study whether the organizational structures of the group were flexible and effective enough to cope with the situation; and (3) to investigate whether the information circuits and authority lines, up to the highest level, were adequately structured for the present tasks. The committee would make no decisions but would advise the board. Any publicity was to be avoided.[10]

---

[8] PPSF, Box 1981–91, "Plan de redressement," 19 Oct. 1981; ACS, Organisation, Paul Washer, "Bilan économique 1968–1988. Essai de diagnostic et conclusions," 27 May 1988; Cayez (1988), 300–1; Abelshauser (2002), 559.

[9] ACS, MoB, 23 Nov. 1981, 25 Jan. 1982; ACS, 1001-40-15, "Situation nette consolidée – Debt ratios," 14 Dec. 1981; interview Paul Washer, 29 Nov. 2007; interview Pierre Casimir-Lambert, 21 Apr. 2011; database of the University of Antwerp, Studiecentrum voor Onderneming en Beurs (SCOB).

[10] ACS, CdL, "Projet de création d'un Comité de liaison," 17 Mar. 1982; ACS, MoB, 22 Mar. 1982.

TABLE 20.1. *Performance of the Solvay Group, 1980–1989*

Year	Annual Growth of Sales (%)	Annual Growth of Net Profit (%)	Annual Growth of Cash Flow (%)	Cash Flow as % of Sales	Net Profit as % of Sales	Debt Ratio (%)	Personnel
1980	14.4	−61.5	−19.2	7.5	1.4	40.2	49,057
1981	13.7	−138.1	−23.6	5.1	−0.5	42.5	48,237
1982	12.9	444.8	59.5	7.2	1.5	43.3	45,369
1983	11.4	102.3	22.4	7.9	2.6	44.1	44,186
1984	13.3	53.5	21.6	8.4	3.6	39.2	43,537
1985	0.8	1.1	1.2	8.5	3.6	35.7	44,461
1986	−4.0	22.0	19.7	10.6	4.6	34.5	44,787
1987	3.4	22.5	15.8	11.9	5.4	36.8	44,957
1988	13.4	24.2	25.6	13.2	6.0	35.3	44,301
1989	1.3	10.6	−5.3	12.3	6.5	31.2	45,011

Source: Calculated on the basis of ARS, 1980–1989.

During these difficult times, some family shareholders raised doubts over whether Jacques Solvay was the right man to help Solvay through the crisis. In their views an excellent alternative was available: Jean Gandois, Jacques Solvay's successor as president of CEFIC and until July 1982 chairman and CEO of Rhône-Poulenc. Gandois, *polytechnicien*, had made a career in the steel industry before he joined Rhône-Poulenc in 1976. Soon, he made great impression by restructuring the ailing fibers activities of the company, and he became its chairman in 1979. In that role he effectively turned around the product portfolio of the French chemical group, steering his company toward high-value-added products, pharmaceuticals and agrochemicals in particular. High debts accumulated over the years made Rhône-Poulenc vulnerable, though. In February 1982 the group was nationalized by the French socialist government – these were the days of Pierre Mauroy and François Mitterand – and soon Gandois, who was a convinced liberal, ran into conflict with the French state over the strategy of his company. In July 1982 he resigned. In November 1982 the Liaison Committee held two meetings in which only nonexecutive directors were present. Obviously, the performance at the "highest level" of the company was then discussed. During these final meetings, the committee confirmed the leadership of Jacques Solvay.[11]

When presenting its conclusions, the Liaison Committee was satisfied with respect to its first mission. It had a better understanding of the causes of the crisis, and it agreed with the actions taken by the Executive Committee. Loutrel's analysis that the two oil shocks had totally changed the world of petrochemicals had made a great impression in particular. In 1972 the price of ethylene accounted for about 30 percent of the sales price of polyethylene, but in 1981 that figure had grown to more than 70 percent; for PVC it had grown to 60 percent. The second oil shock had reversed the balance of power: polyethylene and cracking were almost totally dependent on petroleum. That made Solvay vulnerable in the field of polyolefins, in which seemingly only the oil companies had a future. The board therefore agreed with Jacques Solvay that the group should protect itself by improving its ethylene supply and reducing its exposure in plastics.[12]

With respect to the other two missions the committee did not have final solutions, but it formulated a number of recommendations for the Executive Committee to work out and implement in the following year. Financial results would be communicated more quickly and more precisely to the Executive Committee. Also, the international legal structure of the company would be simplified, by integrating subsidiaries into larger national entities, so that

[11] ACS, CdL, letter Paul Janssen to J. Solvay and Y. Boël, 3 Mar. 1982; ACS, MoB, 22 Nov. 1982; "Mutations au CEFIC." *Revue Solvay*, (1982) (2); *Innovating* (1995), 101, 106–9, 120–4; Bower (1986), 64, 140–1, 212, 215; oral communication Daniel Janssen, 30 Mar. 2011; interview Pierre Casimir-Lambert, 21 Apr. 2011. During an interview on 21 Nov. 2011, Paul Washer expressed doubts about whether Jean Gandois ever was a serious candidate. He never heard his name mentioned in this respect.

[12] ACS, CdL, "Mémorandum sur notre développement aux USA," 15 Feb. 1982; id., "Conclusion du Comité de Liaison au Conseil d'Administration," 22 Nov. 1982; ACS, MoB, 22 Nov. 1982.

TABLE 20.2. *Solvay's Financial Results in Plastics, 1981–1983 (in million BEF)*

Year	CCPC	PE/PP USA	PE/PP Europe	PVC Europe	Processing
			Net Industrial Result		
1981	−1,150	−1,400	−800	−2,800	−900
1982	−1,450	−150	−160	−2,770	+40
1983	−2,200	+400	+100	−300	+40
			Cash Flow		
1981	−1,100	−850	−400	−1,950	+100
1982	−1,410	+550	+400	−1,890	+1,220
1983	−2,200	+1,200	+700	+600	+1,800

Sources: ACS, 1020–10, "Plan Financier," 16 Mar. 1982; id., "Plan Financier," 14 Mar. 1983; id., "Plan Financier," 12 Mar. 1984.

greater flexibility could be achieved with respect to the pooling of liquidity and fiscal optimization.

Together, these conclusion and recommendations set the agenda for the years to come. Geographical expansion, emphasized in June 1982 by the Corporate Planning Department, would become an issue. Corporate organization and financial accounting became important, too. And finally, reducing exposure in plastics by divesting large parts of it returned to the agenda time and again in the board meetings.

20.2   REDUCING EXPOSURE IN PLASTICS

Apart from CCPC, there were three major plastics domains in which Solvay lost money during 1981 and 1982: PVC in Europe, polyolefins in the United States, and polyolefins in Europe (see Table 20.2). In all those domains the company had to reevaluate its strategy and decide whether the activity should be divested.[13] In PVC the losses were enormous; and, during 1981 and 1982, they were twice as large as the losses on CCPC (see Table 20.2). But PVC was so strongly integrated with the rest of the company, upstream (electrolysis) and downstream (plastics processing), that it was decided not to sell the PVC activities but to rationalize the sector and try to find an oil company that would be willing to become a partner to reduce the vulnerability of the ethylene supply.

Before any significant initiatives could be started, the immediate problem that had to be solved was the supply of funds to the Solvic companies that were suffering huge cash drains. ICI – Solvay's partner in Solvic that owned 25 percent of shares – refused to supply any cash. In the negotiations that followed, it was decided that ICI would withdraw from Solvic – an option already contemplated before – so that Solvay would get total ownership and be able to fully integrate the Solvic companies into the Solvay organization.

[13] ACS, 1001–26-1, "Problèmes à long terme," 15 Feb. 1982, 49–50.

In 1984 and 1985 Solvic Italy, Solvic Belgium, and Solvic France were successively integrated into Solvay. Hispavic followed in 1990.[14]

In the spring of 1982 Solvay started talks with Shell about a joint venture in VCM and PVC, but nothing concrete emerged from that. After 1983 the results quickly improved, and in 1987 there were again high profits in PVC.[15]

Selling the polyolefins activities in the United States was not a high priority either. The United States was a major oil-producing country, so its petrochemical industry was less vulnerable than its counterpart in Europe, and in HDPE Solvay had a large market share. More important, Solvay's policy of geographical risk spreading centered on expansion in the United States would certainly not be helped by selling Soltex. It was decided, therefore, to continue as a producer of HDPE and PP in the United States. From 1986, large profits were made that swept the divestment issue completely from the table, for the time being at least.[16]

Therefore, all emphasis was on the divestment of the European polyolefins business. Sarralbe was vulnerable, because it was completely dependent on one cracker, owned by CdF Chimie. Rosignano was more flexible, with transport overseas, but its position was inferior to that of Deer Park. After November 1982, the nonexecutive directors time and again raised the issue of divesting the polyolefins in Europe. Not all Executive Committee members felt the same sense of urgency, and there was uncertainty about the best timing of the divestment. From 1984 to 1986 Solvay negotiated with the Dutch company DSM and, later, with the Italian company Enichem, but in both cases without final results.[17]

By the summer of 1987, the revenues on polyolefins had greatly improved. The years 1986–1988 were excellent for these plastics, and the Executive Committee started to reevaluate its strategy. At a board meeting in September 1987, Daniel Janssen sketched the importance of HDPE for return on equity and the growth of the group. Solvay was fifth in Europe and third in the United States, but if one took a global perspective, it appeared that Solvay was the second-largest producer in the world. So in the context of a global strategy, the HDPE business certainly was an option for the company, especially because the sales of its interest in CCPC, in July 1987, had reduced Solvay's exposure in the field of petrochemicals considerably (see Chapter 18). The board agreed on a strategy to enlarge the market share in the United States and to focus on HDPE resins for special applications (fuel tanks especially) in Europe and Brazil.

[14] ACS, MoE, 17 June 1980, 16 Dec. 1980, 16 Mar. 1982, 7 Feb. 1984, 5 Feb. 1985, 10 Apr. 1985, 25 July 1989, 24 Oct. 1989, 27 Feb. 1996; ACS, MoB, 22 Mar. 1982, 26 Mar. 1984, 26 Nov. 1984, 15 Apr. 1985; ACS-CR, letter ICI to Solvay, 9 July 1982; id., sales of ICI's share in Hispavic to Solvay, 3 May 1990; Rapaille (1990), 123.

[15] ACS, MoE, 18 May 1982, 28 June 1982; ACS, MoB, 22 Mar. 1982, 23 Nov. 1987; [Daniel Janssen], "Discours de fin d'année," inserted in the *Revue Solvay* (1987) (1).

[16] ACS, CdL, "Programmation à long terme," 8 June 1982; ACS, 1001–26, "Orientations stratégiques pour nos lignes de produits," 29 Sept. 1983, 56–61; ACS, MoB, 28 Sept. 1987, 23 Nov. 1987.

[17] ACS, MoB, 22 Mar. 1982, 26 Nov. 1984; ACS, 1001–26, "Orientations stratégiques pour nos lignes de produits," 29 Sept. 1983, 59–60; ACS, MoE, 4 Dec. 1984, 2 July 1985, 3 Sept. 1985, 29 Jan. 1986; ACS, 1001–26-1, "Politique générale du groupe," 1 Apr. 1985.

The divestment of the polyolefins business had been removed from the table, but it remained present and reappeared at board meetings ten years later (see Chapter 22).[18]

On 6 June 1988 Paul Washer, who had reached the age limit for membership of the Executive Committee, stepped down from active management. He presented a lengthy "business testament" to his colleagues in which he evaluated the development and strategies of the company from 1968 to 1988. The tone was a bit pessimistic. Washer concluded that apart from the previous two to three years, in which profits had grown and debts had been reduced, little progress had been made. Calculated in 1987 Belgian francs, the financial situation of the company in 1986 was not very different from that of 1968. In Washer's view the lack of progress was mainly caused by three constraints: (1) Solvay's being a family business; (2) the vulnerability of plastics; and (3) the structure of Solvay's activities, which were too energy intensive, too capital intensive, and too overstaffed. There certainly is a degree of truth in these observations, but if one looks from another angle at this history, one could also say that Washer's observations are a perfect illustration of the difficult times of the European chemical industry in general between 1969 and 1986, a period that largely coincided with the leadership of Jacques Solvay.[19]

Ironically, Washer's "balance report" also contained statistics on the evolution of the personnel figures at Solvay between 1968 and 1987. It appeared that between 1980 and 1984, divestments, automation, and efficiency measures led to a reduction from 49,200 to 43,500 staff. So, the reduction by 5,000 employees had been realized even without Washer's views being adopted.

The note also advised the company to continue vigorously Solvay's geographical diversification to Japan, Southeast Asia, and the United States. In Washer's view, the share of the European sales in the total sales should be reduced to 50–60 percent. That would indeed become one of the aims that would occupy the company during the last fifteen years of the twentieth century.

20.3   SOLVAY GOES TO ASIA

Early in 1984, Executive Committee member Claude Loutrel contacted the Parisian consulting firm X,A Descourt – founded in 1980 by Robert Descourt, a *centralien* like Loutrel himself – with the request to develop for Solvay a strategy to set up production facilities in the Far East. During the weeks before, the Executive Committee had concluded that Southeast Asia and Japan had enormous growth potential, so that Solvay should intensify its business with that region and, more specifically, establish sales offices and plants.[20]

---

[18] ACS, 1001–26-1, "Politique générale du groupe," 17 Mar. 1987; id., 14 Mar. 1988; ACS, MoB, 27 July 1987, 28 Sept. 1987, 23 Nov. 1987; ACS, MoE, 8 Sept. 1987, 6 Oct. 1987.

[19] ACS, Organisation, Paul Washer, "Bilan économique 1968–1988. Essai de diagnostic et conclusions," 27 May 1988; "Allocution de Monsieur Yves Boël...3 juin 1991," insert in the *The Solvay Review* 2/91, 8.

[20] ACS, 1001–26-1, letter Robert Descours to Mr. Loutrel, 22 Feb. 1984; interview Olivier Monfort, 21 Apr. 2011.

Some competitors, such as the large German companies and ICI, were already present in Asia for a long time. Since the 1970s, though, when several industrial sectors (e.g., textiles, automobile, electronics) started moving from Europe to Asia, other American and European chemical companies (e.g., Akzo, Dow, Rhône-Poulenc, Degussa, DuPont, FMC) decided to follow their customers or at least intensify their exports to the Asian region. Triggered by the crisis of the early 1980s, Solvay followed.[21]

When Solvay in 1981 asked Henri Vander Eycken, professor of business economics and strategic management at the Université Libre de Bruxelles and Vrije Universiteit Brussel, what Solvay's policy should be in a context of weak European economic growth and which product groups should be developed, the consultant pointed to some important geographical trends. In his "Reference Scenario for the Chemical Industry" he argued that the basic chemical industry would increasingly move to member states of the Organization of the Petroleum Exporting Countries, with their cheap oil resources, and to the newly industrializing countries of Latin America and Southeast Asia, with their low labor costs. On the basis of Vander Eycken's report, in September 1983 the Corporate Planning Department of Solvay – under the supervision of Jean-Jacques Van de Berg, who just had entered the Executive Committee in June 1982 – formulated a consistent set of strategies for all products. The report explicitly mentioned the option to move some Solvay plants to the newly industrializing countries, but no concrete proposals were made. Shortly thereafter, Claude Loutrel, board member of Interox, concluded that the peroxides joint venture should become more active in Asia and that Solvay should take the lead to push Interox in that direction. For a world leader in hydrogen peroxide and perborates such as Interox, a stronger presence in Asia was important. But at the same time, it would be a good opportunity to test the waters for Solvay's own expansion in Southeast Asia. In late 1983 a team was formed in Solvay, led by Claude Loutrel and assisted by Michel Bonnefoy and Albert Rampelberg.[22]

When the Asia plan began in 1984, Solvay did not completely start from zero. In Japan, from about 1960 the sales of Solvay products had been granted to the trading company Marubeni. Together with Marubeni, Solvay founded in 1975 Solvay-Marubeni Chemicals for the sales and distribution of the highly active catalyst to the Japanese licensees of Solvay's polypropylene process. Solvay also had a 10 percent stake in a HDPE producer in Taiwan, as a result of licensing. Also, Solvay was mainly present in high-value-added products that had been globalized early, such as pharmaceuticals, veterinary products, and peroxides. Kali-Chemie, Duphar, and Salsbury all had local sales offices in the region (e.g., India, Japan, Philippines, Indonesia, Singapore), and Interox

---

[21] ACS, 1001-26-1, "Politique générale," 3 Apr. 1981; Jacques Solvay, "Discours de fin d'année," insert in the *Revue Solvay* (1983) (3); *Innovating* (1995), 120, 161–7; Spitz (2003), 126, 247–82.

[22] ACS, MoE, 17 June 1980, 4 Oct. 1983; ACS, CdL, "Programmation à long terme," 8 June 1982; ACS, 1001-26, H. Vander Eycken, "Un scénario de référence pour l'industrie chimique," Nov. 1982; id., "Orientations stratégiques pour nos lignes de produits," 29 Sept. 1983; ACS, 1001-26-1, Van de Berg, "Politique groupe," 8 Mar. 1983; id., letter Michel Bonnefoy to Robert Descours, 28 Feb. 1984; interview Jean-Marie Chandelle, 15 June 2011.

was present in Australia, India, and Japan. In addition, there were the usual overseas exports in alkalis, polyolefins, peroxides, veterinary products, and barium and strontium derivatives of Kali-Chemie that were used in television screens produced in growing numbers in the Far East. Despite all these activities, Asia accounted for only about 2 percent of Solvay's total sales.[23]

After several months of study, Robert Descourt in July 1984 concluded that the economic importance of the region was still modest but would grow considerably over the following ten to fifteen years; that Solvay was not too late, but its Asia presence and trade were lacking coordination; and that it would be important to establish local offices in the region and then gradually start industrial activities. He sketched a development plan for the region, starting from bridgeheads in Hong Kong and Singapore. In September 1984, the Executive Committee adopted Descourt's conclusions and asked Jean-Pierre Van Halteren and Jacques Mortier to set up offices in Singapore and Hong Kong, under the supervision of Loutrel and Rampelberg, and to investigate the prospects of production plants of Solvay in different countries. The Asia Division was born.[24]

Many inside Solvay were very cautious as regards the erection of plants in the Far East. The cultural climate in those countries was so different from that of Europe, and there were doubts about whether the right staff and work force could be found for modern Solvay plants. More important, there was still a dominant engineering philosophy of large-scale and low-cost production inside the company. Wouldn't it be better to have world-scale production plants in Europe to supply the Asian market? Also the Corporate Planning Department had a very cautious attitude; it advised starting with very small investments, for instance in animal health and plastics processing, but not in peroxides or PVC.[25]

From 13 January to 20 February 1985 Van Halteren and Mortier made their first trip through the region. They visited Hong Kong, China, Taiwan, Thailand, Singapore, Malaysia, and Indonesia, and they spoke with several businesspeople, agents, clients, bankers, other European companies, local authorities, and Belgian diplomats. A second trip was made a few months later. On the basis of these explorations, it was decided to first establish an office at Singapore. It started in the summer of 1985, incorporated as Solvay (South East Asia) Pte Ltd. (SEA), headed by Van Halteren. The next year also a small office at Hong Kong was created. In the summer of 1987 two additional sales offices were

[23] ACS, MoE, 6 Nov. 1974, 3 Dec. 1974, 17 Sept. 1975, 17 June 1980; "Solvay-Marubeni Chemicals filiale Japonais," *Revue Solvay* (1975) (6): 18; ACS, 1001–26-1, letter Michel Bonnefoy to Robert Descours, 28 Feb. 1984; "Voyage du Comité Exécutif en Asie," *Revue Solvay* (1989) (1): 28–9; *Solvay* (1988), 17, 21.

[24] ACS, 1001–26-1, letter Bonnefoy to X.A. Descours, 7 June 1984; id., [X,A Descours], *Eléments d'une strategie dans la zone Est/ Sud-Est Asiatique*, Solvay & Cie (July 1984); id., Claude Loutrel and Albert Rampelberg, "Développement dans la zone est/sud-est asiatique," 5 Sept. 1984; ACS, MoE, 10 Sept. 1984.

[25] ACS, 1001–26-1, J. Solvay, "Note aux Directions Centrales, Directions Nationales, Administration des Filiales," 2 Oct. 1984; ACS, MoE, 5 Feb. 1985; interview Daniel Janssen, 13 Nov. 2007.

opened in Seoul (Korea Branch of Solvay SEA) and in Tokyo (Nippon Solvay KK). Within three years, Solvay had established itself in East Asia.[26]

Starting industrial activities was of course far more complex. On the basis of their first mission, Van Halteren and Mortier saw several possibilities in China, Taiwan, and Indonesia. During the months following their trip, Interox took the lead. Competitors were constructing peroxides plants in the Asian region, so it was important that Interox act quickly. From early 1985 Interox worked on projects for hydrogen peroxide plants in Indonesia and Malaysia. Parallel to that, in mid-1986 Solvay established contacts in Malaysia to construct a PVC plant in a petrochemical complex near Singapore. In August 1986 Claude Loutrel and Albert Rampelberg made a tour through the region. In Bangkok they met Belgian ambassador Patrick Nothomb, who was passionate about the business opportunities in Thailand and who convinced Loutrel that the country deserved a careful investigation by Interox and Solvay. The political situation was rather stable, there was great freedom of enterprise, and the economy was growing. During the following months, both the Indonesian peroxide project and the new Thai peroxide project were studied. But by the end of 1986 it was decided to first erect a hydrogen peroxide plant in Thailand. Problems concerning corruption in Indonesia were one reason not to start industrial activities there. Also the Malaysian PVC project did not materialize. It would be Thailand again that would become the new location for that Solvay activity.[27]

Thailand

In March 1987 Claude Loutrel visited Thailand. With the help of Ambassador Nothomb he was able to contact many Thai businesspeople and politicians, and the idea to start a hydrogen peroxide plant in Thailand was generally received well. The next month Interox sent a mission to Bangkok to prepare the project and raise interest among Thai authorities. That mission team included Jacques Seressia and Jean-Marie Chandelle of Solvay and Malcolm Smith and Peter Lee of Laporte. They had first negotiated the construction of a hydrogen peroxide plant in Indonesia, and when that project stagnated, they were sent to Thailand to convince the Board of Investment (BOI) to grant a promotion certificate. On

[26] ACS, 1001-26-1, "Mission Est/Sud-Est asiatique," 4 Mar. 1985; id., Van Halteren and Mortier, "Note pour le Comité Exécutif. Implantation du Groupe Solvay en Asie," 28 Mar. 1985; id., "Développement des activités du Groupe en Asia," 11 Apr. 1985; ACS, MoE, 22 Feb. 1985, 30 July 1985, 1 July 1985, 27 Apr. 1987, 30 June 1987; ACS, MoB, 1 July 1985, 27 July 1987; Jacques Solvay, "Discours de fin d'année," insert in the *Revue Solvay* (1985) (3): 1–6; "Solvay dans le Far East," *Revue Solvay* (1986) (1): 18–21; "Solvay en Asie," *Revue Solvay* (1989) (3): 3; *Solvay* (1988), 17, 19, 21

[27] ACS, 1001-26-1, "Développement des activités du Groupe en Asia," 11 Apr. 1985; id., fax J.P. Van Halteren to Messrs. Secousse and Christiaens on: "Indonésie – Résumé de l'étude realize par PTT," 9 June 1989; ACS, MoE, 6 Mar. 1986, 2 Sept. 1986, 18 Nov. 1986, 15 Dec. 1987; ACS, MoB, 30 June 1986; Daniel Janssen, "Discours de fin d'année." insert in the *Revue Solvay*, (1987) (1): 1–5; "La Thaïlande: Land of the Free," *Revue Solvay* (1989) (3): 1–10; interview Daniel Janssen, 13 Nov. 2007; interview Claude Loutrel, 31 Jan. 2008; telephone conversation with Claude Loutrel, 26 May 2011; interview Jean-Marie Chandelle, 15 June 2011.

28 October 1987 permission was granted, after contacts by Loutrel with the vice prime minister of Thailand, Major General Chatichai Shoonhavan, and other high officials, under the condition that Solvay and Laporte would not own more than 49 percent of shares.[28]

In the meantime, Thai Peroxygen Chemicals Ltd. was created in July 1987; a few months later its name was changed into Peroxythai Ltd. A site was leased at Map Ta Phut, south of Bangkok, where after the discovery of natural gas in the Gulf of Thailand in the early 1980s, the Thai government had taken the initiative to develop a petrochemical complex. Interox planned to construct a hydrogen peroxide plant with a capacity of ten thousand tons per year (calculated as the 100 percent pure substance) to serve growing markets in Thailand, Malaysia, and elsewhere, in textiles, tanning, paper recycling, and rubber. Between November 1987 and June 1988, Solvay and Laporte were able to find seven Thai partners and a company of Thai "nominees" informally controlled by Interox to acquire 11 percent of shares. As a result, directly and indirectly Interox controlled 60 percent of its new subsidiary in Thailand. In the autumn of 1988 construction of the plant began. Thai personnel were trained at the Interox plant at Warrington, United Kingdom, and Loutrel's assistant Michel Bonnefoy was appointed managing director. The plant started up almost on schedule, in April 1990. Solvay had realized its goal of becoming a producer in Asia.[29]

Parallel to the preparation and construction of the hydrogen peroxide plant, Solvay developed plans for the construction of PP and PVC plants in Thailand. When Loutrel visited the country in the summer of 1987, he heard that the Thai government had the intention to develop a second petrochemical complex, NPC 2, near Map Ta Phut. Van Halteren and Loutrel immediately laid down a claim to lease a piece of land in the new complex. Two months later, to speed up things at the BOI, Loutrel decided to use the plans for a new PVC plant that Solvay just had developed for Rosignano but that would not be built (see Chapter 21). In December 1987 Solvay submitted an ambitious plan that implied a total investment of US$330 million: first a PVC plant of 135,000 tons per year would be constructed; later, when the ethylene supply could be guaranteed, a VCM plant and an electrolysis unit would follow. Solvay received authorization in July 1988, again with the condition of searching for Thai partners, and with the obligation to sell 20 percent of shares to the public within five years after starting up.[30]

[28] ACS, MoE, 10 Mar. 1987, 17 Nov. 1987; "Peroxythai: une initiative Interox en Thailande," *Revue Solvay* (1989) (3): 6–8.
[29] ACS, MoB, 27 July 1987; ACS, MoE, 28 July 1987, 22 Sept. 1987, 17 Nov. 1987, 23 Feb. 1988, 15 Nov. 1988, 3 Feb. 1989, 15 May 1990, 24 July 1990; ACS-CR, Shareholders Agreement Peroxythai, 27 May 1988; "Thailande: Interox inaugure Peroxythaï," *Revue Solvay* (1990) (2): 25; Spitz (2003), 272–3; interview Jean-Marie Chandelle, 15 June 2011; personal communication by Claude Loutrel, 14 Sept. 2011.
[30] ACS, MoE, 8 Sept. 1987, 17 Nov. 1987, 29 Mar. 1988, 5 July 1988; ACS, 1001–26-1, letter C. Loutrel to Mr. Korn Dabbarandi, Deputy Minister of Industry, 1 Oct. 1987; ACS, MoB, 25 July 1988; "Vinythai: Étappe majeure de l'implantation de Solvay en Thaïlande," *Revue Solvay* (1989) (3): 9–10.

FIGURE 20.2. Daniel Janssen (middle) and H. E. Patrick Nothomb (ambassador of Belgium to Thailand, left) visiting the king of Thailand, Bhumibol Adulyadej, in 1989. (Daniel Janssen Archives.)

In the summer of 1988, on the occasion of Solvay's 125th anniversary, Daniel Janssen, Claude Loutrel, and Jean-Pierre Van Halteren made a "charm offensive" through East Asia, together with their spouses, during which they visited Thailand as well. Janssen spoke to Major General Chatichai, who had become prime minister in the meantime, and with other high officials. Together with Ambassador Nothomb, he also made a courtesy visit to King Bhumibol. Through visits like these and Loutrel's frequent presence, Solvay succeeded in building up a strong network of relations with Thai politicians and businesspeople. As a result, after it had found Thai partners, the company again received the promotion certificate and its many privileges in April 1989.[31]

For the PVC business Solvay created the company Vinythai Ltd. in 1988. A little later an agreement was reached with a Thai partner, the Charoen Pokphand Group, which had started in the agro-food business but later diversified into plastics. This time Solvay would own 49 percent of the shares of Vinythai, Charoen Pokphand would acquire 45 percent, and the remaining 6 percent would be divided among smaller Thai partners. Sergio Sardano, a chemical engineer who had been the commercial leader of Solvay Italy, was appointed managing director. When the construction of the plant started in 1990, eight Thai engineers from the University of Chulalongkorn were sent for a year to

[31] ACS, MoE, 6 Sept. 1988, 21 Apr. 1989; "Voyage du Comité Exécutif en Asia," *Revue Solvay* (1989) (1): 28–35.

Tavaux to learn about all aspects of PVC manufacture. Unfortunately, after their return several of them accepted better-paid jobs at plants of Solvay's competitors, but some stayed and helped get the plant on stream in 1992. For the housing of the personnel Vinythai created a *cité* (company town), as was usual at the old Solvay plants in Europe.[32]

During the first few years, the monomer VCM for the PVC plant was bought "at sea," that is, on the global VCM market. When the date of the start-up of the cracker of NCP 2, in 1995, was approaching, Solvay started planning electrolysis and VCM plants. In 1994 Solvay and Charoen Pokhand succeeded in obtaining a funding package of US$276 million from a consortium of five Thai banks and twelve international banks to extend the Map Ta Phut complex. To secure the supply of salt to the electrolysis unit, Vinythai integrated backward. It associated itself with two Thai companies that belonged to the Japanese Asahi Glass group and established the joint venture Pimai Salt Company Ltd. to exploit a saline at Pimai in Thailand. After the electrolysis and VCM plants had come on stream, in April 1996, Vinythai not only had guaranteed a cheaper supply of monomer to the PVC plant but also had become a producer of caustic soda, used in many industries. Soon it was decided to start construction phase 3, again led by Vincent De Cuyper, to extend the Map Ta Phut complex. In 2000 – after the serious Asian economic crisis of 1998 – production approached 175,000 tons per year. Within ten years Solvay certainly had succeeded in establishing itself robustly in Thailand.[33]

South Korea

When in April 1990 Solvay's first plant in Thailand came on stream, the company already had two running plants in Korea. Development of this "second industrial pole" of Solvay in Asia had taken place rapidly.[34]

On 22 October 1986 Daniel Janssen, Albert Rampelberg, and Jean-Jacques Van de Berg traveled to Hanover for a meeting with the *Vorstand* of Kali-Chemie. During that meeting it appeared that KC's important business in barium and strontium carbonates, in which it was the world leader, was losing ground. These salts were used in television screens and other electronic products, and the business was transferred increasingly to Asia, especially to South Korea, where Samsung-Corning was a large producer of such screens. Stimulated by the Executive Committee members, Cyril Van Lierde and his colleagues in the KC-*Vorstand* contacted the Korean firm and by June 1987 a major

---

[32] ACS, MoE, 6 Sept. 1988, 24 Jan. 1989, 21 Feb. 1989, 23 May 1989, 4 July 1989, 19 Dec. 1989, 29 May 1990; ACS-CR, Shareholders Agreement Vinythai, 14 Feb. 1989; " Eight Thai Engineers in Tavaux," *The Solvay Review* (1990) (1): 38–9; interview Daniel Janssen, 13 Nov. 2007; conversation with Jacques Tétu, Tavaux, 4 May 2011.

[33] ACS, MoE, 29 Aug. 1989, 24 Nov. 1995; PR, 5 Aug. 1994, "Solvay: Set Up of a Joint Venture and Investment for the Exploitation of Salt in Thailand"; D. Dussard, "Vinythai Opens Up its Share Capital," *Solvay Live* 23 (1) (Summer 1995): 20; J.-P. Pleska and G. Couppey, "Vinythai: Instilling a New Spirit, Step by Step," *Solvay Live* 63 (Spring–Summer 1999): 16; interview Claude Loutrel, 31 Jan. 2008.

[34] ACS, 1001–26-1, "Politique générale du groupe," 14 Mar. 1988; ACS, MoB, 25 July 1988.

contract with Samsung-Corning had been signed. The leaders of Kali-Chemie were not inclined to erect a plant in South-Korea. In their view, Samsung-Corning should be supplied by their two European barium and strontium carbonate plants at Bad Hönningen, Germany, and Massa, Italy. This view was in total contradiction to the new Asia policy of the Solvay leaders. A more global view was needed. Kali-Chemie thereupon renegotiated the matter with Samsung-Corning, and on 7 August 1987 an agreement was signed by Van Lierde and by Kun-Hee Lee, chairman of the board of the Samsung Group. Both companies would establish in South Korea a 50–50 joint venture for the production of barium and strontium carbonates, named Daehan Specialty Chemicals Co. Ltd. (DSC), which would construct a plant with a capacity of forty thousand tons of carbonates per year.[35]

After twelve Korean process engineers, superintendents, and other technicians were trained in 1989 at the Kali-Chemie plant at Bad Hönningen, the Daehan plant, at Onsan on the southeastern coast of South Korea, came on stream during the first months of 1990. Onsan was the third plant of Kali-Chemie for the production of barium and strontium carbonates and, as such, was part of a worldwide system of production planning and distribution. The decision to start producing in Korea obviously was a good one, because after initial troubles due to crisis in the electronic industry and extremely difficult cooperation of the Korean partners, the capacity was soon enlarged to seventy thousand tons per year. In 1999 Solvay succeeded in acquiring a 60 percent majority of shares, in line with its enhanced global strategy.[36]

Almost simultaneous to the negotiations between Kali-Chemie and Samsung-Corning, Albert Rampelberg was involved in the establishment of a plastics processing plant in South Korea. Early in 1987 Solvay was approached by Kasaï, a subsidiary of the Nissan group, to erect a joint venture in South Korea for the production of Wood-Stock, a composite from polypropylene and wood fibers, or sawdust, well suited for the production of molded parts of cars, such as dashboards, door panels, and rear shelves. Rampelberg was enthusiastic about the proposal. He also saw it as an opportunity to send Maximilian Hotter, who in 1984 had opened a sales office of Alkor in Singapore that later had been integrated into Solvay (SEA), to South Korea to establish a sales office in Seoul. Hotter would become known as "Mr. South Korea," and with his knowledge of plastics processing, he seemed to be the right person to help introduce Solvay's Wood-Stock to the expanding South Korean car industry. The sales office opened June 1987, but finding the right partner for Wood-Stock in Korea took some time. When by March 1988 a partner had been found, it was not Nissan but the Korea Plastics Industry Corp. (KPIC), a subsidiary of the Korea Explosives Group. The 50–50 joint venture, named

[35] ACS, MoE, 2 Sept. 1986, 4 Nov. 1986, 5 Apr. 1987, 28 July 1987; ACS, MoB, 19 Mar. 1987, 23 Nov. 1987, 25 July 1988; "A giant step into the Far East. Kali-Chemie in the land of the morning calm," *The Solvay Revue* (1988) (1): 20–5.
[36] ACS, 1805-37, Advisory Committee Solvay/Kali-Chemie Coordination, 2 Feb. 1989, 30 Oct. 1989, 4 May 1990, 5 Dec. 1990; ACS, MoE, 28 June 1994, 28 Feb. 1997, 27 July 1999; PR, 16 Sept. 1999, "Recent strategic developments of Solvay in Asia."

Hanyang Polymer Co. Ltd., started producing a few months later. Within a year the plant had to be enlarged. After the Korea Explosives Group in 1993 had changed its name to Hanwha Corporation, the name of Hanyang Polymer was changed to Hanwha Advanced Materials.[37]

When Daniel Janssen, Claude Loutrel, and Jean-Pierre Van Halteren visited Korea in the summer of 1988 as part of the Asian charm offensive, they met, among others, N. G. Sung, vice chairman of the Korea Explosives Group, and they were invited for a visit to their home by Mr. and Mrs. K. H. Lee, chairman of Samsung. Also in the case of Korea the Solvay network in Asia started to take shape. The development of a large second industrial center, next to Thailand, stayed a bit behind expectations, though. Serious plans in 1988–1989 to create a joint venture with Samsung for the production of HDPE and PP did not materialize, nor did other projects that Solvay would have liked to develop together with Samsung (e.g., epichlorohydrin).[38]

Japan, India, and China

When Solvay asked for the advice of Robert Descourt at the start of its Asia policy, Japan was deliberately left out. There were already several contacts with Japanese firms, mainly on technological issues concerning polymers. These contacts with Japan had been maintained by Jacques Viriot, and when he left the Executive Committee in 1984 they became the domain of Jean-Jacques Van de Berg. After a visit to Japan together with Viriot, from 9 to 14 December 1984, Van de Berg argued in the Executive Committee that the relations between Solvay and Japan should be intensified, by appointing a liaison officer in Japan as well as a coordinator at Brussels for new activities in Japan.[39]

During the following years, Van de Berg would travel many times to Japan, where, helped by Marubeni, he built quite a network of contacts with Japanese chemical firms. The good reputation of Solvay's highly active PP catalyst opened many doors. Initially, these Asian activities led to some friction with Claude Loutrel when Van de Berg suggested that Loutrel, Van Halteren, and Mortier limit their activities strictly to Southeast Asia and not include Japan, India, and China, thereby implying that this would be his domain. The issue was soon settled, but for a while Japan was handled quite separately from the rest of the Asia policy of Solvay. In 1985 Van de Berg gave the head of the license department at Brussels, R. Eischen, the task of monitoring Japanese technological developments and coordinating contacts between Solvay and Japanese firms.

[37] ACS, 1001–26-1, "Asie – Politique des produits Tr," 20 Feb. 1987; id., "Note pour Monsieur Rampelberg – Mission en Corée du Sud," 14 Apr. 1987; ACS, MoE, 6 Jan. 1987, 8 Jan. 1988, 24 Jan. 1989, 20 June 1989; ACS, MoB, 25 July 1988; PR, 1 Mar. 1988, "The Solvay Group to form another joint venture in South Korea."

[38] ACS, MoE, 1 Mar. 1988, 21 Feb. 1989, 21 Apr. 1989, 29 Aug. 1989; ACS, 1001–26-1, fax M. Hotter to J. P. Van Halteren, 20 May 1988; ACS, MoB, 25 July 1988; "Voyage du Comité Exécutif en Asia," *Revue Solvay* (1989) (1): 30–3; ACS, 1805–37, Advisory Committee Solvay/Kali-Chemie Coordination, 2 Feb. 1989, 30 Oct. 1989, 22 Jan. 1990.

[39] ACS, 1001–26-1, letter Bonnefoy to Mr. Descours, 28 Feb. 1984; id., letter R. Descours to Loutrel, 21 Sept. 1984; ACS, MoE, 19 Dec. 1984.

A Japanese subsidiary was created, Solvay Development (Japan) Ltd., which would be a bridgehead in Tokyo with respect to technology transfer and licensing. From about 1987 Jean-Pierre Golstein was appointed head of that firm, and he became the liaison officer and technical interface between Solvay and its Japanese partners. Together, Eischen, Golstein, and Van de Berg were able to establish useful contacts with Japanese chemical firms, mainly in the field of technopolymers, but also in ceramics and the new membrane technology for electrolysis that had been developed by Asahi. Solvay took out licenses and introduced several special polymers to the European market: Ixef and Nyref (aromatic polyamides), licensed by Mitsubishi Gas Co.; PPS (polyphenylen sulfide), licensed by Tohpren; and Primef and some other materials (see Chapter 21).[40]

In addition to technology transfer, Solvay's policy with respect to Japan rested on two pillars: pharmacy and trade. In pharmaceuticals and related products Duphar was already importing in Japan since 1954. Kali-Chemie followed in 1967. After the acquisition of Duphar by Solvay, the Japanese activities of Duphar and Kali-Chemie were united from 1 July 1981 within Kali-Duphar KK, headed by Duphar's longtime agent in Japan, Shogo Shibuya. Kali-Duphar was trading many different products, but it was not well suited to introduce completely new pharmaceuticals, such as fluvoxamine (Luvox), to the Japanese market and to take care of the registration procedure. Therefore, Solvay decided to establish the joint venture Solvay-Meiji Yakuhin KK in 1989, together with Meiji Seika Kaisha Ltd., a large company in foodstuffs and pharmaceuticals. Four years later, Solvay intensified its presence in the Japanese pharmaceutical market by the acquisition of Kowa Yakuhin Kogyo. It changed the name of that pharmaceutical company to Solvay Seiyaku KK. With this Solvay also had its own production facilities in this second-largest pharmaceutical market. In 1999 Jürgen Ernst, then head of Solvay's pharmaceutical sector, integrated the activities of Solvay-Meiji Yakuhin into Solvay Seiyaku.[41]

Supported by Daniel Janssen, Loutrel and Van Halteren decided in the second part of 1986 that the time had come to extend the commercial activities of the Singapore office to South Korea and Japan. On 1 July 1987 Nippon Solvay KK was created in Tokyo for the sales of basic chemicals, plastics, and other Solvay products on the Japanese market. It was headed by Shibuya, who combined this new position with the management of Kali-Duphar. Nippon Solvay was not responsible, though, for the growing supplies of KC's barium and strontium carbonates to Japanese producers of television screens

[40] ACS, 1001-26-1, "Développement au Japon," 15 Jan. 1985; id., "Politique générale du groupe," 1 Apr. 1985; id., letter J.-J. van de Berg to J. Mortier, 28 Feb. 1986; id., "Note de dossier – Territoires et produits de la compétence de la mission Solvay dans le sud-est asiatique," 17 Mar. 1986; id., "Technolopolymeres – Asie," meeting 8 Oct. 1986; ACS, MoE, 22 Jan. 1985, 2 July 1985, 17 June 1986, 7 Nov. 1989; ACS, MoB, 23 Sept. 1985, 27 July 1987; J. J. Durré, "The Specialist in the Japanese Market," Solvay Review (Jan. 1991): 24; interview Aloïs Michielsen, 21 Apr. 2011; personal communication by Claude Loutrel, 14 Sept. 2011.

[41] ACS, 1001-26-1, "Implantation du Groupe en Asia," Sept. 1986; id., "Politique générale du groupe," 17 Mar. 1987; ACS, MoE, 15 Dec. 1987, 6 Dec. 1988, 23 Oct. 1992, 23 Dec. 1993, 31 Aug. 1999; ACS, MoB, 25 July 1988; interview Claude Loutrel, 31 Jan. 2008.

and electronic components. Kali-Chemie had granted the import and distribution of those products to a Japanese merchant firm. From the viewpoint of the Solvay top management that wanted to integrate Kali-Chemie fully into Solvay (see Section 20.4), that situation certainly was an anomaly. Moreover, the cash flow generated by the sales of barium and strontium carbonates was of great importance to Nippon Solvay. Therefore, in 1990 a delicate operation started to transfer the import and distribution of barium and strontium derivatives to Nippon Solvay. It would take three years before all activities were fully transferred.[42]

When Jacques Solvay in 1990 characterized the move of his company to Asia, he left no doubts about Solvay's major loci of activity: Thailand, Korea, and Japan, and in that order. Commercially, Solvay was present in many other Asian countries, though, and in some industrially as well. Between 1986 and 1988 Solvay negotiated, for instance, with Indian partners to establish plants for the production of poultry vaccines and polypropylene. Albert Rampelberg took the lead in the first area, and Jean-Jacques Van de Berg in the second. On 31 August 1987 Van de Berg signed a contract with Kanoria Chemicals to create the joint venture Polypropylene India Ltd. that would construct a PP plant with capacity of thirty thousand tons per year not far from Delhi. Start-up was scheduled for 1990, but in 1991 it still had not happened. In April 1988 Rampelberg also announced the creation of Solvay B.E. Animal Health Ltd. in Hyderabad, a joint venture between Solvay (40 percent) and Biological E. Ltd. (60 percent), a producer of human vaccines and other pharmaceutical and biological products owned by the Raja family, which for many years had been a partner in the Indian subsidiary of Duphar. The joint venture was divested when Solvay sold all its animal health activities in 1996.[43]

If doing business in Asia was difficult sometimes, this was a fortiori the case in China. After Deng Xiaoping had initiated China's "policy of opening to the world," between 1980 and 1984 several special economic zones were established in towns such as Shenzhen and Zhuhai. Many European and American firms held great expectations concerning these developments, but they soon discovered that it was extremely difficult to start joint ventures in which Western partners could exercise control. When Van Halteren and Mortier visited Zhuhai in early 1985, they concluded that the possibilities were enormous but that negotiations would take a very long time. Solvay decided to take no concrete industrial initiatives but to invest in long-term

---

[42] ACS, MoE, 2 Sept. 1986, 30 June 1987, 15 May 1990; "A giant step into the Far East. Kali-Chemie in the land of the morning calm," *The Solvay Revue* (1988) (1): 20–5; "Voyage du Comité Exécutif en Asia," *Revue Solvay* (1989) (1): 28–9; ACS, 1805–37, Advisory Committee Solvay/Kali-Chemie Coordination, 30 Oct. 1989, 4 May 1990, 5 Dec. 1990; personal communication by Daniel Janssen, 1 Sept. 2011.

[43] ACS, MoE, 1 July 1986, 6 Jan. 1987, 28 July 1987, 19 Jan. 1988, 6 Sept. 1988, 27 Aug. 1991, 29 Aug. 1995; ACS, MoB, 26 Jan. 1987, 25 July 1988; PR, 31 Aug. 1988, "Solvay enters into partnership for polypropylene production in India"; PR, 15 Apr. 1988, "The Solvay Group and Biological E. Ltd. Set up a joint venture in India in the animal health sector"; "Solvay in the Asia-Pacific: full of eastern promise," *Solvay Life* (Summer 1997): 4–5.

relations with China, by supplying products and giving technical aid. Large amounts of caustic soda and, later, barium and strontium carbonates were exported to China. Also, the company received numerous Chinese requests to grant licenses on several important Solvay technologies, mostly soda ash. Early in 1987, a Chinese delegation of the Dalian Chemical Industrial Corporation visited four Solvay plants in Europe, as well as the research laboratories at NoH, but without immediate results. Solvay's main negotiator regarding soda ash technology, Claude Boulvin, learned Chinese to do a better job. He succeeded in establishing agreements in 1988 and 1989 to provide technical support to three Chinese soda ash plants, in Dalian, Canton, and Jilantai. During the 1990s, Boulvin continued providing technical assistance to the Chinese soda ash industry in cooperation with the Belgian-Chinese trading firm of Henri Lederhandler, until Solvay's soda ash department in 1997 concluded that all help to the Chinese soda ash industry should be stopped immediately. Making Chinese soda ash producers more competitive had pushed the American companies partly from the Asian market, and as a result, they had turned their stern to Europe, where they were spoiling Solvay's own soda ash business.[44]

Apart from Boulvin's activities and some investigations, together with Charoen Pokphand, on constructing a PVC plant in China, not much took place until the Executive Committee decided in the mid-1990s to intensify the company's growth in Asia, in China in particular. Solvay Biosciences (China) Ltd. was successfully created in 1994 for the sales of veterinary products. In October 1995 Solvay finally succeeded in establishing its first joint venture in China: the Changzhou Wood-Stock Ltd. Co., together with the China Automotive International Corporation and the Changzhou General Plastic Plating Factory. When in 1997 Hong Kong became part of China, Solvay moved its trading office, headed by W. Lalande, to Beijing, and after the Asian crisis of 1998, Solvay created new Chinese subsidiaries with increased speed. In 1999 alone, three new agreements were concluded on joint ventures in PVC blends and compounds, in pipes and fittings, and in barium and strontium carbonates. Although these activities were still modest, Solvay certainly had gained momentum in China at the start of the twenty-first century.[45]

---

[44] ACS, 1010–10, report by Mr. Vinçotte, 12 May 1980; Jacques Solvay, "Discours de fin d'année," insert in *Revue Solvay* (1983) (3); ACS, 1001–26-1, letter M. Bonnefoy to X. A. Descours, 7 June; id., "Mission Est/Sud-Est asiatique. Resumé et conclusions"; id., "Note pour le Comité Exécutif – Vente de technologie soudière à la Chine." 30 May 1988; ACS, MoB, 1 July 1985; ACS, MoE, 7 Jan. 1986, 2 June 1987, 26 July 1988, 29 Jan. 1997; "Solvay dans le Far East," *Revue Solvay* (1986) (1): 18–21; "Visite d'une délégation Chinoise," *Revue Solvay* (1987) (1): 24; interview Olivier Monfort, 21 Apr. 2011.

[45] ACS, 1001–26-1, "PVC – Voyage en Chine, du 26.02.89 au 08.03.89," 9 Mar. 1989; ACS, MoE, 18 Apr. 1990, 24 July 1990, 27 Apr. 1994, 9 Mar. 1995, 24 Nov. 1995, 22 Dec. 1995, 14 May 1996, 12 Jan. 1999, 27 July 1999, 24 Nov. 1999; PR, 27 Oct. 1995, "Solvay and the rapidly developing Chinese Automotive Industry: a new joint venture"; "Tiger gets the flu, but Solvay just sneezes," *Solvay Live* (Summer 1998): 14; W. Lalande, "Solvay in China," *Solvay Live* (Winter 1998–1999): 11.

The Cumulative Effect of National Activities

When Solvay started its Asia policy in 1984, total sales in Asia were about US$80 million, a mere 2 percent of total sales. Intensifying Solvay's presence in the region by establishing sales offices in Singapore, Seoul, and Tokyo had immediate results. In 1988 total sales almost tripled to US$220 million, about 4 percent of total sales. During the following years several plants came on stream, but the effect on total sales was at first only modest. In 1990, the share of Asia in Solvay's total sales had fallen again to less than 3 percent because of several factors, including China's decision to stop all imports of (heavy) chemicals, the lack of supplies from Solvay plants in Europe due to great demand at home, the crisis in the electronics industries, and the falling exchange rate of the dollar. In 1994–1995 sales had grown to about US$350 million to US$400 million, then about 5 percent of the total sales.[46]

Halfway through the 1990s, Solvay was present in nine countries in the Asia-Pacific region, with twenty-four subsidiaries. Nevertheless, the Executive Committee concluded that reinforced investments in Asia were needed to improve the geographical spread of the company. Daniel Janssen, chairman of the Executive Committee, formulated the ambition to double Asia's share of total sales in ten years' time. Then, in the late summer of 1997, suddenly the Asia crisis broke out. Sales stagnated, and Asia's share of Solvay sales dropped again. Thereafter, the share of the Asia sales in the total sales started to climb, partly as a result of the selling of Solvay's polyolefins business to BP, that impacted mainly the other regions (see Chapter 22). In 2005 the target of 10 percent was not reached, but progress had been made, which was continued during the years 2005 to 2009, when the share of Asia climbed to 9–10 percent. The selling of the pharmaceutical activities to Abbott, early in 2010 (see Chapter 22), had a dramatic effect on geographical diversification of the company. With a 14 percent share in 2010, Asia had become an important part of the business.[47]

20.4 REORGANIZING SOLVAY GERMANY AND GOING EAST

When the Liaison Committee in November 1982 advised simplifying the international legal structures and merging subsidiaries into larger national entities, the situation in Germany certainly was the most striking example of how things could go wrong. In that country, Solvay had two subsidiaries of almost equal size: one, DSW, was a national stronghold in the field of basic chemicals and plastics, and the other, Kali-Chemie, was a highly diversified multinational, largely owned by DSW but not effectively controlled by it. As a result, there

---

[46] ACS, MoE, 2 Sept. 1986; 24 Nov. 1995; Daniel Janssen, "Discours de fin d'année," insert in *Revue Solvay* (1987) (1): 1–5; ACS, MoB, 25 July 1988; ACS, 1001-26-1, "Asie – Vente des Produits Chimiques et Plastiques – Stratégie et Procédures," 21 June 1990.

[47] "Rencontre avec: Le Président de Solvay: Les modes manageriales passent, l'ethique reste," *Usine Nouvelle* (10 Oct. 1996); "Solvay in the Asia-Pacific: Full of eastern promise," *Solvay Life* (Summer 1997): 4–5; ARS 1987–2010.

were two large central administrations in Germany, in Solingen and Hanover, respectively, with their own legal, technical, environmental, personnel, and sales departments. This was, of course, highly inefficient. In 1978 it was estimated that in case of a merger probably 100 to 150 staff members could be lost by the elimination of duplication. When a little later the economic circumstances got worse, these inefficiencies became a growing nuisance. It is therefore no surprise that in a presentation on long-term developments, Georges Vanden Berghen, head of corporate planning, in 1980 spoke of "the problem of Germany": the high costs of a dual organization, the lack of control and coordination, and the insufficient payments by the German subsidiaries to the Central Administration in Brussels.[48]

Ever since on 1 January 1966 a new German law on joint stock companies had come into force that gave more freedom to the executive boards of subsidiaries that were not completely owned, Solvay tried to increase its control over Kali-Chemie. The law of 1966 defined an instrument for that purpose, the so-called Control Agreement (*Beherrschungsvertrag*), that could be closed between the parent company and the subsidiary under some strict conditions: 75 percent of the votes at a general assembly should agree with it; the parent company should do a public offer on the remaining shares; and for the minority shareholders who did not want to accept the public offer, a handsome dividend should annually be guaranteed. During the following years, the issue was considered time and again, but no acceptable solution could be found.[49]

A new situation emerged when after the Ronnenberg disaster, DSW succeeded in acquiring more than 78 percent of the shares of Kali-Chemie (see Chapter 19). Solvay (via DSW) was in a position to push a control agreement through the general assembly. Moreover, the need for improved coordination had only grown, in pharmacy and biotechnology especially. More frequent meetings between the leaders of Kali-Chemie and the Executive Committee were organized, but again Solvay's German confidants – Hilmar Kopper of Deutsche Bank and the lawyer Harro Gurland – advised not going one step further by enforcing a control agreement. Moreover, with Solvay in 1981 in deep crisis, it would have been too costly to buy the minority shareholders out. Kopper then got the brilliant idea to avoid painful legislation and lack of motivation among KC personnel by establishing a personal union between the executive boards of DSW and KC. At the end of 1981 Heinz Blessmann, member of the *Geschäftsführung* of DSW, was also appointed member of the *Vorstand* of KC; Günther Wehrmeyer, member of the KC *Vorstand*, was also appointed *Geschäftsführer* of DSW; and Herman Geuens, general manager of Duphar, was also appointed member of the KC *Vorstand*, so that the

[48] ACS, 1805-37-34, "La Kali-Chemie: Réflections sur sa position au sein du groupe Solvay"; ACS, 1001-26-1, "Problèmes à long terme," 4 Feb. 1980.
[49] ACS, 1805-37-2, "Contrat d'entreprise éventuelle entre D.S.W. et Kali-Chemie," 26 Nov. 1965; ACS, 1805-37-34, letter Albert Rampelberg to Solvay & Cie, 3 Oct. 1966; id., "Note pour M. Swolfs. Fusion éventuelle DSW-KC," 28 Oct. 1976; id., "Note pour M. Swolfs," 8 Nov. 1976; ACS, MoE, 30 July 1974.

coordination between Duphar and Kali-Chemie in the field of pharmaceuticals was improved as well. A few months later, Cyril Van Lierde, chairman (*Vorstandssprecher*) of Kali-Chemie, also became chairman of DSW.[50]

During the following years, Van Lierde and his collaborators gradually tried to intensify the dialogue between DSW and KC, to improve the psychological climate, and to strengthen the feeling among the personnel of DSW and KC of belonging to one group. On 1 April 1984 the sales departments of both companies in the field of soda ash were united at Solingen. Three years later, this culminated in the acquisition by DSW of KC's soda ash plant at Heilbronn.[51]

In this way the cooperation between the two German companies improved, but collaboration between Kali-Chemie and Brussels still left much to be desired. Outside the fields of peroxides, soda ash, and pharmacy, KC was running numerous businesses without much involvement of the Solvay headquarters: catalysts, fluorine compounds, barium and strontium carbonates, and several biological products. When Daniel Janssen became chairman of the Executive Committee in June 1986, ending that situation certainly was one of his priorities. The quasi autonomy of Kali-Chemie inevitably gave rise to frictions on both sides, for instance regarding the investments in production facilities for barium and strontium carbonates in Korea, or KC's divestment of its pharmaceutical subsidiary in Mexico without the consent of the Executive Committee. People at KC, in turn, were not happy with the transfer of the Heilbronn plant to DSW.[52]

Very discreetly and with the help of Deutsche Bank, Solvay started gradually buying shares of Kali-Chemie on the stock market. At the same time the department Alkalis, Chlorine, and Derivatives (Produits Alcalis et Derivés, PrAD) started to involve itself with the managerial coordination of the non-Solvay products of Kali-Chemie (Produits Kali-Chemie, PrKC), with the exception of the biological products, which were coordinated by the Animal Health Department (Departement Santé Animale, DSA) of Solvay. From early 1988 the Advisory Committee for the Solvay/Kali-Chemie Coordination started to meet

[50] ACS, 1805-37-34, "La Kali-Chemie: Réflexions sur sa position au sein du groupe Solvay," 9 May 1978; id., "Kali-Chemie. Points essentiels pour une prise de contrôle," 1978; id., "Propositions pour une définition du domaine d'activité a choisir pour le développement de Kali-Chemie," 19 Oct. 1978; id., "Kali-Chemie," meeting 24 Oct. 1978; ACS, MoE, 1 July 1980, 28 July 1981, 28 June 1982; AHR, PD Geuens, "DSW – KC – Nomination," 14 Sept. 1981; ACS, MoB, 28 Sept. 1981; "Une meilleure collaboration entre les DSW et la Kali-Chemie." *Revue Solvay*, (1982) (1): 4–5; ACS, 1020–10, meeting Executive Committee with Mr. Van Lierde," 29 June 1982.

[51] ACS, 1020–10, meeting Executive Committee with Mr. Van Lierde, 14 Dec. 1982; id., meeting, 18 Oct. 1983; ACS, 1805–37-4, "Engineering à la Kali-Chemie et coopération avec les DSW," Oct. 1984; ACS, MoE, 5 Feb. 1985, 30 July 1985, 2 Sept. 1986, 5 May 1987; "La chimie à une longue tradition en Allemagne," *Revue Solvay* (1985) (2): 1–17; ACS, 1805–37-34, letter Cyril Van Lierde to Solvay & Cie, 8 Aug. 1986; PR, 14 Apr. 1987, "The Solvay-Group: regrouping the sodium carbonate-activities in Germany."

[52] ACS, 1805-37-4, "Zusammenfassende Darstellung des Rechtsgutachtens von Herrn Dr. Gurland"; id., letter Cyril Van Lierde to Solvay & Cie, SG, 8 Aug. 1986; ACS, MoE, 2 Sept. 1986, 27 Apr. 1987, 19 May 1987, 2 June 1987; interview Daniel Janssen, 13 Nov. 2007; interview Cyril Van Lierde, 13 Oct. 2008.

about four times a year, with three Solvay members (Loutrel; Jean Christiaens, head of PrAD; and Alfred Hoffait, head of DSA) and three representatives of Kali-Chemie (Van Lierde, Günther Tilk, and Günther Wehrmeyer – all members of the *Vorstand*). After having been majority shareholder of Kali-Chemie for more than thirty years, Solvay finally started to really involve itself in the miscellaneous products of KC, thereby pushing hard to enhance its global presence. The committee functioned until the end of 1990, when Kali-Chemie was fully integrated into the Solvay Group.[53]

The Creation of Solvay Deutschland

During the end of 1988 and the first part of 1989, Hilmar Kopper and Daniel Janssen made a plan for the restructuring of Solvay's German operations. The idea was to create the holding company Solvay Deutschland GmbH, to which Solvay would transfer all its shares of DSW, and that would conclude a *Beherrschungsvertrag* with Kali-Chemie. That finally, after twenty-five years, that crucial step was made, was certainly helped by the fact that Solvay had acquired in the meantime 89.7 percent of the share capital of KC. Doing a public offer on the remaining shares was feasible. The *Vorstand* of Kali-Chemie agreed with the conclusion of a control agreement, and on 17 November 1989 the establishment of Solvay Deutschland, operational as of 1 January 1990, was publicly announced, as was a cash offer to the minority shareholders of KC. In January 1990 an extraordinary general assembly of KC accepted the control agreement, with only 0.3 percent of the votes against the proposal. A number of minority shareholders went to court, though. Litigation started that lasted until 1999, when Solvay offered a settlement.[54]

An ingenious financial arrangement was a crucial part of Operation Solvay Deutschland. For BEF 53 billion (about DM 2.5 billion) Solvay sold all its parts in DSW to Solvay Deutschland. About 41 percent of those parts had been held by the Mutuelle Solvay, which was liquidated for that occasion, to reduce the fiscal effects of the operation in Belgium. In its turn, Solvay Deutschland – which had received a loan of DM 1.6 billion from a consortium led by Deutsche Bank – transferred DM 1.7 billion in cash to Solvay. On the level of the consolidated results of the Solvay Group, almost nothing happened, but the practical effects of the operation on the balance sheet and the cash movements were large. After

[53] ACS, 1001-26-1, "Politique générale du groupe," 26 Mar. 1986; ACS, MoE, 21 Oct. 1986, 6 Oct. 1987, 9 Nov. 1987, 15 Dec. 1987; ACS, MoB, 23 Nov. 1987, 25 Jan. 1988; ACS, 1805-37, "Gestion de PrKC – Création d'un Comité consultative de coordination Solvay/Kali-Chemie," 11 Dec. 1987; id., letter Daniel Janssen to Cyril Van Lierde, 18 Dec. 1987; interview Daniel Janssen, 13 Nov. 2007.

[54] ACS, MoE, 21 Feb. 1989, 12 Sept. 1989, 9 Jan. 1990, 3 Dec. 1991; ACS, 1805–37-1, letter Vorstand Kali-Chemie to Solvay & Cie, 14 Nov. 1989; PR, 17 Nov. 1989, "Solvay & Cie establishes Solvay Deutschland to regroup its interests in the Federal Republic of Germany (FRG)"; ACS, 1805-40-24, "Note pour monsieur Friesewinkel – L'impact de la cession de filiales Kali-Chemie (ou certaines de leurs activités) sur les procédures entamées contre Kali-Chemie par certain de ses actionnaires minoritaires"; ACS, 1805–49-2, Aufsichtsrat of Kali-Chemie AG, 25 June 1999; interview Daniel Janssen, 13 Nov. 2007.

many years of getting often too little money out of the German operations, Solvay could suddenly cash in its German assets, thereby doubling its equity from BEF 55 billion to BEF 111 billion (US$3 billion). On the German side there were large fiscal effects. In 1990 it was estimated that Solvay Deutschland would get a tax reduction of DM 30 million each year.[55]

When the preparations for Operation Solvay Deutschland were in full swing, the Berlin Wall fell on 9 November 1989. Soon it appeared that the costs of an eventual German unification would be gigantic. Interest rates started to climb. Naturally, the financial burdens of Solvay Deutschland grew as well. Aggravated by a general economic stagnation in Germany, which in 1993 also hit the Solvay Group hard (see Chapter 21), Solvay Deutschland had several years of losses. This would last until the summer of 1996, before a solution was found when Solvay succeeded in renegotiating the conditions of the loans with the Deutsche Bank and its consortium.[56]

During these years, another delicate operation had to be executed: the actual integration of the DSW and KC organizations. It was clear that much efficiency could be gained by merging the two central administrations. But the overall organization of both companies was so completely different that also on the level of the production plants and sales organizations, a totally new start was needed. DSW had a Solvay culture, with large plants run by engineers, within a matrix framework, whereas KC was run by chemists in charge of smaller-scale units, along the traditional German model of top-down product divisions. Shortly before the creation of Solvay Deutschland, strategic business units (SBUs) had been introduced at Solvay's German plastics subsidiary Alkor, which had split its business into industrial foils (Alkor Kunststoffe) and consumer products (Alkor Markenhandel). The managers of these departments received full responsibility over production, marketing, sales, and research. The first experiences with this new form of organization were positive. Michielsen, then head of Solvay's processing sector, became an ardent defender of the SBU concept and introduced it later at Solvay (see Chapter 21).[57]

In the course of 1990 the Executive Committee, together with leading executives of Solvay Deutschland and advised by Arthur D. Little, designed an organizational structure in which all the operational activities of DSW and KC

[55] ACS, 1284-40-2, letter Jacques Lévy-Morelle to Executive Committee, 29 Nov. 1989; ACS, MoE, 5 Dec. 1989, 9 Jan. 1990; "Solvay Deutschland regroups all Solvay's activities in the Federal Republic of Germany (FRG)," *Solvay Review*, (1990) (1): 32–3; PR, 21 June 1991, "An agreement has been entered into by the Belgian state and Solvay S.A. regarding the refund to Solvay of BEF 5.7 billion"; *Mutuelle* (2000), 13–14; interview Daniel Janssen, 13 Nov. 2007.

[56] ACS, 1284-37-1, minutes meeting Solingen, 6 Nov.1990; ACS, 1284-40-2, "Gesell-schafter beschluss der Solvay Deutschland, Solingen," 20 Jan. 1992; ACS, MoE, 3 Nov. 1992; PR, 2 Mar. 1993, "Kapitalerhöhung bei Solvay Deutschland"; PR, 29 Aug. 1996, "Solvay Group: project to substitute some existing borrowings"; interview Daniel Janssen, 13 Nov. 2007.

[57] "A reshuffled national management," *Solvay Live* (Summer 1993): 4–7; ACS, 1284-37-1, letter Dr. Bernd Jürgen Tesche to Aloïs Michielsen, 4 Nov. 1993; interview Alois Michielsen, 16 Apr. 2008, 21 Apr. 2011; interview Claude Thibaut de Maisières and Michel Bande, 2 May 2011; interview Georges Theys and Michel Bande, 6 June 2011.

were transferred to Solvay Deutschland starting 1 January 1991 and brought under fourteen, and later fifteen, "product companies," or business units, following the Alkor example, and then progressively integrated into the Brussels-based Solvay sectors. At the request of the Executive Committee, most product companies had the word *Solvay* in their name. Some, such as Solvay Alkali GmbH, Solvay Salz GmbH, and Solvay Kunststoffe GmbH, were the continuation of previous DSW activities, but most product companies had their roots inside Kali-Chemie. The new organization aimed to bring Solvay closer to the customers, and to change the perception of Solvay to that of a more dynamic company. Managers of the product companies were made fully responsible for their business, both in Germany and abroad.[58]

Parallel to these reorganizations in the field of production and sales, the central services were also reorganized. Some members of the Executive Committee seem first to have been in favor of concentrating all services at the DSW central office at Solingen, which had been constructed in the mid-1970s, but the new top managers of Solvay Deutschland (Henri Lefèbvre and Bernd Tesche), supported by the consulting firm of A. D. Little, were able to convince Janssen and Michielsen that Hanover was better placed and had a lower risk that many valuable staff members would leave the company. Moreover, after the fall of the Iron Curtain, Hanover had a central position in unified Germany and was close to Bernburg and Berlin. As a result, the central services were mainly concentrated in Hanover. As part of the operation, administrative personnel were reduced by about one hundred. During the following two years, a further reduction of two hundred staff members would be achieved.[59]

Retrieving Bernburg

Bernburg had been one of the largest soda ash plants of the Solvay Group. After World War II, the works encountered the unhappy fate of being situated in the Russian-occupied zone. The soda ask works were demolished and later reerected as VEB Sodawerke "Karl Marx" (see Chapter 13). After a merger with the nearby soda ash plant at Stassfurt, in 1965, the company was renamed VEB Vereinigte Sodawerke "Karl Marx" Bernburg-Stassfurt. Under that name it survived in East Germany. When the Berlin Wall fell, the works were a large plant with a production capacity of more than five hundred thousand tons per year and almost 1,800 employees.[60]

---

[58] ACS, MoE, 6 Feb. 1990, 9 Oct. 1990, 20 Nov. 1990, 26 Mar. 1991; [ACS, 1284–37-1, minutes meeting Solingen, 6 Nov. 1990; "Réorganisation de nos activités allemandes," *Solvay Flash* (19 Dec. 1990); ACS, 1284–37-1, Extraordinary General Assembly of Kali-Chemie, 28 Dec. 1990; "Reorganization of Solvay's German activities," *Solvay Review* (Jan. 1991): 25; "Report on Germany," *Solvay Live* (Summer 1993): 1–25.

[59] ACS, 1284–37-1, Van Lierde and Lefèbvre, "Organisation des serves administratives de Solvay Deutschland déménagement à Hanovre," 15 Oct. 1990; ACS, MoE, 20 Nov. 1990; ACS, 1282–40, "Note pour le Comité Exécutif," 17 Feb. 1993; id., "Étude Roland Berger sur optimization de certain services centraux de Solvay Deutschland GmbH," 4 Oct. 1993; "A reshuffled national management," *Solvay Live* (Summer 1993): 4–7.

[60] ADSW, 110, Gedanken am 13. Oktober 1962; id., Argumentationsmaterial zur Entwicklung des VEB Vereinigte Sodawerke "Karl Marx" Bernburg-Stassfurt anlässlich der Parteiwahlen 1988; [Autorenkollektiv] (1983); [Kemper and Lorenz] (2008), 34–47.

Contrary to the situation with respect to Hungary, Czechoslovakia, Poland, and other Eastern European countries, the German Democratic Republic never had paid any compensation to Solvay after the war. Solvay, assisted by the Belgian government, had negotiated several times with the East German authorities but unsuccessfully. Shortly after the notorious day of 9 November 1989, Solvay therefore again put forward a claim that all its former properties in East Germany should be returned to the company.[61]

The first priority was to retrieve Bernburg. Daniel Janssen took the political lead and appointed Pierre De Bruecker, head of the Corporate Planning Department, to coordinate the negotiations. Formal negotiations were started with the East German authorities and later with the so-called Treuhandanstalt, created 1 March 1990. Discrete and direct contacts were established with the manager of the Bernburg plant, Walter Thiele, and his colleagues. In April 1990 a Solvay delegation visited Bernburg. On the basis of those contacts, the employees at Bernburg decided to lift the Bernburg plant out of the *Kombinat* with Stassfurt and to continue as a separate legal entity, which after German reunification on 3 October 1990 was formalized as Sodafabrik Bernburg GmbH. In the meantime negotiations between the Belgian and German governments, as well as between Solvay and the Treuhandanstalt, were difficult and tardy. Solvay insisted that the plant be returned to Solvay without payment, and that the plant would be profitable again in 1991. In practice, that meant that the personnel numbers would be reduced greatly before Solvay would take over the plant. Already during 1990 Thiele was able to reduce the work force to 1,200 heads. But Solvay argued that a plant of similar size managed by Solvay would run with 400 to 500 people.[62]

Early in 1991 Solvay reached a verbal agreement in Berlin with Detlev Rohwedder, president of the Treuhandanstalt, but on 1 April of that year he was assassinated by members of the Red Army Faction terror group. The Treuhandanstalt kept its promise, though, and in the summer of 1991 a final agreement was concluded. Solvay would get the plant back on 1 September 1991, without payment, but it promised to invest at least DM 200 million during the following five years in the modernization of the soda ash plant and in the erection of a large hydrogen peroxide plant with a capacity of fifty thousand tons per year. These investments guaranteed employment in the Bernburg region; but the work force of 950 people was reduced to fewer than 600 within a few years.[63]

Well before the takeover of the Bernburg plant, the product companies of Solvay Deutschland had started to become commercially active in the territory of former East Germany. A sales organization was set up for that region. The

[61] ACS, MoE, 9 Jan. 1990; ACS, 1001–1, "Eléments de réponse aux questions du Professeur Jean Salmon au sujet des Deutsche Solvay-Werke (périodes nazie, d'occupation soviétique et RDA)," 15 Mar. 1990; PR, 15 Mar. 1990, "Solvay and Eastern Germany."

[62] ADSW, *Informatsblatt der Direktion* (11 May 1990); ACS, MoE, 24 July 1990, 26 Mar. 1991; "Retour à Bernburg," *Revue Solvay* (Autumn 1991): 3–5; [Kemper and Lorenz] (2008), 48–9, 52; http://de.wikipedia.org/wiki/Treuhandanstalt.

[63] PR, 20 Aug. 1991, "Solvay recovers its plant at Bernburg, in the east of Germany"; "Retour à Bernburg," *Revue Solvay* (Autumn 1991): 3–5; PR, 22 Jan. 1992, "Interox invests in Bernburg"; [Kemper and Lorenz] (2008), 50–2.

great dream of Solvay with respect to Bernburg was that is not only would supply the markets in eastern Germany but also would serve as a bridgehead for the conquest of the markets in other countries in Central and Eastern Europe. Reality was less rosy, though. The change from the communist economic planning systems to the modern Western capitalist market economy proved a difficult and painful process. The industry in the former East Germany collapsed completely. Previously, in the German Democratic Republic, a market existed that consumed 500,000 tons of soda ash a year, but demand fell back within a few years to 150,000 tons per year. Moreover, the subsidized plant nearby at Stassfurt appeared to be a nasty competitor. As a result, Solvay in May 1993 announced that it was considering closing the soda ash plant at Heilbronn (see Chapter 21). Investments in Bernburg appeared to be much greater than expected, or at least than as first announced. Between 1991 and late 1996 more than DM 700 million were invested in Bernburg, making it one of the most modern and well-equipped plants of its kind. The heavy soda ash plant came on stream in 1994 and the hydrogen peroxide plant in 1995. It would take some time, though, before the plant became a full economic success.[64]

The Return to Central Europe

The changing political conditions in Central and Eastern Europe inevitably confronted the Executive Committee with the question of whether to invest in the countries of the former Soviet bloc. In late 1989 and early 1990 the issue was discussed in the Executive Committee, as well as with Solvay's board member and German adviser Helmut Kopper, with the conclusion that there were still many uncertainties and that the situation in the different countries varied so much that a general "East policy" was not appropriate. Hungary and Czechoslovakia seemed to promise the best prospects. In February 1990 a delegation from technical universities from Hungary, East Germany, Yugoslavia, the Soviet Union, Poland, Bulgaria, and Czechoslovakia visited Solvay's research center at NoH. "Tomorrow we will again go to Eastern Europe," prophesized Solvay's chairman Jacques Solvay on the first general assembly after the fall of the Berlin Wall. That fit excellently, he argued, in the global strategy that Solvay had also brought to the United States, Brazil, Thailand, Korea, and Japan.[65]

In September 1990 Solvay and its Austrian partner Wienerberger announced that they had taken a 50 percent interest in the Hungarian company Pannonpipe, a large local producer of plastic pipes and fittings. After an absence of more than forty years, Solvay had returned to the region. In 1991, sales offices were established in Budapest and Prague, and in 1993 in Warsaw and

---

[64] ACS, 1284-37-1, minutes meeting Solingen, 6 Nov.1990; "Retour à Bernburg." *Revue Solvay* (Autumn 1991): 3–5; PR, 24 May 1993, "Solvay to stop soda ash production at Couillet (Belgium) and considers closing its soda ash plant at Heilbronn (Germany)."

[65] ACS, MoE, 12 Dec. 1989, 9 Jan. 1990; ACS, 1001-1, "Nationalisations des avoirs Solvay en Bulgarie et Roumanie," 6 Feb. 1990; id., "Bref historique de la nationalisation des avoirs de Solvay & Cie. S.A. en Yougoslavie (1946)," 16 Feb. 1990; "Allocution de Monsieur Solvay,...31 mai 1990," *Revue Solvay* (1990) (2): 10–11.

Bratislava, but no large investments were made for a while. During the crisis of the early 1990s, Solvay needed to give much attention to the reorganization of its existing business, as well as to making Bernburg a profitable plant. The expansion in Eastern Europe slowed. Negotiations with the Polish authorities on the return of Solvay's former soda ash plants in Poland dragged on for years, but without a positive result. At the end of 1996, after four years of negotiations, Solvay finally could announce a great success: there was an agreement with the Bulgarians that Solvay would take an interest in the huge soda ash plant at Devnya (see Chapter 21). This was a breakthrough, which definitively put Solvay on the map in Central and Eastern Europe.[66]

At the end of the 1990s, Solvay's globalization policy drove in a higher gear. Just like in Asia at the same time, as well as in Argentina (see Chapter 21), within a few years several acquisitions and investments were made in Central and Eastern Europe. In September 1997 a representation office was opened in Moscow, followed shortly thereafter by sales offices in Romania, Bulgaria, and Croatia. The following few years, joint ventures were created in Poland and Romania, especially in plastics processing to supply car manufacturers in those countries. Before the end of the century, a joint venture in epichlorohydrin was created in Poland as well. A beginning had been made. In the twenty-first century, Solvay would also invest in Russia on a large scale (see Chapter 21).[67]

---

[66] PR, 14 Sept. 1990, "Solvay's industrial come back to Central Europe"; "In Eastern Europe: Dear Cousins," *Solvay Review* (June 1991); "Solvay sur la mer Noire?" *Solvay Live* (Winter 1996–1997): 26; J.- P. Van Halteren and Annie Gaudy, "How's Your Czech?" *Solvay Live* 63 (Autumn 1999): 7–9; interview Olivier Monfort, 21 Apr. 2011.

[67] PR, 26 Aug. 1997, "Solvay opens sales representation office in Moscow (Russia)"; PR, 2 Mar. 1998, "Solvay and Organika Zachem envisage to create a production joint venture in Poland for epichlorohydrin and allyl chloride"; F. Schouppe, "SPE-B in Russia – A new market in the pipeline," *Solvay Live* (Summer 1998): 16–17; PR, 28 Sept. 1998, "Continued expansion of Solvay's automotive activities – Creation of 'Solvay Automotive Polska' (Poland)"; PR, 22 Dec. 1999, "The Solvay Group reinforces its presence in Central Europe: Solvay and Pannonplast create a joint venture Pannon Aldra, industrial sheet manufacturer in Hungary."

FIGURE 21.1. As a result of the increased focus on product strategies, on 1 January 1995 all general product managers entered the Executive Committee, without becoming board members. The Executive Committee doubled in size. In this picture from 1997, seated from left to right, are Jean-Jacques Van de Berg, board member; Aloïs Michielsen, vice chairman; Daniel Janssen, chairman; and René Degrève, finance and corporate planning. Standing, from left to right, are Jean Christiaens, chemicals; Christian Jourquin, plastics processing; Henri Lefèbvre, plastic resins; and Jürgen Ernst, pharmaceuticals. In the background is a painting of Ernest Solvay (Solvay Archives).

21

Toward Sustainable Product Leadership

After the crisis of the early 1980s, the years 1987–1990 were excellent for the chemical industry. Oil prices stayed at a low level, and inflation and interest rates in the industrial countries dropped. The plastics business boomed, especially in the United States. In 1988 Solvay achieved an astonishing return on investment (ROI) of more than 65 percent in its plastics sector. Over the years 1987–1989 the company realized an average ROI of more than 40 percent in plastics and more than 30 percent in alkalis. Because of these large cash flows, the financial position of the group improved greatly. The debt ratio fell to about 30 percent (see Table 20.1). Large sums were available that were used for the acquisition of shares of Kali-Chemie, DSW, the Société Générale de Banque, and Sofina, for large and growing R&D budgets (e.g., pharmaceuticals, special polymers), for acquisitions, and for the enlargement of plants. A substantial part of these sums was used to strengthen Solvay's position in bulk plastics: the acquisition of the PVC producer Brasivil in Brazil, the construction of the Vinythai complex, enlargements of other PVC plants, the construction of a large DCE (dichloroethane) plant at Antwerp, the construction of PP and HDPE plants at Antwerp, and the enlargement of other PP and HDPE plants in Europe and the United States to improve competitiveness.[1]

In late 1989 the economic tide started to turn. The Gulf War of 1990, and the short but heavy oil shock that resulted from it, produced in 1990–1991 a short recession in the United States that soon went over to Europe. The low dollar gave American companies an advance to compete on the European market. At the same time, the German reunification of 1990 required large sums of money, which inevitably led to high interest rates, with a strong deutschmark and an even lower dollar as a result. It also pushed up unemployment. Together with the unstable and uncertain situation in postcommunist Eastern Europe, the unusually tight European monetary policies, and a crisis of the European Monetary System, all ingredients for economic decline were there. By 1992 the British economy had moved into a recession, Germany followed soon, and in

---

[1] Spitz (b) (2003); ACS, 1001-26-1, "Politique générale du groupe," 17 Mar. 1987; ACS, MES 1997/1, B. de Laguiche, "Evolution des resultats et ROI sur 10 ans," 20 May 1997; ACS, [C. Nanquette], "Achats d'actifs à tiers et prises de participations dans des sociétés non consolidees liees au Groupe," 31 May 1994.

1993 Europe encountered one of its most serious economic crises since World War II.[2]

The chemical industry was hit hard, particularly petrochemicals. Like Solvay, other producers had enlarged their plastics capacities considerably. Market prices were falling rapidly. A purchasing stop in 1989 by one of the largest consumers, China, led to overproduction. The cyclic character of the bulk plastics economy operated again full swing, aggravated by general economic decline. Although it had been stated in March 1989 that Solvay had become less vulnerable in the plastics field, with positive results even in bad circumstances, in 1992 negative results were reported. The ROI in plastics went down from 22 percent in 1990 to −5.8 percent in 1993. With bad results in alkalis as well, 1993 became the worst year in Solvay's history. Daniel Janssen decided to restructure massively and to book as many restructuring costs as possible, so that the company could start its way up after the crisis with a clean slate. As a result, the group had a consolidated net result of minus BEF 6.9 billion (US$200 million) in 1993.[3]

21.1 IMPROVING COMPETITIVENESS IN DIFFICULT TIMES

After the invasion of Kuwait by Iraq, on 2 August 1990, oil prices went up immediately. The Executive Committee reacted quickly by adapting the investment plans for the years 1991–1995: the average annual sum for investments was lowered, and instructions were given to keep personnel numbers and salary costs as low as possible. The Executive Committee also initiated measures to bring down the costs of the Central Administration in Brussels.[4]

In the course of 1991 it appeared that this was not enough; each month Solvay's results were lower again. To turn the tide, a far more stringent companywide recovery plan was initiated in November 1991. That plan included earlier measures taken, together with stricter implementation targets at all levels: to reduce investments, lower the R&D budget, cut general overheads, and limit the growth of salaries. These measures implied in practice considerable reductions of the work force and a number of drastic reorganizations. In 1992 the work force was reduced by 1,700 heads, and in 1993 by another 2,500. Thereafter, Solvay continued downsizing the organization. Between the start of 1992 and the beginning of 1996, the total head count of the entire Solvay group went down from 45,600 to 38,600 (by 15 percent). By 1998, a further reduction to 33,100 persons had been achieved.[5]

---

[2] "After Two or Three Years" (1992); Battiloso, Foreman-Peck, and Kling (2010).

[3] Spitz (b) (2003); ACS, MoB, 22 Mar. 1989, 8 Apr. 1992, 29 Sept. 1993; ARS 1993: 4–5.

[4] ACS, MoE, 28 Aug. 1990, 22 Jan. 1991; ACS, MoB, 27 Sept. 1990; ACS, [Daniel Janssen], "Lignes de conduite pour le Groupe suite à l'invasion du Koweit," 31 Aug. 1990.

[5] ACS, MoE, 5 Nov. 1991, 29 Jan 1992, 13 May 1992, 30 Apr. 1996; ACS, MoB, 27 Nov. 1991; "Strategie. Solvay et les cycles économiques," *Revue Solvay* (Autumn 1991): 10–11; "Avis No. 265 relatif à la reunion extraordinaire du Conseil d'Entreprise de Solvay Bruxelles du 13.02.1992," *Solvay Hebdo* (14 Feb. 1992); ACS, 1020–10, "Exposé du Baron Daniel Janssen – Le redressement," 23 Nov. 1994.

Closing Couillet – The Ancestral Plant

Among the most drastic measures taken were the shutting down of plants and the closures of complete sites. During 1991–1993 the Executive Committee restructured the sulfur business in France and shut down the glycerin plant at Tavaux, part of the chlorinated solvents production at Jemeppe and Tavaux, the installations for chlorate and hydrogen peroxide at Linne-Herten, the PVC plant at Hallein, the soda ash factory at Heilbronn, and – the most difficult decision of all – the soda ash plant at Solvay's oldest site, Couillet, after almost 130 years.[6]

That last decision especially was one of great symbolic significance. Solvay, as a family firm, had a long and strong tradition of taking care of its personnel, and only on rare occasions had closed important plants or sites. So many drastic steps having to be taken in such a short time, with the closure of the ancestral plant among them, certainly showed that times in the chemical industry had changed. Even as a world leader in soda ash, Solvay was losing large sums of money in its smaller and older plants because of fierce competition from American, Polish, and Bulgarian competitors.

Plans to shut down Couillet were not new. In Europe, the soda ash market was hardly growing, and in Belgium the glass industry – a major consumer of soda ash – was downsizing. Couillet lost several of its traditional customers. During the crisis of 1980–1982 the closing down of the Couillet soda ash plant was discussed, but Solvay decided in the interest of the employees to first shut down the soda ash plant at Sarralbe, where workers could be engaged in the polyolefins plants. After the shutdown of Zurzach, a few years later, Couillet was the least competitive of Solvay's soda ash plants by far. It was too small, obsolete, overstaffed, and in a far-from-ideal location with respect to raw materials supply and transport of products.[7]

In the framework of the recovery plan, Solvay in June 1992 announced a drastic reorganization of the Couillet plant. Before July 1994 about 25 percent of the more than 400 workers, employees, and staff members would be sent into early retirement. This was only the prelude to more dramatic measures. "After having studied all the options," Daniel Janssen said, he decided to close Couillet: "This was the most painful decision of my career." On 24 May 1993 the end of soda ash production at Couillet was announced. This time, dismissal of personnel (about 250 heads) or transfer to other Solvay sites (about 30 heads) was inevitable. Naturally, there was strong opposition from politics and the labor unions, and there were strikes by workers whose fathers and grandfathers had often also worked for Solvay. After four months of negotiations by the general manager for the Benelux, Jacques Van Bost, agreement could be reached about the social plan. Shortly before, as a gesture

[6] ACS, MoE, 22 Nov. 1991, 25 Apr. 1993; ACS, MoB, 8 Apr. 1992, 6 Apr. 1993; Bloemen, Lemmen, and de Wilde (2000), 43.

[7] ACS, 1010–10, presentation Mr. Vinçotte, 12 May 1980; ACS, 1001–26, "Orientations stratégiques pour nos lignes de produits," 29 Sept. 1983; ACS, 1001–26-2, presentation Mr. Loutrel on soda ash strategy, 30 Jan. 1991; ACS, 1059-2-6, "Le carbonate de soude en Europe – Situation début 1992," 11 Feb. 1992; interview Olivier Monfort, 21 Apr. 2011.

to the Walloon community, Solvay had donated the fifty-hectare estate of Alfred Solvay at Parentville, near Couillet, to the Université Libre de Bruxelles, which wanted a foothold near Charleroi. Van Bost succeeded in finding jobs for many employees within a year. Part of the social plan also implied that about forty workers would (temporarily) be engaged in other plants at the site. But during the following years these plants were shut down: the sodium silicate plant in 1996 and the calcium chloride plant in 1998. That was the end of Solvay's Couillet site.[8]

New Strategies and Structures

When, after the deep crisis of 1993, Solvay came back on track in 1994, the Executive Committee decided to continue with the recovery plan. Apart from problems associated with the business cycle, there were indeed fundamental structural problems that the European chemical industry had to face. Since 1984 the Solvay group had witnessed almost no growth, in real terms, and during the 1990s net profits and ROI never reached the levels of the golden years of 1986–1989 (see Table 21.1). The same was true for many other chemical companies. Markets in Europe stagnated. Partly because they were saturated, given limited population growth, economic problems, and maturity of substitution markets, but also because of ecological considerations. For example, PVC bottles were replaced by PET bottles, and glass – the largest market for soda ash – was increasingly being recycled, to mention just two examples. To profit from markets with larger growth figures, Solvay had therefore moved to the United States, South America, and Asia, but American and Japanese companies had entered the Asian and European markets as well. As a result, by the early 1990s competition in the chemical industry was increasingly acquiring a global character. Just like other European chemical firms, Solvay's cost structure compared unfavorably with that of the US chemical companies. Moreover, the traditional defense mechanism of agreements with colleagues, to keep the prices at an acceptable level, was undermined by an energetic antitrust policy in the European Community. Between 1983 and 1990 Solvay was part of investigations against producers of peroxides, polypropylene, PVC, and soda ash, and it was sentenced to pay (high) penalties, which it sometimes successfully appealed. Independent of those appeals, the issue illustrates that the conditions of competition in Europe were changing. During the 1990s processes of liberalization and globalization of markets gained momentum: the creation of a unified European market by the Maastricht treaties of 1992, the establishment of the NAFTA economic zone in North America in 1993, and, on the global level, the various agreements reached during General Agreement on Tariffs and Trade negotiations.[9]

---

[8] ACS, MoB, 26 Jan. 1993, 6 Feb. 1997; ACS, MoE, 31 Aug. 1993, 2 Dec. 1996, 16 Dec. 1997, 5 Dec. 2000; PR, "Solvay to stop soda ash production at Couillet (Belgium) and considers closing its soda ash plant at Heilbronn (Germany)," 24 May 1993; Fouyon (1994); interviews Daniel Janssen, 16 Oct. 2007, 13 Nov. 2007.

[9] ACS, MoB, 26 Nov. 1984, 2 June 1986, 19 Mar. 1987, 30 Jan. 1990, 28 Sept. 1994, 27 Nov. 1995; PR, "Polypropylene: Solvay appeals against the Commission's decision," 3 July 1986; PR,

TABLE 21.1. *Performance of the Solvay Group, 1989–1997*

Year	Annual Growth of Sales (%)	Annual Growth of Net Profit (%)	Cash Flow as % of Sales	Net Profit as % of Sales	ROI (%)	EBIT as % of Sales	Total Personnel
1989	1.3	10.6	12.3	6.5	20.8		45,011
1990	-0.6	-4.8	12.3	6.2	18.1		45,671
1991	-0.2	-21.8	11.8	4.9	7.9	5.9	45,585
1992	-0.1	-20.6	11.5	3.9	6.3	5.5	46,858
1993	-4.1	-170.0	5.0	-2.8	2.3	3.0	43,163
1994	7.4	215.2	10.3	3.0	8.1	6.8	39,874
1995	4.2	57.1	11.3	4.6	12.6	9.5	38,616
1996	3.2	9.0	11.7	4.8	12.0	7.6	35,400
1997	10.3	1.0	10.9	4.4	10.5	7.1	34,445

Sources: Calculated on the basis of annual reports, Solvay & Cie, 1989–1997 [R. Degrève], "Aux members du Comité Exécutif – 15 Années de chiffres du Groupe Solvay," Note DCFi-CP 24 June 1998 (MES1998/1).

By about 1990 many multinational chemical companies realized that they were facing structural problems in their industry: low growth, increasing competition, falling prices, and low revenues. To find a way out, most of them embraced new strategies and adapted their organizational structures. Instead of the diversification strategies of the 1980s, the choice was made to focus on global leadership positions in so-called core businesses in which economies of scale and other cost advantages could be realized. In practice, this meant that noncore businesses were divested to companies that could obtain leadership by combining their own business with that of a "colleague" business. A permanent reshaping of the chemical landscape was the result (see Section 21.4). On the organizational level, the achieving of drastic cost reductions by introducing lighter, leaner, and meaner organizations was a main target. Matrix organizations were mostly replaced by product-oriented organizations that were well in line with the new strategy of product leadership.[10]

21.2 FROM MATRIX ORGANIZATION TO BUSINESS UNITS

Since its introduction in 1968, Solvay functioned internally as a matrix organization in three dimensions, with functional departments (e.g., technology, personnel, finance), product departments (e.g., alkalis, peroxides, plastics, pharmacy), and national organizations (e.g., France, Spain, Germany, Benelux) (see Chapter 17).

The Reorganizations of the Mid-1980s

In the wake of the conclusions of the Liaison Committee, two partly interconnected questions were tackled: How could the implementation of Solvay's strategy be improved, which businesses should be developed, and which businesses should Solvay divest? And how could the functioning and cost-effectiveness of the Solvay organization be enhanced? As a solution to both problems, Jacques Viriot and Jean-Jacques Van de Berg in December 1982 proposed to introduce strategic business units (SBUs), an organizational concept first developed in 1968 by the American giant General Electric, advised by the Boston Consulting Group and McKinsey. An SBU-based company organization would facilitate the development of specific strategies on the level of product groups and would simplify the company structure from a three-dimensional matrix to a one-dimensional product-based organization.[11]

In the Executive Committee, these ideas did not find a warm welcome. Jacques Solvay, who had introduced the matrix organization together with Dick Paget, was a true believer in its positive aspects. "I am quite convinced,"

"Soda ash: The EC Commission fines Solvay for ECUs 30 million," 19 Dec. 1990; "Allocution de Monsieur Solvay . . . 31 mai 1990, *Revue Solvay* (1990) (2): 10–11; Frieden (2006), 378–91; interview Jacques Lévy-Morelle, 7 Sept. 2010.

[10] Hill (1982); ACS, 1001-26-1, "Politique générale du groupe," 14 Mar. 1989; *Innovating* (1995), 112–13; Chandler (2005), 30–1, 50–2, 59–62, 122–4, 130–3, 138–40; Schröter (2007), 71–9.

[11] ACS, Organisation, "Étude de notre organization," 3 Dec. 1982; Ocasio and Joseph (2008).

he argued a few years later, "that the humanist philosophy of Ernest Solvay will continue to hold up when confronted with all the ruthless competition that we see;... one significant example [is] our matrix organization.... It is quite difficult to make such a matrix organization work, since it needs a climate of trust and reliance: this is a basic tenet of Solvay's company culture and thus we manage well with this type of organization and we have no desire to alter it."[12] In his view the matrix organization fitted perfectly well with the family feeling that he liked to cultivate inside the company. Also, Claude Loutrel and Albert Rampelberg did not agree with the novel ideas on SBUs. In their view, the matrix organization should be maintained, but the product departments should have priority in (strategic) decisions. Operational tasks, though, should be delegated to the national organizations.[13]

In the autumn of 1983, the SBUs were again put on the agenda in an extensive report by Corporate Planning on the product strategies of Solvay, the first of its kind. Ten SBUs were introduced, but they were, with minor exceptions, in fact no more than the six traditional main lines of strength (see Chapter 19), to which four new product areas were added (i.e., pharmacy, veterinary products, specialties, and miscellaneous products of Kali-Chemie). In the Executive Committee the strategic ideas on the product strategies were largely approved, but not many words were spent on the SBU concept. It died in silence. When Daniel Janssen became chairman of Executive Committee in June 1986, he abolished the division of the six traditional and four diversified product groups and created five product sectors – alkalis, chlorine, and derivatives; peroxides; plastics; plastics processing; and health – each one was tasked with developing its own specialties. With this operation, he also initiated the integration of the KC products into the group (see Chapter 20).[14]

Parallel to the work on product strategies by Corporate Planning, a task force chaired by Georges Theys was inaugurated that undertook a detailed screening of the Solvay organization within the framework defined by Loutrel and Rampelberg. Between mid-August and mid-November 1983, 250 persons from all middle and top levels of the Solvay organization in several countries were interviewed, and the development and use of management information systems was studied in the United States. By December 1983, the task force concluded that there was a lack of entrepreneurial spirit among staff members and that the matrix organization functioned less well than it should. The role of the functional departments had been weakened, the national managers were far too powerful, and the functioning of the product departments was ambiguous. Apart from the technical reporting systems – such as the comparative production tables (see Chapter 2) – there were no systematic reporting practices. There was an informal network that partly compensated these deficits, but it functioned only between the French-speaking staff in the traditional product

[12] ARS 1990: 6–7.
[13] ACS, Organisation, "Organisation: Réunion des Directeurs Centraux et Nationaux à Bruxelles, le 24 mai 1983."
[14] ACS, 1001–26, "Orientations stratégiques pour nos lignes de produits," 29 Sept. 1983; ACS, MoE, 4 Oct. 1983, 4 Dec. 1984, 1 Oct. 1986.

sectors. All later acquired subsidiaries (e.g., Kali-Chemie, Duphar) were outside that network. Staff members in those firms did not have a strong feeling of belonging to the group.[15]

The task force came up with numerous suggestions for improvement, the most crucial of which was the establishment of a separate management department for information systems (Direction Centrale des Systèmes Informatique, DCSI) under Theys. Together with McKinsey, the department developed within ten months a computerized uniform accounting information system for the entire group – called SIR, for Système d'Information Rapide. Despite much resistance from within the group, the system was improved over the years. This system informed the Executive Committee far more quickly than before on sales figures as well as on results by country and by product group.[16]

The start of DCSI was realized soon, but several other suggestions by the task force – concerning the national organizations, the reduction of general costs and personnel numbers, an improved marketing orientation, and the introduction of quality improvement procedures – were implemented only slowly, if at all. Probably, the sense of urgency to further improve the organization diminished during the golden years of 1986 to 1989. Personnel numbers, for instance, which had been reduced from 49,000 to 43,500 between 1980 and 1984 (see Chapter 20), went up to almost 45,700 in 1990.

Introducing Total Quality Management

Systematic attention to quality improvement of all the aspects of production and organization goes mainly back to American business scholars of the 1940s and 1950s, such as W. Edwards Deming, Joseph M. Juran, and Armand V. Feigenbaum. Their ideas were assimilated and put into practice in Japan during the 1950s and 1960s, where they were developed theoretically by Kaoru Ishikawa and others. Hand in hand with the global business successes of the Japanese automobile and electronics firms, the organizational and quality management practices of these companies were copied elsewhere. During the 1980s, the idea of total quality management (TQM) started its march through the industry of the United States, where Ford Motor Company was one of the successful early adopters. Crucial to TQM is the idea that the quality of products and processes is the responsibility of everyone in the organization and the supply chain. In practice, this meant that companies such as Ford were putting pressure on their suppliers to deliver products of uniform high quality.[17]

As a supplier to the car industry and the electronic industries, Solvay naturally became involved in the drive to define and improve quality standards. This

[15] ACS, MoE, 25 May 1983, 4 Oct. 1983; ACS, "Task Force Systèmes de communication et organization," 30 Nov. 1983; interview Georges Theys and Michel Bande, 6 June 2011.

[16] ACS, Organisation, "Adaptation de notre organization – recommandatios," 30 Dec. 1983; id., "Adaptation de l'organisation du Groupe," 27 Jan. 1984; id., J. Solvay, "Note aux Directions Nationales et Administrations des Filiales," 25 June 1984; ACS, MoE, 20 Jan. 1984, 8 May 1984, 16 June 1984, 4 Dec. 1984; interview Georges Theys and Michel Bande, 6 June 2011.

[17] Juran (1995).

happened first in the United States, where Solvay made special electronic-grade hydrogen peroxide for its customers and where it produced plastic fuel tanks and other technical parts for car companies such as Ford and Chrysler. The Quality Services Department was established at Soltex in January 1989. Environmental and safety aspects were also increasingly involved in TQM. This implied a responsibility for the company's products from production through to consumption and waste. During the late 1980s the American chemical industry, including Solvay America, embraced the Responsible Care Program, which included aspects such as these (see Section 21.3).[18]

When competition in the global chemical industry increased, raising product quality to a higher and uniform level evolved into a key issue in relation to large and crucial customers. Several of these customers had become global players, which implied that they wanted to have the same high-quality supplies in all their factories across the globe. At Solvay, several quality-improvements projects were going on in various plants and in relation to specific customers, but without central coordination. In 1989 the Executive Committee realized that more coordination was needed, and it decided to start the Quality Action Plan for the entire company. Michel Boulerne was tasked with advising on the development of a comprehensive implementation plan and the budgets required. He then was involved in the quality management of the production of fuel tanks at the Société de Transformation des Matières Plastiques (STMP) in France, where, like in other plants working for automotive, the highest quality standards within Solvay had to be met. In March 1990 his report was ready. It proposed to implement before 1993 the total quality management model internationally at all levels, to change the company culture, and to induce quality awareness and a customer orientation among all Solvay personnel. When in 1992–1993 the mission, strategy, and structure of Solvay were redefined, the provision of "quality... chemicals, pharmaceuticals and related products and services" became an explicit part of Solvay's mission.[19]

The quality drive between 1990 and 1993 would be the start of a continuing series of management interventions to change Solvay's company culture into a more customer-oriented direction. After 1993 the total quality management program was continued as an effort "to establish a slimmer, more participative and more entrepreneurial organization, focusing on... business units." When that large organizational change had been completed by 1997, a new program focusing on innovation was introduced to further change the company culture. At the same time, advised by the consultant Jean-Pierre Bizet, Freddy Declerck, Frank McKevitt, and Jacques Van Bost continued Boulerne's efforts to increasingly improve quality management at Solvay and to further simplify the organization.[20]

---

[18] *Today Solvay America* 1 (3) (Sept. 1989).

[19] ACS, MoE, 6 June 1989; 27 Mar. 1990, 14 May 1991; PPSF, Jacques Solvay, "Family Business Network: Enhancing excellence of family business," 9 Nov. 1992; interview Jacques Van Bost, 19 July 2011; personal communication by Jacques Lévy-Morelle, 1 Sept. 2011.

[20] M. Boulerne, "Business units – Snapshot of a responsive structure," *Solvay Live* 24 (1) (Spring 1996): 4–5; ACS, MoE, 26 Mar. 1997, 29 July 1997; interview Jacques Van Bost, 19 July 2011.

The Change to Strategic Business Units

With the unified European market approaching, the Solvay leadership reflected on the future sales organization for Europe. Operational tasks such as marketing, sales, and logistics had traditionally been executed by the national organizations. In May 1990, therefore, the Executive Committee invited the consultant Arthur D. Little (ADL) to study Solvay's sales organizations for alkalis, peroxides and plastics, and to come up with proposals for future European-wide sales organizations in those fields. When ADL's report was ready at the end of 1990, it suggested introducing business units as part of the solution. According to the consultancy firm, Solvay had a long tradition of leadership and strong national organizations, but it was in danger of losing that position to other chemical groups that had adapted their organizations better to changes in the European and global markets. The growing importance of the five product sectors had not yet been translated to new organizational structures. "Many staff members," the report concluded, "are spending a lot of time on managing 'the system' instead of their products." For ADL, the introduction of a business-unit organization was inevitable.[21]

Parallel to the study by Arthur D. Little-France, a German office of the same company advised on the implementation of the merger of DSW and Kali-Chemie with Solvay Deutschland, and on the implied organizational changes (see Chapter 20). As a result, ADL proposed splitting DSW and Kali-Chemie into product companies or business units. These developments were limited to Germany, though, and therefore did not strongly interfere with the international organization of the group into separate national entities, which was a key aspect of Solvay's matrix structure. The same was true for the (partial) introduction of business units in the domains of plastics processing and health during the early 1990s, initiated by Michielsen. These two sectors stood quite apart from the rest of the Solvay organization. Changes in these sectors did not have a great impact on the entire group.

Despite serious objections by some members of Executive Committee to an organization based on business units, for two important reasons the issue returned on the agenda in the course of 1992. In the first place, total quality management demanded that Solvay would formulate a coherent and transparent mission, strategy, and structure that would give a clear sense of direction to all Solvay employees. In the second place, the recovery plan of November 1991 put cost reduction at center stage and was therefore a strong incentive for attempts to arrive at a lighter and leaner organization. Between 7 February and 2 April 1992, therefore, Daniel Janssen spoke personally to all central and national general managers on the functioning of the structure of the group. It appeared that all managers found the matrix structure indispensable, but the product managers were strongly in favor of a structure in which the five sectors would become more autonomous divisions. The national managers were

[21] ACS, MoE, 15 Sept. 1990, 18 Dec. 1990; ACS, 1001–26-1, [Arthur D. Little], *L'Organisation Commerciale des DPrA, DPrO et DPrP*, 25 Jan. 1991; interview Aloïs Michielsen, 16 Apr. 2008.

mostly opposed to that idea, whereas the functional managers were moderately in favor of a matrix in which product divisions would play a role.[22]

During the summer of 1993, using the crisis as an opportunity, finally some consensus was reached about the introduction of a lighter and more market-oriented divisional structure, under which decentralized business units would reside while keeping "the matrix spirit" at the same time. Local business units such as the PVC business unit at Ferrara and a calcium chloride business unit at Couillet were created in the existing matrix structure. At the same time, parallel to these developments, Michielsen continued the further articulation of the business-unit organization within the plastics-processing sector.[23]

To emphasize the growing role of the product departments, from 1 January 1995, all general product managers became members of the Executive Committee, without being board members at the same time. In 1994 it also was decided that the matrix organization would gradually be replaced by an organization based on business units. In April 1994 Aloïs Michielsen was appointed vice chairman of the Executive Committee and chief operating officer (COO); as such, he had general supervision over all five product sectors. In this role as COO, Michielsen pushed forward the creation of business units with a global scope, replacing or supplementing the local business units.[24]

The first of these international business units – soon called strategic business units (SBUs) – was that of fluorinated products, created early in 1994. Building on first steps like these, as well as on the German examples, Frank McKevitt, a former coworker of Sadler in the United States; Michel Boulerne; and others worked in November 1994 to embark on studies of introducing new budgeting systems for overhead costs, the decentralization of general services, the accountability of business units in multisectoral plants, and the definition of financial objectives for the business units and remuneration of managers. Between 1994 and 1996 these problems were gradually sorted out, and a business unit organization was put in place. By mid-1996 there was a leaner organization with twenty SBUs with global responsibility, a number of regional business units (RBUs), local operating units (OUs), and service units (SUs), all varying in scope and mission. At a meeting in the Maison d'Ernest Solvay in May 1996, the new organization was discussed extensively and, finally, accepted by the central and national general managers of the group.[25]

---

[22] ACS, letter from Executive Committee to the general managers, 19 Apr. 1992; ACS, MoE, 13 May 1992; personal communication by Daniel Janssen, Aug. 2011.

[23] ACS, "Mission, strategy and structure of the Group Solvay," 19 Mar. 1993; ACS, MoE, 15 June 1993, 31 Aug. 1993; ACS, Minutes of a meeting of the Working Party, 30 Aug. 1993; ACS, Exposés Directeurs 1994/3, Dossier Loutrel, "Exposé du Baron Daniel Janssen – Le redressement," 23 Nov. 1994; interview Aloïs Michielsen, 21 Apr. 2011; interview Claude Thibaut de Maisières, 2 May 2011.

[24] ACS, MoE, 9 Nov. 1993; ACS, 1284-37-1, "Notice pour Monsieur Van de Berg," 19 Nov. 1993; ACS, MoB, 29 Nov. 1993, 28 Nov. 1994; interview Aloïs Michielsen, 16 Apr. 2008.

[25] ACS, MoE, 26 Nov. 1983, 25 Aug. 1994, 8 Nov. 1994, 30 May 1995, 7 Nov. 1995, 30 Apr. 1996; ACS, MoB, 28 Sept. 1994, 24 Jan. 1995; ACS, 1073-1-1, letter Whitson Sadler to Frank McKevitt, 19 Oct. 1994; ACS, 1001–26-1, letter Daniel Janssen to the central and regional managers, 20 June 1996.

Parallel to the introduction of the business units, the importance of the central and national organizations was gradually reduced. After having been in power for more than a century, the central role of DCT inside Solvay had definitely ended. On the geographical level, significant milestones were the step-by-step subordination of different national organizations under a single leadership. Several tasks were transferred from the national organizations to the SBU's, and, as a result, fewer high quality people were needed to manage them. Already early in 1989 Serge Forthomme, general manager for Austria, had also become responsible for Switzerland. The same happened two years later in Spain and Portugal, under the single leadership of Christian Jourquin. The crucial change took place in 1996, though, when Jacques Thoelen was appointed general manager for Germany, Austria, and Switzerland, and Georges Theys for Italy and France. In 2002–2003, finally, the European Regional Board was created, chaired by Jacques Thoelen; the board coordinated policies for Europe. In most cases, though, a true merger of national organizations did not take place. Under a single leadership, small national organizations continued to operate in different countries.[26]

Outside Europe, a regional organization had existed in Asia since the start of Solvay's active presence in the region in late 1984 (see Chapter 19). Early in 1991, Whitson Sadler, head of Solvay America, was also made responsible for Canada and Mexico, and Jean-Pierre Lapage, general manager for Brazil, also received responsibility for Argentina. About ten years later these two regional organizations would evolve into organizations for the NAFTA region and Mercosur, respectively.[27]

Looking back on the introduction of the SBUs at Solvay, one can conclude that they were successful in giving the company a sharper strategic focus and a leaner organization. The reduction of personnel realized between 1993 and 1997 was substantial. But there was also a negative side: SBUs tried to keep their highly experienced people, so that the circulation of personnel through the Solvay organization declined; it was more difficult to start new businesses outside the strategic domains of the SBUs; and finally, the reduced importance of the national organizations had adverse effects on the contacts between Solvay and local politicians. When these flaws in the new organization were discovered, remedies such as competence centers and the multidisciplinary advisory councils Technology and Information, Knowledge Management and Organization Development, Human Resources, and New Business Development were introduced. In that modified form the Solvay organization entered the twenty-first century.[28]

[26] "Le Groupe Solvay en Autiche," *Revue Solvay* (1989) (1): 2–5; ACS, MoE, 12 Sept. 1989, 18 June 1991, 23 Oct. 1992; ACS, MoB, 26 July 1995; ACS, MES meeting 4–5 Dec. 1996; interview Aloïs Michielsen, 21 Apr. 2011; interview Georges Theys, 6 June 2011; interview Jacques Van Bost, 19 July 2011.

[27] ACS, MoE, 22 Jan. 1991; ARS 2002: 7.

[28] "Savoir gére, gérer le savoir," *Solvay Live* 65 (Feb. 2001): 4–11; interview Jacques Van Bost, 19 July 2011.

21.3 CHLORINE CHEMISTRY UNDER ATTACK

With the change toward greater importance of the product organization, the sectors and SBUs during the 1990s increasingly articulated their own strategies (see Section 21.4). But there was one issue that became more important for all of them: the environment.

Public awareness of environmental problems greatly increased during the 1960s, when unprecedented economic growth led to growing industrial emissions into the water, air, and soil. Rachel Carson's famous book *Silent Spring*, on the dangers of chlorinated pesticides, was only the spark that ignited the fire of public protest and new legislative activity. During the 1960s and 1970s many environmental protest groups were created in Europe, the United States, and Japan, and increasing legislative activity took place. Symbolic milestones of note were the proclamation of the European Year of Nature Conservation, in 1970, and the United Nations Conference on the Human Environment, held in Stockholm in June 1972.[29]

At Solvay, apart from safety issues in the plants, two problems had caught the attention already for some time: the calcium chloride and salty wastes of the soda ash plants and the mercury emissions of the electrolysis units. However, systematic attention to environmental issues was lacking until 1970. Then, Solvay erected commissions for the protection of the environment in all its large plants and a coordinator for environmental issues; Roger Loché, former plant manager of Couillet, was appointed in 1971 at the Central Administration. In 1970 the protection of the environment was addressed for the first time in Solvay's annual report.[30]

During the 1970s, four partly new problems received much public attention and occupied the Solvay leadership: the chloride emissions in the rivers Sambre (Couillet), Meurthe (Dombasle), Sarre (Sarralbe) and Rhine (Rheinberg); the growing problems concerning plastic wastes (packaging); the destruction of chlorinated organic substances by incineration on a ship at the North Sea; and the toxicity of vinyl chloride (see Chapter 16). Moreover, after the oil crisis of 1973, improving the energy efficiency of the plants became of prime importance. Internally, Solvay worked hard to solve these issues, but in external communication – similar to other chemical companies at that time – the importance of the issues was often played down. In the late 1970s environmental issues again disappeared from the Solvay annual reports. When the task force of 1983 evaluated Solvay's environment policies, it characterized them as too defensive. A more proactive approach was advocated, and in 1984 a new organization on "security, health and the environment" was put into place.[31]

---

[29] Homburg, Travis, and Schröter (1998), 121–200; Van der Heijden (2004); Hünemörder (2004).

[30] "Le Service de Sécurité à Neder-over-Heembeek," *Revue du Personnel* 12 (3) (1963): 25–9; ACS, MoE, 15 Nov. 1967, 5 Dec. 1972; PR, "Calcium chloride, Soudière Suisse," 28 May 1969; ARS 1970: 14–15; id. 1971: 21–2; "Un problème d'actualité: l'Environnement," *Revue Solvay* (1971) (6): 3–5.

[31] ARS 1972: 32–3; id. 1973: 32–3; id. 1974: 30–1; ACS, MoE, 15 Feb. 1972, 5 Mar. 1974, 28 Oct. 1974, 2 Sept. 1975; "Allocution du Comte Boël...14 juin 1971," *Revue Solvay* (1971) (4): 4–7; "Polluante, l'industrie chimique?" *Revue Solvay* (1972) (5): 14–15; ACS, file De Bois,

Actions against PVC and Chlorine Chemistry

During the late 1970s and mid-1980s, a number of events occurred that placed the chemical industry firmly in the spotlight of the general public and the authorities: the dioxins accident at Seveso, Italy, in July 1976; the deadly gas cloud released by an accident at a pesticides factory of Union Carbide at Bhopal, India, in December 1984; and the chemical spill from an agrochemical storehouse of Sandoz near Basel in November 1986 that heavily polluted the river Rhine. At Solvay, the Executive Committee responded immediately to the Bhopal and Sandoz tragedies. It started safety audits of all plants and improved communication procedures on safety issues.[32]

As chlorinated organic chemicals had been involved in two of the cases, environmental protest groups intensified their campaigns against these chemicals and against the massive use of PVC in particular. In 1983 intense campaigns started in Germany against Solvay's wood-protection product Xylamon, and lawsuits followed. During the same years, the dump of chlorinated waste products by Duphar, though dating from before Solvay's ownership, received significant media exposure in the Netherlands (see Chapter 19). In several European countries environmental protest groups focused their actions against plastics waste increasingly on PVC. They argued that during burning of PVC in waste incinerators, considerable amounts of dioxins were released. Associating PVC with the "horror chemical" dioxin seemed an effective strategy to kill any further public disputes on dangers. In 1985 chlorinated fluorocarbons (CFCs) – produced by Solvay in Germany and Spain – were suspected of destroying the ozone layer (see Section 21.4). Two years later, Greenpeace started to campaign against chlorinated organic chemicals. One of the organization's first targets was the Solvay plant at Jemeppe, where Solvay operated a pilot plant for the incineration of chlorinated by-products.[33]

Confronted with attacks like these, the leaders of chemical companies first seemed a bit embarrassed by the aggression against their industry. Soon the industry organized its defense, though. In response to the transnational campaigns of Greenpeace and other activist groups, Solvay and other chlorine producers participated actively in the European Year of the Environment 1987. They united themselves in 1991 in Euro-Chlor, a federation aimed at informing politicians and journalists about the facts of chlorine technology, such as the amounts of PVC waste, the industry's efforts in the field of recycling, and the negligible traces of dioxins that were produced during incineration. The

---

"Defense des bouteilles en PVC pour l'emballage de l'eau minerale," 21 Jan. 1975; ACS, "Task Force Systèmes de communication et organization," 30 Nov. 1983; *Het zout in de Rijn* (1986); interview Jacques Lévy-Morelle, 10 Sept. 2010.

[32] ACS, MoB, 25 Mar. 1985, 24 Nov. 1986; ACS, MoE, 28 Mar. 1986, 4 Dec. 1987; "Discours de fin d'année du baron Daniel Janssen," insert in *Revue Solvay* (1986): 1–6; interview Daniel Janssen, 13 Nov. 2007.

[33] Groen (1983), 12–14; Zapke (1996); ACS, MoE, 16 Apr. 1985, 18 June 1985, 21 Oct. 1987; ACS, 1001-26-1, "Politique générale du groupe," 14 Mar. 1988; "Switzerland – Un treno che non scoppia di salute," *Revue Solvay* (1990) (2): 19; Tukker (1998), 174–81, 243–5; http://archive.greenpeace.org/toxics/reports/restrictions.pdf; Beukers and van den Tweel (2006), esp. 115–35.

message they tried to get across was that the chlorine business was a safe and responsible industry. Before that message was received, though, during the late 1990s a heated controversy between the industry and environmental groups took place, in which the different companies had to campaign energetically in their home countries: Atochem in France, Shell and Akzo in the Netherlands, Hoechst and Bayer in Germany, Norsk Hydro in Norway and Sweden, and Solvay in Belgium.[34]

The actions against the chlorinated organics industry culminated by 1990 in transnational campaigns in almost all Western European countries, in which Greenpeace especially played a leading role. Solvay and other manufacturers defended themselves not only in extensive publicity campaigns but also in increased technological activity to replace end-of-pipe solutions with cleaner production processes, for instance for VCM (oxychlorination with oxygen instead of air) and electrolysis (with membranes instead of mercury), and to improve recycling technologies. In 1989 the Conseil Européen des Fédérations de l'Industrie Chimique (CEFIC), introduced the Responsible Care Program in Europe, which had been developed in Canada and the United States. In January 1991 Daniel Janssen, then president of CEFIC, signed the Responsible Care Charter on behalf of Solvay.[35]

Despite these improvements, the industry was still on the defensive when in September 1992 seven Belgian political parties agreed to introduce an "eco-tax" on PVC bottles. Solvay started a vigorous counterattack, because it thought a specific tax on PVC was discriminatory and totally unjustified. In January 1992 a demonstration of workers of PVC plants and chemical factories was held in Brussels in which six thousand workers took part, joined by the retired Jacques Solvay and his wife. Following that demonstration, workers in the chlorine and PVC industries of Belgium and the Netherlands organized themselves into the action group the Chlorophiles, which campaigned against Greenpeace for several years.[36]

The confrontations between Solvay and Greenpeace reached a climax in 1993. Greenpeace wanted chlorine chemistry to be phased out before the year 2000, and it started aggressive actions against Solvay and other producers on a broad front. On 24 March 1993 Greenpeace activists from different countries

---

[34] ACS, 1020–10, presentation Mr. Van Lierde, 6 Nov. 1984; "Matières Plastiques et environnement," *Revue Solvay* (1985) (3): 34–8; ACS, MoE, 24 Nov. 1986; "Solvay et la protection de l'environnement," *Revue Solvay* (1987) (1); ACS, MoE, 21 Oct. 1987, 15 Mar. 1988, 3 Nov. 1992; Mr. Delatte, "Chlor-Alkali symposium – Let's talk about it," *Solvay Live* (Winter 1993): 28–9; Tukker (1998); interview Daniel Janssen, 13 Nov. 2007.

[35] "PVC" special issue, *The Solvay Review* (1990) (1); Tukker (1998), 181–8; Beukers and Van den Tweel (2006), esp. 118–33; ACS, MoE, 20 Dec. 1988, 20 Nov. 1990, 13 May 1992, 15 June 1993; "Responsible care," *The Solvay Review* 2/91; "More than one life for plastics!" *The Solvay Review* 2/91: 27–31; P. Coërs, "Responsible care policy: Performing better for the environment," *Solvay Live* (Fall 1992): 14–17; CEFIC (1992): 14–15; interview Daniel Janssen, 13 Nov. 2007.

[36] PR, "Solvay Belgium considers unjustified and discriminatory the green taxes imposing the beverages sold in PVC containers," 9 Dec. 1992; ARS 1992; Beukers and Van den Tweel (2006), 130; http://nl.wikipedia.org/wiki/Chlorofielen; http://home.scarlet.be/chlorophiles/nl/nl_index.html.

FIGURE 21.2. Double-decker bus, with the slogan "Greenpeace is fooling itself – Greenpeace is fooling you – Solvay informs you," which followed the *Beluga* boat of Greenpeace in 1993 to inform the public about the statements on dioxins distributed by Greenpeace and about Solvay's efforts in the field of recycling. (Solvay Archives.)

moored their action vessel *Solo* in front of the Solvay plant at Antwerp-Lillo, to block the salt supply to the plant. Some activists chained themselves to cranes; others welded a large container onto the railroad access to the plant, with slogans such as "Chlorine kills" and "Stop chlorine – Zero 2000." Solvay immediately went to court to stop this illegal action. It also demanded that Greenpeace's bank accounts and other Belgian assets be frozen. On 27 March the court decided in favor of Solvay, and the following two days police removed the activists.[37]

Although the Antwerp-Lillo action was the most radical by far that Solvay had encountered, it was only one of a whole array of confrontations initiated by Greenpeace that year. Activists intervened at Solvay's general assembly in Brussels and at public hearings and meetings at Martorell and Jemeppe, they blocked chlorine rail transportation to and from Hallein and Linne-Herten, and they infiltrated the sites at Tavaux and Jemeppe. Finally, in November and December 1993 Greenpeace made a big protest tour and media event with its vessel *Beluga* along the river Meuse in Belgium and the Netherlands.

[37] Beukers and Van den Tweel (2006), 125–7; "Solvay and Greenpeace – Much ado about a molecule," *Solvay Live* 21 (3) (Winter 1993–1994): 19.

This time Solvay's management for the Benelux countries, weary of all these attacks, decided that the time for unconventional counteractions had come. It hired a double-decker bus, with the slogan "Greenpeace is fooling itself – Greenpeace is fooling you – Solvay informs you," to follow the track of the *Beluga* via the road and inform the public about the false statements on dioxins distributed by Greenpeace and about Solvay's efforts in the field of recycling.[38]

Although Greenpeace's antichlorine campaigns continued for at least another two years, they did not succeed in convincing political circles, or the public at large, of the alleged dangers of chlorine chemistry, and by the end of the 1990s, the public debate had died out. In 1999 Solvay broadened its responsible-care efforts to include sustainable development, a key concept that still guides Solvay's activities today. During these first years of the twenty-first century, Solvay intensified its efforts in the field of recycling. Early in 2002 an industrial-scale recycling plant, using Solvay's Vinyloop process, came on stream at Ferrara. Solvay also continued the gradual replacement of its mercury-cell electrolysis plants with units using the membrane technology, licensed from Asahi Glass. By 2011 almost all of Solvay's electrolysis plants had been converted to the membrane process.[39]

21.4 SUSTAINING LEADERSHIP

The year 1993, when the actions by Greenpeace against Solvay reached a climax, was also economically one of the most difficult years in Solvay's history. Since late 1991, the Solvay leadership had tried to overcome the growing crisis by reducing costs, adapting the organization, and refocusing its strategy on pharmaceuticals and products in which Solvay was among the leaders worldwide.

In a way, that focused strategy was a return to Solvay's traditional policy of concentrating on a limited number of main lines of strength. During the 1980s this had been followed by a strategy phase of diversification, in animal health, pharmaceuticals, and specialties, and after the crisis of 1980–1982 in new directions such as technopolymers and composites, biotechnology, electronic chemicals, and neo-ceramics. The Lazard brothers and the company Rain Hill were contacted to help Solvay in searching for acquisitions in these

---

[38] PR, "Open letter from Solvay to Greenpeace," 7 June 1993; J. Lampe, "PVC & dioxins," *Solvay Live* (Summer 1993): 30–1; ACS, MoB, 29 Sept. 1993; Bloemen, Lemmen, and de Wilde (2000), 47; interview Daniel Janssen, 13 Nov. 2007.

[39] ACS, MoE, 12 Apr. 1995; PR, "No to a strategy of fear!" 1 June 1995; J.-M. Chandelle, "The precautionary principle: Wisdom or paralysis," *Solvay Live* 24 (1) (Spring 1996): 18–19; Tukker (1998), 205–13, 268–75; Beukers and Van den Tweel (2006), 129–35; J.-M. Yernaux and H. Leitner, "Recyclable and recycled," *Solvay Live* (Dec. 1997): 6–7; Ch. Tahon, M. Delattre, and P. Coërs, "Product stewardship: Responsibility throughout the product life-cycle," *Solvay Live* 62 (Winter 1998–1999): 18–19; PR, on new recycling channel, 21 Sept. 1999; J.-M. Yernaux, "The Vinyloop process," *Solvay Live* 63 (Autumn 1999): 10; PR, "Yet another solution for recycling PVC," 15 June 2000; ACS, MoB, 27 July 2000; PR, on mercury electrolysis, 8 Dec. 2006; interview Thierry Lefèvre and Michel Bande, 8 July 2010; interview Georges Theys and Michel Bande, 6 June 2011. Cf. Yarime (2009).

TABLE 21.2. *Product Leadership Ranking of Solvay, 1994*

Product	Europe	World
Alkalis		
Soda ash	1	1
Salt	1	2
Caustic soda	1	3
Barium and strontium carbonates	1	1
Peroxides		
Hydrogen peroxide	1	1
Persalts	1	1
Plastics		
PVC	2	3
HDPE	5	1
Plastics processing		
HDPE fuel tanks	2	1
Health		
Digestive products	1	1
Laxatives	1	2
Hormone treatments	2	4
Vaccines (human health)	–	3
Vaccines (poultry, pigs)	–	1

Source: Adapted from ARS 1994, 7. Sectors are in italics.

areas in the United States. A few activities were established and acquired in the field of electronic chemicals, but during the 1990s these activities in electronic chemicals were cut back again.[40]

When in 1986 Daniel Janssen became chairman of the Executive Committee, he focused Solvay's business not only on the five sectors, mentioned already, but especially on areas with great potential of profitable and noncyclical growth. In practice, that meant giving priority to the health sector and to special polymers.[41]

The mission and strategy of 1993 explicitly formulated the aim "to be a World leader in selected areas where we have a competitive advantage."[42] These were the core activities of the group. The products in which Solvay was leading in Europe and worldwide are shown in Table 21.2. Here, we discuss the leadership strategies of some of these products in more detail, including the fluorinated chemicals in which Solvay was not yet leading in 1994 but

[40] ACS, 1001–26, "Politique groupe," 8 Mar. 1983; id., "Diversification – Réunion avec Rain Hill," 21 Dec. 1984; id., "Electronic Materials – Meeting held at NoH on Feb. 28, 1985"; id., "Politique industrielle – Produits pour l'eclectronique," 23 May 1985; id., "Politique générale du groupe," 26 Mar. 1986; id., "Diversification des principales sociétés chimiques dans les domains où Solvay envisage de se diversifier," 29 May 1986; id., "Politique générale du groupe," 17 Mar. 1987; ACS, MoE, 14 May 1991.

[41] ARS 1986: 6–7; ACS, MoE, 29 July 1986, 15 Mar. 1988; ACS, MoB, 28 Mar. 1988.

[42] ARS, 1994, 1.

would obtain world leadership in later years. Polyolefins and pharmaceuticals are discussed in Chapter 22.[43]

One of the most important elements of the new strategy was the practice of regularly evaluating the competitive performance of the Solvay products and to withdraw from fields in which Solvay did not have a real competitive edge internationally. More than ever before, divestments and the termination of activities became an integral part of Solvay's business policy. As a result, Solvay's product mix changed drastically during the 1990s. The largest changes were in the health sector, where fine chemicals, crop protection, industrial enzymes, and animal health were sold (see Chapter 19). The revenues of these transactions were reinvested in the accelerated growth of (human) pharmaceuticals. There were also great portfolio changes in plastics processing. Additional great changes in the portfolio in plastics (e.g., polyolefins, special polymers), chemicals (e.g., fluorinated chemicals, salt), and pharmaceuticals would take place after the start of the new century. They are partly discussed in the next chapter. Taken together, they completely revolutionized Solvay's product mix.[44]

Soda Ash: Defending Leadership

For decades soda ash was one of the most important cash cows of Solvay. In addition to being the largest soda ash producer in the world – with a global market share of more than 16 percent in the 1960s – Solvay especially had an extremely strong position in Western Europe, with market shares ranging from 60 percent in France and Germany to almost 100 percent in Belgium, Austria, Italy, and Spain.[45]

Since about 1975, that situation had gradually started to change. Market conditions in Europe, the United States, and Japan deteriorated as a result of slowed economic growth, but also because of specific causes such as the growing recycling of glass, changing laundry practices, the partial substitution of caustic soda for soda ash, and the growing global power of Solvay's major customers in glass manufacture (e.g., Saint-Gobain, Asahi) and detergents (e.g., Procter and Gamble, Unilever). Growing imports from Central and Eastern Europe, often from former Solvay plants, as well as from the United States, made the situation worse. Stimulated by overcapacity in the United States and helped by a low dollar, American producers of natural soda entered the European market in 1978 and had become by 1980 a dangerous threat. Soda ash prices in Europe went down, and several of the smaller Solvay plants were producing losses.[46]

[43] ARS 1990: 6–7; id. 1992: 4–5; ACS, 1001–26, letter from Daniel Janssen to members of Executive Committee, 25 Aug. 1992, with five articles on the chemical industry; ACS, MoE, 3 Nov. 1992.

[44] ACS, MoB, 30 Nov. 1992, 6 June 1994, 25 Jan. 1995; ACS, [C. Nanquette], "Desinvestissements du groupe entre 1985 et 1993, et desinvestissements prevus en 1994," 20 May 1994; ARS 1994: 8–9; id. 1997: 8; interview Michielsen, 16 Apr. 2008.

[45] ACS, CdG, 24 Sept. 1958; "Parlons produits: Le carbonate de soude (Na2CO3), matière fondamentale," *Revue Solvay* (Mar.–Apr. 1969): 5–8.

[46] ACS, 1010–10, presentation Mr. Vinçotte, 12 May 1980; E. Coppens and H. Dessart, "Adapting to the new conditions of the sodium carbonate market," *Revue Solvay* (1983) (2): 17–19; ACS,

To defend its leading position, Solvay did all it could to reduce its production costs, mainly by improving the energy efficiency of the plants and by closing the smallest plants and concentrating production capacity in the larger ones. Between 1981 and 1991, all soda ash units in which caustic soda from diaphragm electrolysis was converted into soda ash were closed, despite being rather new (see Chapter 15). In addition, Solvay decided to close the soda ash plants at Sarralbe (1983) and Zurzach (1987) and to enlarge the soda ash plants at Rosignano and Torrelavega, both of which were close to the sea.[47]

As a result of these measures, a higher dollar, and special contracts with large customers, for which the company later was fined by the European Commission, Solvay succeeded in improving its results in soda ash considerably during the second part of the 1980s. From 1988, though, when the dollar began to fall again, Solvay was increasingly threatened by imports from natural soda ash from the United States, in a declining market. Imports to the European Community from the United States and from Central Europe grew from 4 percent of the market in 1990 to 14 percent in 1992. As a result, Solvay's soda ash position deteriorated within a few years, especially in Northern Europe, and Solvay's return on investment in soda ash and its derivatives declined from 34.3 percent in 1990 to a mere 3.5 percent in 1993.[48]

This time, Solvay's answer to these attacks on its leadership was not only defensive, such as the closing down of Couillet and Heilbronn; it was also offensive. New technology (e.g., gas turbines with cogeneration) was introduced to reduce the energy costs; prices of soda ash were lowered in Northern Europe, a great departure from usual practices, to compete with Akzo and Brunner Mond; and most important, three new large-scale soda ash plants were acquired at Bernburg in Germany (1991), at Green River in the United States (1992), and at Devnya in Bulgaria (1997). The strategic significance of these three acquisitions was great. Bernburg was well situated in relation to the Central European markets, but at first it had a difficult time, given overproduction in Western Europe and the collapse of the Eastern economies. The acquisition of the large Green River plant of Tenneco was the culmination of many efforts over more than four years to again gain a foothold in soda ash in the United States. Despite the high price of US$500 million, it greatly improved Solvay's global position in soda ash. It not only helped reduce the import pressure on Solvay's European home market but also proved a bridgehead for the markets of Asia and Latin America. Within a few years the capacity of the

---

1001–26-1, "Note au Comité Exécutif – Proposition de strategie carbonate 1995–2000," 2 May 1994.

[47] ACS, 1020–10, "Reflexions sur l'actuelle situation de crise," 19 Oct. 1981; PR, "The European Community lifts antidumping rights applicable to soda ash imports from the U.S. – Solvay's viewpoint," 16 Oct. 1990; ACS, MoE, 5 Nov. 1991.

[48] ACS, MoB, 28 Nov. 1988, 29 Nov. 1993; PR, "Soda ash: The EC Commission fines Solvay for ECUs 30 million," 19 Dec. 1990; ACS, 1001–26, presentation Mr. Loutrel, 30 Jan. 1991; ACS, MoE, 25 Nov. 1992; PR, "Memorandum: Solvay's soda ash market," 14 Dec. 1993; ACS, MES meetings, B. de Laguiche, "Evolution des resultats et ROI sur 10 ans," 20 May 1997.

FIGURE 21.3. The Devnya, Bulgaria, plant bought by Solvay was the pride of the country: it appeared on ten-leva Bulgarian banknotes from 1974 to the early 1990s. (National Bank of Bulgaria).

Green River plant was expanded from 1.8 megatons per year to 2.4 megatons per year.[49]

With the acquisition of the modern soda ash plant at Devnya – with a capacity of 1.2 megatons per year, the largest single-unit plant in Europe – Solvay had similar aims as with Green River: reducing pressure in its home market and gaining market share elsewhere in the world. Since the start of the dramatic changes in the former communist countries, Solvay had tried to reacquire one of its former Polish plants at Podgórze and Inowrocław, but unsuccessfully. A new option opened up when in early 1996, following high inflation in Bulgaria and pressed by the International Monetary Foundation, the Bulgarian government decided to privatize the gigantic Sodi soda ash plant at Devnya, one of the few soda ash plants in the world with a harbor that could receive large seaborne vessels. Despite the risks involved – the plant was performing badly – Solvay decided to acquire 60 percent of shares, and the rest were reserved for local shareholders. When a US firm offered US$160 million, Solvay raised its bid just in time, and supported by its long-term Austrian partner Credit-Anstalt, the European Bank for Reconstruction and Development (EBRD), and the Turkish producer Sisecam, it succeeded in acquiring the package for sale. In April 1997 a final agreement was reached, and the name of the new company was changed to Solvay Sodi. One-quarter of the product was marketed by Sisecam in Turkey; the remaining three-quarters were sold by Solvay to Eastern Europe, Central Asia, the Middle East, and elsewhere. Devnya, located close

---

[49] ACS, MoB, 27 July 1987, 30 Jan. 1990, 29 Jan. 1992, 27 Nov. 1995; ACS, MoE, 28 July 1987, 4 July 1989, 17 Dec. 1991; ACS, 1001–26, "Politique générale du groupe," 14 Mar. 1988; ACS, 1059-2-6, "Le carbonate de soude en Europe – Situation début 1992," 11 Feb. 1992; PR, "Solvay Minerals, Inc.: Capacity expansion," 12 July 1995; PR, "Solvay Minerals expands soda ash in Wyoming, USA to 3,5 million short tons/year," 24 July 1996; O. Montfort, "Solvay, soda ash and trona . . . ," *Solvay Live* (Autumn 1996): 10–11.

to the Black Sea, was an excellent location for export. Solvay decided to invest heavily in the plant, as well as in securing its supply of raw materials (e.g., salt, limestone, steam, electricity).[50]

Through these acquisitions and large investments, Solvay succeeded in raising its competitiveness in soda ash within a few years. With growth of its production capacity from 4.6 megatons to 7.5 megatons between 1991 and 1997, despite the closure of two plants, Solvay remained the undisputed global leader in soda ash. When in early 1998 the incoming chairman of the Executive Committee, Aloïs Michielsen, looked back on what had been achieved, he called Solvay's European soda ash strategy a model on how to become as competitive as its American peers, which could serve as an example for the other SBUs. In the twenty-first century, Solvay entered alliances and joint ventures in soda ash in China and acquired the Alexandria Sodium Carbonate company in Egypt (2008). However, it could not realize its attempt to regain control, after almost a century, of Solvay's plant at Berezniki, Russia.[51]

Hydrogen Peroxide: From Specialty to Bulk Product

The formation of the Interox group in 1970–1971 created an industrial player in the field of peroxides with a dominant position in many European national markets, and global aspirations from the start. From the date of its creation, Interox energetically continued its international expansion. New hydrogen peroxide plants soon came on stream, partly in collaboration with third parties, in several countries, and in 1979 in Deer Park, Texas, the largest plant of all (see Chapters 15 and 18). As a result, by 1979 the Interox group consisted of eleven companies and eight associated companies, which operated twenty-two industrial sites in sixteen different countries. In the meantime, Solvay enlarged its shareholding in Laporte to 10 percent in 1974, and then, after delicate talks with banks, Laporte, and the British government, gradually to 25 percent by 1990. Reasons for this policy were not only to have a greater say in decisions concerning peroxides but also because of Laporte's titanium dioxide business, which Solvay wanted to acquire.[52]

[50] ACS, MoE, 25 Nov. 1992, 26 Sept. 1995, 27 Feb. 1996; ACS, 1001-26-1, "Note au Comité Exécutif – Proposition de strategie carbonate 1995–2000," 2 May 1994; ACS, MoB, 12 Dec. 1996, 31 July 1997, 23 Mar. 2000; PR, "Solvay signs a preliminary agreement with Bulgarian authorities on acquisition of 60 percent of Sodi shares," 19 Dec. 1996; PR, "Solvay Group finalises deal with Bulgarian authorities on the acquisition of Sodi Devnya," 15 Apr. 1997; O. Monfort, "Solvay-Sodi, in Bulgaria, on the Black Sea – Solvay moves Eastward," *Solvay Live* (Summer 1997): 16–17; PR, "Solvay Sodi takes control of three Bulgarian suppliers," 3 Aug. 2000.

[51] ARS 1997: 5–9; O. Monfort, "Soda ash and derivatives SBU: Strategy of world leader," *Solvay Live* 63 (Spring-Summer 1999): 20–1; PR, Press release, alliance with NCI, Sinopec in China, 13 May 2004; PR, acquisition of Alexandria Sodium Carbonate company in Egypt, 17 Oct. 2008; PR, Acquisition of Berezniki Soda Ash plant cannot be finalized, 10 June 2010.

[52] PPSF, Org 70–71, meeting Jacques Solvay and Paul Washer in Lisbon, 24–26 July 1971; ACS, MoE, 7 Mar. 1972, 17 July 1973, 3 Sept. 1974, 21 Jan. 1975, 17 Mar. 1975, 29 July 1975; "Collaboration renforcé entre Solvay & Laporte," *Revue Solvay* (June–July 1975): 18; "Interox:

During the 1970s and 1980s growth prospects were generally good, given the replacement of chlorine by hydrogen peroxide in the bleaching of paper pulp, as well as the growth of paper manufacture in general. The only worry was the domination of small plants in the Interox group, whereas competitors such as Degussa and Oxysynthèse (Atochem/Air Liquide) had constructed plants of far-larger magnitude. For a while, this had no great consequences in the still rather compartmentalized European market. With a global market share of 26 percent in hydrogen peroxide in 1983, and 46 percent in persalts, the position on Interox remained strong. During the second part of the 1980s, Interox further strengthened its global position by commissioning new plants in the Americas and Asia: a second plant in Brazil came on stream in Curitiba in 1988; a second plant in the United States, in Longview, Washington, started a year later; and in 1990 the plant at Map Ta Phut, Thailand, became operational.[53]

By 1988, with the unified European market approaching, the hydrogen peroxide market in Europe started to change rapidly. The European Commission took action against manufacturers after it discovered that there was almost no international trade in peroxides, whereas the national markets were controlled by local producers. An outsider, Kemira, entered the business by constructing hydrogen peroxide plants in Finland and later the Netherlands. The existing manufacturers responded vigorously. Interox's partner in Finland doubled its capacity to 30 kilotons, and the Interox plant in Jemeppe was enlarged to 50 kilotons. Degussa, in turn, decided to bring its plant in Antwerp to 105 kilotons, a world record in those days. In the early 1990s the lowering of cost prices through scaling up moved as an epidemic through the industry. Solvay-Interox decided to construct a 50 kilotons plant at Bernburg and greatly enlarged several of its other plants. Other producers did the same. In just a few years the Continental European market, Germany especially, was totally spoiled by huge overcapacities. Hydrogen peroxide that just a few decades before had been a delicate and precious chemical that produced high revenues suddenly had become a commodity produced on ever-larger scales.[54]

Staying competitive in such a market required huge investments. On that point, the visions of Solvay and Laporte diverged considerably. Improving the global position of a bulk product such as hydrogen peroxide fit well in Solvay's overall strategy. Laporte, by contrast, was more inclined to focus its business on specialties such as organic peroxides and persulfates. In 1991 it was therefore decided to end cooperation and to split the Interox business into two parts: the hydrogen peroxide, persalts, and caprolactone activities would become part of Solvay; the far smaller activities in organic peroxides and persulfates went

un groupe en pleine croissance," *Revue Solvay* (1979) (3): 13–14; PR, "Solvay Group – Increased holding in Laporte Industries (Holdings) PLC," 24 Oct. 1986.

[53] ACS, 1010–10, presentation PrO, 14 Apr. 1980; ARS 1983: 21; id. 1985: 20–1; ACS, MoB, 26 July 1989; PR, "Interox plants commissioned in Brazil and Finland," 6 July 1988; "Interox: Opening the Longview plant," *The Solvay Review* (1990) (1): 36–7.

[54] PR, "Interox to increase European peroxide capacity," 13 Sept. 1990; PR, "Interox increases European peroxide capacity," 4 Feb. 1991; PR, "Interox invests in Bernburg," 22 Jan. 1992; ACS, Exposés Directeurs 1994/1, "Note de dossier – L'activité peroxyde en Europe," 5 May 1994.

to Laporte. To account for the great difference in assets and sales, Solvay transferred about two-thirds of its shareholding in its British partner (16.5 percent of total shares) to Laporte. The remaining 8.5 percent of shares were sold to institutional investors, giving Solvay cash revenue of BEF 4.7 billion (US$140 million). After the deal, which became effective as of 1 January 1992, Solvay changed the name of the Interox group and its companies to Solvay Interox.[55]

Between 1992 and 1994 the price of hydrogen peroxide in Europe dropped by more than 50 percent as a result of overcapacities, the general recession, and the pressure on prices from Degussa. For Solvay no profitable business was possible at that market price. Following the advice by A. D. Little, Solvay Interox Europe was created to improve service to customers and to reorganize existing plants. Large plants were scaled up, and small, noncompetitive and obsolete plants were closed: Linne-Herten in September 1993, Höllriegelskreuth in October 1994, Tavaux at the end of that year, and in September 1995 the plant at Bad Hönningen. As other producers were facing the same problems, some talks took place between 1994 and 2000 to stop the erosion of prices. After Degussa had informed the European Commission on this practice, thereby avoiding a penalty itself, the other manufacturers were sentenced in 2006 to heavy fines, €167.1 million in the case of Solvay. During most of the 1990s, prices of hydrogen peroxide in Europe stayed under severe pressure, though. In the meantime, Solvay selectively continued its expansion outside Continental Europe and increased its production of specialties, such as ultrapure hydrogen peroxide for the semiconductor industry.[56]

As a result of all these measures, Solvay confirmed its global leadership. The commoditization of hydrogen peroxide continued. Large plants at Deer Park (85 kilotons), Bernburg (70 kilotons), and Curitiba (90 kilotons) were shadowed by the huge projects initiated after the year 2000. Between 2004 and 2008 Solvay, together with BASF, prepared and constructed a 230-kilotons megaplant at Antwerp that made use of the new the "high-productivity hydrogen peroxide process" developed by Solvay. It delivered the feedstock to a large propylene oxide (PO) plant constructed by BASF and Dow on the site. In 2007, Solvay and Dow decided to construct an even larger 330-kilotons

---

[55] ACS, MoE, 15 May 1990, 17 Dec. 1991, 11 Feb. 1992, 24 Mar. 1992; ACS, MoB, 27 Nov. 1991, 1 June 1992; PR, "Solvay and Laporte in serious discussions about an agreement to reorganize the Interox businesses," 28 Nov. 1991; PR, "Solvay – Laporte agreement regarding Interox companies," 24 Mar. 1992; "Warrington 3rd of June 1992: Speech by Baron Daniel Janssen...," insert in *Solvay Live* (June 1992).

[56] "Interview: Marc Duhem, General Manager of Solvay Interox," *Solvay Live* (June 1992): 2–3; PR, "Solvay Interox – start of construction of a new hydrogen peroxide plant at Bernburg and creation of a new Pan-European operations organisation," 6 Oct. 1992; ACS, Exposés Directeurs 1993/1, presentation Ph. Deroisy, 26 Jan. 1993; ACS, Exposés Directeurs 1994/1, "Note de dossier – L'activité peroxyde en Europe," 5 May 1994; ACS, MoB, 28 Sept. 1994; PR, "Solvay announces... the construction of a new 85,000 tonnes/year hydrogen peroxide plant at Deer Park," 1 Sept. 1995; D. Samson and L. Signorini, "L'eau oxygénée et l'infinement petit," *Solvay Live* (Winter 1996–1997): 6–7; PR, "Solvay Interox to close research site at Widnes (U.K.)," 20 Nov. 1997; http://fr.transnationale.org/entreprises/solvay.php; http://www.chemie.de/news/d/54481/.

plant in Thailand, again to supply a PO plant to be constructed by BASF and Dow, which came on stream in October 2011. Two more initiatives for joint ventures in hydrogen peroxide followed the 2007 decision: in China in 2009 and in Saudi Arabia in 2011.[57]

Barium and Strontium Carbonates: From Bulk Products to Specialties

The production of barium and strontium carbonates started at Solvay when the Belgian company succeeded in 1953 in obtaining the majority of shares of Kali-Chemie (KC). At one of the many KC plants, Bad Hönningen, barium and strontium derivatives had already produced since the establishment of that plant in 1890. The traditional uses of barium and strontium carbonates were in relatively low-tech ceramics applications. When it was discovered that barium and strontium had useful properties (shielding X-rays) in the screens of cathode-ray tubes for televisions and later computers, their demand grew hand in hand with the use of those products. In 1963 Kali-Chemie acquired the Italian company Società Bario et Derivati (Sabed), with a plant for barium derivatives at Massa di Carrara and a barite mine in Spain. With that acquisition Kali-Chemie had become the largest manufacturer of barium and strontium carbonates in the world. In 1988 it had a global market share of 45 percent.[58]

When the production of television and computer screens increasingly moved from Europe to Asia, Kali-Chemie set up the joint venture Daehan Specialty Chemicals Co. Ltd., together with Samsung, with a plant in Onsan, Korea, where production started in 1990 (see Chapter 18). In 1989 Kali-Chemie also succeeded in acquiring an interest in the Mexican producer of strontium carbonates Sales y Óxidos (Syosa), situated in Villa de García, near Monterrey.[59]

During the early 1990s the barium and strontium business struggled with a serious overproduction crisis for several years, to which Solvay partly responded by moving to the production of highly pure grades and other specialties. When the economy recovered, a new and far-greater problem appeared: the television and computer manufacturers tended to choose flat screens over cathode-ray tubes. At first the situation was uncertain, but after

---

[57] PR, "Peróxidos do Brasil starts to expand its hydrogen peroxide production to 90,000 tonnes per year," 1 Dec. 2000; PR, Solvay confirms intention to create Hydrogen Peroxide joint venture with BASF, 2 Sept. 2004; PR, BASF, Dow, Solvay partnership breaks new ground with innovative HPPO technology in Antwerp, 27 Sept. 2006; PR, Solvay and Huatai to jointly build hydrogen peroxide plant in China, 8 Oct. 2009; PR, Solvay to form Joint Venture with Sadara to build Hydrogen Peroxide plant in Saudi Arabia, 28 July 2011.

[58] Rüsberg (1949), 39–43, 57–8, 65; ACS, 1805–40-24, visit Messrs. Lega, Proyard, and Dr. Rüsberg to the Minas de Baritina (Spain), 23–24 May 1979; ACS, 1805–37, Advisory Committee Solvay/Kali-Chemie Coordination, 30 June 1988; ACS, MoB, 28 Nov. 1988; N. Trevisan, "SABED – Barium, strontium and...chianti," *Solvay Live* 24 (1) (Spring 1996): 8–9.

[59] ACS, MoE, 5 May 1987; ACS, MoB, 27 July 1987; ACS, 1805–37, Advisory Committee Solvay/Kali-Chemie Coordination, 14 Oct. 1988, 30 Oct. 1989, 22 Jan. 1990, 4 Oct. 1990; PR, "Solvay Group: Investment in Mexico," 8 May 1989.

a few years it appeared that flat screens would become the trend, with a negative impact on the demand for barium and strontium carbonates. It took a while before Solvay took the market signals seriously enough. At first it decided to stick to its strategy of global leadership and to strengthen especially its position in Asia through alliances and joint ventures in China and India. When by 2004 the production of cathode-ray tube screens suddenly collapsed, Solvay decided to join forces with one of its US competitors, Chemical Products Corporation (CPC). But by then only the niche markets for high-purity and ultrafine grades were left. Solvay had to learn the hard way that when you do not listen to the market well enough, you are too late to gain market share in upcoming new technology (flat screens). In 2006 the SBU of barium and strontium was merged with the SBU of advanced functional materials. The products had lost their special status and visibility within the company.[60]

The Fall and Rise of Fluorinated Chemicals

Like barium and strontium derivatives, fluorine compounds entered the Solvay business via Kali-Chemie. Late in 1960, Kali-Chemie took an interest of 50 percent in the Saline Ludwigshalle at Bad Wimpfen, in southern Germany, an enterprise that had exploited salt and fluorspar (CaF_2) deposits since the early nineteenth century. Kali-Chemie decided to extend the business on the site for its own account with the production of organic fluorine derivatives. In December 1961 a license agreement was concluded with Allied Chemical that gave Kali-Chemie the right to produce and sell in Continental Europe Allied's Genetron chlorofluorocarbons (CFCs), called Kaltron by KC. In 1963 the Kaltron plant at Bad Wimpfen came on stream. The products were mainly used in aerosols and to a lesser extent as refrigerants and solvents. Business went very well. By the 1980s Kaltron production at Bad Wimpfen had grown tenfold. Kali-Chemie also constructed a Kaltron plant in Spain, on Solvay's site at Torrelavega.[61]

In 1973 Kali-Chemie succeeded in obtaining a majority interest in Saline Ludwigshalle and started to further integrate the inorganic and organic activities. A central role in the plant was played by the production of hydrogen fluoride (HF) from fluorspar. It was the key intermediate for all other products of the plant: inorganic fluorine compounds, mainly used in metallurgy and in the treatment of surfaces; organic fluorine derivatives, such as the Kaltrons and

---

[60] ACS, "Vision stratégique," 13 May 1996; ACS, MES meeting, 27–28 May 1998; PR, "Solvay Group strengthens its position in the field of barium and strontium carbonates production and marketing," 17 Dec. 1998; Paul Dandoy, "La galaxie Baryum Strontium," *Solvay Live* 65 (Feb. 2001): 28–9; PR, Solvay and Chemical Products Corporation seek to create global barium strontium joint venture, 24 Nov. 2004; PR, Solvay and Chemical Products Corporation launch global barium strontium joint venture, 18 Nov. 2005.

[61] ASD, Prüfungsbericht KC 1960: 9, id. 1962: 6–8; ACS, RdG, 16 Feb. 1961; ACS, 1805–37, Advisory Committee Solvay/Kali-Chemie Coordination, 30 June 1988; "L'Usine de Torrelavega développe ses installations," *Revue du Personnel* (1967) (3): 10; http://www.solvay. de/standorte/badwimpfen/wissenswertes/0,,49935-4-0,00.htm.

the "halons" used in fire extinguishers; and finally sulfur hexafluoride, a product used in high-voltage switch gears. Profits grew successfully during most of the 1980s.[62]

Then there appeared a dark cloud in the sky. In 1974 the chemists Mario J. Molina and F. Sherwood Rowland published a paper in which they argued that CFCs destroyed stratospheric ozone, a gas layer that shields Earth from ultraviolet radiation. It aroused much interest, and in 1978 the US government decided to ban CFCs as propellants for nonessential aerosol sprays. The industry was quick in steering its CFCs production to new outlets, such as blowing agents for polyurethane foams, refrigerants, and solvents. In 1985, though, British scientists published their discovery of a hole in the ozone layer over the Antarctic. For years this became a great issue in the media, in politics, and in debates among environmentalists. At an international conference at Montreal, in September 1987, a protocol was signed that demanded a 50 percent reduction before 1998 of the use of CFCs, as well as some other chemicals that destroyed the ozone layer. During conferences in London (1990) and Copenhagen (1992), this was later changed to a total ban by 1996.[63]

The industry responded with a double strategy. On the one hand, it emphasized all the scientific uncertainties of the issue and lobbied in political circles for temporization and for a less inclusive and less stringent character of possible measures. On the other hand, it immediately started to prepare for the future and embarked on research on alternatives for the CFCs and other substances hit by the ban. Research on new products and processes was mostly done by each company individually, but on toxicological and environmental issues there was cooperation. In December 1987, sixteen of the leading CFC producers, including Solvay, started the Program for Alternative Fluorocarbon Toxicity Testing (PAFT). And the following year eleven manufacturers, again including Solvay, embarked on the Alternative Fluorocarbon Environmental Acceptability Study (AFEAS). In house, Solvay quickly started research at Hanover, NoH, and Tavaux on hydrochlorofluorocarbons (HCFCs), second-generation CFC alternatives, which had a lesser impact on the ozone layer. Solkane 142b and Solkane 141b, two intermediates of VF2 production at Tavaux for the special polymer PVDF, were soon promoted as possible alternatives.[64]

From about 1988, Solvay took measures to phase out the chemicals hit by the ban, as well as by additional regulations in several countries, step by step and mostly ahead of the official schedule. Between November 1991 and May 1994, production of halons and Kaltrons at Torrelavega and Bad Wimpfen was stopped. In the meantime, CFCs were replaced with the previously mentioned products and with third-generation alternatives such as hydrofluorocarbons

[62] G. Grunghard, "Introducing fluorine," *Solvay Live* (Fall 1992): 8–9; Eberhard Piepho, "L'avenir au fluor," *Solvay Live* 64 (Summer–Autumn 2000): 10–11; ACS, 1055-2-1, "Produits Fluorés – Environnement, Santé et Réglementation," 27 Feb. 2002.

[63] ACS, MoE, 4 June 1985, 5 May 1987; ACS, MoB, 19 Mar. 1987, 28 Nov. 1988; see also Cagin and Dray (1993); Anderson and Sarma (2002); Oreskes and Conway (2010), 107–35.

[64] ACS, 1805-37, Advisory Committee Solvay/Kali-Chemie Coordination, 14 Mar. 1988, 14 Oct. 1988, 22 Jan. 1990, 29 May 1990; ACS, MoE, 20 June 1989; ACS, MoB, 29 July 1989, 6 Mar. 1990; Anderson and Sarma (2002), 199–204, 216, 264–5.

(HFCs), which contained no chlorine. Solvay was actively involved in research on those third-generation substances. During the early 1990s, more than half of the research budget of the broad alkalis sector was spent on researching halogenated organic chemicals alone. Between 1992 and 1995 several new products were introduced to market, first as refrigerants and later for foams and aerosols. All these HFCs had no impact on the ozone layer, but unfortunately it appeared that they contributed to the greenhouse effect, a worry that had gone public in the meantime. Therefore, Solvay spent four years of research at Hanover and NoH developing Solkane 365mfc, a substance with a favorable eco-balance. It was introduced as a foaming agent on pilot-plant scale in 1999 and on an industrial scale three years later.[65]

In the middle of the crisis of the early 1990s, when Solvay started to critically evaluate the global potentials of all its businesses, the company got an offer from a firm that wanted to buy Solvay's fluorine business. The members of the Executive Committee seriously considered selling it, because at that time Solvay's fluorine activities were quite behind companies such as DuPont, ICI, and Atochem. The issue was complicated, though, because the minority shareholders of Kali-Chemie might go to court and force Solvay to reinvest revenues from the sale in Kali-Chemie. At an Executive Committee meeting in November 1993, Eberhard Piepho, general manager of the fluorine activities, convinced Executive Committee members to keep the business and develop it. In 1995 the fluorine SBU got a first foothold in the United States, where the company Advanced Research Chemicals Inc. was acquired, with a plant at Catoosa, Oklahoma. The following year, Solvay took over the HCFC and HFC activities of the German giant Hoechst, with production facilities at Frankfurt, Germany, and Tarragona, Spain. In 1997 the security of raw materials supply was greatly improved when Solvay acquired the important fluorspar mine at Okurusu in Namibia, with reserves for at least twenty years. At that stage, Piepho and Jean Christiaens, head of the chemicals sector, thought a great leap forward should be made, in line with Solvay's global leadership strategy, by joining forces with DuPont or ICI. Talks and negotiations with DuPont, by far the largest company in the field, followed, but no final agreement could be reached.[66]

[65] ACS, 1805–37, Advisory Committee Solvay/Kali-Chemie Coordination, 4 May 1990; ACS, MoE, 20 Nov. 1990, 4 June 1996; PR, "Substitutes for CFC's – Further progress at Solvay," 2 Apr. 1991; ACS, MoB, 1 June 1992, 11 Feb. 1999; PR, "Solvay: Definitive stop of CFC's and launch of new substitutes of the 3rd generation," 14 June 1994; PR, "International Ozone Day – Solvay's contribution towards a solution of the problem," 16 Sept. 1995; F. Delplanque, "HFC: Solvay finds missing pieces in the CFC substitute puzzle," *Solvay Life* (Summer 1997): 24–5; ACS, Exposés Directeurs 1997, presentation SBU-F, 2 Dec. 1997; Eberhard Piepho, "L'avenir au fluor," *Solvay Live* 64 (Summer–Autumn 2000): 10–11; PR, "Solvay reinforces fluorine specialties: New production plant for Solkane 365 MFC is operational," 24 Mar. 2003.

[66] ACS, MoE, 9 Nov. 1993, 20 Jan. 1998, 2 Apr. 1999; ACS, MoB, 26 July 1995, 30 Mar. 1999, 3 June 1999; PR, "CFC Substitutes: Solvay intends to acquire the Hoechst fluorocarbons business," 2 Feb. 1996; PR, "Solvay acquires Hoechst fluorocarbons business," 4 June 1996; "An African dream – Solvay acquires a mine in Namibia," *Solvay Live* (Dec. 1997): 15.

Early in 2000 Solvay acquired Norfluor SA, a producer of hydrogen fluoride (HF) in Ciudad Juárez, Mexico, as well as Chemtech Products of St. Louis, Missouri, a producer of inorganic fluorine compounds. In this way, the fluorine SBU greatly strengthened its position in North America. Two years later, the largest purchase by the Solvay group to that point took place when Solvay acquired the Italian company Ausimont, a producer of fluorinated polymers and fluorine compounds (see Chapter 22). Talks had started almost immediately after the negotiations with DuPont were cancelled. In May 2002 they were concluded successfully. From then on Solvay was ranked second in the world in fluorines, and first in Europe, completely in line with Solvay's leadership strategy.[67]

Over the following few years Solvay's fluorine business expanded mainly in Asia, in the field of high-tech inorganic fluorines. In the field of organic fluorinated chemicals, Solvay could not compete with cheap Chinese manufacturers, though, who in 2006 suddenly started to flood the global market. In 2007 a major reorganization was carried out that involved a loss of around 250 jobs in five sites: Hanover, Bad Wimpfen, Frankfurt, Porto Marghera (Italy), and Tarragona. The HCFCs were taken out of production, but the inorganic fluorinated specialties continued to play an interesting role.[68]

Leading in Fuel Tanks – A Story of Growth and Divestment

When Solvay built up its plastics-processing activities during the late 1950s and 1960s, developments occurred in all possible directions. As a result, by 1980 Solvay's processing sector included plants in fields as diverse as packaging (e.g., bottles, food packaging), construction (e.g., wood protection, corrugated PVC sheets, paint and coatings, special cements, window frames), and calendering (e.g., industrial foils; interior decoration, including wallpaper; adhesive foils; automotive products), as well as more recent acquisitions in foams, pipes and fittings, and injection and blow-molded technical parts for the automobile industry, including fuel tanks (see Chapter 16).

After the crisis of the early 1980s, Solvay decided to improve the focus of its processing sector. Activities in the fields of foams (1985), paints and coatings (1986–1987), packaging (1986–1992), wood protection (1994), and special cements (1994) were divested because of their low return on investment and little prospect for improved results. By contrast, acquisitions and investments

---

[67] ACS, MES meeting, 8–9 Dec. 1999; PR, "Solvay Fluor Business: Acquisitions in USA and Mexico," 10 Jan. 2000; ACS, MoB, 9 Feb. 2000; PR, "Solvay grows further in fluorinated specialities," 26 July 2000; PR, Solvay successfully completes acquisition of Ausimont, confirms leadership in fluorinated specialties, 7 May 2002.

[68] PR, Solvay to launch production of fluorine specialties in Asia, 22 June 2005; PR, Solvay to launch fluorochemicals production in China, 21 Aug. 2006; PR, Solvay takes steps to restore competitiveness of its Fluor Chemicals business, 29 Oct. 2007; PR, Solvay expands its high-purity wet chemicals business in the Chinese electronic market, 5 Sept. 2010; PR, Solvay acquires a Bulgarian fluorspar mine, 22 Feb. 2011.

were concentrated in fields that depended on advanced technical know-how, such as special products for the automobile industry and industrial sheets and foils, or products that consumed much PVC and HDPE, such as pipes and fittings. In 1989 the 50–50 joint venture Pipelife was created with the Austrian company Wienerberger, which over the course of the 1990s would greatly expand its activities all over Europe. When in 1996 the SBUs were introduced, the plastics-processing sector concentrated its activities in four SBUs: interior decoration, automobile, industrial foils, and pipes and fittings. A further focus took place in 2001 when the interior decoration SBU was sold to the German company Langbein-Pfanhauser Werke (LPW).[69]

From the 1960s, the automobile industry increasingly had started to substitute metallic and textile parts of cars for parts made of plastics. This started with objects such as chair covers, trim parts for doors, and dashboards. More technically complicated parts followed. Especially after the two oil crises, automobile manufacturers realized that substituting metals by plastics could reduce the weight of cars and, by implication, the consumption of gasoline. The automobile industry therefore became a huge market for plastics-processing firms. Solvay had created already in June 1972 a specific Automobile Division that developed close relations with French and foreign car manufacturers.[70]

As part of Solvay's broader strategy to reduce cyclicality, the Corporate Planning Department by 1979 had advised focusing car-related activities on more technically sophisticated products, such as fuel tanks made of HDPE. In 1979 Solvay created the joint venture Creaplast, together with the French company STMP, which specialized in high-tech car parts. The plant was at Laval, close to a site of a French car manufacturer. In 1981 Solvay acquired the majority of STMP shares. Later that year, the company Société des Plastiques d'Alsace (Sodepa) at Pfastatt, near Mulhouse, was included in the business as well, and another production location for fuel tanks, run by Solvay's subsidiary Sociedad General de Hules, was opened at Barcelona. For these fuel tanks special qualities of HDPE were needed, with very high molecular weights. That fit perfectly with Solvay's strategy to develop its vulnerable polyolefins business in the direction of special grades with higher value-added. After some difficult first years, given the recession of the car industry, a good synergy emerged between Solvay's HDPE production and the production of fuel tanks. A large contract was concluded with Renault in 1983. Every year Solvay's fuel tank had to meet higher-quality standards set by car manufacturers, and

[69] ACS, Organisation, "Tr. dans le cadre d'une revision de l'organisation du groupe," 9 May 1983; ACS, MoB, 25 July 1988, 28 Nov. 1994; ACS, binder "La Transformation," "Strategy – Giving more focus to processing," Mar. 1990; ACS, [C. Nanquette], "Desinvestissements du groupe entre 1985 et 1993, et desinvestissements prevus en 1994," 20 May 1994; PR, "Solvay Group – joint venture with Wienerberger in the field of pipes," 29 May 1989; ACS, Michel Bilquin, "Solvay et les activités Décoration – Histoire et leçons d'une croissance et d'un decline," 18 Oct. 2002.

[70] "Le department auto-Europe," *Actualités TrC* (Feb. 1973): 8–9; M. Catalon, "La crise de l'industrie automobile," *Actualités TrC* (Mar.–Apr. 1974): 4–5.

therefore production robots and automated systems were soon introduced to its manufacturing lines in France and Spain. In the second part of the 1980s a large modern production line was also constructed at Hedwin's plant at South Bend, Indiana, between Chicago and Detroit, which produced tanks for the new Ford Thunderbird.[71]

The 1980s were a learning period for Solvay in the field. It succeeded remarkably well. Within ten years the company was able to manufacture fuel tanks in France, Spain, and the United States of the highest quality, and an important network with car manufacturers was established. On that basis, Solvay decided in the late 1980s to expand its fuel-tank business geographically. In 1988 a company was created in Great Britain. The following year, production of HDPE fuel tanks also started at Solvay's subsidiary Hanyang Polymer Co., in South Korea. Halfway through 1990, Solvay strengthened its position in the North America market considerably with the acquisition of the plastics operations of the Kuhlman group, with manufacturing activities in Canada, the United States, and Mexico. In 1992 the company was the second-largest producer of fuel tanks in Europe and, with its interests in Korea and North America, the largest in the world. It frequently manufactured fuel tanks and technical parts for specific models of Citroën, Peugeot, Renault, Ford, Chrysler, General Motors, and Volkswagen, to name just a few, with which the company closely cooperated. At the request of customers, Solvay delivered the tanks just in time, within a few hours after the order.[72]

Just-in-time delivery sometimes required that Solvay construct a new factory close to a manufacturing site of a car company. In 1995, to serve Chrysler, then Solvay's largest customer, Solvay constructed a new plant at Adrian, Michigan. After the mid-1990s internationalization continued at a faster pace, with acquisitions and joint ventures in Italy (1995), Germany (1996), Argentina (1996), Poland (1998), Japan (1998), and Romania (1999). Commenting in 1998 on the power of the automobile manufacturers, Aloïs Michielsen, Solvay's new CEO, remarked: "A French manufacturer ... is asking Solvay to follow it to Russia, and another wants us in Argentina." What should we do?[73]

---

[71] ACS, MoE, 7 Oct. 1980, 15 Feb. 1982, 19 Nov. 1985, 28 July 1987, 2 June 1988; ACS, MoB, 24 Nov. 1980, 28 Sept. 1981; ACS, CdL, "La transformation: Ses caracterisques – Ses problèmes – Son apport," 9 June 1982; interview Aloïs Michielsen, 24 Sept. 2008.

[72] ACS, MoE, 17 May 1988, 5 Dec. 1989, 6 Feb. 1990, 14 Apr. 1990, 3 July 1990, 20 Nov. 1990, 14 May 1991, 3 Dec. 1991, 27 Sept. 1994, 25 Nov. 1994, 24 Mar. 1995; ACS, MoB, 26 July 1989, 28 Nov. 1994; PR, "Solvay strengthens its position in the field of plastic specialties for the automotive industry," 20 July 1990; "Automobiles and automobile markets," *Solvay Live* 22 (2) (Winter 1994): 1–17.

[73] ACS, MoE, 3 May 1995, 29 June 1995, 22 Dec. 1995, 14 May 1996, 20 June 1996, 24 July 1996, 1 Oct. 1996, 13 May 1997, 2 Dec. 1997, 28 July 1998, 9 Mar. 1999; PR, "Solvay-Group acquires fifty percent of the Italian automotive components company 'Safiplast,'" 29 Nov. 1995; PR, "Solvay acquires major German automotive supplier," 11 Mar. 1996; PR, "Solvay creates automotive joint venture in Argentina," 4 July 1996; ACS, MES meeting, 28–29 May 1997, "Liste des 25 plus gros clients de Solvay"; C. Thibaut de Maisières, "Automotive SBU: Thinking global," *Solvay Live* (Summer 1997): 8–9; PR, Solvay (Belgium) and Subansamble (Romania) decide to create a joint venture in the field of plastic fuel systems, 6 May 1999.

In the light of these powerful customers, as well as growing overcapacities, Solvay in 1999 decided to join forces with one of its strongest competitors, the French company Plastic Omnium – founded by Pierre Burelle in 1947 – which had entered the fuel-tank business in 1986. After careful negotiations, Inergy Automotive Systems, the 50–50 joint venture between Plastic Omnium and Solvay Automotive, took off in July 2000. With sales of about €1 billion in 2001, 3,300 employees, a global market share of 40 percent, and thirty-three sites in seventeen different countries, Solvay's world leadership in this field was considerably strengthened. Expansion in Asia, South America, and Central Europe ranked high on the agenda. Within a month, Inergy took over Nissan's fuel-tank business in Japan. Plants in Korea, Slovenia, Thailand, and South Africa followed.[74]

In the second part of the 2000s, Inergy also succeeded in gaining a foothold in important fast-growing automobile markets such as China, Russia, and India. Despite that, the business became increasingly difficult, with lower margins, given powerful customers. Inergy closed several sites in countries with high labor costs, so that by 2010 only twenty-four sites in eighteen countries were left. That year, Solvay decided to sell its stake in Inergy for €270 million to its partner Plastic Omnium. It needed the money for expansions in new directions, after the sale of the pharmaceuticals business. Moreover, after selling its HDPE business to BP in 2005 (see Chapter 22), there was no internal synergy inside Solvay between resins and processing in the field. For the same reason, Solvay in 2012 also sold its 50 percent interest in Pipelife to its partner Wienerberger. With that last divestment, Solvay's involvement in plastics processing had come to an end, after an involvement for more than fifty years.[75]

PVC: Continued Leadership by Scaling Up and Joining Forces

Starting from the excellent ICI technology in the field of PVC, and supported by its own strong R&D efforts and technical service, the Solvay company had acquired a leading position in PVC in Europe in a remarkably short time (see Chapter 15). With the expected saturation of the Western European markets and the growing criticism of PVC from European ecologists, Solvay's strategy focused on following the growth of Western European

[74] ACS, Exposés Directeurs 1998, "Transformation," 8 Apr. 1998; ACS, MoE, 28 Apr. 1998, 29 Sept. 1998, 24 May 2000; ACS, MoB, 16 Dec. 1999, 5 June 2000; PR, "Inergy Automotive Systems: Birth of a world leader in fuel systems," 17 July 2000; Laure-Ève Monfort, "Inergy tient la route," *Solvay Live* 65 (Summer–Autumn 2001): 8–9; http://www.plasticomnium.com/en/inside-pastic-omnium/the-company/history.html.

[75] PR, Inergy Automotive Systems deploys its fuel systems business in China, India, and Russia, 7 May 2007; PR, Inergy Automotive Systems starts operations in China, 26 June 2008; PR, Inergy Automotive Systems is building new factories in China and India to serve growing automotive markets, 18 June 2009; PR, Inergy Automotive Systems starts producing fuel systems in its new plant in Stavrovo, Russia, 4 Nov. 2009; PR, Plastic Omnium will acquire Solvay's shares in Inergy Automotive Systems for EUR 270 million, 28 July 2010; PR, "Wienerberger will acquire Solvay's stake in Pipelife," 15 Feb. 2012.

markets, reducing production costs as much as possible, and developing its business more vigorously in the much faster-growing Brazilian and Asian markets.

In 1992 the PVC plant at Map Ta Phut became operational and was enlarged to a fully integrated electrolysis, VCM, and PVC complex in 1996. In Brazil, in 1989 Solvay acquired a majority shareholding in the company Brasivil Resinas Vinilicas SA, which operated a PVC plant close to Solvay's site at Elclor in Santo Andre. In the following years the South American market developed favorably, but Solvay do Brasil was handicapped with respect to its supply of ethylene. An excellent opportunity to improve that situation appeared in 1995, when Jean-Pierre Lapage, Solvay's national manager in Brazil, informed Solvay leaders that the government of Argentina had decided to privatize its petro-chemical and plastics businesses and to become part of the Mercosur economic area (Brazil, Argentina, Uruguay, and Paraguay). Solvay succeeded in obtaining a 51 percent shareholding in the company Indupa, which produced chlorine, caustic soda, VCM, and PVC in a chemical complex at Bahia Blanca, which had access to important natural gas reserves nearby. Soon Solvay decided to expand the electrolysis and the VCM and PVC plants considerably. By the end of 1997 the Brazilian caustic soda, VCM, and PVC activities were inte-grated into Indupa, under the leadership of Lapage. Solvay was better equipped to face growing competition in Mercosur by producers from the US Gulf Coast.[76]

In Europe, the golden years of 1987 and 1988 led to ambitious plans to install new capacity. To reduce transportation of VCM from Northern Europe to Ferrara, as well as exports of PVC to Italy, Solvay planned a new VCM-PVC complex at Rosignano. At the end of 1988 it appeared, though, that the municipality of Rosignano did not agree. A new plan to construct the complex at Ravenna could not be realized because no agreement could be reached concerning the ethylene supply. As a result, Solvay decided to raise its capacity via removing bottlenecks at existing plants and by constructing a 250 kiloton per year ethylene dichloride (EDC) plant at Solvay's site at Lillo near Antwerp, which could supply EDC to Solvay's VCM plants.[77]

With hindsight it was a good thing, perhaps, that the Rosignano investment was cancelled – soon the market circumstances deteriorated. Huge overca-pacities in the United States and Eastern Europe led to growing imports into Western Europe, and prices fell by almost 40 percent. In the years 1991–1993

---

[76] ACS, MoE, 21 Mar. 1989, 20 June 1989; ACS, MoB, 26 July 1989, 8 Feb. 1996, 27 Sept. 1997, 15 Dec. 1997; PR, "Solvay Group in Brazil: acquisition in the PVC field," 31 July 1989; ACS, 1061–2-1, "Exposé stratégie dans les Plastiques," 28 Nov. 1994; PR, "Solvay: Major expansion in South America," 9 Feb. 1996; PR, "Solvay Group: Continued expansion in Mercosur with USD 66 million investment in Indupa plant at Bahia Blanca (Argentina)," 3 June 1997; PR, "Solvay expands position as leading PVC producer in Mercosur," 16 Sept. 1997; PR, "Indupa . . . decides the acquisition of similar activities from Solvay do Brasil," 23 Dec. 1997.

[77] ACS, "Reflexions sur l'implantation de nos futures unites Plastiques Europeennes," 30 Aug. 1988; ACS, MoE, 6 Dec. 1988, 20 June 1989; ACS, 1001–26-1, "Politique générale du groupe," 14 Mar. 1989; personal communication by Claude Loutrell, 14 Sept. 2011.

Solvay was losing money on PVC. To consolidate its position, Solvay modernized and scaled up its installations to lower production costs as much as possible. At the end of 1993 Solvay also decided to close its small and unintegrated suspension plant at Hallein, as part of a reorganization project of European manufacturers. Moreover, Solvay decided to restructure and modernize its emulsion polymerization plants directed at the production of special grades. The emulsion units at Ferrara, Jemeppe, and later at Martorell were shut down, and all production was concentrated at Tavaux and Rheinberg. By measures such as these, Solvay succeeded in surviving the crisis of the early 1990s and increased its competitiveness – it ranked second in Europe after EVC (later Ineos). On a global scale Solvay surpassed EVC, though, because of its plants in South America and Thailand. It was ranked third in the world, after Formosa Plastics, from Taiwan, and the Japanese firm Shin-Etsu.[78]

The recovery of the mid-1990s was short lived. Business cycles in plastics seemed to become shorter, and results in PVC went down again in 1996. With a low dollar and very low local prices of ethylene, producers situated on the Gulf Coast – subsidiaries of Formosa Plastics and Shin-Etsu among them – could export VCM and PVC at competitive prices to Latin America and Europe. Only fully integrated electrolysis-VCM-PVC of about 250 kilotons per year could compete, which meant that further rationalizations and restructuring were necessary. After confidential negotiations during 1998 and 1999 by Henri Lefèbvre, then head of the plastics sector, and Jacques van Rijckevorsel, head of PVC, and a long antitrust investigation by the European Commission, Solvay and BASF on 1 August 1999 merged their European PVC and PVDC activities into the joint venture SolVin (75 percent to Solvay and 25 percent to BASF). This perfectly illustrates, just like Inergy Automotive Systems, Solvay's new strategy of the late 1990s of concluding partnerships to strengthen its position in specific areas. Important technical and economic synergies were a valuable part of the deal: SolVin would get access to ethylene supplied by the steam crackers of BASF at Ludwigshafen and Zandvliet, near Antwerp, and the by-product hydrochloric acid produced by BASF's isocyanate plant at Zandvliet would serve as cheap feedstock for SolVin's EDC plant at that site. To further compete, Solvay also closed its suspension PVC plant at Ferrara and its relatively new EDC plant at Lillo, and BASF in turn closed its VCM and PVC plants at Zandvliet. To compensate for these losses of capacity, the bottlenecks were removed at the remaining VCM and PVC plants (i.e., Jemeppe, Rheinberg, Tavaux, Ludwigshafen). The merger of the PVC activities again reduced the number of producers. Of the twenty-seven Western European PVC producers in the 1970s, only ten were left. At the end of 2005 SolVin also closed the

[78] ACS, MoE, 22 Oct. 1991, 9 Nov. 1993, 24 Nov. 1995; ACS, 1061-2-1, "Le secteur plastiques de Solvay de 1970 à 1991," 14 July 1992; id., "Note au Comité Exécutif – PVC Resins Europe – Proposition d'un plan de redressement emulsions," 13 Nov. 1995; "Exposé stratégie dans les Plastiques," 28 Nov. 1994; id.; ACS, MoB, 29 Sept. 1993, 30 Sept. 1998; PR, "Solvay rationalizes its PVC activities in Austria," 5 Nov. 1993.

relatively small plant at Ludwigshafen, which was one of the oldest PVC plants in Europe, dating from before World War II. As a result, only fully integrated large-scale plants were left. Jemeppe and Rheinberg grew to PVC plants of more than 300 kilotons per year each. By 2009 Jemeppe had enlarged to 475 kilotons per year.[79]

Spain was left out of the agreement with BASF. In that country Solvay's subsidiary Hispavic cooperated with Atochem in the VCM joint venture Viniclor at Martorell (65 percent to Solvay and 35 percent to Atochem). In response to the difficulties of the European PVC business, Solvay and Atochem in 1998 decided to restructure their Spanish activities. They pioneered a so-called production agreement, in which both partners cooperated in the production of PVC but were autonomous in marketing, sales, distribution, and R&D. To achieve economies of scale, Atochem closed its PVC plant and took an interest of 35 percent in Hispavic's PVC plant at Martorell, which was enlarged to a more competitive scale. In 1999 Solvay and Atochem also succeeded in acquiring together a 60 percent shareholding in the huge VCM plant of Shell Chemicals (375 kilotons per year) at Fos in southern France (the remaining 40 percent was held by Atochem), as well the total ownership of Shell's suspension PVC plant at nearby Berre. Again, Solvay and Atochem concluded a production agreement that left both partners free in all other domains. In 2002 Solvay's 65 percent share in the VCM and PVC plants at Martorell was integrated into SolVin. The contracts with Atochem (later Arkema) remained unaffected. In 2010 SolVin and Arkema decided to end their minority cross-holdings in these Spanish and French businesses. SolVin became the sole owner of the VCM and PVC plants at Martorell, and Arkema got full control over the two plants in France.[80]

As a result of these partnerships with BASF and Atochem, Solvay was able to greatly improve its competitive position in Europe. Between 2001 and 2009,

[79] ACS, MES meeting, B. de Laguiche, "Evolution des resultats et ROI sur 10 ans," 20 May 1997; id., "Exposé de B. de Laguiche," 29 May 1997; ACS, MoB, 27 Sept. 1997, 30 Sept. 1998, 14 Dec. 1998, 14 Dec. 2000; ACS, 1092–66-2, "Allucution du Baron Daniel Janssen . . . à l'occasion du Centenaire de l'usine de Jemeppe-sur-Sambre le 3 octobre 1997"; ACS-CR, contracts between BASF and Solvay, 12 Feb. 1998, 30 Sept. 1998, 2 Apr. 1999; ACS, MoE, 3 June 1998, 23 Feb. 1999, 28 June 2000; PR, "Solvay intends to stop PVC production in Ferrara (Italy)," 2 Oct. 1998; E. Breny, "PVC: A Solvay joint venture with BASF," *Solvay Live*, 62 (Winter 1998–1999): 15; PR, Vinyls venture company SolVin, rationalization of EDC-VCM-PVC units in Antwerp, 8 Mar. 1999; PR, "SolVin commercial start-up," 27 July 1999; PR, SolVin implements industrial plan, 30 Mar. 2001; PR, SolVin invests EUR 50 million to concentrate vinyl production on global size plants, 11 May 2006; PR, Solvin moves to reap sustainable benefits from dynamic vinyls market, 24 July 2007.

[80] ACS, MES meeting, 27–28 May 1998; ACS, MoB, 4 June 1998, 30 Sept. 1999; ACS-CR, contracts between Hispavic, Elf Atochem/Atofina, and Shell, 3 Feb. 1999, 7 July 1999, 1 Oct. 1999, 22 Dec. 1999, 25 Jan. 2000, 1 July 2002, 8 July 2002; PR, "Solvay and Elf Atochem to reorganize their PVC production in Spain," 9 Feb. 1999; ACS, MoE, 23 Feb. 1999; PR, "Solvay and Elf Atochem confirm the acquisition of VCM and PVC production of Shell in France," 23 Dec. 1999; PR, SolVin takes over Solvay's PVC interests in Martorell, Jan. 2002; PR, Solvay and Arkema to untie vinyls production joint ventures in France and Spain, 25 June 2010.

the worldwide PVC business expanded greatly. During these good years Solvay kept pace in Western Europe, as sketched out earlier, but the largest expansion took place outside that area. In the second part of the decade, Solvay Indupa modernized and enlarged its plant at Santo Andre, Brazil, to a large integrated VCM-PVC plant. About the same time, Vinythai doubled its VCM plant and enlarged its PVC plant. The most interesting development of all took place in Russia, where the market for PVC products was growing quickly and where Solvay in 2003 had set up a joint venture for PVC compounds with the Nikos group at Tver, returning to that country after an absence of almost ninety years. Together with Sibur LLC, an affiliate of Gazprom, Solvay in 2007 decided to create a fully integrated electrolysis-VCM-PVC complex in Russia, run by the 50–50 joint venture RusVinyl. A 330-kiloton-per-year PVC plant, including the associated VCM and electrolysis facilities, was constructed at Kstovo, in the Nizhny Novgorod region.[81]

Looking back on the development of Solvay's PVC business over the past twenty years, one may note that the difficult 1990s, in which not only the profits were low but also the product was heavily attacked by environmentalist, were followed by years in which PVC consumption grew tremendously again, especially in Latin America and Asia. By focusing on large and integrated PVC-VCM-electrolysis complexes, as well as on perfecting products, Solvay succeeded in remaining one of the largest high-quality PVC companies in the world. Because of the dependence of PVC sales on the economic cycle (e.g., housing, car industry), 2011 was again a difficult year, though, in Europe especially.[82]

Special Polymers: Starting Small, Growing Great

Special polymers form a heterogeneous class of materials that have in common properties that make them suited for interesting applications, such as specific electrical or mechanical properties (e.g., engineering polymers, technopolymers) or the property of being able to form films that cannot be penetrated by oxygen, which makes them suited for packaging material for foodstuffs (e.g., barrier polymers). Often, they are made in far-smaller quantities than bulk polymers such as PVC and HDPE, and mostly much larger profits per unit can be gained.

Solvay entered this field in the 1950s when it started to investigate in its laboratory, in addition to the polymerization of vinyl chloride, which leads to

---

[81] ARS 2003: 24; id., 2004: 33; PR, Solvay Indupa launches plan to expand and upgrade vinyls production in Brazil, 30 Aug. 2006; PR, Solvay Indupa will produce bioethanol-based vinyl in Brazil, 14 Dec. 2007; PR, Vinythai to double VCM capacity, 10 Nov. 2004; PR, Vinythai: Solvay's vinyls affiliate in Thailand expands upstream capacity, 28 Feb. 2005; PR, Vinythai: Solvay's vinyls affiliate in Thailand increases PVC production capacity, 11 Sept. 2008; PR, Solvay and SIBUR sign join venture agreement to build Russia's first world-scale vinyls production plant, 28 June 2007; PR, EBRD invests EUR 52 million in Russian integrated PVC producer RusVinyl, 27 July 2010.

[82] PR, "4th Quarter and full year 2011 Results," 17 Feb. 2012.

PVC, the polymerization of vinylidene chloride, which leads to PVDC. That polymer had already been produced by the German chemical industry and by Dow, but Felix Bloyaert was able to file a few patents for Solvay that gave the company entry into the field. Production started at Tavaux in 1956–1957 on a semi-industrial scale. The product was marketed under the trade name Ixan, and industrial production started in 1961 and 1962, also at Tavaux. Later, PVDC developed into a successful barrier polymer for packaging foodstuffs.[83]

After Kali-Chemie acquired a stake in Saline Ludwigshalle, Felix Bloyaert and his coworkers at NoH started investigating the polymerization of vinylidene monomers in which chorine was replaced by fluorine. That led to the polymer PVDF, with interesting properties as a barrier polymer and for technical applications. In 1972, the research at NoH was complemented by development work at Tavaux. From 1974, batches of PVDF, commercialized under the trade name Solef, were sent to specific customers. In the mid-1980s the market had been developed to such an extent that an industrial plant was constructed at Tavaux.[84]

Hand in hand with Solvay's growth in plastics processing, the central research laboratory at NoH investigated several classes of polymers for specific applications. During the 1970s there was energetic activity at NoH (research) and Tavaux (development) on polyacrylonitril polymers (PAN), commercialized as Soltan, suited for beer and other sparkling drink bottles. A plan to construct a PAN plant at Deer Park in 1975 did not become reality. By contrast, another polymer, Ixol, was successfully developed as a fire protector for polyurethane (PUR) foams. A plant was constructed in 1980 at Tavaux.[85]

In all these cases the development and (early) commercialization were coordinated by Solvay's R&D Department. Starting in 1979, as discussed in Chapter 19, the Specialties Department was established under Luciano Balducci, which from then on would take care of the commercialization of specialties. To develop Solvay's specialties business rapidly, it would not be enough to wait for the results of research. Between 1979 and 1986, therefore, several licenses for Europe on special polymers were taken out, mainly from Japanese companies. In this way, Solvay was able to develop its portfolio of special polymers in the direction of high-stiffness polymers suited for engineering purposes. In 1979 a license was taken out on the engineering polymer Arylef from the Japanese firm Unitika. In 1983 licenses on the polyarylamide polymers Ixef and Nyref

[83] Kline Rooney, Crawford, Love, and Curtis (n.d.); Brandt (1997), 79, 232, 288–9, 335; ACS, CdG, 9 Dec. 1954, 24 Feb. 1955; Ducordeaux, Robin, Tétu, and Amiot (2005), 170–1.

[84] ACS, RdG, 2 June 1964; ACS, CdG, 11 June 1964; ACS, MoE, 20 Mar. 1973, 4 Nov. 1975, 9 Apr. 1987; ACS, MoB, 24 Sept. 1982, 26 Nov. 1984, 28 Jan. 1985, 27 Jan. 1986; ACS, 1020–10, presentation Mr. Bloyaert, 15 Jan. 1979.

[85] ACS, MoE, 3 Dec. 1974, 18 Feb. 1975, 29 July 1975; ACS, 1294–53-2, Soltex Board of Directors, 30 Nov. 1976; ACS, 1020–10, presentation Mr. Bloyaert, 12 Jan. 1981; ACS, MoB, 8 Apr. 1992.

followed, both licensed from the Mitsubishi Gas Co. Nyref was not a success, but Ixef was developed into the successful commercial product MXD6, which was manufactured at Solvay's plant at Rheinberg. Finally, in 1987 a license was acquired from the Japanese company Tohpren for the technical polymer PPS, commercialized under the name Primef.[86]

By taking out such licenses, Solvay was able to obtain a position in the field of special polymers in a short time. There was also a novelty from research: (poly)ethylene vinylalcohol (EVOH), commercialized as Claren. It was produced in a pilot plant at Tavaux in 1982, and on a commercial scale by 1985 at Rosignano. This was too quickly. There were numerous technical and commercial problems, and in 1991 the Executive Committee concluded that production and marketing of Claren should be stopped.[87]

Despite some disappointments like these, there was great confidence among Solvay's leadership that special polymers were a viable option for the future. In 1986, and again in 1989, it was concluded that special polymers should become a growth area of Solvay. At NoH, then, 160 of 950 R&D workers were focusing on special polymers. Special attention was given to the United States, also as part of the strategy to develop special polymers on the basis of PP and HDPE. The 50–50 joint venture in polypropylene compounds for automobile applications, set up with Dexter in 1990, fit perfectly with that strategy.[88]

The crisis of the early 1990s hit this part of Solvay's business hard. In those years, PVDF, which had flourished during the 1980s, and which would become the flagship of Solvay's special polymers business later, was in serious decline. In 1994 the company even contemplated selling the entire PVDF business to the American 3M group. The transaction did not take place, though. And in 1998 Solvay cooperated with 3M's subsidiary Dyneon in setting up a joint venture for the production of the monomer VF2 at 3M's site in Decatur, Alabama. Solvay also constructed a PVDF plant at that site.[89]

The big leap forward in this field happened in the twenty-first century during two major deals that are described in the next chapter. In November 2001,

[86] PR, "Solvay-Unitika agreement," 5 June 1979; ACS, 1001-26-1, "Politique générale du groupe," 1 Apr. 1985; ACS-CR, agreement with Tohpren, 1 Apr. 1987; PR, "Solvay introduces a new engineering thermoplastic," 9 June 1987; PR, "Solvay sells – polyarylamide new plant," 17 Dec. 1987; ACS, MoE, 12 Oct. 1998, 27 July 1999; interview Jacques van Rijckevorsel, 6 Nov. 2008.

[87] ACS, MoE, 19 June 1984, 30 Apr. 1991; "Discours de fin d'année du baron Daniel Janssen," insert in _Revue Solvay_ (1986); ACS, Exposés Directeurs 1990/1, presentation Y. Secousse, 14 May 1990; PR, "Solvay withdraws from EVOH market," 10 July 1991.

[88] ACS, MoE, 29 July 1986, 21 Mar. 1989; ACS, MoB, 17 Apr. 1989, 22 Sept. 1989; PR, "Solvay and Dexter intend to collaborate in the field of polypropylene compounds," 21 Dec. 1989.

[89] ACS, MoE, 5 Nov. 1991, 23 Jan. 1995; ACS, [C. Nanquette], "Desinvestissements du groupe entre 1985 et 1993, et desinvestissements prevus en 1994," 20 May 1994; ACS, MoB, 6 June 1994, 15 Dec. 1997; PR, "Joint venture with US-company 'Dyneon' for VF2-monomer production and new PVDF Solef-plant in Decatur (Alabama, USA)," 29 Jan. 1998.

Solvay acquired the engineering polymer activities of BP, which were produced at several sites in the United States. And a few months later Solvay absorbed the fluoropolymers and elastomers of Ausimont. As a result of these two deals, Solvay advanced to the first rank worldwide in special polymers.[90]

---

[90] PR, Solvay's agreement with BP enters into force: Strenghtening of Solvay's position in high-margin specialty polymers, 1 Nov. 2001; PR, Solvay Solexis: Birth of a global leader in fluorinated materials, 28 Nov. 2002.

FIGURE 22.1. Since 2004 Solvay has been one of the main sponsors of Bertrand Piccard and André Borschberg's Solar Impulse project to develop an airplane that can fly around the world solely on solar energy. In July 2010 the airplane flew for more than a day for the first time. Solvay contributed extensively to that development through its research efforts, and its fluoropolymers and engineering plastics for batteries, photovoltaic cells, and lightweight constructive parts. This photo shows the training flight of the solar plane, piloted by André Borschberg, in April 2011. (Copyright: Solar Impulse/Stéphane Gros.)

22

Chemicals and Plastics of the Future

Major Turning Points at the Start of a New Century

After the crisis of 1991–1993 the global economy developed well, in general. In the United States these were the Clinton years, with lower state deficits and booming stock markets, especially in ICT shares and equity funds investing in newly industrializing countries. In 1998, though, the Asian economic crisis broke out, and two years later the dot-com bubble collapsed. Shortly thereafter, on 11 September 2001, the world order was shaken by Al Qaida's attacks on the United States, which led to the invasion of Afghanistan and the war in Iraq. The first decade of the twenty-first century therefore started off full of uncertainties. At the same time, though, there were also signs of a promising future, in Europe especially. The euro had been introduced in banking and at the stock exchange in January 1999, and the coins and notes were circulating since 1 January 2002. The Central and Eastern European economies started to recover. In most European countries the economy grew greatly in 1999–2000 and again in 2006–2007, with moderate growth during the years in between. The rate of the dollar went down in relation to the euro, and oil and energy prices went up, a result of economic growth in China especially, as well as the war in Iraq.[1]

In this economic landscape, full of tensions and paradoxes, Solvay performed well. The development of the earnings before interest and tax (EBIT) may serve as a convenient proxy. During the difficult early part of the 1990s, EBIT had been about 5 percent of sales. Then a number of years followed during which the EBIT hovered around 8 percent (1994–2001). From 2002 to 2007, with an EBIT greater than 10.5 percent on continuing operations, the company did much better. Obviously, the introduction of a leaner organization in the 1990s and, especially, an increased focus on pharmaceuticals and other high-value-added products started to pay off. This made the first decade of the twenty-first century one of the most profitable periods for Solvay since the first oil crisis of 1973.[2]

At the end of the decade, the economic climate changed dramatically. The cumulating state deficits in the United States; the increased competition in the

---

[1] Frieden (2006), 389–91, 399; http://en.wikipedia.org/wiki/Dot-com_bubble; http://www.solvay. com: "Speech by Mr. Aloïs Michielsen ... to the General Shareholders' Meeting of May 11, 2010"; http://epp.eurostat.ec.europa.eu/tgm/table.do?tab=table&plugin=1&language=en& pcode=tsieb020.

[2] ARS 1991–2010.

banking sector, which seduced some banks to introduce some risky derivates; and finally, the collapse of the housing bubble in the United States, led in the fall of 2008 to one of the most serious banking crises since the Great Depression. An economic recession followed in all sectors. Many governments had to further increase their indebtedness to protect crucial systemic banks against total collapse. In Belgium and the Netherlands, the Fortis group, in which Solvay had a large interest, was in great trouble.[3]

After a brief recovery in 2010 and early 2011, accumulated public debts in several European states led again, starting in the summer of 2011, to a slowdown in the euro zone and to a recession in some European countries. With a recession in 2008–2009 and a serious slowdown in 2011–2012 following each other so closely, high demands were posed to the Solvay leadership; more so because these external threats intersected with enormous changes inside the company.

During no other decade of its history, perhaps, Solvay witnessed greater changes in its product portfolio than during the first ten years of the new millennium. As will be described here, Solvay first in 2001 sold its large polyolefins business to the oil company BP Amoco, and acquired in its turn important activities in special polymers from BP and Montedison. At the end of the decade Solvay divested its pharmaceutical activities, which had been Solvay's antidote against economic cyclicality for so many years, for €5.2 billion to the American company Abbott. A year after selling its pharmacy sector to Abbott, Solvay reinvested €6.6 billion into the acquisition of the French firm Rhodia, thereby almost doubling its personnel from about 16,800 to more than 29,100. With the inclusion of Rhodia – active in markets such as consumer goods and automotive – Solvay completed the turnaround of its portfolio. The Solvay of 2011 differs in many respects from the Solvay of 2000.[4]

Despite all these drastic changes, there was also great continuity. Solvay, after 150 years, is the main chemical group in Europe that has preserved its character as a family firm.

22.1   THE ROLE OF THE FOUNDING FAMILIES

Until the transition of Solvay from a simple partnership to a joint-stock company in 1967, the Solvay family both owned the business, together with other founding families, and managed it. The *gérance* was totally composed of family members. Soon after 1967 that situation would change, though (see Chapter 17). For almost fifteen years, only Jacques Solvay and Paul Washer represented the Solvay family in the day-to-day management of the company.[5]

Understandably, there was a preference among family shareholders that at least the chairman of the Executive Committee would be a member of the Solvay family. But leadership qualities were a prerequisite. When René Boël

---

[3] McDonald and Robinson (2009); Smit (2008), 425–38.
[4] E-mail from Bernard de Laguiche to the author, 3 Nov. 2011; ARS 2011.
[5] In this section, "Solvay family" describes the descendants of Ernest and Alfred Solvay and their sisters. It therefore includes the Boëls, Janssens, Washers, Delwarts, Semets, and Laguiches. It excludes the families of the *commanditaires*: Pirmez, Nélis, Lambert, and their descendants.

stepped down in 1971, some family members contemplated promoting a non-family member to the rank, but Jacques Solvay was chosen. When the latter approached the age limit for Executive Committee members (sixty-five), several family members were taken into consideration, but the appointment of a non-family member was again investigated seriously as well. After a careful search it was a relief for the family that in 1984, Daniel Janssen, an engineer and descendant of Ernest Solvay with rich managerial experience in the pharmaceutical and chemical industries, was willing to exchange his leading position at UCB for a future chairmanship of the Executive Committee of Solvay. In 1986 he succeeded Jacques Solvay.[6]

In 1998 Solvay would for the first time hire a CEO who was not a member of the Solvay family. Aloïs Michielsen, who succeeded Daniel Janssen, was born into an entrepreneurial family himself and therefore had a good feeling for the culture of family business. After studying chemical engineering at Louvain and a PhD program in business administration at the University of Chicago, Michielsen had entered the Solvay company in 1969. He first worked in the Marketing Department and then became personal assistant to Paul Washer. Thereafter, he made his career mainly in plastics processing, until he was appointed member of the Executive Committee in 1990. Asked about his role as first nonfamily CEO, after 135 years, Michielsen in 2008 emphasized the importance of the trust he received from two generations of major shareholders: Paul Washer, Jacques Solvay, Yves Boël, Paul-Emmanuel Janssen, and Daniel Janssen. The latter especially, who in 1998 succeeded Yves Boël as chairman of the board of directors, had always given great support to Michielsen's policies and decisions. Janssen managed the relations with the other family shareholders and took on board much of the external relations, such as contacts with industrial federations, the Trilateral Commission, the Bilderberg group, and with governments.[7]

The fact that Michielsen first made a long career inside Solvay certainly helped in creating a relation of trust with members of the Solvay family. The same is true of Michielsen's successor, Christian Jourquin, who became CEO in 2006. Michielsen then succeeded Daniel Janssen as chairman of the board. For the first time in Solvay's history, both top positions in the company were occupied by nonfamily members.[8] Jourquin, educated as a commercial engineer at the École de Commerce Solvay (now the Solvay Brussels School of Economics and Management) of Brussels University, entered the Solvay company in 1971. After having worked in Italy and Switzerland, he became personal assistant to Albert Rampelberg and was then appointed to the managerial board of Duphar. He worked in pharmaceuticals for ten years. In 1991 he became general manager of Solvay's business in Spain and Portugal, before he entered the Executive

---

[6] PPSF, Jacques Solvay, "Family Business Network: Enhancing Excellence of Family Business," 9 Nov. 1992; interview Paul Washer, 29 Nov. 2007; interview Albert Rampelberg, 4 Apr. 2008.

[7] Interview Aloïs Michielsen, 16 Apr. 2008; interview Daniel Janssen, 23 Jan. 2008; ACS, MoB, 31 July 1997, 5 Feb. 1998.

[8] PPSF, Denis Solvay, "Solvay Group/Leveraging Family Ownership," presentation to the Family Business Forum, 7 June 2007.

Committee as head of the peroxides sector in 1996. Later, he also managed the plastics processing and chemicals sectors, and thereby gained an all-round view of Solvay's businesses. When Jourquin succeeded Michielsen in 2006, he, significantly, was the first CEO of Solvay, since its foundation in 1863, to have an economic training instead of a technical engineering background.[9]

Since Paul Washer's departure in June 1988, only one member of the Solvay family was part of the Executive Committee – first Daniel Janssen, then Bernard de Laguiche – of the six to eight nonfamily members. Parallel to that reduced family influence in the Executive Committee, the position on the board of directors was strengthened. During the early 1980s, most decisions were in fact taken by the Executive Committee and then later approved by the board. Since the intervention by the Liaison Committee, in 1982–1983, the timely distribution of information to nonexecutive board members gradually improved. Between 1980 and 2000, the number of truly external board members increased from two to four. Until January 1995 the Executive Committee was composed of board members only. After that date, the heads of the product sectors became members of the Executive Committee without being board members at the same time (see Chapter 21). When he became chairman of the board in 1998, Daniel Janssen greatly improved the functioning of the board, as well as the transparency of the division of labor between the board and the Executive Committee. As a result of all these changes the board of directors was strengthened, and therefore, indirectly, so was the position of the family shareholders, who occupied more than half of the seats as a result of their shareholding.[10]

Since the transformation to a joint-stock company, shareholding by the founding families gradually decreased. Nevertheless, in 1982 it still was about 64 percent. The following year, Solvac was created in an attempt to improve the position of the Solvay share at the stock exchange while at the same time creating the conditions for the founding families to stay in control (see Chapter 17). From 23 percent in 1983, Solvac raised its shareholding in steps to 27 percent in 2003. Expected new European legislation that obliged shareholders to do a public offer on all the remaining shares when they would raise their interest in a company to greater than 30 percent induced Solvac in 2006 to acquire a little more than 30 percent of Solvay before the new legislation became effective. Shareholders that already held 30 percent or more were exempted from a mandatory takeover bid. Shares of Solvac, which are all registered, can only be held by physical persons. By 2010, about 80 percent of Solvac shares were held by family members of the founders of Solvay. It is estimated that members of those families, about 2,500 in total, also owned about 25 percent of the shares of Solvay directly. This means that, directly or via Solvac, the founding families still control more than 50 percent of shares of Solvay.[11]

---

[9] In 2012 Aloïs Michielsen reached the age limit for directors (seventy years). He was replaced by Nicholas Boël.

[10] Interviews Daniël Janssen, 13 Nov. 2007, 23 Jan. 2008; ACS, MoB, 29 Nov. 1993, 28 Nov. 1994, 4 June 1998, 14 Dec. 1998.

[11] ACS, "Actionnaires Solvay & Cie. S.A. – Interlocuteurs possible des différents groupes familiaux – 1er septembre 1982"; ACS, MoE, 18 Oct. 1983; ARS 1999: 8–11, 23; id. 2001:

The large role of the descendants of the founders of the company makes Solvay less vulnerable to the dynamics of financial markets, but it also requires intense and transparent communication between the company and the family shareholders. In the 1960s it was René Boël who took care of that communication, then Jacques Solvay and, later, Daniel Janssen. Since 2006, Denis Solvay, a descendant of Alfred Solvay and deputy chairman of the board of directors, has taken care of the relations with the family shareholders on issues such as representation in governing bodies, assisted by Jean-Pierre Delwart and Bernard de Laguiche. All this "is conducted very discreetly, very humanely, very friendly," Daniel Janssen declared in 2007.[12] A typical career of a family member goes as follows: first he, or (recently) she, would be appointed at young age in the supervisory board of the Mutuelle Solvay; then, after some years of experience, he or she would advance to the board of directors of Solvac. From that board, finally, family members on the board of Solvay are recruited.[13]

Altogether, about twenty-five seats are occupied by family members. From the number of seats occupied by the different family branches, it appears that family shareholding is remarkably stable.[14] During the past fifteen years, on the board of Solvac four seats were occupied by descendants of Ernest Solvay; two by those of Pirmez; and one each by those of Alfred Solvay, Delwart-Solvay, Semet-Solvay, Nélis and Lambert, despite changes of directors during those years. On the board of Solvay – in the same period – four seats were occupied by descendants of Ernest Solvay, two by those of Alfred Solvay, one by those of Pirmez, and one by members of either the Nélis or the Lambert family (together about 50–57 percent of seats). This astonishing degree of stability of family shareholdings is partly attributable to Solvay's consistent dividend policy since the late 1980s – raising the dividend whenever possible, never lowering it, with payments spread throughout the fiscal year. But other factors have played a role as well. "If you are born with the shares in your cradle," Aloïs Michielsen concluded, "you are more tolerant to losses. The stability is then higher. . . . But, as a CEO, you have to deserve the confidence of the family shareholders" by producing good financial results. Daniel Janssen, in his turn, pointed to the rather conservative outlook of the families involved. "Many of them are wealthy for more than hundred years, [and] have a great part of their fortune in the form of Solvay shares. They own forests and farms" that give revenues only in the long run. "The culture is not going for quick money. They are long term oriented. . . . Most of them keep their Solvay shares, that they

10–11, 73; id. 2003: 5, 85–86; id. 2006: 121; id. 2008: 133; id. 2010: 171; ACS-CR, Convention between Solvac and Fortis Bank on a roll-over credit of €400 million, 14 Sept. 2006; interview Daniel Janssen, 16 Oct. 2007; interview Paul Washer, 29 Nov. 2007; interview Aloïs Michielsen, 16 Apr. 2008.

12　Interview Daniel Janssen, 16 Oct. 2007.

13　Interview Daniel Janssen, 23 Jan. 2008; interview Paul Washer, 29 Nov. 2007. See Van Driessche (2010).

14　Traditionally a calculation scheme was practiced in which a seat in the Solvay Board was good for 10 points, a seat in the Board of Solvac counted for 5 points, and a position in the Supervisory Board of the Mutuelle Solvay for 1 point. Posts were allocated depending on the total shareholding of each family branch.

have received from their parents and that they will give to their children." As a result, Solvay is more long-term oriented, he stated, than companies that are fully dependent on the capital market.[15]

To protect the company from unfriendly takeovers, the large shareholding of Solvac and the great loyalty of the family shareholders were important assets, of course. Nevertheless, extra precautions were taken. In 1988–1989 at Janssen's initiative, Solvay took, via the Mutuelle Solvay, a substantial interest in Sofina and an increased interest in the Société Générale de Banque (see Chapter 21), and at the same time it issued a debenture loan with warrants. The entire loan was subscribed to by Solvac, Sofina, Deutsch Bank, and Crédit Suisse. In 1998 this "poison pill" construction was extended for another five years, but with Fortis Bank instead of Crédit Suisse. Solvay then also changed its statutes, so that it could purchase, if needed, up to 10 percent of its own shares (since May 2009, up to 20 percent). When the agreement expired in October 2003, it was not renewed. Probably, the growing shareholding of Solvac, together with the option to purchase 10 percent of Solvay's own shares, was considered a sufficient defense against hostile takeover.[16]

Evaluating the changing role of the traditional families of shareholders inside Solvay, one can conclude that the recent situation with the two top-positions occupied by nonfamily members has not been a revolution but rather the outcome of a gradual process. Both Aloïs Michielsen and Christian Jourquin stayed in close touch with Denis Solvay and other leading members of the shareholding families. The symbiosis clearly benefits both parties. Stability of the shareholding permitted Solvay's top management to contemplate long-term strategies. "Most of the time," Michielsen said, "one can reach a consensus in the Board, between family members and the others, even if it's not always easy. It never happened that family directors and nonfamily directors diverged completely on big strategic issues."[17] In the interest of long-term value creation, members of the shareholding families certainly have not been risk averse. But there have also been limits to the risk taking. Solvay's equity has always grown at a rate at which the family shareholders could stay in control. It remains speculation whether Solvay would have grown faster under different conditions of ownership. That it then would have been a very different company can be counted as a certainty.[18]

[15] J.L. Anspach, "The mystery of the dividend," *Solvay Live* (Fall 1992): 24–5; ARS, 1990–2010; interview Aloïs Michielsen, 16 Apr. 2008; interview Daniel Janssen, 16 Oct. 2007.
[16] ACS, [C. Nanquette], "Achats d'actifs à tiers et prises de participations dans des sociétés non consolidees liees au Groupe," 31 May 1994; ACS-CR, convention between Solvay & Cie, Solvac, Sofina, Deutsche Bank and Crédit Suisse, 5 June 1989; id., "White knights" convention among Solvay, Solvac, Sofina, Deutsche Bank, and Générale de Banque, 26 May 1998; id., convention between Solvac and Fortis Bank, 7 May 2003; ARS 1988: 11; id. 1999: 11; id. 2001: 11; id. 2003: 5, id. 2006: 122–3; ACS, MoB, 5 Feb. 1998, 18 Feb. 2009.
[17] Interview Aloïs Michielsen, 16 Apr. 2008.
[18] Interviews Daniel Janssen, 16 Oct. 2007, 23 Jan. 2008; interview Paul Washer, 29 Nov. 2007; interview Aloïs Michielsen, 24 Sept. 2008; personnal communication by Jean-Marie Solvay, 1 Sept. 2011.

22.2 FROM BULK PLASTICS TO SPECIAL POLYMERS

At a meeting of the board of directors of Solvay on Thursday, 28 September 2000, Aloïs Michielsen proposed new strategic orientations that signified one of the most radical reorientations of his company in many years. During the summer of 2000, members of the Corporate Planning and Financial Departments of Solvay had carefully analyzed the prospects of a set of new projects, their financing, and their effects on the growth of Solvay's results. The impressive package included many different elements: the divestment of Solvay's salt business, which had been part of the company for more than one hundred years; the divestment of plastic products for homes (decoration); the divestment of the polypropylene business to BP Amoco; the establishment of two joint ventures in polyethylene, together with BP Amoco; the acquisition of the engineering polymers business of BP Amoco; the acquisition of the Italian chemical company Ausimont, producer of fluorinated polymers and chemicals; the divestment of Ausimont's peroxides business, in line with the competition policy of the European Commission; and a reduction of the investments in pharmaceuticals from €200 million to €100 million over five years. The major operation within this package was the shift from the highly cyclical bulk plastics (HDPE and PP) to the far less cyclical special polymers (from BP Amoco and Ausimont).[19]

The roots of the decision to step out of the polyolefin business lay in the mid-1990s. In the aftermath of the crisis of 1991–1993, the board of Solvay asked to investigate the possible divestments of the polyolefins. On the basis of the financial figures of the previous fifteen years and a study by A. D. Little, it was again concluded that despite the cyclicality, the average results of the bulk plastics were above the average of the rest of the business. The plastics sector of Solvay was generally strong and the company policy was that it should keep its position.[20]

When the report by ADL was discussed, in 1994 and 1995, the situation had already started to change. Intense competition led to extensive consolidation in the sector through joint ventures, strategic alliances, and acquisitions, which often involved a large oil company that controlled the ethylene and propylene feedstocks. Shell took over the PE and PP activities of Montedison, and OMV and Borealis announced a joint venture, as did BASF and Hoechst. Moreover, Exxon developed a class of highly successful so-called metallocene catalysts and almost monopolized that technology through an extensive carpet-bombing of patents. Alfred Hoffait, head of research, and others at Solvay started to become a bit worried about the situation. Solvay

---

[19] ACS, "New strategic orientation for Solvay," 28 Sept. 2000; ACS, MoB, 27 July 2000, 28 Sept. 2000; ACS, letter Aloïs Michielsen and Daniel Janssen to the members of the board of directors, 13 Sept. 2000; ACS, MoE, 25 July 2000, 12 Sept. 2000; ACS, "Nouvelles orientation stratégiques pour Solvay," 6 Sept. 2000.

[20] ACS, green folder "Les Plastiques," "Note à M. Janssen – Renseignements pratiques sur trois consultants," 15 Sept. 1994; id., Project proposals by Maurice Olivier, Arthur D. Little International Inc., Brussels, to Mr. Secousse, 4 Nov. 1994; ACS., MoB, 28 Nov. 1994; 30 Mar. 1995, 27 Nov. 1995.

was lagging behind with respect to the metallocenes and was surrounded by a growing number of strong competitors. The year 1996 again showed bad results. Solvay had been the global leader in HDPE in 1994–1996 but had fallen back to the third place by 1998. In PP Solvay's position deteriorated in those years from the seventh to the tenth position. In the fall of 1997, René Degrève, Bernard de Laguiche, and Guy Veulemans spoke with experts of the London office of Goldman Sachs on Solvay's position in the polyolefins industry. "Over the last few years," the consultants concluded, "Solvay's competitors have changed dramatically. In polypropylene and high-density polyethylene, your company is competing head-to-head with fully-integrated players, namely the oil 'majors' and chemical companies focusing exclusively on commodity products."[21] According to Goldman Sachs, Solvay should therefore enter into strategic alliances with oil companies, or with other dominant players that had access to ethylene and propylene. The company took the advice seriously and started to investigate the creation of alliances in Europe and the United States.[22]

The candidate of choice in Europe was the Belgian oil company Petrofina. Yves Boël, chairman of Solvay's board of directors, was on the board of Petrofina, as was Solvay board member Étienne Davignon. Moreover, collaboration with Petrofina embodied the dream of creating a strong, integrated Belgian petrochemical company. The Belgian oil company had acquired a position in the field of the metallocenes. Already, earlier in the 1990s Aloïs Michielsen and Daniel Janssen had started negotiations with Petrofina's CEO François Cornelis and with Axel de Broqueville, Petrofina's head of chemicals, but an agreement had been blocked by the Board of Petrofina. In 1998 the head of Solvay's plastics sector, Henri Lefèbvre, resumed negotiations and succeeded in arriving at two agreements, which were signed by October 1998. Petrofina gave Solvay global access to its metallocene technology for polypropylene, and Solvay, in turn, gave Petrofina a global license on its chromium catalysts. In addition to a research agreement, both companies also decided to collaborate in the construction of two large HDPE plants in Belgium, to better coordinate the extension of capacities, one in Antwerp, run by Solvay, and another run by Petrofina.[23]

Selling Solvay's polyolefins activities to Petrofina was also discussed, but on 1 December 1998, the Belgian oil company was absorbed by the French oil company Total. A huge reshuffling took place in the oil industry, because the same month BP merged with Amoco. In early 2000 the company TotalFinaElf was formed. Solvay, which had many relations as client and competitor with Fina and Elf's subsidiary Atochem, was suddenly confronted with a far

[21] ACS, 1061-2-1, fax Peter D. Sutherland, Goldman Sachs International, to Daniel Janssen, 27 Oct. 1997.

[22] ACS, MoB, 25 July 1996; interviews Aloïs Michielsen, 24 Sept. 2008, 17 Aug. 2011.

[23] ACS, green folder "Evolution du secteur Plastiques," note by Janssen to Loutrel on Petrofina, 17 Nov. 1993; ACS-CR, agreement with Petrofina on the supply of ethylene and propylene, 29 Sept. 1997; ACS, MoB, 30 Sept. 1998; PR, "Belgium: Fina and Solvay announce polyethylenes co-operation agreements," 1 Oct. 1998; ACS, MES-meeting, 9–10 Dec. 1998; interview Daniel Janssen, 13 Nov. 2007; interview Aloïs Michielsen, 17 Aug. 2011.

stronger party, and therefore closer collaboration was not possible. When Solvay later joined forces with BP, the agreements of October 1998 were included in the joint venture. The same was true for a similar alliance that Solvay concluded in August 1999 with Phillips Petroleum Co. in the United States.[24]

The Portfolio Swap with BP

Although these alliances were steps in the right direction, they did not solve Solvay's problems concerning the supply of olefins, the cyclicality of the business, and the deteriorating situation of PP. Moreover, tolerance for cyclical business was diminishing at Solvay. When Michielsen became chairman of the Executive Committee in June 1998, he announced that reducing cyclicality would be among his priorities. In early 2000, an interesting opportunity presented itself when BP Amoco approached Solvay to purchase the polyolefins plants at Deer Park. BP Amoco had two polyolefins plants in Europe, at Grangemouth in Scotland and Lavera in France, but no plants in the United States. As part of a global strategy, having a plant in the United States was an absolute necessity, and Solvay's Deer Park HDPE plant was one of the best in the country. However, it was not an option for Solvay to sell the American business and keep the far weaker European polyolefins activities; by selling the HDPE and PP plants at Deer Park, Solvay would lose much added value in the United States, which would undermine its strategy of geographical diversification. Therefore, Solvay soon put two cards on the table: BP Amoco should also take over Solvay's European activities and sell to Solvay its engineering polymers, which were concentrated in the United States. In July 2000 the contours of a possible deal already became visible: BP would buy Solvay's PP activities; it would sell its engineering polymers business to Solvay; and Solvay and BP would create two joint ventures for HDPE – a 50–50 venture in Europe and a 51–49 venture in the United States, with the option that Solvay would exit those joint ventures after some time.[25]

After the approval by Solvay's board of directors, Henry Lefèbvre in Europe, and Whitson Sadler and Roger Kearns in the United States, entered very difficult and lengthy negotiations with BP, which had put almost sixty lawyers on the case. Several competitors were also interested in BP Amoco's engineering polymers. Moreover, the polyolefin business suddenly deteriorated, which made fixing the values difficult. In December 2000, finally, a memorandum of understanding could be signed on the main aspects of the contract and on

---

[24] ACS, MoB, 29 July 1999, 16 Dec. 1999; ACS, MoE, 27 July 1999, 7 Dec. 1999, 24 May 2000; PR, "Phillips and Solvay Group announce construction of shared U.S. High-Density Polyethylene plants," 30 Aug. 1999; PR, "Solvay Polymers and Chevron Phillips Chemical Company confirm the construction of new U.S. High-Density Polyethylene plant," 12 Sept. 2000; interview Daniel Janssen, 13 Nov. 2007; interview Aloïs Michielsen, 17 Aug. 2011.

[25] ACS, MES-meeting, 27–28 May 1998; ACS, MoB, 16 Dec. 1999; ACS, MoE, 28 June 2000, 25 July 2000, 12 Sept. 2000; ACS-CR, letter agreement with BP Amoco on polyolefins, 12 July 2000; ACS, MoB, 27 July 2000, 28 Sept. 2000; "Nouvelles orientation stratégiques pour Solvay," 1 Sept. 2000; interviews Aloïs Michielsen, 16 Apr. 2008, 24 Sept. 2008, 17 Aug. 2011.

FIGURE 22.2 In August 2001 Solvay concluded a deal with BP. After a successful record in this field for more than forty years, Solvay sold all its polyolefins activities to the British oil company and acquired the promising engineering plastics of BP in return. (*From left to right*) Henri Lefèbvre, head of Solvay's plastics sector; Byron Elmer Grote, executive director of BP; Aloïs Michielsen, CEO of Solvay; and Michael Buzzacott, head of the petrochemicals sector of BP. (Henri Lefèbvre Collection.)

the monetary values of BP's and Solvay's polyolefins business (€430 million versus €1.760 million), as well as of BP's engineering polymers (US$700 million). Solvay would exit the HDPE joint ventures after four years, for a price that would be fixed via a put-and-call procedure. After a meeting of the board of Solvay, one of the directors gave Aloïs Michielsen the strong advice to fix the final exit price before the contract would be signed, or else the powerful BP "could kill Solvay" during the times of the joint venture.[26] Again, tough negotiations followed. Binding contracts were signed in early August 2001, and the deal became effective as of 1 October of that year. Solvay had made an important step in the growth of its special polymers activities and had started its withdrawal from the polyolefins. It was a fantastic deal for Solvay. When Solvay in January 2005 left the HDPE activities completely to BP for the price agreed to in 2001, the market value of the business had declined considerably. Not much later BP sold all its polyolefins activities to Ineos.[27]

---

[26] Interviews Alois Michielsen, 16 Apr. 2008, 17 Aug. 2011.

[27] ACS, MoE, 17 Oct. 2000, 5 Dec. 2000; ACS, "Note au Conseil d'Administration," 7 Dec. 2000; ACS, MoB, 14 Dec. 2000, 26 July 2001; PR, "Major activity exchange between Solvay and BP," 19 Dec. 2000; PR, Signature of final contracts with BP, 6 Aug. 2001; PR, Solvay finalizes sale of interest in BP Solvay Polyethylene joint ventures to BP, 7 Jan. 2005; interview Daniel Janssen, 13 Nov. 2007; interview Alois Michielsen, 24 Sept. 2008.

The Acquisition of Ausimont

At an early stage, the strategic operation with respect to BP got somewhat intertwined with Solvay's attempts to acquire Ausimont. If both operations would succeed, Solvay would advance to leading global position in special polymers; moreover, the expected gains from the put-and-call procedure with BP could serve as a security in financing the Ausimont deal. The Italian company came into the picture at the end of 1999 after Solvay's attempt to join forces with DuPont in fluorinated chemicals had failed (see Chapter 21). Eberhard Piepho, the leader of Solvay's fluorine activities, thereupon drew attention to Ausimont, a subsidiary of Montedison that had not only an interesting business in fluorinated chemicals but also substantial sales in fluorinated polymers. Solvay was larger in fluorinated chemicals, Ausimont in fluorinated polymers. It fit in an excellent manner with Solvay's strategy to grow in special polymers.[28]

To express Solvay's interest in Ausimont, Aloïs Michielsen and Jean Christiaens, head of the Chemicals Sector, flew to Milan to have lunch with Enrico Bondi, the CEO of Montedison. They got the feeling that the Italian company would be willing to sell its subsidiary, but Solvay did not hear anything about the issue for months. Then suddenly, in August 2000, Bondi phoned Michielsen, came to Brussels, and made clear that he wanted to sell for €1.2 billion. The business appeared to be more profitable than Solvay had initially assumed, with plants in the United States that made it extremely attractive. Ausimont thereupon was included in the master plan that Michielsen presented to the board in September 2000.[29]

In the fall of 2000 a Solvay delegation, led by Bernard de Laguiche, investigated the figures in detail. Solvay formulated a bid of €1.15 billion and a number of conditions, but these were not acceptable to Montedison. In early December the Italian company withdrew Ausimont from the sale. That disappointing outcome for Solvay was also caused by the unstable situation of Montedison itself. The Italian company was a conglomerate of agribusiness, chemicals (Ausimont), and energy activities (Edison), controlled mainly by the bank Mediobanca. On 1 July 2001 Fiat and Electricité de France, joining forces in Italenergy, launched a hostile takeover bid on the remaining shares, with the aim of taking over the energy activities. They succeeded in acquiring 52 percent in a short time. The affair stirred Italian politics considerably but also offered new chances for Solvay. On 16 July a confidentiality agreement among Solvay, Montedison, and Ausimont was signed, and negotiations started again.[30]

---

[28] ACS, MoB, 30 Mar. 1999, 3 June 1999; ACS, MES-meeting, 8–9 Dec. 1999; interviews with Aloïs Michielsen, 16 Apr. 2008, 17 Aug. 2011.

[29] ACS, "Polymères speciaux – Interets compares des projets Ose et Celsius," 6 Sept. 2000; ACS, "New strategic orientation for Solvay," 28 Sept. 2000; interviews Alois Michielsen, 24 Sept. 2008, 17 Aug. 2011.

[30] ACS, MoE, 22 Nov. 2000, 5 Dec. 2000; ACS, "Note au Conseil d'Administration," 7 Dec. 2000; ACS, MoB, 28 Sept. 2000, 14 Dec. 2000, 26 July 2001; ACS-CR, confidentiality agreement Montedison-Solvay, 16 July 2001; "Solvay to acquire Ausimont?" *Chemical Week*, 18 July 2001; Pat Regnier, "The End of the Affair," *Time Magazine World*, 23 July 2001; interviews Alois Michielsen, 24 Sept. 2008, 17 Aug. 2011.

It would take several months before a final agreement could be reached. Montedison had opened a tender in which about twenty bidders took part. By October 2001, Solvay was among the last few bidders. But Mediobanca was blocking the sale. During lunch with the board of directors, Michielsen inquired whether any of them had good contacts at Fiat. Daniel Janssen was well acquainted with Umberto Agnelli and contacted him. Jean-Marie Solvay, in turn, asked his father, who had been a personal friend of Fiat patriarch Gianni Agnelli since his student days in Switzerland, to draft a personal letter in which the aspects of family business were emphasized and in which Solvay's interest in Ausimont was expressed. On receipt, Gianni Agnelli immediately phoned Jacques Solvay to discuss the situation. Shortly thereafter, the blockade by Mediobanca was lifted and talks on Ausimont were resumed. On 21 December 2001 an agreement was reached. Solvay would buy Ausimont for €1.3 billion, subject to the approval of the antitrust authorities in Europe and the United States. In the financing of that acquisition, the largest in Solvay's history to date, Solvay's recent deal with BP played an important part. The money that would be generated by the selling of the HDPE business to BP in 2005 could already be put to use as a security.[31]

The European authorities decreed the selling of Ausimont's Italian peroxides activities. In December 2002 they were sold to Degussa. The US authorities demanded the divestment of Solvay's PVDF production in Decatur, Alabama. It was sold to Solvay's business partner Dyneon. After approval by the authorities, Solvay had acquired a company with 2,700 employees and sales of about €600 million, which fit perfectly with its strategy to grow in specialties and special polymers. The company had become one of the world leaders in fluoric products. On 1 January 2003 the fluoric polymers of Solvay and Ausimont merged into a new company, Solvay Solexis, under the leadership of Bernard de Laguiche.[32]

The combined BP-Ausimont operation produced a revolution in Solvay's product portfolio. Of Solvay's total capacity of bulk plastics in 2000 of about 4.2 million tons (1.9 million PVC, 1.5 million HDPE, and 0.8 million PP), 1.5 million tons were divested in 2001 (all PP and half of HDPE) and another 0.8 million tons in 2005 – altogether a 55 percent reduction in Solvay's total bulk capacity. This was replaced by a whole array of new advanced polymer varieties. To Solvay's traditional special polymers PVDC, PVDF, and poly-arylamide (IXEF), the acquisition of BP Amoco's engineering polymers – which had become Solvay Advanced Polymers – added the polysulfones, in which the company was a world leader; high-performance polyamides; liquid crystals; and other polymers – all produced in the United States. Next to PVDF, which Ausimont also produced, the Italian company added to this package a series

---

[31] ACS, MoB, 1 Oct. 2001, 18 Oct. 2001, 17 Dec. 2001; PR, Solvay enters into one-to-one talks with Montedison, 28 Nov. 2001; PR, "Agreement to buy Ausimont is major thrust in Solvay's strategy to boost high-value specialties," 21 Dec. 2001.

[32] PR, Solvay successfully completes acquisition of Ausimont, 7 May 2002; PR, Solvay in agreement with Dyneon to sell Solvay Fluoropolymers, 27 Aug. 2002; PR, Solvay Solexis: Birth of a global leader in fluorinated materials, 28 Nov. 2002; PR, Solvay wraps up acquisition of Ausimont, 13 Dec. 2002.

of new fluoropolymers (e.g., PTFE, MFA, PFA, ECTFE) and fluoroelastomers (Technoflon), produced in Italy and the United States. Although Solvay lost much production capacity in the United States, in terms of tons, total added value was only slightly affected because of the acquisition of the American production plants of BP and Ausimont. In just two years (2001–2002) special polymers had become one of Solvay's foremost activities, with world leadership in fluoromaterials and ultra-high-performance engineering polymers.[33]

22.3 INNOVATING IN NEW DIRECTIONS

During the second part of the 1990s, two new initiatives emerged within Solvay that later would become increasingly intertwined: New Business Development and a drive to boost innovation. New Business Development (NBD) was mainly a by-product of the introduction of strategic business units (SBUs). To avoid Solvay's horizon completely narrowing down to the short- and medium-term interests of the SBUs, in 1998 head of research Alfred Hoffait set a portion of his budget aside for the development of new technologies, products, and businesses that fell outside the scope of the SBUs. The NBD organization focused, technologically speaking, on inorganic and organic chemistry and on polymers. Pharmacy fell outside Hoffait's jurisdiction.[34]

The innovation drive at Solvay, though related to the introduction of total quality management and the SBUs (see Chapter 21), had its roots in the general perception that Europe was lagging behind the United States with respect to innovation. Several companies introduced award schemes and other measures to increase their innovativeness. At Solvay, the first local initiatives were taken by Whitson Sadler (United States), Georges Theys (Italy and France), and Marc Duhem (Spain and Portugal). Daniel Janssen broadened these initiatives to the entire group. He wrote the note "Growth through Innovation" that was discussed by all top managers in May 1997. The following year, the all-encompassing campaign Passion for Innovation was rolled out in the group, coordinated by Bernard de Laguiche. As member of the European Round Table of Industrialists, Daniel Janssen then also organized the European conference "Innovation, Employment, and Competitiveness" and initiated the establishment of the Solvay Chair for Technological Innovation at the Solvay Business School at Brussels and INSEAD, Fontainebleau. When Aloïs Michielsen succeeded Janssen in June 1998, he continued those activities to promote innovation.[35]

---

[33] ACS, "Polymères speciaux – Interets compares des projets Ose et Celsius," 6 Sept. 2000; ACS, 1055-2-1, "Produits Fluorés – Environnement, Santé et Réglementation – Présentation au Comex, NoH," 27 Feb. 2002.

[34] A. Hoffait and M.-L. Miserque, "The skills clash is the mother of invention," *Solvay Live*, 25 (2) (Summer 1997): 12; ARS 1998: 38; id. 2000: 40–1; ACS, MoB, 30 Mar. 1999; M.-L. Miserque, L. Lerot, P. Baekelmans, and L. Ninane, "New Business Development: donner une suite aux bonnes idées," *Solvay Live* 64 (Summer–Autumn 2000): 16–17; "Savoir gérer, gérer le savoir," *Solvay Live* 65 (Feb. 2001): 11.

[35] Homburg (2000): 125–6, 143; ACS, MES-meeting, 4–5 Dec. 1996; id., 28–29 May 1997; ACS, MoE, 9 Mar. 1998, 25 June 1998, 31 Aug. 1998; "Who are you, Mr. Michielsen?" *Solvay Live*

Among these initiatives was the inauguration of the Innovation Trophy for excellent innovative ideas, the Innovation Scorecard to monitor innovations, and several measures to include innovation in Solvay's job evaluation systems. De Laguiche was succeeded in 2001 as innovation sponsor by Jacques van Rijckevorsel, who also introduced the Innovation Charter. Moreover, the group organized periodically "Sciences for Innovation" conferences, to which Nobel laureates and others were invited to discuss key technologies of the future, such as nanomaterials. Open innovation was embraced as a leading concept. At least 50 percent of all projects should be developed in a structured partnership with external partners; 30 percent of the group's income needed to result from new products and technologies, preferably related to sustainable development.[36]

The Solar Impulse initiative is the symbolic figurehead of these innovation efforts and targets; it is a project devoted to the construction on an airplane that can fly around the world without any fuel, powered solely by solar energy. The initiative was started in 2003 by Bertrand Piccard, grandson of the famous Auguste Piccard, who visited the Solvay Conferences during 1922 and 1933. Bertand Piccard had flown with a balloon around the world. In December 2003 he was invited by Solvay to give a speech at a presentation of the Innovation Trophy. With strong words of support by Jacques van Rijckevorsel, in 2004 the Executive Committee decided to sponsor Piccard's project. Solvay thus became the first main partner in the project. Later, Piccard succeeded in also engaging Omega, Deutsche Bank, and Schindler, as well as a number of other companies, in lesser roles. Solvay's main contribution was not only by funding the project but also through its scientific expertise, as well as its products. After seven years of development, construction, and testing, the plane – with a wingspan of more than sixty meters and a weight of only 1,600 kilos – flew for the first time, for twenty-six hours, on 8 July 2010. Solvay products that made possible that achievement were mainly fluoropolymers and engineering plastics, used partly for the plane's lightweight construction but also in connection to batteries and photovoltaic cells. The project was a great success and generated much publicity for Solvay.[37]

Several products used in the Solar Impulse airplane also played a role in Solvay's New Business Development. When the NBD plan started in 1998,

62 (Summer 1998): 4–5; B. de Laguiche, and M. Bilquin, "A passion for innovation," *Solvay Live* 62 (Summer 1998): 6–8; PR, Inauguration of the Solvay chair for technological innovation at the Solvay School of Commerce of ULB and at Insead," 10 June 1999; interview Daniel Janssen, 16 Oct. 2007; interview Jacques van Rijckevorsel, 6 Nov. 2008; interview Georges Theys and Michel Bande, 6 June 2011.

36 ACS, MoE, 9 Feb. 1999, 29 June 1999, 7 Dec. 1999, 6 June 2000, 7 Nov. 2000; "Solvay Innovation Trophy with Innovatrix," *Solvay Live* 63 (Spring–Summer 1999); PR, Solvay's innovation trophy 2000 rewards four projects, 9 Feb. 2001; PR, Solvay Science for Innovation Conference focuses on the creation of novel, complex materials, 30 Nov. 2007; interview Jacques van Rijckevorsel, 6 Nov. 2008; personal communication by Jacques van Rijckevorsel, 3 Oct. 2011; personal communication by Jean-Marie Solvay, 14 Oct. 2011.

37 PR, Solvay is Solar Impulse's technological partner, 13 June 2005; PR, Solar Impulse's maiden flight was made possible by Solvay's innovative materials and knowhow, 7 Apr. 2010; "Wings of the future," *Solvay Live* (Sept. 2011): 30; interview Aloïs Michielsen, 17 Aug. 2011; personal communication by Jacques van Rijckevorsel, 3 Oct. 2011.

it first developed in all directions: biodegradable polymers, plastics recycling, fluorine chemistry for optical fibers and lithium batteries, peroxide chemistry and catalysts, water treatment, and membranes for fuel cells, to mention some examples. Narrowing down the options took several years. In 2004 the New Business Board was created, which apart from the heads of the product sectors and the head of research and technology, also included three external members: Philippe Busquin, former European commissioner for research; Marcel Crochet, honorary rector of the University of Louvain-la-Neuve; and board member Jean-Marie Solvay. They decided to take "megatrends" in society – issues concerning energy, food, and water, especially – as starting points for the choice of projects, taking Solvay's specific competences into account. Against that broader background two competence centers were created, one technology driven (advanced technologies), focusing on nanotechnologies and renewable chemistry, and the other business driven (future businesses), focusing on organic electronics and sustainable energy.[38]

The theme of sustainable energy consists of two platforms, one devoted to energy generation (e.g., fuel cells, organic photovoltaic) and one devoted to storage (lithium batteries). Attention to fuel cells already dates from the early days of the NBD initiative. When Solvay acquired Ausimont in 2002, it appeared that the Italian company was also working on fluorinated membranes that could be used as selective barriers in fuel cells. In October 2004 Solvay took a stake in Conduit Venture, a capital fund that was operating in that area. About a year and a half later, Solvay and the Belgian multinational Umicore created the joint venture SolviCore to produce membrane-electrode assemblies, which play a key role in fuel cells. Umicore had important know-how on catalysts for fuel cells; Solvay could offer its membrane technology. Aloïs Michielsen and Umicore CEO Thomas Leysen, who used to meet at several occasions, decided to join forces. A development station was created at Umicore's German research-and-development center at Hanau. Solvay gradually broadened its involvement in this area by taking a stake in the British fuel-cell developer Acal at the end of 2008 and by constructing a large test fuel cell that can generate one megawatt at SolVin's plant at Lillo, near Antwerp.[39]

Also, Solvay's interest in lithium and lithium batteries has a long history, but recently the successful application of fluorinated polymers and fluorine chemicals in these batteries has given the company a stronger position. In 2009

[38] ARS, 1998: 38; id. 2000: 40–1; id. 2002: 30–1; ACS, MoB, 30 Mar. 1999; M.-L. Miserque, L. Lerot, P. Baekelmans, and L. Ninane, "New Business Development," *Solvay Live*, 64 (Summer–Autumn 2000): 16–17; ACS, letter M. Washer to A. Michielsen, "Stratégie du Groupe Solvay . . ., 25 Jan. 2005; "Solvay overleeft," (2009); personal communication by Jacques van Rijckevorsel, 3 Oct. 2011; personal communication by Jean-Marie Solvay, 14 Oct. 2011.

[39] ARS, 2001: 28–9; PR, Solvay joins Conduit Venture Limited, 19 Oct. 2004; PR, Umicore and Solvay launch Solvicore, 25 July 2006; Brion and Moreau (2006), 432–5; PR, Solvay takes stake in fuel cell developer ACAL, 3 Dec. 2008; PR, Solvay has successfully commissioned the largest PEM fuel cell in the world at SolVin's Antwerp plant, 6 Feb. 2012; note Jacques van Rijckevorsel to authors, 4 Nov. 2008; interview Aloïs Michielsen, 17 Aug. 2011; personal communication by Jacques van Rijckevorsel, 3 Oct. 2011.

a plant for the production of a fluorine chemical used in these batteries started at Solvay's site at Onsan, South Korea, to serve the booming Asian market.[40]

In 2006 Léopold Demiddeleer, general manager of New Business Development at Solvay, also decided to fund research on organic light-emitting diodes (OLEDs) at the Georgia Institute of Technology, in the United States. This was the start of an extensive involvement of Solvay in organic electronics, which branched out to printable electronics (e.g., OLEDs, organic memories, sensors) and sustainable energy (e.g., organic photovoltaics). Solvay started collaborating with the Norwegian company Thin Film Electronics (in organic memories) and with the American firm Plextronics, a leading company in printed electronics and in organic photovoltaic technology. Given the large estimated market growth in solar cells and printable electronics, Solvay is clearly building a wide network to profit from that growth when it takes place.[41]

As a result of the Horizon project (see Section 22.5), the innovation drive and New Business Development were merged into one organization. The Innovation Center was created, headed by Pierre Joris, with Léopold Demiddeleer as responsible manager for future business. The New Business Board was replaced by the Innovation Board, chaired by Jacques van Rijckevorsel. The integration with the innovation and business development activities of Rhodia (see Section 22.5) definitely will be the next great challenge.[42]

22.4   SOLVAY PHARMA: FROM PRIORITY BUSINESS TO DIVESTMENT

During the 1990s, most sales in pharmaceuticals were realized in well-established products that had already been marketed by Kali-Chemie and Duphar for years, or even decades (see Table 22.1). There were great expectations from the start for the antidepressant Fluvoxamine, introduced in Europe in 1983. Under the name Luvox, Solvay wanted to sell it in the United States, the world's most important pharmaceutical market. Registration by the powerful Food and Drugs Administration (FDA) did not go very smoothly, though, given Eli Lilly's blockbuster Prozac. That was a significant handicap for Solvay, because the FDA was not convinced that Luvox was a better medication (see Chapter 19). After several years, the FDA finally approved Luvox in 1994 as a

[40] ACS, 1001–26-1, "Groupe Solvay – Stratégie d'ensemble," Mar. 1984; A. Hoffait and M.-L. Miserque, "The skills clash is the mother of invention," *Solvay Live* 25 (2) (Summer 1997): 12; ARS 2000: 40–1; PR, Solvay's new PVDF significantly increase power capacity lithium-ion batteries, 27 Aug. 2009; PR, Solvay inaugurates production unit in Korea for a new additive for Lithium ion batteries, 1 Dec. 2009.

[41] PR, Solvay joins advanced materials venture capital fund, 31 Aug. 2006; PR, Solvay and Thin Film Electronics sign agreement to develop and optimize materials for printed memories, 14 June 2007; PR, Solvay expands printed electronics development platform with investment in Plextronics, 30 Aug. 2007; Jacques van Rijckevorsel, "New Business initiatives: 4 themes – 6 platforms," ca. 2011; personal communication by Jacques van Rijckevorsel, 3 Oct. 2011.

[42] "Innovation Center: A springboard for new business," *Solvay Live* (Sept. 2011): 23–5; personal communication by Jean-Marie Solvay, 14 Oct. 2011.

TABLE 22.1. *Sales of Five Major Solvay Pharmaceutical Products (1995–2004) in Millions of Euros*

Name	Creon	Serc	Duphalac	Fluvoxamine/Luvox	Estratest
Origin	Kali-Chemie	Duphar (Unimed)	Duphar	Duphar	Reid-Rowell
Solvay Since: (origin)	1954 (1900)	1980 (1970)	1980 (1977)	1983	1986 (c. 1970)
Therapeutic Area	Gastro	Cardio/mental	Gastro	Mental	HRT
1995	68	58	74	86	37
1996	76	64	78	126	50
1997	89	69	77	167	72
1998	99	69	82	188	96
1999	112	70	81	228	124
2000	119	72	81	271	145
2001	131	77	80	147	199
2002	140	80	83	96	207
2003	137	86	76	80	131
2004	130	96	78	77	100

Note: Gastro = gastroenterology; cardio = cardiology; mental = mental health, psychiatry, central nervous system; HRT = hormone replacement therapy, women's health, and men's health.
Source: Annual Reports Solvay, 1995–2004.

drug for use in treating only obsessive-compulsive disorders, a far smaller market than that for antidepressants. Solvay's strategy in pharmaceuticals was to improve geographical diversification through enhanced expansion in the United States, Japan, Canada, and Central Europe, and to focus research, production, and sales on a limited number of therapeutic areas: cardiovascular diseases, gastroenterology, psychiatry and the central nervous system, hormone replacement therapies for women (and later men), and immunology (vaccines). The company also decided to be more present with the Solvay name in the pharmaceutical market. In 1991 Kali-Chemie Pharma was renamed Solvay Pharma Deutschland, Reid-Rowell became Solvay Pharmaceuticals Inc., and Duphar was renamed Solvay-Duphar.[43]

During the mid-1990s, the deregulation of health-care systems and the strong desire of governments to stop increasing costs in the medical sector put a strong pressure on market prices. By contrast, because of ever-stricter regulations,

---

[43] ARS, 1987–1995; ACS, MoE, 15 Mar. 1988, 14 May 1991; ACS, MoB, 22 Sept. 1989, 1 June 1992, 27 Nov. 1995; Le Fanu (1999), 219–20; PR, "Solvay acquires Kingswood Canada Inc. in the field of human health," 22 Oct. 1990; PR, "Pharmaceutical strategic alliance between Upjohn and Solvay," 21 May 1991; PR, "Solvay purchases the Japanese company Kowa Pharmaceutical Industry Ltd.," 30 Nov. 1992; J. Wegener and B. Kwist, "Human Health: Target 2000," *Solvay Live* (Winter 1993–1994): 2–4; PR, "Health: Solvay receives the approvable letter from FDA (USA) for Luvox-TM (OCD indication)," 2 Sept. 1994; PR, Solvay Pharmaceuticals Inc. Suspends sales of LUVOX in the USA after FDA exclusivity expiration, 23 May 2002.

research costs and development times increased. Important competitors drastically reorganized their pharmaceutical business. Chemical giants such as Dow, DuPont, and ICI decided to set each of their pharmaceutical divisions at arm's length, or even completely apart, as in the case of ICI (Zeneca, 1993). Several major acquisitions and mergers took place, such as those of Rhône-Poulenc and Rorer (1990), Glaxo and Wellcome (1995), and Hoechst and Roussel Uclaf (1996). In the midst of that storm, Solvay had to define its position. Several financial analysts thought that Solvay's pharmaceutical business was too small, and they doubted whether "in the long term . . . Solvay is the best home for this business." Partly in response to that, the Solvay leadership decided in 1994–1996 to divest crop protection, enzymes, and animal health and to focus completely on human health (see Chapter 19). In 1996 the growth of the pharmaceutical business of Solvay became the top priority, not only in absolute terms but also relative to other sectors. A target to grow within five years to 20 percent of the total sales was set, and indeed it was reached in 2001 (see Table 22.3). To achieve that goal, it was decided to invest €200 million each year in research and acquisitions. In 1997 about 53 percent of the total research budget of Solvay was spent on pharmacy alone; in 2000 this had grown to 69 percent.[44]

There certainly was a great need to intensify research. In this highly competitive market, the life cycles of new products tended to become ever shorter. Table 22.1 nicely illustrates this phenomenon for Luvox and Estratest, where sales after a high peak went into rapid decline. In order to grow, then, Solvay had to replace those products with new ones. Inside Solvay's pharmaceutical research departments in Hanover, Weesp, and the United States there were several promising products in the pipeline, but by 1997 they were not advanced enough to put them on the market. The company therefore acquired licenses on hormone replacement products: Prometrium from Schering-Plough and Estrogel from La Salle Laboratories. In 1999 a license from SmithKlineBeecham was obtained for the cardiovascular drug Teveten. The same year, Solvay also successfully launched a tender offer on the shares of Unimed Pharmaceuticals Inc. in Chicago, a company that had the promising hormone preparation AndroGel for men in its pipeline. These were important decisions. Teveten and AndroGel proved successful acquisitions, with high sales figures during the 2000s (see Table 22.2). They more than compensated for the declining sales of Luvox and Estratest.[45]

[44] Chandler (2005), 52, 62, 71, 124, 126, 132, 140, 187, 202, 205, 210–11, 227, 239–42, 248, 250–2, 254, 256; ACS, MoB, 1 June 1992, 27 Nov. 1995, 25 July 1996, 15 Dec. 1997; ACS, green folder "Evolution du secteur Plastiques," Report on Solvay by the Swiss Bank Corporation, 1993; J. van Randen and A. de Jonge, "The race to develop the medicines of the future," *Solvay Live* (Autumn 1996): 17; ACS, MES-meeting, 29 May 1997; ACS, 1061-2-1, fax Peter D. Sutherland, Goldman Sachs International, to Daniel Janssen, 27 Oct. 1997.

[45] ACS, MoB, 5 June 1997, 3 June 1999, 16 Dec. 1999; ACS, MES-meeting, 27–28 May 1998; id., 9–10 Dec. 1998; id., 16–17 May 1999; "Aceon et Teveten: à la conquête du coeur des Américains," *Solvay Live* 63 (Winter 1999–2000): 8–9; PR, Approval by US FDA for Androgel, first gel to treat male testosterone deficiency, 29 Feb. 2000; Roger Bickerstaffe, "Pharma : Alliances stratégiques," *Solvay Live* 65 (Summer–Autumn 2001): 10–12.

TABLE 22.2. *Sales of Five Major Solvay Pharmaceutical Products (2000–2009) in Millions of Euros*

Name	Creon	Influvac	Teveten	AndroGel	TriCor/Lipanthyl
Origin/License	Kali-Chemie	Duphar	SmithKline Beecham	Unimed	Fournier
Solvay Since: (origin)	1954 (1900)	1980 (1950)	1999	1999	2005
Therapeutic Area	Gastro	Vaccines	Cardio	HRT	Cardio
2000	119	51	16	29	
2001	131	56	35	129	
2002	140	60	53	196	
2003	137	68	66	250	
2004	130	76	72	231	
2005	162	100	91	239	(185)
2006	191	118	95	275	413
2007	198	127	106	308	433
2008	217	116	116	337	511
2009	268	162	110	452	453

Note: Gastro = gastroenterology; cardio = cardiology; HRT = hormone replacement therapy, women's health, and men's health. TriCor's results for 2005 are from 1 August.
Source: Annual Reports Solvay, 2000–2009.

There was one dark cloud on the horizon, though. During the 1990s, a research worker at one of Solvay's US laboratories had manipulated his figures for more favorable results. This had been discovered by the FDA, which in September 1997 started an Application Integrity Programs (AIP) procedure against Solvay. This was very serious matter, because not many companies have survived the procedure. The FDA took its time, and as a result it also took up the time of the head of pharmaceuticals, Jürgen Ernst, and other Solvay managers for many years. During that time, registration of new drugs in the United States had to be handled with the utmost care, and it was often postponed. This was one reason that in 2000 Solvay decided to reduce over five years its annual investments in pharmacy from €200 million to €100 million. The money could better be used to acquire Ausimont.[46]

After the AIP procedure had been settled, Solvay resumed its expansion in the pharmaceutical sector. As research results continued to lag behind expectations, the company decided to reinforce growth by means of acquisitions and more energetic marketing efforts. In late 2004 Solvay launched a successful bid on the shares of the Swedish company NeoPharma, which had developed the anti-Parkinson's drug Duodopa. In the autumn of 2005 Solvay introduced Duodopa in several European countries. By then, Solvay had also bought the far-larger French company Fournier Pharma, which was integrated into Solvay

[46] ACS, MES-meeting, 16–17 May 1999, "Solvay Assembee Générale, Juin 1998, Stand by Statement"; id., 6 Dec. 2001; ACS, MoB, 5 June 2000, 7 June 2001, 17 Dec. 2001; ACS, "Nouvelles orientation stratégiques pour Solvay," 1 Sept. 2000; interview Alöis Michielsen, 17 Aug. 2011.

TABLE 22.3. *Division of Sales and Rebit Across Different Product Groups, 1999–2010 (%)*

Year	Chemicals		Plastics (including processing)		Pharmaceuticals	
	Sales	Rebit[a]	Sales	Rebit[a]	Sales	Rebit[a]
1999	31	33	52	43	17	24
2000	29	35	53	45	18	20
2001	32	46	48	22	20	32
2002	33	31	43	39	24	31
2003	33	29	43	34	24	37
2004	34	22	43	49	24	29
2005	33	29	41	40	27	31
2006	32	27	40	35	28	38
2007	32	28	41	36	27	37
2008	33	24	39	26	28	50
2009	32	25	35	8	33	67
2010	44	46	56	54	0	0

[a] 1999–2001 earnings before interest and taxes.

Source: *Annual Reports Solvay*, 1999–2010.

Pharmaceuticals starting on 1 August 2005. With a price of €1.2 billion, it was one of Solvay's largest acquisitions. A major reason to acquire Fournier was a very successful cardiovascular product from its own research. It was marketed as Lipanthyl, but as TriCor in the United States by Abbott. It soon became Solvay's major cash cow in the pharmaceutical sector.[47]

In the framework of the integration of Fournier into Solvay Pharmaceuticals, Werner Cautreels, who had succeeded Jürgen Ernst as head of the Pharma Sector, launched an ambitious strategic program Inspire that apart from the Fournier operation was directed at cutting fixed costs, more focused research, and more energetic sales efforts. The latter part of the program was particularly successful. Within a few years, Solvay was able to considerably raise the sales figures of products such as Creon and Influvac, which Solvay Pharmaceuticals and its predecessors had already been selling for more than fifty years. Between 2004 and 2009, the share of pharmaceuticals in Solvay's total sales grew by these efforts from 24 percent to 33 percent, and its contribution to the profits (Rebit) from about 30 percent to more than 50 percent. This remarkable success in pharmaceuticals changed completely the profile of the Solvay group (see Table 22.3): it was much less cyclical, far less capital intensive, more research intensive, and it featured stronger profit growth, a much higher return on equity, and increased share prices.

---

[47] PR, Solvay Pharmaceuticals launches bid to acquire NeoPharma in Sweden, 10 Dec. 2004; ARS 2004: 19; id. 2006: 7, 9–10, 19; PR, Solvay Pharmaceuticals completes acquisition of NeoPharma in Sweden, 21 Jan. 2005; PR, Solvay Pharmaceuticals completes market authorization in 28 European countries for Duodopa, 28 Nov. 2005; PR, Solvay finalizes agreement to buy Fournier Pharma, 12 July 2005.

With results as excellent these, it is almost impossible to understand why Solvay would sell its pharmaceutical sector only a few years later. For that one has to look to the prospects in the longer run. Two products in particular, the gastroenterological product Cilansetron and the antipsychotic drug Bifeprunox, had accumulated high expectations for quite some time. Cilansetron had been developed by Solvay since the early 1990s. In 2000 the research entered phase 3, the last phase of clinical research before registration. Early in 2004 it was announced that the product would probably launch in 2005. In April 2004 it was offered for registration to the Medicine and Healthcare Regulatory Agency (MHRA) in the United Kingdom, which was the reference country for Europe, and on 1 July 2004 to the FDA. It appeared, though, that the MHRA had tightened procedures for clinical trials. In June 2005 it informed the Belgian company that additional information was required. A few months later, Solvay decided to suspend the registration in the United States as long as discussions with the European authorities were going on. That appeared to be the end of the story. A short message in the 2006 annual report was the last public statement made.[48]

Even higher expectations were connected to Bifeprunox, a drug for schizophrenia. Research and development had been done by Solvay Duphar during the 1990s, and it was subsequently developed since 2000 with the Danish company H. Lundbeck AS. In September 2003 it entered phase 3, and half a year later Solvay signed a cooperation agreement with the large American pharmaceutical company Wyeth. In July 2004 Wyeth and Solvay announced that Bifeprunox could become a blockbuster, with a sales figure of more than US$1 billion. Then, first results of phase 3 were below expectations. Whereas a market introduction first had been planned in 2006, Solvay and Lundbeck announced that additional phase 3 trials would be needed. Despite this, Solvay and Wyeth submitted the registration files in October 2006 to the FDA. In August 2007 the FDA requested additional information, and in February 2008 Wyeth announced that it had ended the collaboration with Solvay in this field. Solvay and Lundbeck continued cooperation for a while but stopped all activities in 2009. After the failures of Cilansetron Bifeprunox, Solvay had to draw the unpleasant conclusion that, after the introduction of Fluvoxamine in 1983, its own pharmaceutical R&D laboratories in fact had not succeeded in bringing a high-sales drug to the market.[49]

---

[48] [Urban] (2005); ARS, 1992: 24; id. 2000: 23; id. 2002: 16; id. 2004: 1, 18, 21; id. 2006: 24, 27; ACS, MoB, 14 Dec. 2000; PR, Solvay Pharmaceuticals moves ahead in irritable bowel syndrome with Cilansetron, 18 July 2001; PR, Solvay Pharmaceuticals Inc. submits new drug application to the United States Food and Drug Administration for Cilansetron, 1 July 2004; PR, MHRA Requests further information on Cilansetron, 30 June 2005; PR, Cilansetron; Solvay Pharmaceuticals suspends registration activities in the US, 29 Nov. 2005.

[49] [Urban], (2005); ARS, 2000: 22–3, 25; id. 2003: 13, 17–19; id. 2005: 20, 23; id. 2007: 1, 6, 26–7, 29; PR, Solvay Pharma and Lundbeck move into clinical phase III with joint schizophrenia treatment, Bifeprunox, 2 Sept. 2003; PR, Solvay Pharmaceuticals and Wyeth announce submission of new drug application for Bifeprunox to treat schizophrenia, 12 Oct. 2006; ACS, MoB, 26 Feb. 2008, 11 Dec. 2008; PR, Solvay Pharmaceuticals S.A. acknowledges decision of Wyeth Pharmaceuticals to terminate the collaboration agreement on bifeprunox, 29 Feb. 2008; "Lundbeck, Solvay stopped bifeprunox studies," *Reuters News*, 30 July 2009.

Solvay was not unique in that respect. Other pharmaceutical companies were facing the same problem of diminishing returns on research, as well as increased difficulties in convincing the registration authorities. Mergers and acquisition were taking place at an increased magnitude, to profit from the pipelines of other companies. In 1999 a mega-merger took place between Rhône-Poulenc and Hoechst Marion Roussel to create Aventis, which five years later was followed by an even larger merger between Aventis and Sanofi-Synthélabo, creating Sanofi-Aventis. In 2000 the giants Glaxo Wellcome and SmithKline Beecham merged to GlaxoSmithKline (GSK). Pfizer, already a huge company by 1999, has since absorbed several large companies: Warner-Lambert (2000), Pharmacia Corp. (2004), and Wyeth (2009). After the bank crisis of late 2008, Merck & Co. merged with Schering-Plough, which two years earlier had taken over Organon from Akzo-Nobel. Often, several dozens of billions of dollars were involved in these transactions. Solvay was only a modest player in that world.[50]

As a result of these consolidations in the industry, the increasing pressure on the sales prices, ever-higher regulatory barriers, rising R&D costs, the (costly) increasing personalization of therapies, and the possibility that Solvay's largest cash cow TriCor would soon be attacked by producers of generics, Solvay in late 2007 identified its pharmaceutical business as a risk factor and decided to analyze its future. Solvay Pharmaceuticals was smaller than the critical size needed to address the previously mentioned changes in the environment. For R&D, maximum budgets were available that were too small to adequately fill all phases of the R&D pipeline in the therapeutic areas selected by Solvay. Under the supervision of Aloïs Michielsen, Christian Jourquin, and Bernard de Laguiche, several investigations were carried out in 2008 and 2009 under the code names Parthénon and Apollo.[51]

On 1 April 2009 the *Financial Times* published the news that this critical evaluation was going on, and a little later the Belgian press reported that Solvay had given a mandate to Citigroup, Morgan Stanley, and Rothschild to sell the pharmaceutical activities to the highest bidder. Since then, the financial circles and the financial press carefully monitored all possible signals. Persistent rumors indicated that Solvay would sell its pharmaceutical activities to the Swiss company Nycomed, but on 28 September 2009 Solvay disclosed that the buyer would be Abbott, one of the ten largest pharmaceutical companies in the world. Then the public was informed that several options had passed in review: (1) keeping the status quo; (2) going public with the pharmaceutical sector; (3) doing an acquisition; (4) engaging in a merger of partnership; and finally (5) divesting the business. The last option was finally chosen, because of disadvantages associated with the first four alternatives, and because only that option would generate the financial means needed for sustainable,

---

[50] Chandler (2005), 68, 124, 227, 240, 249–50, 253, 256.
[51] ACS, MoB, Jourquin, "Solvay Group Strategy," Dec. 2007; id., 30 July 2008, 29 Oct. 2008, 18 Feb. 2009; id., Cautreels, "Solvay Pharmaceuticals Plan 2009–2013," 11 Dec. 2008; http://www.solvay.com: Address by Christian Jourquin...to the Solvay General Shareholders' Meeting, May 11, 2010.

long-term development of the chemical and plastics businesses. The fact that the entire evaluation lasted more than a year was not only caused by its complexity but probably also by the existence of different views on the issue inside Solvay.[52]

After approval by the US and European competition authorities was received, the deal was concluded on 15 February 2010. Solvay sold its pharmaceutical activities to Abbott for a value of about €5.2 billion, €4.8 billion in cash and €0.4 billion to take over certain debts and obligations. About 9,000 employees were transferred from Solvay to Abbott. On 31 December 2009 Solvay had a total workforce of 28,204 according to the annual report; and a year later this was 16,785. Solvay had become a totally different company, standing on two legs – chemicals (44 percent) and plastics (56 percent) – instead of three (see Table 22.3). The reasons for choosing Abbott were, apart from the price, the existing relationship, Abbott's good knowledge of Solvay's products, its good standing in the industry, and Abbott's strategic intentions. Nevertheless, in September 2010 the American company announced that it would cut 3,000 jobs of its 93,000 employees, with 500 in Weesp and 300 in Hanover, mainly in research. Also Solvay's former US headquarters in Marietta, Georgia, was closed. Obviously, consolidation of the pharmaceutical industry was still going on.[53]

22.5   MOVING FORWARD IN TIMES OF CRISIS: THE FRIENDLY TAKEOVER OF RHODIA

Already well before the agreement with Abbott in September 2009, the management of Solvay was thinking deeply about the future of the company after the sale of its pharmaceutical activities. During 2008 the company reoriented its strategy, hand in hand with a reflection on possible acquisitions. The reason for the strategic reorientation was the conviction that fundamental changes, or paradigm shifts, were taking place in the external world. The trends identified included climate change and the growing influence of ecological issues on business in general; increased competition for energy sources and raw materials; globalization of the economy; the rising power of the BRIC countries (Brazil, Russia, India, and China); and finally, the accelerating pace of technical innovation. Against that background, investigations and projections were made of Solvay's future at its 175th anniversary in 2038, culminating in a strategy discussion at Hanzinelle Castle, near Charleroi, in September 2008. Following the footsteps of other chemical companies, it was decided to take sustainable development as the key concept for Solvay's future. In the view of Solvay's

---

[52] PR, Solvay confirms it is proceeding with an analysis of various options for its pharmaceutical activities, 1 Apr. 2009; ACS, MoB, 12 May 2009; PR, Note about the press release published on 1 Apr. and 22 Apr. 2009; "Nycomed Said to Be Close to Getting Debt Funding for Solvay Bid," *Bloomberg press release*, 11 Sept. 2009; PR, Decision to Sell Pharmaceuticals Sector to Abbott, 28 Sept. 2009.

[53] http://www.solvay.com: Presentation "Strategic refocus, Pharmaceuticals divestment," 28 Sept. 2009; PR, Solvay closes EUR 5.2 billion sale of Solvay Pharmaceuticals to Abbott, 16 Feb. 2010; Press Review Solvay, 17 Feb. 2010.

leadership, chemistry and the life sciences could offer important solutions to the problems sketched above, but it implied at the same time that Solvay should reduce its environmental footprint, spare natural resources and energy, and be faster and more agile in responding to shorter product life cycles. Together with continued attention to product leadership, orientation toward activities with lower cyclicality, and an increased presence in emerging regions with high growth, these would be the search criteria for businesses that could replace Solvay's pharmaceutical sector after its divestment.[54]

When these studies and discussions on Solvay's future strategy were going on, the subprime mortgage crisis in the United States was growing in magnitude; it had started to infect several US banks and soon the entire global banking system. During the second half of 2008, the economy moved into a recession, and at the end of the year demand in several industrial sectors stagnated. Decreasing gross domestic product in Europe and the United States continued during most of 2009. Also, Solvay's operational results went down for more than a year, but they did not turn into negative figures. The company was better equipped to withstand a severe crisis than it had been in 1981 and 1993. It could also bear a loss of more than €300 million on its shareholding in the Fortis bank. This had been a shareholding with a long history, dating from the times of the Société Belge de Banque (see Chapter 10) and, later, the Générale de Banque. In the latter, the Mutuelle by 1998 still had a stake of 3 percent, which was substantial in a bank of that size. That year, Solvay supported an unfriendly takeover of the Générale de Banque by Fortis, and it succeeded in realizing a considerable surplus value on that transaction. The company remained a Fortis shareholder, with an interest of 0.8 percent when Fortis shares completely collapsed in September 2008, with subsequent interventions by the Belgian and Dutch governments. To survive the crisis, the Solvay management decided in the autumn of 2008 to solidify the company's finances: the investment budget was cut by 30 percent, large investments in Russia and Brazil were postponed, and working capital was limited to a minimum.[55]

From February 2010, with the Abbott deal closed, Solvay had €4.5 billion in extra cash on its accounts. This was invested prudently in state bonds, but it was clear from the outset that the money should be reinvested in industrial chemistry. Soon the names of several possible targets started to circulate in the press: the Belgian company Umicore, the Swiss chemical firm Clariant, the German producer of fragrances and flavors Symrise, the Dutch chemicals

54 ACS, MoB, "Solvay Group Strategy," Dec. 2007; id., 30 July 2008, 11 Dec. 2008; ACS, "Hanzinelle 4 – "Solvay 175" – Sustainable development: A key driver for innovation and value creation," 4 Sept. 2008; PR, Solvay sets ambitious goals for its Sustainable Development, 15 Oct. 2008; ACS, MoB, "Solvay Group Strategy," 9 Dec. 2008; ARS 2008: 2–3; id. 2009: 2–6; http://www.solvay.com: Address by Mr. Christian Jourquin . . . at the year-end gathering at Neder-over-Heembeek, 17 Dec. 2009.

55 ARS 2007: 7; PR, First quarter 2008, 13 May 2008; ACS, RdG, 12 May 1964; ACS, MoB, 5 Feb. 1998, 4 June 1998, 29 Oct. 2008, 11 Dec. 2008; PR, "Solvay contributes to creation of European banking group around Générale de Banque and Fortis," 18 May 1998; ACS, MoE, 3 June 1998; ACS, MoB, "Solvay Group Strategy," 9 Dec. 2008; PR, 2008 Results, 19 Feb. 2009; PR, First quarter 2009 results, 12 May 2009; PR, First half 2009 results, 30 July 2009.

and life sciences company DSM, the German companies Wacker Chemie and Cognis, and the Danish producer of food ingredients and enzymes Danisco, to mention a few.[56]

In the meantime, Solvay's CEO Christian Jourquin started a radical restructuring of Solvay's organization, prepared by McKinsey, under the banner of the Horizon project. It was Solvay's answer to both the economic crisis and a possible acquisition. Similar to the reorganization of the 1990s (see Chapter 21), Horizon aimed at making the Solvay organization lighter, more efficient, more agile and responsive, and closer to the customer. Moreover, Solvay's learning capacities were to be improved, and the company was to become more Asian-like. In line with that last target, Solvay early 2010 announced the creation of three research, development, and technology centers in India, South Korea, and China. Half a year later, the contours of the new organization were made public. In specialty chemicals and polymers, global business units (GBUs) were set up, whose headquarters were moved from Solvay's corporate headquarters in Brussels. The main office for special chemicals was created at Seoul, South Korea, and the headquarters for specialty polymers at Bollate, Italy. In essential chemicals (e.g., soda ash, peroxides) and plastics (e.g., vinyls), regional business units (RBUs) were created in Solvay's major markets – Europe, North America, Mercosur, and Asia-Pacific – also with separate headquarters. As a result, the size of Solvay's headquarter in Brussels was greatly reduced. Solvay, which had cultivated its tradition for such a long time, even decided to leave its office spaces at the Rue Prince Albert, where the headquarters had been housed for about 125 years, and move the corporate departments to its Research and Technology Center at Neder-over-Heembeek, on the outskirts of Brussels. During the entire operation, which was planned to be finished by the end of 2012, about 800 jobs would be made redundant, on top of the 1,630 positions that had already disappeared during the 2008–2009 crisis.[57]

Just before Christmas in 2010, Christian Jourquin announced that the group was "preparing to take one of the biggest steps in its history."[58] The acquisition he had in mind did not fly, though. At the end of January 2011, five new alternative acquisitions were investigated. The most attractive among them appeared to be the French company Rhodia. Jourquin immediately started

[56] ACS, MoB, 11 Dec. 2008, 12 May 2009; "Solvay overleeft," (2009); http://www.solvay.com: Presentation "Strategic refocus, Pharmaceuticals divestment," 28 Sept. 2009; ARS 2009: 2–6; "DSM must become predator or risk becoming prey," *Reuters News*, 9 Mar. 2010; "Mysterie rond Solvay wordt groter – Chemiebedrijf verkoopt belangen in automobile-joint venture – logische zet of geld voor grote overname?, *De Tijd*, 18 June 2010; interview Pierre Casimir-Lambert, 21 Apr. 2011.

[57] http://www.solvay.com: Address by Mr. Christian Jourquin...at the year-end gathering at Neder-over-Heembeek, 17 Dec. 2009; ARS 2009: 2–6; PR, Solvay launches three Research, Development & Technology centers in Asia, 11 Feb. 2010; http://www.solvay.com: Address by Christian Jourquin...to the Solvay General Shareholders' Meeting, 11 May 2010; PR, Solvay details a new organization project to secure sustainable growth, 23 Sept. 2010; "The New Solvay – Horizon, Rhodia...a new momentum," *Solvay Live* (Sept. 2011): 12–15; interview Christian Jourquin, 27 Sept. 2010.

[58] http://www.solvay.com: Address by Mr. Christian Jourquin...at the year-end gathering at Neder-over-Heembeek, 22 Dec. 2010.

talks with its CEO, Jean-Pierre Clamadieu. The idea to join forces was received positively. Within about five weeks an agreement would be reached. On 4 April 2011 Solvay and Rhodia announced that, after permission was given by the authorities, Solvay would make a friendly cash offer for Rhodia's shares. Although not all analysts were enthusiastic about the deal, signals from the stock market were definitely positive. Within a few days, Solvay shares went up from €83.86 to €91.41.[59]

Rhodia

Rhodia had been created in January 1998, but it roots went back well into the nineteenth century, to just before the founding date of Solvay. In 1857 the young chemist Prosper Monnet established at Lyons one of the earliest French aniline dye companies, the firm Monnet & Dury. The French patent monopoly of the notorious dye firm La Fuchsine forced Monnet to stop by 1864, but a few years later he reestablished himself in Switzerland as P. Monnet & Cie., with the help of the wealthy Lyons merchant Marc Gilliard. After a second plant had been established in France, the firm was renamed in 1886 into Gilliard, Monnet et Cartier, which in 1895 transformed into a joint-stock company, the Société Chimique des Usines du Rhône. Next to dyes, that company produced chemicals for dyeing and tanning, pharmaceuticals, synthetic flavors, and other organic chemicals and specialties. In 1928 the Société Chimique des Usines du Rhône merged with the Établissement Poulenc Frères, of Ivry-sur-Seine, near Paris, to the company Rhône-Poulenc. Poulenc Frères, which produced mainly inorganic chemicals, including medicines, also had a long history; it was established in 1859.[60]

During the early twentieth century, the Société Chimique des Usines du Rhône expanded to other product areas and to foreign countries. In 1902 the trademark Rhodia was introduced for some of its products. After World War I, that name was also given to foreign subsidiaries created in Brazil (1919) and the United States (1919). Three years later, the company, together with the Comptoir des Textiles Artificiels (CTA), founded Rhodiaceta, which would become a large producer of acetate rayon, in France, in many other European countries, and in Latin America and the United States. Poulenc Frères, in turn, took in 1927 a majority interest in the British pharmaceutical company May & Baker.

After the merger, Rhône-Poulenc continued its expansion in pharmaceuticals and synthetic fibers, and after World War II in petrochemicals, polymers, agrochemicals, and other product groups. Through a series of mergers, it developed into the largest chemical company in France. During the 1970s,

[59] ARS 2010: 2–7; PR, Solvay to create with Rhodia a major player in Chemicals, 4 Apr. 2011; Solvay Press Review, 8 Apr. 2011.
[60] Homburg (1983); Cayez (1988); *Innovating* (1995); *International Directory of Company Histories*, vol. 38 (St. James Press, 2001), at http://www.fundinguniverse.com/company-histories/Rhodia-SA-Company-History.html.

under the leadership of Wilfrid Baumgartner and Renaud Gillet, the chemical divisions of Progil and Péchiney-Saint-Gobain were absorbed in stages. During the same decade, a deep crisis in synthetic fibers brought Rhône-Poulenc into deep trouble. Under the leadership of Jean Gandois (see Chapter 19), the company divested its petrochemicals and bulk polymers and decided to move energetically toward products with high value-added. After nationalization in 1982, the company's turnaround continued. When in 1993 Rhône-Poulenc was privatized again, its portfolio included many new or recently acquired products.

The great restructuring taking place in the pharmaceutical industry during the 1990s did not leave Rhône-Poulenc untouched. In 1990 its pharmaceutical business merged with the US company Rorer, and at the end of the decade, after a deep crisis in the company, it was decided that Rhône-Poulenc would be split into two parts: in January 1998 the Chemicals Division and the Fibers and Polymers Division were set apart to form the company that received the (old) name Rhodia, whereas the pharmaceuticals and similar businesses continued as Rhône- Poulenc, until that company merged with Hoechst in 1999, thereby creating Aventis.

In 1999, with the creation of Aventis, Rhône-Poulenc sold off its position and made Rhodia an independent company. Its CEO, Jean-Pierre Tirouflet, started an ambitious restructuring and acquisition program. Titanium dioxide activities were divested, and several polyester plants were shut down. In 1999 Rhodia acquired the British firm Albright & Wilson, which dated from 1856. It was one of the world's largest producers of phosphates and phosphorous-based products. One year later, the American producer of fine chemicals ChiRex was bought. The company also greatly invested in the Asia-Pacific region in those years, where Rhône-Poulenc's pharmaceutical activities had already been present for many decades.

With these actions the company succeeded in strengthening its leadership and becoming less cyclical. But the costs of the acquisition had been high, leading to enormous debts. During the difficult business years from 2001 to 2003, Rhodia balanced on the edge of the abyss. In 2003 Jean- Pierre Tirouflet was replaced as CEO by Jean-Pierre Clamadieu, who turned around and restructured the company. Between 2000 and 2011, the total work force of Rhodia worldwide was reduced from around thirty thousand to fourteen thousand.[61]

At the moment of Solvay's cash offer for Rhodia's shares, the French company owned some sixty-five production sites in nineteen different countries, with a strong presence in Asia and Latin America in particular. It had sales subsidiaries in many more countries. Five research centers were situated in France (Lyons and Aubervilliers), the United States, Brazil, and China. The company was particularly strong in consumer goods and automotive markets,

---

[61] http://www.rhodia.com/en/news_center/news_releases/ (1998–2011). See Bálint (2011), 178–80.

and it had leading global positions in surfactants, phosphorus chemistry, high-performance silica, rare-earth-based formulations, diphenols, polyamides, and cellulose acetate tow. Total sales were €5.2 billion in 2010.[62]

Solvay and Rhodia – Continuing to Travel Together

Rhodia and Solvay were remarkably complementary in many respects, and they had a good cultural fit. Several arguments were in favor of the deal. In the first place, Rhodia met criteria that had been formulated in advance: it was present in emerging regions, was leading in several products, had many high-value-added products, and was striving to become more sustainable. Second, it also greatly enlarged Solvay's size. The headcount would grow again from sixteen thousand to almost thirty thousand, and the annual sales figure from €7.1 billion in 2010 to €12.7 billion in 2011. Third, together a broader basis in global leadership could be obtained: Solvay would contribute leadership positions in specialty polymers, peroxides, and minerals (soda ash), whereas Rhodia would add positions in polyamide materials, consumer chemicals (e.g., surfactants, phosphorous), and advanced materials (e.g., silica, rare earths). Fourth, a better geographical balance would result. Solvay was stronger in Western Europe but Rhodia in Asia. The share of Asia and Eastern Europe in Solvay's sales, which had been about 19 percent in 2010, would move to 25 percent after the acquisition. Also, the dependence on final markets would be better balanced. Solvay had a good position in the construction and automotive markets, but it was weak in consumer goods, a market that was Rhodia's largest market by far, followed by automotive. A last important feature was the innovation and technology focus that characterized both companies. All these arguments certainly were of importance, but the strong will of both parties to make the cooperation a success counts perhaps even more.[63]

In June 2011 Solvay launched its takeover bid for Rhodia's shares, and on 31 August 2011 it announced that the tender offer had been a success. More than 95 percent of shares had been acquired. Rhodia was added as a third sector of Solvay's product organization, next to chemicals and plastics. On 8 September two Rhodia executives were added to the Executive Committee, Gilles Auffret, Rhodia's former COO, as head of the Rhodia Sector, and Rhodia's former CEO Jean-Pierre Clamadieu, as deputy CEO of Solvay. Already during the negotiations in February and March, it had been agreed that Clamadieu would succeed Jourquin as CEO of Solvay at Jourquin's retirement in 2013, but later it was announced that the succession would take place one year earlier, on 10 May 2012. As a result, Clamadieu became the first CEO who had not made his career inside Solvay, thereby following the footsteps of several other major companies, such as Unilever (Polman), Philips (Boonstra), Bayer (Dekkers),

---

[62] *Rhodia overview 2010* (Paris: Rhodia, 2010); "The New Solvay – Horizon, Rhodia . . . a new momentum," *Solvay Live* (Sept. 2011): 16–19.

[63] http://www.solvay.com: "Opening New Frontiers – Roadshow presentation 1Q11 results," 9 May 2011; id., Address by Christian Jourquin . . . to the Solvay General Shareholders' Meeting 10 May, 2011; PR, "4th Quarter and full year 2011 Results," 17 Feb. 2012.

and AkzoNobel (Van Lede and Wijers). But at the same time, Nicholas Boël also succeeded Aloïs Michielsen as chairman of the board, thereby securing the leadership by the founding families.[64]

The integration of two companies of that size certainly will take time. During the past ten years, this chapter has shown, Solvay has changed dramatically. Further changes as a result of the integration with Rhodia will be one of the great challenges of the future.

---

[64] PR, Total success of Solvay recommended tender offer for Rhodia, 31 Aug. 2011; PR, Solvay recommended tender offer for Rhodia: Implementation of a squeeze-out, 13 Sept. 2011; PR, Appointment of the future Chairman of the Board of Directors of Solvay, 27 Oct. 2011; PR, "Appointment at Solvay's Top in 2012," 17 Jan. 2012.

FIGURE 23.1. Solvay leaders at the bell ceremony organized for the introduction of the Solvay share at the Paris Stock Exchange on 23 January 2012. Solvay joined the listed companies that make up the "CAC 40" in September 2012. (*Left to right*) Bernard de Laguiche, Christian Jourquin, and Jean-Pierre Clamadieu. (Copyright Solvay.)

23

Conclusion of Part 3

After the turmoil of two world wars and the Great Depression, the decades following 1950 were of almost idyllic peace. Yet apart from the founding years of the company, there has been no period in which Solvay's product portfolio and organization changed more deeply. In 1950 Solvay was devoted almost completely to the production of chemicals. More than 80 percent of its production was still in alkalis, the core business since Solvay's creation in 1863. Although the company remained number one in the world in that area, sixty years after 1950 the production of alkalis had dropped to less than 30 percent of total sales. Instead, Solvay had become one of the world leaders in PVC, special polymers, and peroxides – products that, apart from small amounts of PVC, the company did not even make before 1950. Moreover, between 1950 and 2010 Solvay established a profitable pharmaceutical business, developed it, and sold it again. It also started the production of high-density polyethylene (HDPE), became the world leader in that field, and then divested that business. These brief references to major movements in the product portfolio illustrate some of the dramatic developments at Solvay during the past sixty years. This, though, is only the tip of the iceberg, because Solvay's organization, culture, and geographical presence changed deeply as well. This all happened in three quite different stages: a period of growth from 1950 to the late 1970s; a transitional period from the late 1970s to the mid-1990s; and a period since about 1995 with enhanced global competition, in which Solvay's sales stagnated but profitability grew (see Table 23.1).

23.1 GROWING IN PLASTICS

The years between 1950 and 1980 were a period of strong growth for Solvay. Total sales, corrected for inflation, quadrupled between 1955 and the late 1970s; the total workforce grew from about twenty thousand to almost fifty thousand; and Solvay greatly diversified into plastic resins (e.g., PVC, polyolefins), plastics processing, and peroxides. Although at the start of the period Solvay almost exclusively produced chemicals, by 1980 that production sector was reduced to 50 percent, because of the growth of plastics at Solvay and, to a lesser extent, pharmaceuticals.

The growth of the postwar consumer markets was the main driver of that spectacular development. But without the vision of René Boël, Henri Delwart, and Jacques Solvay, Solvay would not have diversified organically

TABLE 23.1. *Development of Solvay, 1950–2010*

Year	Employees (x 1000)	Soda Ash (Mt)	PVC (kt)	Infl. Corr. Sales (M€) (1)	ROE (%) (2)	Sales Europe (%)	Sales Chem. (%)	Sales Plastics (%)	Sales Health (%)
1950	19.4	2.1	1	136	8.5		99	1	0
1955		2.6	22	270	12.4		92	8	0
1960	29.9	2.9	100	361	9.3		82	17	1
1965	37.8	3.0	239	523	5.2		69	30	1
1970	42.9	3.6	424	704	7.6	86	61	37	2
1975	42.7	3.5	592	899	7.3	81	55	41	4
1980	49.1	4.1	747	1,139	4.6	79	48	46	6
1985	44.5	3.8	750	1,323	13.1	73	44	45	11
1990	45.7	4.0	964	1,347	15.8	77	40	47	13
1995	38.6	5.6	1,088	1,278	10.8	68	34	50	16
2000	32.3	6.5	1,562	1,540	10.9	59	29	53	18
2005	28.7	7.4	1,915	1,339	17.8	56	33	41	26
2010	16.8	6.6	1,868	1,005	16.4	55	44	56	0

Note: The financial figures have been corrected for inflation, using 1953 as the year of reference. See http://economie.fgov.be/en/binaries/cpi.histr920.tcm327–65934.xls. Three years' averages, ROE 1950–1965 Solvay & Cie, 1970–2010 consolidated figures Solvay Group.

Sources: ARS 1967–2011; PDO. Cf. Appendices A2 (a)–(b) and A3.

into plastics, peroxides, and plastics processing, and it would have missed great opportunities. To pick the fruits of growing demand, permanent investments are needed. Self-financing, facilitated by profits made during the late 1950s and early 1960s, was the first source of capital. A second important injection into the company's growth came from the portfolios of ICI and Allied shares, which in fact were reserves generated during the late nineteenth and early twentieth centuries. Between 1960 and 1980 both shareholdings were largely sold, and they helped finance Solvay's expansion. A third important mechanism for expansion derived from cheaper loans, made possible by Solvay's transition from a limited partnership into a joint-stock company in 1967. Together, these three financial sources drove forward Solvay's expansion in PVC, from a dwarf to a European giant (see Table 23.1).

That Solvay succeeded so much in its diversification was largely because of the excellence of its engineers, its international organization, and its close relation to ICI. Engineers dominated Solvay's culture and organization until the 1990s. They were convinced that they could solve any technical problem, and with that spirit they succeeded remarkably well in PVC, where a position of leadership was achieved within ten years. They were very successful also in peroxides, as well as in HDPE and PP, where they discovered highly active new catalysts that greatly strengthened Solvay's technological position in these fields.

During the 1950s and 1960s, ICI was Solvay's "big brother." It was its major competitor and at the same time its closest partner. Until that cooperation formally ended in July 1981, Solvay was frequently in touch with ICI managers and technicians in the fields of alkalis, PVC, polyethylene, and crop protection. In 1954, when Jacques Solvay was preparing himself for a future position in the *gérance*, he worked during two weeks in several of ICI's departments. But it was also the end of an era; he was the last of the Solvay leaders who would be trained like that.

Solvay's rapid international expansion into new product groups was certainly greatly supported as well by the company's excellent international organization. Because of its soda ash and electrolytic plants, the company was present in many European countries and in Brazil. It often had good relations with local politicians and businesspeople. Building on these local positions of strength in alkalis, PVC was rolled out in Belgium, Austria, Italy, France, Brazil, Spain, and Germany, and the same pattern was followed in peroxides. As a result, Solvay became number one on the Continent in these fields in a short time. One should not be blind to the fact, though, that this was a process of growth via the multiplication of relatively small units. When later the European Community began to increasingly develop toward a unified market, Solvay's position turned into a disadvantage: several plants had to be closed down, and others to be expanded, to supply a larger market at lower costs.[1]

---

[1] Cf. Jones and Miskell (2005).

23.2   A PERIOD OF DIVERSIFICATION AND TRANSITION

During the 1970s, economic growth in Western Europe and the United States started to slow. Already during the early 1970s this was felt in the soda ash market; a decade later in PVC. Between 1970 and 1980 return on equity declined (see Table 23.1). Under the leadership of Jacques Solvay and, later, Daniel Janssen, Solvay responded to the oil shocks and the saturation of markets in a number of ways: it started to diversify geographically, first to the United States, and then to Asia, Central Europe, and Latin America; it started to diversify into new domains of animal health and (human) pharmaceuticals, which were unrelated to Solvay's organic growth patterns to that point; and it entered a process of organizational change, in which a product-based organization gradually replaced a country-based organization, and in which the accounting systems were adapted to that new structure.

With hindsight, the period from the late 1970s to the mid-1990s can be characterized as a transitional one. At the start of it, Solvay still was a very European company, with 80 percent of its sales in Europe. Fifteen years later, despite geographical diversification, Europe still accounted for about 70 percent of sales. Only after the mid-1990s did non-European markets become truly important. The sales in the NAFTA region climbed between 1995 and 2000 from 19 percent to 28 percent of Solvay's total sales. It declined again during the following decade as a result of divestments in petrochemicals and pharmaceuticals. Between 1995 and 2010 the importance of the Asian market for Solvay grew from 5 percent to 14 percent, and Mercosur from 6 percent to 11 percent. It was therefore mainly during this period that Solvay's internationalization really gained momentum.

The same applies to a certain extent to Solvay's product diversification. Given the expansion of Kali-Chemie's pharmaceutical activities and the acquisition of Salsbury (1979), Duphar (1980), and Reid-Rowell (1986), the relative size of Solvay's human health and animal health activities grew fourfold between the late 1970s and 1995, from about 4 percent to 16 percent of Solvay's sales. That was spectacular, no doubt, but at the same time, by 1995 Solvay was still dominated by its far-larger plastics and chemicals sectors. Only during the early twenty-first century did Solvay's pharmaceutical activities account for a large part of sales and, even more so, profits (see Table 22.3).

Although Solvay did relatively well between 1970 and 1987 as compared to other major chemical companies, it cannot be denied that in real terms the growth of Solvay's sales between 1980 and 1995 was modest compared with growth during the first period. Solvay was certainly not unique in that respect. The saturation of markets in Western Europe, the United States, and Japan hit the entire chemical industry and led to ongoing restructurings in the sector.[2]

Milestones in Solvay's fast growth during those years undoubtedly were the acquisition of the Deer Park plant and the HDPE activities of Celanese, in late

---

[2] Reuben and Burstall (1973), 128–31; Aftalion (1988), 375–7.

1974. These were also the years in which Solvay still could inject revenues from sales of its Allied shares into its expansion. During the 1980s the Allied tap dried up, and after the crisis of 1981, with the first net losses in Solvay's history, competition was increasingly felt in the unifying European market. Solvay started to close down plants, first in causticization – Torrelavega (1977), Ebensee (1978), and Povoa (1986) – after earlier shutdowns during the 1960s (see Chapter 15). Shutdowns in diaphragm electrolysis followed – Rosignano (1981), Jemeppe (1982), and others. And then soda ash – Sarralbe (1983), Zurzach (1987), and Tavaux (1991) – culminating in the closing down of Heilbronn and Couillet in 1993 and finally in PVC, in Torrelavega (1983), Hallein (1994), and Ferrara (1998). In the case of soda ash and PVC, the lost capacity was largely replaced by the expansion of other plants that could produce at lower production costs.

23.3 REAPING THE FRUITS OF FOCUSING ON LEADERSHIP AND PROFITABILITY

During the past fifteen to twenty years, global competition has intensified greatly. That in real terms Solvay's total sales declined between 2000 and 2010 was mainly caused by two major divestments: the selling of the polyolefins business in 2001 and of the pharmaceuticals sector in 2010. But price erosion in all bulk sectors – soda ash, PVC, peroxides – also played a role. Table 23.1 clearly shows that after 1995, because of the acquisition of Green River and Devnya in soda ash, and the collaboration with BASF in PVC, the growth of soda ash and PVC production gained new momentum, which clearly distinguishes the third period from the earlier transitional period. Solvay operated with a leaner organization, based on strategic business units and more focused on products that were number one, two, or three in their markets globally. Under the leadership of Aloïs Michielsen and, later, Christian Jourquin, Solvay grew especially in the field of highly sophisticated engineering plastics and fluorinated polymers, in which it became a world leader. The decline of sales, in real terms, hides the fact that, generally speaking, the past fifteen years, until the financial crisis of 2008, had been a period of good profits, far higher at least than during the years 1980 to 1995. Between 1995 and 2010 return on equity as percentage of sales almost doubled, mainly as a result of the excellent profitability of the pharmaceuticals sector, which grew to the highest levels in Solvay's postwar history (see Tables 22.3 and 23.1).

Solvay's top management gave priority to the acquisition and development of products with high value-added, leading to the growth of profits and return on equity rather than to the growth of sales. The fact that the company still is a family firm, which sets limits to its indebtedness, presumably plays a large role in that respect. This is reflected in comparisons with other companies in the sector. In terms of sales growth, Solvay between 1987 and 2007 performed less well than several of its competitors.[3] But with the acquisition of Rhodia in

---

[3] Aftalion (1988), 375–7; on the ICIS top-100, see http://www.icis.com/Articles/2007/09/17/9062496/top-100-global-chemical-companies.html; see also Baker (2010): 8.

2011, the company surely is opening a new chapter. It has almost doubled again its sales and its workforce, and it will continue to grow in highly specialized fields in which it is a world leader.

Being a family firm in the highly competitive twenty-first century has favorable and less favorable sides. It is good for a robust dedication to long-term strategies, including a commitment to research and development. But at the same time, this leads to the avoidance of risks. Moreover, limits are set to raising equity through a public offering, and therefore to growth of sales, as long as the founding families want to keep the present level of their interest in Solvay. Just before World War I, Solvay was among the three largest chemical companies in the world. Between the two world wars it was among the ten largest companies. But during the past few decades – until the sales of the pharmaceutical business in 2010 – it mostly hovered around number twenty-five. As a consequence, as argued already, Solvay focuses increasingly on the profitability of its business units. It is to be expected that in the coming years the combined Solvay-Rhodia group will increase again its focus. The recent divestment of Solvay's last remaining plastics-processing business – in pipes and fittings – illustrates the course that will be taken.[4]

4 PR, "Wienerberger Will Acquire Solvay's Stake in Pipelife," 15 Feb. 2012. See: www.solvay.com.

Appendix A

TABLE A.1. *Solvay Leadership (1863–2012)*

Executive Presidents (1863–2012)

Name	Title	Dates
Ernest Solvay	Founding *gérant*	26/12/1863–26/05/1922
Alfred Solvay	Founding *gérant*	26/12/1863–23/01/1894
Armand Solvay	President of the *gérance*	26/05/1922–02/02/1930
Louis Solvay	President of the *gérance*	02/02/1930–05/05/1947
Ernest-John Solvay	President of the *gérance*	05/05/1947–31/12/1963
René Boël	President of the *gérance*	01/01/1964–30/06/1967
	President of the ExCom	01/07/1967–14/06/1971
Jacques Solvay	President of the ExCom	14/06/1971–02/06/1986
Daniel Janssen	President of the ExCom	02/06/1986–04/06/1998
Aloïs Michielsen	President of the ExCom	04/06/1998–09/05/2006
Christian Jourquin	President of the ExCom	09/05/2006–10/05/2012
Jean-Pierre Clamadieu	President of the ExCom	11/05/2012–//

Note: Excom = Executive Committee; // = ongoing mandate in 2013.

Gérants (1863–1967)

Name	Dates
Ernest Solvay	26/12/1863–26/05/1922
Alfred Solvay	26/12/1863–23/01/1894
Prosper Hanrez	21/06/1880–05/07/1886
Louis Semet	04/07/1887–06/05/1907
Fernand Van der Straeten	07/05/1894–05/05/1913
Armand Solvay	07/05/1894–02/02/1930
Georges Querton	06/05/1907–28/06/1914
Edgar Hulin	06/05/1907–01/07/1919
Édouard Hannon	06/05/1907–04/05/1925
Louis Solvay	06/05/1907–05/05/1947
Émile Tournay	01/05/1916–05/05/1947
Emmanuel Janssen	01/05/1916–04/05/1931
Ernest-John Solvay	04/05/1925–31/12/1963
Robert Gendebien	03/05/1926–16/12/1953
Philippe Aubertin	09/07/1928–31/12/1958
René Boël	04/05/1931–30/06/1967
Henri Delwart	31/07/1945–30/06/1967
Pierre Solvay	05/05/1947–30/06/1967
Jacques Solvay	16/12/1955–30/06/1967
Paul Washer	12/12/1960–30/06/1967

Executive Committee (1967–2012)

Name	Dates
René Boël	01/07/1967–14/06/1971
Henri Delwart	01/07/1967–12/06/1972
Pierre Solvay	01/07/1967–01/01/1970
Jacques Solvay	01/07/1967–02/06/1986
Paul Washer	01/07/1967–06/06/1988
Albert Bietlot	01/01/1968–12/06/1978
Édouard Swolfs	01/01/1968–25/06/1979
Jacques Viriot	14/06/1971–04/06/1984
Claude Loutrel	01/01/1975–30/09/1995
Albert Rampelberg	12/06/1978–31/05/1990
Jean-Jacques Van de Berg	07/06/1982–04/06/1998
Daniel Janssen	04/06/1984–04/06/1998
Aloïs Michielsen	31/05/1990–09/05/2006
Robert Friesewinkel	01/06/1992–30/09/1993
René Degrève	06/06/1994–13/06/2008
Jean Christiaens	01/01/1995–29/02/2000
Marc Duhem	01/01/1995–31/12/1995
Yves Secousse	01/01/1995–31/03/1996
Victor Dierinckx	01/01/1995–30/06/1997
Jürgen Ernst	01/01/1995–01/12/2004
Christian Jourquin	01/01/1996–10/05/2012

(continued)

Executive Committee (1967–2012) (continued)

Name	Dates
Henri Lefèbvre	01/04/1996–01/06/2004
Bernard de Laguiche	01/03/1998–//
Luigi Belli	04/06/1998–31/08/2007
Jacques van Rijckevorsel	01/03/2000–//
Werner Cautreels	01/01/2005–15/02/2010
Vincent De Cuyper	01/05/2006–//
Jean-Michel Mesland	01/09/2007–//
Roger Kearns	01/07/2008–//
Jean-Pierre Clamadieu	08/09/2011–//
Gilles Aufret	08/09/2011–//

Note: // = ongoing mandate in 2013.

Chairmen of the Board of Directors (1967–2012)

Name	Dates
René Boël	01/07/1967–14/06/1971
Jacques Solvay	14/06/1971–03/06/1991
Yves Boël	03/06/1991–04/06/1998
Daniel Janssen	04/06/1998–09/05/2006
Aloïs Michielsen	09/05/2006–08/05/2012
Nicolas Boël	08/05/2012–//

Board of Directors (1967–2012)

Name	Dates
René Boël	01/07/1967–14/06/1971
Henri Delwart	01/07/1967–12/06/1972
Pierre Solvay	01/07/1967–10/06/1974
Jacques Solvay	01/07/1967–03/06/1991
Paul Washer	01/07/1967–06/06/1988
Albert Bietlot	01/01/1968–06/06/1983
Édouard Swolfs	01/01/1968–06/06/1983
Valentin Casimir-Lambert	10/06/1968–14/06/1971
Hugues le Hardÿ de Beaulieu	10/06/1968–31/05/1990
Roger Janssen	10/06/1968–03/07/1975
Pierre de Laguiche	10/06/1968–26/02/1981
Jean-Louis Semet	10/06/1968–10/06/1974
Guido Colonna di Paliano	08/06/1970–12/06/1978
Wilfried Guth	08/06/1970–02/06/1986
Jacques Viriot	14/06/1971–04/06/1984
Pierre Casimir-Lambert	14/06/1971–05/06/2003

(continued)

Board of Directors (1967–2012) (continued)

Name	Dates
Yves Boël	14/06/1971–04/06/1998
André Ganshof van der Meersch	10/06/1974–05/06/1997
Claude Loutrel	10/06/1974–30/09/1995
Paul-Emmanuel Janssen	24/11/1975–04/06/1984
Albert Rampelberg	12/06/1978–31/05/1990
Lord Ezra	25/06/1979–31/05/1990
Hubert de Wangen	29/06/1981–12/05/2009
Jean-Jacques Van de Berg	07/06/1982–05/06/2000
Daniel Janssen	04/06/1984–09/05/2006
Étienne Davignon	03/06/1985–05/06/2003
Hilmar Kopper	02/06/1986–05/06/2003
Solvac (represented by Paul Washer until 1993, then by André Ganshof van der Meersch)	06/06/1988–06/06/1996
José del Marmol	31/05/1990–06/06/2002
John Milne	31/05/1990–06/06/1996
Aloïs Michielsen	31/05/1990–08/05/2012
Jean-Marie Solvay	03/06/1991–//
Robert Friesewinkel	01/06/1992–30/09/1993
Guy de Selliers de Moranville	07/06/1993–//
Édouard de Royère	06/06/1996–30/10/2002
Kenneth Minton	06/06/1996–09/05/2006
Denis Solvay	05/06/1997–//
Nicolas Boël	04/06/1998–//
René Degrève	04/06/1998–28/02/2006
Jürgen Ernst	04/06/1998–31/12/2004
Whitson Sadler	01/01/2002–11/05/2010
Jean van Zeebroeck	06/06/2002–//
Jean-Marie Folz	30/10/2002–//
Jacques Saverys	05/06/2003–08/05/2007
Karel van Miert	05/06/2003–22/06/2009
Uwe-Ernst Bufe	05/06/2003–12/05/2009
Christian Jourquin	02/06/2005–10/05/2012
Bernard de Laguiche	01/03/2006–//
Bernhard Scheuble	09/05/2006–//
Anton van Rossum	09/05/2006–//
Charles Casimir-Lambert	08/05/2007–//
Hervé Coppens d'Eeckenbrugge	12/05/2009–//
Petra Mateos	12/05/2009–//
Yves-Thibault de Silguy	11/05/2010–//
Évelyn du Monceau	11/05/2010–//
Jean-Pierre Clamadieu	08/05/2012–//

Note: // = ongoing mandate in 2013.

Chairmen of the Conseil de Surveillance (1883–1967) and Collège des Commissaires (1967–1986)

Name	Family Group	Dates
Eudore Pirmez	Pirmez	02/07/1883–02/03/1890
Henri Pirmez	Pirmez	05/05/1890–03/05/1897
Léon Mondron	Lambert	03/05/1897–06/05/1912
Paul Misonne	Pirmez	06/05/1912–07/08/1926
Joseph Libbrecht	Nélis	02/05/1927–05/02/1928
Maurice Pirmez	Pirmez	07/05/1928–22/12/1928
Paul Casimir-Lambert	Lambert	06/05/1929–07/12/1939
Jean de Dorlodot	Pirmez	06/05/1940–14/06/1954
Arthur Fallon	Pirmez	14/06/1954–17/07/1961
Léon Coppens d'Eeckenbrugge	Nélis	12/06/1962–30/06/1967
		01/07/1967–09/06/1969
Bernard de Meester de Ravenstein	Pirmez	09/06/1969–12/06/1978
José del Marmol	Pirmez	12/06/1978–02/06/1986

Note: There was no chairman before 1883.

Appendix B

TABLE B.1(a). *Financial Perimeter and Performance of Solvay & Cie (1865–1966)*
(in million BEF)

Year	Total Assets	Equity	Net Profit	Return on Equity (%)
1865	0.3	0.2	0.0	−15.9
1866	0.3	0.2	0.0	0.0
1867	0.3	0.2	0.0	2.7
1868	0.4	0.2	0.0	22.1
1869	0.5	0.3	0.1	30.7
1870	0.7	0.3	0.1	43.2
1871	0.9	0.3	0.2	95.3
1872	1.1	0.3	0.3	117.9
1873	−	1.2	0.3	27.0
1874	−	1.5	0.4	31.0
1875	3.8	1.7	0.5	30.2
1876	4.6	2.1	0.9	44.1
1877	5.5	2.9	1.5	52.6
1878	6.7	4.0	1.6	40.4
1879	10	5.1	2.4	47.0
1880	12	7.0	3.1	44.4
1881	16	9.4	3.6	37.7
1882	22	13	4.5	34.1
1883	28	17	5.2	31.4
1884	34	22	5.0	23.0
1885	33	23	3.8	16.2
1886	34	26	3.5	13.6
1887	36	30	1.8	6.1
1888	37	31	3.3	10.8
1889	37	31	5.0	16.5
1890	45	30	6.6	21.7
1891	43	32	7.3	22.8
1892	50	32	13	41.3
1893	53	33	11	33.5
1894	53	37	9	24.6
1895	55	39	9	22.6
1896	61	41	12	28.6
1897	64	44	11	24.5
1898	70	47	11	23.3
1899	78	53	11	20.7
1900	82	54	14	26.0

Year	Total Assets	Equity	Net Profit	Return on Equity (%)
1901	83	57	11	19.9
1902	87	59	16	27.6
1903	97	64	19	29.0
1904	102	69	19	27.9
1905	111	76	20	26.5
1906	119	82	21	26.0
1907	127	89	22	25.2
1908	n.a.	n.a.	n.a.	n.a.
1909	141	n.a.	n.a.	n.a.
1910	153	110	n.a.	n.a.
1911	166	119	26	22.0
1912	176	128	26	20.6
1913	184	137	26	19.1
1914–16	n.a.	n.a.	n.a.	n.a.
1917	324	164	n.a.	n.a.
1918	410	230	n.a.	n.a.
1919	400	235	26	11.2
1920–31	n.a.	n.a.	n.a.	n.a.
1932	2,166	1,544	322	20.8
1933	2,693	1,803	259	14.4
1934	2,783	1,905	239	12.5
1935	3,171	2,001	334	16.7
1936	3,279	2,143	322	15.0
1937	3,228	2,276	267	11.7
1938	3,288	2,369	235	9.9
1939	3,455	2,459	340	13.8
1940	3,506	2,650	201	7.6
1941	3,848	2,744	208	7.6
1942	4,585	2,870	157	5.5
1943	4,654	2,955	74	2.5
1944	4,144	3,122	55	1.8
1945	4,920	3,659	86	2.3
1946	4,776	3,342	227	6.8
1947	6,671	5,183	268	5.2
1948	7,288	5,372	511	9.5
1949	7,086	5,526	316	5.7
1950	7,638	5,643	522	9.2
1951	8,175	5,888	623	10.6
1952	8,506	6,125	503	8.2
1953	9,420	6,759	819	12.1
1954	9,854	7,197	967	13.4
1955	11,313	7,864	944	12.0
1956	12,160	8,263	983	11.9
1957	12,709	8,645	993	11.5
1958	13,079	9,033	891	9.9
1959	13,782	9,356	1,004	10.7
1960	14,474	9,639	1,108	11.5
1961	24,757	19,401	1,126	5.8
1962	26,658	20,031	1,094	5.5
1963	28,963	21,061	894	4.2
1964	31,109	21,679	1,138	5.3
1965	32,420	22,195	1,211	5.5
1966	34,303	22,496	1,091	4.9

Note: Amounts are in constant million BEF. Data could not be found for some years (n.a. = not available). Between 1865 and 1896 (inclusive), accounting periods are 1 May–30 April; from 1897, 1 January–31 December. For turnover figures from 1955 to 1966, see Table 17.1. Turnover in 1950 was BEF 5 billion.
Sources: ACS, AG, reports by the *gérance* 1865 to 1919; AFi, annual fiscal declarations 1932 to 1966.

TABLE B.I(b). *Financial Perimeter and Performance of the Solvay Group (consolidated), 1967–2010 (in million €)*

Year	Total Assets	Turnover	Net Profit	Equity	Return on Equity (%)	Persons Employed
1967	1,177	725	33	753	4.4	39,878
1968	1,213	812	42	755	5.6	39,475
1969	1,264	936	77	743	10.3	41,611
1970	1,422	1,042	51	795	6.5	42,914
1971	1,629	1,121	48	803	6.0	43,716
1972	1,752	1,289	56	837	6.7	44,701
1973	1,871	1,581	63	897	7.0	44,274
1974	2,088	1,943	74	1,023	7.2	44,467
1975	2,274	1,990	30	1,084	2.8	42,706
1976	2,285	2,178	121	1,012	12.0	44,109
1977	2,372	2,245	66	1,052	6.3	44,857
1978	2,481	2,358	81	1,048	7.7	44,967
1979	2,861	2,999	117	1,064	11.0	46,214
1980	3,056	3,432	49	1,157	4.2	49,057
1981	3,354	3,902	− 19	1,277	− 1.5	48,237
1982	3,762	4,407	64	1,384	4.6	45,369
1983	4,245	4,911	130	1,465	8.9	44,186
1984	4,610	5,545	200	1,598	12.5	43,527
1985	4,572	5,589	202	1,621	12.4	44,461
1986	4,512	5,362	246	1,639	15.0	44,787
1987	4,923	5,543	302	1,684	17.9	44,957
1988	5,735	6,283	375	2,003	18.7	44,301
1989	6,038	6,366	414	2,273	18.2	45,011
1990	6,840	6,327	394	2,306	17.1	45,671
1991	6,868	6,316	308	2,533	12.2	45,585
1992	6,510	6,308	245	2,649	9.2	46,858
1993	6,652	6,052	− 171	2,436	− 7.0	43,163
1994	6,551	6,500	197	2,432	8.1	39,874
1995	6,496	6,776	310	2,469	12.6	38,616
1996	7,018	6,990	338	2,877	11.7	35,400
1997	7,799	7,709	341	3,236	10.5	34,445
1998	3,293	7,451	378	3,293	11.5	33,104
1999	3,670	7,869	423	3,670	11.5	32,834
2000	3,974	8,863	433	3,974	10.9	32,294
2001	3,939	8,725	403	3,939	10.2	31,413
2002	3,346	7,919	494	3,346	14.8	30,302
2003	3,510	7,557	430	3,510	12.3	30,139
2004	3,792	7,271	541	3,792	14.3	26,926
2005	3,920	8,562	816	3,920	20.8	28,730
2006	4,456	9,299	817	4,456	18.3	29,258
2007	4,459	9,572	828	4,459	18.6	28,340
2008	4,745	9,490	449	4,745	9.5	29,433
2009	5,160	8,485	553	5,160	10.7	28,204
2010	14,014	7,109	1,823	6,839	26.7	16,785
2011	19,437	12,693	784	6,653	11.8	29,121

Note: Amounts are in constant million €, with the exchange rate of 1€= 40.3399 BEF. Return on equity for 2010 is unusually high because of the incidental sales of the pharmaceutical sector to Abbott, which brought extraordinary results.

Sources: ARS 1967 to 2010.

Appendix C

TABLE C.1. *Production of Major Products of the Solvay Group, in Kilotons per Year, 1866–2011*

Year	Soda Ash Solvay	Brunner, Mond/ICI	SPC/ Allied	Caustic Soda Causticization	Electrolytic	PVC	HDPE	PP	H_2O_2
1866	0.2	–	–	–	–	–	–	–	–
1867	0.5	–	–	–	–	–	–	–	–
1868	1	–	–	–	–	–	–	–	–
1869	1	–	–	–	–	–	–	–	–
1870	2	–	–	–	–	–	–	–	–
1871	3	–	–	–	–	–	–	–	–
1872	3	–	–	–	–	–	–	–	–
1873	4	–	–	–	–	–	–	–	–
1874	5	2	–	–	–	–	–	–	–
1875	8	3	–	–	–	–	–	–	–
1876	12	5	–	–	–	–	–	–	–
1877	19	10	–	–	–	–	–	–	–
1878	25	13	–	–	–	–	–	–	–
1879	32	17	–	–	–	–	–	–	–
1880	43	20	–	–	–	–	–	–	–
1881	53	24	–	–	–	–	–	–	–
1882	68	47	–	–	–	–	–	–	–
1883	88	58	3	0.2	–	–	–	–	–
1884	109	66	12	0.3	–	–	–	–	–
1885	141	84	20	1	–	–	–	–	–
1886	162	93	34	2	–	–	–	–	–
1887	181	111	40	3	–	–	–	–	–
1888	193	129	51	4	–	–	–	–	–
1889	209	136	53	5	–	–	–	–	–
1890	235	150	68	8	–	–	–	–	–
1891	250	159	73	8	–	–	–	–	–
1892	278	174	83	14	–	–	–	–	–
1893	292	174	85	19	–	–	–	–	–
1894	293	189	105	20	–	–	–	–	–
1895	307	206	113	25	–	–	–	–	–
1896	363	191	127	29	–	–	–	–	–
1897	361	183	167	25	–	–	–	–	–
1898	382	182	205	29	0.3	–	–	–	–
1899	424	201	259	33	1	–	–	–	–

(continued)

TABLE C.I *(continued)*

Year	Soda Ash			Caustic Soda		Plastics			H_2O_2
	Solvay	Brunner, Mond/ICI	SPC/ Allied	Causticization	Electrolytic	PVC	HDPE	PP	
1900	456	227	300	47	2	–	–	–	–
1901	474	223	264	46	3	–	–	–	–
1902	483	234	351	45	4	–	–	–	–
1903	523	245	323	48	5	–	–	–	–
1904	551	260	346	52	6	–	–	–	–
1905	582	281	310	54	7	–	–	–	–
1906	650	304	397	61	7	–	–	–	–
1907	709	319	421	62	7	–	–	–	–
1908	738	288	355	70	8	–	–	–	–
1909	772	322	368	75	8	–	–	–	–
1910	837	332	414	95	9	–	–	–	–
1911	884	360	448	95	9	–	–	–	–
1912	960	389	463	122	10	–	–	–	–
1913	988	421	476	141	12	–	–	–	–
1914	827	437	459	127	9	–	–	–	–
1915	846	498	511	145	8	–	–	–	–
1916	1,022	478	753	192	9	–	–	–	–
1917	846	470	879	137	4	–	–	–	–
1918	696	494	855	107	4	–	–	–	–
1919	527	487	581	82	1	–	–	–	–
1920	734	672	801	114	3	–	–	–	–
1921	734	432	412	129	4	–	–	–	–
1922	1,029	620	685	179	7	–	–	–	–
1923	1,013	690	796	150	9	–	–	–	–
1924	1,225	754	644	198	9	–	–	–	–
1925	1,385	700	678	243	10	–	–	–	–
1926	1,492	592	n.c.	266	9	–	–	–	–
1927	1,595	760	n.c.	288	11	–	–	–	–
1928	1,800	829	n.c.	332	15	–	–	–	–
1929	1,857	800	n.c.	320	20	–	–	–	–
1930	1,708	845	n.c.	305	19	–	–	–	–
1931	1,438	740	n.c.	252	19	–	–	–	–
1932	1,454	858	n.c.	236	18	–	–	–	–
1933	1,400	855	n.c.	274	18	–	–	–	–
1934	1,511	920	n.c.	286	18	–	–	–	–
1935	1,619	1,004	n.c.	314	21	–	–	–	–
1936	1,782	1,005	n.c.	357	26	–	–	–	–
1937	2,067	1,140	n.c.	422	30	–	–	–	–
1938	1,999	951	n.c.	403	32	–	–	–	–
1939	2,246	1,192	n.c.	518	56	–	–	–	–
1940	2,042	1,301	n.c.	467	53	–	–	–	–
1941	2,054	1,303	n.c.	457	63	–	–	–	–
1942	1,887	1,307	n.c.	411	66	–	–	–	–
1943	1,675	1,233	n.c.	394	71	–	–	–	–
1944	1,195	1,234	n.c.	224	44	–	–	–	–
1945	506	1,252	n.c.	102	17	–	–	–	–
1946	1,314	1,320	n.c.	257	50	–	–	–	–
1947	1,723	1,159	n.c.	430	68	–	–	–	–

| Year | | Soda Ash | | Caustic Soda | | Plastics | | | |
	Solvay	Brunner, Mond/ICI	SPC/Allied	Causticization	Electrolytic	PVC	HDPE	PP	H$_2$O$_2$
1948	2,010	1,467	n.c.	497	68	–	–	–	–
1949	1,955	1,457	n.c.	494	58	–	–	–	–
1950	2,128	1,619	n.c.	509	75	1	–	–	–
1951	2,615	1,797	n.c.	687	98	2	–	–	–
1952	1,995	1,485	n.c.	464	96	3	–	–	–
1953	2,352	1,575	n.c.	596	102	14	–	–	–
1954	2,517	1,767	n.c.	641	135	17	–	–	–
1955	2,570	1,827	n.c.	602	162	22	–	–	–
1956	2,768	1,908	n.c.	660	176	34	–	–	–
1957	2,592	1,852	n.c.	606	210	46	–	–	1
1958	2,463	1,649	n.c.	531	234	57	–	–	1
1959	2,657	1,854	n.c.	526	294	82	1	–	6
1960	2,896	1,869	n.c.	593	362	100	3	–	10
1961	2,844	1,712	n.c.	501	389	122	5	–	11
1962	2,837	1,737	n.c.	402	422	143	7	–	13
1963	2,945	1,658	n.c.	403	467	184	10	–	17
1964	3,131	1,703	n.c.	398	550	227	12	–	19
1965	3,030	1,792	n.c.	256	609	239	15	–	24
1966	3,073	n.c.	n.c.	225	667	248	22	–	31
1967	3,155	n.c.	n.c.	241	771	272	33	–	35
1968	3,177	n.c.	n.c.	115	848	345	n.c.	–	34
1969	3,456	n.c.	n.c.	126	1,013	375	n.c.	–	39
1970	3,567	n.c.	n.c.	122	1,133	424	48	–	41
1971	3,622	n.c.	n.c.	128	1,209	499	62	–	83
1972	3,784	n.c.	n.c.	120	1,293	576	87	–	90
1973	3,936	n.c.	n.c.	57	1,504	703	123	–	96
1974	4,036	n.c.	n.c.	68	1,517	656	130	–	101
1975	3,515	n.c.	n.c.	72	1,198	592	256	–	95
1976	3,607	n.c.	n.c.	57	1,409	703	336	1	111
1977	3,524	n.c.	n.c.	13	1,340	682	394	15	114
1978	3,483	n.c.	n.c.	9	1,350	708	437	33	122
1979	3,934	n.c.	n.c.	9	1,502	814	483	75	142
1980	4,084	n.c.	n.c.	10	1,379	747	473	89	135
1981	3,685	n.c.	n.c.	9	1,325	647	427	104	146
1982	3,517	n.c.	n.c.	11	1,287	657	485	108	156
1983	3,487	n.c.	n.c.	10	1,377	701	553	158	167
1984	3,884	n.c.	n.c.	11	1,457	690	608	185	172
1985	3,847	n.c.	n.c.	8	1,448	750	640	199	160
1986	3,794	n.c.	–	4	1,482	807	664	257	192
1987	3,848	n.c.	–	–	1,610	905	763	293	227
1988	3,933	n.c.	–	–	1,684	942	798	331	235
1989	4,012	n.c.	–	–	1,681	959	763	319	254
1990	3,951	n.c.	–	–	1,551	964	863	365	282
1991	4,088	n.c.	–	–	1,426	956	891	363	289
1992	4,965	n.c.	–	–	1,430	984	906	363	310
1993	4,725	n.c.	–	–	1,357	1,048	912	403	310
1994	5,136	n.c.	–	–	1,499	1,127	993	473	335
1995	5,635	n.c.	–	–	1,523	1,088	1,041	469	396

(*continued*)

TABLE C.1 *(continued)*

Year	Soda Ash Solvay	Brunner, Mond/ICI	SPC/ Allied	Caustic Soda Causticization	Electrolytic	Plastics PVC	HDPE	PP	H$_2$O$_2$
1996	5,645	n.c.	–	–	1,665	1,209	1,144	496	358
1997	6,501	n.c.	–	–	1,764	1,319	1,260	628	399
1998	6,285	n.c.	–	–	1,692	1,195	1,217	654	391
1999	6,020	n.c.	–	–	1,836	1,282	1,311	693	409
2000	6,451	n.c.	–	–	1,825	1,562	1,402	619	453
2001	6,962	n.c.	–	–	1,735	1,727	1,328	579	436
2002	6,895	n.c.	–	–	1,792	1,770	–	–	453
2003	6,973	n.c.	–	–	1,781	1,830	–	–	488
2004	7,212	n.c.	–	–	1,837	1,920	–	–	555
2005	7,387	n.c.	–	–	1,934	1,915	–	–	562
2006	7,017	n.c.	–	–	1,960	1,896	–	–	610
2007	7,290	n.c.	–	–	2,051	1,887	–	–	638
2008	7,208	n.c.	–	–	1,907	1,735	–	–	637
2009	5,806	n.c.	–	–	1,859	1,720	–	–	638
2010	6,573	n.c.	–	–	2,010	1,868	–	–	776
2011	7,056	n.c.	–	–	1,988	1,812	–	–	880

Note: Solvay's soda ash and caustic soda series include production from Solvay & Cie, DSW, SW, and Lubi-moff as long as their plants were part of the group. Until 1925 and 1965, respectively, figures of SPC/Allied and of Brunner, Mond/ICI were registered by Solvay's statistical department. Up to these dates, Solvay considered those productions as belonging to the Group. After these dates, they were not communicated anymore (n.c.). Chlorine is not mentioned in this table. The total amount of chlorine products (e.g., chloride of lime, PVC), calculated as pure chlorine, is equivalent to the total amount of electrolytic caustic soda (roughly 1 kilogram of chlorine for 1.1 kilogram of caustic soda). The figures of electrolytic caustic soda combine the three types of electrolysis: mercury cells, membrane cells, and diaphragm cells. From 1965, caustic soda produced through the diaphragm process was not sold as such but was transformed to soda ash. For those years, total alkali production therefore cannot be calculated by simply adding the figures for soda ash and caustic soda. From 1992 the Solvay soda ash column includes natural dense soda ash produced from trona at Green River, Wyoming. PVC = polyvinyl chloride, HDPE = high-density polyethylene, PP = polypropylene, and H$_2$O$_2$ = hydrogen peroxide.
Sources: ART–PDO Solvay & Cie, SPC, BM, SW, DSW.

Sources and Bibliography

(1) Abbreviations Used in the Footnotes

ABM   Archives Brunner, Mond & Co., in ICI archives, Public Records Office –
Cheshire, United Kingdom

ACo   Archives of the Solvay Couillet Plant – Bois-du-Luc, Belgium

ACS   Archives of the Solvay Corporate Secretariat – Brussels

ACS-CR   Solvay Contracts Room, inside ACS – Brussels

ACS-O   Old Archives of the Solvay Corporate Secretariat – Brussels

ADSW   Archives of Deutsche Solvay Werke – Bernburg, Germany

AES   Archives of Ernest Solvay, inside ACS – Brussels

AFi   Archives of the Solvay Financial Department – Brussels

AG   Assemblées Générales Solvay – Brussels

AHR   Archives of the Solvay Human Resources Department – Brussels

AL   Archives of the Solvay Legal Department – Brussels

ARS   Annual Report Solvay (officially published English version, unless otherwise
stated)

ART   Archives of the Solvay Research and Technology Department – Brussels

ASD   Archives Solvay Deutschland – Hanover, Germany

ASPC   Archives of the Solvay Process Co. – Syracuse, New York, United States

ASSR   Archives of the Solvay Rosignano plant, Italy

AT   Archives of the Solvay Tax Department – Brussels

ATo   Archives of the Solvay Torrelavega plant, Spain

CdG   Conseil de Gérance of Solvay, inside ACS – Brussels

CdL   Comité de Liaison of Solvay, inside ACS – Brussels

CdS   Conseil de Surveillance of Solvay, inside ACS – Brussels

DS   Dossiers Spéciaux of Solvay, inside ACS – Brussels

HC   Historical Collection of Solvay (Sanctuaire) – Brussels

MES   Maison Ernest Solvay – Brussels

MoB   Minutes of the Board of Directors of Solvay, inside ACS – Brussels

MoE   Minutes of the Executive Committee of Solvay, inside ACS – Brussels

NAB   National Archives of Belgium – Brussels

NARA   National Archives and Records Administration – College Park, Maryland,
United States

NdG   Notes de la Gérance of Solvay, inside ACS – Brussels

PD   Solvay Personal files (dossiers personnels), inside AHR

PDO   Productions depuis l'Origine, Solvay statistical file – Brussels

PPSF   Private papers Solvay Family – La Hulpe, Belgium

PR   Press releases, inside Solvay Publicity Department – Brussels

RBHC   *Revue Belge d'Histoire Contemporaine*

RdG   Réunions de Gérance of Solvay, inside ACS – Brussels
RMES   Registre Maison Ernest Solvay, inside ACS – Brussels

(2) Interviews and Personal Communications

(All interviews were held in Brussels, unless otherwise stated; personal communications are indicated by "pc.")

- Christiane Baleux, NoH, 10 September 2009 (pc)
- Michel Bande, 8 July 2010, 2 May 2011, 6 June 2011, 19 July 2011
- Jean-Pierre Bindelle, 4 May 2010
- Félix Bloyaert, 26 March 2009, 13 April 2009 (pc)
- Mathilde Boël, 27 November 2007
- Yves Boël, 22 November 2007 (pc), 2 June 2009 (pc to Jean-Marie Solvay)
- Pierre Casimir-Lambert, 23 May 2008, 22 June 2009, 21 April 2011, 27 January 2012
- Hervé Coppens d'Eeckenbrugge (pc), 6 January 2009
- Jean-Marie Chandelle, 15 June 2011
- René Degrève, 2 December 2008, 12 May 2010
- Patrice Ducordeaux, Tavaux, 4 May 2011 (pc)
- Robert Friesewinkel, 13 December 2007 (pc), 2 October 2008, 2 November 2010 (pc)
- Auguste Gosselin, 3 November 2009, 27 November 2009
- Alfred Hoffait, 14 May 2009
- Daniel Janssen, 16 October 2007, 13 November 2007, 23 January 2008
- Christian Jourquin, 27 September 2010, NoH, 21 November 2011
- Elisée Lamborelle, 23 January 2008
- Thierry Lefèvre, 8 July 2010
- Henry Lévy-Morelle, 9 November 2007
- Jacques Lévy-Morelle, 7 September 2010, 10 September 2010
- Claude Loutrel, 31 January 2008, 26 May 2011 (pc), 14 September 2011 (pc)
- Aloïs Michielsen, 16 April 2008, 24 September 2008, 21 April 2011, 17 August 2011
- Olivier Monfort, 21 April 2011
- Albert Rampelberg, Uccle, 4 April 2008
- Whitson Sadler, 12 May 2010
- Jean-Pierre Schrayen, Tavaux, 3 May 2011 (pc)
- Jacques Solvay, La Hulpe, 27 November 2007; La Hulpe, 16 January 2008
- Jean-Marie Solvay, 14 October 2011 (pc)
- Jacques Tétu, Tavaux, 4 May 2011 (pc)
- Georges Theys, 6 June 2011
- Claude Thibaut de Maisières, 2 May 2011
- Jacques Van Bost, 19 July 2011
- Cyril Van Lierde, 13 October 2008
- Jacques Van Rijckevorsel, 4 November 2008 (pc), 6 November 2008, 3 October 2011 (pc)
- Jacques Viriot, Paris, 10 August 2009
- Paul Washer, November 2007 (pc), 29 November 2007, December 2007 and 9 January 2008 (pc), 20 May 2011 (pc), 22 June 2011 (pc), 8 and 11 July 2011 (pc), 21 November 2011, 7 December 2011 (pc)
- Pierre Weekers, 8 April 2008 (pc), 8 April 2008, 21 December 2010 (pc), 4 March 2011 (pc)

(3) Archives Consulted

Belgium

Solvay Headquarters, Brussels-Ixelles (moved to NoH in 2012)

- Archives of the Corporate Secretariat (ACS)
- Archives of the Financial Department (AFi)
- Archives of the Tax Department (AT)
- Archives of the Legal Department (AL)
- Archives of the Human Resources Department (AHR)
- Historical Collection (Sanctuaire), Brussels (HC) (moved to MES in 2011)

Maison d'Ernest Solvay, Brussels-Ixelles

- Historical Collection (MES)

Solvay Research and Technology, Neder-over-Heembeek

- Archives of the Research and Technology Department (ART)
- Library Solvay Research and Technology
- Documentation Patent Department

National Archives of Belgium, Brussels (NAB)

- Archives of the Comité National de Secours et d'Alimentation (CNSA)

Ecomusée du Bois-du-Luc, La Louvière

- Archives of the Couillet Plant (ACo)

Solvay family, La Hulpe

- Private Papers Solvay Family (PPSF)

Germany

Solvay Deutschland, Bernburg

- Archives of Deutsche Solvay Werke (ADSW)

Solvay Deutschland, Headquarters, Hanover

- Archives Solvay Deutschland (ASD)

Italy

Solvay plant, Rosignano

- Archives of the Rosignano plant (ASSR)

Spain

Solvay plant, Torrelavega

- Archives of the Torrelavega factory (ATo)

United Kingdom

Public Records Office – Cheshire, Chester

- Archives Brunner, Mond & Co., in ICI archives (ABM)

United States

Public Library, Solvay village, New York

• Archives of the Solvay Process Co. (ASPC)

Rhode Island Historical Society, Providence, Rhode Island

• Solvay Process Company Records and Hazard family papers

(4) Unpublished Memoirs, Reports, and Brochures

Belgian and American CRB Fellows, Biographical Directory, 1920–1950. New York: Commission for Relief of Belgium, 1950.

Brion, René, and Jean-Louis Moreau. *Historique sommaire de la Société Belge de Banque S.A.* Brussels: BNP Paribas Fortis Historical Center, 2008.

Casimir-Lambert, Pierre. *Aperçus historiques sur Solvay & Cie.* Typescript, summer 1967.

CEFIC: 20 Years of Progress and the Challenges of the Future. Brussels: European Chemical Industry Council, 1992.

Cinquantenaire de la Société Solvay & Cie, 1863–1913, Discours. Brussels, 1913.

Discours d'Ernest Solvay à l'occasion du 25e anniversaire de Solvay & Cie, 1888.

Eilsberger, Ernst (a). *Deutsche Solvay-Werke Aktiengesellschaft Bernburg: Ihre Enstehung und erste Wirksamkeit, 1880–1930.* Bernburg: Privately printed, n.d. [1930].

Eilsberger, Ernst (b). *Deutsche Solvay Werke AG: Sa naissance et son activité première, 1880–1930.* Bernburg: Privately printed, n.d. [1930].

Fouyon, Dominique. *La fermeture de la soudière Solvay Couillet.* MA thesis, Université Libre de Bruxelles, Institut du Travail, 1994.

Glasscock, William F. *The Commercial History of the Ammonia Soda Process.* ICI internal report, 1969.

Istituzioni assistenziali, sociali e dopolavoristiche – Solvay & Cie. Trieste Italy: Arti Grafiche L. Smolars & Nipote, 1934.

Masson-Solvay, Marie. *Les débuts de la Société Solvay & Cie, mémoire intime.* Internal Solvay publication, Brussels, May 1915.

Mioche, Philippe. *Quand Solvay conquiert la France (1870–1914).* Unpublished research report, 2008.

Mioche, Philippe. *Fabriquer de la soude pendant le fascisme et le franquisme? Solvay en Espagne (1908–1945) et en Italie (1918–1945).* Unpublished research report, 2009.

Mutuelle Solvay, 1914–2000: Histoire. Internal publication, Mutuelle Solvay & Janssen, Brussels, 2000.

Pelseneer, Jean. *Historique des Instituts internationaux de Physique et de Chimie Solvay depuis leur Fondation jusqu'à la deuxième Guerre Mondiale.* Manuscript, Archives ULB, Brussels, 1975.

Praml, Yvonne. *Solvay Hallein in der Zeit des Nationalsozialismus.* Solvay Österreich AG, internal publication, Vienna, 1998.

Soltex: 20 Years in Deer Park. Deer Park, TX: Soltex, 1977.

Solvay & Cie. S.A. Stabilimenti di Rosignano. Rosignano, Italy: Solvay, n.d. [1977].

Sougnez, Ernest. *Ernest Solvay, industriel pendant la guerre 1914–1918.* Typed report, October 1936.

Tassel, Emile. *Notes sur les travaux poursuivis par Ernest Solvay de 1857 à 1914.* Brussels: Imprimerie G. Bothy, 1920.

Timeline Poster 25 Years of Solvay Polymers, 1974–1999/Company Milestones Calendar. Deer Park, TX: Solvay Polymers, 2000.

Trump, Edward N. *Looking Back at 50 Years in Ammonia Soda and Alkali Industry.* Typescript, Syracuse, NY, 1935.

Trump, Edward N. *Early History of the Solvay Process Company.* Typescript, Allied Library, Solvay Village, NY, n.d.

Washer, Paul. *Memento à l'usage des historiens chargés d'écrire l'histoire de Solvay SA.* Typescript, Brussels, November 2007.

Watts, J. *The First Fifty Years of Brunner, Mond & Co 1873–1923.* Privately printed, Derby: Bemrose, 1923.

Het zout in de Rijn: Reinwaters akties tegen de Rijnverzilting. Amsterdam: Stichting Reinwater, 1986.

(5) Bibliography

Abelshauser, Werner, ed. *Die BASF: Eine Unternehmensgeschichte.* Munich: C. H. Beck, 2002.

Abelshauser, Werner, Wolfgang von Hippel, Jeffrey A. Johnson, and Raymond G. Stokes. *German Industry and Global Enterprise: BASF – The History of a Company.* Cambridge: Cambridge University Press, 2004.

Accarain, Michel. *La société Lubimoff, Solvay & Cie, par Wladimir Orlow.* Louvain-la-Neuve, Belgium: Presses Universitaires de Louvain, 2002.

Aftalion, Fred. *Histoire de la chimie.* Paris: Masson, 1988.

Aftalion, Fred. *A History of the International Chemical Industry: From the "Early Days" to 2000.* 2nd ed. Philadelphia: Chemical Heritage Press, 2001.

"After Two or Three Years of Restructuring in a Climate of Increased Competition – Daniel Janssen: The Growth of the Chemical Industry Will Be Served by European Unification." *L'Echo (Brussels),* 10 Dec. 1992.

Aiken, William Earl. *The Roots Grow Deep: The Story of Captain Ford, His Son Edward and Their Contributions to America's Glass Industry.* Cleveland, OH: Lezius-Hiles Company, 1957.

Ainsworth, Susan J. "Solvay America's Chief Sees Stable Presence, Long-Term Growth for Firm." *Chemical & Engineering News* 70 (28 Sept. 1992): 17–20.

Albright, Lyle F. "Vinyl Chloride Processes." *Chemical Engineering* 74 (1967): 123–30.

Álvarez Quintana, Covadonga, Faustino Surez Antuña, and Óscar Caso Roiz. *Solvay-Lieres, Conjunto Industrial Minera, 1903–2003.* Lieres, Spain: UV Lieres/Solvay, 2003.

Amatori, Franco, and Bruno Bezza. *Montecatini 1888–1966: Capitoli di storia di una grande impresa.* Bologna, Italy: Il Mulino, 1990.

Anderson, Stephen O., and K. Madhava Sarma. *Protecting the Ozone Layer: The United Nations History.* London: Earthscan, 2002.

Audoin-Rouzeau, Stéphane, and Christophe Prochasson, eds. *Sortir de la grande guerre: Le monde et l'après-1918.* Paris: Tallandier, 2008.

[Autorenkollektiv]. *Von der "Buckauer" zum Volkseigener Betrieb "Karl Marx": Aus der einhundertjährigen Geschichte des Sodawerkes Stassfurt.* Stassfurt, Germany: Betriebsparteiorganisation der SED des VEB Vereinigte Sodawerke "Karl Marx," Bernburg-Stassfurt, 1983.

Baillot, Rémi. *Georges Claude, le génie fourvoyé: Créateur de l'Air liquide, du tube au néon, de l'énergie thermique des mers...* Bonchamps-Lès-Laval, France: EDP Sciences, 2010.

Bairoch, Paul. *Mythes et paradoxes de l'histoire économique*. Paris: La Découverte, 1999.

Baker, John. "The Decade's Climbers and Fallers." *ICIS Chemical Business* (13–19 Sept. 2010), 8. http://www.icis.com.

Bálint, Anna. *Clariant clareant: Die Anfänge eines Spezialitätenchemiekonzerns*. Frankfurt: Campus Verlag, 2011.

Baptista Robert J., and Anthony S. Travis, "I.G. Farben in America: The Technologies of General Aniline & Film." *History and Technology* 22 (2) (2006): 187–224.

Barjot, Dominique, ed. *International Cartels Revisited: Vues nouvelles sur les cartels internationaux (1880–1980)*. Proceedings of the Caen Preconference, 23–25 September 1993. Caen, France: Éditions-Diffusion du Lys, 1994.

Barkan, Diana K. "The Witches' Sabbath: The First International Solvay Congress in Physics." *Science in Context* 9 (1993): 59–82.

Barré, C. "Azote et carbochimie." *Revue Arts et Manufactures* 105 (Jan. 1961): 14–17.

Bartl, Heinz, Günter Döring, Karl Hartung, Christian Schilder, and Rainer Slotta. *Kali im Südharz-Untrut-Revier*. Bochum, Germany: Deutsches Bergbau-Museum, 2003.

Battiloso, Stefano, James Foreman-Peck, and Gerhard Kling. "Business Cycles and Economic Policy." In Stephen Broadberry and Kevin H. O'Rourke, eds., *The Cambridge Economic History of Modern Europe*. Vol. 2, *1870 to the Present*. Cambridge: Cambridge University Press, 2010, 360–89.

Baudhuin, Fernand. *Histoire économique de la Belgique, 1914–1939*. Vols. 1 and 2. Brussels: Bruylant, 1946.

Baumgarten, Ferdinand, and Arthur Mezlény. *Kartelle und Trusts: Ihre Stellung im Wirtschafts- und Rechtssystem der wichtigsten Kulturstaaten*. Berlin: Liebmann, 1906.

Bensaude-Vincent, Bernadette, and Isabelle Stengers. *Histoire de la chimie*. Paris: La Découverte, 1993.

Berend, Ivan T. *An Economic History of Twentieth-Century Europe*. Cambridge: Cambridge University Press, 2006.

Berghahn, Volker R. *Modern Germany: Society, Economy, and Politics in the Twentieth Century*. Cambridge: Cambridge University Press, 1982.

Berghahn, Volker R. *The Americanisation of West German Industry, 1945–1973*. Royal Leamington Spa, UK: Berg, 1985.

[Bertoni, Roberto, Sergio Foschi, Dina Guerra, and Bruno Zannoni, eds.]. *Ferrara e il suo petrolchimico: Il Lavore e il territorio – Storia, cultura e proposta*. Ferrara, Italy: CdS Edizioni, 2006.

Bertrams, Kenneth. *Universités & Entreprises, Milieux académiques et industriels en Belgique, 1880–1970*. Brussels: Le Cri, 2006.

Bertrams, Kenneth. "Converting Academic Expertise into Industrial Innovation: University-Based Research at Solvay and Gevaert, 1900–1970." *Enterprise and Society* 8 (4) (2007): 807–41.

Bertrams, Kenneth. "De l'action humanitaire à la recherche scientifique: La Commission for the Relief in Belgium et la création du Fonds National de la Recherche Scientifique en Belgique, 1914–1930." In Ludovic Tournès, ed., *Philanthropie et américanisation: Les fondations américaines et leurs réseaux en Europe (1900–2000)*. Paris: Ed. Autrement, 2010, 43–61.

Bertrams, Kenneth. "Caught Up by Politics? The Solvay Councils on Physics and the Collapse of Neutrality." In Rebecka Lettevall, Geert Somsen, and Sven Widmalm, eds., *The Science, Culture and Politics of Neutrality in Twentieth-Century Europe*. London: Routledge, 2012, 190–219.

Beukers, Eelco, and Harry van den Tweel. *Onder druk wordt alles vloeibaar: een geschiedenis van het chloortransport in Nederland.* Utrecht, the Netherlands: Matrijs, 2006.

Blackford, Mansel G., and K. Austin Kerr. *BF Goodrich: Tradition and Transformation 1870–1995.* Columbus: Ohio State University Press, 1996.

Bloemen, Annie, Paul Lemmen, and Louis de Wilde, eds. *De Soda.* Roermond, the Netherlands: Solvay Chemie BV, 2000.

Bolle, Jacques. *Solvay, L'invention, l'homme, l'entreprise industrielle.* Brussels: Weissenbruch, 1963.

Bougeard, Robert, Benedito Libeiro, and Regina Lorch, eds. *Quem controla o que.* São Paolo: Banas, 1961.

Bower, Joseph L. *When Markets Quake: The Management Challenge of Restructuring Industry.* Boston: Harvard Business School Press, 1986.

Brandt, E. B. *Growth Company: Dow Chemical's First Century.* East Lansing: Michigan State University Press, 1997.

Brauman, Annick, and Marie Demanet. *Le Parc Léopold 1850–1950, le zoo, la Cité scientifique et la ville.* Brussels: Archives d'Architecture Moderne, 1985.

Brion, René. "Hanrez Famille." In Ginette Kurgan-van Hentenryk, Serge Jaumain, and Valérie Montens, eds., *Dictionnaire des patrons en Belgique: Les hommes, les entreprises, les réseaux.* Brussels: De Boeck Université, 1996a, 349–51.

Brion, René. "Lepage Louis." In Ginette Kurgan-van Hentenryk, Serge Jaumain, and Valérie Montens, eds., *Dictionnaire des patrons en Belgique: Les hommes, les entreprises, les réseaux.* Brussels: De Boeck Université, 1996b, 429–30.

Brion, René, and Jean-Louis Moreau. *La Société Générale de Belgique, 1822–1997.* Antwerp, Belgium: Mercator, 1998.

Brion, René, and Jean-Louis Moreau. "Jalons pour une histoire du gaz en Belgique aux XIXe et XXe siècles." In S. Paquier and J.-P. Williot, eds., *L'industrie du gaz en Europe aux XIXe et XXe siècles, L'innovation entre marchés privés et collectivités publiques.* Brussels: Peter Lang, 2005, 197–224.

Brion, René, and Jean-Louis Moreau. *Van mijnbouw tot Mars: De ontstaansgeschiedenis van Umicore.* Tielt, Belgium: Lannoo, 2006.

Brooks, Nathan M. "Munitions, the Military, and Chemistry in Russia." In Roy MacLeod and Jeffrey A. Johnson, eds., *Frontline and Factory: Comparative Perspectives on the Chemical Industry at War, 1914–1924.* Dordrecht, the Netherlands: Springer, 2006, 75–101.

Brown, Michael. "Setting Occupational Health Standards: The Vinyl Chloride Case." In Dorothy Nelkin, ed., *Controversy: Politics of Technical Decisions.* Beverly Hills, CA: Sage, 1979, 125–41.

Brüll, Chrisoph. *Belgien im Nachkriegsdeutschland: Besatzung, Annäherung, Ausgleich (1944–1958).* Essen, Germany: Klartext-Verlag, 2009.

Bruyneel, André. "The Belgian 'Commission Bancaire': Functions and Methods." *Journal of Comparative Corporate Law and Securities Regulation* 1 (1978): 187–209.

Buchmann, Walter. *Eigenschaften von Polyvinylchlorid-Kunststoff.* Munich: J. F. Lehmanns Verlag, 1944.

Bud, Robert. *The Uses of Life: A History of Biotechnology.* Cambridge: Cambridge University Press, 1993.

Buijs, Goof, Stephanie Kaars, and Jeroen Trommelen. *Gifpolder Volgermeer van veen tot veen.* Wormerveer, the Netherlands: Noord-Holland, 2005.

Cacheux, Emile. *Etat des habitations ouvrières à la fin du XIXᵉ siècle; étude suivie du Compte-rendu des documents relatifs aux petits logements qui ont figuré à l'Exposition universelle de 1889.* Paris: Baudry, 1891.

Caesar, H. M. *PVC and Chain Management: A Starting Point for PVC Chain Management in the Netherlands.* Woerden, the Netherlands: Nederlandse Federatie voor Kunststoffen, May 1990.

Cagin, Seth, and Philip Dray. *Between Earth and Sky: How CFCs Changed our World and Endangers the Ozone Layer.* New York: Pantheon Books, 1993.

Carls, Stephen D. *Louis Loucheur, ingénieur, homme d'État, modernisateur de la France, 1872–1931.* Villeneuve d'Ascq, France: Presses Universitaires du Septentrion, 2000.

Caron, François, Paul Erker, and Wolfram Fischer, eds. *Innovations in the European Economy Between the Wars.* Berlin: De Gruyter, 1995

Cassis, Youssef. *Big Business. The European Experience in the Twentieth Century.* Oxford: Oxford University Press, 1999.

Cassis, Youssef. *Capitals of Capital: The Rise and Fall of International Financial Centres, 1780–2009.* Cambridge: Cambridge University Press, 2010.

Cassis, Y., and P. L. Cottrell, eds. *The World of Private Banking.* Farnham, UK: Ashgate, 2009.

Castel, Odile. *Histoire des faits économique: La dynamique de l'économie mondiale du XVe siècle à nos jours.* Rennes, France: Presses Universitaires de Rennes, 2005.

Cayez, Pierre. *Rhône-Poulenc 1895–1975. Contribution à l'étude d'un groupe industriel.* Paris: Armand Colin/Masson, 1988.

Celati, Giampiero, and Leo Gattini. *Sale e pietra, 1912–1925: Quaderni di storia Rosignano XX Secolo.* Pisa, Italy: Giardini, 1993.

Celati, Giampiero, and Leo Gattini. *La cimineria dimezzata: Quaderni di Storia Rosignano XX secolo.* Vol. 3, 1926–1944. Pisa, Italy: Istituti Editoriali e Poligrafici Internazionali, 1998.

Cent ans de droit social en Belgique, 1886–1987. Brussels: Ministry of Labor, 1987.

Chadeau, Emmanuel. "International Cartels in the Interwar Period: Some Aspects of the French Case." In Akira Kudo and Terushi Hara, eds., *International Cartels in Business History.* Tokyo: University of Tokyo Press, 1992, 98–113.

Chandler, Alfred D., Jr. *Strategy and Structure: Chapters in the History of the American Industrial Enterprise.* Cambridge, MA: MIT Press, 1962.

Chandler, Alfred D., Jr. *Scale and Scope: The Dynamics of Industrial Capitalism.* 7th ed. Cambridge, MA: Harvard University Press, 2004.

Chandler, Alfred D., Jr. *Shaping the Industrial Century: The Remarkable Story of the Evolution of the Modern Chemical and Pharmaceutical Industries.* Cambridge, MA: Harvard University Press, 2005.

Chandler, Alfred D., Jr., and Herman Daems, eds. *Managerial Hierarchies.* Cambridge, MA: Harvard University Press, 1980.

Chauveau, Sophie. "Mobilization and Industrial Policy: Chemicals and Pharmaceuticals in the French War Effort." In Roy MacLeod and Jeffrey A. Johnson, eds., *Frontline and Factory: Comparative Perspectives on the Chemical Industry at War, 1914–1924.* Dordrecht, the Netherlands: Springer, 2006, 21–30.

Chiousse, Casimir. *Les œuvres sociales à l'Exposition universelle de Paris 1900.* Paris: Bibliothèque de la Fédération des Sociétés Coopératives de Consommation des Employés des Chemins de Fer P. L. M., 1901.

Coenjaers, Tony, and Guy Legrand. "Jacques Solvay: La stratégie des point forts." *Trends/Tendances* 9 (192) (12 Oct. 1984): 30–3, 36.

Cohan, William D. *The Last Tycoons: The Secret History of Lazard Frères & Co.* New York: Doubleday, 2007.

Coleman, Donald. "Man-Made Fibres before 1945." In D. Jenkins, ed., *The Cambridge History of Western Textiles*. Vol. 1, Cambridge: Cambridge University Press, 2003, 933–47.

Colli, Andrea. *The History of Family Business, 1850–2000*. Cambridge: Cambridge University Press, 2003.

Cominolli, Rita. *Smokestacks Allegro: The Story of Solvay, a Remarkable Industrial/Immigrant Village (1880–1920)*. New York: Center for Migration Studies, 1990.

Conrad, Christoph. "La naissance de la retraite moderne: l'Allemagne dans une comparaison internationale (1850-1960)." *Population* 45 (3) (1990): 531–63.

Constas, Muriel, Didier Devriese, and Kim Oosterlinck, eds. *Solvay Business School, 1903–2003*. Brussels: Archives de l'Université Libre de Bruxelles, 2003.

Conway, Martin. *Collaboration in Belgium: Léon Degrelle and the Rexist Movement, 1940–1944*. New Haven, CT: Yale University Press, 1993.

Conway, Martin. "Belgium." In T. Buchanan and M. Conway, eds., *Political Catholicism in Interwar Europe, 1918–1965*. Oxford: Oxford University Press, 1996, 187–218.

Cook, Warren A., Paul M. Giever, Bertram D. Dinman, and Harold J. Magnuson. "Occupational Acroosteolysis. II. An Industrial Hygiene Study." *Archives of Environmental Health* 22 (1971): 74–82.

Cordier, J. M., C. Fievez, M.J. Lefèvre, and A. Sevrin. "Acroostéolyse et lésions cutanées associés chez deux ouvriers affectés au nettoyage d'autoclaves." *Cahiers de Médecine du Travail* 4 (1966): 14.

Creech, J. L., and M. N. Johnson. "Angiosarcoma of the Liver in the Manufacture of Polyvinylchloride." *Journal of Occupational Medicine* 16 (1974): 150–1.

Crombois, Jean-François. *L'univers de la sociologie en Belgique, 1900–1940*. Brussels: Ed. de l'Université Libre de Bruxelles, 1994.

Crombois, Jean-François. "La pensée morale, sociale et politique d'Ernest Solvay." In Andrée Despy-Meyer and Didier Devriese, eds., *Ernest Solvay et son temps*. Brussels: Archives de l'Université Libre de Bruxelles, 1997, 209–20.

Czichon, Eberhard. *Der Bankier und die Macht: Hermann Josef Abs in der deutschen Politik*. Cologne, Germany: Pahl-Rugenstein, 1970.

Daumalin, Xavier, Olivier Lambert, and Philippe Mioche. *Une aventure industrielle en Camargue: Histoire de l'établissement Solvay de Salin-de-Giraud (de 1895 à nos jours)*. Vol. 1. Aix-en-Provence, France: Mémoire Industrie & Patrimoine Provence, 2007.

Davidson, A., T. N. Blockley, and B. Vigers, *Hydrogen Peroxide Works of Otto Schickert & Co. at Bad Lauterberg and Rhumspringe* British Intelligence Objective Sub-Committee Final Report No. 294. London: HM Stationery Office, [1946].

Davies, Duncan S. "Chemical Industry in its Historical Context." In D. H. Sharp and T. F. West, eds., *The Chemical Industry*. Chichester, UK: Ellis Horwood, 1982, 40–61.

Daviet, Jean-Pierre. *Un destin international: La Compagnie de Saint-Gobain de 1830 à 1939*. Paris: Édition des Archives Contemporaines, 1988.

Daviet, Jean-Pierre. *Une multinationale à la française, Saint-Gobain 1665–1989*. Paris: Fayard, 1989.

de Kerchove, Charles. *L'industrie belge pendant l'occupation allemande, 1914–1918*. Paris: Presse Universitaire de France; New Haven, CT: Yale University Press, 1927.

De Schaepdrijver, Sophie. *La Belgique et la Première Guerre mondiale*. Brussels: PIE-Peter Lang, 2004, 69–79.

De Schaepdrijver, Sophie. "A Civilian War Effort: The Comité National de Secours et d'Alimentation in Occupied Belgium, 1914–1918." In *Remembering Herbert Hoover and the Commission for Relief in Belgium*. Brussels: Fondation Universitaire, 2006, 24–37.

DeBell, John M., William C. Goggin, and Walter E. Gloor. *German Plastics Practice*. Springfield, MA: DeBell and Richardson, 1946.

Delaet, Jean-Louis. "La mécanisation de la verrerie à vitres à Charleroi dans la première moitié du XXe siècle." In Ginette Kurgan and Jean Stengers, eds., *L'innovation technologique, facteur de changement (XIXe-XXe siècles)*. Brussels: Ed. de l'Université Libre de Bruxelles, 1986, 113–52.

Delaet, Jean-Louis, and Valérie Montens. "Pirmez Famille." In Ginette Kurgan-van Hentenryk, Serge Jaumain, and Valérie Montens, eds., *Dictionnaire des patrons en Belgique: Les hommes, les entreprises, les réseaux*. Brussels: De Boeck Université, 1996, 514–17.

Depoortere, Rolande. "Theunis Georges." In Ginette Kurgan-van Hentenryk, Serge Jaumain, and Valérie Montens, eds., *Dictionnaire des patrons en Belgique: Les hommes, les entreprises, les réseaux*. Brussels: De Boeck Université, 1996, 574–6.

Despy-Meyer, Andrée, and Didier Devriese, eds. *Ernest Solvay et son temps*. Brussels: Archives de l'Université Libre de Bruxelles, 1997.

Despy-Meyer, Andrée, and Valérie Montens. "Le mécénat des frères Ernest et Alfred Solvay." In Andrée Despy-Meyer and Didier Devriese, eds., *Ernest Solvay et son temps*. Brussels: Archives de l'Université Libre de Bruxelles, 1997, 221–45.

Devos, Greta. "International Cartels in Belgium and the Netherlands during the Interwar Period: The Nitrogen Case." In Akira Kudo and Terushi Hara, eds., *International Cartels in Business History*. Tokyo: University of Tokyo Press, 1992, 117–38.

Devriese, Didier, and François Frederic. "Ernest Solvay: De la réalité au mythe." In Andrée Despy-Meyer and Didier Devriese, eds., *Ernest Solvay et son temps*. Brussels: Archives de l'Université Libre de Bruxelles, 1997, 321–46.

[Diaféria, Lourenço]. *Solvay do Brasil S.A. Sua origem: Sua história (50 Anos)*. São Paulo: Solvay do Brasil SA, 1991.

Dienel, Hans-Liudger. *Linde: History of a Technology Corporation, 1879–2004*. New York: Palgrave Macmillan, 2004.

Donnelly, James. "Consultants, Managers, Testing Slaves: Changing Roles for Chemists in the British Alkali Industry, 1850–1920." *Technology and Culture* 35 (1) (1994): 100–28.

Dormois, Jean-Pierre. *La défense du travail national? L'incidence du protectionnisme sur l'industrie en Europe (1870–1914)*. Paris: Presses Université Paris-Sorbonne, 2009.

Douglas, William O., and George E. Bates. "The Federal Securities Act of 1933." *Yale Law Review* 43 (2) (1933): 171–217.

Dreyfus, Michel. "Mutualité et organisations politiques et sociales internationales (1889–1939)." *Vingtième siècle: Revue d'histoire* 48 (Oct.–Dec. 1995): 92–102.

Drouard, Alain. *Une inconnue des sciences sociales: La Fondation Alexis Carrel, 1941–1945*. Paris: Maison des Sciences de l'Homme, 1995.

Drucker, Peter F. *The Age of Discontinuity: Guidelines to Our Changing Society*. London: Heinemann, 1969.

Dubois, Léon. "Evence II Coppée." *Biographie Nationale* (Académie Royale de Belgique). Vol. 44, fasc. 1. Brussels: Bruylant, 1985, 306–24.

Duchene, Vincent. "De l'alchimie traditionnelle à la chimie industrielle: L'industrie chimique belge au XIXe siècle." In Bart Van Der Herten, Michel Oris, and Jan

Roegiers, eds., *La Belgique industrielle en 1850: Deux cent images d'un monde nouveau*. Antwerp, Belgium: Crédit Communal, 1995, 285–95.

Ducordeaux, Patrice, Marcel Robin, Jacques Tétu, and Yvon Amiot. *Solvay Tavaux: Une usine et des hommes*. Dole, France: Dmodmo, 2005.

Dumoulin, Michel. *Petrofina: Un groupe pétrolier international et la gestion de l'incertitude*. Vol. 1, *1920–1979*. Louvain, Belgium: Ed. Peeters, 1997.

Dumoulin, Michel, and Anne-Myriam Dutrieue. *La Ligue Européenne de Coopération Économique (1946–1981): Un groupe d'étude et de pression dans la construction européenne*. Bern, Switzerland: Peter Lang, 1993.

Dutrieue, Anne-Myriam. "Boël Famille." In Ginette Kurgan-van Hentenryk, Serge Jaumain, and Valérie Montens, eds., *Dictionnaire des patrons en Belgique: Les hommes, les entreprises, les réseaux*. Brussels: De Boeck Université, 1996, 60–4.

Dyer, Davis, and David B. Sicilia. *Labors of a Modern Hercules: The Evolution of a Chemical Company*. Boston: Harvard Business School Press, 1990.

"ECN 25th Anniversary: A Quarter Century of Change within the Industry as Reported in European Chemical News." *European Chemical News* 25 (19 Jan. 1987): 24–56.

Eichengreen, Barry. *The European Economy since 1945*. Princeton, NJ: Princeton University Press, 2007.

Eilsberger, Hellmut. "Eilsberger, Ernst." *Neue Deutsche Biographie* 4 (1959): 392.

Exposition Universelle de Paris 1867: Rapports du jury international publiés sous la direction de M. Michel Chevalier. Vol. 7, *Group V, Classes 44 to 46*. Paris: Imprimerie administrative de Paul Dupont, 1868.

Ferguson, Niall. "Public Debt as a Postwar Problem: The German Experience after 1918 in Comparative Perspective." In C. Levy and M. Roseman, eds., *Three Postwar Eras in Comparison: Western Europe 1918-1945-1989*. London: Palgrave, 2002, 99–119.

Freeman, Chris, and Luc Soete. *The Economics of Industrial Innovation*. 3rd ed. Cambridge, MA: MIT Press, 1997.

Fridenson, Patrick, ed. *The French Home Front, 1914–1918*. Providence, RI: Berg, 1992.

Frieden, Jeffrey A. *Global Capitalism: Its Fall and Rise in the Twentieth Century*. New York: W. W. Norton, 2006.

Friedrich, Volker, Adam Hehn, and Rolf Rosenbrock. *Neunmal teurer als Gold: Die Arzneimittelversorgung in der Bundesrepublik*. Reinbek bei Hamburg, Germany: Rowohlt, 1977.

Gadisseur, Jean. "Le triomphe industriel." In *L'industrie en Belgique: Deux siècles d'évolution 1780–1980*. Brussels: Crédit Communal, 1981, 51–70.

Galambos, Louis, Takashi Hikino, and Vera Zamagni, eds. *The Global Chemical Industry in the Age of the Petrochemical Revolution*. New York: Cambridge University Press, 2007.

Galbraith, John K. *The Age of Uncertainty*. Boston: Houghton Mifflin, 1977.

Gall, Lothar. "Hermann Josef Abs and the Third Reich: 'A Man for All Seasons?'" *Financial History Review* 6 (1999): 147–202.

Gall, Lothar. *Der Bankier Hermann Joseph Abs: Eine Biographie*. Munich: C. H. Beck, 2004.

Gall, Lothar, and Manfred Pohl, eds. *Unternehmen im Nationalsozialismus*. Munich: C. H. Beck, 1998.

Galvez-Behar, Gabriel. *La République des inventeurs: Propriété et organisation de l'innovation en France (1791–1922)*. Rennes, France: Presses Universitaires de Rennes, 2008.

Giannetti, Renato, and Valentina Romei. "Appendix: The Chemical Industry after World War II – A Quantitative Assessment." In Louis Galambos, Takashi Hikino, and

Vera Zamagni, eds., *The Global Chemical Industry in the Age of the Petrochemical Revolution*. New York: Cambridge University Press, 2007, 407–52.

Gillingham, John. *Belgian Business in the Nazi New Order*. Ghent, Belgium: Jan Dhondt Foundation, 1977.

[Gintl, Wilhelm]. *Der Öesterreichische Verein für chemische und metallurgische Production, 1856–1906*. Prague: A. Haase, 1906.

Godfrey, John F, *Capitalism at War: Industrial Policy and Bureaucracy in France, 1914–1918*. Hamburg, Germany: Berg, 1987.

Godineau, Laure. "L'économie sociale à l'Exposition universelle de 1889." *Le Mouvement social* 149 (Oct.–Dec. 1989): 71–87.

Gotovitch, José. "La Belgique et la guerre civile espagnole: un état des questions." *Revue Belge d'Histoire Contemporaine* 14 (3–4) (1983): 497–532.

Groen, Maurits. *Internationaal Water Tribunaal: Op weg naar schoner water*. Lelystad, the Netherlands: Stichting IVIO, 1983.

Gubin, Eliane, and Valérie Piette. "Une histoire de familles." In Andrée Despy-Meyer and Didier Devriese, eds., *Ernest Solvay et son temps*. Brussels: Archives de l'Université Libre de Bruxelles, 1997, 95–136.

Haber, L. F. *The Chemical Industry during the Nineteenth Century*. Oxford, UK: Clarendon Press, 1958.

Haber, L. F. *The Chemical Industry, 1900–1930: International Growth and Technological Change*. Oxford, UK: Clarendon Press, 1971.

Hannah, Leslie. "Visible and Invisible Hands in Great Britain." In Alfred D. Chandler Jr. and Herman Daems, eds., *Managerial Hierarchies*. Cambridge, MA: Harvard University Press, 1980, 41–76.

Hardach, Gerd. "Industrial Mobilization in 1914–1918: Production, Planning, and Ideology." In Patrick Fridenson, ed., *The French Home Front, 1914–1918*. Providence, RI: Berg, 1992, 57–88.

Hardie, D. W. F. *Castner-Kellner Alkali Company, Fifty Years of Progress (1895–1945)*. Birmingham, UK: Imperial Chemical Industries, 1947.

Hardie, D. W. F. *Electrolytic Manufacture of Chemicals from Salt*. London: Oxford University Press, 1959.

Hauzeur de Fooz, Carlos, *Étude synthétique sur l'industrie chimique et sur l'industrie des métaux non ferreux en Belgique*. Brussels: GIG, 1951.

Hayes, Peter. "Zur umstrittenen Geschichte der I.G. Farbenindustrie AG." *Geschichte und Gesellschaft* 18 (1992): 405–17.

Hayes, Peter. "Big Business and 'Aryanization' in Germany, 1933–1939." *Jahrbuch für Antisemitismusforschung* 3 (1994): 254–81.

Hayes, Peter. *Industry and Ideology: IG Farben in the Nazi Era*. New York: Cambridge University Press, 2001.

Hayes, Peter. *From Cooperation to Complicity: Degussa in the Third Reich*. New York: Cambridge University Press, 2004.

Haynes, Williams, ed. *American Chemical Industry: The Chemical Companies*. Vol. 6. New York: Van Nostrand, 1954.

Héger, Paul, and Charles Lefébure. *Vie d'Ernest Solvay*. Brussels: Lamertin, 1929.

Heinrich, Oswald J. "The Manufacture of Soda by the Ammonia Process." *Transactions of the American Institute of Mining, Metallurgical and Petroleum Engineers (AIME)*, 7 (May 1878–Feb. 1879): 294–8.

Hennebicque, Alain. "Albert Thomas and the War Industries." In Patrick Fridenson, ed., *The French Home Front, 1914–1918*. Providence, RI: Berg, 1992, 89–133.

Henry, Albert, *L'œuvre du Comité National de secours et d'alimentation pendant la guerre*. Brussels: Office de Publicité, 1920.

Henson, J. H. L., and A. Whelan, eds. *Developments in PVC Technology*. London: Applied Science Publishers, 1973.

Hexner, Erwin. *International Cartels*. London: Sir Isaac Pitman, 1946.

Hiebert, Ray Eldon. *Courtier to the Crowd: The Story of Ivy Lee and the Development of Public Relations*. Ames: Iowa State University Press, 1966.

Hill, Roy. "BASF Rethinks Its Top Management Chemistry." *International Management* (March 1982): 12–16.

Homburg, Ernst. "The Influence of Demand on the Emergence of the Dye Industry: The Roles of Chemists and Colourists." *Journal of the Society of Dyers and Colourists* 99 (1983): 325–33.

Homburg, Ernst. "The Emergence of Research Laboratories in the Dyestuffs Industry, 1870–1900." *British Journal for the History of Science* 25 (1992): 91–111.

Homburg, Ernst. "Epiloog: DSM Research op weg naar de 21ste eeuw." In H. W. Lintsen, ed., *Research tussen vetkool en zoetstof: Zestig jaar DSM Research 1940–2000*. Zutphen, the Netherlands: Walburg Pers, 2000, 116–35.

Homburg, Ernst. *Groeien door kunstmest: DSM Agro 1929–2004*. Hilversum, the Netherlands: Verloren, 2004.

Homburg, Ernst, and Arjan van Rooij. "Die Vor- und Nachteile enger Nachbarschaft: Der Transfer deutscher chemischer Technologie in die Niederlande bis 1952." In Rolf Petri, ed., *Technologietransfer aus der deutschen Chemieindustrie (1925–1960)*. Berlin: Duncker & Humblot, 2004, 201–51.

Homburg, Ernst, Aat J. van Selm, and Piet F. G. Vincken. "Industrialisatie en industriecomplexen: de chemische industrie tussen overheid, technologie en markt." In Johan Schot, Harry Lintsen, Arie Rip, and Adri Albert de la Bruhèze, eds., *Techniek in Nederland in de twintigste eeuw*. Vol. 2. Zutphen, the Netherlands: Walburg Pers, 2000, 376–401.

Homburg, Ernst, Anthony S. Travis, and Harm G. Schröter, eds. *The Chemical Industry in Europe, 1850–1914: Industrial Growth, Pollution and Professionalization*. Dordrecht, the Netherlands: Kluwer Academic Publishers, 1998.

Hong, Young-Son. *Welfare, Modernity, and the Weimar State, 1919–1933*. Princeton, NJ: Princeton University Press, 1998.

Hou, Te-Pang. *Manufacture of Soda, with Special Reference to the Ammonia Process*. New York: Chemical Catalog Company, 1947.

Hounshell, David, and John K. Smith, Jr. *Science and Corporate Strategy: Du Pont R&D, 1902–1980*. Cambridge: Cambridge University Press, 1988.

Hünemörder, Kai F. *Die frühgeschichte der globalen Umweltkrise und die Formierung der deutschen Umweltpolitik (1950–1973)*. Stuttgart, Germany: Franz Steiner, 2004.

Innovating for Life: Rhône-Poulenc 1895–1995. Paris: Albin Michel, 1995.

An Inside Look at Allied Chemical: Centennial Celebration September 12, 1981. Solvay, NY: Allied Chemical Co., n.d. [1981].

Jackson, Melissa H. "The New Chairman of the Board Brings His Vision of Pride and Purpose to Overseeing CMA's Passage into Becoming the American Chemistry Council." *CMA News* (June 2000): 9–11.

James, Harold. *The Nazi Dictatorship and the Deutsche Bank*. Cambridge: Cambridge University Press, 2004.

Johnson, Jeffrey A. "The Academic-Industrial Symbiosis in German Chemical Research, 1905–1939." In John E. Lesch, ed., *The German Chemical Industry in the Twentieth Century*. Dordrecht, the Netherlands: Kluwer, 2000, 15–56.

Johnson, Jeffrey A., "Technological Mobilization and Munitions Production: Comparative Perspectives on Germany and Austria." In Roy MacLeod and Jeffrey A. Johnson, eds., *Frontline and Factory: Comparative Perspectives on the Chemical Industry at War, 1914–1924*. Dordrecht, the Netherlands: Springer, 2006, 1–20.

Johnson, Jeffrey A., and Roy MacLeod. "The War the Victors Lost: The Dilemmas of Chemical Disarmament." In Roy MacLeod and Jeffrey A. Johnson, eds., *Frontline and Factory: Comparative Perspectives on the Chemical Industry at War, 1914–1924*. Dordrecht, the Netherlands: Springer, 2006, 221–45.

Joly, Hervé. "Famille Gillet." In Jean-Claude Daumas, Alain Chatriot, Danièle Fraboulet, and Hervé Joly, eds., *Dictionnaire historique des patrons français*. Paris: Flammarion, 2010, 326–30.

Jones, Geoffrey, and Peter Miskell. "European Integration and Corporate Restructuring: The Strategy of Unilever, c. 1957–c. 1990." *Economic History Review* 58 (1) (2005): 113–39.

Jones, Isabelle. "La mission économique belge à Londres (20 juillet-31 décembre 1940)." *Cahiers du Centre de Recherches et d'Études Historiques de la Seconde Guerre Mondiale* 11 (1988): 187–206.

Jühe, Susanne, and Günther Veltmann, "Zur Klinik der sogenannten Vinylchlorid-Krankheit (Sklerodermie-ähnliche Veränderungen bei Arbeitern der PVC-herstellenden Industrie)." *Medichem: Erstes internationales Symposium der Werkärzte der Chemischen Industrie, 27–29.4.1972, Ludwigshafen* 1 (1972): 267–76.

Juran, Joseph M., ed. *A History of Managing for Quality: The Evolution, Trends, and Future Directions of Managing for Quality*. Milwaukee, WI: ASQC Quality Press, 1995.

Karlsch, Rainer. "Capacity, Losses, Reconstruction and Unfinished Modernization: The Chemical Industry in the Soviet Zone of Occupation (SBZ)/GDR, 1945–1955." In John E. Lesch, ed., *The German Chemical Industry in the Twentieth Century*. Dordrecht, the Netherlands: Kluwer, 2000, 375–92.

Kaufman, Morris. *The History of PVC: The Chemistry and Industrial Production of Polyvinyl Chloride*. London: Maclaren and Sons, 1969.

[Kemper, Doris, and Volker Lorenz]. *125 Jahre Solvay Bernburg: Festschrift Solvay Bernburg 1883–2008*. Bernburg, Germany: Solvay Chemicals GmbH and Werk Bernburg, 2008.

Kennedy, Carol. *ICI: The Company That Changed Our Lives*. London: Hutchinson, 1986.

Kevles, Daniel J. "'Into Hostile Political Camps': The Reorganization of International Science in World War I." *Isis* 62 (1971): 47–60.

Keynes, John M. *The Economic Consequences of Peace*. New York: Harcourt Brace, 1920.

Kline, G. M., J. H. Rooney, J. W. Crawford, T. Love, and F. J. Curtis. *Investigation of German Plastics Plants, 17 May–3 June 1945*. n. p., Combined Intelligence Objectives Sub-Committee report XXIX-62.

Kobrak, Christopher. *National Cultures and International Competition: The Experience of Schering AG, 1851–1950*. Cambridge: Cambridge University Press, 2002a.

Kobrak, Christopher. "Politics, Corporate Governance, and the Dynamics of German Managerial Innovation: Schering AG between the Wars." *Enterprise and Society* 3 (2002b): 429–61.

Krause, Wolfgang, and Douglas J. Puffert. "Chemicals, Strategy and Tariffs: Tariff Policy and the Soda Industry in Imperial Germany." *European Review of Economic History* 4 (2000): 285–309.

Kreikamp, Hans-Dieter. "Die Entflechtung der I. G. Farbenindustrie A. G. und die Gründung der Nachfolgegesellschaften." *Vierteljahrshefte für Zeitgeschichte* 25 (1977): 220–51.

Kuhlmann, Heide, and M. A. Rudmann, eds. *The Magic Potions in the Belly Gland: The Story of Research into the Exocrine Pancreas and the Active Substance Pancreatin – A Century of Pankreon.* Hanover, Germany: Solvay Pharmaceuticals, 2000.

Kuisel, Richard. *Capitalism and the State in Modern France.* Cambridge: Cambridge University Press, 1981.

Kurgan-van Hentenryk, Ginette. "Le patronat et la mise en œuvre du pacte social (1945–1954)." In Dirk Luyten and Guy Vanthemsche, eds., *Het Sociaal Pact van 1944. Oorsprong, betekenis en gevolgen.* Brussels: VUB Press, 1995, 211–23.

Kurgan-van Hentenryk, Ginette. "Sabatier, Gustave." In Ginette Kurgan-van Hentenryk, Serge Jaumain, and Valérie Montens, eds., *Dictionnaire des patrons en Belgique: Les hommes, les entreprises, les réseaux.* Brussels: De Boeck Université, 1996, 539–40.

Kurgan-van Hentenryk, Ginette. "La Société Générale, 1850–1934." In Erik Buyst, Isabelle Cassiers, Helma Houtman-De Smedt, Ginette Kurgan-van Hentenryk, Herman Van der Wee, Guy Vantemsche, et al., eds., *La Générale de Banque, 1822–1997.* Brussels: Racine, 1997, 63–285.

Kurgan-van Hentenryk, Ginette. "Jewish Private Banks." In Y. Cassis and P. L. Cottrell, eds., *The World of Private Banking.* Farnham, UK: Ashgate, 2009, 213–30.

Kurgan-van Hentenryk, Ginette, Serge Jaumain, and Valérie Montens, eds. *Dictionnaire des patrons en Belgique: Les hommes, les entreprises, les réseaux.* Brussels: De Boeck Université, 1996.

Lambert, Franklin J. "Internationalisme et révolution quantique: Les premiers Conseils Solvay." *Revue Germanique Internationale* 12 (2010): 159–73.

Lamirand, Georges. *Le rôle social de l'ingénieur: Scènes de la vie d'usine.* Paris: Plon, 1932.

Landes, David. *The Unbound Prometheus: Technological Change and Industrial Development in Western Europe from 1750 to the Present.* 2nd ed. Cambridge: Cambridge University Press, 2003.

Langlinay, Erik. "Kuhlmann at War, 1914–1924." In Roy MacLeod and Jeffrey A. Johnson, eds., *Frontline and Factory: Comparative Perspectives on the Chemical Industry at War, 1914–1924.* Dordrecht, the Netherlands: Springer, 2006, 145–66.

Le Fanu, James. *The Rise and Fall of Modern Medicine.* London: Little, Brown, 1999.

Lederer, Emil. *State of the Masses: The Threat of the Classless Society.* New York: Norton, 1940.

[le Ricousse, Gilles]. *L'industrie au regard de l'environnement: Fabrication du chlorure de vinyle monomère et du chlorure de polyvinyle.* [Paris]: Ministère de l'Environnement et du Cadre de Vie, Direction de la Prévention des Pollutions, Service de l'Environnement Industriel, August 1980.

Lesch, John E., ed. *The German Chemical Industry in the Twentieth Century.* Dordrecht, the Netherlands: Kluwer, 2000.

Les Soudières réunies 1855–1955. Paris: Office de Publicité Générale, 1955.

Levinson, Charles. *PVC zum Beispiel: Krebserkrankungen bei der Kunststoffherstellung.* Reinbek bei Hamburg, Germany: Rowohlt, 1975.

Lévy-Leboyer, Maurice. "The Large Corporation in Modern France." In Alfred Chandler and Herman Daems, eds., *Managerial Hierarchies.* Cambridge, MA: Harvard University Press, 1980, 117–60.

Lindner, Stephan. *Inside IG Farben: Hoechst during the Third Reich.* Cambridge: Cambridge University Press, 2008.

Lisagor, Nancy, and Frank Lipsius. *A Law unto Itself: The Untold Story of the Law Firm Sullivan & Cromwell.* New York: Paragon House, 1989.

Lischka, J. R. *Ludwig Mond and the British Alkali Industry.* New York: Garland, 1985.

Littmann, William. "Designing Obedience: The Architecture and Landscape of Welfare Capitalism, 1880–1930." *International Labor and Working-Class History* 53 (Spring 1998): 88–114.

Lucion, René. *La grosse industrie chimique en Belgique*. Brussels: Fédération pour la Défense des Intérêts Belges à l'Étranger, 1908.

Lunge, Georg. "La grande industrie chimique." *Revue générale des sciences pures et appliquées* 4 (1893): 107–15.

Lunge, Georg, and J. Naville. *La grande industrie chimique: Traité de la fabrication de la soude et de ses branches collatérales*. Vol. 3. Paris: Masson, 1881.

Luyten, Dirk. "Wetgevende initiatieven met betrekking tot bedrijfsorganisatie in de dertiger jaren in België." *Revue belge d'histoire contemporaine* 19 (3–4) (1988): 587–654.

Luyten, Dirk. *Burgers boven elke verdenking? Vervolging van de economische collaboratie in België na de Tweede Wereldoorlog*. Brussels: VUB Press, 1996.

Luyten, Dirk. "Prosecution, Society and Politics: The Penalization of Economic Collaboration in Belgium after the Second World War." *Crime, History and Societies* 2 (1) (1998): 111–33.

Luyten, Dirk. "The Belgian Economic Elite and the Punishment of Economic Collaboration after the Second World War: Power and Legitimacy (1944–1952)." *Jahrbuch für Wirtschaftsgeschichte* (2) (2010): 95–105.

MacLeod, Roy, and Jeffrey A. Johnson, eds. *Frontline and Factory: Comparative Perspectives on the Chemical Industry at War, 1914–1924*. Dordrecht, the Netherlands: Springer, 2006.

Maier, Charles S. *Recasting Bourgeois Europe*. Princeton, NJ: Princeton University Press, 1975.

Maier, Charles S. "The Two Postwar Eras and the Conditions for Stability in Twentieth-Century Western Europe." *American Historical Review* 86 (2) (1981): 327–52.

Maltoni, Cesare, and Giuseppe Lefemine. "Carconogenicity Bioassays of Vinyl Chloride: I. Research Plan and Early Results." *Environmental Research* 7 (1974): 387–405.

Marage, Pierre, and Grégoire Wallenborn, eds. *The Solvay Councils and the Birth of Modern Physics*. Basel, Switzerland: Birkhäuser, 1999a.

Marage, Pierre, and Grégoire Wallenborn. "Physics Prior to the First Council." In Pierre Marage and Grégoire Wallenborn, eds., *The Solvay Councils and the Birth of Modern Physics*. Basel, Switzerland: Birkhäuser, 1999b, 70–94.

Marsch, Ulrich. *Zwischen Wissenschaft und Wirtschaft: Industrieforschung in Deutschland und Grossbritannien, 1880–1936*. Paderborn, Germany: Schöningh, 2000.

Martin, Heinz. *Polymere und Patente: Karl Ziegler, das Team, 1953–1998: Zur wirtschaftlichen Verwertung akademischer Forschung*. Weinheim, Germany: Wiley-VCH, 2002.

Mazower, Mark. *Dark Continent: Europe's Twentieth Century*. London: Penguin, 1999.

McCaffray, Susan. "Origins of Labor Policy in the Russian Coal and Steel Industry, 1874–1900." *Journal of Economic History* 47 (4) (1987): 951–65.

McDonald, Lawrence G., and Patrick Robinson. *A Colossal Failure of Common Sense: The Inside Story of the Collapse of Lehman Brothers*. London: Ebury, 2009.

Metzner, Alfons. *Die chemische Industrie der Welt*. Vols. 1 and 2. Düsseldorf, Germany: Econ-Verlag, 1955.

Milward, Alan S. *War, Economy, and Society, 1939–1945*. Berkeley: University of California Press, 1977.

Mioche, Philippe. "Jean Monnet, homme d'affaires à la lumière de nouvelles archives." *Parlement[s]* (2007) (3): 60–8.

Mittmann, Detlef. *Die chemische Industrie im nordwestlichen Mitteleuropa in ihrem Strukturwandel.* Wiesbaden, Germany: Franz Steiner, 1974.

Mond, Ludwig. "On the Origin of the Ammonia Soda Process." *Journal of the Society of Chemical Industry* 4 (9) (1885): 527–9.

Moorman, Jenny. *Two Men and a Fish: The Story of Rowell Laboratories.* Baudette, MN: Reid-Rowell, 1987.

Morris, Peter J. T. *The Development of Acetylene Chemistry and Synthetic Rubber by I.G. Farbenindustrie A.G., 1926–1945.* Ph.D. diss., University of Oxford, 1982.

Motta, Massimo. *Competition Policy: Theory and Practice.* Cambridge: Cambridge University Press, 2004.

Moureu, Charles. *La chimie et la guerre: Science et avenir.* Paris: Masson & Cie, 1920.

Musset, René. "Le pétrole dans la Basse-Seine." *Annales de Géographie* 68 (1959): 409–23.

Nash, George H. *The Life of Herbert Hoover: The Humanitarian, 1914–1917.* New York: W. W. Norton, 1988.

Nefors, Patrick. *La collaboration industrielle en Belgique, 1940–1945.* Brussels: Racine, 2006.

Nelson, Daniel. *Managers and Workers: Origins of the Twentieth-Century Factory System in the United States, 1880–1920.* 2nd ed. Madison: University of Wisconsin Press, 1995.

"A New Look for European Old-Timer: Solvay Float First Bond Issue, Moves Deeper into Plastics." *Chemical Week* (29 Sept. 1971): 29–31.

Noiriel, Gérard. "Du 'patronage' au 'paternalisme': La restructuration des formes de domination de la main-d'œuvre ouvrière dans l'industrie métallurgique française." *Le Mouvement social* 144 (Jul.–Sep. 1988): 17–35.

Notes, lettres et discours d'Ernest Solvay. Vols. 1 and 2. Brussels: Lamertin, 1929.

Nuwer, Michael. "From Batch to Flow: Production Technology and Work-Force Skills in the Steel Industry, 1880–1920." *Technology and Culture* 29 (4) (1988): 808–38.

Ocasio, William, and John Joseph. "Rise and Fall – or Transformation? The Evolution of Strategic Planning at the General Electric Company, 1940–2006." *Long Range Planning* 41 (2008): 248–72.

Oreskes, Naomi, and Erik M. Conway. *Merchants of Doubt: How a Handful of Scientists Obscured the Truth on Issues from Tobacco Smoke to Global Warming.* New York: Bloomsbury Press, 2010.

Overy, Richard. *War and Economy in the Third Reich.* Oxford, UK: Clarendon Press, 1994.

Paolini, Gabriele. *Novant'anni di movimento sindacale alla Solvay di Rosignano (1913–1993).* Rosignano-Solvay, Italy: Tipografia Nuovo Futuro, 2007.

Peeters Wim, and Jérôme Wilson. *L'industrie belge dans la Russie des Tsars.* Liège, France: Ed. Du Perron, 1999.

Perales, José L. Ruiz. *Cien años del servicio médico Solvay en Barreda-Torrelavega, 1904–2004.* Torrelavega, Spain: Solvay Química, 2004.

Perrot, Michelle. "The Three Ages of Industrial Discipline in Nineteenth-Century France." In John Merriman, ed., *Consciousness and Class Experience in Nineteenth-Century Europe.* New York: Holmes and Meier, 1979, 149–68.

Petri, Rolf. "Cartels and the Diffusion of Technologies: The Case of Hydrogenation and Catalytic Refining." In Dominique Barjot, ed., *International Cartels Revisited. Vues nouvelles sur les cartels internationaux (1880–1980).* Caen, France: Éditions-Diffusion du Lys, 1994, 287–300.

Petri, Rolf. "Technical Change in the Italian Chemical Industry: Markets, Firms and State Intervention." In Anthony S. Travis, Harm G. Schröter, Ernst Homburg, and Peter J. T. Morris, eds., *Determinants in the Evolution of the European Chemical Industry, 1900–1939: New Technologies, Political Frameworks, Markets, and Companies.* Dordrecht, the Netherlands: Kluwer, 1998, 275–300.

Petri, Rolf. *Storia economica d'Italia: dalla Grande Guerra al miracolo economico (1918–1963).* Bologna, Italy: Il Mulino, 2002.

Petri, Rolf, ed. *Technologietransfer aus der deutschen Chemieindustrie (1925–1960).* Berlin: Duncker & Humblot, 2004a.

Petri, Rolf. "Zwischen Konkurrenz und Kooperation: Die deutsche Chemieindustrie und das technologische Aufholen Italiens." In Rolf Petri, ed., *Technologietransfer aus der deutschen Chemieindustrie (1925–1960).* Berlin: Duncker & Humblot, 2004b, 253–90.

Petri, Rolf. "Intervento pubblico ed espansione della chimica italiana fino all 'miracolo economico.'" In G. Pizzorni, ed., *L'industria chimica italiana nel Novecento.* Milan: Franco Angeli, 2006, 107–12.

Pirenne, Henri. *La Belgique et la guerre mondiale.* Paris: Presse Universitaire de France; New Haven, CT: Yale University Press, 1928.

Pistor, Gustav. *Hundert Jahre Griesheim 1856–1956: Ein Beitrag zur Geschichte der chemischen Industrie.* Tegernsee, Germany: Griesheim, 1958.

Pizzorni, G., ed. *L'industria chimica italiana nel Novecento.* Milan: Franco Angeli, 2006.

Pizzorni, Geoffrey J. "Caratteri e sviluppi dell'industria chimica italiana nella prima metà del Novecento." In G. Pizzorni, ed., *L'industria chimica italiana nel Novecento.* Milan: Franco Angeli, 2006, 53–8.

Plessis, Alain. "The Parisian 'Haute Banque' and the International Economy in the 19th and Early 20th Centuries." In Y. Cassis and P. L. Cottrell, eds., *The World of Private Banking.* Farnham, UK: Ashgate, 2009, 127–40.

Plumpe, Gottfried, *Die I.G. Farbenindustrie AG. Wirtschaft, Technik, und Politik 1904–1945.* Berlin: Duncker & Humblot, 1990.

Pound, Arthur. *Salt of the Earth: The Story of Captain J. B. Ford and Michigan Alkali Company.* Boston: Atlantic Monthly Company, 1940.

Puig, Núria. "Auslandsinvestitionen ohne Technologietransfer? Die deutsche Chemieindustrie in Spanien (1897–1965)." In Rolf Petri, ed., *Technologietransfer aus der deutschen Chemieindustrie (1925–1960).* Berlin: Duncker & Humblot, 2004, 291–322.

Puig, Núria. "The Global Accommodation of a Latecomer: The Spanish Chemical Industry Since the Petrochemical Revolution." In Louis Galambos, Takashi Hikino, and Vera Zamagni, eds., *The Global Chemical Industry in the Age of the Petrochemical Revolution.* Cambridge: Cambridge University Press, 2007, 368–400.

Puig, Núria. "Foreign Firms, National Business Groups, and the Making of the Spanish Chemical Industry." *History of Technology* 30 (2010): 154–66.

Rabinbach, Anson. *The Human Motor: Energy, Fatigue, and the Origins of Modernity.* Berkeley: University of California Press, 1992.

Raff, R. A. V., and J. B. Allison. *Polyethylene.* New York: Interscience, 1956.

Ranieri, Liane. *Émile Francqui ou l'intelligence créatrice, 1863–1935.* Paris: Duculot, 1985.

Ranieri, Liane. *Dannie Heineman: Un destin singulier, 1872–1962.* Brussels: Racine, 2005.

Rapaille, Maxime. *Solvay, a Giant: From the Banks of the Sambre to the Edges of the Earth.* Brussels: Didier Hatier, 1990.

Rapport général sur le fonctionnement et les opérations du Comité National de secours et d'alimentation. Vol. 1, *Le Comité National. Sa fondation, son statut, son fonctionnement.* Brussels: Vromant, 1921.

Reader, W. J. *Imperial Chemical Industries, A History.* Vol. 1, *The Forerunners 1870–1926.* London: Oxford University Press, 1970.

Reader, W. J. *Imperial Chemical Industry, A History.* Vol. 2, *The First Quarter-Century 1926–1952.* London: Oxford University Press, 1975.

Reich, Cary. *Financier: The Biography of André Meyer – A Story of Money, Power, and the Reshaping of American Business.* New York: Quill, 1983.

Reid, Donald. "Industrial Paternalism: Discourse and Practice in Nineteenth-Century French Mining and Metallurgy." *Comparative Studies in Society and History* 27 (4) (1985): 579–607.

Rency, Georges. *La Belgique et la guerre.* Vol. 1, *La vie matérielle de la Belgique durant la guerre mondiale.* Brussels: Henri Bertels, 1920.

Reuben B. G., and M. L. Burstall. *The Chemical Economy: A Guide to the Technology and Economics of the Chemical Industry.* London: Longman, 1973.

Ricci, Steven. *Cinema and Fascism: Italian Film and Society, 1922–1943.* Berkeley: University of California Press, 2008.

Romano, Sergio. *Giuseppe Volpi et l'Italie moderne.* Rome: École Française de Rome, 1982.

Rupprecht, Anja, ed. *Salz, Soda, Solvay: 100 Jahre Solvay in Rheinberg, 1907–2007.* Hanover, Germany: Solvay Chemicals GmbH, 2007.

Rüsberg, F. *Fünfzig Jahre Kali-Chemie Aktiengesellschaft; Zugleich ein Beitrag zu der Geschichte der chemischen Industrie und der Kali-Industrie Deutschlands, insbesondere der Anfänge der Soda-Industrie.* N.p.: [1949].

Saelens, Christian. "Le P.O.B. et la reconnaissance de Burgos: rupture ou continuité." *Revue belge d'histoire contemporaine* 18 (1–2) (1987): 291–314.

Salmon, Jean. "La reconnaissance du Gouvernement de Burgos." *Revue belge d'histoire contemporaine* 18 (1–2) (1987): 125–55.

Salvati, Mariuccia. "The Long History of Corporatism in Italy: A Question of Culture or Economics?" *Contemporary European History* 15 (2) (2006): 223–44.

Sánchez Landeras, José Luis. *1908–1998: Solvay Torrelavega – Nueve décadas construyendo su futuro.* Torrelavega, Spain: Solvay Química, 1998.

Sarralbe 1885–1985: Centenaire de l'usine Solvay. Sarreguemines, France: Pierron, 1986.

Schallermair, Christian. "Die deutsche Sodaindustrie und die Entwicklung des deutschen Soda-aussenhandels 1872–1913." *Vierteljahrschrift für Sozial- und Wirtschaftsgeschichte* 84 (1) (1997): 33–67.

Schloessing, Théophile, and Eugène Rolland. "Mémoire sur la fabrication du carbonate de soude." *Annales de chimie et de physique* 4 (14) (1868): 5–63.

Schmaltz, Florian, and Karl-Heinz Roth. "Neue Dokumente zur Vorgeschichte des I.G. Farben-Werks Auschwitz-Monowitz: Zugleich eine Stellungnahme zur Kontroverse zwischen Hans Deichmann und Peter Hayes." *1999. Zeitschrift für Sozialgeschichte des 20. und 21. Jahrhunderts* 13 (2) (1998): 100–16.

Schreib, H. *Traité de la fabrication de la soude d'après le procédé à l'ammoniaque.* Paris: Librairie Polytechnique, 1906.

Schreiber, Jean-Philippe. "Philippson Famille." In Ginette Kurgan-van Hentenryk, Serge Jaumain, and Valérie Montens, eds., *Dictionnaire des patrons en Belgique: Les hommes, les entreprises, les réseaux.* Brussels: De Boeck Université, 1996, 507–10.

Schreier, Anna Elisabeth, and Manuela Wex. *Chronik der Hoechst Aktiengesellschaft 1863–1988.* Frankfurt : Hoechst AG, 1990.

Schröter, Harm G. "The International Potash Syndicate." In Dominique Barjot, ed., *International Cartels Revisited: Vues nouvelles sur les cartels internationaux (1880–1980)*. Caen, France: Éditions-Diffusion du Lys, 1994, 75–92.

Schröter, Harm G. "Cartelization and Decartelization in Europe, 1870–1995: Rise and Decline of an Economic Institution." *Journal of European Economic History* 25 (1) (1996): 129–53.

Schröter, Harm G. "Competitive Strategy of the World's Largest Chemical Companies, 1970–2000." In Louis Galambos, Takashi Hikino, and Vera Zamagni, eds., *The Global Chemical Industry in the Age of the Petrochemical Revolution*. Cambridge: Cambridge University Press, 2007, 53–81.

Sermon, Lucien L. "Métamorphoses de la concurrence." *Revue de la federation des industries belges* (Dec. 1960): 817–25.

Sharp, D. H., and T. F. West, eds. *The Chemical Industry*. Chichester, UK: Ellis Horwood, 1981.

Silverman, Milton, and Philip R. Lee. *Pills, Profits, and Politics*. Berkeley: University of California Press, 1974.

Sirjacobs, Isabelle. "Solvay-Couillet: Histoire d'un site industriel." In Andrée Despy-Meyer and Didier Devriese, eds., *Ernest Solvay et son temps*. Brussels: Archives de l'Université Libre de Bruxelles, 1997, 299–317.

Smit, Jeroen. *De prooi: Blinde trots breekt ABN Amro*. Amsterdam: Prometeus, 2008.

Smith, John K, Jr. "National Goals, Industry Structure, and Corporate Strategies: Chemical Cartels between the Wars." In Akira Kudo and Terushi Hara, eds., *International Cartels in Business History*. Tokyo: University of Tokyo Press, 1992, 139–58.

Snyder, Timothy. *The Reconstruction of Nations: Poland, Ukraine, Lithuania, Belarus, 1569–1999*. New Haven, CT: Yale University Press, 2003.

Société belge de l'azote et des produits chimiques du Marly. Liège, France: Sape, [1955].

Solvay & Cie: La chemie au service de l'industrie. N.p.: N.d. [1958].

The Solvay Story. N.p.: Allied Chemical, Solvay Process Division, n.d. [1964].

Solvay: 1863–1988. 125ème anniversaire. Brussels: Solvay & Cie, 1988.

"Solvay en France depuis cent quinze ans." *Revue du Groupe Solvay en France "Catalyse."* (Sept. 1988).

"Solvay overleeft niet zonder nieuwe activiteiten." *Trends*, 30 July 2009.

Solvay, Ernest (signed "a doctor"). *Science contre religion au point de vue social, ou Faut-il avancer ou reculer*. Brussels: Privately printed, 1879.

Solvay, Ernest. *Notes sur le Productivisme et le Comptabilisme*. Brussels: Lamertin, 1900.

Solvay, Ernest. "Coup d'œil rétrospectif sur le procédé de fabrication de la soude à l'ammoniaque." *Extrait du rapport du Ve congrès international de chimie appliquée*. Berlin, 1903, Vol. 1, 1904, 108–17.

"Sowjetzone: Enteignet den Sodakönig." *Der Spiegel* 4 (28) (13 July 1950): 7–8.

Spitz, Peter H. *Petrochemicals: The Rise of an Industry*. New York: John Wiley & Sons, 1988.

Spitz, Peter H. (a), ed. *The Chemical Industry at the Millennium: Maturity, Restructuring, and Globalization*. Philadelphia: Chemical Heritage Press, 2003.

Spitz, Peter H. (b) "Restructuring: The First Wave." In Peter H. Spitz, ed., *The Chemical Industry at the Millennium: Maturity, Restructuring, and Globalisation*. Philadelphia: Chemical Heritage Press, 2003, 9–50.

Spoerer, Mark, and Jochen Fleischhacker. "Forced Laborers in Nazi Germany: Categories, Numbers, and Survivors." *Journal of Interdisciplinary History* 33 (2) (2002): 169–204.

Sprenger, R. M. *"Ten behoeve van de gezondheid van mens, dier en plant": De geschiedenis van Duphar 1930–1980.* Weesp, the Netherlands: Solvay Duphar BV, 1992.

Steen, Kathryn. "German Chemicals and American Politics, 1919–1922." In John E. Lesch, ed., *The German Chemical Industry in the Twentieth Century.* Dordrecht, the Netherlands: Kluwer, 2000, 323–46.

Stengers, Isabelle. "La pensée d'Ernest Solvay et la science de son temps." In Andrée Despy-Meyer and Didier Devriese, eds., *Ernest Solvay et son temps.* Brussels: Archives de l'Université Libre de Bruxelles, 1997, 149–65.

Stokes, Raymond G. *Divide and Prosper : The Heirs of I.G. Farben under Allied Authority, 1945–1951.* Berkeley: University of California Press, 1988.

Stokes, Raymond G. *Opting for Oil: The Political Economy of Technological Change in the West German Chemical Industry, 1945–1961.* Cambridge: Cambridge University Press, 1994.

Stokes, Raymond G. "Flexible Reaktion: Die Bedeutung des Technologietransfers für die deutsche Chemieindustrie (1925–1961)." In Rolf Petri, ed., *Technologietransfer aus der deutschen Chemieindustrie (1925–1960).* Berlin: Duncker & Humblot, 2004, 49–57.

Szöllösi-Janze, Margit. "Losing the War, but Gaining Ground: The German Chemical Industry during World War I." In John E. Lesch, ed., *The German Chemical Industry in the Twentieth Century.* Dordrecht, the Netherlands: Kluwer, 2000, 91–121.

Taylor, Alan J. P. *The Habsburg Monarchy, 1809–1918: A History of the Austrian Empire and Austria–Hungary.* 7th ed. London: Macmillan, 1961.

Teichova, Alice. *An Economic Background to Munich: International Business and Czechoslovakia, 1918–1938.* Cambridge: Cambridge University Press, 1974.

Tester, D. A. "The Pattern of Usage of PVC." In J. H. L. Henson and A. Whelan, eds., *Developments in PVC Technology.* London: Applied Science Publishers, 1973, 1–16.

The History of Coke Making and of The Coke Ovens Managers' Association. Cambridge, UK: W. Heffer and Sons, 1936 (electronic edition, 2002).

Thiel, Jens. *"Menschenbassin Belgien": Anwerbung, Deportation und Zwangsarbeit im Ersten Weltkrieg.* Essen, Germany: Klartext, 2007.

Tilman, Samuel. *Les grands banquiers belges (1830–1935): Portrait collectif d'une élite.* Brussels: Éditions de l'Académie, 2006.

Toca, Angel. *La introducción de la gran industria química en España: Solvay y su planta de Torrelavega (1887–1935).* Santander, Spain: Universidad de Cantabria, 2005.

Tooze, Adam. *The Wages of Destruction: The Making and Breaking of the Nazi Economy.* London: Penguin, 2007.

Torkelson, T. R., F. Oyen, and V. K. Rowe. "The Toxicity of Vinylchloride as Determined by Repeated Exposure to Laboratory Animals." *American Industrial Hygiene Association Journal* 22 (1961): 354–8.

Travis, Anthony S. "High Pressure Industrial Chemistry. First Steps, 1909–1913, and the Impact." In Anthony S. Travis, Harm G. Schröter, Ernst Homburg, and Peter J. T. Morris, eds., *Determinants in the Evolution of the European Chemical Industry, 1900–1939: New Technologies, Political Frameworks, Markets, and Companies.* Dordrecht, the Netherlands: Kluwer, 1998, 3–21.

Travis, Anthony S., Harm G. Schröter, Ernst Homburg, and Peter J. T. Morris, eds. *Determinants in the Evolution of the European Chemical Industry, 1900–1939: New Technologies, Political Frameworks, Markets, and Companies.* Dordrecht, the Netherlands: Kluwer, 1998.

Trempé, Rolande. "2e partie 1871–1914." In Claude Willard, ed., *La France ouvrière: Histoire de la classe ouvrière et du mouvement ouvrier français.* Vol. 1. Paris: Éditions de l'Atelier, 1995, 221–410.

Tukker, Arnold. *Frames in the Toxicity Controversy, Based on the Dutch Chlorine Debate and the Swedish PVC Debate.* PhD diss., Tilburg University, 1998.

[Urban, Judith]. *"Geboren uit een lamp": Solvay Pharmaceuticals 75 jaar.* Weesp, the Netherlands: Solvay Pharmaceuticals, n.d. [2005].

Van Belle, Jean-Louis, ed. *Solvay et Cie: Recueil d'archives inédites relatives à la société en commandite, 1862–1890.* Braine-le-Château, France: La Taille d'Aulme, 2008.

Van Belle, Jean-Louis, ed. *Addendum au Recueil d'archives inédites relatives à la société en commandite Solvay et Cie. 1862–1890.* Braine-le-Château, France: La Taille d'Aulme, 2010.

Van Daele, Jasmien. "Engineering Social Peace: Networks, Ideas, and the Founding of the International Labour Organization." *International Review of Social History* 50 (2005): 435–66.

van de Kasteele, R. P. *Het kunststoffengebied: Chemie, grondstoffen en toepassingen.* Amsterdam: Wed. J. Ahrend & Zoon, 1949.

Van Driessche, Luc. "Solvay, Boël, Janssen: Chimie, acier, finance: l'Histoire imbriquée de trois piliers de l'industrie Belge." *L'Echo (Brussels)*, 26–28 June 2010, 37.

Vanden Driessche, M. "La prudence, comme première strategie." *Le Soir (Brussels) – Supplement Economie* (31 Oct.–1 Nov. 1985).

Van der Heijden, Hein-Anton. "De milieubeweging in de twintigste eeuw." *BTNG/ RBHC* 34 (3) (2004): 445–83.

van der Vleuten, E. B. A. "In Search of the Networked Nation: Transforming Technology, Society and Nature in the Netherlands in the 20th Century." *European Review of History* 10 (2003): 59–78.

Van Langenhove, Fernand. *L'action du gouvernement belge en matière économique pendant la Guerre.* Paris: Presse Universitaire de France; New Haven, CT: Yale University Press, 1927.

Van Langenhove, Fernand. "Dannie Heineman. La vocation internationale d'un grand ingénieur au siècle de l'électricité." *Bulletin de la Classe des Lettres et des Sciences Morales et Politiques* (Académie Royale de Belgique), 5th ser., 68 (1977): 13–56.

Vanpaemel, Geert. "The Organisation of Science in the 19th Century." In Pierre Marage and Grégoire Wallenborn, eds., *The Solvay Councils and the Birth of Modern Physics.* Basel, Switzerland: Birkhäuser, 1999, 55–70.

van Rooij, Arjan. *The Company That Changed Itself: R&D and the Transformation of DSM.* Amsterdam: Amsterdam University Press, 2007.

Van Tiggelen, Brigitte. "Les premiers Conseils de chimie Solvay (1922–1928): Entre ingérence et collaboration, les nouvelles relations de la physique et de la chimie." *Chimie nouvelle* 17 (Dec. 1999): 60–8.

van Zanden, Jan Luiten, Joost Jonker, Stephen Howarth, and Keetie Sluyterman. *A History of Royal Dutch Shell.* Vol. 2, *Powering the Hydrocarbon Revolution, 1939–1973.* New York: Oxford University Press, 2007.

Verg, Erik, Gottfried Plumpe, and Heinz Schultheis. *Meilensteine: 125 Jahre Bayer 1863–1988.* Leverkusen, Germany: Bayer AG, 1988.

Viola, Pier Luigi. "Canceragenic Effect of Vinyl Chloride." In R. Lee Clark, ed., *Proceedings of the 10th International Cancer Congress, Houston 1970: Abstracts.* Chicago : Year Book Medical Publishers, 1970, 29.

Viola, P. L., A. Bigoti, and A. Caputo. "Oncogenic Response of Rat Skin, Lungs, and Bones to Vinyl Chloride." *Cancer Research* 31 (1971): 516–22.

Viré, Liliane. "La Cité scientifique du Parc Léopold." *Cahiers bruxellois* 19 (1974): 86–180.

Wagner, Bernd Christian. *IG Auschwitz: Zwangsarbeit und Vernichtung von Häftlingen des Lagers Monowitz, 1941–1945.* Munich: K. G. Saur, 2000.

Warren, Kenneth. *Chemical Foundations: The Alkali Industry in Britain to 1926.* Oxford, UK: Clarendon Press, 1980.

Warren, Kenneth. "Technology Transfer in the Origins of the Heavy Chemicals Industry in the United States and the Russian Empire." In David J. Jeremy, ed., *International Technology Transfer, Europe, Japan and the USA, 1700–1914.* Aldershot, UK: Elgar, 1991, 153–75.

[Wertz, William C., ed.]. *Phillips: The First 66 Years.* Bartlesville, OK: Phillips Petroleum Company, 1983.

West, Carolyn V. *1700 Milton Avenue, the Solvay Story (1881–1981).* Solvay, NY: Allied Chemical Co., 1981.

Westermann, Andrea. "PVC, Dynamit Nobel und die Stadt Troisdorf: Lokale Deutungen von industriellen Gesundheitsgefahren und ihre Verallgemeinerung." In F.-J. Brüggemeier and I. Engels, eds., *Natur- und Umweltschutz nach 1945: Konflikte, Konzepte, Kompetenzen.* Frankfurt am Main: Campus, 2005, 249–67.

Westermann, Andrea. *Plastik und politische Kultur in Westdeutschland.* Zürich: Chronos, 2007.

Whitlock, Brand. *Belgium under the German Occupation: A Personal Narrative.* London: W. Heinemann, 1919.

Wilkins, Mira. *The History of Foreign Investment in the United States, 1914–1945.* Cambridge, MA: Harvard University Press, 2004.

Wurm, Clemens. "The Politics of International Cartels: Great Britain, Steel and Cotton Textiles in the Interwar Period." In Dominique Barjot, ed., *International Cartels Revisited: Vues nouvelles sur les cartels internationaux (1880–1980).* Caen, France: Éditions-Diffusion du Lys, 1994, 255–64.

Yarime, Masaru. *From End-of-Pipe Technology to Clean Technology: Environmental Policy and Technological Change in the Chlor-Alkali Industry in Japan and Europe.* Saarbrücken, Germany: VDM Verlag Dr. Müller, 2009.

Zapke, Volker. "Und dann bin ich richtig zusammengebrochen: Ich hab also wirklich gedacht, ich muß sterben – Das schmutzige Geschäft mit Holzschutzmitteln." In Antje Bultmann, ed., *Vergiftet und alleingelassen Die Opfer von Giftstoffen in den Mühlen von Wissenschaft und Justiz.* Munich: Droemersche Verlagsanstalt, 1996, 67–118.

Index